ABOUT THE HOLLAND HANDBOOK

Welcome, expat, to the Netherlands! We are proud to present you this seventeenth edition of *The Holland Handbook*, which we hope will prove to be as good a friend to you during your stay in the Netherlands as it has been to numerous other expats over the past sixteen years.

This book has been compiled for a very mixed group of readers who have one thing in common and that is that they want to find their way in the Netherlands: the expat employee, the expat partner, foreign entrepreneurs, and the many foreign students who come to the Netherlands to train or study. Also for those involved in expatriate affairs who want to keep abreast of the latest developments in their various areas of interest, this book has proven to be a very welcome source of information. Last but not least, this book is a wonderful reminder, including beautiful photographs, of life in the Netherlands for those who are moving on to their next posting – or back home.

The Holland Handbook is the result of the enthusiastic efforts of more than 20 authors, organizations and proofreaders of various nationalities and with very different backgrounds. Most of them are specialists who work for international companies and organizations and who have an impressive amount of know-how when it comes to providing expatriates with information.

The diversity of the editorial team makes reading this book a journey in itself. You will find technical information on practical subjects interspersed with personal experiences, background information and columns – all written in each contributor's personal style. With so many topics to cover, *The Holland Handbook* may at times take an unexpected turn – however, as this book is primarily meant as a reference book and not as a book to be read in one go, you can simply select the topic you want to read up on, even if you only have a few minutes to spare.

Though *The Holland Handbook* contains a wealth of information, we do not have the illusion that it is at all complete. It is meant as an introduction, or orientation if you will, into the various subjects that can be of interest to you. By referring you to the relevant literature, addresses and websites, we have provided you with as many sources of additional and/or more in-depth information as we can think of. Undoubtedly we have forgotten a few subjects, websites or books. If you feel that we have left out something that should not have been missed, we would greatly appreciate it if you let us know about this, for instance by sending an e-mail to editor@xpat.nl.

We hope you have a pleasant, enriching and successful stay in the Netherlands.

Bert van Essen and Gerjan de Waard
Publishers

  www.facebook.com/XPatMedia

THE HOLLAND HANDBOOK

YOUR GUIDE TO LIVING IN THE NETHERLANDS

INTRODUCTION

Art, music, architecture, folklore, foods and dress, our roles and relationships, body language, gestures, greetings and partings, all weave together to form a rich cultural diversity. Every culture is the outcome of centuries of social interaction, a shared history, religious norms and experience – however, it is only when we are among people of a different culture that we really become aware of how much we are the product of those shared elements ourselves. It is just as important to realize that the majority of the people in our host culture are also not aware of how their shared background influences their own behavior – and of how unfamiliar and uncomfortable this behavior may be for us (or perhaps, how reassuringly similar!). When attempting to understand and survive in another culture, there are many areas where we need to pause and consider how our own culture and the host culture differ. This takes time, patience, and some sense of adventure. The first step in achieving this is realizing that neither way of living is wrong or right – it's just... different.

A New Life in the Netherlands
Adapting to a New Country and a New Culture

BY DIANE LEMIEUX

So you decided to come live in the Netherlands. You may have been tantalized by the idea of exploring old-world Europe with its architecture and museums. Or maybe it was the possibility of viewing kilometers of flower beds and sand dunes from the seat of a bicycle that attracted you to this country. Perhaps the adventure of undertaking something new, something different is what tipped the balance for you. Whatever it was that made you say *yes* to a move to the Netherlands, here you are and the country is just outside your door, waiting to be discovered.

But now, instead of having time to visit, like a tourist on an extended trip, you are faced with the task of undertaking all of life's daily chores in an entirely new environment. Whereas at home you did most of these things without thinking, you must now spend time and energy discovering where to buy milk and how to pay the phone bill. The climate is different, you need to get used to the types of products that you can and cannot find at your local grocers', and you have to orient yourself using street signs and product labels you do not understand. You suddenly discover that English is used far less than you had expected, and that Dutch is far harder to learn than you had hoped.

This is the process of adaptation, of creating a new home in this foreign country. Eventually you will be settled in a new house, and will have established routines that make life seem more normal; you will have identified a favorite grocery store or market, know where to purchase your home-language newspaper, and may even have discovered a favorite café for your usual Sunday morning breakfasts. This book will help you with this process of adapting to this country you have adopted, however briefly, as your home.

But this book also has a different focus; to describe the culture of the people who live here, as well as the practicalities of life in the Netherlands. The word 'culture' as it is used here is not about the artistic and historic expressions of culture you find in museums. It is about everyday behavior, the glue that binds communities, the norms and values that regulate social life. The Dutch culture is expressed through language, through social structures and habits, through the way people communicate with each other. This culture is subtle and you will discover it slowly over time, as you increasingly deal with the 'locals'. It is something you will piece together as you interact with your neighbors, as you watch your colleagues at work, from the way you are treated in the shops or when taking the train.

The Dutch, of course, are not explicitly aware of their culture, just as we are not aware of our own. It is only because we are here as foreigners, observing another culture, that we become aware of the differences between the way members of the host culture react, and our own expectations of how one 'should' act. We came, expecting certain patterns of behavior from our hosts: the stereotypes typify the Dutch as being tolerant, frugal and hardworking. From the stories of the red light district you may expect a very liberal society and, knowing of the reputation the country has as a leader in graphic design and architecture, you may expect an innovative attitude to life and work. And yet you will also find conservative attitudes and behaviors.

Dutch society is a highly complex, multi-cultural mix of historic and modern influences, whose daily practice and social behavior may not live up to the values and etiquette that you are accustomed to. Your daily chores bring you into a series of intercultural encounters with the Dutch which sometimes leave you wondering 'what just happened?' It is this process of accumulated 'incidents' that we call 'culture shock' and that is blamed for much of the strife associated with expatriate living.

It is popularly understood that culture shock is a process, containing a set of phases which will all pass, eventually leading you to return to your normal, happy state as a well-adjusted individual. What is not often explained is that culture shock is experienced differently by every individual, depending on their own culture, attitudes, expectations, and previous international experience. Furthermore, moments of frustration and anger may occur at any time during a stay in a foreign country and are a normal part of adjustment. However, culture shock is also a process which can be controlled and minimized.

The advice given by most intercultural or adaptation specialists is to get to know your host culture. Understanding the underlying reasons for the behavior of the Dutch helps to see them as individuals and not as a global 'them'. *The Holland Handbook* has been written by both Dutch individuals and expatriates with years of experience in living with and explaining the Dutch to foreigners. They describe the historic and cultural aspects that influence the behavior you observe, making it more comprehensible and logical. You don't have to like everything about the Dutch culture or adapt to every aspect of it either. But with a bit of understanding and good will you will most probably come to find at least a few friends in this society, people who will make the experience of having lived in the Netherlands a memorable one.

What does it mean to be in the Netherlands? You crawl ahead on the highway behind laboring windshield wipers, watching the ragged horizon of apartment buildings go by as the gray clouds are chased along by a strong south-western wind.

As the slowly moving traffic jams come to another halt, you have the chance to focus on your fellow drivers. Your first conclusion is obvious: you are in a wealthy country. This is evident from the newness of the cars and the fact that, despite the economic crisis, the number of traffic jams has remained daunting. So much so that radio announcers have long since stopped listing all of them and simply recite the longest – and their total length, which often exceeds 90 kilometers. No wonder, as this country welcomed its 8 millionth car in 2016. Meanwhile, as you will surely notice, the government is working hard at widening the highways, or laying new ones – a cause of considerable temporary inconvenience. Though the government decided, in 2012, to reduce the budget for road construction / improvement, it is still considerable. Towards the end of 2015, for instance, it opened an addition to the A4, which connects The Hague and Rotterdam, thanks to which these two cities – which are only 20 kilometers apart – will be linked by two highways instead of one. They will also soon be starting on the construction of a new tunnel underneath the Nieuwe Waterweg, west of Rotterdam, as well as tackling the bottlenecks around Utrecht. Another innovation that is on the agenda is the replacement of gasoline by electricity in order to reduce the emission of CO_2 – however, this is coming about rather slowly, despite political ambitions to rid the country of gas stations by the end of last year.

Stuck among the traffic are many trucks, which are well-kept and loaded with valuable goods. These goods are seldom raw materials, but rather finished industrial goods. The prominent phone numbers and e-mail addresses that can be found on the sides of the trucks are testimony to the fact that this country has a good network of electronic communication and that the electronic highway is fully operational. You can't see this from behind your steering wheel, but these past years the chances that the trucks are carrying products that have been manufactured in the Netherlands are small. Already at the start of this century, the Dutch government decided that this country is a post-industrial services economy. The throughput of goods – entering and leaving the country through harbors such as Rotterdam as well as the airports – has become an important sector of the Dutch industry. At the same time, the Netherlands is among the top four food exporters in the world, not to mention being a top exporter of plants and flowers. You can also see an interesting new development: Eastern European URLs on the sides of trucks bearing Eastern European license plates (from Poland, Hungary and Rumania). The wages in these countries are lower, so that these transportation companies can offer their services at lower rates, forcing more and more Dutch transportation companies to move their business to Eastern Europe. A similar step to what the shipping companies ended up doing during the second half of the former century when their ships started bearing Panamanian and Liberian flags.

Yet, there is an apparent contradiction to the perceived wealth, if you look around you: the cars are far from luxurious. You are surrounded by middle-class cars, and you can see how strongly the Asian market is represented on the European car market as, these past few years, the Dutch have embraced smaller, more economic cars – due to the crisis and the accompanying tight pockets, but also thanks to the temporary introduction of fiscal measures aimed at stimulating the purchase of environmentally-friendly cars. (When, in 2014, the fiscal incentives for buying partially electric cars were so high that the purchase price enjoyed a 70% subsidy, these measures were terminated.) And, trust the Dutch merchant mentality, which motivated some to buy these relatively cheap electric cars locally and sell them at an attractive price abroad. But, where are the Rolls Royces, Cadillacs, Daimlers and Jaguars? In the Netherlands, if you want to see one of these cars, you will have to visit a dealer's showroom. On the road, the most expensive cars you will see are the standard Mercedes, Audis and BMWs and the occasional secondhand Jaguar. And, should you actually spot a Rolls Royce trying to make its way through traffic, you will notice that it does not really command any respect. To the contrary. It will even seem as if the middle class cars think it inappropriate for such a showpiece to be on the road and will want to prove, by the way they drive, that they are worth just as much as the fellow in the Rolls.

SELF-DRIVING CARS

Traffic experts in the Netherlands insist that tackling bottlenecks and other issues will never be enough to rid this country of its traffic jams, because there are still simply too many cars. Which is why the Dutch Minister of Traffic and Water Affairs, Melanie Schultz van der Hagen, is such a fan of self-driving cars. If these niftily computerized vehicles manage to maintain a steady speed at a fixed distance from the cars around them, then the Dutch roadways will prove to have sufficient capacity. She has taken legal measures to make experiments on the Dutch roads possible and hopes that the Netherlands will be a forerunner in this area.

Things are going fast and it would appear that self-driving cars will be the norm sooner than we currently think. An additional benefit is that computers allow a more efficient use of the roads than humans tend to show, meaning that less asphalt will be needed to accommodate the nation's traffic. A fleet of self-driving cars could then eliminate the need for many planned road-widening projects.

TRAFFIC FINES

Your fellow drivers, incidentally, appear to be talking to themselves. You can see that they are keeping it short. Probably they are telling someone that they will be late, due to traffic. In the past, they would have reached for their mobile phones, but they don't do that anymore – it is no longer allowed. Nowadays, you are expected to use a hands-free system, or else the police will redirect you to a road stop, where they will present you with a hefty fine after having courteously introduced themselves and shaken your hand. It must be noted, incidentally, that recently they having been clamping down on a variety of activities that could cause you to drive without exercising due care – such as eating a sandwich while driving...

Failing to drive hands-free can prove to be expensive for another reason, as well. Before you know it, you might have missed a speed limit reduction. On many parts of the highway, you can now drive 130 kilometers an hour – but these have proven to be limited. Every 15 minutes or so, there will be a sign reducing the maximum velocity for some or other reason – to, for instance, 120, 100, 80 or even 70 kilometers an hour. And everywhere, there are cameras ready to snap a picture of a 'traffic-sinner'. Who is sure to receive a considerable fine. In 2014, almost 10 million fines were paid, yielding the nation's coffers € 627 million. In 2010, this had been € 525 million. It should come as no surprise therefore, if you run into a disgruntled Dutchman who is expressing his suspicion that the fines have nothing to do with enforcing safety but rather with reinforcing the nation's wallet.

The overall picture, however, becomes a quite different when you look at the distribution of wealth. The richest 1% of the population owns 25% of the nation's wealth, which, in 2014, amounted 1.116 billion euros. Yet, trust the Dutch: this concentration of wealth in the bank accounts of just a few was just not right, according to the majority, and they immediately started to plead for a raising of the wealth tax. Die-hard socialists? One of them was a card-carrying Liberalist.

Five years after being hit quite hard by the oil crises in 1974 and 1979, the Netherlands resumed its growth – which was only interrupted by the dotcom crisis in 2001 and then again by the credit crisis in 2008. Already in the first months of the crisis, the government appointed a great number of commissions whose task it was to determine how – wherever possible – government expenditures could be reduced by 20%, for when the time comes that the economy recovers and the mile-high bill for the emergency measures is due. For, when push comes to shove, the Netherlands is a country that wants to make sure that its household budget is balance. For instance, the cabinet that was formed in 2010, expressed plans to reduce government spending by € 18 billion. At first, it seemed that this measure would be sufficient to tackle the country's economic challenges, but in 2011 the economy took another nosedive, requiring the government to cut expenditures by another € 12 billion, in order to reduce the 4.5% financial deficit to 3% – the maximum for members of the European Union. The Dutch government had no choice but to do this as it had taken a strict line vis-à-vis the upholding of this limitation when the southern European countries – particularly Greece – were facing the pos-

sibility of bankruptcy. When it became clear that this would not be enough, the government did not even hesitate to cut another € 18 billion, plus schedule another € 4 billion cut for the year 2014.

The Dutch population accuses the government of making sweeping cuts that are damaging to the economy, but the answer of the government is short, based on an expression they feel the Dutch might have forgotten: frugality and hard work make houses like castles. If we pay the price now, says the country's liberal Prime Minister Rutte, then "the crisis will have made us stronger". "And more social," adds Diederik Samsom, leader of Rutte's coalition party, the social-democratic Labor Party. At the start of 2014, it seemed as if they might be proven right. The economy showed a slight upswing and the asking prices of houses started going up – after having gone down 20% over the past years. In 2015 and 2016, this upswing appeared to be here to stay, though politicians, professors and representatives of the various industries warned that the recovery is and remains fragile. One should keep in mind that, in Europe, a growth percentage of 1.5-2% is already considered quite positive.

Han van der Horst (1949) is an historian. He worked for the Communications Directorate of Nuffic, the Netherlands Organization for International Cooperation in higher education. He is a prolific author on Dutch history and culture. Among expatriates, his best-known book is 'The Low Sky – Understanding the Dutch'.

MONEY GRABBERS

The 2008 financial crisis had its repercussions not only for the banks, but also for the housing corporations and project developers that had been created out of the privatized associations and foundations for affordable living in the '90s of the previous century. These corporations and project developers had grossly exceeded their limits by going into office real estate, the construction of villas and even activities abroad. When this went wrong, it turned out that the managing directors of these corporations – just like their colleagues at the banks – had awarded themselves generous salaries. In order to answer the public indignation that followed, the government decided that persons in (semi) public office may never earn more than the Prime Minister (€ 180,000 a year). Anyone who does, public office or not, is quickly accused of being a money-grabber. The Dutch do, however, distinguish between entrepreneurs who bear their own (considerable) risk and those who don't and who therefore are 'merely' employees. Unless proven otherwise, the latter are automatically labeled money-grabbers.

This is what happened to the members of the Board of Directors of the ABNAmro Bank, which had been saved and nationalized in 2008. In March 2015, these members (with the exception of the president)

awarded themselves a raise of € 100,000 a year to compensate them for the fact the government had abolished the system of bonuses – which it had done for the purpose of curtailing irresponsible speculation and risk-taking.

The dismay among politicians and the people was so great that the Directors paid the raise back – thus avoiding the beginning of a run on the bank. Their colleagues with the competitor, ING, which has paid off all its state support, awarded themselves an even greater raise – which they kept. More than ever before, bankers are perceived as incorrigible money grabbers. Should this come up at a party, there will undoubtedly be someone who will point out the fact that all the other employees of the banks haven't received a raise in years, while the members of the Boards of Directors initiated one series of dismissals after the other. This policy of reducing the number of employees is seen as anti-social in the Netherlands, unless there is absolutely no other way to stop a company from going under. Talk of terms of employment in keeping with the rest of the labor market for all levels of a company are dismissed summarily by people who, by American standards, would be considered very conservative.

URBANIZED CENTER

The Randstad, in the provinces of North-Holland, South-Holland, Utrecht and Flevoland, is strongly urbanized. There are no real metropolises with millions of people in Holland. The largest city, Amsterdam, does not have more than about 823,000 inhabitants. Still, Holland is a highly urbanized country. Every few kilometers, there is an exit to one, two or three municipalities that have a couple of thousand to not many more than 100,000 inhabitants. These cities and towns all have their own character and are all equally picturesque. In the urban areas you will find neither hovels nor palaces. What you will find are primarily middle class houses. Even Wassenaar, Aerdenhout or Rozendaal, the Dutch equivalents of Miami Beach and Beverly Hills, look comparatively modest. There is an undeniable air of wealth, but none of the glitter of excessive opulence.

Particularly the cities of the Randstad – Rotterdam, Delft, The Hague, Leiden Haarlem, Amsterdam, Hilversum, Utrecht, and Gouda – are an almost continuous circle or half-moon. The Dutch call this a 'rand', or 'edge', hence the name Randstad. In this middle lays a green

area, with small and medium-sized villages. Together with the Southeastern area of Brabant, this area is the country's economic powerhouse, where the majority of companies are located, money is made and culture is generated.

You will also not find harbors filled with expensive yachts. Those who buy a pleasure yacht in the Netherlands will have a hard time finding a spot for it, as the harbors are all filled. Not with luxurious threemasters and a regular crew, however, but rather with motor and sail boats of all shapes and sizes. And should there be one that sticks out above the rest, chances are it is flying a foreign flag.

You would almost think that socialism reigns here, even more so than in the countries of the former East Bloc. A conclusion several conservative as well as liberal bloggers would be happy to support. However, economic statistics show the opposite. When it comes to per capita income, the Netherlands is securely situated towards the top of the European Union. After all, the wage system is pretty balanced and there are no extreme differences.

THE NETHERLANDS

WADDEN ISLANDS

WADDEN SEA

Leeuwarden

Groningen

Den Helder

Assen

IJSSELMEER

Emmen

NORTH SEA

Hoorn

Alkmaar

Zwolle

Lelystad

Hengelo

Haarlem

Amsterdam

Almere

Amersfoort

Apeldoorn

Enschede

Leiden

Utrecht

Den Haag
(The Hague)

Zoetermeer

Gouda

Arnhem

Delft

Rotterdam

Nijmegen

GERMANY

's-Hertogenbosch

Breda

Tilburg

Middelburg

Eindhoven

Venlo

Duisburg

Essen

Antwerp

Düsseldorf

Mönchengladbach

BELGIUM

	Highway
	Road
✈	Airport
●	Main City

Brussels

Cologne

Heerlen

Maastricht

Luik

Aachen

THEY MUST BE GIANTS BY STEVEN STUPP

One of my first observations about the Netherlands was how tall the Dutch are. Actually, tall doesn't do them justice. They are really tall. Damn tall. I am not used to thinking of myself as short; I'm above the average, adult-male height in my native land. But after a few introductions, where I looked up and found myself staring the person in the throat, the point hit home.

According to the statisticians, the Dutch are currently the tallest people in the world. The average height for men is 6 foot, 0.4 inches (1.84 meters); the women come in at a respectable 5 foot, 7.2 inches (1.71 meters). Cold averages, however, don't convey the entire picture. Connoisseurs of numbers know to look at the tails of a distribution. There are quite a few Dutch men, and even a few women, who are over seven feet tall (2.10 meters). This poses some interesting problems. For example, they are taller than the height of many doorways in the Netherlands; I have no doubt that the risk of accidental concussions is now a painful reality. On the other hand, size does offer some advantages: the Dutch are already a volleyball powerhouse, and if basketball ever catches on in the somehow misnamed Low Countries, they'll give the Michael Jordans of this world a run for their money.

What is truly remarkable is that the Dutch are getting taller. While the average height in all first-world countries increased dramatically over the last century, this growth spurt has slowed down of late and seems to be leveling off. The increase in the average height of the Dutch, however, shows no sign of abating. In the last decade alone, the average height of 18 to 39-year-old men and women has increased by 0.9 inches (2.3 centimeters) and almost 0.7 inches (1.7 centimeters), respectively. It is in this context that height has taken on an interesting significance in Dutch society. Enhancing one's stature has become surprisingly important. Techniques range from the large hats Dutch policewomen wear – it makes them appear taller – to surgery.

The Dutch are often critical – and rightly so – of cosmetic surgery, such as face-lifts, tummy-tucks and breast implants. That stated, every once in a while a particularly short Dutch man or woman (typically, shorter than five feet tall or some 1.5 meters) undergoes a fairly radical surgery called the Ilizarov procedure, in which a patient's femurs are broken and the bone ends are separated using a metal frame. Over time, the bones grow together and fuse, thereby increasing the patient's height. Aside from the pain and the risk of infection, there is nothing fundamentally wrong with the procedure and the patients usually seem pleased with the results. A similar technique is used in other countries, but it is reserved for cases of exceptional dwarfism. What defines that, I suppose, is a question of perspective.

Male tourists will encounter this quote-unquote difference in perspective the first time they go into a public bathroom. The urinals are mounted sufficiently high on the walls to make it almost impossible to use them, unless you stand on your tiptoes. Unfortunately, there are no boxes or phone books in the bathrooms to level the porcelain playing field and to give foreigners a much-needed leg up! As a consequence, I always enjoy the look of shock on the faces of many male visitors in the Netherlands as they return from the *wc* (the Dutch phrase for toilet).

An exchange I once had with a Dutch friend is also illustrative. She was reading a Dutch magazine when I suddenly heard "Tsk, tsk, tsk, tsk, tsk." (A sound the Dutch like to make. In this case it conveyed sympathy.) "That's terrible," she said. I asked her what was wrong. "There's a letter here from a mother whose daughter is only twelve years old and is already 183," she replied. That seemed unremarkable, so I asked, "Pounds or kilograms?" A bewildered look crossed her face and her head recoiled in shock. It took a few seconds for what I had said to sink in. Finally, she blurted out, "No, centimeters!" (While there is nothing inherently wrong with being very tall, the Dutch mother was concerned that her daughter might be teased or could encounter other social problems.)

That conversation also emphasizes the fact that, no matter how hard you try, you remain a product of your country of origin. People in many countries (in particular, Americans), even if they don't have the problem personally, are obsessed with weight. The Dutch are plagued by their size, although they seem to deal with their affliction better than most. As an aside, the Dutch still don't really have a weight problem. While there are overweight people in the Netherlands (the overall trend mirrors that found in other countries), obesity is less prevalent, and frankly, is never carried to the extremes that occur in places like the United States. How is this possible? Simple: they don't eat as much and what they do eat contains a lot less sugar and fat. If anything, some of the Dutch have the opposite problem with regard to weight. I know a few Dutch women, and even a few men, who are not anorexic, but do have an odd problem: they can't gain weight. They eat lots of junk food and still can't gain weight. What do you say to someone who tells you, with complete sincerity, that they have always wanted to know what it feels like to go on a diet? Welcome to a different world.

Aside from the general improvement in the standard of living over the last half-century and the more even distribution of wealth in Dutch society, the best explanation I've come across for the remarkable growth spurt in the Netherlands is their diet. Specifically, the infant diet. In a laudable program, the government-subsidized *Consultatiebureau* provides regular advice to parents about their children's health and nutrition through four years of age. The objective is to improve the well-being of newborns. It has been an admirable success. The hypothesized impact on the height of the general population is apparently unintended. Alternatively, in a new twist to the age-old, survival of the fittest argument, a few British colleagues once proposed a theory over a couple of beers in a pub. "It's all a simple matter of natural selection," they said. "How's that?" I asked. To which they answered: "What with all of those floods, only the tall could survive."

Steven Stupp is the American author of the book *Beneden de zeespiegel* (literally translated: Underneath the Sea Level). He resided in the Netherlands for several years, and in this book he tells us, with characteristic dry humor, about the cultural shock of living here, while sharing what he got to know about the country and her inhabitants.

CHAPTER 1

The windmills of your mind are not playing tricks on you. You have (or your Dearly Beloved has) accepted that job in the Netherlands. The dust, created by the whirlwind consequences of this decision, has started to settle and you are beginning to wonder what type of country you have come to. Having read about culture shock in the preceding introduction, you now know that the best step towards familiarizing yourself with this new culture is knowing more about it. First off, relax in the knowledge that the Netherlands has one of the highest standards of living in the world. But what about their government and politics, economy, the climate, and their religion? This chapter will tell you about how history and living below sea level helped shape the politics of this nation.

CONTRIBUTING AUTHORS STEPHANIE DIJKSTRA AND HAN VAN DER HORST

HISTORY AND ITS INFLUENCE ON THE DUTCH OF TODAY

In the Middle Ages, there were many countships and the occasional duchies on the territory of the Netherlands, which for the larger part coincide with the current provinces. By way of a long historic process, the King of Spain inherited all of these in the second half of the 16th century. However, his hands were tied by the many privileges that the cities and rural districts had acquired in the time of the counts and dukes. These had to do with autonomy and other regulations, as a result of which the King was obligated to appoint the local governors from a predetermined select group of persons, recommended by the prominent local families.

Philip II's intention was to end these privileges. For his day and age, he was a modern ruler who believed in a powerful central authority that maintained the same procedures everywhere, and who based his decisions on the ethical and ideological principles of one sole religion, that of the Roman Catholic Church. However, in the Netherlands, there was much sympathy for Protestantism, especially that of John Calvin.

Philip II's ideas were therefore not met with much enthusiasm. There was a successful uprising – in which a central role was played by William of Orange, the patriarch of the Dutch royal family. William of Orange was a stadtholder – a representative of the king – in several of these countships, including Holland, and he found he could not agree with the loss of the existing privileges nor with the persecution of the Protestants, which was a central element in the royal politics.

The uprising against Philip II resulted in the Republic of the Seven United Netherlands, in which the old privileges and local autonomy remained of central importance. This republic could be seen as a union of states, something like the European Union, in which the independent states worked together closely without relinquishing their sovereignty. In this system, no one could muster enough power to conquer a position of dominance in this republic and, if one was too much of a braggart or made too much of a show of wealth and power, one only succeeded in creating enemies. A politically high-ranking position could only be based on influence and not on power. Even the stadtholders, who were always recruited from the House of William of Orange – and who managed to make their position a hereditary one – were unable to acquire very much power. Though they might have had the authority vested in them by Philip II, this was subject to the many constraints that also came with the system of privileges and old rights.

To get something done in the old Republic required the formation of coalitions with others, while also making sure not to unnecessarily offend one's opponents. Central conditions to being successful were: respect for others, a modest life style, a willingness to listen and the capacity to restrain oneself. Calvinism, the source of this philosophy, was embraced in a liberal way by a majority of the elite, and was very influential.

The Netherlands is no longer a union of states, but instead a democratic state whose unity is symbolized by the King – a descendant of William of Orange's older brother Jan. However, the mentality of the Dutch has remained the same. Even though Dutch society has become strongly secularized, it is still greatly influenced by Calvinistic philosophies. Still evident today is the strong Protestant work ethic characterized by overtones of moderation in all aspects of life, decision-making by consensus, and the stymieing of individualism. The Netherlands is a country where ostentatiousness and boastfulness are akin to sinfulness, and where orderliness and cleanliness are next to godliness. Showing off your wealth is still considered equal to showing a lack of respect, and secretiveness is looked upon with suspicion – hence the open curtains after dark, serving a triple purpose: to demonstrate a lack of ostentatiousness, the evidence of orderliness and to show that there are no secrets. The Protestant work ethic is further reflected in the way in which the country is run, a system generally referred to as the 'Poldermodel'.

POLDERMODEL

A piece of land that is completely surrounded by a dike for the purpose of protecting it against high waters is called a polder in Dutch. You can find them in all shapes and sizes. The largest in the Netherlands, Flevoland (large enough to have become the Netherlands' youngest province), measures 48,000 hectares. The management of such a polder requires a tight cooperation between the users. The smallest mistake can result in disaster, as a dike is only as strong as its weakest point.

Life behind the dikes has influenced the Dutch culture. It might be going too far to say that it is solely responsible for making the Dutch a democratic people, however, it is clear that they are partial to detailed agreements, to which they must strictly adhere – for all are responsible for 'their part of the dike'. Foreigners never fail to notice the large degree of organization and planning in Dutch society.

This coming together to reach a consensus, this give and take in all the various areas, all characterize Dutch society and Dutch politics. It has resulted in, for instance, the downward adjustment of wage demands, the tolerance of drugs and the legalization of prostitution. This attitude can be summarized in a 'new' word, invented by the British press in 1997: poldermodel.

THE NETHERLANDS WITHOUT DIKES

The Netherlands literally means Low Lands: 40% of this nation's land lies below sea level. Dunes, dikes, dams and delta works protect us against the water of the sea and the rivers. Without these barriers, the Netherlands would become largely immersed under water.

This poldermodel has not been consistently popular, however. During the first years of the 21st century, the Dutch themselves started to have their doubts about it – led by the suddenly very popular newcomer Pim Fortuyn, who appeared almost as if out of nowhere in the political arena, but was shot to death on May 6, 2002 – before he could truly embark on a political career. Fortuyn and his followers were of the opinion that all this poldermodel-consulting and searching for consensus only distracted people from the real problems in society and was keeping them from making important decisions that were long overdue. The economic recession, the increasing unemployment, and the reduction in income of the average Dutch citizen further fed the criticism of the poldermodel and the subsequent cabinets, led by CDA-Christian Democrat Jan Peter Balkenende, were strongly influenced by this train of thought. However, more than 10 years later, setting aside Dutch nature in favor of a different approach has proven to be harder than initially anticipated and the Dutch appear to have re-embraced their old tradition of consultation and detailed agreements (you can read more about this in *And the Dutch Politicians Plod On* on page 24).

THE DUTCH POLITICAL SYSTEM IN BRIEF

THE GOVERNMENT

The Dutch government is what one calls a 'monarchical government', meaning that it is not only comprised of the ministers and the state secretaries, but also the monarch, King Willem-Alexander. Another term for describing this is: a constitutional monarchy with a parliamentary system, whereby the constitution has determined how the powers are divided between the monarch and the other institutions of the government. For instance, the Parliament has been given certain rights allowing them to check the power of the government (listed further on in this chapter). Notably, though the ministers are accountable to Parliament, the King, who has no political responsibility, is not. In fact, since 1848, the person of the king is inviolable. The ministers are responsible for everything he does or says. This puts him in a delicate position; the King, the Queen and their princesses cannot make any public statements without consulting with the Prime Minister first.

THE CABINET

The cabinet's responsibilities are: preparing and implementing legislation, overseeing the local government, carrying out the day-to-day business of government and maintaining international relations. The observant follower of Dutch politics will notice that the number of ministers tends to change from one cabinet to the next. This can be due to the introduction of a new post that resorts under an existing ministry, but that is considered sufficiently important under the current circumstances to warrant its own minister. Sometimes, the reason behind the addition to, or reduction in, the number of ministers or state secretaries is merely a political one. The numeric distribution of the members of the cabinet must reflect the representation of the coalition partners in the

Parliament as closely as it can. Otherwise one of the coalition partners might feel sold short, which could eventually lead to the fall of the cabinet.

THE PARLIAMENT

The Netherlands has a representative democracy and its Parliament (*Staten Generaal*) is made up of two chambers: the Upper House (*Eerste Kamer*), whose 75 members are elected by the members of the provincial councils; and the Lower House (*Tweede Kamer*, or Second Chamber), whose 150 members are elected directly by the people.

The two Houses of Parliament have been given four rights: the right to set a budget; the right of interpellation; the right to put questions before the ministers and state secretaries; and the right of inquiry. The Lower House has been given two further rights: the right of amendment and the right to propose legislation.

Until 1917, the Netherlands made use of the district system for elections. This was then replaced by proportional representation, making the country, province or municipality one single borough. And then there is the quota; if you divide the total number of votes collected by the number of seats in the representative body, you have a quota. In order to win a seat, you must attain this quota. For instance, the Lower House has 150 seats; in order to win a seat, one has to have won 1/150 of all votes. In this system, voters vote for a party that submits a list of candidates. It is possible, however, to vote for a particular candidate. Though this will always count as a vote for the party, those who receive more than 25% of the party's quota for a seat are guaranteed a seat in the Parliament. The other seats are divided according to the order in which the party candidates appear on the list. Prime Minister Mark Rutte would like to reduce the number of parliamentary members to 100, in order to cut costs.

However, this requires an amendment to the Constitution. And this takes time – and requires a two-thirds majority in parliament.

The elections for the Second Chamber (by the people) and the Upper House (by the members of the Provincial States) do not take place simultaneously. In fact, they are separated by a number of years. This means that a government can have a majority in the Second Chamber, without having one in the First. This is the case for the second Rutte Cabinet, as a consequence of which the ministers find themselves in a position that they have to make concessions in order to garner the support of the members of the Upper House that are in the opposition – thus muddying the waters a bit. To combat this, the cabinet managed to build up a reasonably stable relationship with the opposition parties D66, ChristenUnie and SGP IN 2013. In return for a number of concessions, they helped the Parliament secure a majority in the Upper House. Finance Minister Dijsselbloem even arranged to consult the leaders of these parties when drawing up the budget. These three parties have since earned the name 'favorite opposition parties' in the Dutch world of politics, while the other opposition parties are finding themselves sitting it out in the dugout. Not everyone is in agreement with the actions of the Upper House. They feel that the senators should limit themselves to judging the quality of the legislation, maintaining a largely un-political stance. However, there is nothing in the Dutch constitution to support the demands for this more modest role.

All in all, the election of the Provincial States in 2015 had plenty of political significance. The outcome would determine the composition of the First Chamber. No one talked about province-related issues. The focus was solely on the Cabinet's policy, about which the party leaders – none of whom was a candidate in these elections – debated on television. The outcome of the elections was not positive for the Cabinet: it had lost its majority in the First Chamber.

AND THE DUTCH POLITICIANS PLOD ON

Those who visit the restaurants and cafés surrounding Binnenhof, the nerve center of Dutch politics in The Hague, are quite likely to stumble across Prime Minister Mark Rutte – usually in a lively discussion with one of his many acquaintances. This does not surprise anyone.

In a country in which the main social rule is 'act normal, and you will be acting crazy enough', this type of behavior is greatly appreciated. Grandstanding is generally frowned upon. Even when Willem-Alexander's inauguration was approaching, the Prime Minister immediately declared that we were going to have a great, albeit *sober*, party.

'Sober' has become a key issue in Dutch politics. Former State Secretary Teeven of Justice wants to make the jail facilities more 'sober'. His colleague Jetta Klijnsma, of Social Affairs, wants to cut down on a number of benefits, such as the one for widows. These are tough times, which means there is not enough money to fund generous provisions. An important characteristic of the Dutch word 'sober' is that it has a certain element of 'precisely enough'. Anything more would constitute unnecessary luxury.

Already in 1991 the founders of the euro – including the Netherlands – agreed that they would not tolerate a government budget deficit that exceeded 3% and that the ultimate goal would be a budget surplus. This would allow them to shore up the value of the new currency.

And that is what is making things difficult now. Until the 2008 credit crisis, the budgets of the European countries appeared reasonably solid. However, rescuing the banks cost so many billions of euros that the deficits shot up. Plus there was the reduction in tax revenues due to the shrinking economy.

Yet the European governments are holding on to the 3%-principle. In this respect, Germany and the Netherlands have been the strictest and the firmest these past years. Whenever a country started floundering, the EU was willing to help avoid immediate bankruptcy by means of billion-euro loans (not gifts), under the condition of severe cut-backs in government expenditures – even if this impacted the economy in steps of full percentages.

Consequently, the rich countries of the north could not morally afford to disregard the 3%-rule – which proved a problem for the Netherlands as it was having trouble keeping its budget within these limitations.

In October 2010, Mark Rutte's first cabinet took over at the helm. It was a coalition of the conservative-liberal VVD and the Christian Democrat CDA. As this coalition did not yet represent a parliamentary majority, Rutte entered into an agreement with Geert Wilders, the leader of the Party for Freedom (PVV) – which hates immigrants (particularly Muslims), the European Union, and what they refer to as 'the leftist elite'. In return for a number of concessions, Wilders promised not to trip up the cabinet. These concessions included a very strict immigration policy and cuts in what he calls the 'hobbies' of the leftist elite: art, culture and developmental aid. And the environment.

The Rutte cabinet expected to be able to keep the Netherlands under the 3%-limit by structurally cutting back € 18 billion of government expenditures. The citizens of the Netherlands felt this in their wallets when the health insurance deductible went up, the pensionable age was raised, etc. Also the arts suffered greatly – to the joy of the PVV.

However, in 2012, it became apparent that the state coffers were not filling quickly enough so that the deficit, instead of going down, went up to 4.5%. Rutte got together with Geert Wilders and Sybrand Buma (of the CDA) to negotiate a new series of cuts. Three weeks later, Wilders left the negotiating table in a huff.

Rutte tendered the resignation of his cabinet and new elections were scheduled for September 2012. In the interim, the Prime Minister reached an agreement with the progressive liberal D66, GroenLinks and the ChristenUnie in order to collect the € 12.4 billion necessary to stop the gap. This was achieved, among others, through an increase in taxes and a raising of the pensionable age.

The outcome of the September 2012 elections was a political landslide in favor of the VVD and the Social Democratic PvdA. Accompanied by loud applause, the second Rutte cabinet entered the political arena, made up of ministers supplied by these two parties.

The aim of this coalition of liberals and social democrats was to cut back € 18 billion in hopes of reaching that mythical 3%-limit. By March 2013, it became clear that these measures would not be enough to achieve this. Partly because the Minister of Finance, Dijsselbloem, had found himself forced to nationalize the SNS-bank in order to avoid a 'Cypriote' situation, but also because the Dutch economy was still shrinking. So they decided to cut back another € 4 billion – at the expense of facilities for the elderly, mortgage options, unemployment support and the widows' benefit.

THE POLITICAL PARTIES

The Dutch Lower House of Parliament is elected by proportional representation and currently there are 16 political parties in the Lower House. Traditionally, the three largest are the PvdA (or Labor Party), a social democratic party that has its roots in the trade union movement; the CDA (Christian Democrats), a merger of three confessional parties that bases its ideas on religious principles; and the VVD, a liberal party. However, as of the most recent election, the three largest parties are VVD, the PvdA, and instead of the CDA; the PVV and the SP.

As noted earlier, there are also several other parties, whose popularity waxes and wanes in accordance with the political climate in the country, and some of which last only a few years, while others have been around for decades. An example of the latter is the D66, a progressive liberal party that was founded in 1966 and which has fruitlessly been campaigning for the introduction of the district system and the election of mayors. Having gone from three to 12 seats between 2006 and now, it appears to have regained the confidence of the voters. The other smaller parties that can be found in Parliament are Groen Links, the fundamentalist protestant parties SGP and ChristenUnie, and the Partij voor de Dieren (PvdD, or Party for Animals).

This all goes very much against the grain of the Dutch tradition, which built an extensive welfare state during the second half of the 20th century. The motto used to be: "We take care of you, from the cradle to the grave". And they did. Parents received a Child Benefit. The unemployment benefit made sure that the loss of a job did not lead to immediate financial disaster. And the Disability Act paid out a benefit to all those who for health reasons were no longer able to work. And then there was the Exceptional Medical Expenses Act which ensured that the elderly did not have to worry about their exceptional expenses in connection with health care. This act has been abolished and has been replaced by one containing stricter rules.

In 2013, the impact of these plans started to become increasingly clear and the government's popularity reached an all-new low. The polls showed that, in particular, the PvdA's social-democrats were losing their support. The rightist-liberal VVD had already been known for its impatience with the country's status as a welfare state, but this attitude was costing the PvdA – the protector of the weak – its voters. In the polls, it saw itself reduced to 10 or 11 seats, while the VVD – though not terribly popular itself – still retained its 21 seats. The fact that the parties' constituents were serious became evident during the municipal and provincial elections held in 2015: the PvdA and the VVD were given a clobbering. At the same time, very few people went to the voting booth; increasingly, they seem to be tired of politics altogether – something that in the long term could prove a threat to democracy.

So the question arises as to whether the Dutch population will be willing to go along with the government's 'soberness' for very long. Will it tolerate the fact that both of Rutte's cabinets are using the financial crisis to convert the Netherlands from a country with protective (social) measures into a society in which individuals have to take responsibility for their own welfare, requiring them to make their own buffers to help them cope with the whims of mercy? This would require not only a new political mind-set, but a new social-cultural one as well.

These new economic measures have not only come under sharp criticism from the 'usual suspects' – leftist interest groups and unions – but also from the corporate world. In April 2013, the unions and the employee organizations came up with a wide 'social plan' – full of proposals on how to postpone or even foil the plans of the government by means of their own measures.

A first, it seemed as if the Cabinet had no choice but to reach an agreement with the social partners – the name given to the organizations of employers and employees in the Netherlands – but as time passed, the ministers became more adept at playing the Hague political game, and they found their allies. As mentioned earlier, the government has a generous majority in the Lower House, but not so in the Upper House; in order to attain a majority there, they had to reach an agreement with the opposition – at a price. The machinations surrounding the new pension plans was an excellent illustration of what happened if they failed to do this – relying instead on their ability to convince. The majority in the Upper House was so opposed to the plans that the Lower House chose to withdraw their proposal rather than suffer defeat. Instead, they entered into negotiations with the opposition and proved their willingness to make adjustments. Thanks to the support of the aforementioned 'favorite opposition parties' – D66, ChristenUnie and SGP – the Cabinet eluded the grip of the unions and employer organizations, and was also able to see its budget passed. This situation was almost identical to that of the first Rutte-Cabinet – only with a different 'favored' opposition.

Interestingly enough, these 'favorite opposition parties' seem immune to the current Cabinet's unpopularity; they are doing well in the polls and booked great – D66 even spectacular – success in the municipal and provincial elections of 2015.

THE SMALLER PARTIES

The SGP, which has had two or three seats in the Parliament since 1920, is part of national folklore. Its constituents are among the most orthodox protestants of the country; many of them still reject television and consider the taking out of insurance as an unlawful way of escaping God's hand. Until recently, the SGP also still rejected female suffrage. This past decade, the party and its principles have been under fire, as some of its views are considered inappropriately close to Muslim fundamentalism – a globally hot topic at the moment. Still, its members appear to be loosening up somewhat; recently its parliamentary members even appeared in political TV programs – something that until very recently would have been seen as akin to consorting with the devil.

GroenLinks started out as a merger of several parties that represented a combination of greens, pacifists and communists. Its popularity was at its highest in 1998, when it won 11 seats in the elections. Its focus is on environmental issues, and a just division of power, knowledge, property, labor and income and is best summarized as leftist-liberal. After the last elections, in 2012, it saw itself reduced to four parliamentary seats, though it is said that, were there to be elections this year (2016) it would obtain 16 seats.

The ChristenUnie was founded in 2000, and is a merger between

LEAN YEARS

2013 was a bad year. Unemployment went up and the economy continued its slump, causing critics to feel confirmed in their criticism. However, towards the end of the year, things started to improve; there was a slight upswing in the economy which continued on into the start of this year, while the Central Bureau of Statistics showed that the budget deficit had gone down to 1.8% – well below the 3%-limit set by the EU for its members. And not only that; even the housing market started to show recovery – causing politicians to carefully suggest that the worst of the crisis was over. In 2015, the signs were even more positive. The Netherlands profited from the growth that occurred most of Europe, strongly boosted by interest rates that were rapidly approaching 0% and had not been this low since the 16th century (!). Furthermore, the European Central Bank started stimulating the economy by, on a large scale, purchasing obligations. However, the money came into the hands of banks that did not appear eager to lend it to investors or companies. Still, the threat of deflation appeared to have been countered by the spring of last year. It was not hard for the Minister of Finance, Jeroen Dijsselbloem of the Social Democrats, to present budgets with a deficit easily under 3%. In the meantime, the stock markets went up. In April of that year, the Dutch AEX exceeded 500 points. This had not happened since 2007 and was a doubling of where it had been at its lowest point since the 2008 crisis. There were nonetheless plenty of people who were afraid that this was merely a new bubble, while the positive development did not much affect the number of jobs on the market.

Let's keep in mind what the Dutch would say: "One swallow does not a summer make". The fact that seven lean years have gone by does not mean that we are now entering seven fat years – though the Dutch politicians, with an eye on the upcoming elections in 2017, are certainly hinting that this might indeed the case.

key to the European Union. Wilders started a new, rightist, political party aimed at enticing Pim Fortuyn-voters (see further on), and his propaganda mainly focuses on his rejection of Islam; he wants to close the borders to newcomers, particularly those of Muslim conviction. He has since received so many threats, that he currently lives under strict personal protection. The party's other policies include a rejection of bureaucracy and a system of social provisions that does not show a lot of common sense. It is still quite successful, however. In 2010 it won 23 seats, which were later reduced to 15 after it supported Rutte's unpopular cabinet – though polls show that it now stands at 37 seats if there were to be elections.

In 2012, a new party, 50 Plus, also managed to win two seats in the Dutch Parliament. Many of the older generation are furious about the lowering of the pensions and fear that they are the ones who are going to end up paying the price for the economic crisis.

To explain the term 'Pim Fortuyn-voters' (under PVV): in the 2002 elections, newcomer Pim Fortuyn's party – Pim Fortuyn himself was murdered by an environmental activist just days before the elections took place – emerged as the great victor with 26 seats. The LPF, as this party was called, booked a lot of success with its rightist-populist program, which greatly focused on traditional Dutch 'norms and values'. However, within just a few months, the party fell apart due to personal infighting. When new elections were held towards the end of 2002, the party was brought back to just eight seats, and no longer held any political clout. Now, the LPF is no longer represented in the Parliament at all. Political polls show that the voters have indeed turned towards Geert Wilders.

The number of parties in the current Second Chamber has risen to 16, due to the fact several rebel members of parliament have left (or been forced to leave) their original parties and start a new one. Which is permitted in the Netherlands. A notable example of this is Geert Wilders' PVV, but also the VVD and the PvdA have lost a few members this way.

FORMING A CABINET

Because there are so many political parties in the Netherlands, there are numerous coalition possibilities. Consequently, several months generally pass after the elections, during which, after extensive deliberation, a cabinet is formed with a program to which the majority of the members of Parliament can give their approval. In the meantime, the Prime Minister tenders the resignation of the entire cabinet – which the King 'answers' by requesting the cabinet to stay on until there is a new one.

Does this mean that the Netherlands does not have a government in the interim? Of course not. After the cabinet's resignation, the incumbent ministers continue to run the country – until the new cabinet is formed. However, decisions that might lead to extensive discussions in Parliament are delayed until the new cabinet is in power.

Any policies that the Parliament approved before the elections are continued, but this seldom gives rise to any problems. In fact, it has often happened that the government that was on the way out approved a new budget, though more often than not this has proved to be a colorless document, meant to be 'colored in' when the 'real' cabinet then entered into power. (The entering into power of the new cabinet, incidentally, happens from one day to the next, making it seem as if the 'old' ministers have but a morning to clear out their desks.)

two religious parties. It wants to balance the tendency towards materialism and individualism, by focusing on a joint responsibility within society for each other.

The Netherlands is the only country in the world with a Party for the Animals; Partij voor de Dieren. The party has two seats in the government and its two parliamentary members focus on supporting animal rights, fighting the inhumane treatment of animals in the bio-industry, and creating an ecologically-based policy. They are professional politicians who are taken seriously by their colleagues and who have ensured that animal well-being is a recognized action item for the Dutch government.

The Party for Freedom (PVV) revolves around the dissident VVD-member of Parliament Geert Wilders, who, at the start of 2004, was forced to leave his party when he refused to accept his party's policy on non-Dutch nationals and their support for the admission of Tur-

THE THREE LEVELS OF GOVERNMENT

The Netherlands not only has a central government, but also provincial and municipal governments and the water boards. The central government occupies itself with matters of national interest. The provincial governments concern themselves with social work, cultural affairs, environmental management, spatial planning, energy and sports. The municipal governments occupy themselves with traffic, housing, social services, health care, sports, culture, the water supply, public schooling and recreation. In order to help fund these activities, the provinces and municipalities receive government funding and levy their own local taxes. You can read more about the local taxes that may affect you on page 96. The last elections for the water boards took place this year, at the same time as the elections for the Provincial States – they yielded no major shifts.

VOTING AND STANDING FOR ELECTION AS A NON DUTCH NATIONAL

Voting

If you are an EU citizen, you are allowed to vote in municipal elections under the same conditions as Dutch nationals. This means that you must be at least 18 years of age on the day of the election and you must be a resident of a particular municipality on the day on which the candidates are nominated. If you are a non-EU national, you may vote under the same conditions; however, you must also have been a legal resident of the Netherlands for a continuous period of at least five years. To vote for the water boards, you must be living in a 'watership', at least 18 years of age, and have Dutch/ EU nationality or – if you are of another nationality – be a legal resident of the Netherlands. Only those of Dutch nationality may vote in the Provincial States-elections. For more information on whether you can be considered a legal resident for voting purposes, you can call the Ministry of Home Affairs (see the end of the chapter).

If you are a member of consular or diplomatic staff, you are not allowed to vote in the Netherlands, nor is your spouse/partner or children (if they are members of your household).

If you are an EU citizen, and a resident of the Netherlands, you are allowed to vote in elections for the *European Parliament* provided you do not vote in the same election in your home country, are 18 years of age or older, and are not disqualified from voting in the Netherlands or your home country.

Only Dutch nationals may vote in elections for the Second Chamber of the Parliament (the members of the First Parliament are elected by the members of the Provincial States) and the Provincial States.

Standing for Election

You can stand for election to municipal councils under the same conditions as stated above for voting. The only difference is that you must satisfy these conditions not on the day of nomination, but on the day you are admitted to the municipal council. You can also stand for election in Dutch elections to the European Parliament, provided you do not stand for election elsewhere.

Only Dutch nationals may stand for election for the First and Second Chamber of the Parliament, as well as for the Provincial States.

A NEW PHENOMENON: THE REFERENDUM

Towards the end of the 18th century, when the Netherlands was still under the influence of the French Revolution, a number of referendums were held in order to approve the constitution. They soon proved impractical, however, and that was that. Generally speaking, the Dutch politicians were not great fans of referendums. They believed in the system of representatives of the people, who – without having to refer to their constituents – made their decisions, based on their conscience, common sense and the direction indicated by these same constituents. Referendums and plebiscites were seen as the instruments of demagogues. The fact that Switzerland was showing differently failed to convince them otherwise; the exception, to them, just proved the rule.

During the '60s of the previous century, this conviction became less solid. The new party for young innovative liberals – D66 – gave referendums a prominent position in their program, which reintroduced the concept of plebiscite on the agenda. Yet it would take another half a century for the legislative bodies to do something with the idea. Also the populists that surrounded Geert Wilders and the PVV applauded the idea of a referendum that would give the common people a chance to give 'the elite' the finger. Slowly but surely, the phenomenon gained momentum and in 2005, the government – more or less as an experiment – organized a referendum on the so-called European constitution, a somewhat foggy name for an extensive treaty that gave expression to the ideas behind the European Union. The call for the referendum was heeded by 63.3% of the population, 61.6% of whom expressed their disapproval. Prime Minister Balkenende somberly announced that the outcome would be respected. After which the Netherlands signed the Treaty of Lisbon, which replaced the European constitution, but was awfully similar. This caused quite some bitterness among the naysayers. The pressure among the people to make the referendum a fixed part of the Dutch political process became stronger.

Of all the political parties, the conservative VVD continued to take a strong stand against referendums. In the 'factory' of the poldermodel, the issue of the referendum was mixed, mangled and reshaped into something with – so hoped, without a doubt, many supporters in the Lower House – unsurmountable barriers. For starters, they were to be advisory in nature, allowing politicians to merely consider them advice to change their course. Referendums would therefore only be allowed regarding laws or treaties that parliament had already passed. There were a few exceptions to this, the most important ones being: changes to the constitution, to tax legislation and regarding the form of state. A plebiscite regarding the monarchy would be unlawful, as would be multiple referendums regarding the same topic. Anyone who wanted to request a referendum had to follow two steps. First, they had to submit an introductory request with the government, accompanied by 10,000 signatures. Then they would have to be able to submit at least 300,000 additional signatures – all on paper and to be handed in to the Electoral Council. This law entered into force towards the end of 2014. A referendum would only be taken into account if more than 30% of the voters voted. And the consequences? The government would have to reconsider the issue in parliament. They could even try to have the parliament reapprove the original proposal. After all, the referendum was to be considered advisory only, and not 'corrective'.

Expectations were very modest.

Until a populist/rightist website found a way to legally collect the necessary signatures for the introductory request and the subsequent 300,000 additional signatures online, and to print them out in one go, after which the paperwork could be submitted to the Electoral Council. Together with two groups of rightist intellectuals, GeenStijl chose a topic that would bring the government maximum embarrassment and that could exploit any skepticism

ECONOMY

The Netherlands is in the world's top ten in export volume and ranks in the world's top twenty for GNP, even though, in terms of square kilometers, it is one of the smallest countries in the world. Though it is true that, in population density, it is on a par with countries such as India and Japan, nonetheless this only amounts to a population of 17 million.

GATEWAY TO EUROPE
The Netherlands owes its favorable ranking, among others, to its advanced transportation infrastructure, with, at its hub, both the port of Rotterdam (fourth largest seaport in the world in terms of container activity) and Schiphol Airport (the fourth largest airport in Europe). Also the country's advanced telecom infrastructure and its extensive (hi-speed) railway network help support the Netherlands' position as 'the gateway to Europe'.

Traditionally, the Netherlands has been a country that other countries are eager to invest in, which has been reflected by the huge investments made in the Dutch economy and Dutch companies over the years. This willingness to invest in the Dutch economy is largely due to the country's stable and flexible work environment (thanks to the Poldermodel), its central geographic location, its well-educated multilingual work force and the amount of know-how available here.

Individuals, often enticed while traveling here to stay and find a job, are as motivated as companies are to settle in the Netherlands, particularly since the opening of the frontiers within the European Union. The Dutch government, recognizing the value of top-notch specialists who contribute to the knowledge pool and economy of the Netherlands, has also introduced a number of tax measures aimed at making it more attractive for non-Dutch nationals to come and work here (you can read more about this in chapter 5). Also the bureaucratic red tape has been simplified, reducing the number of hoops employers and employees have to jump through to obtain the necessary papers.

regarding the European Union. The government was about to ratify a treaty of association with Ukraine, after a successful parliamentary debate on the topic. So these groups requested a referendum. They 'informed' the people about the threat posed by the Brussels juggernaut and claimed – entirely incorrectly – that this treaty represented a first step towards full membership of the European Union, allowing millions of Ukrainians to eat out of the Western European trough. This way, they easily collected the initial 10,000 signatures, followed by an additional 450,000. The referendum became inevitable.

During the months preceding the referendum, most politicians – except for those of the rightist/populist PVV, the leftist/ socialist SP, and the Party for the Animals – supported a "yes", albeit by means of rather meek propaganda. At the same time, they declared – as did Prime Minster Rutte – that the outcome would be honored. This was seen as a promise that the advice of the people would be heeded.

Opinion polls indicated that it was unsure whether the required 30% of voters would show up. Many yes-voters and people who were not great supporters of the referendum decided to stay home despite repeated requests from the politicians not to do so. They felt that the politicians who were in favor of the treaty could hardly openly encourage people to stay home, but that, in their heart of hearts, these politicians secretly hoped that it would all blow over.

It did not. The electoral threshold was met – just barely – and more than 61% voted 'no'. This put the government in a difficult position. All the European countries, with the exception of the Netherlands, had already ratified the treaty. Two million people had voted against it – but there are more than half a billion EU residents. Formally, the Netherlands could choose *not* to ratify the treaty of association, as a consequence of which, formally, it would no longer be an option. Put mildly, this would 'surprise' the other EU member states who might be disinclined to support the Netherlands should it require their support for something of economic importance to the country in the future. Furthermore, and this is only human, the voters had publicly embarrassed the Prime Minister and his Cabinet. Any time they showed up at one of the many European Ministerial Councils – the place where real decisions are made – they would be tainted by the stain of this 'no'. Contrary to what most people think, the important decisions are made by the Ministerial Councils and not the European Parliament or the European Commission.

The simplest solution would have been to ignore the outcome of this advisory referendum, but the politicians had already closed the door to this option themselves. Prime Minister Rutte therefore opted for another approach. He attempted to qualify the voters' 'no', trying to explain what lay at the root of their decision, and what their objections were. If these objections could be dealt with, then perhaps the treaty could be ratified with a few minor changes. Thus the 'no' was converted into a 'no, unless'. Some politicians pointed to the modest turnout and stated that the opinion of those who had stayed home should also be taken into account. This is a prime example of the Dutch poldermodel and policy of compromise. It is quite similar to how the thorny issue of the European constitution had been dealt with. Also then, they claimed that the naysayers had been satisfied by the (rather comparable) Treaty of Lisbon, in which, for example, the article on the European anthem – Beethoven's famous *All Men Shall Be Brothers* – could no longer be found.

All in all, this does not foster a general faith in politics. The groups behind this referendum have stated that they have acquired a taste for more, while the goings-on surrounding this first referendum gave the outcome far more weight than had been legislatively intended. And now local initiatives for referendums are popping up left and right.

RANDSTAD

After Paris, London and Milan, the Randstad (the area including, and between, Amsterdam, The Hague, Rotterdam and Utrecht) is the largest economic urban area in the EU, measured in terms of gross domestic product. This is largely due to the strong presence of financial and commercial services; which happens to be one of the motors of Dutch economy.

SECTORS

Though the economy of the Netherlands is relatively resilient, it is nonetheless dependent – as a country of trade, which accounts for 60% of the country's GNP – on the economy of the rest of the world. It might not drop as quickly as the overall economy, but it will not bounce back as quickly either, due to the relatively high costs of labor (wages and pension premiums). The most important trade commodities for the Netherlands are machinery and transportation equipment, followed by chemical and mineral products.

As the 'gateway to Europe', the Netherlands' most dominant sector is the services sector, accounting for approximately two-thirds of both its GNP and its work force. Another dominant sector is that of mineral extraction, particularly the production of natural gas. Other sectors that consistently contribute to the Dutch economy are the restaurant, trade, and repair services sector, and the health care and related services sector. A final important sector is the agricultural and food sector; it generates approximately 10% of the GNP; 75% of the agricultural produce is exported.

The Dutch economy benefits greatly from the fact that the world's largest chemical companies are based here, while the Netherlands is one of Europe's largest suppliers of high-tech goods for both the industrial and the consumer market. As mentioned earlier, this country is also Europe's largest producer of natural gas, as witnessed by its reserves in the north of the country, while Rotterdam imports and refines huge amounts of crude oil that is shipped to the rest of western Europe. Thanks to these offshore installations and refineries, the Netherlands has many activities in the oil and gas industries, including a strong research and development technology and a specialized construction industry.

A little aside: in confirmation of the country's reputation as the nation of tulips, the Netherlands exports 4 billion flower bulbs a year, mostly tulips. 60% of these go to Germany, the UK, France and Japan, though the U.S. is their top destination, with 900 million bulbs making their way across the Atlantic.

WELFARE

All in all, this makes the Netherlands a wealthy country, with a high per capita GDP boosted by social security measures guaranteeing a minimum income, health care and education.

THE YEAR 2015

At 2%, the growth of the Dutch economy over 2015 was twice that of 2014, and exceeded that of the Eurozone (1.6%). Had it not been for the fact that, due to earthquake problems, the government decided to cut back on the extraction of gas in Groningen and to import more, the economy would have grown by 2.4%. While the reduction in the production of gas constituted a considerable setback for the government coffers, its debt as well as its deficit went down – though some wonder how much the low interest rates have contributed to creating this situation/illusion. (Another important consequence of the reduction of the production of gas is the increased use of coal in the production of electricity, increasing the country's CO_2-output, which is in conflict with the plans articulated by the Paris summit in 2015).

Still, there are a number of observations that have been made surrounding this improvement in the Dutch economy. For one, there are still 600,000 unemployed persons (614,000 on average over 2015, or 6.9%, down from 7.4%). Though there are more people working, they occupy temp positions, while there is a significant increase in self-employed positions. This means that jobs are being filled by flexible workers and self-employed persons rather that full-time employees. All with the accompanying possible impact on household consumption and pension build-up. Even without this factor, pension providers are facing tough choices: due to the historically low interest rate they are forced to increase their reserves – and to possibly increase premiums or decrease pension payments; which could once again influence household consumption. All in all, not quite a stable situation yet.

Furthermore, the sharp reduction in the oil price, causing a reduction in the price of fossil fuels and products whose price is largely dictated by energy prices, has caused a reduction in inflation, while also other products are experiencing a price reduction. Though, as yet, there does not appear to be a downward wage-price spiral, the question arises as to whether this will nonetheless lead to postponement of expenditures and constitute a threat to the economy.

The 2015 growth of the Dutch economy was largely due to investments (10.3%), domestic consumption (1.5%: appliances, home decoration, clothing, going out, recreation and cultural activities) and government consumption (just a small fraction). Where did the investments go? Particularly to housing market and the automobile industry: as the BPM for cars (Vehicle Tax) was due to rise by January 1, 2016, people and companies decided to buy their car before that date, as well as trucks, trailers, etc. Further investments were made in machines and telecommunica-

tion. As for the housing market, the construction of new houses, as well as the increased purchase of existing houses – and the related desire to fix 'm up – has given the construction market a boost. And not only the construction market; anything related to interior decorating - DIY, furniture, kitchens, bathrooms and, last but not least, gardens - is along for the ride.

As for sectors: since 2013, the construction, commercial services and industry sectors have shown a clear upswing; agriculture, forestry and fishery showed a slight decrease since 2014, while mineral extraction has experienced a significant downturn.

Though exports increased over 2015, the positive effect of exports (+5.3%) was countered by the negative effect of imports (+6.4%). Particularly the decreased production of natural gas and the related necessity to import more (in order, among others, to meet supply obligations abroad) was a contributing factor. Another factor was the increased need to import investment and consumption goods in order to meet the local demand for more of these, and an 11%-increase in the import of services – particularly business services. Exports experienced a growth particularly in services (+12.3%), while that of goods only experienced a growth of 3.4% – with re-exports exceeding the export of locally-produced goods. Exports to Russia suffered the most – in large part due to the boycott in connection with the situation in Ukraine, but also to a decrease in the export of machines, trailers and tractors. Despite China's decrease in economic growth, exports to the country increased by 9%, while exports to Belgium, Germany and the U.K. increased (by 7%, 2% and 6% respectively), and exports to the U.S. decreased by 4%.

While the government found itself struggling to meet the European norm for government deficits over 3% of the gross national product between 2009 and 2012, it managed to reduce it to 1.8% over 2015, down from 2.4% over 2014 – so it appears to be getting this under control. This was largely due to an increase in tax revenue, thanks to the improved economy, in combination with an increase in tax rates – enough to compensate for the decrease in natural gas-generated income and the lower fossil fuel prices. Also the listing of the ABN AMRO on the stock exchange in November and the sales of interest rate derivatives helped pull the Dutch government out of its struggles.

The real disposable income of households went up by 2.1% over 2015 – an increase this nation had not seen since 2001 and one that is thanks to an increase in employee wages (collective labor wages went up by 1.4%) as well as in number of employees / self-employed persons (up by 73,000). Also the amount represented by household savings, pensions and stocks went up over 2015, despite negative stock market fluctuations in the second and third quarters. As 16% more houses were sold over 2015 (ranging from 7% in Zeeland to almost 20% in South Holland), at an average price increase of 2.9% (from 0.4% in Zeeland to 5.3% in North Holland, particularly Amsterdam – bringing the prices there almost back up to those of 2008), this means that total mortgage debts increased over 2015 by € 4 billion.

Over the past years, more companies have been started than terminated, bringing the number of companies from 1.1 million in 2008 to 1.5 million now, whereby 77% (!) are one-person operations. Twelve thousand of the newly founded companies in 2015 offer management consultancy, while there are 8,000 new web shops. Of the companies that ceased to exist, 7,000 were in management consultancy and 5,000 were web shops, too. Not all of these are due to bankruptcy; the number of bankruptcies was 21% lower than the preceding year and the lowest in seven years. Only 12.2% of these bankruptcies took place among sole proprietors. Most bankruptcies were in trade – wholesale, retail and the automobile trade – followed by financial services.

The number of jobs in employment went up by 76,000 to 7.8 million in 2015, while the number of jobs in self-employment went up by 33,000 to 2.1 million – amounting to a total of approximately 9.9 million jobs for 8.8 million people. Especially in the hotel and restaurant business, trade and temp jobs, the increase was felt. A decrease was notable in the health care sector and, until the fourth quarter, the construction sector. Forty-nine percent of employees work part-time, 51% full-time, of which 74% of men and 25% of women.

It looks like the Dutch economy is climbing out the valley, along with many – but unfortunately not all! – other countries. Let's keep our fingers crossed for the worldwide economy.

CLIMATE

BORING!

Unfortunately, the Netherlands simply does not have the most exciting of climates. Granted, there are magnificent winter and glorious summer days but, sadly, not very many. This can be very hard to take for those who have not grown up here (and even for those who have!). Many expats comment on how the gray and dreary skies and constant rainfall make it all that much harder to be motivated to get out of bed in the morning and that the only thing that makes it even harder in the winter is that the sun comes up so late. So, what are the facts and how do you get through this?

WINTER

Let's take December. During the last three decades of the 20th century, the average temperature during the month of December was 4° C – hardly North Pole conditions. The last very cold December days of that century were in 1995, when the average temperature was -0.9° C (also not very shocking). Of course, when it does decide

to dip below zero, it goes way down below: in the winter of 2001-02 and the next, the temperature somewhere in Groningen did go down to a frigid -17° C...

And how about January? January is known as the month of ice – but does it deserve this name? Not according to the Dutch Weather Institute (KNMI); only the occasional January has been good and cold – notably in 1996 and 1997, giving the Netherlands its last Elfstedentocht (11-town ice-skating tour that only takes place when the water freezes over on all the lakes and canals in Friesland solidly enough to support thousands of ice-skaters and spectators).

In fact, it can be concluded that Dutch winters have been heating up over the course of the 20th century. This is blamed on the uncommon strength of the western winds, which allow the warm temperatures of the seas (7° C) to influence the winter temperature, rather than the winds that come in from the north-east. Unfortunately, this also means more precipitation, which, in combination with mild winters, amounts to an awful lot of rain. Hence the dreary, bleak, rainy, wimpy winters.

SUMMERS

And the summers? The Netherlands is known for its wishy-washy summers in two senses; warm and dry one year, cool and wet the next – or warm and dry this *week*, cool and wet the next. Whether or not you can pack up your tent and enjoy the local vacation spots depends entirely on your luck. A note: though cool and wet summers immediately spark the global climate change discussion, Dutch summers have been this way since before the Middle Ages, the KNMI (Dutch Meteorological Institute) assures us.

On a positive note; 2003's summer was so sunny that it broke all records since 1901, while 2005 is on a shared fifth place on this list! Also the '90s saw a couple of record-breaking, top-of-the-list summers, while, in fact, during the 21st century so far, the average annual temperature has exceeded the 300-year history of the Dutch weather institute's recordings, so let's enjoy this upswing while it lasts ...

SURVIVING

So, how do you survive? Step one is to simply accept the facts, rather than fight them or hope for anything else. As for the summers,

you simply make a choice: either you go find a place where the sun is guaranteed to shine (home?) or you decide you want to see more of the country and will take the weather as it comes. As for the winters; December is easy. This is the month of lights and candles for the holiday season – and they will presumably brighten your spirits considerably. And January, February and March? If you are not off skiing or vacationing, this is a good time to light the fire in the fireplace (if you have one) and settle down for some good reading. Get together often with friends, eat good hearty meals, turn on all the lights, and splash a bit of color on your walls to liven things up. In short, go in search of, or create some of your own, *gezelligheid*. (For things to do with kids, check out chapter 8). And spend a lot of time by the window. Though this will unfortunately expose you to the gray winter skies, it will also expose you to whatever sunlight there is to be had – an absolutely necessary ingredient in combating the winter blues.

And whenever the sun comes out: go for it!

2015

Once again, we experienced a year that that ended up in the top-ten of 'good' ones since 1901, thanks largely not so much to a warm summer as to an exceptionally mild November and December. The year also started out quite mild; with friendly temperatures in January and February – but followed by a cool spring. Summer was pretty ordinary – with the exception of a sweltering heat wave from June 30 to July 5. Imagine the luck of the DIY-chain that – having been tipped by the weather gods in advance as to what was in store – purchased air conditioners in bulk and offered them at attractive prices just at the start of six-day heat blast. In all of the Netherlands, nary an air conditioner could be found in the stores halfway this period. April, May, June, July and August proved to be quite sunny, and were followed by a cold start to the fall season. Despite this cold start, the fall proceeded to become quite mild and December became the mildest December month since 1706. Whether or not you experienced 2015 as a wet year, depended on where you lived: the Veluwe (in the eastern part of the country) welcomed a lot of rain, while in the south-east the year qualified as a dry one.

And now, our usual overview of numbers:
- 0 day of ice (maximum temperature < 0° C) (0 in 2014; normal: 8)
- 40 days of frost (minimum temperature < 0° C) (27 in 2014; normal: 58)
- 69 warm days (maximum temperature > 20° C) (110 in 2014; normal: 85)
- 29 summer days (maximum temperature > 25° C) (23 in 2014; normal: 26)
- 5 tropical days (maximum temperature > 30° C) (2 in 2014; normal: 4)

RELIGION

Although modern Dutch society is very secular, and not many Dutch people identify with an organized religion, you will see plenty of churches and other places of worship, and you will have plenty of opportunity to practice your own religion if you wish.

THE CHURCHES YOU SEE

Before the Protestant Reformation, most Dutch people were Roman Catholics. Churches were built as Catholic churches; full of altars, images and decoration.

The religious reforms of the 16th century took place in the Low Countries against a background of resistance against Spanish domination. The Spanish were militant Catholics, and their persecution of Protestant 'heretics' sharpened the economic and political conflict. It also sharpened the fury with which the Dutch reformers stripped their churches of all the trappings of the Catholic Church. All statues and decorations were removed, and altars were either removed or replaced by burial monuments for leading citizens. Only the pulpits were left standing. These more sober and democratically furnished interiors suited the beliefs of the Calvinists better. Today most of the churches built before the Reformation are still Protestant and sober, having been stripped of their Catholic 'frills'. Only in the southern provinces, where Catholics accounted for a larger percentage of the population, did they suc-

ceed in regaining control of the old churches.

The people who remained Catholic after the Protestant Reformation were never systematically persecuted in the Netherlands, but they were discriminated against and hindered in the practice of their religion. For centuries they kept a low profile, getting together for services in hidden, or semi-hidden churches. They were called Papists (*Papen*), and even today you see traces of their neighborhoods reflected in the names of streets and towns. Only in the middle of the 19th century, with the start of the industrial revolution, did the Catholics have enough confidence and resources to start building their own large churches again. Most of these were built in neo-Gothic style. Their newer-looking, machine-made bricks distinguish them from the older churches.

Except for Maastricht and other cities in the south, nearly all large churches you see in Dutch city centers fall into one of these two categories: Protestant and dating from between the 13th and 16th centuries, or Catholic and dating from the 19th century. Churches that date from the 17th, 18th or 20th centuries were usually built on a modest scale.

DUTCH DENOMINATIONS

The southern provinces of Brabant and Limburg are predominantly Catholic, and the other provinces are predominantly Protestant. Of the Dutch people who nowadays claim church affiliation, only about 5% of the population attends services regularly, and though there are more registered members of the Roman Catholic Church (4.2 million) than of the Protestant Church (1.7 million), only 6.3% of the Catholics go to church regularly, while 22% of the Protestants do.

PROTESTANTS

At the time of the Reformation, some Dutch Protestants followed the teachings of Martin Luther, but most followed the more radical John Calvin, of France. The main feature of Calvinism, in addition to its sobriety, was its belief in predestination – the belief that some people are destined for a place in heaven and others are not. These ideas have evolved, and different streams and communities have developed throughout the years.

The two main categories of Protestantism in the Netherlands today are *Nederlands Hervormd* (Dutch Reformed) and *Gereformeerd* (Reformed). But there are other groups as well – Evangelical, Lutheran, Baptist, Apostolic, Pentecostal and many more.

CATHOLICS

In the 1960s and 1970s, the Dutch Catholic Church was extremely progressive. A series of conservative appointments by subsequent Popes has made it less so, but you can still find a full range of communities – at one end of the spectrum parishes still using the Latin liturgy, and at the other end parishes committed to the most modern ideas and practices. There are also Byzantine Catholic communities.

A little-known group is the so-called Old Catholics; in 1723 – in protest against the concentration of power in Rome – they 'broke' with the city by choosing their own bishop. When, in 1870, the infallibility of the Pope was announced, many Old Catholics and others of similar conviction came together and, in 1889, formed the Union of Utrecht. Currently, the Old Catholic Church has approximately 5,800 members in 26 parishes in the Netherlands, however, worldwide there are over 500,000 members.

PHILOSOPHICAL GROUPS

Instead of being members of churches, some people in the Netherlands belong to groups that share a particular philosophical outlook on life. There are of course many of these, but the main ones that are also known outside the Netherlands are: Anthroposophists, Humanists, New Age and the Sufi Movement.

ISLAM

With approximately 660,000 (practicing) Muslims living in the Netherlands (4.9 % of the population), Islam has become one of the country's main religions. Mosques have been built in most of the larger cities by communities of immigrants from Turkey, Morocco and Indonesia, and the Dutch public is gradually learning more about Islam – enough to make allowances for colleagues and pupils who are fasting for Ramadan, for example.

Though many believe that Islam is the fastest-growing religion in the Netherlands, that is not necessarily the case; the method of counting applied to the group of Muslims and the group of Christians is different. Only church-registered Christians are taken into account, versus all immigrants from Muslim-countries. If Christians (immigrants) were to be counted in the same manner, then this would prove to be the fastest-growing religious group. The prediction has been made that by the year 2020 Islam will be the second largest religion in the Netherlands, with 7% of the populace being Muslim, and only 10% Catholic. Looking at the numbers for 2013, however, with Roman Catholics making up 25% of the population, and Protestants 10.5%, it is hard to believe that these predictions will actually pan out. Perhaps the percentage of Muslims will equal the percentage of Protestants, but that will still leave the country with 35% registered Christians, while also among Muslims, second and third generation 'immigrants' are becoming more secularized.

JUDAISM

Before and during the Second World War, when Hitler's anti-Semitism took hold in Europe, many Jews came to the Netherlands. Aside from the fact that there already was a large Jewish community in the Netherlands, this country had remained neutral during the First World War, and more importantly, had (has) a centuries-long tradition of religious tolerance. The Jews hoped that these factors would allow them to find a safe haven here – but unfortunately the Netherlands was occupied during the war and could not be the safe haven they had hoped for. In fact, only 13% of the Jewish population of the Netherlands, which had been at 140,000, survived the Second World War. This has since grown to approximately to a sizeable Jewish community, of around 35,000 members, remains in the Netherlands, of which the center is in Amsterdam, though synagogues can also be found in other cities.

OTHER RELIGIONS

Other religious affiliations that have active communities in the Netherlands include Hinduism, Buddhism and Baha'i. For addresses, check the end of this chapter.

YOU CAN'T FIND A COMMUNITY THAT PRACTICES YOUR RELIGION?
Try contacting the Netherlands Center for Foreigners (NCB or *Nederlands Centrum voor Buitenlanders*) in Utrecht, Amsterdam, Rotterdam, Leiden or Tilburg (www.ncbnet.nl).

SOME STATISTICS AND FACTS ON THE NETHERLANDS

- The total land surface area is 33,948 km²/21,218 mi². This excludes all inland and territorial waters wider than 6 meters/20 feet. If all the water surface area is included, the Netherlands has an area of 41,526 km²/ 25,954 mi²
- The Netherlands' North Sea coastline is longer (642 km) than its border with either Belgium (407 km) or Germany (556 km)
- About 60% of the population lives below sea level
- The highest point in the Netherlands is the Vaalserberg in the province of Limburg; is 321 meters/1,053 feet above sea level
- The lowest point in the country is 6.76 meters/ 22.18 feet below sea level.

- It is in the Prince Alexander Polder northeast of Rotterdam (Nieuwerkerk a/d IJssel)
- Head of State: King Willem-Alexander
- Type of state: constitutional monarchy
- Seat of government: The Hague
- Capital: Amsterdam
- Population: 17 million
- 'Non-Western' non-native Dutch: 2.1 million
- 'Western' non-native Dutch: 1.66 million
- Number of households: 7.67 million
- Average life expectancy men born now: 79.2 years, women: 82.9 years
- Average age: 40.1 (gradually increasing: in 1990, it was 36.6)
- Population growth: 79,000

- Number of marriages/registered partnerships: 78,002
- Number of gay marriages: 1,810
- Number of divorces: 35,946
- Healthy to very healthy: 80.3%
- Immigrants: 202,647
- Emigrants: 146,279
- Asylum-seekers: 47,764 (including 11,440 children)
- Countries of origin of asylum-seekers: mostly Syria (44%) and Iraq (9%)
- Labor force: 7.89 million
- Unemployment: 680,000 (6.9% of the labor force) (January 2016: 6.5%)
- Predicted unemployment 2016: 6.7%
- Unfit for work: 776,000
- No. of jobs: 10 million
- No. of self-employed persons: 1.2 million

- Inflation 2015: 0.6%
- Economic growth 2015: 2%
- Predicted economic growth 2016: 2.1%
- Budget deficit: 1.8%
- Gross National Product per capita: € 39,300
- Religion: 4 out of 10 persons profess to being religious
- Exports: +5.3%
- Imports: +6.4%
- Household consumption: +2.1%
- Consumer confidence: 6
- Most important trade partner: Germany
- Average income: € 35,500 gross
- Average price of a house: € 227,000

HOLLAND OR THE NETHERLANDS?

Now there's a good question: why is this country sometimes referred to as Holland and sometimes as the Netherlands? The official name of the country you have come to live in is the Netherlands, or 'Low Lands'; a country where 60% of the people live below sea level.

Then why is this country so often referred to as Holland? The answer to this question lies in its history. A few centuries ago, the province of Holland (which included today's North and South Holland provinces) was economically the strongest of all the Dutch provinces, and the one from which virtually all foreign trade originated. Most of the Dutchmen that foreign traders dealt with were Hollanders, literally from Holland. Hence, when talking about the Netherlands, this became the accepted way of referring to the country and its people. Over the years, both names have come to be accepted, although the official name, of course, remains the Netherlands.

SENSITIVITY

Though it is generally accepted that the Netherlands is referred to as Holland, those who are not from the provinces of North or South Holland do not like to be referred to as Hollanders, or to have their language referred to as *Hollands*. The other Dutch provinces are: Friesland, Groningen, Drenthe, Limburg, Utrecht, Gelderland, Overijssel, Noord-Brabant, Zeeland and Flevoland (the latter came into existence only 28 years ago and consists entirely of reclaimed land).

Holland in the Netherlands

RANDSTAD

Nowadays, it is of course – long since – no longer the case that the Holland provinces are the most advanced, though most businesses are still located in the provinces of North and South Holland and Utrecht – an area that is commonly referred to as the Randstad. The rest of the Netherlands is just as well-developed and houses many international businesses and expatriates, and the infrastructure (road, rail, water and telephone) is excellent, all across the country.

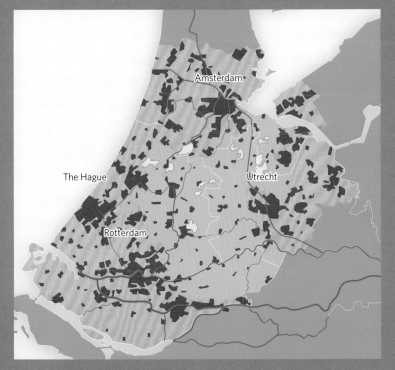

The Randstad

REFERENCES

THE NETHERLANDS – GENERAL

www.dutchnews.nl – English-language news from business and politics to sport. Plus features, opinion and debate

www.expatica.com – News and community portal for expats in Europe

www.holland.com – For useful and fun information on what's on in the Netherlands

www.iamexpat.nl – News, life style, housing, career and education in the Netherlands

www.xpat.nl – The information platform for expatriates in the Netherlands with an event calendar, news, and an archive of articles and books on the Netherlands

DUTCH GOVERNMENT

www.overheid.nl – access to the websites of the Dutch Government Departments and Ministries.

THE DUTCH ROYAL FAMILY

www.koninklijkhuis.nl/english

WEATHER INFORMATION

www.knmi.nl
www.weer.nl
www.weathernews.nl
www.buienradar.nl

DUTCH HISTORY

THE LOW SKY

By Han van der Horst
Published by Scriptum
The book that makes the Netherlands familiar. A detailed exploration of the reasons for desire of the Dutch for independence, their sense of respect and their business sense
www.scriptum.nl

LOGBOOK OF THE LOW COUNTRIES

by Wout van der Toorn
Published by Seaside Publishing
A handy and Informative book to make comparisons between the history of the Low Countries and the wider world.
www.seasidepublishing.com

RELIGION

AFRIKAANSE KERK (SOUTH AFRICAN CHURCH)

Gruttersdreef 106, 7328 DN Apeldoorn
Tel.: 055 543 18 93
www.afrikaansekerk.nl

ANGLICAN CHURCH – CHRIST CHURCH

Groenburgwal 42, 1011 HW Amsterdam
Tel.: 020 441 03 55
www.christchurch.nl

THE BAHA'I FAITH NATIONAL CENTRE

Riouwstraat 27, 2585 GR The Hague
Tel.: 070 517 80 24
www.bahai.nl

ENGLISH REFORMED CHURCH AMSTERDAM

Begijnhof 48, 1012 WV Amsterdam
Tel.: 020 624 96 65
www.ercadam.nl

ENGLISH AND AMERICAN EPISCOPAL CHURCH OF ST. JOHN & ST. PHILIP

Ary van der Spuyweg 1, 2585 JA The Hague
Tel.: 070 355 53 59
www.stjohn-stphilip.org

THE BLESSED TRINITY

Zaaiersweg 180, 1097 ST Amsterdam
Tel.: 020 465 27 11
www.blessedtrinity.nl

JEWISH COMMUNITY

Van der Boechhorststraat 26,
1081 BT Buitenveldert, Amsterdam
Tel.: 020 646 00 46
www.nihs.nl

AMERICAN PROTESTANT CHURCH

Esther de Boer van Rijklaan 20,
2597 TJ The Hague
Tel.: 070 324 44 90
www.apch.nl

CROSSROADS INTERNATIONAL CHURCH OF THE HAGUE
Bezuidenhoutseweg 249,
2594 AM The Hague
Tel.: 070 322 24 85
www.crossroadschurch.nl

ENGLISH SPEAKING CATHOLIC CHURCH OF THE HAGUE – CHURCH OF OUR SAVIOUR
Parish House
Ruygrocklaan 126, 2597 ES The Hague
Tel.: 070 328 08 16
St. Aloysius College
Oostduinlaan 50, 2596 JP The Hague
Tel.: 070 328 08 16
www.parish.nl

CHURCH OF CHRIST
De Gaarde 61, 2542 CH The Hague
Tel.: 070 329 73 80
www.gemeentevanchristus.nl/denhaag

LIBERAL JEWISH COMMUNITY OF THE HAGUE
Prinsessegracht 26, 2514 AP The Hague
Tel.: 070 365 68 93
www.ljgdenhaag.nl

BAPTIST COMMUNITY
Vier Heemskinderenstraat 91,
2531 CA The Hague
Tel.: 070 380 03 18

REFORMED COMMUNITY THE HAGUE
Diamanthorst 187, 2592 GD The Hague
Tel.: 070 385 87 07

TRINITY BAPTIST CHURCH
Bloemcamplaan 54, 2244 EE Wassenaar
Tel.: 070 517 80 24

TRINITY INTERNATIONAL CHURCH
Gruttolaan 23, 2261 ET Leidschendam
Tel.: 070 517 80 24
www.trinitychurch-nl.org

THE ENGLISH CHURCH OF ST. JAMES
Koninklijke Marinelaan 53, 2251 BA Voorschoten
Tel.: 071 561 15 28
www.stjames.nl

THE SCOTS INTERNATIONAL CHURCH ROTTERDAM
Schiedamsevest 121, 3021 BH Rotterdam
Tel.: 010 412 47 79
www.scotsintchurch.com

HOPE INTERNATIONAL BAPTIST CHURCH
Schiedamse Vest 121, 3021 BH Rotterdam
Tel.: 010 888 90 46
www.hope-baptist-church.com

ST. MARY'S ANGLICAN EPISCOPAL CHURCH OF ROTTERDAM
Pieter de Hoochweg 133, 3024 BG Rotterdam

Tel.: 010 476 40 43
www.stmarys.nl

HOLY TRINITY CHURCH
Van Hogendorpstraat 26, 3581 KE Utrecht
Tel.: 030 251 34 24
www.holytrinityutrecht.nl

TRINITY CHURCH EINDHOVEN
Pensionaat Eikenburg, Aalsterweg 289, 5644 RE Eindhoven
Tel.: 040 244 81 49
www.trinitychurcheindhoven.org

CHAPTER 2

Now that you have learned more about the history of this country and its political system and climate, you might be wondering about the people you are sharing this country with. What kind of people are the towering Dutch? What about their customs and etiquette, particular ways of celebrating holidays and special occasions, and their oh-so-challenging language? This chapter will help you navigate through some of the canals of these riddles. In the end, the effort you put into rowing through uncharted territory will matter more than which way the wind is blowing.

CONTRIBUTING AUTHORS STEPHANIE DIJKSTRA, ARNOLD ENKLAAR AND BEN VAN DER HAVE

CUSTOMS AND ETIQUETTE

Before you put your proverbial foot in your proverbial mouth, here are some lessons picked up at the school of hard knocks, where the price of tuition is a lot higher than learning it here.

PERSONAL SOCIAL SPACE

Dutch social space is determined in great part, it is deemed, by the lack of physical space that is available in Holland. Granted, everything and everyone *is* very close together: Holland has one of the highest average population densities in the world; 408 inhabitants per km².

Theory has it that the Dutch compensate for this lack of physical space by making their personal social space wider, so that they can better deal with the problems of living in such a crowded society.

Observe, for instance, the Dutch standing in line, if you can find one. They normally stand much closer together than Americans do. Americans tend to feel uncomfortable if you stand that close to them in line. American social connections, on the other hand, are much more intimate than Dutch social connections. While Americans interact with people with seeming informality and call everyone by his or her first name, Dutch interaction is generally stylized and formal. Calling a Dutch person by first name when you are not supposed to is like talking to an American with your nose three inches from his. You are invading his space and that makes him feel uncomfortable.

The extended Dutch social space is viewed by many foreigners as standoffishness, but to the Dutch it is just a way of coping with life in a shoebox. As long as you are polite enough to respect other people's social space, they will politely respect yours and tolerate almost anything you want to do – testimony to a nation dually praised and criticized for its tolerance – as long as you keep it inside your social and personal space and out of theirs.

GETTING A WORD IN EDGEWISE

Oddly enough, the amount of time that the Dutch pause at the end of a sentence to indicate that they have finished talking and that someone else can take a turn is a lot shorter than it is in English. Even when they speak English, the Dutch still use the same short 'change-speakers' pause to give others a chance to join the conversation. Until you get used to it, you may not get much said, because you may not recognize the shorter pause as a signal to say something, and thereby miss your turn, feeling like they're rudely cutting you off. The cue to change speakers is something that you normally perceive subconsciously, based on years of experience listening to other people talk. Just being aware that there is a difference between cultural modes is usually all you need to reset the length of time that you recognize as a change-speakers' cue, so that you can get a word in edgewise.

VISITING

Generally, the Dutch do not like company to stop by informally, if they just happen to be 'in the neighborhood'. If you know someone very well, you can call in the morning to ask if you can come by that evening, but normally you should call further in advance. The greater the social distance between you, the longer in advance you need to call. Grown children even call their parents – and vice versa – to see if it is all right to come by for a visit.

FASHIONABLY LATE

Conversely, do not invite Dutch acquaintances to 'drop by anytime'. Set a specific time and date, and specify what you intend to serve. 'Come by next Tuesday at two for coffee' and they will be there at the stroke of two. 'Fashionably late' in Holland is waiting for the bell on the tower clock to finish ringing before you ring the doorbell.

COFFEE

Since the Dutch do not like 'surprise' company, the coffee will be ready to pour when you arrive. Yours should be too. An offer of coffee (or tea) is the absolute minimum expected when someone visits your home. Even the workmen who come to fix a leaky faucet will be offered a cup of coffee. Suffice it to say that there will also be cookies, or, if this is a special occasion like a birthday or anniversary, pastries. ALWAYS WAIT TO BE SERVED. It's considered very impolite to help yourself. Conversely, do not forget to offer your Dutch guests a second round of coffee, tea, or cookies; they will not help themselves.

A couple we know, who speak no Dutch, went to visit friends in Holland and when they came back, they were proud to announce that they had learned the Dutch word for 'Hello'. *Koffie?* he said with no accent at all, and he was right. The first thing any Dutch host(ess) says when someone comes into the house is not 'Hello', but: '*Koffie?*' (Do you want a cup of coffee?).

HOSPITALITY GIFTS

A visit to someone's home invariably calls for a hospitality gift. Flowers, cookies, or candy are almost always appropriate. If you think that your host(ess) might be dieting or diabetic, take flowers. Flowers are quite inexpensive in Holland, as this is the world's largest flower exporter, and are a welcome present.

(Hint: buy flowers with the blooms still closed. Not only do they last longer, but fully open flowers have an aura of cheapness about them. The impression will either be that the florist took advantage

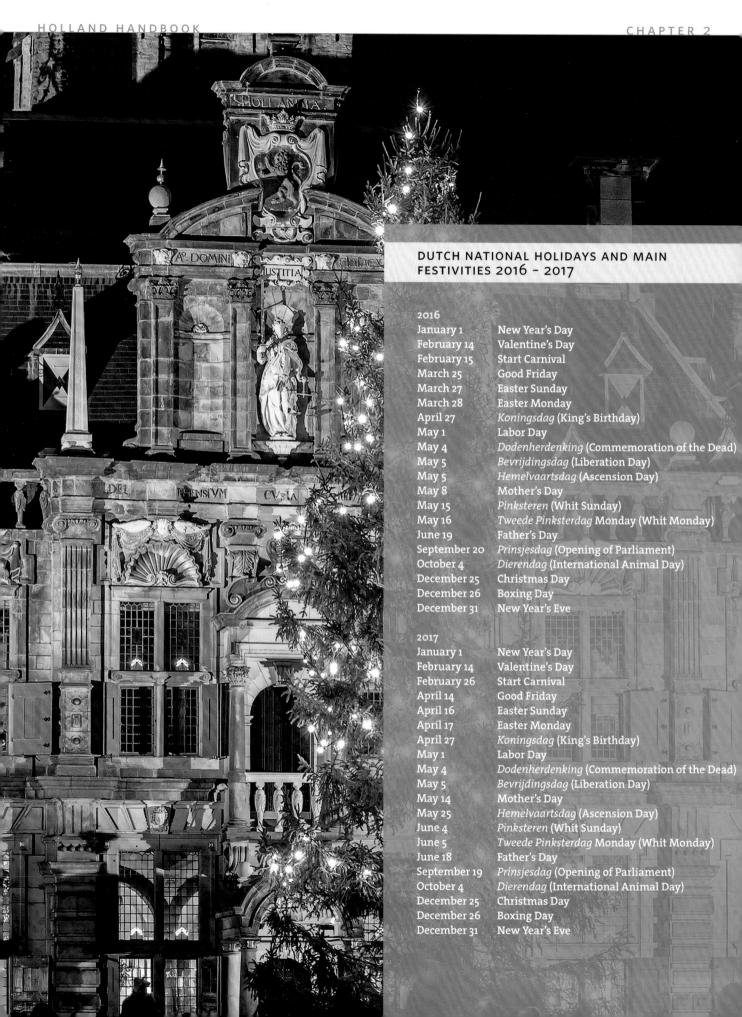

DUTCH NATIONAL HOLIDAYS AND MAIN FESTIVITIES 2016 – 2017

2016

January 1	New Year's Day
February 14	Valentine's Day
February 15	Start Carnival
March 25	Good Friday
March 27	Easter Sunday
March 28	Easter Monday
April 27	*Koningsdag* (King's Birthday)
May 1	Labor Day
May 4	*Dodenherdenking* (Commemoration of the Dead)
May 5	*Bevrijdingsdag* (Liberation Day)
May 5	*Hemelvaartsdag* (Ascension Day)
May 8	Mother's Day
May 15	*Pinksteren* (Whit Sunday)
May 16	*Tweede Pinksterdag* Monday (Whit Monday)
June 19	Father's Day
September 20	*Prinsjesdag* (Opening of Parliament)
October 4	*Dierendag* (International Animal Day)
December 25	Christmas Day
December 26	Boxing Day
December 31	New Year's Eve

2017

January 1	New Year's Day
February 14	Valentine's Day
February 26	Start Carnival
April 14	Good Friday
April 16	Easter Sunday
April 17	Easter Monday
April 27	*Koningsdag* (King's Birthday)
May 1	Labor Day
May 4	*Dodenherdenking* (Commemoration of the Dead)
May 5	*Bevrijdingsdag* (Liberation Day)
May 14	Mother's Day
May 25	*Hemelvaartsdag* (Ascension Day)
June 4	*Pinksteren* (Whit Sunday)
June 5	*Tweede Pinksterdag* Monday (Whit Monday)
June 18	Father's Day
September 19	*Prinsjesdag* (Opening of Parliament)
October 4	*Dierendag* (International Animal Day)
December 25	Christmas Day
December 26	Boxing Day
December 31	New Year's Eve

of your being a foreigner and palmed them off on you, or you took advantage of their lower price to skimp on your hospitality gift.)

KISSING

The arrival ritual for good friends and family members at a Dutch home catches many foreigners by surprise. Ladies enter first to a round of three – the number is significant – kisses on the cheek (right-left-right) with each person there. The men follow, shaking hands with the other men and fashionably kissing all the ladies lightly on the cheek three times (right-left-right). As a foreigner you can get by with shaking hands instead of kissing.

Stating your name – both first and last or just first or last name only – as you greet someone is considered basic protocol. Understanding the name that they've just told you is another matter.

SPECIAL OCCASIONS – THE DUTCH WAY

BIRTHDAYS

Nearly all Dutch people celebrate all of their birthdays with great enthusiasm. On that day they can usually expect family and friends to visit them at home, or to telephone or send a birthday card. It is considered rather anti-social for a person to ignore his or her own birthday (*verjaardag*). Contrary to American custom, for example, where the birthday celebrant is catered to, the Dutch celebrant plans and hosts the festivities, inviting and catering to friends and family, most often at home. The custom in the workplace is to bring pastries for colleagues at work to enjoy over coffee. Likewise, children bring treats to school for all their classmates.

Birthday calendars (*verjaardagkalenders*), which are usually hung prominently in the bathroom, help people keep track of the dates on which they have to pay visits or send cards. A word of advice: don't overlook a Dutch person's birthday; such forgetfulness borders on insolence.

Curiously, it is customary to congratulate not only the person whose birthday it is, but also his or her relatives, friends and even neighbors. To say 'Congratulations (*Gefeliciteerd!*) on the birthday of your brother-in-law' would be quite normal. By the same token, don't be caught off guard if someone congratulates *you* whenever it's your spouse's or child's birthday. You'll now understand what you did to deserve the kudos!

TURNING FIFTY: 'ABRAHAM AND SARA'

The 50th birthday is a milestone that the Dutch are particularly keen to celebrate. The person in question is then referred to as Abraham (for men) or Sara (for women), a tradition that originates from a reference to the Bible where Jesus is explaining that Abraham had 'seen' the day on which Jesus would become the Messiah. Skeptics thought he meant that he had actually 'met' Abraham and sarcastically said, 'Not yet 50 years of age, but already you have met Abraham!' Hence the tradition in the Netherlands that, when you reach the age of 50, you see Abraham or Sara. A life-size doll, with a big sign hung from its neck indicating one or the other constituent, is often placed in front of the celebrant's house. Unlike some cultures that tend to hide or bury the aging process, the Dutch seem uncharacteristically proud of reaching a ripe old age. In their view, the more years the merrier.

WEDDINGS

The pre-wedding custom of a bridal shower is one that supposedly originated in Holland. It is said that the daughter of a miller wanted to marry a man her father didn't approve of, and he wouldn't provide her with a dowry. The villagers took pity on the girl and 'showered' her with gifts, enabling her to marry the man of her choice. If this is true, however, it is certainly one custom that left the Netherlands along with settlers to the New World, as it definitely does not exist in the Netherlands of today.

Strangely enough, a church ceremony alone does not constitute a legal marriage here. A civil ceremony, often conducted in the town hall by a local official, is required for a couple to be legally married (see more on page 115). As such, a Dutch wedding could easily consist of both a civil and a church wedding in one day. Following the ceremony, the celebrations may take place in three parts: a *receptie*, *diner*, and a *feest* (reception, dinner and party). Unusual as it may seem, it is quite common to invite different people to different parts of the celebrations. Family and very close friends may be invited to everything, whilst colleagues and neighbors may be invited to the *receptie* only.

WEDDING ANNIVERSARIES

Though not always customary, the Dutch will at times succumb to the temptation to celebrate a wedding anniversary with a large group of friends and family, usually on the 12 1/2, 25th or 50th anniversary. In such cases, the appropriate gifts are typically flowers, wine or a joint gift given by a group of friends, colleagues or relatives. Often you are approached in a letter by one of the children or a family friend, inviting you to sing a song, give a speech or contribute to a joint gift.

BIRTHS

That pink or blue balloon-decked stork in your neighbor's garden means that a new baby boy or girl has arrived. Friends, colleagues and relatives, even those that the parents may have long since forgotten, call to make an appointment, no less, to come and admire the little darling, and bring along a gift – usually a toy or some item of clothing. Visitors are served tea or coffee and *beschuit met muisjes*; rusks or crisp-bread covered with sugared aniseeds (sweets resembling mice); pink for girls and blue for boys. (You can read more about this on page 190.)

GIFTS, CARDS AND PARTY ETIQUETTE

Dutch people routinely give each other gifts on various occasions. These include birthdays, visits to someone's home for a meal, and parties to celebrate weddings, anniversaries and graduations. Gifts are generally small and not lavish, unless they are for a family member. Bouquets of flowers, bottles of wine and boxes of chocolates are common gifts. In fact, a group of friends might even put their money together and buy what is considered a larger gift, such as a book or a CD.

A Dutch person generally presents a gift as soon as he sees the recipient, and the recipient generally opens the gift immediately. Not to do so would be considered impolite. Don't, however, expect effusive thanks, as the Dutch are not generally known for their ebullience. Over-enthusiasm can be viewed as pretentious behavior.

Greeting cards are sent on many occasions. In addition to birthday cards, there are cards of congratulations for events such as

passing exams, moving to a new home, and taking early retirement. Millions of postcards are also sold, and not just to tourists. While people on holiday send postcards to family and friends back home, many Dutch people also send them as thank-you cards after they have enjoyed a meal at a friend's home, for example.

DEATHS

When a member of the family passes away, the family sends out cards, usually with gray borders, announcing the death, and often place an obituary in the newspaper. When you hear about the death of a friend, or a dear one of a friend, it is greatly appreciated if you write a short note of condolence. If the friend is a close one, you can visit the family to pay your respects (do not do this unannounced) or give them a short phone call. The Dutch traditionally go to the funeral service (which is most often held in the funeral home and not in a church) and, depending on their close ties with the deceased, have a flower arrangement delivered by a florist, to be placed on the casket, to which a ribbon or card is attached with a few final words and the names of the sender(s). Sometimes, the announcement already states that the family does not wish to be disturbed before the funeral (*bezoek is niet gewenst* – we would prefer no visitors) or that the funeral will be held for only the immediate family (*de overledene wordt in besloten kring begraven*). Some families prefer that you donate money to a charity rather than give flowers, and the card will then suggest the charity of choice. After the funeral, a reception is held, where you will be given the opportunity to pay your condolences in person to the family.

TYPICAL DUTCH FESTIVITIES

CARNIVAL – FEBRUARY

Carnival, the Dutch either love it or hate it. Those who live *beneden de rivieren* (below the rivers, in other words in Noord-Brabant or Limburg) love it and celebrate it with a passion. Virtually all businesses close (except cafés and restaurants of course) in a three-day celebration of life, spring, beer and friendship, though in the province of Limburg there is an added element of poking fun at the government and politics. In the provinces *boven de rivieren* (above the rivers) the general attitude towards carnival is one of aloofness – adding to their reputation among the Southerners as a dour and 'un-fun' people – a gray dividing line that, some would say, smacks of a still Protestant-based north and a predominantly Catholic south.

Dutch carnival has the same origins as carnival in Rio (the period of excess preceding the period of self-deprivation of Lent) and is about as wild, though you must bear in mind of course, that it is celebrated by the 'cold-blooded' Dutch rather than the 'hot-blooded' Brazilians, not to mention the general difference in temperature at that time of year! People get dressed up and go from café to café, singing songs, participating in parades and consuming large quantities of beer. There is no need to be afraid of this being a local festivity at which strangers are not accepted: strangers are welcome, and it is a great way to meet new people. Breda, Maastricht and 's Hertogenbosch are three of the major venues.

APRIL 27: KING'S (BIRTH)DAY

Although not necessarily known to be royalists, the Dutch are extremely fond of their Royal Family. Throughout history, the Dutch Royal Family has been very popular and the Family's birthdays have been celebrated with enthusiasm. As of 1898, Queen Wilhelmina's 18th birthday, the holiday has been officially referred to as *koninginnedag* (literally Queen's Day). April 30th officially became *koninginnedag* when Queen Juliana changed the date to her own birthday. Queen Beatrix, whose birthday is actually on January 31st, left April 30th as the official day to celebrate her birthday as the weather would then (theoretically) be much better than at the end of January.

As of 2014, the King celebrates his birthday on April 27, but the festivities will remain the same – at least that's what we've been told.

You can celebrate the King's birthday either by visiting the town or city the King visits on this day – and witness traditional entertainment and games – or you can visit some of the bigger cities. Amsterdam, in particular, goes all out on this day, with a *vrijmarkt*, a free market that fills the streets in the center of Amsterdam with stands run by people age 5 – 105, selling anything and everything. People from all across the world come to Amsterdam (including an annual influx of gays from San Francisco hyped on the suggestive nomenclature of *Queens'* Birthday, as it used to be called until Queen Beatrix abdicated the throne) to enjoy this special atmosphere. Another option is to visit the traditional *koningsmarkt* (King's Market) of your own town, where the locals sell just

about anything for a song, a great opportunity for bargain hunters and antique buffs – but be there early for the best values (6 A.M.)!

COMMEMORATING THE DEAD: MAY 4TH

More a day of national significance than of festivity, May 4th is initially the day on which the Dutch remember those who died during the Second World War: soldiers, people in the Resistance and those who did not survive concentration camps in Europe as well as in Indonesia. Since 1961, it commemorates all war victims in the years since the start of the Second World War in general. Between 8 P.M. and 8:02 P.M., a two-minute silence is observed nationally. People stop whatever they are doing (often pulling their cars over to the side of the road) to reverently remember those who did not make it through the war. Even local radio and television broadcasts are halted. In many municipalities, people come together for short ceremonies, particularly in The Hague, on the Waalsdorpervlakte, and in Amsterdam, on the Dam Square. Flags are hung half-mast throughout the country.

LIBERATION DAY: MAY 5TH

Following the sober day of May 4th, the Dutch celebrate their total liberation from the occupying forces in 1945 (some parts of the Netherlands had been liberated in November 1944) on Liberation Day, May 5th. Flags are hung full-mast and the streets take on a festive look. Because commemorating the dead and celebrating liberation deserve individual and equal attention, they have been set on different days. Unfortunately, this memorable day is not celebrated as extensively as it used to be: some businesses and most government offices are closed for the day (in keeping with the collective labor agreement), but most are not. However, there is always some celebration going on somewhere, while movies and documentaries about this period on TV provide you with the opportunity to learn a little bit about (recent) Dutch history if you want.

TRICK OR TREATS – SINT MAARTEN

Increasingly, the trick or treats day of November 11 is being reintroduced. On this day, children (often accompanied by parents) come by your door, carrying lanterns and singing songs such as '*Sint Maarten, Sint Maarten, de koeien hebben staarten, de meisjes hebben rokjes aan, daar komt Sint Martinus aan*' (St. Martin, St. Martin, the cows have tails, the girls wear skirts, there comes St. Martin – who *knows* what the one has to do with the other). This day is a 'treats'-day – no tricks – the treats being anything from tangerines to cookies to candy. The children do not get dressed up for this occasion, either; it is a simple – though friendly and *gezellige* – neighborhood event. In some cities, due to the exposure to other cultures, rather than with Sint Maarten on November 11, children go trick or treating on October 31, Halloween.

SINTERKLAAS

You may have already met up with a typical Dutch personality called Sinterklaas, or St. Nicholas. You may too have observed that he has many similarities with that white-bearded, red-clothed man you tend to run into towards the end of December in other countries (as well as in the Netherlands). However, Sinterklaas has made considerably better arrangements for himself. Santa Claus may live on the North Pole, but Sinterklaas lives in the South of Spain. Santa Claus flies in from the North Pole on his sleigh, high through the freezing skies; Sinterklaas takes a leisurely cruise from the South of Spain to the Netherlands (hence the song: *Zie ginds komt de stoomboot uit Spanje weer aan* – or, 'Look, there comes the steamboat from Spain'). Santa Claus has to squeeze down and back up all those chimneys himself; Sinterklaas has a whole crew of helpers named Zwarte Pieten, or Black Petes, to do that for him.

The phenomenon of Zwarte Piet is an element that tends to surprise visiting foreigners. In this era of post-anti-apartheid and desegregation, what exactly do the Dutch think they're doing with black-face-painted helpers? Well, Sinterklaas's Zwarte Pieten actually represent the Moors of Spain; chased into the Sierra Nevada by the Catholic Spaniards in the 15th century, they apparently sought gainful employment in the services of St. Nicholas. As a matter of fact, and this is the God's honest truth, if you drive along the coast of Southern Spain, between Motril and Málaga, you run into a tiny little sign, pointing up a narrow winding road into the hills, saying San Nicolás.... Incidentally, there is no evidence whatsoever that the presence of Zwarte Piet at Sinterklaas' side has in any way influenced children's perception of people of another race. However, we refer you to page 52 for more on this topic.

December 6th is St. Nicholas's birthday (or as some claim, the anniversary of his death, the 5th being his birthday) when, according to legend, this 4th-century Saint gave gifts of gold to three poor girls for their dowries, a tradition the Netherlands emulates (children still receive chocolate coins around this time). Throughout the centuries, Sinterklaas has been considered the patron saint of children (as well as of traders). Consequently, on December 5th, he brings them gifts that are surreptitiously dropped off in a sack on the doorstep of each household. During the evening, families exchange gifts, and traditionally drink hot chocolate and eat *banketstaaf*, made of puff pastry and almond paste. On December 6th, as a birthday present to himself, some would say, Sinterklaas high-tails it back to warm, sunny Spain for another 11 1/2 months.

Sinterklaas's birthday is not only a holiday for children; grown-ups like to participate in the fun by means of a gift (serious, silly or, often, homemade, called a *surprise*) with an accompanying poem that summarizes the receiver's past year, intermingled with surprising habits and silly mistakes – often in a slightly ridiculing tone. (Bear in mind that the Dutch love to tease and the more they make fun of you, the more they like you, although it has been known to happen that the unsuspecting receiver of such a lovingly and amusingly composed poem has rushed out of the room in tears.)

For more on Sinterklaas, see page 191.

CHRISTMAS DAY AND NEW YEAR'S EVE

Christmas Day itself is normally reserved for religious observances and family get-togethers (see more about this on page 191), increasingly combined with gifts. Likewise, the stroke of midnight on New Year's Eve signals that it's time to pay a quick visit to your neighbors with good wishes for the coming year. New Year's Day is a quiet continuation of the same. This all sounds rather tame and civilized, but don't worry; there are plenty of wild parties on New Year's Eve for those who care to go all out!

THE DUTCH LANGUAGE

First off, be thankful that almost everyone speaks virtually fluent English in the Netherlands. The Dutch are enviable linguists who switch from one language to another with the greatest of ease. In the beginning, the Dutch think it's perfectly fine if you speak English, and they will respond in English. But don't be fooled into thinking that their own language is not so important to them. If, after a year, your Dutch is still non-existent or barely so, they will become considerably less tolerant. Thinking that you are not doing your best to accept their culture, they may hold this against you – either explicitly or implicitly.

Like it or not, you must realize that *you* are a guest in *their* country, not the other way around, and that, by right, you should learn your host's language if you're going to live here for any length of time.

WHY SHOULD YOU LEARN DUTCH?

Maybe you think: 'I'm only going to be in Holland for a few years, and everyone understands me at work – why should I make the effort of learning a language I am not going to need for the rest of my life?' Experience shows that you will not only feel more acclimated if you learn the language of your host culture, but that you will generally be more accepted and appreciated for having made the effort, especially with such an obscure and sufficiently difficult language.

Moreover, if you are the partner or spouse of an employee who has been placed in the Netherlands, your life is probably quite different. If you do not have a job, you run more of a risk of becoming

isolated, particularly if you can't speak the local language. If you remain an outsider, you will miss out on the finer subtleties of the language and, therefore, the culture itself. In short, you will simply feel more comfortable with your life in Holland if you can understand what's going on around you. You'll quickly realize that having a command of the Dutch language will go a long way towards being able to decipher all those packages in the supermarket, for example, not to mention being able to read the local newspaper. Learning Dutch may, consequently, be of unexpected significance to both you and your children, though they will most likely pick up the language more easily through immersion in daily life, or what seems to adults as pure osmosis. Survival of the fittest is key to any expatriate experience, and language adaptation is no exception.

HOW DIFFICULT IS DUTCH?

Dutch is not an easy language for English speakers – we simply do not have the capacity for those throaty, guttural sounds on which Netherlandish children are weaned. Sentence structure is awkwardly reversed, and the Dutch seem to have imposed no limit on word length. (*Levensverzekeringsmaatschappijen*, translated as 'life insurance companies', and *projectontwikkelingsmaatschappijen*, meaning 'property development companies', at 32 and 34 letters each, are the two longest official words in the Dutch language, although there are even much longer unofficial, makeshift conglomerations of words used in everyday language.) If your native language is similar to Dutch, or you've studied a parallel language, you'll be one step ahead of the game.

THE FIRST STEPS

Decide whether you would prefer to follow an established course or take private lessons. The Netherlands has a national network of language institutes that offer courses in Dutch to foreigners (usually, these courses are referred to as NT2, *Nederlands als tweede taal* – Dutch as a second language). The local city or town hall will advise you as to where the nearest institute is, so that you can make an appointment. During an interview, they will probably ask you what type of school you went to at home, what diplomas you have, whether you interact with a lot of Dutch people, whether you have time to go to a school and to do homework, etc. They may also ask you to take a placement exam to determine what level you should pursue. Depending on your specific needs, the institute may suggest an intensive course for quicker immersion.

Caution: don't be tempted to buy a Dutch phrasebook, as these are generally geared to tourists and often don't accurately reflect common usage. Invest instead in a good Dutch dictionary and a basic 'Dutch for beginners' book to get you started.

Of primary importance is learning the numbers in Dutch, as you'll quickly discover that such everyday tasks as shopping and making appointments rely on this basic knowledge. Dutch numbers require some mental gymnastics – '21' is expressed as 'one and twenty', for example – so be prepared.

SOME PRELIMINARY WORDS OF ADVICE

- *Let everyone know that you don't (or hardly) speak any Dutch* Do this before the other overestimates your capacity to understand him or her, and starts off too quickly and with too complicated a vocabulary. Don't, however, insist on only English conversation as you'll never learn Dutch that way. Simply employ the following sentence if need be: *Ik wil Nederlands leren* (I want to learn Dutch). The reactions will vary. Some will turn up the volume, others will revert to a type of pidgin Dutch, as if talking to a child. Don't be offended; it's a natural reaction.
- *Do not be afraid to make mistakes* Many expatriates want to master Dutch as well as they do their native language – and it annoys them if they can't converse quickly. Though this is understandable, patience is of the essence. Fluency takes much time, and all that matters at first is basic communication.
- *Don't make it unnecessarily hard* Try to avoid difficult subjects at first. Keep your initial conversations simple.

TWELVE CLUES TO UNDERSTANDING THE DUTCH MENTALITY BY ARNOLD ENKLAAR

At first sight, the Dutch appear to be like many other normal Europeans. But those of you who have lived here longer and have worked with the Dutch, will have found dramatic differences. In order to avoid irritation or surprises, it might be good to know a little more about the Dutch culture. In these paragraphs, you will find a short overview of the 12 principles or values that rule Dutch society, from politics, work, and school, to the most intimate parts of family life.

The first four values come straight from Christianity:

1 SALVATION Your sacrifices and efforts will be rewarded in the future
2 GUILT You are responsible for the good and bad things that are the consequences of your acts
3 LOVE THY NEIGHBOR You should be concerned about the welfare of others
4 TRUTH You should always tell the bare facts

In the first place, the Dutch, just as other people who live in Christian cultures, are strongly oriented towards the future. Progress and innovation are important issues. Secondly, they are always worrying whether they did things right or wrong. The degree of personal responsibility is high. Thirdly, the Dutch feel greatly involved with people who have troubles, or who are suffering – whether close to home or on the other side of the world. This is evident from the country's extensive social security system and its high budget for developmental aid. Fourthly, the Dutch put a lot of stock in the objective truth and the bare facts. They find it more important to tell someone else exactly what they think than to be polite.

The next five values follow from Protestantism:

5 WORK It is good to work
6 ORDER & TIDINESS You should be well-organized
7 UTILITY Everything you do, must have a purpose, you may not waste
8 RELIABILITY You must do what you promised
9 MODERATION You must exercise self-control, and must not overdo

The Dutch think that it is better to work than to idly sit by. The higher they are on the corporate ladder, the harder they work. They appreciate an organized life that is dictated by the clock and their agenda, and think that a house should be neat and clean. The Netherlands is a relatively clean and well-organized country, in which a lot of big and little rules tell you how to behave. Also abroad, the Dutch are known for their tightness. One thing is certain; they hate waste; of money, time or anything else. Don't be surprised if they ask you what purpose your proposal serves. Couldn't it be done more efficiently, or perhaps effectively? The Dutch are very literal about their agreements and promises; if you agree to do something, then you must actually do it, or they will conclude that you are unreliable. In daily life, the Dutch hate extremes and exaggeration, they applaud self-restraint and frown upon expressing strong emotions. Only under certain conditions (a soccer match, carnival, at a disco), do they ever let it rip.

All this may sound pretty familiar to people from other Christian or Protestant countries. But the difficult part is still to come. The last three principles are typically Dutch and explain why certain things are done differently here or are found to be different than they are in the surrounding countries.

10 CONSENSUS You should always try to compromise

The Dutch dislike conflict and aggression, and consistently strive for consensus and harmony, which they refer to affectionately as 'gezelligheid'. They devote quite a bit of time to meetings and discussions, in order to make sure that all disagreements have been resolved. Instead of letting the democratic majority rule the minority, they prefer to find a solution that appeals to everyone; a compromise. A compromise that everyone will then stick to, for fear of conflict. This is often referred to as the 'poldermodel'. Consequently, the Netherlands has a relatively peaceful, non-violent society, in which strikes end rather quickly in compromise and the police apply a de-escalating approach to handling skirmishes.

So what was going on, these last couple of years, when so many Dutch gave heed to the calls of radical politicians such as Fortuyn and Wilders and started agitating harshly against immigrants in general and Muslims in particular? Precisely because the political elite had spent years ignoring certain problems and societal discontent, for fear of uncomfortable discussions, the proverbial camel's back had to break some day. And when this happens, also the goody-goody Dutch can become hostile and unreasonable. Luckily, the atmosphere is changing again, measures have been taken to deal with the problems and most Dutch have resumed their normal, peaceful and consensus-oriented attitude.

11 EQUALITY You should not think that you are better than anyone else

In the Netherlands, all hierarchy and differences in social status are carefully smoothed over and disguised. It is painful to give direct instructions to someone who is under you, such as your cleaning lady. You can't just say: "Daisy, clean up the kitchen and the bathroom!" To the Dutch, this is a brusque order against which they rebel immediately. Instead, they formulate it as a polite question: "Would you perhaps be willing to do the kitchen and the bathroom today?" It sounds like a suggestion, but to the Dutch, this already feels like giving / receiving an order. The Dutch do not apply politeness towards superiors, but rather reverse politeness towards inferiors. You must, at all cost, avoid the impression that you think you might be superior to the other (even if you are a minister or have won the Nobel prize). It is perfectly easy to manage the Dutch, provided you treat them as equals and disguise every instruction as a friendly request.

The Dutch are allergic to people who toot their own horn; they expect modesty and if you fail to act like a 'normal' person, then you will be mowed down. You are not only not allowed to be openly proud of your achievements, the same applies to being proud of your country and your history. To many Dutch people, nationalism is a cardinal sin. This is not to say that the Dutch are not proud of their country; they just cannot say so openly.

12 SELF-DETERMINATION I will decide what I do – not my father, boss or government

The Dutch find it more important that people be allowed to make their own choices, than to tell them what to do. Their motto is: everyone should decide for themselves what to do, as long as what they do doesn't interfere with my life. This is the basis for Dutch tolerance: it is not so much that they understand people who think differently, as that they are pragmatic; if you leave me alone, I will leave you alone. This explains why the Dutch tolerate the use of soft drugs, abortion and euthanasia. It does not so much mean that they 'do' it, but rather that they feel that whether or not someone else does, is their personal choice and none of anyone's business. This explains why so many different lifestyles can coexist in such a small country, from extravagant gay people who marry, to black-clad orthodox protestants who go to church three times every Sunday.

Children are not so much raised to respect their elders or general moral principles – but to think for themselves and speak for themselves. Dutch employees are expected to demonstrate a high degree of responsibility and initiative. Do take into account therefore that all Dutch people, be they young or old, have an opinion on everything and want to be heard. After which they will call a meeting, to reach a compromise!

- *Don't pretend to understand* If the other person has already explained something twice and you still don't understand, the temptation is great to nod enthusiastically as if you get it. You do not want to appear stupid or impolite. However, it is best to admit defeat; have them repeat it again. Who knows what you will learn?
- *Absorb all day* As you hear Dutch in your daily activities, pay attention to what others are saying and how they say it. If you don't know the words, look them up for future reference and try to use them yourself. Attempt to read local or national newspapers and to decipher Dutch television. It's a great way to practice.

WHICH DUTCH?

Not all Dutch people speak the same Dutch language. There is a standard language: *Algemeen Beschaafd Nederlands* (ABN), which translates into the somewhat pompous-sounding 'General Civilized Dutch'. Well-educated Dutch people who live in the Randstad (the area comprising Amsterdam, The Hague, Rotterdam, Utrecht and everything in between) speak this, as it is the old dialect of the District of Holland, which was once the most powerful province. *Hollands* thus became the most widespread dialect and the basis for the standard language that is spoken by the Royal Family, the members of Parliament, teachers and preachers, and on radio and television.

The other regions in the Netherlands speak the same language, but the pronunciation can be quite different and hard to understand at first: there is *Zeeuws* (spoken in Zeeland), *Twents* (spoken in Twente – in the east), *Gronings* (spoken in Groningen), *Drents* (spoken in Drenthe), *Brabants* (spoken in Noord-Brabant) and *Limburgs* (spoken in Limburg) – and even within these dialects, there can be considerable variation. And then the people from the various cities all have their very distinct way of pronouncing the language as well. The Dutch can tell within a sentence whether someone is from The Hague, or Amsterdam, or Limburg or Groningen.

In Friesland, a province in the northwest of Holland, there is a wholly different language called 'Fries', or Frisian, which is spoken in addition to Dutch. Though perhaps many of the words used are the same – but pronounced differently – they also have a whole unique vocabulary. An interesting factoid to note is that Frisian is considered, historically, to be closer to the English language than Dutch is. Unless you're a die-hard linguist, however, it would be highly unlikely for you to need or want to learn this unique language unless, of course, you intend to live in that region for a lengthy period of time. Even then, Dutch would suffice, as everything is signposted in both languages there.

YOUR AIM

In the end, how far you progress with Dutch will depend on the amount of time you put into it, your ambition and your talents. You might attain the highest level: speaking with ease, making virtually no mistakes, understanding complicated speeches and articles and writing a nearly faultless proposal. Or maybe you will never get any further than a sort of tourist Dutch enabling you to at least carry on a semblance of a conversation. In a country where English is second nature, it will require some determination on your part to plunge hook, line and sinker into learning Dutch. Chances are you won't regret it.

THE ROYAL FAMILY

THE MEMBERS

The Dutch Royal Family and the 'Royal House' are not the same. Not every member of the Orange Nassau family is a member of the Royal House. The Royal Family is made up of the former Queen and her sisters, their spouses and their children, King Willem-Alexander, his brothers, their spouses and their children and grandchildren. Who becomes a member of the Royal House – and therefore could theoretically become the monarch – has been determined by law and consists of the Head of State King Willem-Alexander, his wife Queen Máxima, their children and their spouses and grandchildren, his mother (formerly Queen Beatrix), as well as his brother Prince Constantijn and his wife Princess Laurentien, and his aunt Princess Margriet and her husband Pieter van Vollenhoven.

Members of the Royal House who marry without the official approval of the Parliament, lose the right to succeed to the Throne – an issue that came to bear when Crown Prince Willem-Alexander announced his engagement in 2001 and again when and his late brother Johan Friso announced his engagement in 2003. Johan Friso as well as two of Queen Beatrix's sisters lost the right to the throne by marrying without this permission.

POLITICAL POSITION

The King, together with the ministers, form the government. It was determined in 1848 that the ministers, and not the King, are responsible for acts of government. Laws that have been passed by the Parliament, and Royal Decrees, are signed by both the King (Queen) and the minister in question, lending them the authority of the Head of State and placing the responsibility for them with the minister.

Until 2012, after elections, the then-Queen, upon the recommendation of the Vice President of the Council of State, the Presidents of both Houses of the States-General, the presidents of the Parliamentary groups of the political parties and sometimes the Minister(s) of the State, appointed the so-called (in)formers (*formateurs* or *informateurs*) who were to form a new cabinet, based on the outcome of the election. In 2012, the Dutch Parliament decided that it was perfectly capable of appointing its own (in)formers. Consequently, the King no longer plays a role in the formation of the cabinet other than its swearing in – which is merely a ceremony.

Every year, on the third Tuesday of September, called *Prinsjesdag*, the King and members of his family ride in the royal Golden Coach from the palace on the Noordeinde to the Binnenhof, where the government is housed. Here the King holds his famous speech, called the *Troonrede*, before the members of the Upper and Lower House, in which the government's policies for the coming year are set out. Prinsjesdag is a popular outing for schools, but also for grown-ups and tourists, who come to The Hague to admire the beauty of the royal procession and taste a bit of the atmosphere of yesteryear.

In the early '50s of the previous century, Queen Juliana started a new tradition of Christmas speeches that were broadcast on the radio and television. In these speeches, she emphasized the unity of the country and the fact that all the Dutch should look out for each other. She also commemorated national tragedies, if there had been any, while she clearly expressed her religious devotion, without specifying her denomination. King Willem-Alexander has chosen to continue this tradition with passion and enthusiasm.

TRAGEDIES

These past years, the Royal Family has been hit by two tragedies. In 2009, there was an attempt on the lives of the members of the Royal Family on Queen's Day. Every year, on April 30 (as of 2014; April 27), the members of the Family visit a municipality and participate in the festivities. In 2009, they visited Apeldoorn. After the festivities, they boarded a bus (in stereotypical Dutch fashion; let's not get too fancy) and were heading towards the Palace 't Loo when a Suzuki Swift drove into the crowds in an attempt to hit the bus. It crashed into a monument and the driver died later that day. Before lapsing into a coma, however, he told a police officer who was on the scene that he had wanted to hit the Royal Family. Seven onlookers had been killed. The Royal Family expressed their sympathy and the Queen gave an impassioned speech on the tragedy the next day.

The second tragedy took place in February of 2012, when, during their annual ski vacation in Lech, Austria – a place the Family has been visiting for decades and where they are considered honorary citizens – Prince Friso, the Queen's second son, was hit by an avalanche. Though he survived the incident, he remained

in a coma until he passed away on August 12, 2013. The ceremony of his funeral was impressive, but in consultation with, and out of respect for, the Royal Family, the Dutch broadcasting companies only televised a few moments of it.

THE KING AND QUEEN

In 2010, Queen Beatrix celebrated her 30th anniversary as Queen of the Netherlands and speculation abounded as to whether or not she planned to abdicate. Finally, in 2013, on January 28, the Queen announced her plan to abdicate on April 30 of that year – the day on which she normally would have celebrated her birthday. The Dutch public expressed its appreciation of the pride and sense of duty of the Queen and felt she deserves some peace and quiet. She has been succeeded by King Willem-Alexander to universal acclaim. Willem-Alexander has had plenty of opportunity to practice for his royal position through his activities which focused on two main issues: sports, and water and its role in the Netherlands and the world. He was sorry to have to abdicate from the Olympic Committee as this cannot be combined with the position of Head of State. The same goes for his position of stimulator and Chairman of the Dutch water sector.

Almost from the beginning, the King's Argentinean wife Máxima has been involved in all sorts of activities aimed at integrating non-native Dutch women into Dutch society and – on a worldwide level – in initiatives providing micro-credit as an instrument of developmental aid. In 2009, the royal couple made a well-documented trip to the South Pole, where they – from the depths of a glacier – expressed their concern about the climate crisis. As Queen, she can continue these activities as she, contrary to husband, does not fulfill an official position – as determined by the Constitution of the Netherlands.

Willem-Alexander, who is not planning on limiting himself to a merely ceremonial role, has announced that he will fulfill the position of monarch on his own, and not share the job with the new Queen – in keeping with the constitution. Yet he also said that his demeanor will be less formal and majestic than that of his mother. Queen Beatrix had always been a somewhat stand-offish monarch, who adhered strictly to protocol. Only when she visited the victims of disasters to offer consolation and sympathy on behalf of the Dutch population

did this stand-offishness disappear. Willem-Alexander is far more jovial and Queen Máxima also contributes a certain Latin American savoir vivre to their public appearances. This already became clear during the inauguration. As the new Royal Family sailed down the IJ in Amsterdam, the new King moored his boat to visit the podium where world-famous DJ Armin van Buuren was playing. Queen/Princess Beatrix would have been more likely to visit the Nederland Dans Theater ballet, or a concert of classical music. After the inauguration, the royal couple visited various parts of the country, once again showing his more informal demeanor. The King also considers himself an ambassador of the Dutch economy and, like his grandfather Prince Bernhard, wishes to support the Dutch commerce by means of marketing activities – provided of course, that this does not damage his constitutional position as Head of State. During several state visits, the King has demonstrated how he plans to do this, to the general appreciation of society and the business community.

At the start of 2016, Willem-Alexander had been king for 1,000 days – cause for reflection on his performance. The opinion was unanimously positive. In the eyes of the royalty watchers, the King is a nice guy, who – contrary to his somewhat formal and standoffish mother, is quick to put his subjects at ease with a quip. On the other hand, he is definitely capable of displaying royal dignity when so required; during official speeches, state visits

and ceremonies. He visibly enjoys decorating brave soldiers who have put the lives of their comrades above their own in the line of duty. Máxima still shines, albeit slightly more in the background now that her husband wears the crown. The princesses are adorable – as they should be. It is already clear that Princess Amalia is aware of the responsibilities to which she will be called in the future. She reminds the Dutch of her grandmother, from whom she appears to be learning on a daily basis. And of course, the King moves within the limits set by the Dutch constitution.

PRINCESS INSTEAD OF QUEEN

Upon abdicating, Queen Beatrix did not become Queen Mum but rather Princess, as did her grandmother Wilhelmina and her mother Juliana before her. Princess Beatrix moved to her historic mansion Drakenstein, in Lage Vuursche, near Utrecht. This is where she spent the first happy years of her marriage to Prince Claus van Amsberg and this is where her sons were born. The local population looked forward to her return. They are proud that she is able to walk around their village like any normal local, without having to be reminded of her special status. In 2015, it was decided Princess Beatrix, as her sisters, would no longer participate in the official King's Day celebrations.

KING'S DAY

The Dutch are not quite yet used to the new word; *Koningsdag*. It means King's Day and

refers to His Majesty's birthday. Until King Willem-Alexander became King, it was called *Koninginnedag* – Queen's Day – a name it had had since 1890, when the nation's last king – Willem III – passed away. Since that day, there had only been women on the throne.

On Queen's Day, or Kings' Day, the Dutch through their affection for the throne. Almost every municipality has an 'Orange Association' of diehard monarchists who work together with the municipality to arrange a number of festivities that involve a lot of folklore and children's games. Wherever you go, you hear the thump of marching bands and other music. In Amsterdam, people come together to sell their secondhand items on the so-called Free Market (*Vrijmarkt*). This custom has spread across the nation the past 30 years to almost all municipalities, meaning that you will likely run into your neighbors' kids selling their old toys on that day, which they have spread out on an old rug on the street. They will be flanked by grown-ups who are selling old percolators and other household items for a song. Don't hesitate to encourage your children to join in and develop their marketing qualities. Or to 'take to the streets' with your own obsolete household items. The Dutch will be sure to appreciate and applaud your initiative, taking into account the fact that you are an expatriate. Koningsdag is the nation's largest public party, even more widespread than carnival.

On her birthday, Queen Juliana used to stand on the steps of her palace and 'Orange Associations' from across the nation would parade by. Queen Beatrix would take a helicopter or royal bus (typical Dutch: a bus, rather than a cavalcade of limousines) to visit two municipalities. There, the local population would arrange traditional games and art forms, and the Royal Family would join in on the fun. Once, King Willem-Alexander, who was still Crown Prince at the time, found himself obligated to join in on a game of toilet bowl throwing.

After his inauguration, the King introduced a number of changes. He only visits one single municipality and the idea is that this municipality present things of which it is proud. As the visit is televised live, this is an opportunity for the municipality to intensively market itself. And this is precisely in line with how the new business-like King wishes to fulfill his position – for this is how he himself refers to it.

PROSTITUTION, DRUGS AND EUTHANASIA

High on the to-do list of every visitor to the Netherlands, right up there with the famed museums, is a walk on the wild side of seemingly sedate Dutch society: a tour of the red-light district in Amsterdam. The *wallen* ('the walls'), as that part of town is known, lives up to its billing. Everything you expect is there. Teeming crowds juxtaposing businessmen and tourists; prostitutes publicly ensconced in the windows of the numerous business establishments; the quote-unquote coffee shops that sell everything from Thai stick to space cakes – coffee definitely not being the specialty of the house.

POINT OF VIEW

After soaking in the sights for a few minutes, you may notice an unexpected aspect of human nature: the only thing that makes the goings-on into a spectacle is your point of view. Having spent some time in the Netherlands, you probably aren't surprised that everything is well-organized (the Dutch police even have an English-language how-to guide to help tourists safely explore the steamier side of the city); but you probably did not expect it to be 'dead normal', as the Dutch say. The only difference between the streets of the red-light district and other shopping districts in the city is the merchandise. While there are prostitutes and drugs in every large city, Dutch or otherwise, in the Netherlands both businesses are given an air of legitimacy that exceeds that found in most other countries. Like so many other visitors, you marvel at the tolerant Dutch in action.

CLICHÉS

Noting that the Dutch are tolerant, however, is not exactly a radical discovery. Social experiments in the Netherlands are sufficiently renowned that such comments are almost clichés. But there is more to this than just being open-minded. Most visitors are shocked when they learn that until recently prostitution was illegal and that the possession or sale of recreational drugs remains against the law. After one day in Amsterdam, it is hard to believe that any of this ever was a criminal offense – which, in a sense, is correct: even when illegal, these activities occurred and thrived with the tacit approval of the local community and the Dutch government.

TURNING A BLIND EYE

How does one reconcile the contradiction? Activities were or are illegal yet officially tolerated at the same time. The superficial answer, in a tradition that is centuries old, is that the laws in the Netherlands are intentionally enforced in a selective manner via a practice called *gedogen*, which means something like turning a blind eye. When it comes to social policy, the underlying motive is the Dutch are not just tolerant; they are incredible pragmatists.

TOLERANCE VS. ACCEPTANCE

Don't confuse Dutch realism with loose mores. As individuals, most are principled; a fair number are very religious. When asked, the overwhelming majority indicates that they don't use drugs or prostitutes, and the statistics bear this out. Remarkably, the Dutch make a distinction between their values and what they expect from others. While there is general agreement that recreational drugs and prostitution are social evils, there is also a strong consensus that they are going to occur whether they are illegal or not and that prosecution often results in social ails worse than the original malady. Thus, it is better to mitigate the negative aspects of these activities with regulation (what could be more Dutch than that?) than to drive them underground through futile attempts at eradication. That these vices were or are still technically illegal is mostly a reflection of the consensus-building that is implicit to Dutch public policy: it is one thing to passively accept certain activities as inevitable; it is another to actively endorse them. In short, there is a big difference between tolerance and acceptance.

A WORK IN PROGRESS

Sounds great. But how well do these Dutch approaches work? The answer depends on your priorities. In the case of prostitution, the public-health accomplishments are impressive. Thanks to access to medical care and routine testing, the physical well-being of most prostitutes and their clients is significantly better in the Netherlands than in many other countries. Unfortunately, rules only protect those who are a part of the system, and even then, only those who are able to understand and use them. In particular, many of the prostitutes are thought to be illegal immigrants, including an unknown number who were coerced into the trade and work in de facto slavery. Due to fear of reprisals or deportation, it is less likely that foreign prostitutes will contact the authorities for help if they need it. Recent attempts to expand government control by legalizing brothels may have made things worse: the added expense has driven some activity underground. While such problems are not unique to the Netherlands, the abuse of these individuals, in spite of the existing rules and regulations, is, to say the least, extremely troubling to the Dutch.

DRUG TOURISM

There are also some notable achievements associated with the recreational drug policies. While the drug business undoubtedly accentuates the petty theft that is prevalent in the Netherlands (Hey! Where's my bicycle?!?), the fears of critics have not come to pass. The streets of the country are not clogged with addicts; and while most Dutch teenagers go through a period of exploration, where some experiment with drugs, most move on: teenage and adult drug usage rates are relatively low. The biggest problems with Dutch drug policy are associated with foreigners, including a thriving business in drug tourism. Many of these visitors are the source of much of the drug-related theft and the less frequent acts of violence. Other countries in the European Union that have stricter drug policies have pressured the Dutch to modify their approach. To date the Dutch have largely resisted these demands. However, they have introduced a new regulation regarding the purchase of soft drugs in the so-called 'coffee shops'. All you have to do is prove that you are a legal resident and older than the age of 18, by means of proof of registration with the municipality you live in and an ID, WHILE, officially, tourists are banned from purchasing soft drugs at a coffee shop. However, the mayor of Amsterdam has already publicly stated that visitors will not be refused. See also page 165.

EUTHANASIA

New ground-breaking social policies, often controversial and influential, continue in the Netherlands. A recent example is the legalization of euthanasia. Legislative experiments in this regard date back more than two decades. The old law offered the usual subtle compromises, where euthanasia was technically illegal but physicians were rarely prosecuted. Once again, the fears of critics were largely unfounded: euthanasia was reserved as a treatment option of last resort (most were terminally ill cancer patients) and studies confirmed that there was no systematic abuse of the system. However, the same studies showed that the majority of euthanasia cases went unreported, presumably out of fear of prosecution. The new law attempts to correct these and other deficiencies. While the requirements are similar, oversight is now after the fact and a doctor's actions are now presumed legal unless there is evidence that the guidelines have been severely violated. As with some other recent Dutch experiments, the efficacy of the new law remains to be seen.

TOO PRAGMATIC?

All of this leads some to conclude that the Dutch are too pragmatic. The foreign press invariably carries stories that make you shake your head in wonder, such as the one about the Dutch parents who ran the coffee shop in their town: if their children were going to experiment with controlled substances, they felt better knowing who was selling them the drugs! Nonetheless, in spite of the occasional excesses and the remaining problems, rational social policies as well systematic and open education on sex, drugs as well as alcohol have successfully encouraged responsible behavior. As a consequence, most Dutch teenagers choose abstinence or practice safe sex, as evidenced by the low rates of sexually transmitted diseases, teen pregnancies and abortions. (Even dictionaries for Dutch tourists propagate the party line. When it comes to sex, the content is restricted to such useful phrases as 'Only with a condom' and 'Let's not take any chances'.)

While it may not be politically or culturally feasible for other countries to adopt these policies or approaches, one cannot help but admire what the Dutch have accomplished.

ALL OF A SUDDEN ZWARTE PIET IS A CONTROVERSIAL CHILDREN'S FRIEND

While all across the world Christmas decorations are being unpacked, they remain in their boxes for another couple of weeks in the Netherlands. Here, the shop windows are inhabited by two unusual figures: a bishop with a long white beard and his pal, a black servant, dressed up like a 16th-century nobleman, wearing poofy pants and a cap with a feather. These men are Sinterklaas (or Sint Nicolaas) and Zwarte Piet. Sint Nicolaas rides a white horse, his servant goes on foot. And together, they visit almost every house in the Netherlands on December 5 to drop off bags of presents. Sometimes they hand them over personally – but most of the time they just bang on the windows and leave the bag by the door.

Sint and Piet arrive in the Netherlands halfway November, and are officially welcomed to each town and city by the local mayor. Every year, one of these official 'processions' is televised. Preceding this day, Dutch television brings us three weeks' worth of the Daily Sinterklaas

News. Sinterklaas lives in Spain and travels to the Netherlands by ship, meeting all sorts of challenges along the way; for instance, he loses his book, in which he has noted which child gets which gifts. However, after a series of cliffhangers, he makes it just in time for his official entry into the country. And you might notice that there is more than one Zwarte Piet. By now, Sinterklaas is accompanied by hundreds of them, all of whom help the gift distribution company of Sinterklaas operate effectively.

During his procession through town, Sint Nicolaas tells the children that they can place their shoe by the chimney. In this shoe, they place bread and/or a carrot for his horse. And they place a cup of water next to it. All of this will be gone the next morning, as Sinterklaas and his helpers travel across the roofs, whereby Zwarte Piet goes down the chimney and leaves behind a gift, taking the bread and water back up for Sinterklaas' horse.

The big party however, as said earlier, is December 5. On this day, a bag of presents is produced that has surprises in it – also the Dutch call them, literally, 'surprises'; pronounced surpreezes. A large 'surprise' could contain only a very small present – such as a single candy. Many of these surprises have been made with a lot of dedication and hard work and have been given the shape of an animal or some other object. Often Sint and Piet have added a poem to the gift, in which the receiver is gently teased. It is of great essence that the no one is able to link the gift to the real giver.

December 6 marks the end of this period. Sinterklaas vanishes without a trace and the next day all store windows reflect the Christmas spirit while the newspapers carry one last-ditch headline: "Once again, Sinterklaas proved his generosity". In 2013, Sinterklaas revenue amounted to more than half a billion euros – on a population of fewer than 17 million. It also brought the 500 millionth Internet payment via Ideal. Without a doubt, Sint and Piet have thus acquired substantial economic significance. In 2014, the Saint and his helpers spent € 530 million, placing the majority of their orders on the Internet.

And now these festivities are brought into disrepute – all because of Zwarte Piet. To the Dutch people of Caribbean heritage, this fairytale figure is a racist caricature. They connect Zwarte Piet with the transatlantic period of slavery, in which the Netherlands played a significant role. Approximately 15% of slaves on the Middle Passage were transported by Dutch ships. Most of them were brought to Surinam or the island of Curaçao before the coast of Venezuela, where they were sold on to other parts of Latin America and the Caribbean area. Currently, Curaçao is an autonomous part of the Kingdom of the Netherlands.

These opponents of Zwarte Piet are getting a lot of support from abroad. The Americans see 'blackface' in him; part of their vaudeville tradition in which white people with partially blackened faces played clownesque roles. Since the '70s, blackface has been considered beyond the pale.

In the fall of both 2013 and 2014, artist Quinsy Gario got a lot of publicity when he criticized Zwarte Piet. He bluntly called the Sinterklaas festivities racist, meant to undermine the position of black people. Only the complete eradication of Zwarte Piet would cleanse the festivities and make them suitable for the 21st century.

This brought about a storm of protest. Most Dutch parents had never seen anything of evil in this important child benchmark of the year. And now they were being told that they were tolerating racist activities in their very own homes. In 2013, the Piet-ition, a special Facebook-page created by a small advertising agency in Roosendaal, already garnered more than two million likes. And not only that. Geert Wilders and his PVV immediately came to the defense of Zwarte Piet. The children's friend became a political issue. On the one side of the spectrum he was portrayed as a symbol of racism while on the other side – the extreme right – he was elevated to the status of icon of authentic Dutch culture. The discussion in the media soon became venomous. Anyone who dared to say that Zwarte Piet was a symbol of white hegemony and white privilege was told that he could pack his bags and get lost if he didn't like it here. Or, at the very least, that Zwarte Piet's face had become blackened by the soot in the chimney.

The traditional answer to any type of discussion of this nature in the Netherlands is, of course... compromise. Concessions are made in order to remove any dissatisfaction. The suggestion that Zwarte Piet could be given another color – say, a rainbow Piet – were immediately rejected, however, by the radical opponents of his very existence: the entire symbol of slavery had to be eradicated. The mayor of Amsterdam decreed that during Sinterklaas' procession through Amsterdam, the Zwarte Pieten were not to wear golden hoops in their ears. In March 2014 it was discovered that undercover negotiations were going on, attended by a council member of Amsterdam's GroenLinks, in search of a solution. These negotiations were also being attended by Gario and his supporters as well as the Sint Nicolaas Committee – great supporters of Zwarte Piet. How democratic these talks were was not clear nor was it clear whether the solution they might come up with would prove to be acceptable to the general public.

At the same time, a trial took place. Opponents of the Zwarte Piet-phenomenon argued that the official arrival of Sinterklaas should be abolished, on the grounds that the racist nature of this event constituted a threat to certain ethnic groups. At first, a judge ruled that some people might indeed feel restricted in their freedom by the performance of Sinterklaas' black-faced helpers. The mayor of Amsterdam appealed this decision as he feared that the same arguments might be used by opponents of other manifestations, such as Gay Pride. The highest court for these types of cases, agreed with him. It decided that mayors should only focus on threats to the public order. This was a clever way of avoiding the issue of whether or not the existence of Zwarte Piet could be considered racist. In the fall of 2014, it became clear where this was all heading. On television, the Sinterklaas-News program for children showed an old factory in which candidates for the position of Zwarte Piet had to go down a chimney – after which they reemerged with black soot on their faces. The Zwarte Pieten who had already qualified for the position in previous year kept their blackened faces. And the soot-faced Pieten opened the possibility to other colors in the future – which were already present at a variety of Sinterklaas parades across the country.

During the official arrival of Sinterklaas – televised nationally – Zwarte Piet's opponents held a silent protest on the square where the mayor was to welcome Sinterklaas. As this was prohibited, they were removed by the police with the necessary force, which led to a lot of commotion and a very emotional discussion on the Internet. In 2015, the demonstrators got a better spot to show their dismay with what they perceive to be a racist tradition.

It would appear that the controversy surrounding Zwarte Piet will probably rear its ugly head a couple of more times during the years to come. Particularly as there are so many angles to it. And also particularly because his opponents have decided to be principled and uncompromise, on the issue. The fact that Zwarte Piet can be linked to racial practices and customs, also makes it hard for his supporters to compromise: for if they were to do this, they would implicitly be admitting that they had (subconsciously) been acting in a racist manner themselves. A concept that makes them unwilling to make any concessions at all.

It is unclear how this is all to end. Only one thing is beyond discussion: Zwarte Piet is to the Dutch, what the bullfights are to the Spaniards. Or, as critics of his appearance like to say, he has lost his innocence forever.

SINTERKLAAS AND ZWARTE PIET, A EUROPEAN TRADITION

The Sinterklaas-festivities are not purely Dutch. He appears in a number of European countries, but is hardly a saint there. And nowhere does his existence have any implications for commercial enterprises, while here it constitutes a large portion of their sales.

In other parts of Europe, Saint Nicholas is a frightening figure whose hideous sight intimidates people, with the help of a black creature who is dressed like the devil – known in Germany and Austria as Krampus. Young children hide behind their mothers' skirts when he rattles his chains.

It isn't even always a children's festivity. There are towns in Switzerland in which young men from different neighborhoods battle each other, led by their own personal Sinterklaas. The ambulances and other health services are on the alert during these battles, but everyone is willing to make this sacrifice for this tradition. Despite the blood and violence.

On the Dutch Wadden Island of Ameland there is another ancient tradition. It clearly has its own fifty shades of grey as outsiders (such as tourists) are strongly advised to leave the island around December 6, as infractions of these rules are not tolerated by anyone. First, in all the villages, the women and children are chased into their houses. The streets are ruled by Sundeklazen, the men of the villages who are dressed up as unrecognizable Sinterklaas-like appearances. They are armed with sticks. The houses in which the women are waiting, are unlocked. The men 'force' their way inside and make the women jump over their sticks and dance with them. If they do not obey, they are swatted on their shins. Sometimes, a woman will disguise herself as a man and mix with the male Sinterklazen. If they are caught, they are given a beating or made to sit on a pile of dung. The Amelanders are very close-lipped about this tradition, and both the men and women are fond of it. They are only moderately willing to explain it to outsiders and will simply not tolerate any criticism.

From this all, it is clear that Sinterklaas has his origins in very old, heathen traditions that could be thousands of years old. We know that missionaries converted Europe to Christianity approximately 1,500 years ago, implementing one of Pope Gregory the Great's instructions: to not eradicate any of the heathen traditions, but to give them a Christian sauce. For instance, cult places where the people had worshiped Freya, goddess of fertility, became places where Jesus's mother Maria was worshiped – which they remain to this day. Saint Nicholas is the Christian version of the German god Wodan. Why Nicholas and not someone else? He is the patron saint of merchants, fishers and seamen – which basically just about covers all of the Netherlands.

Wodan rode his eight-legged horse Sleipnir along the heavens and used his one eye (the sun) to peer down the chimneys of the Germans and into their houses to ensure that they were making the right sacrifices. Sinterklaas riding his horse on the roofs can clearly be led back to this god, as can the bread and carrots by the chimney be led back to the sacrifices. Wodan was accompanied by a goblin-like fertility god, who is conceivably the origin of Krampus and Zwarte Piet. Particularly if you take into account the fact that Zwarte Piet not only carries a bag, but also a cane – former instruments of punishment.

In the 19th century, the Netherlands went through a large-scale civilization process. The builders of this nation created not only a liberal constitution, but also a national system of education, in which the national language and the nationally 'accepted' norms, values and traditions were taught. This included the tradition of Sinterklaas, but without the wild, heathen and Dionysian elements. In the western part of the Netherlands, the Sinterklaas festivities already represented a long-standing tradition of being a children's party in which the Saint handed out gifts and Zwarte Piet 'threatened' the children with his cane – without really carrying out the threat. Something they did fear however, along with a sack of salt instead of gifts or – worst of all – being carried off in the sack. Where to? Spain, as this is where legend had it that he lived.

An Amsterdam-bred teacher, Schenkman, canonized Sinterklaas somewhere around 1850 in a book of rhymes, in which the saint and his helper feature. The text makes no mention of the skin color or name of the helper. The illustrators were the ones who gave him a black complexion. In the first edition of Schenkman's book on Sinterklaas, Zwarte Piet is dressed as an Ottoman prince, in the second edition, as a 16th-century page. He rode horse, just like Sinterklaas. It is clear that he is not a slave, but rather a type of Middle Age squire. This is the Zwarte Piet that has evolved into the current jolly children's friend.

Opponents of Zwarte Piet claim that the black helper is some sort of racist symbol. Some go as far as to claim that the teacher also meant him to be a slave – the Netherlands only abolished slavery in the colonies in 1863 – but this is highly unlikely. In Schenkman's social circle, slavery was very controversial. Nor do his appearance and position point to slavery.

This does not take away the fact that if your frame of reference is formed by a history of slavery, this might by be painfully triggered by Zwarte Piet's appearance. Which is invoked by his opponents as an argument for changing him or abolishing the Sinterklaas festivities altogether – nor does it sound completely unreasonable. On the other hand, the Netherlands has more than one tradition that is not understood, or misunderstood, outside certain circles. If Zwarte Piet were to disappear because certain categories of the population found him offensive, this could also have consequences for other customs and festivities.

Still, it would appear as if Zwarte Piet is slowly but surely on his way out. This is the consequence of how the Dutch authorities have taken their familiar path of compromise, introducing a soot-faced Piet or a rainbow Piet – who acquired his color as the ship sailed underneath a rainbow.

SUPPORT ORGANIZATIONS

ACCESS
A volunteer not-for-profit organization that serves the needs and interests of the international community in the Netherlands. Its dedicated volunteers, representing an impressive cultural and linguistic variety, work to:
- provide guidance, advice, information to help individuals with settling, and/or living and working in the Netherlands
- promote friendship, understanding and well-being of the members of the international community in the Netherlands
- contribute to community development through skill training schemes and courses
- serve as a bridge between local and international communities

Laan van Meerdervoort 70, 2517 AN The Hague
0900 2 222 377 (€ 0.20/min) www.access-nl.org
Or visit The Hague International Centre – the City Hall Atrium, 9 A.M. – 5 P.M. Mon-Fri

OUTPOST THE HAGUE
(AT SHELL HEADQUARTERS)
The center of a worldwide spouse-to-spouse network that provides Shell families with practical information about living conditions in expatriate locations around the world. All Outpost locations provide career and development resources and relocation resources to Shell expatriates and repatriates.
Postal address: P.O. Box 162, 2501 AN The Hague
Visiting address: Carel van Bylandtlaan 16, HAG C30, 2596 HT The Hague
Tel.: 070 377 65 30
https://the-hague.globaloutpostservices.com

OUTPOST THE HAGUE (IN RIJSWIJK)
Kesslerpark 1, 2288 GS Rijswijk
Tel.: 070 447 57 85
https://the-hague.globaloutpostservices.com

OUTPOST AMSTERDAM
Grasweg 31, 1031 HW Amsterdam
Tel.: 020 630 21 56
https://amsterdam.globaloutpostservices.com

OUTPOST ASSEN
Schepersmaat 2, 9400 HH Assen
Tel.: 0592 363 064
https://assen.globaloutpostservices.com

STICHTING JAPANESE HELPDESK
www.jadesas.or.jp

EXPATRIATE ARCHIVE CENTRE
The Expatriate Archive Centre welcomes contributions from retired, repatriated or current expatriates and their children.
Paramaribostraat 20, 2585 GN The Hague
Tel.: 070 427 20 14
www.xpatarchive.com

EXPAT DESKS

EXPATCENTER AMSTERDAM
WTC Amsterdam, D-tower 2nd Floor
Strawinskylaan 39, 1077 XW Amsterdam
Tel: 020 254 79 99
www.iamsterdam.com/expatcenter

THE HAGUE INTERNATIONAL CENTRE
The Hague City Hall, Atrium
Spui 70, 2511 BT The Hague
Tel.: 070 353 50 43
Open Monday to Friday from 9 A.M. to 5 P.M.
E-mail: internationalcentre@denhaag.nl
www.thehagueinternationalcentre.nl

ROTTERDAM INFO EXPATDESK
Coolsingel 195 – 197, 3012 AG Rotterdam
Tel.: 010 790 01 90
E-mail: expatdesk@rotterdam.info
www.rotterdam.info/expatdesk

EXPAT CENTER LEIDEN
Stationsweg 41, 2312 AT Leiden
Tel.: 071 516 60 05
www.expatcenterleiden.nl

HOLLAND EXPATCENTER SOUTH
Vestdijk 27a, Eindhoven
Tel.: 040 238 67 77
Mosae Forum 10, Maastricht
Tel.: 043 350 50 10
Stadhuisplein 128, Tilburg
Tel.: 040 238 67 77
www.hollandexpatcenter.com

EXPATDESK NIJMEGEN
Stadswinkel, Marienburg 75
6511 PS Nijmegen
Tel.: 024 329 22 408
www.nijmegen.nl/expats

EXPAT CENTER UTRECHT
Utrecht City Hall
Stadsplateau 1, 3521 AZ Utrecht
Tel.: 030 286 58 20
www.utrecht.nl/english/expatcenter

WELCOME FAIRS

I AM NOT A TOURIST FAIR
Information fair for expats organized yearly in the Fall at the Beurs van Berlage, Amsterdam
and in June in Eindhoven
www.expatica.com/iamnotatourist

FEEL AT HOME IN THE HAGUE
Event for the international community in the Hague region
www.feelathomeinthehague.com

IAMEXPAT FAIR
Expat fair organized in Spring in the Westergasfabriek, Amsterdam
www.iamexpatfair.nl

CULTURE TRAINING

ROYAL TROPICAL INSTITUTE (KIT)
Intercultural Management & Communication
Offers various group programs designed for foreign employees and their partners who are posted to the Netherlands.
Linnaeusstraat 35F, 1093 EE Amsterdam
Tel.: 020 568 83 19
www.interculturalprofessionals.nl

RECOMMENDED READING

GENERAL

THE HOLLAND GUIDE APP
Published by XPat Media
The Holland Handbook on your iPad
With extra features, almost a thousand live references and hundreds of stunning photos
Available in the App Store
www.xpat.nl/hollandguide

THE LITTLE ORANGE HANDBOOK,
HOLLAND FOR NEWCOMERS
Published by XPat Media

This book offers, compact, clear and to-the-point information on the Netherlands. A practical and quick introduction to a country in which at times it is easy to get lost in a maze of rules, regulations and laws.
www.xpat.nl
To order: www.hollandbooks.nl

THE UNDUTCHABLES
By Colin White and Laurie Boucke
Published by White – Boucke Publishing Inc.
A tongue-in-cheek observation of the Netherlands, its culture and its inhabitants.
www.undutchables.com

THE LOW SKY, UNDERSTANDING THE DUTCH
By Han van der Horst
Published by Scriptum
The book that makes the Netherlands familiar. A detailed exploration of the reasons for desire of the Dutch for independence, their sense of respect and their business sense
www.scriptum.nl

DEALING WITH THE DUTCH
By Jacob Vossestein
Published by KIT Publishers
The cultural context of business and work in the Netherlands
www.jacobvossestein.nl
To order: www.hollandbooks.nl

THE DUTCH AND THEIR DELTA
Living Below Sea Level
By Jacob Vossestein
Published by XPat Media
The fascinating account of how the Dutch manage to live below sea level
www.jacobvossestein.nl
To order: www.hollandbooks.nl

HOW TO BE DUTCH, THE QUIZ
By Gregory Shapiro
Published by XPat Media
The questions that SHOULD be on the Dutch citizenship exam according to an American Netherlander who's been in the country for 20 years.
www.howtobedutch.nl
To order: www.hollandbooks.nl

DISCOVERING THE DUTCH
By Emmeline Besamusca & Jaap Verheul
Published by Amsterdam University Press

This updated edition tackles the heart of the question of Dutch identity through a number of essential themes that span the culture, history and society of the Netherlands.
To order: www.hollandbooks.nl

BEAUTIFUL HOLLAND
A book about the Netherlands' past, present and future with 288 pages of beautiful photos. Including 40 layar movies to view on your smart phone
Available in ten languages: Dutch, English, German, French, Italian, Spanish, Portuguese, Japanese, Chinese and Russian
www.beautifulholland.nl
To order: www.hollandbooks.nl

READY STEADY, GO DUTCH
Published by ACCESS an Dutchnews.nl
A must-have resource for anyone planning on settling in the Netherlands, or who has been here a little longer.
The book has been compiled from the experiences of some 150 people from all over the world.
To order: www.access-nl.org or www.dutchnews.nl

STUFF DUTCH PEOPLE LIKE
By Colleen Geske
A study of all things orange. It investigates and highlights the idiosyncrasies of the Dutch culture and their uncanny ability to talk on a mobile phone, while carrying 2.5 children, 6 bags of groceries, a television set, and a mattress balanced on a gear-less bicycle,
www.stuffdutchpeoplelike.com

HOW TO SURVIVE HOLLAND
By Martijn de Rooi
The author manages with quick wit, sarcasm and slightly self-deprecating humor to more than adequately convey a rather candid assessment of the Dutch people as a whole.
www.dutchshop.nl or www.hollandbooks.nl

NEW VISIONS OF THE NETHERLANDS
Photography: Frans Lemmens
Text: Martijn de Rooi
Like a consummate Dutch old master, photographer Frans Lemmens has painted a rich and colorful portrait of this often-surprising country, the people who live in it and the places and things worth seeing.
www.dutchshop.nl or www.hollandbooks.nl

OVER HOLLAND
Photography Karel Tomeï
Published by Scriptum
Previously unpublished work by Holland's most renowned aerial photographer, Karel Tomeï. Humorous and refreshingly different: spectacular and surprising photographs are combined with work by Dutch writers, cabaret artists, poets, actors and aphorists.
www.scriptum.nl

HOLLAND BOOKS
Features a wide range of books and travel guides on Holland: www.hollandbooks.nl

CULTURAL TRANSITION

THE ART OF CROSSING CULTURES
By Craig Storti
Published by Intercultural Press
www.interculturalpress.com

THE PSYCHOLOGY OF CULTURE SHOCK
By Colleen Ward, Stephen Bochner, Adrian Furnham
Published by Routledge
www.routledge.com

CULTURESHOCK! NETHERLANDS
A survival guide to customs and etiquette
By Hunt Janin
Published by Marshall Cavendish Editions
www.marshallcavendish.com

A MOVEABLE MARRIAGE
Relocate your Relationship Without Breaking it
by Robin Pascoe
Published by Expatriate Press Ltd.
www.expatexpert.com

HOMEWARD BOUND
A Spouse's Guide to Repatriation
By Robin Pascoe
Published by Expatriate Press Ltd.
www.expatexpert.com

THE MOBILE LIFE
Published by XPat Media
By Diane Lemieux & Anne Parker
A new approach to moving anywhere.
www.themobilelife.eu

BLACK AND ABROAD
By Carolyn Vines

Published by Adelaar Books
Experiences and perspectives of a black American woman traveling and living abroad.
www.blackandabroad.com

DUTCH LANGUAGE

THE DUTCH TONGUE
By Ben van der Have
Written in the form of a conversation between a student of the Dutch language, Nancy, and her local linguistic expert, Thomas, Ben van der Have takes the reader on a journey of language-learning which goes far beyond the rules of grammar and vocabulary teaching.
www.scriptum.nl

DUTCH FOR EXPATS
By Maik Klaassen

Published by VanDorp Educatief/XPat Media
A comprehensive course book intended for adults living and working in the Netherlands who need to learn and practise the essential communication tools of the Dutch language in a limited timeframe. CD-rom included.
www.nederlandsalstweedetaal.nl

DUTCH FOR SELF-STUDY
By Hinke van Kampen
Published by Het Spectrum
This book and two cd-roms provide the basic structures of the Dutch language
www.spectrum.nl

DUTCH LANGUAGE TRAINING
www.berlitz.com
www.britishschool.nl/languagecentre
www.directdutch.com
www.dnalanguages.nl

www.dutchindialogue.com
www.dutchforexpats.com
www.ita-talen.nl
www.kickstartschool.nl
www.kit.nl
www.koentact.nl
www.learndutch.org
www.lexicon.nl
www.linguarama.nl
www.nt2digitaal.nl
www.nederlandsalstweedetaal.nl
www.nedles.nl
www.pcilanguages.com
www.reginacoeli.nl
www.taalthuis.nl
www.taaltaal.nl
http://tornantetrainingen.nl
www.toptaal.com
www.volksuniversiteit.nl
www.volksuniversiteitamsterdam.nl

CHAPTER 3

Many of you have come to the Netherlands as an expatriate – placed or transferred here by your employer – so that most of the important things have been taken care of for you. On the other hand, many of you have not come here with the full company support system behind you. If this is the case, there are a number of things you need to know before entering the job market, such as: the make-up of the Dutch employment market, finding a job here as an expatriate, Dutch labor law, the Dutch social security system, the possibilities of continuing the social insurance legislation of your country of origin in the Netherlands and how to go about setting up your own business.

Going through this chapter will help you prepare for your ventures, by giving an overview of these topics as well as, on the reference page, the addresses, phone numbers and websites of those organizations that can help you along the way.

Working in the Netherlands

CONTRIBUTING AUTHORS STEPHANIE DIJKSTRA, HAN VAN DER HORST, PETER KRANENBURG, ARJAN ENNEMAN, NANNETTE RIPMEESTER AND LIANE VAN DE VRUGT

THE DUTCH EMPLOYMENT MARKET

The Netherlands is known for its tulips and windmills but is far more diverse and pluralistic than one might expect. It offers international job seekers endless possibilities and has plenty to offer foreign students as well. Despite the lingering worldwide economic crisis, the country still has a relatively low unemployment rate, and is a comparatively large economic player, with its two international mainports and its longstanding tradition as a nation of trade. It also has a strong educational system and great internship arrangements. Below you will find information on the labor market of this small country with its international and impressively diverse job market.

THE DUTCH WORKFORCE

The Dutch unemployment rate is one of the lowest in the EU and is considered moderately low on a worldwide scale, which is quite remarkable given the recent worldwide economic downturn and its effect on the Dutch market, which historically relies on international trade. At the end of 2015, the total labor force shrank to approximately 7.9 million, with an unemployment rate of 6.8% in December – a considerable improvement over the 7.4% rate in 2014. Although at the moment not many sectors are looking to fill vacancies, there are still opportunities in the commerce, health care and manufacturing sectors for those wishing to find a job in this country, which we can see further on in this chapter.

Part-time employment in the Netherlands is rather high; reports state that part-time employment constitutes nearly 40% of total Dutch labor force. Accordingly, almost 31% of total job vacancies are posted for part-time employment. Gender difference in employment participation is quite high; approximately 75% of Dutch women work fewer than 35 hours a week, while only 25% of Dutch males hold part-time positions (Eurostat, 2015). Most people work directly for an employer, though a considerable and growing number are self-employed; according to the Dutch Bureau of Statistics CBS, in 2015 more almost 1.2 million persons claimed self-employment (referred to as *Zelfstandige Zonder Personeel*, or *ZZP-ers*), which is nearly 10% of the labor force. Compared to other European countries, this level of self-employment is quite high, particularly among younger people. The development of self-employment remains hard to predict, however, and is always prone to fluctuation – though, at least for the Dutch market, it appears to be here to stay. The amount of flexible contacts also continues to grow, especially among young people. In 2013, 55% of the population between the ages of 15-24 held flexible employment contracts. If you compare this to those aged 28 and older, where approximately 10% has a flexible work contract, this would appear to either be pointing towards a trend among the younger work population to focus more on a life/work balance or else simply towards a streamlining of business in order to cope with the financial crisis.

The education level of those working in the Netherlands has been rising steadily over the past decade: one in every three high school graduates continues their education at a research university or a university of applied sciences (you can read more about the distinction between these two in chapter 9).

Though traditionally the Netherlands was a country where employees worked for the same employer their whole life, this changed dramatically during the '90s when, due to the flourishing economy, the age of job-hopping arrived. This development came to a severe halt with arrival of the economic crisis, as a consequence of which competition for jobs increased considerably.

On the bright side though, the Dutch labor market seems to have recuperated and the outlook for the employment sector is rather positive. Figures for 2014 and 2015 indicate a general downturn in unemployment, while labor participation has gone up. Youth unemployment in the Netherlands has also gone down and is currently below EU average, signifying that more young professionals have been able to find employment after completing their education than their peers in other Member States. Overall, the number of job vacancies has significantly increased across many sectors compared to previous years, which will be discussed in the next section.

SECTORS

The commercial services sector remains the largest employer in the Netherlands, and has been for several years, closely followed by the health care and manufacturing industries. The number of vacancies remained relatively stable over 2012 and 2013, but in 2014 and 2015 there has been a marked increase in jobs openings in the trade, transport, financial services and information technology sectors (and some analysts say that that the trade sector may show further improvement over the coming years). Currently, science & engineering is the only sector showing a constant and steadily increasing need for international and capable workers in areas such as water management, green and renewable energy, as well as logistics.

EMANCIPATION?

The Netherlands is viewed by those abroad as an 'emancipated' country, where women share an equal standing with men. To a large degree this is true; in fact, many expats comment on how the Dutch women are the ones 'who wear the pants at home' – to use a Dutch expression. However, the workforce does not reflect this

emancipation, particularly not in the full-time and/or highest paid job sectors. The cause for this can presumably be found in the fact that, aside from there being relatively little government support for child care, Dutch social values dictate that women spend more time with their children. Although Dutch society is egalitarian by nature, on average the more traditional role definition still holds true; men work full-time, women part-time, and the women play a greater part in the raising of the children. Based on a study conducted by the Central Bureau for Statistics, more women (especially with a higher education) expect that their career opportunities will be negatively affected once they have children. Fifty-eight percent of working women without children say that they expect motherhood to harm their career. Men, interestingly, agree that becoming a parent has a more significant effect on women's career paths compared to theirs. This having been said, in reality the percentage of households in which the man is the sole earner and the woman does not work at all is only 20%. One could argue that it is the 'glass ceiling' that keeps the women in the Dutch labor market from progressing up the career ladder, yet, the 'sticky floor' may be of importance here too.

Expat women are often greatly surprised at this huge inequality and are quite dismayed at how few women are in top positions – nonetheless, the number of women in employment increased from 52% in 1997 to 63% in 2012 and is currently heading towards 70%. The aim of the Dutch government was to have 65% of the women working at least 12 hours a week by 2010. This target was not met, however – though the numbers have clearly continued to rise while this issue remains on the political agenda.

As yet, as mentioned earlier, most women are in part-time positions, with around three-quarters of women of working age working part-time, and only 19% of employed mothers working over 35 hours a week. Less than 10% of women in the Netherlands work full-time, as a consequence of which few of them are in the business's top echelons or among the top earners. Only approximately 20,000 full-time working mothers held management positions in 2014, compared to more than 130,000 full-time working fathers (CBS, 2015). Perhaps crucially, an increasing number of young women receive temporary or flexible contracts compared to their male peers. Whether this is through choice, other factors, or a combination of those or other issues is hard to determine. Yet, lately, there has been a steady increase among the number of women on management boards. The Dutch Women's Board Index shows that, in 2014, 15% of all directors were female (99 women among a total of 757 directors). Among those women, the majority occupied non-executive managerial positions, which is 19.5% of the number of board members in the Supervisory or Executive Boards studied. The percentage of women in Boards of Directors has steadily increased from 10.4 in 2012 to 13.3 in 2013, whereby four companies reached the European quota of 40% in 2014. A law, enacted in 2012, mandated that Dutch companies fill 30% of their executive positions with women by January 2016. However, on that date, no company that publicly traded on the Dutch stock exchange had reached that target. There is currently a proposal to extend the target date to January 2019. Notably, women are far better represented in the non-profit sector than they are in the business sector, which has been to their advantage, as the number of jobs available in health care, education and the public sector, though feeling the pinch at the moment, are likely to keep growing over the years to come.

All in all, nonetheless, it can be said that Dutch women – reflective of the country's overall population average – generally enjoy a high standard of living and material satisfaction. As well as highlighting the very equitable distribution of wealth found in the Netherlands, this points to the general acknowledgement that these women – with their flexible attitude towards work – are an integral part of the country's solid financial structure.

DUTCH EMPLOYMENT LAW

As many of you will not have moved to the Netherlands on an expat contract governed by your home country laws, the rules that apply to those employed directly by a Dutch employer can be of great importance to you. Even expatriates, whose contract explicitly states that a foreign law applies to the employment relationship, will find that they are subject to mandatory rules of Dutch employment law and/or Dutch rules of public order by means of binding allocation rules of international private law. For this reason, we include an overview of the main issues contained in this law:

PROBATION PERIOD

Type of Contract	Maximum Duration of Probation
Contract for less than 6 months	no probation period
Contract between 6 months and for 2 years	1 month
2-year or permanent contract	2 months

As of January 1, 2015, new legislation, the 'Wet Werk en Zekerheid', entered into force. With regard to probation periods in short-term contracts, this new law includes some clear changes. For any temporary employment contract with a total duration of less than six months, a probation period is no longer permitted.

CHAIN CONTRACTS

An employment contract for a fixed period of time ends automatically by operation of law (van rechtswege) on the agreed end date. However, under the new legislation (applicable to contracts starting February 1, 2015), this only applies to a contract of a maximum of six months. For every other length of contract, the employer is required to specify a month in advance what will happen on the official end date. The new law also has consequences for 'chain contracts' (keten contracten). Under the previous legislation, you could be employed on a fixed-term contract basis for three consecutive contracts and/or for a maximum period of three years. This 'chain' could be broken if, during a period of three months, the employee was not in the employment of the employer in question. As of July 1, 2015, after three consecutive fixed-period contracts – or if the fixed-term contracts exceed two years – the employment contract is deemed to be a contract for an indefinite period of time, even if it is explicitly stated that it is a fixed-term contract. Under the new legislation the 'chain' is only broken after a minimum break of six months.

MINIMUM/MAXIMUM DURATION CONTRACT

If you work on call and you are not certain about the number of hours that you are working on a weekly or on a monthly basis, your employer can offer you a min/max contract (with a minimum as well as a maximum number of hours – do note that the minimum number of hours per call is three) or a 'nul-uren contract', which offers great flexibility, but does not have the minimum number of hours as a prerequisite and can only be offered for a maximum of six months.

TERMINATING AN EMPLOYMENT CONTRACT

As of July 1, 2015, there are two options for an employer who wishes to terminate an employment contract, depending on the reason for the termination. If the work relationship is damaged, an employer can only terminate an employment contract via the sub-district sector of the District Court (or Cantonal Court). In case of economic reasons or in case of illness of the employee, the employment contract can be terminated via the UWV. For employees who have been employed for a minimum of two years, a so-called transition compensation is due. See below. (See more on dismissal on page 66.)

NOTICE PERIOD

When terminating an employment contract, an employer must apply the following notice periods (these do not apply when the employment contract is dissolved by the courts):

Length of employment period	Notice period
0 – 5 years	1 calendar month
5 – 10 years	2 calendar months
10 – 15 years	3 calendar months
> 15 years	4 calendar months

The above notice periods apply to contracts for an indefinite period of time. In the case of other contract forms, such as a temporary employment contract, the employer must notify the employee one month in advance of his intentions – if the contract is for six months or more. For 'temp' contracts with a duration of less than six months, termination is/can be with immediate effect.

For an employee, the notice period is always one month, unless, either in the employment contract or in a separate written agreement, the employer and the employee agree upon a different notice period. Whereby it should be noted that any personally agreed-upon notice period for the employee is doubled for the employer (i.e. if an employee agrees to a two-month notice period at the beginning of their contract, the employer must agree to give four months' termination notice to said employee). Collective agreements can provide for different (and even equal) notice periods to be observed.

SEVERANCE PAYMENT

Severance payment can be granted either as a lump sum (known as a 'golden handshake'), or as a periodically paid supplement to the unemployment benefit (for more on this benefit, see page 72) or lower wages in the next job. In the case of collective dismissals or highly paid individuals, the payment is usually in the form of a lump sum. At the end of 2013, a new regulation was passed that abolished the option of deferring taxation on a golden handshake. Starting January 1, 2014, the lump sum is taxed, at a rate that takes into account the total amount earned during that year. There has been much upheaval about the severance payment of some highly paid senior managers, causing the Dutch government to rethink the dismissal process in the Netherlands. Nonetheless, no changes have been made as yet and a commission has been asked to advise on the issues at stake.

These past years, a number of changes have been introduced, making it possible to take into account the labor market perspective of the dismissed employee, the employee's behavior, and the financial situation of employee and employer. Also, short-term contracts are better covered by the new model. As of July 1, 2015, employers will owe compensation if they terminate a permanent contract or a temporary contract that lasted more than 24 months. This transition payment (*transitievergoeding*) replaces the existing cantonal court formula (*kantonrechtersformule*), according to which the employee is awarded one, one-and-a-half or two months' salary per year of employment, depending on their age. Regardless of the termination route (UWV or Distric Court/Cantonal Court), a severance payment must be paid by the employer, to a maximum of € 75,000. Specifically, the new severance payment is calculated as follows: 1/3 of their monthly salary is granted to employees for every year of employment if they were employed for a period shorter than 10 years in total, or 1/2 of their monthly salary for every year of employment that exceeds the ten years. For more information, you can consult www.ontslag-krijgen.nl ('being fired').

WORKING THROUGH AN EMPLOYMENT AGENCY

The Netherlands, where the first temporary employment agencies started over 30 years ago, was also one of the first countries where these agencies were very successful. They still remain important players on the labor market, and currently the top agencies are: Randstad Nederland, Start People Netherlands, Unique Nederland, Luba Uitzendbureau, Tempo-Team and Adecco.

There are two main Temporary Workers unions; the ABU and NBBU. These unions are governed by their own collective labor agreement (CAO), in which various regulations are given on (but not limited to), such subjects as:

- statutory number of vacation days
- holiday allowance
- national holidays
- salary statement specifications
- working overtime
- illness/sick pay
- the 'Phase system' and 'Chain system'.

Not all employment agencies have joined a Union for Temporary Workers, as membership is not obligatory. Nonetheless, as of September 17, 2005, all employment agencies must conform to the legally binding aspects of the ABU Collective Agreement for Temporary Employees 2009 – 2014 (to which slight changes were introduced in 2010). Only a few agencies are exempt from this CAO (e.g. those who are a member of the NBBU). For more specific information, see the English website of the ABU, www.abu.nl.

FOREIGN TEMPS

(Some provisions of) the Collective Agreement for Temporary Employees (ABU Collective Agreement) apply/applies to all employment agencies, thus also to (foreign) employment agencies that place employees on the Dutch labor market from abroad. Keep in mind that nationals of the European Economic Area (EEA) can move to the Netherlands for work and enjoy the same conditions as Dutch nationals in areas such as access to housing, wages and social security – among others.

MULTILINGUAL JOBS

When looking for employment in the Netherlands whereby you can work in your native language, you can either register with various specialized employment agencies (a listing of these can be found at the end of this chapter) or you can apply directly with companies where the business language is your native language. The job market for foreign staff encompasses a wide spectrum of professions including, but not limited to: administration, secretarial, IT, finance, marketing, support staff, sales, logistics, middle and senior management, etc.

After the UK, Germany and France, most 'multilingual' jobs are to be found in international call and shared service centers located in the Netherlands. There are over 150 of these multilingual service centers in the country, most of which are located in the Randstad region (the triangle between, and including, Utrecht, Rotterdam, The Hague, and Amsterdam). However, you will find more and more pan-European centers in Maastricht, Arnhem and other cities, particularly near the border. Within these organizations, English is usually the business language.

Most Dutch people speak more than one foreign language to some extent (usually the Dutch rate their own language skills a lot higher than they actually should!), yet the international centers and companies have a preference for native speakers. Please do read the paragraph on *Protection Labor Market*, further on, however.

LANGUAGE

It is still pretty common for foreigners to live and work in the Netherlands for years without learning the language, however, we cannot emphasize enough the importance of learning Dutch; this will not only be beneficial within the work place but also during your day-to-day endeavors in the Netherlands. Far too many foreigners make no effort to learn even the basics, but the Dutch always appreciate and respect those who make an effort to learn their language. Dutch is not the easiest language to learn, and it can be very difficult for those who live in the Randstad to find the opportunity to practice their Dutch language skills, as the helpful Dutch will almost invariably switch to English once they detect an accent. But, please persevere; the effort will pay off in the end, especially for those who plan on staying in the Netherlands for a longer period of time. The good thing about learning Dutch is that the Dutch do not have a problem with other people's grammatical mistakes – they still get the point you are trying to make. Do ask them to correct you though; otherwise you will keep making the same mistakes!

PROTECTION LABOR MARKET

When applying for a work permit, beware of the stringent legal protection of the Dutch labor market, making it difficult for non-EU/EEA/ Swiss nationals to receive such a permit (you can read more about this on page 112). If the job you are applying for meets the criteria for the so-called Highly Skilled Migrant Program, do note that the IND provides your prospective employer with a simplified application procedure, as the aim is to attract talent to the Netherlands and retain it here. Certain salary requirements apply – you can read more about this on page 113. For EU/EEA and Swiss nationals, freedom of movement applies, in keeping with the Freedom of Labor Act (Wet Arbeid Vreemdelingen, or WAV). This means that they do not need a work permit to work here. It also means that, when seeking to fill a job opening, employers in the Netherlands must prioritize not only Dutch applicants over foreign applicants, but also EU/EEA applicants over non-EU/EEA/ Swiss applicants. However, these privileges do not yet extend to citizens of Croatia, who will still need to wait until 2018, before they gain freedom of movement. Being a native speaker of a particular language will no longer automatically qualify you, if the Dutch authorities are of the opinion that your prospective employer should be able to find a Dutch/EU/EEA/Swiss employee who can also speak your language.

Please also note that when faced with the choice, the employer, who will be the one applying for your work permit, might well choose an employee who does not need a work permit over you (if you do need one) – as the application process is a time-consuming one. This may seem unfair – yet is something you should realistically take into account. With any luck, the new regulations, aimed at simplifying and shortening this procedure, will succeed in leveling this aspect of the playing field.

SALARIES

In general, you may be surprised at the salaries in the Netherlands compared to those in your country of origin. Salaries are always commensurate with the general cost of living and pay parity is generally only reached at very senior management levels. However, you will find that, in fact, the net wages are comparable as most expenses and some allowances are tax-exempt.

Furthermore, a statutory holiday allowance (minimum of 8% of a gross annual salary), usually paid in the month of May, is awarded to each individual pro-rated to the number of months worked.

(COMPULSORY) HEALTH INSURANCE

All residents of the Netherlands working and paying taxes in the Netherlands must arrange private health care insurance (there is sometimes the option of participating in a collective insurance arranged by the employer). This form of private insurance is known as *Zorgverzekering* (or '*care insurance*'); for more information on insurances, see page 124).

HOW TO FIND A JOB

The Dutch economy is recovering from the recession. Since early 2015 this has been the same for the employment market, though improvement remains modest. The prognosis for the 2016 labor market remains slightly positive, yet the number of job seekers remains high, so there is much competition from other candidates.

Despite the possible language barrier, the Dutch employment market offers foreigners plenty of career opportunities. There is a growing demand for professionals and starting graduates in a number of industries and functional areas, such as: health care, engineering, ICT, Internet / social media, high-tech, technical positions, legal and tax professionals, interim managers, education, science, and non-industrial positions.

It is for this reason that the Dutch government has introduced the concept of knowledge migrants – a tax measure created to make working here attractive for high-earning professionals recruited abroad, as well as highly educated graduates from abroad who are searching for a first employment position in the Netherlands. You can read more about this on page 131-132. Having said this, the following sectors are still struggling and not hiring many new employees: banking, real estate, the government, NGOs, non-profit organizations, and the manufacturing sector.

The unemployment rate was 6.5% at the start of this year, which is almost 1% lower than last year, while currently the length of the average job search is about three to four months. As mentioned earlier, however; you can expect a lot of competition from other candidates; it is not unusual for more than 100 candidates to apply for a specific vacancy!

Because the Dutch economy is very internationally-oriented, the ability to speak English – fluently – is an important requirement when looking for a good job. However, this is primarily the case for commercial companies and less so for certain sectors, such as the health sector, non-profit organizations, NGOs, and governmental organizations. Remember also that it is not easy to find a part-time job of fewer than 30 hours a week (particularly if you don't speak Dutch).

THE FIRST STEP

There are four ways to find a job:
- through ads on the Internet (both on jobsites and on the websites of the employers) and in the printed press
- through employment and recruitment agencies
- by means of an open application
- by networking.

In principle, you should try all four and not limit yourself to one of these.

Furthermore, in the Netherlands, only half of the vacancies are published in the media/Internet or offered through agencies. This means that more than 50% of the vacancies are part of what we call the 'hidden job market', and are only visible to insiders. That is why it is very important that you approach employers directly (with an open application) and that you quickly start working on building your own network.

JOBSITES

The most relevant jobsites are:
- www.linkedin.com
- www.monsterboard.nl (in Dutch)
- www.intermediair.nl (in Dutch)
- www.iamexpat.nl/career/jobs-netherlands
- www.stepstone.nl (in Dutch and English)
- www.expatica.com (in English)

- www.englishlanguagejobs.com (in English)
- www.togetherabroad.nl (in English)
- www.oneworld.nl (in Dutch)
- www.jobbird.com (in Dutch)
- www.nationalevacuturebank.nl (in Dutch)
- www.fd.nl (in Dutch).

NEWSPAPERS

The best newspapers for jobs are the Saturday editions of the national and regional newspapers, for commercial and administrative/clerical jobs, and the free news-tabloid *Metro*.

EMPLOYMENT AND RECRUITMENT AGENCIES

For those who do not have sufficient (job-specific) work experience, *uitzendbureaus* (employment or temp agencies) are a good first step, but be clear about the type of job you do and do not want. If you have more than three years' (specific) work experience, then you should also approach the specialized recruitment agencies, but ask in advance whether or not a command of the Dutch language is a requirement.

At the moment, in certain industries, there are a lot of job seekers out there, so keep in mind that the employment agencies are getting a lot of calls from a lot of candidates. Consequently, these agencies are *only* interested in candidates who fit the profiles for the vacancies they have. Keep this in mind when composing your cv: they will want to see it first, before deciding whether or not to meet you in person. Beware that agencies are normally not interested in candidates who need a work permit to work in the Netherlands. If you need a work permit, your best chance is through contacting companies directly and not through an agency (you can read more about when you need a work permit and the complicated legal rules around obtaining one on page 112).

OPEN APPLICATIONS

Open applications are also a good way of finding a job, though possibly not the quickest. Especially small and medium-sized organizations appreciate the attention they receive and the willingness to take the initiative that you thus demonstrate. You should of course orient yourself on the organizational structure, the department and the positions. Do not be vague about what you want and what you have to offer. Furthermore, it is always advisable to address a specific person in your application, preferably the manager of the department for which you want to work or the human resource manager who is responsible for recruitment.

NETWORKING

Networking can also help you find a suitable job, and, in this tough employment market, it is often the only successful method. It is important to follow a certain strategy in doing this. To start with, you should make an overview of your network (on paper) and consciously set about expanding upon it. The most important thing to keep in mind is that you should clearly and concisely communicate what you are looking for and what you have to offer to every person you meet. Good networkers know when, and how, to come to the point. Find out whether there is an organization of professionals within your line of work in the Netherlands that you can join and make sure to use social media such as LinkedIn or Facebook to expand upon your network. Especially LinkedIn has

become embedded in Dutch culture and is used by many Dutch professionals, recruiters and employers.

TIPS FOR WRITING YOUR RESUME

First of all: a resume is called a 'curriculum vitae' (or cv) in Europe. In the Netherlands, employers prefer a concise cv (one or two pages, preferably with a photo) that has been tailor-made for the position within the organization. Always start with your work experience, unless you have just graduated and do not yet have any work experience – and list your achievements. Arrange your experience in reverse chronological order, starting with the most recent experience. Pay special attention to the job titles of the positions you held: is the job title the same in the Netherlands as in the country you are from? Do not forget to have your diplomas evaluated by the IDW (www.idw.nl, see the end of the chapter) so that your employer knows what the comparable Dutch diploma is. Also make clear if you have lived/worked/studied in more than one country, as today's employers are often specifically looking for employees who have international experience. Last but not least, clearly specify your language abilities.

And don't forget that that employers will 'google' you and check out your LinkedIn or Facebook profiles before inviting you for an interview.

TIPS FOR WRITING A COVER LETTER

Always send a cover letter along with your cv, in which you state why you are applying for this position. It goes without saying that it is important to know about the organization to which you are applying and in your cover letter it is always a good idea to include one or two sentences on what you expect to contribute to the company. Employers appreciate it when you try to place yourself in their (customers') shoes and try to anticipate their wishes. And use the same type of language and vocabulary used on the company's website and in the job description.

BE FLEXIBLE

Aside from showing your knowledge and abilities, it is important to be flexible, particularly when it comes to the type of employer that you want to work for. You will be missing opportunities if you insist on focusing on certain sectors (industries); many expats want to work in the creative sector or consumer goods (such as personal care products, advertising or fashion) and overlook the business-to-business sectors (such as chemicals, engineering or energy). You should take into account that the competition is great in the creative and consumer goods sectors and the number of job openings limited, as these companies are not expanding quickly, certainly not compared to certain business-to-business sectors.

And of course, do not forget: don't choose an employer, choose your boss.

FINDING A JOB VIA THE INTERNET

Nowadays, about 95% of the jobs that are posted publicly are posted on the Internet and only 5% in the printed media. Of course, the advantages are plentiful. Job seekers can apply to jobs all across the world, without having to find a way to buy a local newspaper (say, you live in Brussels and are considering looking for a job in Hong Kong). And, once you have found a company you are interested in, all you have to do is visit its Internet site to find out more about it. However, keep in mind that, as it is so easy to send your cv via the Internet, employers receive a shipload of cvs from all across the world. Consequently, they sometimes doubt the seriousness of the jobseekers, as many cvs are of the dime-a-dozen variety (see more about setting up your cv further on, under *Key Words*). A good idea would be for you to make an initial or follow-up phone call to your prospective employer. Also here, remember that employers will 'google' you before you will be invited for an interview.

KEY WORDS

There are a number of issues you should keep in mind. Firstly, precisely because information on your potential employer is so easy to find via the Internet, the employer expects you to know more about the company once you come in for a job interview. Secondly, you should not only work on composing an attention-grabbing personal letter, but you should also focus on using key words. You are looking for a job in Off-Shore Construction, you are applying for their position in Hong Kong, you have five years' experience in Airport Sites, you speak three languages, including Cantonese. As your potential employer is likely to sort your letter according to the key words, make sure you don't make any typos when typing in these words – else your application will simply never be picked up. To avoid this, make use of the 'spell-checker', but don't forget to use your own, ever-critical, eye.

As mentioned earlier, thanks to the discovery of the convenience of Internet job applications, employers probably receive dozens of applications a day. So make sure you distinguish yourself through your cv, cover letter and (online) profiles: keep it concise and to-the-point, making it clear that you are applying for this job with this company (and why) – and what you have to offer them.

E-MAILING YOUR RESUME/CV

A word of advice for those sending their resume via e-mail: do not include your letter as a separate attachment, but (also) make it part of the e-mail message. And include a photo. Or send a link to your online cv on, for instance, LinkedIn.

E-LANCERS

The Internet has made it very easy to work from your own home (or wherever you are) and has led to the phenomenon of e-lancing. E-lancing allows you to work and still be there for your family, to take on that one essential job when on vacation and, in certain countries, being a self-employed e-lancer allows you to benefit from great reductions for tax purposes, allowing you to convert a considerably higher amount of your gross income into net income. This is certainly the case for the Netherlands; if you want to know more about setting up your own business, we refer you to page 74.

INTERNET ADDRESSES

You will find a selection of useful websites at the end of the chapter.

CITIZEN SERVICE NUMBER

Everyone who is employed legally has a 'social-fiscal' number – the Citizen Service Number, or *burgerservicenummer* – for tax purposes. Without this number, your employer cannot properly pay out your salary for tax purposes or credit your contributions for your benefits. Also expat family members need to obtain a Citizen Service Number. They will need this number – and proof that they are staying here legally, such as a residence permit or a valid passport – to arrange their obligatory health insurance (you can read more about this on page 124). You also need a Citizen Service Number when you register with temporary job agencies.

In November 2007, the Citizen Service Number was officially introduced to replace what was then still called the sofi-number. This unique number – which, if you already had a sofi-number, remained the same – is issued to those persons who in one or other way have to deal with government organizations (for instance, for benefits, rent subsidy or educational purposes, to name a few). If you are going to reside in the Netherlands for longer than four months, you have the legal obligation to register with the municipality – BRP, or *Basis Registratie Personen* – within five days of your arrival. You will then receive your personal Citizen Service Number straight away. Some municipalities send it to you within a few days, by mail.

If you are not a resident of the Netherlands or will be staying here fewer than four months, you do not have to register with the BRP. However, you can opt to register with the BRP voluntarily so that you are issued a *burgerservicenummer*. You are then registered with the RNI, or Register for Non-Residents (*Register Niet Ingezetenen*). This can come in handy if you need to arrange tax-related matters, your pension, or benefits, such as the General Old Age Pension (AOW), if you live abroad.

If your stay here extends beyond the initially-intended four months, you are de-registered with the RNI, and registered as a resident. Your *burgerservicenummer* stays the same. In principle, you will have this *burgerservicenummer* for the rest of your life, even if you move to another country.

DISMISSAL

A chapter dedicated to the mechanisms of the Dutch labor market should also include information on the unique dismissal system of this country. There are few countries where employees enjoy as much protection against dismissal as they do in the Netherlands.

Here a short overview of the rules and regulations governing this subject.

FIXED VS. INDEFINITE CONTRACT

When explaining the rules on dismissal, a distinction should be made between an employment agreement for a fixed period of time and an employment agreement for an indefinite period of time. An employment agreement for a fixed period of time ends automatically (under certain conditions) by operation of law upon expiration of the agreed-upon period. The fixed period does not necessarily refer to a particular date. It can also be linked to the occurrence of a particular objectively assessable circumstance. For instance; the completion of a project, or the return of a sick or pregnant employee (who was being replaced).

An agreement for an indefinite period of time is terminated by either giving notice of termination or by a dissolution decision given by the court. You can read about both procedures in the following paragraphs.

Other ways to terminate an employment agreement for a fixed period of time or an employment agreement for an indefinite period of time are: by mutual consent, during the probationary period, or through summary dismissal for 'urgent cause'. Also these will be described in more detail in the following paragraphs.

THE WORK AND (SOCIAL) SECURITY ACT

On June 10, 2014, the Dutch Senate passed the Work and (Social) Security Act (Wet Werk en Zekerheid). This Act substantially changed the rules on flexible employment, dismissal and the Dutch Unemployment Insurance Act (ww). The new rules have been implemented in three phases, specifically on January 1, 2015, July 1, 2015, and April 1, 2016.

The new rules on flexible employment are aimed at reinforcing the legal position of flexible workers. Most of the rules entered into effect on January 1, 2015.

Probationary Period

All employment contracts entered into on or after January 1, 2015, may no longer include a probationary period if the employment contract is entered into for a period of six months or less. Any probationary period agreed upon will be deemed null and void.

Non-Compete Clause

Non-compete clauses may no longer be included in employment contracts for a fixed period of time (regardless of the duration), unless the employer indicates in writing in the employment contract why compelling business or operational interests require such a clause. If no written reasons are given, the clause is void. These compelling business or operational interests must still exist when the clause takes effect, i.e. the termination date of the employment contract.

The new rules apply to all employment contracts entered into on or after January 1, 2015. Non-compete clauses in contracts for a fixed period of time entered into before this date will remain valid.

Notification Obligation

The Act also introduces a notification obligation for employment contracts for a fixed period of time of six months or longer. No later than one month before the employment contract for a fixed period expires, the employer must notify the employee in writing whether or not the employment contract will be extended and, if so, on what terms. If the employer does not notify the employee at all, the employee is entitled to a compensation of one month's gross salary. If the employer fails to notify the employee about the termination or extension on time, the employee is entitled to a pro rata compensation. The notification obligation does not apply to employment contracts that do not end on a specific calendar date (such as a project or the replacement of a sick employee), nor to temporary agency contracts containing an assignment clause (*uitzendbeding*).

The Obligation to Continue to Pay Salary

The new Act limits the possibility of excluding the obligation to continue to pay salary in the absence of work. Before January 1, 2015, the obligation to continue to pay salary could be excluded in writing during the first 26 weeks of the employment contract and, if a Collective Labor Agreement (*Collectieve Arbeidsovereenkomst*,

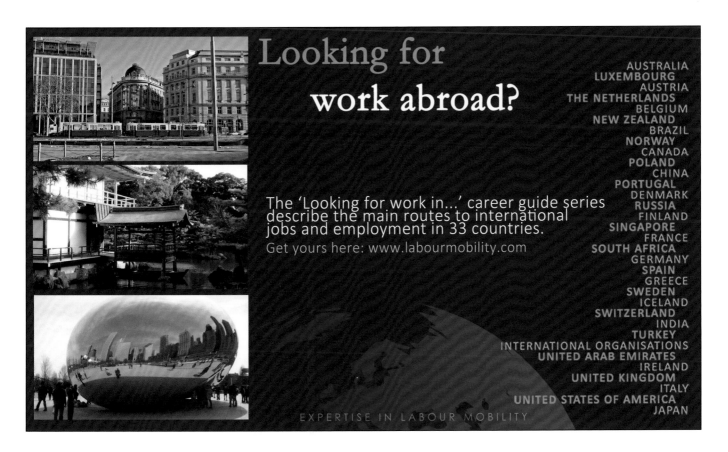

CAO) applied, the 26-week statutory period could be extended indefinitely. Under the Act and only if a CAO applies, after the initial 26-week period, this period may only be extended for positions which by their nature involve occasional rather than permanent work.

The new rules apply to employment contracts entered into on or after January 1, 2015. Existing deviations from this, contained in CAOs will, however, remain valid for the remaining period, but only until July 1, 2016.

Main Rule 'No Work, No Pay' Reversed

The current main rule – 'no work, no pay' – has been abolished as of April 1, 2016. At the same time the so-called risk rule, which was an exception to this main rule, has been amended. According to this risk rule, an employee retains the right to pay if he has not been able to work due to a cause which should reasonably be for the account of the employer. Although the Minister explained that no major changes were envisaged, the majority is of the opinion that, as of April 1, 2016, the burden of proof will be reversed to the employer: the employer will be obliged to pay salary if the employee does not perform any work, *unless* the employer can prove that this should reasonably be for the account of the employee. Examples of such a situation might be participating in a strike, not arriving at work on time or serving a prison sentence.

The Chain Rule

The so-called chain rule stipulates that employment contracts for a fixed period of time will be converted by operation of law into indefinite employment contracts at some point in time. The Act reduces the maximum period for successive employment contracts for a fixed period of time from three to two years. The maximum number of contracts that may be concluded within this period will still be three. For employment contracts to be considered successive, the permitted interval between them will be increased from three to six months. The Act also limits the possibility of deviating from the chain rule by means of a CAO. Only in the case of a temporary agency contract, or if the intrinsic nature of the business operations so requires, may the maximum period for successive temporary employment contracts be extended to four years and the maximum number of temporary contracts be increased to six.

Certain categories of employees are excluded, such as employees younger than 18 years of age who, on average, do not work for more than 12 hours, and other groups to be designated by the Minister.

The new rules apply to employment contracts entered into on or after July 1, 2015. Extensive and difficult transitional rules apply to ascertain whether or not an employment agreement for an indefinite period of time is deemed to exist if a new employment contract is entered into on or after July 1, 2015. Existing deviations in CAOS will remain in effect until the CAO ends, but these will no longer apply after July 1, 2016.

DISMISSAL

The Act also provides for major changes in the rules for dismissal as of July 1, 2015. The old rules will remain in effect for termination procedures commenced before this date. The most important changes are set out below.

Imperative Dismissal Route

It will no longer be possible for the employer to choose between the two dismissal routes, via the Employee Insurance Agency (UWV) or the subdistrict sector of the District Court. If an employer wants to dismiss an employee for business economic reasons or due to long-term incapacity for work, the employer must apply for a dismissal permit with the UWV. If the dismissal is based on other reasons, such as unsatisfactory performance or a damaged working relationship, the employer must go to the subdistrict sector of the District Court.

Training Obligation

The Act also introduces an obligation for the employer to enable employees to take training courses required to perform their work. This obligation plays an important role for both the UWV and the court when deciding whether an employee may be dismissed or not: if the employee can be reassigned to a different, suitable position, with or without training, or if this would be the more logical course of action, dismissal will be denied nor may an employee whose performance is unsatisfactory be dismissed if it turns out that his underperformance is the result of the employer not complying with above obligation.

Notice Period

The notice period for termination will remain the same, but the time taken for proceedings before the UWV or the subdistrict sector of the District Court may be fully subtracted from the notice period provided that at least a one-month notice period remains. The Court is not required to take the notice period into account in the event of a serious culpable act or omission by the employee.

Transitional Payment

Severance pay based on the so-called Cantonal Court formula no longer applies as of July 1, 2015. Proceedings based on 'manifestly

unreasonable dismissal' and the fair compensation that can be awarded in such proceedings will also be a thing of the past. Instead the so-called transitional payment (*transitievergoeding*) has been introduced. An employee will be entitled to a transitional payment if the employer either terminates the employment contract, gives notice to terminate or does not renew it AND the employee has been employed for at least 24 months in total. The employee will also be entitled to a transitional payment if he himself dissolves, terminates or does not renew the employment contract due to a serious culpable act or omission by the employer.

The amount of the transitional payment will depend on the number of years of service and the employee's monthly salary. An employee accrues a transitional payment of 1/6th monthly salary after every period of six months of service, hence 1/3rd of the monthly salary after every year of service (12 months). An employee who has worked for more than 10 years accrues a transitional payment of 1/4th of his monthly salary after every subsequent six months of service, i.e. half a month's salary after every year of service for those years he has worked beyond 10 years. The transitional payment is only accrued after every full period of six months, i.e. the 6-months' period of service will not be rounded up. No transitional payment is accrued if an employee is not employed for a full period of six months. The maximum statutory transitional payment will be € 76,000 gross or one year's salary (if this is higher than € 76,000). The employer and employee may agree on higher payments in the employment contract (golden parachutes).

In the event of a serious culpable act or omission by the employer, the Court may grant an extra compensation (or 'fair payment') to the employee.

The transitional payment will not be due if the employer:
- is declared insolvent
- is granted a suspension of payments, or
- is subject to debt rescheduling.

A transitional payment does not need to be paid either if the employee:
- is not yet 18 years of age and works 12 hours per week or less
- has reached retirement age, or
- is guilty of a serious culpable act or omission.

Transitional Scheme for Employees Aged 50 Years and Older
For employees aged 50 years or older, who have been employed for over ten years, a transitional scheme applies until January 1, 2020. For every six-month period that this person over 50 was employed by the employer after reaching the age of 50, he will receive half a month's salary. This scheme for people over 50 does not apply to companies employing fewer than 25 people.

Deduction of Transitional and Employability Costs
An employer may deduct so-called transitional and employability costs from the transitional payment. Transitional costs are costs incurred in connection with terminating or not extending an employment contract, which are aimed at preventing or curtailing unemployment, e.g. training and outplacement costs, as well as costs for observing a notice period that is longer than what is applicable between the parties, while the employee is free to look for another job. Employability costs are costs incurred during employ-

ment and aimed at increasing employability. Costs incurred for increasing possibilities for internal reassignment, or which are directly connected with the employee's current responsibilities, may not be deducted from the transitional payment, nor may employability costs be deducted if they have been incurred more than five years prior to the termination date.

An employer may only deduct transitional and employability costs with the employee's consent. That consent is not required if arrangements are made in a CAO.

Appeal
The Act introduces the possibility of filing an appeal (or even an appeal in cassation) against a dissolution decision of the subdistrict sector of the District Court. At present, this possibility is only very limited. A decision in first instance is not, initially, suspended by an appeal or an appeal in cassation. In addition, as of July 1, 2015, a decision made by the UWV is open to appeal. For instance, if the UWV does not grant a dismissal permit, an employer can still appeal to the subdistrict sector of the District Court to terminate the employment contract with the employee. Should the UWV have granted a dismissal permit, it is the employee who can appeal and claim reinstatement of his employment contract.

Any claims relating to termination of the employment contract must be filed in court by means of an application. The summons, as used for example with salary claims today, will disappear.

TERMINATION WITHOUT THE COURT OR THE UWV
Probationary Period
During and even before the start of the probation period, either party may terminate the employment contract with immediate effect without stating any reasons. A probationary period is only valid when it has been agreed upon in writing.

Termination by Mutual Consent or Agreement
An employment contract may only be terminated without the involvement of the UWV or the subdistrict sector of the District Court:
- by giving notice to terminate and the employee gives his consent, or
- where a settlement agreement has been reached.

The employee will have two weeks to reflect and to either retract his consent or dissolve the settlement agreement. The employer must notify the employee of this statutory period of reflection and retraction in writing. If the employer fails to inform the employee in writing of this right of reflection and retraction, the period will be extended to three weeks.

If the employee retracts his consent or revokes the settlement agreement, the employer must follow the imperative dismissal route or try to reach a new settlement agreement. Special rules apply with respect to managing directors.

If a settlement agreement is entered into, the employer is not obliged to pay the statutory transitional payment. Parties are free to make their own arrangements regarding a severance payment. The employee is, however, not likely to accept an amount that is lower than the transitional payment. Please note, that if the employer gives notice to terminate the employment agreement with the consent of the employee, he is still obliged to pay a transitional payment if the total years of service amount to more than 24 months.

Urgent Cause

Sometimes, an urgent situation can arise in which either the employer or the employee cannot reasonably be expected to continue the employment. If this situation has been caused by the employee, the employer is entitled to terminate the employment agreement without notice and with immediate effect. He does not have to follow the imperative dismissal route. The Dutch Civil Code gives a number of examples of what constitutes urgent cause, such as misleading or false statements, theft, fraud, breach of trust, gross negligence, etc.

The urgent cause must be sufficiently urgent to warrant immediate and irrevocable termination and must be communicated to the employee without delay, stating the exact reasons for termination, preferably in writing. In general, a delay will be regarded as evidence that the cause was not urgent.

If the court is of the opinion that the cause was not urgent enough to justify an immediate termination, it can declare the dismissal void. Since no prior approval of either the Court or the UWV was obtained, the employee will then in principle be entitled to receive his salary as of the date of the nullified termination until the employment agreement is properly terminated.

30%-RULING

Losing your job need not have consequences for the application of the 30%-ruling in the future; if you find a new employer within three months and all other conditions for application of the ruling are still met, you will be able to apply for the ruling again and benefit from it for the remainder of the applicable period.

PENSION

One of the things you will want to arrange when you come to work in the Netherlands, is your old age pension. The easiest would be for you to be able to continue participating in your existing pension scheme back home (or your former country of employment). However, for this to be without negative tax consequences, your pension scheme must 'qualify'.

QUALIFYING PENSION SCHEME

In general, foreign (non-Netherlands) pension schemes do not 'qualify' for Dutch tax purposes. However, according to Dutch law, a foreign pension scheme can be approved by the Dutch tax authorities as a qualifying pension scheme if it meets the following conditions:

- you are working in the Netherlands on a temporary basis
- you and your employer jointly file a request with the Dutch tax authorities to have the scheme deemed a qualifying scheme
- your Dutch employer has granted pension rights/entitlements to you under the foreign pension scheme
- you were already participating in the foreign pension scheme before your assignment here
- the foreign pension scheme is a common pension scheme in its country of origin
- the foreign pension scheme meets several Dutch statutory conditions for qualifying pension schemes
- the pension fund or pension insurance company is a professional insurance company in accordance with Dutch tax law.

Pension contributions you pay to a qualifying pension scheme are deductible for Dutch tax purposes and the pension contributions paid by your employer are not considered taxable wages. The pension benefits you receive at a later date are subject to wage tax. This is called the 'rule of reversal'. If you are participating in a pension scheme arranged by a Dutch employer, then in all likelihood, it is a qualifying pension scheme.

If you contribute to a pension scheme that does not qualify, your contributions are not tax-deductible, nor are your employer's contributions considered non-taxable income. The actual pension benefit payments, however, will be tax-free.

AFTER LEAVING THE NETHERLANDS

If you leave the Netherlands and have participated in a qualifying (Netherlands or approved foreign) pension scheme, the Dutch tax authorities will impose a so-called protective tax bill (*conserverende aanslag*) on your pension rights. You will, however, not have to pay this tax bill, unless you carry out what is referred to as a 'forbidden act', which could indicate that you have made improper use of your pension insurance. An example of such an act would be commuting the pension, selling it, or using it as security. If, after ten years, you have not done any of this, or if you move back to the Netherlands, then the protective tax bill is revoked and you will not have to pay it. A few years ago, the question arose as to whether the Netherlands, based on European legislation, is actually authorized to levy protective tax bills on pension rights. On June 16, 2009, the Dutch Supreme Court ruled that in certain cases this is indeed the case and the Ministry of Finance immediately came up with legislation to close the loopholes, with retroactive effect. The protective tax bill now relates to the pension premiums for which the employee enjoyed a tax benefit in the Netherlands.

Where your pension payments will be taxed, depends on the applicability and contents of a tax treaty on this matter at the time of payment.

SOCIAL SECURITY

TO WHOM IS IT APPLICABLE

Those who legally reside and/or work in the Netherlands are in principle subject to the Dutch social security system. This legislation is also important for their partners and/or other members of their families, unless they are exempt under EC Regulation 883/2004 (before May 1, 2010, this was EC-Regulation 1408/71) or a bilateral social security treaty (both of which you will read about further on). There are two kinds of compulsory social insurance schemes in the Netherlands; one that is applicable to the population in general (national insurance schemes) and one that is applicable to employees only (employee insurance schemes).

NATIONAL INSURANCE SCHEMES

In principle, the national insurance schemes (*volksverzekeringen*) cover all persons living or working in the Netherlands. The schemes are as follows:

General Old Age Pensions Act (AOW)

Those who are covered by the AOW are entitled to an old age pension upon reaching the age of 65. A legislative proposal has been passed that has resulted in an incremental raising of the pensionable age to 66 by 2018 and 67 by 2021, meaning that the pensionable age has already been raised to over 65. A proposal is pending as a consequence of which, as of 2024, the pensionable age will depend on the average life expectancy. Future recipients of the AOW will be informed five years in advance as to when they can expect to receive it.

General Surviving Relatives Act (ANW)

Those who are covered by the General Surviving Relatives Act (ANW) are entitled to a widow's, widower's or 'dependent children'-benefit. The deceased spouse, partner or parent must have been insured under the ANW at the date of his or her death.

    The amount paid out on the basis of the benefit is a percentage of the minimum wage – however, the actual benefit can be less since the ANW survivor's benefit is income-dependent.

Long-Term Care Act (WLZ)

This act replaces the Exceptional Medical Expenses Act (AWBZ), and makes a provision for those who need intensive care or supervision 24/7. For instance, elderly persons with dementia, or persons with severe mental, physical or hearing/seeing disabilities. This includes treatment and nursing in recognized institutions and nursing homes, personal care and nursing, the supply of artificial appliances, medical care, and transportation to the place of supervision or treatment. In order to receive this care, the person must be approved for it. He is then issued a so-called WLZ-indicatie.

The Health Insurance Act (ZVW)

Everyone who legally resides in the Netherlands and is subject to the Dutch social security system is obligated to have health insurance, to be taken out with a 'private' health insurance company. These companies are obligated to accept everyone for the standard package, irrespective of gender, age, or health. You can choose between two types of insurance policies, or a combination of these two:

- policy in kind: the insurance company enters into several contracts with health care suppliers and pays the insurance companies' bills directly
- restitution policy: the insurant chooses the health care supplier himself, and pays the bills himself, after which he is reimbursed by the insurance company.

You can also take out 'additional' health insurance, if you want to cover more than the standard medical care. However, there is no acceptance obligation for insurance companies in the case of additional insurance.

Child Benefit Act (AKW)

In principle, this benefit (*Kinderbijslag*) is for children under the age of 18. The amount of the allowance depends on the age of the child and special rules apply to children aged 16 and 17.

CONTRIBUTIONS (PAYABLE TO TAX DEPARTMENT)

Contributions for the national insurance schemes are levied on income up to € 33,715 per year (to a maximum of € 9,490), together with the income tax. The percentages are:

	employer	employee
AOW	–	17.90%
ANW	–	0.60%
AKW	–	–
WLZ (FORMERLY AWBZ)	–	9.65%
ZVW	6.75%	

Note: the income-dependent contribution for the ZVW is levied on the employee, but compensated by the employer on a maximum income of € 52,763.

The ZVW (Health Insurance Act) is financed by means of a nominal premium per person of approximately € 1,200 - € 1,450 on average per year (depending on the insurance company) and an income-dependent contribution. If you are an employee, your income-dependent contribution (5.5%) will be compensated by your employer. If you are self-employed or unemployed, you will receive no such compensation. Also if you receive an old-age pension or a benefit, you will pay an income-dependent contribution. Whether or not this is compensated, depends on your pension plan / social security institution. If your income lies below a certain level, you can request the government for financial assistance to help pay your insurance premiums (referred to as the *zorgtoeslag*). Children are covered by the basic insurance, free of charge till the age of 18.

EMPLOYEE INSURANCE SCHEMES

In principle, anyone employed in the Netherlands is compulsorily insured under the employee insurance schemes (*werknemersverzekeringen*). If the total of any of the first three benefits and any other family income is less than the statutory social minimum income, the recipient is entitled to apply to the Social Security Institution for a supplement under the Supplemental Benefits Act (*Toeslagenwet*), which are paid out specifically to help finance rent, health care insurance premiums, daycare for the children of working parents, and general expenses related to the having of children.

    The schemes are as follows:

Sickness Benefits act (ZW) / WULBZ / WVLBZ

Pursuant to the WULBZ (*Wet Uitbreiding Loondoorbetalingsplicht bij Ziekte* – Continuation of Wage Payments during Sickness Act) and the WVLBZ (*Wet Verlenging Loondoorbetalingsplicht Bij Ziekte* – Prolongation of Continuation of Wage Payments during Sickness Act), an employer is obligated to continue paying 70% (up to a maximum of 70% of € 202.17 gross per social security day – i.e. the so-called daily wage) of the employee's salary during the first 104 weeks of sickness, provided the employee is subject to the Dutch social security system or has a contract governed by the Dutch civil code. Depending on the employer, this payment is capped or can even be 100% of the employee's last-earned salary.

    The Sickness Benefits Act (ZW) will only provide a 'safety net' for certain categories of employees, such as employees who do not – or no longer – have an employer (for example temporary workers), and employees who have taken out a voluntary ZW-insurance. Sick pay is usually 70% of the daily wage and is paid out until the employee has been on sick leave for a maximum of 104 weeks.

Female employees are given at least 16 weeks' leave in the event of pregnancy, during which period a pregnancy benefit is paid out by the Social Security Institution (you can read more about this on page 191). The benefit is then 100% of the so-called daily wage, although in practice the employers often pay out the gap between this daily wage and your last-earned salary.

Work and Income According to Labor Capacity Act (WIA)

The WIA applies to all employees who have been disabled for work for more than 104 weeks. The aim of this act is to stimulate 'ability' for work and to make a clear distinction between long-term disability for work (no recovery within five years), temporary complete disability (80-100%) and partial disability for work. Before an employee qualifies for the WIA-benefit, it will have to be determined whether both employer and employee have put enough effort into reintegrating the employee back into the labor process. In the case of complete and permanent disability, this will not be necessary and the employee will have a right to an IVA-benefit (benefit for fully disabled persons), amounting to 75% of the most recent (maximum) daily wage. Those who are less than 80% but more than 35% disabled, have a right to the WGA-benefit (Reintegration Act Partially Disabled Persons). This benefit is at first a salary-related benefit, the duration of which depends on the employment history of the employee in question. At the end of this period, the employee receives either a supplementary allowance or a follow-up allowance. An employee who works and earns at least half of his residual earning capacity (restverdiencapaciteit) is entitled to a supplement of 70% of the difference between his last wage and his residual earning capacity. However, an employee who is unemployed or who earns less than half of his residual earning capacity is entitled to a follow-up allowance of 70% of the legal minimum wage multiplied by a factor that is determined by the percentage of his occupational disability. In principle the employee is entitled to one of these allowances until he/she reaches retirement age.

Disability Insurance Act (WAO)

The WAO will continue to apply to employees who were already receiving the WAO-benefit on January 1, 2006. It entitles employees under the pensionable age to a benefit if they are still at least 15% unfit for work after 52 weeks of disability. The amount of the benefit depends on the degree of disability, the last-earned wage and the age of the employee.

Unemployment Insurance Act (ww)

The ww insures employees against the financial consequences of unemployment. There are a few requirements that must be met for a person to be entitled to a ww-benefit. He/she must:
- have been employed for a period of at least 26 weeks over the 36 weeks immediately prior to becoming unemployed, and
- have received wages over 208 hours or more in at least four of the five calendar years prior to the year in which he/she became unemployed.

DigiD

Perhaps you have heard of it, perhaps you haven't: DigiD. DigiD is your digital identity, consisting of a username and password, which allows you to make use of the electronic services of several government institutions and organizations. You use it, for instance, to file your online tax return, to arrange the Child Benefit, for the online ordering of municipal documents, but also to make an appointment for your driver's exam or to obtain insight into year health care insurance expenditures, etc. You are not required to have a DigiD, as most services can still be arranged by telephone or letter – it is merely a ways of making it possible for you to take care of certain matters online.

To obtain your personal DigiD, you must make sure you are registered with the municipality you live in. Then you visit www.digid.nl, where you fill in your *burgerservicenummer* (see page 66), date of birth, postal code, house number, and e-mail address. Five days after you do this, you will receive your activation code by mail, which you must use within 20 days.

If only the first requirement is met, the employee will receive 75% of the last-earned wage (with a maximum of 75% of € 202.17 gross per social security day – i.e. the maximum daily wage) during the first two months. During the remaining month, he/she will receive 70% of the (maximum) daily wage. If both requirements are met, he/she will receive – in addition to this three-month benefit – a salary-related benefit of 70% of the (maximum) daily wage. The duration of the salary-related benefit depends on the employee's employment record, but can, in total, not exceed 38 months. As of January 1, 2016, the maximum period during which the employee will receive the ww-benefit will be shortened incrementally from 38 months to 24 months (in April, 2019). This can be arranged differently in a collective labor agreement (CAO) and extended to 38 months.

CONTRIBUTIONS

	employer	employee
WAO/WIA basis	5.88%	–
WAO/WIA differentiated*		
ww general	2.44%	–
ww differentiated*		–

* = these percentages vary per company

Contributions for the employee insurance schemes are levied on wages and salaries up to € 52,763 per year.

CONTRIBUTIONS (PAYABLE TO TAX DEPARTMENT)

The contributions for both the national insurance schemes and the employee insurance schemes are levied by the tax department, together with the wage tax.

'DOUBLE' SOCIAL INSURANCES

ANOTHER EU MEMBER STATE
Dutch Social Security
An employee who starts working in the Netherlands is, in principle, subject to the Dutch social security legislation. One of the exceptions to this main rule applies if he has been posted from another EU or EEA (European Economic Area) member state or Switzerland. In the following sections this exception will be discussed in more detail.

Period Shorter than Six Months
Special rules apply to non-residents who carry out work in the Netherlands for a period shorter than six months; they will under certain conditions not be subject to the employee insurance schemes. However, if the income earned in the Netherlands is subject to wage tax here, and the duties are in fact carried out in the Netherlands, they will nevertheless be subject to the national insurance schemes.

Continued Social Security
As of May 1, 2010, EC Regulation 1408/71 has been replaced by EC Regulation 883/2004. This has had a number of consequences for the EU regime on the coordination of social security schemes. Some of the major changes are briefly outlined below.

Transitional Rules
During a transitional period of ten years, the provisions of Regulation 1408/71 will continue to apply to existing situations as long as the facts and circumstances have not changed, unless the employee explicitly requests that the new Regulation be applied.

It is important to note that the provisions of Regulation 1408/71 will continue to apply with regard to non-EU nationals, as the new regulation will only apply to them once the EU Member States have agreed to enlarge the scope of application to this effect. The provisions of Regulation 1408/71 will also continue to apply to nationals of Norway, Iceland, Lichtenstein and Switzerland, as agreements with these countries still have to be concluded with regard to the application of Regulation 883/2004 for workers moving within the EEA and Switzerland.

Assignments
Under Regulation 1408/71, the period during which an employee was eligible for the continuation of the social security scheme of his country of residence while he was on assignment abroad was equal to 12 months with the option of prolonging the secondment with another period of 12 months – provided the host country gave prior approval. Under Regulation 883/2004 this period has been extended to 24 months. This means that the application for a 24 month-assignment will no longer require the intervention of the social security authorities of the host country.

The main conditions for assignment remain unchanged, being:
- the employee is covered by the social security schemes of a member state
- the employee remains in the employment of the company that has assigned him
- the anticipated duration of the assignment does not exceed 24 months
- the employee is not assigned to replace another employee who has completed his maximum term of assignment
- the Dutch company to which the employee is temporarily assigned will not subsequently assign him to work for another company
- the employer usually carries out work on the territory of the assigning state.

If the above conditions are satisfied, the social security legislation of the first member state will remain applicable.

Simultaneous Employment
Under Regulation 1408/71, in the case of simultaneous employment in several states for one and the same employer, an employee was subject to the social security scheme of his country of residence if he carried out part of his activities in the country of residence (in many countries, one day a month on average was considered sufficient in this respect). Under Regulation 883/2004, an employee will only be subject to the social security scheme of his country of residence, in a similar situation, provided he carries out a *substantial* part of his activities in the country of residence. 'Substantial' activities are defined as 25% or more of the working time, remuneration or turnover. This definition could change the social security situation of a number of mobile employees who are working in several countries and who are currently subject to the social security scheme of their country of residence.

In addition, under the new regime, the so-called 'Annex VII situations', whereby an employee may – by way of exception – be subject to two different social security schemes, has been abolished. Anyone who works as an employee as well as a self-employed person in several countries at the same time, will automatically be subject to the social security scheme of the state in which he works as an employee.

Benefits
Specific changes have also been introduced for a number of social security benefits. For instance, the exportation of unemployment benefits is now possible during a period of six months instead of the three months under Regulation 1408/71.

Exceptions
Both Regulations also contain a general exception (article 17 of EC Regulation 1408/71 and article 16 of EC Regulation 883/2004) that can be invoked in those cases in which it is in the interest of the employee to deviate from the mandatory allocation rules, for instance, when it is already clear beforehand that the duration of the assignment will exceed 24 (12) months. In the event of such a request, the two member states concerned will conduct negotiations and, if the request is granted, will reach an agreement. Requests to continue the application of the foreign social security legislation under this provision are generally granted when the anticipated duration of the assignment does not exceed five years. Extensions beyond the five-year period are only very exceptionally allowed.

Conditions

The conditions that must be satisfied may vary slightly from one treaty to another, but will generally comprise the following:

- before being posted abroad, the employee was insured according to the social security legislation of the country from which he is being posted
- the employment with the company in the country from which the person is posted is continued.

Period

The period during which the posting is allowed to continue varies from 12 months to an unlimited period (depending on the treaty) and extension is sometimes possible (also depending on the treaty).

Certificate

It is advisable to apply for a certificate stating which legislation is applicable. In some treaty member states, having this certificate is one of the conditions for posting an employee abroad.

General Rule

If the conditions are not satisfied, the general rule of the relevant treaty takes effect. In all treaties, the general rule is that (the) Dutch social security legislation is applicable if the work is carried out in the Netherlands. Nearly all treaties prevent the simultaneous applicability of the legislation of two countries.

A NON-TREATY MEMBER STATE

Exemption not Possible

If a person is posted from a country with which the Netherlands has not entered into a social security treaty, it is – in general – not possible to obtain an exemption from the Dutch social insurances. As there is no applicable treaty, it is possible that the employee, pursuant to the applicable national social security laws, will have to participate in the social security systems of both countries. This may result both in double liability to pay contributions and double entitlement to benefits.

STARTING YOUR OWN COMPANY

Maybe you came to the Netherlands for the purpose of starting up your own company. Or maybe you came here with your spouse/partner – who was posted here by his or her employer – and want to generate your own income. In either case, you are considering setting up (your own) business in the Netherlands. What are some of the things you have to think of? And who can help you answer the many questions you will have? What diplomas do you need?

There are various organizations that you can turn to for help.

CHAMBERS OF COMMERCE

There are more than 20 regional Chambers of Commerce (Kamers van Koophandel) in the Netherlands. One of their main tasks is to register (practically) all companies based in the Netherlands, whether they are of Dutch origin or foreign. Public and private limited companies, cooperative societies, mutual guarantee associations, sole traders, partnerships and associations of home-owners are obligated to register with the Chamber of Commerce of the district in which they are established, even if they do not carry out

Certificate

An A1-certificate is issued in order to make clear in which country social security contributions are to be paid. In order to actually receive medical care (zvw or wlz) in the Netherlands, in addition to the certificate, a European Health Insurance Card is needed. This is issued by the competent authorities abroad and enables the employee to register with a health insurance company in his country of residence. This is of particular importance if medical care cannot be delayed.

ANOTHER TREATY MEMBER STATE

Social Security Treaty

If a person is assigned from abroad to the Netherlands and the Netherlands has entered into a social security treaty with that other country, the applicable legislation will be determined in accordance with the allocation rules of this treaty. It should first be determined whether the person is covered by the scope of the treaty. For this to be the case, it is generally required that the employee is a national of one of the treaty states and/or was insured in one of the states before being assigned abroad.

Temporary Posting

If the posting is temporary, most treaties allow the continuation of the application of the legislation of the country from which the employee has been posted.

a business. Private persons who work on a free-lance basis and persons who carry out one of the professions specified on the professions list of the Chamber of Commerce, are also obligated to register. The purpose of this registration is to enable third parties to find information on a company – such as who is liable, who can make binding commitments; in other words, the legal structure of a company. The system has been proven to be reliable, transparent and up-to-date.

The Chamber of Commerce is a public institution and the information desk can provide you with information on how to start a business, which diplomas you need for your specific line of business, how to write a business plan to be able to finance your ideas and what (zoning) plans your municipality has within the area in which you want to establish your firm.

MKB-NEDERLAND
Another institution you can turn to for information is MKB-Nederland (Instituut voor Midden- en Kleinbedrijf), an organization that represents the interests of small and medium-sized companies. Various activities are initiated by this institute, aimed at offering its members relevant knowledge and expertise as well as at improving the general position of small and medium-sized companies. You will find its address and telephone number at the end of the chapter.

OTHER INSTITUTIONS
Other institutions that can offer you advice are banks and the national tax office. Both have information desks for people who plan to start their own business and can provide you with the information you need. And last, but not least, all major cities have a business desk at the town hall.

PROOF OF IDENTITY
When an enterprise is started or authorization is given to take responsibility in an enterprise, for example as a private entrepreneur or as director or partner, proof of identity will be required when registering with the trade register. At the counter of the Chamber of Commerce, valid proof of identity together with an original private bank statement or an original extract from the population register (not older than one month) should be presented.

The following documents are accepted as valid proof of identity:
- a valid travel document (Dutch or foreign passport, European identity card)
- a valid Dutch driver's license (a foreign driver's license will not be accepted)
- a residence permit issued by the Dutch aliens police
- a Dutch refugee passport
- a Dutch aliens passport.

SETTING UP ESTABLISHMENT
The Dutch policy of free enterprise entails that there are no specific restrictions for foreign companies who wish to start a business in the Netherlands, nor are there restrictions on the ownership of real estate or on the remission of capital and profits abroad.

There are various ways in which foreign companies can set up permanent establishment in the Netherlands. The Dutch legal system provides a framework with various options, which are described briefly in this section:

- branch office
- *eenmanszaak*: a one-man business
- *maatschap*: partnership – business involving more than one person, usually used by accountants, doctors, etc.
- *vennootschap onder firma* (VOF): general or commercial partnership – business involving more than one person, under a common name, each severally liable
- *commanditaire vennootschap* (CV): limited partnership with managing and 'silent' partners
- *besloten vennootschap* (BV): private company with limited liability
- *naamloze vennootschap* (NV): (public) corporation.

BRANCH OFFICE
A foreign company does not require any prior approval from the Dutch authorities to establish a branch office in the Netherlands. It does have to file various details (i.e. name, trade name, objects, manager) and documents (i.e. articles of association) pertaining to the company and the branch office with the Chamber of Commerce. The local manager of the branch office does not have to be of Dutch nationality. Insofar as the obligation to publish the annual report and accounts also applies under the law of the country of formation of the foreign company, these should be filed with the Dutch Chamber of Commerce as well.

PARTNERSHIP
Under Dutch law it is possible to set up a partnership with two or more partners: the general partnership ('VOF' or *vennootschap onder firma*) and the limited partnership ('CV' or *commanditaire vennootschap*). The basic difference between these two forms of partnership is the partners' liabilities. A limited partnership has one or more managing partners (*beherende vennoten*) and one or more 'silent' partners (*commanditaire vennoten*). The liability of the 'silent' partners is limited to the amount of their capital contributions. Each partner in a general partnership is, in addition to the partnership itself, severally liable for the obligations of the company. Under Dutch law, a partnership is similar to a business under single proprietorship, except that there are two or more owners.

COMPANIES WITH LIMITED LIABILITY
In the Netherlands, corporate law defines two different types of companies with limited liability: the NV (*naamloze vennootschap*), which is a public company with limited liability, and the BV (*besloten vennootschap*), which is a private company with limited liability.

The main differences between the two types of companies are:
- the shares in the NV can be either in bearer or in registered form; the shares in the BV are in registered form only
- the minimum issued and paid up capital of the NV is € 45,000; there is no minimum capital for BVs
- the Articles of Association of a BV must include restrictions for the transfer of its shares; such restrictions are optional for the NV
- the legal limitations regarding the company's purchase of shares in its own capital and regarding financial assistance by the company are stricter for an NV than for a BV
- the BV form is particularly suitable for a wholly-owned subsidiary, joint venture companies and family businesses. The NV is suitable for larger companies whose shares may be listed.

Ask your accountant, legal or financial advisor or the Chamber of Commerce about the legal and fiscal consequences of the above forms.

TAXES SELF-EMPLOYED PERSONS
If you run your own business you can be held liable for the following:
- wage tax
- income tax
- national insurance schemes
- employee insurance schemes (if you have employees)
- VAT (value added tax).

Self-employed persons who have only themselves to think of owe income tax, VAT, and must arrange their own medical insurance, for which they, as does everyone else, owe a fixed contribution and an income-dependent contribution. If their income (if they have a partner for tax purposes; together with their partner) lies below a certain level, they can apply for government assistance in paying for this insurance, called the *zorgtoeslag*. You can read more about this insurance on page 71 and on page 124. Enlisting the services of an accountant will help you benefit from the many deductions that apply to you.

VAT
Those who deliver services and goods in the Netherlands are obligated to charge their customers VAT (*Belasting Toegevoegde Waarde* or BTW), which they subsequently pay to the tax authorities. The general VAT rates are 21% and 6%. They owe this, no matter whether they (aim to) make a profit or not, the moment an invoice is sent out. To the delivery of goods and services outside the Netherlands, other rules apply.

However, the amount of VAT that you have paid to others who deliver their goods and services to you, can be deducted from the amount of VAT you owe. Those whose 'VAT income' does not exceed a certain amount enjoy a full or limited exemption from paying the amount due to the tax authorities.

The amount of VAT due should be reported on the *Aangifte omzetbelasting*, or Turnover Tax Return, on a regular basis (monthly, quarterly or yearly). This is done online, by means of the so-called electronic, or *electronische*, Tax Return. The tax authorities issue you a username and a password to do this.

VAR
Until recently, in order to avoid unpleasant (tax) surprises – for you and your client – you requested the tax authorities to issue you a *Verklaring Arbeidsrelatie* (Statement on Your Labor Relation). This VAR either stated that you were not working in the employment of your client, but for yourself, or that you were working on the basis of a (fictitious) labor relationship. This way, your clients knew upfront whether or not they would have to withhold wage tax or social security contributions on what they paid out to you.

This statement is to be replaced by standard contracts, made up by the tax authorities, which can be downloaded from their site. These contracts are valid for a period of five years and have been drawn up by the various branch organizations for specific professions and will be subject to an independent legal assessment by a panel of experts, since there have been signs that these may – inadvertently – constitute employment contracts under civil law.

The findings of the panel will be published. Since May 1, 2016, the VAR has officially been abolished and the implementation phase has started, which will run until May, 2017. As of that date, the tax authorities will effectively start enforcing the new rules.

You can also draw up your own contract and submit it before the tax authorities for approval. If you base it on a standard contract, you will see which items you should not change if you do not wish to run the risk of being considered to an employee. You are not obligated to make use of such a contract – it just offers you and your clients more clarity and is, in that sense, strongly advisable.

FINANCIAL AID AND DEDUCTIONS
The national tax office can tell you about the Tante Agaath-regulation, a scheme that makes it fiscally attractive for private persons to lend money to those who are setting up a business. Of course, you can approach a bank and see what they can do to help you, too.

When it comes to income tax, entrepreneurs enjoy an additional deduction over and above the levy rebate that every taxpayer has a right to every year of € 7,280, irrespective of the actual profits – though it may not exceed them. To this purpose you must prove that you spent at least 1,225 hours over the past tax year working for your own business (if your spouse works for the same company there are additional rules and possible deductions). Those who are starting up a new business (*startende ondernemers*) have a further deduction, subject to certain conditions, over the first few years of € 2,123. Furthermore, tax credits are available for investments made in cultural investment funds, green funds and socio-ethical funds.

DIPLOMAS / PERMITS
Depending on the type of business you want to start, there are a number of diplomas you might need. For most types of businesses, however, no diploma is required. Furthermore, some businesses are subject to a zoning plan, or require a building permit, environmental permit or establishment permit. Before you start your business, you must make sure you obtain the required permits and/or diplomas, for instance by contacting your municipality.

You can ask at the Chamber of Commerce as to what specific (type of) diploma you will need and how or where you can obtain this. If you have obtained a diploma in another country, this diploma can be evaluated by IDW (see the end of the chapter), to see whether it qualifies.

FREE-LANCING
There are two ways you can go about free-lancing; either as a self-employed person or through an employment agency. In the first case, you can read about some of the rules that apply to you in these paragraphs; in the latter case, you are, in principle, treated as an employee of the employment agency for tax purposes (you can read more about working for an employment agency in the first paragraphs of this chapter).

PERMITS AND CITIZEN SERVICE NUMBER
Note: Every natural person who wants to work in the Netherlands, whether in employment or self-employment, needs to comply with the Dutch entrance requirements set (if any) and needs a Citizen Service Number (*burgerservicenummer*), see page 66 (for Citizen Service Number) and page 111 (for permits).

AT WORK: EGALITARIANISM AND COMPROMISE

EGALITARIANISM

If you were to hear or read an interview with a Dutch captain of industry, you might be surprised to hear him (or her) downplay any central role he might have played in the company's success. He would declare himself a team player and would praise the creativity that is found throughout the company. He would accentuate the fact that all involved carried out the task as a team and that he would of course have accomplished nothing were it not for the energetic input and output of everyone. He would not sell himself as the genius with all the ideas but would describe himself as the coordinator, even if all involved realized deep in their hearts that, without his leadership, the stock value of the company would have long since plummeted.

This all has to do with the great appreciation that the Dutch have for egalitarianism, and their general resistance to being told what to do without any preliminary discussion. And of course, their undeniable need to seek compromise whenever possible. But that's not all. Their ingrained inclination to respect another person will not allow them to give out orders and commands. Conversely, the modern Dutchman likes to 'recognize himself' (his input) – as he puts it – in any decision made. In other words, he expects to be involved in the decision-making. If ministers or CEOs choose to keep a low profile, then this is purely a matter of strategy and tact.

Foreigners who work with Dutch companies – either as a customer or as an employee – are often confused by this egalitarianism. They are amazed at the informality between those who occupy the various rungs on the corporate ladder. Secretaries are on a first-name basis with their bosses. There is little evidence of hierarchy. Even the managers' offices are soberly decorated and visitors are given a modest welcome. It is perfectly normal for the company CEO to stand in line for lunch with the other employees in the company cafeteria – with the visitor right next to him. This does not mean that this visitor is not an honored one, and it gives no indication whatsoever of whether this visit is appreciated. This will only become evident from the meetings themselves and the agreements reached.

COMPROMISE – OVERLEG

Those who work in the Netherlands are often under the impression that a lot of time is wasted on discussions and that these discussions all lead to nothing. There are often meetings, commonly named *overleg* (consultation, or deliberation), with documents, an agenda and a chairman. All those present have their say, after which their remarks are discussed. And all this can be done quite eloquently. At the end, everyone pulls out their *agenda* (calendar), to schedule the next meeting.

He who decides to skip an *overleg* because he has something more urgent to attend to, will soon learn that this is not a wise decision – even if his colleagues were to admit readily that there is much too much *overleg* going on. The interacting that takes place during such a meeting is very important for the general progress. He who does not appear is saying that he does not think that the subject is sufficiently important or, even worse, that he apparently does not take his colleagues seriously. Furthermore, he runs the risk of missing essential information that may become evident during the meeting.

Those who are present during *overleg* show an interest in the problems of their colleagues. They supply suggestions, rather than amendments or commands, and thus declare themselves 'co-responsible'. The Dutch, in their final conclusions, like to use such metaphors as: 'we are all in one line'. Or even: 'our noses are pointing in the same direction again'. Ambitious beginners can also obtain useful information during an *overleg*: for instance, on what the pecking order is within the company.

As the Dutch only consider an idea to be partly theirs if they have been able to exercise influence on it and have been allowed to join the thinking process, it is advisable to take this into account when making plans. When you present a sharply chiseled decision, you will find that everyone has something to say about it and has questions to ask. This is why the Dutch will not be quick to present something as the only, the correct and the true solution. The advantage to this approach is that such an *overleg* will often lead to genuinely valuable suggestions for the improvement of certain aspects of a plan. As a result, the plan will be a joint approach and you will be able to count on everyone's cooperation.

This time-consuming and seemingly useless process of *overleg* helps colleagues become a team. The amount of time that is lost around the table is more than made up for in efficiency and input once everyone goes back to work. Statistics clearly show this. Dutch employees are among the world's leaders when it comes to work productivity.

HARMONIOUS RELATIONSHIPS

You will find this attitude not only on a smaller scale, but also on a larger scale. Dutch business life is generally characterized by harmonious relationships. This is evident from the works council that companies are obligated by law to have and that is elected from and by the employees. Though this council does not have a lot of authority and can not do much more than advise management, management has the obligation to consult it in many situations, such as reorganizations or large investment plans. The relationship between employer organizations and unions are also very harmonious, therefore employees seldom go on strike in the Netherlands. The worst that could happen is that, in the case of wage negotiations, one of the parties involved leaves the negotiation table. Then, after a small concession has been made, the *overleg* will simply resume.

SOCIAL SECURITY

**MINISTERIE VAN SOCIALE ZAKEN EN
WERKGELEGENHEID**
Ministry of Social Affairs and Employment
Anna van Hannoverstraat 4, 2595 BJ The Hague
Tel.: 070 333 44 44
www.rijksoverheid.nl

DE SOCIAAL ECONOMISCHE RAAD (SER)
*The Social and Economic Council of the
Netherlands*
Bezuidenhoutseweg 60, 2594 AW The Hague
Tel.: 070 349 94 99
www.ser.nl

SOCIALE VERZEKERINGSBANK
Social Insurance Bank
Rhijnspoorplein 1, 1091 HG Amsterdam
Tel.: 020 656 52 01
www.svb.nl

UWV
www.uwv.nl

IMMIGRATION/PERMITS

**IMMIGRATIE EN NATURALISATIE DIENST
(IND)**
Immigration and Naturalization Service
Tel.: 0900 123 45 61
www.ind.nl

MINISTERIE VAN BUITENLANDSE ZAKEN
Ministry of Foreign Affairs
Bezuidenhoutseweg 67, 2594 AC The Hague
Tel.: 070 348 64 86
www.government.nl/ministries/bz

NEW TO HOLLAND
www.newtoholland.nl: The official website of
the Netherlands on immigration

PERMITS FOUNDATION
An international corporate initiative to promote the improvement of work permit regulations for the spouses of expatriate employees.
www.permitsfoundation.com

WORK PERMITS
www.workpermit.com/netherlands

DUTCH EXPAT FOUNDATION
An independent interest organization for
expatriates and their Dutch based employers.
www.expatfoundation.org

EUROPE

EURES
European portal for labor mobility of the
European Commission. To find information
on jobs and learning opportunities in Europe.
www.eu.int/eures

**EUROPEAN COMMISION, REPRESENTATION
IN THE NETHERLANDS**
http://europa.eu

TAXES

GENERAL
In Dutch, English and German:
www.belastingdienst.nl

INTERNATIONAL TAX OFFICE HEERLEN
Postal address: P.O. Box 2865, 6401 DJ Heerlen
Visiting address: Kloosterweg 22, 6412 CN
Heerlen (by appointment only)
Tel.: 0800 05 43 (National telephone number)

DUTCH CUSTOMS (DOUANE)
P.O. Box 4486, 6401 CZ Heerlen
Tel.: 045 574 27 00
www.belastingdienst.nl and www.douane.nl

ORGANIZATIONS

MKB-NEDERLAND
*Institute for small and medium-sized
companies*
Brassersplein 1, 2612 CT Delft
Tel.: 015 219 12 12
www.mkb.nl

FENEDEX
Non-governmental export network
Raamweg 14, 2596 HL The Hague
Tel.: 070 330 56 00
www.fenedex.nl

MAJOR CHAMBERS OF COMMERCE

KAMER VAN KOOPHANDEL AMSTERDAM
Amsterdam Chamber of Commerce
De Ruyterkade 5, 1013 AA Amsterdam
Tel.: 020 531 40 00
Team International Trade Information
Tel.: 020 531 44 39
www.kvk.nl

KAMER VAN KOOPHANDEL ROTTERDAM
Rotterdam Chamber of Commerce
Blaak 40, 3000 AL Rotterdam
Tel.: 010 402 77 77
www.rotterdam.kvk.nl
International Business Department
Blaak 40, 3000 AL Rotterdam
Tel.: 010 402 78 90
www.kvk.nl

KAMER VAN KOOPHANDEL DEN HAAG
The Hague Chamber of Commerce
Koninginnegracht 13, 2514 AA The Hague
Tel.: 088 585 15 85
www.kvk.nl

KAMER VAN KOOPHANDEL UTRECHT
Utrecht Chamber of Commerce
Kroonstraat 50, 3511 RC Utrecht
Tel.: 030 236 32 11
www.kvk.nl

INTERNATIONAL CHAMBERS OF
COMMERCE

INT. CHAMBER OF COMMERCE (ICC)
www.iccwbo.org

AMERICAN CHAMBER OF COMMERCE
Scheveningseweg 58, 2517 KW The Hague
Tel.: 070 365 98 08
www.amcham.nl

**BELGISCH-LUXEMBURGSE KAMER VAN
KOOPHANDEL**
Groenmarkt 17, 3311 BD Dordrecht
Tel.: 078 635 19 90
www.nkvk.be

ITALIAN CHAMBER OF COMMERCE
De Ruyterkade 5, 1013 AA Amsterdam
Tel.: 020 751 33 63
www.italianchamber.nl

JAPANESE CHAMBER OF COMMERCE
World Trade Center 8-9, Strawinskylaan 935,
1077 XX Amsterdam
Tel.: 020 662 14 57
www.jcc-holland.nl

NETHERLANDS BRITISH CHAMBER OF COMMERCE
Nieuwezijds Voorburgwal 328,
1012 RW Amsterdam
Tel.: 020 421 70 40
www.nbcc.co.uk

NETHERLANDS CANADIAN CHAMBER OF COMMERCE
Nieuwe Uitleg 26, 2514 BR The Hague
Tel.: 070 363 48 91
www.netherlandscanada.nl

CHAMBER OF COMMERCE NETHERLANDS ISRAEL
Bankrashof 3, 1183 NP Amstelveen
Tel.: 020 503 80 63
www.kvkni.nl

NETHERLANDS GERMAN CHAMBER OF COMMERCE
Nassauplein 30, 2585 EC The Hague
Tel.: 070 311 41 36
www.dnhk.nl

NETHERLANDS FRANCE CHAMBER OF COMMERCE
Wibautstraat 129, 1091 GL Amsterdam
Tel.: 020 562 82 00
www.cfci.nl

NETHERLANDS SOUTH AFRICAN CHAMBER OF COMMERCE
Bezuidenhoutseweg 181, 2594 AH The Hague
Tel.: 070 347 07 81
www.sanec.nl

MAJOR DUTCH BANKS

ABN AMRO BANK
www.abnamro.nl or www.abnamro.com
(international)

ING BANK
www.ing.nl or www.ingbank.com
(international)

RABO BANK
www.rabobank.nl or www.rabobank.com
(international)

SNS BANK
www.sns.nl

TRIODOS BANK
www.triodos.nl

TRADE CENTERS

World Trade Center Business Club:
www.wtcamsterdam.nl
World Trade Center Amsterdam:
www.wtcamsterdam.nl
World Trade Center Almere: www.wtcaa.nl
World Trade Center Schiphol Airport:
www.wtcschiphol.nl
World Trade Center Rotterdam:
www.wtcrotterdam.nl
World Trade Center The Hague:
www.wtcthehague.com

INFORMATION CENTERS

EXPATCENTER AMSTERDAM
WTC Amsterdam, D-tower 2nd Floor
Strawinskylaan 39, 1077 XW Amsterdam
Tel: 020 254 79 99
www.iamsterdam.com/expatcenter

AMSTERDAM AIRPORT AREA
P.O. Box 75700, 1118 ZT Schiphol Airport
Tel.: 020 405 47 77
www.aaarea.nl

WEST-HOLLAND FOREIGN INVESTMENT AGENCY, WFIA
Prinses Margrietplantsoen 25,
2595 AM The Hague
P.O. Box 16067, 2500 BB The Hague
Tel.: 070 311 55 55
www.westholland.nl

THE HAGUE INTERNATIONAL CENTRE
The Hague City Hall, Atrium, Spui 70,
2511 BT The Hague
P.O. Box 12600, 2500 DJ The Hague
Tel.: 070 353 50 43

Open Monday to Friday from 9.00 to 17.00
hours.
www.thehague.com

ROTTERDAM INFO EXPATDESK
Coolsingel 195 – 197, 3012 AG Rotterdam
Tel.: 010 790 01 90
E-mail: expatdesk@rotterdam.info
www.rotterdam.info/expatdesk

EXPAT CENTER LEIDEN
Stationsweg 41, 2312 AT Leiden
Tel.: 071 516 60 05
www.expatcenterleiden.nl

LEIDEN BIO SCIENCE PARK
Poortgebouw Noord
Rijnsburgerweg 10, 2333 AA Leiden
Tel.: 071 524 75 53
www.leidenbiosciencepark.nl

PROVINCE OF UTRECHT – FOREIGN INVESTMENT OFFICE
P.O. Box 80300, 3508 TH Utrecht
Tel.: 030 258 23 96
www.investinutrecht.com

EXPAT CENTER UTRECHT
Utrecht City Hall
Stadsplateau 1, 3521 AZ Utrecht
Tel.: 030 286 58 20
www.utrecht.nl/english/expatcenter

BOM FOREIGN INVESTMENTS
P.O. Box 3240, 5003 DE Tilburg
Goirleseweg 15, 5026 PB Tilburg
Tel.: 088 831 11 20
www.foreigninvestments.eu

BRAINPORT DEVELOPMENT
Emmasingel 11, 5611 AZ Eindhoven
Tel.: 040 751 24 24
www.brainport.nl

HIGH TECH CAMPUS EINDHOVEN
www.hightechcampus.com

EXPAT GUIDE HOLLAND
For internationals who are going to live and
work in the Southeast Netherlands
www.expatguideholland.com

ONTWIKKELINGS MAATSCHAPPIJ OOST NEDERLAND NV
Meander 601, 8625 ME Arnhem
P.O. Box 5215, 6802 EE Arnhem
Tel.: 026 384 42 22
Hengelosestraat 585, 7521 AG Enschede
P.O. Box 5518, 7500 GM Enschede
Tel.: 053 851 68 51

LIMBURGSE ONTWIKKELINGS MAATSCHAPPIJ (LIOF)
Boschstraat 766211 AX Maastricht
P.O. Box 1310, 6201 BH Maastricht
Tel.: 043 328 02 80
www.liof.com

TRADE AND INVESTMENT ORGANIZATIONS

NFIA, NETHERLANDS FOREIGN INVESTMENT AGENCY
Prinses Beatrixlaan 2, 2595 AL The Hague
Tel.: 088 602 80 60
www.nfia.nl

NETHERLANDS ENTERPRICE AGENCY
Prinses Beatrixlaan 2, 2595 AL The Hague
Tel.: 088 602 80 60
www.hollandtrade.com
www.evd.nl

NETHERLANDS COUNCIL FOR TRADE PROMOTION
WTC The Hague
Prinses Beatrixlaan 712, 2595 BN The Hague
Tel.: 070 344 15 44
www.nchnl.nl

BUSINESS CLUBS

THE AMSTERDAM AMERICAN BUSINESS CLUB
A professional networking organization for Dutch and American companies around Amsterdam
Keizersgracht 62-64, 1015 CS Amsterdam
Tel.: 020 520 75 34
www.aabc.nl

CLUB OF AMSTERDAM
An independent, international, future-oriented think tank involved in channeling preferred futures
www.clubofamsterdam.com

COMMERCIAL ANGLO DUTCH SOCIETY
Provides an informal meeting point for Dutch and British professionals
http://cads-amsterdam.org

WTC THE HAGUE INTERNATIONAL BUSINESS CLUB
Prinses Margrietplantsoen 33,
2595 AM The Hague
Tel.: 070 304 36 65
www.wtcthehague.com

CONNECTING WOMEN (THE HAGUE)
A network of professional internationally aware women.
Juliana van Stolberglaan 154,
2595 CL The Hague.
www.connectingwomen.nl

WOMEN'S BUSINESS INITIATIVE INTERNATIONAL
A community of entrepeneurial women.
Laan Copus van Cattenburch 86,
2585 GE The Hague
Tel.: 070 358 85 57
www.womensbusinessinitiative.net

WOMEN'S INTERNATIONAL NETWORK (WIN)
The international networking association for professional women in the Netherlands
www.winconference.net

VOLUNTEER WORK

ACCESS ARE ALWAYS LOOKING FOR NEW VOLUNTEERS
Visit their website for information on the monthly Info Mornings
www.access-nl.org

RECRUITMENT AGENCIES FOR NON-DUTCH NATIONALS

ADAMS MULTILINGUAL RECRUITMENT
Amsterdam, tel.: 020 580 03 40
Rotterdam, tel.: 010 205 27 12
www.adamsrecruit.nl

BLUE LYNX EMPLOYMENT
The Hague, tel.: 070 311 78 22
Amsterdam, tel.: 020 406 91 80
www.bluelynx.com

MADISON PARKER INTERNATIONAL
Voorburg, tel.: 070 387 59 11
www.madisonparker.nl

OCTAGON PROFESSIONALS
Laan Copus van Cattenburch 62,
2585 GC The Hague, tel.: 070 324 93 00
www.octagon.nl

UNDUTCHABLES RECRUITMENT AGENCY
Head Office, tel.: 020 345 51 04
Amsterdam, tel.: 020 623 13 00
Amstelveen, tel.: 020 445 97 38
The Hague, tel.: 070 711 83 00
Utrecht, tel.: 030 238 22 28
Eindhoven, tel.: 040 237 33 95
www.undutchables.nl

JOB SEARCHING WEBSITES

www.linkedin.com
www.monsterboard.nl
www.intermediair.nl
www.iamexpat.nl/career/jobs-netherlands
www.stepstone.nl
www.englishlanguagejobs.com
www.togetherabroad.nl
www.oneworld.nl
www.jobbird.com
www.nationalevacaturebank.nl
www.volkskrantbanen.nl
www.fd.nl

CAREER PORTAL

www.careerinholland.nl

JOB FAIRS

The International Job Fair
Yearly organized in the Beurs van Berlage, Amsterdam
http://jobfair.expatica.com/

DUAL CAREER SERVICE

C&G CAREER SERVICES
Hoogoorddreef 9, 1101 BA Amsterdam Z.O.
Tel.: 020 312 05 40
www.cg-services.com

RECOMMENDED READING

EMPLOYMENT IN THE NETHERLANDS
Published yearly by Loyens & Loeff
Conditions of employment, tax and social security aspects
Available on request by e-mail:
info@loyensloeff.com
www.loyensloeff.com

THE ACCESS GUIDE/WORKING & UNEMPLOYMENT IN THE NETHERLANDS
This guide gives an overview of Dutch Employment Law and information on how to find a job
www.access-nl.org

LOOKING FOR WORK IN THE NETHERLANDS
By Nannette Ripmeester
Published yearly by Expertise in Labour Mobility
If you are looking for work in the Netherlands, this guide provides accurate and practical information on the job hunting process
www.labourmobility.com

DEALING WITH THE DUTCH
By Jacob Vossestein
Published by LM Publishers
The cultural context of business and work in the Netherlands
www.jacobvossestein.nl
To order: www.hollandbooks.nl

A CAREER IN YOUR SUITCASE 4TH EDITION
By Jo Parfitt and Colleen Reichrath-Smith
300 pages of completely revised and updated information for creating and maintaining a career overseas
www.careerinyoursuitcase.com

LEGAL ASPECTS OF DOING BUSINESS IN THE NETHERLANDS
Published yearly by Loyens & Loeff
For entrepreneurs and their legal service providers who are or about to be engaged in business operations in the Netherlands
Available on request by e-mail:
info@loyensloeff.com
www.loyensloeff.com

THE MOBILE LIFE
Published by XPat Media
By Diane Lemieux and Anne Parker
A new approach to moving anywhere.
www.themobilelife.eu

CAREER IN HOLLAND
General information about starting a career in the Netherlands by EP-Nuffic.
www.hollandalumni.nl/career

CHAPTER 4

Before buying or renting a house or apartment in the Netherlands, there are several things you should consider. This chapter offers you practical tips and useful information such as where to buy or rent, selecting an agent, and negotiating the deal. It also points out some of the consequences of your choice in terms of property taxes, waste collection taxes, sewerage taxes, etc., and the taxes (or related exemptions) in connection with the importation of your household goods.

CONTRIBUTING AUTHORS HENK JANSEN, CONNIE MOSER AND ANNETTE DE VREEDE

RENT OR BUY

HOUSING MARKET

During the period preceding 9/11, sales prices doubled in just five years' time in some areas. After that day, they dropped a little and eventually ended up stabilizing shortly thereafter. Then, around 2004-2005, prices started going up again whereby some areas, for instance Amsterdam, saw a spectacular 14%-price increase in 2007. This upward swing in prices continued until mid-2008. Then, in early summer of 2008, as the impact of the subprime mortgage crisis also reached the Netherlands, the housing market went into a decline – a decline that appears to be over, however. Over 2015, house sales went up – in the province of Zuid Holland, even by 20%. Also house prices are going up; by 5.3% in the province of Noord Holland overall, and 10% in the city of Amsterdam. This is the greatest increase in price since 2008, though prices remain 16% lower than they were then.

As interest rates remain at an historic low, people have more disposable income, inflation is low and the job market is looking up, this means that people will continue to buy houses, which will push real estate prices further up. Houses that have been on the market for six or seven years, are being sold now and in some places for more than the asking price, shifting the pendulum towards a seller's market again. No longer can you expect to be the only viewer, or to wait it out and buy the house at the price you set.

It would appear that now is a good time to buy: prices are going up, but are still under the level they were when they were at their peak, and mortgage interests are low. Yet, don't forget to take into account the buyer's costs, see further on, as a consequence of which buying is only attractive if you are planning on staying around for at least four to five years.

Also the rental market is feeling the consequences of the developments on the housing market, with rent prices going up in the vicinity of 2% compared to 2014. Still, though rental prices in the Netherlands might be high compared to some other parts of Europe, they are nonetheless below those of other European capitals such as London or Paris.

FINDING A HOUSE

There is a considerable variety of properties to choose from, although much depends on where you want to live, the living space needed, and your budget. There is a good choice of rental properties in the so-called Randstad area, in the western part of the country, where most international companies are based (Amsterdam, The Hague/Wassenaar, Rotterdam and Utrecht). You can find a house for sale or for rent via advertisements in the newspapers, on notice boards at the women's clubs, international schools or churches, or by driving around and looking out for the signs saying *Te Koop* (for sale) or sometimes *Te Huur* (for rent). Yet the best way to explore the market is by looking at Internet sites such as www.funda.nl (in Amsterdam www.mva.nl), www.jaap.nl, or www.zah.nl.

Though you can go a long way on your own with the help of the Internet, it still remains advisable to contact an agent for the actual house-search and negotiation phase. Most expatriates have never lived in the Netherlands and are therefore not familiar with the price ranges, local contracts, 'invisible' obligations, laws and customs. Using an agent, even though this is more expensive, will help you get a good impression of the living area, speed up the search for suitable accommodation, and get a better deal on the property. Another advantage to using an agent is that they have access to a computerized multiple-listing system which keeps them completely up-to-date on properties available in their district. More on the real estate agent further on.

TO BUY OR TO RENT

Of course, there are a lot of benefits to buying a house. Apart from the fact that you own real estate of which the price may increase again, there is the advantage of a tax relief on the mortgage interest – it is tax-deductible if the house is your principal place of residence, provided you take out an annuity or straight line mortgage (starting last year, new tax measures were introduced that will reduce this benefit incrementally; from 50.5% this year, to 38% by 2041). In addition, a number of the costs related to the financing of the house are also tax-deductible. This means that some of the civil law notary's fees, the closing commission, and the fee for the appraisal of the house are all tax-deductible. Hence, if you are in the highest tax bracket of 52%, the net costs are 48%. (You can read more about the role of the civil law notary on page 122.)

Although at first sight it might seem an attractive option to buy a house, it is a decision that needs serious and careful consideration. A disadvantage when buying real estate in the Netherlands is that you have to pay approximately 6% of the purchase price as one-time buyers' expenses. These expenses consist of a transfer tax of 2%, estate agent fees, civil law notary's fees, a fixed fee for the bank or broker (generally ranging from € 1,500 to € 5,000), etc. In addition to this, home owners must add the so-called deemed rental value (*eigenwoningforfait* – you can read more about this on page 90) to their taxable income and pay taxes over this.

As a result, the break-even point between rent or buy usually occurs after a few years, assuming that housing prices remain constant. Bearing in mind that expatriates usually stay in the Netherlands for a relatively short period of time, this is an important issue to keep in mind. This risk makes buying a medium to long-term decision (five years).

Of course, if you rent a house, you circumvent a lot of the problems and risks, but you also miss out on the possible benefits. And don't forget: rent – though reasonable compared to other European countries – can be high in the Netherlands. You can read more about the tax consequences of renting, and having your rental costs reimbursed by your employer, on page 92.

CHECKLIST OF IMPORTANT ITEMS

If you decide to rent or to buy, make a checklist of items that are important to you and your family and which will influence the location and style of the property. Discuss these with your agent. For example:

- proximity to work and the children's school
- public transportation and school bus routes
- location of shopping centers
- type of neighborhood
- type of house: period or modern
- when renting: is it fully furnished – *gemeubileerd* (all furniture, fixtures and kitchen appliances provided) – or unfurnished.

REAL ESTATE AGENT

Taking into account your likely lack of knowledge of national laws and regulations, you are advised to enlist the services of a real estate agent when looking for a house. Try to find a real estate agent in the city or town you want to buy in. Although some realtors work across a wider area, they may not always be aware of the specific ins and outs of a city, if they do not work there regularly. Things such as bidding systems, zoning plans (*bestemmingsplan*), soil contamination and city council regulations are items that are specific to each city. A local realtor is best equipped to advise you on these.

Real estate agents charge a brokerage fee (*courtage*) for their services. This is usually between 1 to 2 % of the purchase price of the house, though with some realtors the percentage is negotiable. The height of the fee depends the specific services offered; some real estate agencies offer an expat service package.

If you have chosen to rent a property, there are several rental organizations available – which one you choose will depend on where you will be looking for property to rent. Check the resource pages at the end of the chapter.

You can usually find the right agent to suit your needs through word-of-mouth, via the Human Resource Department of the company, via a Relocation Agency or via advertisements in expat journals. Basically every agent connected to the largest trade organization NVM has the same information available through the multiple listing system www.funda.nl, but much depends on how well the agent uses this information and how he goes about selecting the right properties according to the specifications of the lessee or buyer. Therefore, it is important that you feel you can trust your agent. It is practical and saves time and effort to use only one agent. However, if you are not satisfied, if you feel you are not seeing the right properties or that your agent does not understand your needs, get a different one.

AREAS

Most expatriates live in the Randstad, in the area between Amsterdam, The Hague, Rotterdam and Utrecht. There are also many pleasant residential areas near Amsterdam such as Amstelveen, Aerdenhout, Bloemendaal and Heemstede; in 't Gooi (between Amsterdam and Utrecht) which includes Bussum, Hilversum, Naarden, Huizen and Laren; near The Hague around Wassenaar, Voorschoten and Oegstgeest; or in the residential areas of Rotterdam such as Kralingen and Hillegersberg. Of course there are many more smaller villages where pleasant housing can be found.

YOU HAVE DECIDED TO RENT

Types of Rental Properties
Different combinations are possible, depending on the landlord:

- Unfurnished (*Ongemeubileerd*). This offers the barest of necessities – namely, empty. Generally nothing much is included here; no carpeting, no curtains, often a minimum of or no appliances and no utilities.
- Semi-furnished (*Gestoffeerd*). Semi-furnished contains some furnishings and carpeting, and possibly a few appliances. Keep in mind to ask for a complete list of what is included. Utility inclusion or exclusion depends on the landlord.
- Furnished (*Gemeubileerd*). Everything has been taken care of and the apartment is ready to be moved into. It may contain any combination of furniture, appliances, curtains, light fix-

tures, carpets, cutlery and dishes, television, stereo equipment, kitchen appliances such as microwave, dishwasher, refrigerator, and sometimes even bed linens and blankets or down feather beds. Make sure to ask for a complete inventory list before agreeing to anything. If anything is missing, negotiate it before you sign the lease. Utilities are (usually) included.

The Rental Contract
Many rental contracts have been especially designed to meet the needs of expatriates, and include an English translation. A rental contract usually includes the following items:
- rent: the rent is payable one month in advance
- a deposit: one month deposit/bank guarantee is customary; however, some owners demand a 2 or 3-month deposit
- an annual adjustment of the rent, based on increases in the cost of living, as determined by the Central Bureau of Statistics (CBS). This has averaged 1 to 2% over the past years
- user's costs, which are usually not included in the rent, i.e. utilities, municipal levies and garden maintenance
- the so-called diplomatic clause, which gives you the option of terminating the contract by giving two full calendar months' notice if you are transferred abroad (see the following paragraph)
- the brokerage fee, usually one month's rent, excl. 21% VAT
- a clause on minor repairs: the law states exhaustively which minor repairs may be expected and borne by the lessee. If the costs exceed a certain amount, the location of the item that needs repair is hard to reach or if the repair requires specific technical knowledge, then the repair costs are to be borne by the owner
- a clause stating that the lessee is responsible for the yearly cleaning of the central heating system, water boilers, chimneys, gutters and draining pipes
- the obligation to return the property in the same condition, normal wear and tear excepted, at the end of the rental period – or else forfeit (a part of) the deposit.

In connection with repairs, you are advised to do a careful walk-through of the house or apartment you are planning on renting, verifying damages and the need for repairs and improvements – and determining who will be responsible for arranging and paying for these – before you sign on the dotted line.

Diplomatic Clauses in Rental Contracts
A diplomatic clause can be included in the rental contract for the benefit of either both or one of the parties mentioned in the contract. Both the lessor and the lessee may ask for such a clause to be included to ensure that, even though the rental contract may not have expired, the property can be vacated after a notification term mutually agreed upon in advance.

If the lessor has been posted abroad, he may agree to let his property for a specified period. In a diplomatic clause it may be stipulated that should the lessor be relocated to the Netherlands during that period as a consequence of which he will need his property for personal use again, he may terminate the contract before the expiration date – provided the agreed upon notification period is observed.

The lessee may want to take into account the possibility that he could be relocated by his employer – which would entail the need

to move house before the expiration date of the contract. There are various scenarios that come to mind – for instance, the parties may agree to this clause if the lessee is transferred to a place more than 50 km. from the actual residence. Or it may be subject to a stricter condition: the lessee must be transferred abroad before the expiration date of the agreement.

Verbal Agreements
A word of warning: a verbal contract is binding under Dutch law. Therefore, unless you are absolutely sure you will take the property, do not make any written *or* verbal commitment!

Checking In
When the contracts have been signed, and the rent and deposit have been paid into the account of the agent, the lessee will be handed the keys to the property. Ideally, the lessee will be checked in by the owner or his representative, assisted by his own agent. A checklist will be filled out regarding the condition of the house, the furniture, fixtures and fittings belonging to the house, the condition of the exterior/garden, and there will be a check of the inventory. The house should be thoroughly cleaned, including the inside of kitchen and bathroom cabinets. The inspection report as well as the inventory list must be signed by lessee and lessor.

For more on hidden defects, see page 86.

Terminating the Rental Contract
To avoid anxiety and unnecessary costs later, you will need to inform (remind) your landlord well in advance as to what date the contract for your apartment will expire and when you will be leaving. This should be done by way of a registered letter. Depending on your rental contract, there is a notice period to be given before the expiration of the tenancy of:
- at least one calendar month in case the lessee terminates
- at least three months + one month for every year the property has been rented to the lessee with a maximum of six months in case the lessor terminates the contract
- the period specified in the diplomatic clause of the contract.

If you do not specifically stipulate in writing that, after the initial one-year rental period, you will vacate the premises, then the contract undergoes a *stilzwijgende verlenging* or silent continuance whereby you will be liable for a new year of rental fees and you will at the very least forfeit your deposit (usually two months' rent) if you move out anyway. However, after the initial one-year period, if you wish to continue your lease on a month-to-month basis this can be negotiated, depending on your landlord. You may also choose to continue your rental contract for a longer period of time. Either agreement should be confirmed in writing.

Checking Out / Return of the Deposit
Preferably on the last day of the lease period, a check-out is done with all parties concerned. The inventory and condition of the lease property are checked with the checklist made when checking in. If the state of the property is found to be satisfactory and all bills in connection with the property have been paid, the deposit will be paid back within three months after the check-out date. If necessary, the costs of restoring the rental property back to the required state will be deducted from the deposit in accordance with the bills provided by the lessor.

REDOING YOUR HOME

Few people have bought a house of which they thought: 'Yup, *precisely* the way I wanted it,' and left everything the way it was. On the other hand, few people are as notorious for clearing out all but the outside walls and rebuilding from scratch as the Dutch are. Likely, you are somewhere in the middle.

CONTRACTOR – AANNEMER

Should you wish to redo your house (change a wall or two, put in a new bathroom or kitchen, build a fireplace), the person you are looking for is a contractor. Contractors can be found in the Yellow Pages and Internet under the name *aannemers*. There you will find probably at least 100 to choose from – which does not make the choice any easier. A safe bet would be to opt for a contractor who is listed with BouwGarant. Those listed with BouwGarant must meet strict requirements, and can be found on www.bouwgarant.nl and entering your postal code on the home page, where it says *vind een aannemer bij jou in de buurt* (find a contractor nearby you), there you fill in the name of your municipality or your postal code. Otherwise, ask around and see whom others recommend. Be sure to invite a few *aannemers*, as prices can vary considerably, not to mention compatibility: chances are, these people will be running around in your house for weeks, if not months. In March 1, 2013, the VAT for construction costs was brought down from 21% to 6%. Through this applied only until July 1, 2015, there are certain home improvements to which this will continue to apply through 2016 – including, but not limited to, painting, insulation and wall-papering. Additional conditions apply, such as the age of the home and the purpose to which it is used.

OVERSEEING THE PROJECT

The contractor could be a one-man operation or a company (*bouwbedrijf*) ranging in size from two people to several dozen skilled employees. They are responsible for purchasing all the necessary supplies (*bouwmaterialen*) and overseeing the installation of the project, making sure that all of the skilled personnel (a contractor has qualified plumbers, electricians, carpenters, etc. on his payroll) complete their portions of the project at the right moment during the process. They also make sure that the materials used are up to code and meet current safety requirements.

PAPERWORK

All necessary paperwork can also be handled by your contractor. It is best to leave the requesting of building permits and the execution of building plans and blueprints in his hands. Not only does he have ample experience in dealing with the bureaucracy inherent in securing permission, it tends to go much faster than if you attempt to do it yourself.

MONUMENTS

An important matter in this context is the question of whether your house is on the *monumentenlijst* (list of monuments). Houses that are protected under *Monumentenzorg* (Monuments Care) are subject to strict regulations and restrictions regarding maintenance, and any changes have to be approved by a commission representing the Association for the Preservation of Monuments. Even seemingly straightforward matters such as the color of paint used often needs approval. It can take months of waiting for approvals, and in the meantime you are prohibited from making any changes. Your contractor likely knows the best way to approach obtaining permission for any changes you wish to make – and how long it will take. He will also be able to give you a fair idea of what you will be allowed to do.

WORKING 'BLACK'

In order to have a guarantee on your work it is best to work *wit met een bonnetje* ('white with a receipt'). Some tradesmen will work *zwart* ('black'); that is, without a receipt and without adding the 21% VAT (BTW), thus reducing your bill – however, this is illegal and constitutes tax fraud. In addition, you forfeit your right to any claims due to shoddy workmanship or incompletion of the project. Nor will insurance companies cover claims resulting from damages incurred by leaking pipes, electrical fires and the likes. Furthermore, you have no proof regarding the services rendered and materials used.

HANDYMAN

Sometimes people will hire in a handyman (*klusjesman*) who works at the going rate of around € 30 per hour ('ex BTW', meaning that VAT is still to be added to the total bill). Once again, you can probably find a handyman who works 'black' (*zwartwerken*), but if he does, he will not be insured, and any liability claims that could arise from accidents (like his falling off your roof while working) will not be covered and a settlement will not be possible.

A NEW INTERIOR

Though the contractor carries out the project, you yourself will have to select the kitchen cabinets, bathtub, closets, tiles, curtains, carpeting, faucets, paint colors, etc. If you want, you can do this with the help of an interior decorator (see the Yellow Pages, under *binnenhuisarchitectuur* or *interieurontwerpers*). To do it yourself, look under *woninginrichting* (decorating your home) for carpeting, curtains, but also beds and furniture, *keukens* for kitchens, *sanitaire artikelen* for bathrooms, *verf en lak* for paint. Often, your contractor will have reached an agreement with a local bathroom, kitchen or tile specialist regarding deliveries and quality, so you may wish to wait and see whom he recommends – though you are not obligated to go by his recommendations alone.

GARDEN

If you want to do your own garden, you will find what you need at a garden center – to be found in the Yellow Pages under *tuincentra* (for plants and other necessities) or *tuinartikelen* (for garden furniture, sheds, ponds, lighting). If you want to enlist the help of a professional, look under *tuinaanleg en -onderhoud* (garden design and maintenance).

HIDDEN DEFECTS

If it turns out, after you have purchased your house, that there are a number of things that are not in order, you will have to ask yourself what type of 'defect' you are dealing with. In principle, you buy a house 'as it is'; this means, including all visible and invisible defects – and the premise is that you, the new owner, are responsible for all that comes with your new home.

If an invisible defect is considered serious, however, it can qualify as a 'hidden' defect – and there are situations in which the former owner can be held liable (see further on) for the consequences.

OBLIGATIONS REALTOR

Your realtor has an obligation to inform you of known defects of the house. For instance, wooden constructions could be infected with wood rot, mold or fungus growth. Or there could be an oil tank in the back yard, or pests; causing you to run up a hefty bill for extermination. If he fails to inform you of these issues, he can be held liable.

You may expect your realtor to pay attention and be critical – asking the seller pertinent questions that may arise on the basis of his, or your, observations.

REPORTING A DEFECT

In either a rental or purchase property, any discovered hidden defect will need to be reported within a reasonable time frame from the date of purchase. It is best to ask your real estate agent or housing agency what term they apply – case law generally states that this should be two months. For a purchased property, you will have to report any defects or problems to the estate agent who sold you the property and he will negotiate on your behalf with the seller. If the seller is not willing to fix the problem or pay for the damages, you will have to take the matter to the courts.

RESPONSIBILITIES FOR PURCHASED PROPERTY
For the former owner to be held liable, the following conditions must be met:
1. the defect must have been there at the time of the sale and you must be able to prove this
2. you, the buyer, must have inspected the new home. If you *could* have detected the defect during this inspection, but didn't, then this is your responsibility. Some defects occur after the inspection, but before the transfer – these are for the liability of the seller
3. the seller did not inform you of the defects that he was aware of and that could not be detected or were not easy to detect in the case of a normal inspection. The seller must inform you of the defects even if the extent of the defect is not clear – also if it will not influence a normal use of the house
4. the defect must hinder a 'normal' use of (part of) the house – or, put differently, the house must have the qualities that you could expect based on the sales contract.

Another important factor is the age of the house. The older it is, there more you can be expected to have anticipated certain problems.

If you compare points 3 and 4, they would appear to contradict each other. It is clear that there is a gray area there somewhere, so be sure to obtain expert advice in the case of problems. And keep in mind, while looking at a house, that if anything looks fishy (or rickety); ask, take notes, point it out...

NEW PROPERTY
In the case of new property, the contractor is liable for any defects / deficiencies until the moment he delivers the property. He is to take you on an inspection of the property and you must sign a piece of paper stating that you will accept the property as is. Be sure to have an independent professional inspect the property and make a report before you do this! Do not sign a so-called pre-delivery report: new issues might come up that will have to be dealt with. Once the property has been delivered, the contractor has three months in which to fix any issues you note and bring to

his attention. This period stretches out to six months – the so-called maintenance period – for any other problems that may occur. Be sure to keep a written record of everything and to inform the contractor as soon as possible. The contractor has to issue a ten-year warranty on his 'product' and can be held liable for hidden defects for up to 30 years (as can the architect)!

YOU FEEL MISLED
You can also hold the seller of the house responsible if you have been misled regarding (certain parts of) the house and its (their) use. For you to be able to do this, the seller must have been aware of your expectations – which may be hard to prove, certainly if there is nothing in writing or if there are no witnesses (such as your realtor). Another example would be if the realtor (purposely) failed to inform you of the impossibility of your intentions or impressions.

If you were mistaken – but not actively misinformed – regarding the house then though in theory you may seek compensation, this will not be easy. Particularly if the seller was not aware of your expectations or plans. If you want to use the house for special purposes, be sure to include this in your contract, to avoid miscommunication and to make clear who can be held liable for a hidden defect.

PROBLEMS IN THE NEIGHBORHOOD
The seller also has a duty to report beforehand (*mededelingsplicht*) any knowledge of contaminated ground in the neighborhood, or problems in the area, such as wood rot in the foundation poles under the houses. The buyer has a buyer's responsibility to also check to see if there are problems in the area, or if there are any pre-existing building reports (*bouwkundige keuringen*).

RESPONSIBILITIES FOR RENTALS
By law, you should have full, quiet enjoyment of your rental. If there are any defects that impede this legal right, your landlord needs to fix these. You are responsible for small repairs that occur in the course of normal daily life and damages that are not your responsibility can usually be claimed under your household insurance. If you do not have household insurance, keep in mind that you can only hold your landlord liable if he can be held responsible – for instance, if he has carried out sloppy repairs, is behind in his maintenance duties, or has not responded to your complaints, resulting in higher damages.

A general rule of thumb is that anything that is structural is the responsibility of the

party letting out the property (*verhuurder*). Any repairs that lie above a certain cost, require certain technical knowledge or that have to be carried out in a hard-to-reach place, should be paid for by the owner. The best recourse is to be very clear beforehand as to the division of the responsibilities. If you discover problems after you have moved in, you will need to contact the landlord (and/or the housing agency) to notify him of the problem. Hopefully something can be done to solve the problem right away, however, sometimes this is not the case. You may wind up having to pay for the repairman or the exterminator yourself, and then attempting to be reimbursed. To be on the safe side, you can ask the court permission to carry out the repairs / take the necessary measures. Furthermore, you can ask for a rent deduction over the period in which the landlord is in default, or you can start a so-called defect procedure before the rent assessment committee.

INSURANCE
Depending on your realtor, it is possible, in cooperation with your real estate agent, to take out a (maximum) ten-year (depending on the insurer) insurance against hidden mechanical and construction defects. The length of the insurance period depends on the item being insured. If you request such an insurance, the house will be inspected and any defects noted will *not* be covered by the insurance – as they will obviously not constitute 'hidden' defects. Any areas not inspected will also not be covered by the insurance.

WHAT CAN YOU DEMAND?
If you find a hidden defect, you can demand that the situation be restored; in other words, either that you receive compensation of the costs you incur in fixing the problem, or else that the former owner fix it himself. In serious cases, you can demand that the purchase be nullified, or that the purchase price be reduced retroactively.

LEGAL AID
If it turns out that you were not adequately informed, you may have to go to court and let the judge decide about compensation for the reparation of damages. Being as how proving conclusively whether or not one can presume that the selling party knowingly withheld vital information can prove rather hard to do, you may need the services of a lawyer if a timely agreement to remedy the situation cannot be reached (see page 127 for more on legal aid).

YOU HAVE DECIDED TO BUY

Before embarking on the actual process of finding a house to buy, make sure you first contact a bank or mortgage broker to discuss whether you will be able to take out a mortgage here, to what amount you can do this and what the related monthly expenses will be. Having clarified these points will allow you to focus on finding a new home – without being faced with unpleasant surprises just when you think you have found one.

After going into the process of buying a house, we will discuss the available mortgages in more detail.

STEP-BY-STEP

First, a short step-by-step plan of the purchasing process. In the remainder of this paragraph and in other parts of this chapter, insofar as they have not been discussed earlier, we will go into these steps in more detail.

- You select a real estate agent, and discuss what you are looking for, what you need and what is realistic.
- If you have any special wishes regarding the property, make sure your real estate agent and the real estate agent of the seller are aware of this. If they are not, and it turns out your home does not meet these wishes, you cannot hold them accountable for it.
- You contact a mortgage provider, to find out exactly how much mortgage you can take out, whereby you take into account additional expenses involved in the purchase of the home (these are discussed further on).
- You visit property.
- When you have found a home you like, be sure to discuss all issues such as city council regulations, but also issues such as soil contamination.
- If you want this home, you can inform your real estate agent of this verbally.
- Your real estate agent will contact the selling party and relay this message.
- Have a building inspection carried out. If you fail to do this and there is a problem, more likely than not, you will have lost your right to hold the seller accountable.
- Make the purchase of the house contingent upon its passing the building inspection.
- The initial verbal agreement you reach with the seller is put in writing in the preliminary purchase contract. A penalty clause is usually included in case the seller or the buyer does not meet his obligations.
- After being signed by all the parties, the preliminary purchase contract is sent to the civil law notary who deals with the transfer of the title of the house.
- A three-day 'cooling-off' period starts the day after the buyer receives a copy of the signed contract. During these three days the buyer can cancel the deal without any repercussions and without having to state the reason.
- The civil law notary inspects the public registers of the Land Registry regarding mortgages and/or attachments with which the property may be encumbered.
- The transfer of ownership takes place at the civil law notary's office by means of a deed of transfer that is drawn up by the civil law notary and signed by the seller, the buyer and the civil law notary. You will receive a draft of this deed and of the mortgage deed beforehand. Also your agent will receive these and check them.
- The agent will check together with you to see whether the house has been vacated, and is in the agreed condition.
- The civil law notary takes care of the financial settlement of the transaction and ensures that the deed of transfer is entered in the public registers (Land Registry).
- The transfer then becomes official and you receive the keys of your new house.

Points to Watch for When Buying a House:

1. General
When you decide to buy a house, it is doubly advisable to engage an agent, as there are more complicated matters involved than when renting a house. For instance, you need expert advice on matters such as the fluctuation of prices in certain areas, environmental laws, the construction of a house, hidden defects (see page 86), and the issues that need to be taken into account when you buy property on leasehold rather than free-hold.

2. Fixtures and Fittings
When you start negotiating, you should keep in mind that the purchase price excludes furniture, carpets, curtains, light fixtures and sometimes kitchen appliances. You must reach a clear agreement with the seller on which goods are included in the purchase.

3. Deposit
The deposit on the house is generally 10% of the purchase price – due approximately five weeks after the deal has been made – and arranged by the mortgage advisor or the bank itself by means of a bank guarantee issued by a Dutch banking institution. This deposit is to be paid to a civil law notary and can be part of the financing agreement reached for the purchase of the house.

4. Additional Costs
The purchase transaction will cost you an additional approximately 6%. This amount represents a government transfer tax of 2%, land registry expenses, the civil law notary's fees, and the real estate agent's commission – see below.

5. Resolutive Conditions
If you need to obtain a mortgage to finance the purchase, any purchase agreement should be made subject to financing. If necessary, other resolutive conditions should be part of the agreement, such as (if applicable) being able to obtain a permit to occupy the real estate, or even more importantly, the option of having a constructional survey carried out.

THE ACTUAL HOUSE-HUNTING

It is advisable to make sure the agent is well-informed of your specific wishes prior to the actual house-hunting in order for him to select a list of properties that meet your requirements. The agent can also help you become acquainted with the different terms and conditions of contracts and procedures, and check if the specifications you have given are in line with price ranges and the kind of housing available. On the basis of your specific requirements, a selection from the available market supply will be made and a tour of inspection of those residences will be organized. Normally,

more tours will follow until a suitable house is found. It is easier to determine which kind of house suits you best after you have visited several different properties. The average search for the right house will therefore probably take a few months, depending on availability, your needs and market circumstances.

NEGOTIATIONS

Prices and conditions quoted in the listings for sales and rentals are usually negotiable. In close consultation with the agent, price and conditions will be negotiated with the agent representing the owner. These negotiations can consist of several rounds of verbal bidding and counter-bidding.

COSTS

As a general rule, the costs of purchasing a house in the Netherlands amount to approximately 6% of the price of the house (this is not the same as the 10% down payment!). These expenses include:

- appraisal fee (expense for having the house officially appraised in order to secure a mortgage)
- notary costs mortgage deed (*hypotheekakte*)
- cadastral registration fee mortgage deed
- cadastral investigation fee
- administration fee mortgage deed
- structural survey of the house
- bank guarantee fee
- mortgage commission fee (paid either to the bank or the broker)
- National Mortgage Insurance – *Nationale Hypotheek Garantie*
- transfer tax

- estate agent fee
- notary costs for the transfer deed
- interpreter fees.

On a house of € 350,000, your approximate cost would be an additional € 21,000 over and above the € 350,000 purchase price.

TAX-DEDUCTIBLE COSTS

Of interest to know is that the costs listed below are tax-deductible and can be declared (one-time) on your income tax return:

- notary costs mortgage deed (*hypotheekakte*) (VAT/BTW)
- mortgage commission fee (paid either to the bank or the broker)
- cadastral registration fee
- cadastral investigation fee
- appraisal (*taxatie*) fee
- administration fee (*afsluitprovisie*) mortgage deed
- bank guarantee fee.

PRELIMINARY PURCHASE CONTRACT AND TRANSFER OF OWNERSHIP

The verbal agreement is put in writing in the preliminary purchase contract (*voorlopige koopakte*). A penalty clause is usually included in case the seller or the buyer does not meet his obligations. After being signed by all the parties, the preliminary purchase contract is sent to the civil law notary who will deal with the transfer of the title of the house. A three-day 'cooling-off' period starts the day after the buyer receives a copy of the signed contract. During these three days the buyer can cancel the deal without any repercussions and without having to state the reason.

The choice of civil law notary is usually the buyer's. Upon receipt of the preliminary purchase contract, the civil law notary inspects the public registers of the Land Registry regarding mortgages and/or attachments with which the property may be encumbered.

In the Amsterdam area, both parties and their agents often visit the office of the civil law notary together for the signing of the preliminary purchase contract.

The transfer of ownership will take place at the civil law notary's office by means of a deed of transfer to be drawn up by the civil law notary and to be signed by the seller, the buyer and the civil law notary. The civil law notary will first send you a draft of this deed of transfer together with a statement showing the payment due in order to complete the purchase. This statement includes the purchase price, the transfer tax, the cadastral registration fees, notarial fees, the commission on a possible mortgage loan, real estate agent's fees, etc. If there is a mortgage loan, you will receive a draft of the mortgage deed. Your agent will also receive these documents and check them.

Usually on the day of the transfer, the agent will check together with you to see whether the house has been vacated, and is in the agreed condition. It is the task of the civil law notary to take care of the financial settlement of the transaction and to ensure that the deed of transfer is entered in the public registers (Land Registry). The transfer then becomes official and the seller turns over the keys of your new house.

INTERPRETER

If your command of the Dutch language is such that you will be needing the assistance of an interpreter when communicating with the civil law notary, then you are legally required to request the assistance of a sworn interpreter. Depending on your language, this will cost you anywhere between € 150 and € 500.

THE TAX CONSEQUENCES OF RENTING OR BUYING A HOUSE

When moving to a new country, just about the first question you are faced with is; where am I going to live? This decision is, predictably, largely influenced by the decision: am I going to buy a house or am I going to rent one? Many of the issues involved in this choice have been discussed in the preceding paragraphs. However, one important question remains: what are the tax consequences of your decision? This is a complex matter, and we will give a short overview of the topics that will play a role when making your choice.

In some parts, reference will be made to the tax paragraph which you can find in the chapter on *Legal, Tax and Financial Matters*.

BUYING A HOUSE

Mortgage Expenses Deductible

The most important reason to buy real estate – instead of renting it – is most probably the fact that interest paid on a mortgage is deductible when you use the house as your principal place of residence (as of 2014, the rules on deductibility are changing: the maximum rate of deductibility is now 50.5%, but this will decrease by

one percent per year, until it reaches 38% in 2041). Aside from the interest, the one-time expenses related to the mortgage (for example, that part of the civil law notary fee related to the mortgage deed, cadastral registration fee, bank fee and appraisal fee) as well as leasehold are also deductible.

If you decide to take out a higher mortgage than required to finance the purchase of the house itself or for its reconstruction, the related part of the mortgage interest will *not* be deductible. Other expenses related to the house (such as insurance premiums and, of course, capital repayment) are never deductible.

Specific rules apply regarding the deductibility of mortgage interest if you sell a house and buy a new one. As the rules are too complicated to summarize for the purpose of this book, you are advised to consult a specialist should you find yourself in this situation.

In recent years, the government has been re-evaluating its overall mortgage legislation, resulting not only in a lowering of the maximum rate of deductibility, but also in the following measures: mortgage interest is deductible over a maximum period of 30 years, provided the mortgage provides for monthly redemption payments (straight line or annuity), and the maximum mortgage amount will be reduced by 1% per year to 100% of the purchase price of the property by 2018. Consequently, as of that year, buyers will no longer be able to completely finance the additional expenses related to buying a house by means of the mortgage, so that they will ultimately have to bear these costs themselves.

What Type of Mortgage?

You should seek proper advice on the type of mortgage that is suitable in your situation, particularly in view of the limited period of time during which you may need the mortgage. Do not forget to inform the bank if you are benefiting from the 30%-ruling. If the mortgage is linked to a capital insurance, you may be faced with additional tax consequences. Be sure to get expert advice! More on mortgages on page 92.

Deemed Rental Value and woz-Value

Those who own a house and use it as their principal place of residence have to report a certain amount – related to the home ownership – on their income tax return. This amount is a percentage of the value of the house, and is called the *eigenwoningforfait* (or deemed rental value). The *eigenwoningforfait* based on the official value of the house, also known as the woz-value, which is determined every year by the municipality. Every year, the owner receives a so-called *woz-beschikking* (woz-decision, see also page 96), 'confirming' the value of the house, which is used as a basis for determining a number of levies and taxes and has been created in order to rule out the possibility of arbitrariness – as owners used to make their own calculation of the value of their house for tax purposes. woz stands for Wet Waardering Onroerende Zaken, or Value of Immovable Property Act. The general applicable rate of the *eigenwoningforfait* is 0.75% of the woz-value.

The balance of the deemed rental value and the interest can be deducted from your income. You can only deduct your own share in the mortgage. If you are married or if you and your partner are considered fiscal partners (see page 104), you can allocate the mortgage deduction in such a way as to obtain the highest tax relief.

If your partner does not live in the Netherlands, then you can generally deduct only your own share in the mortgage. It would be

a good idea for both of you to look into whether choosing to be treated as a resident taxpayer would be beneficial in your situation.

Preliminary Tax Refund
You can receive a tax refund on the mortgage interest deduction every month by requesting a preliminary negative tax bill from the tax authorities. This is done by means of a special form. The tax authorities will then deposit the refund directly into your bank account.

Real Estate Owned Abroad
If you are a *resident* taxpayer, you cannot deduct the negative income from real estate that is located outside the Netherlands as it is not your principal place of residence. If you are a *non-resident* taxpayer living abroad in your principal place of residence, you can choose to be treated as a resident taxpayer. In that case, you can deduct the mortgage interest (reduced with the deemed rental value) from your Dutch taxable income. However, keep in mind that this option might have – possibly negative – consequences. We recommend that you approach a specialist for advice specifically geared to your situation.

You Don't Live Here, But Own Real Estate Here
You will have to pay tax on a deemed benefit arising from the ownership of the real estate minus the value of the mortgage (a fixed assumed yield) in box 3. This 'benefit' is set at 4% of the market value of the real estate less the debt (the mortgage). The tax rate is 30%. Mortgage interest will no longer be deductible. Each partner has to report his or her own share. If you rent out the real estate, the rental income is free of tax. Any expenses incurred are not tax-deductible.

There are special rules for those who leave the Netherlands only temporarily.

RENTING A HOUSE

Renting a house in the Netherlands is expensive, especially if you need to rent in the western part of the country or close to international schools. There is no tax facility for renting a house whatsoever. With any luck, your employer will choose to compensate you for the housing costs. But in that case, be aware of the tax consequences, see the following paragraphs:

Free Housing Taxable
If you are a resident of the Netherlands (resident taxpayer or partial non-resident taxpayer), any compensation for housing provided by your employer constitutes taxable income. Whether you will have to pay the tax yourself depends on your contract; is it net or gross?

If you are a 'real' non-resident taxpayer, you may benefit from an exemption during a period of two years, under certain conditions.

Special Treatment Under 30%-Ruling
Residents
If you are a resident of the Netherlands (also if you are a partial non-resident taxpayer), in principle the full benefit resulting from the fact that your employer is providing you with housing is a taxable benefit.

If you benefit from the 30%-ruling, special rules apply. A part of the rent may be qualified as an 'extraterritorial expense' (you can read more about this on page 108). That part of the rent can be compensated free of tax (thus reducing the amount of the fixed 30%-allowance!)

Non-Residents
If you are a non-resident of the Netherlands, any compensation of double housing expenses is regarded as compensation for extraterritorial expenses: tax-free, but resulting in a reduction of the 30%-allowance.

TAKING OUT A MORTGAGE

If you have decided to buy a house, you are faced with the question of what will be the most appropriate type of mortgage. The recommended mortgage depends on your special tax position and whether you are likely to move again. In these paragraphs we provide a brief explanation of the relevant types of mortgages available in the Netherlands – whereby we point out that if you take out a new mortgage, you will only be allowed to deduct your mortgage interest from your taxable income if you take out a mortgage with straight line redemption or an annuity mortgage. We will also give a few recommendations as to which types are best suited to your specific tax status.

THE RELEVANT TYPES OF MORTGAGES
Usually a mortgage has a duration of 30 years. Here, we will discuss the three principal types of mortgages and give a brief summary of the mortgages that can no longer be newly taken out.

MORTGAGE WITH STRAIGHT LINE REDEMPTION
The most important characteristic of this mortgage is that the loan is repaid yearly in equal installments (i.e. straight line). As a result of the repayments, the amount of interest payable diminishes every year. Since the interest expenditure decreases steadily, this mortgage is best suited for borrowers who cannot fully benefit from the tax relief on the interest payments.

ANNUITY MORTGAGE
The chief characteristic of an annuity mortgage is that the yearly total of redemption and interest payments remains the same throughout its duration. Although the total remains the same, the mix of interest and redemption of course changes over the years. Owing to this balance between interest and redemption, the redemption is not on a straight line basis.

In the first years, the amount paid by the borrower consists mainly of interest payments. Hence there is a large tax relief in the initial years. Consequently, an annuity mortgage is ideal for people who wish to have a large tax relief in the early years and expect to have a sufficiently high income in later years to be able to make the redemption payments that do not qualify for tax relief.

NATIONALE HYPOTHEEKGARANTIE (NHG)
With a Nationale Hypotheek Garantie (National Mortgage Guarantee), the Stichting Waarborgfonds Eigen Woningen (Homeowners' Guarantee Fund) guarantees payment of the mortgage. In

return for this you pay the NHG a one-time fee (1% for 2016). If you cannot meet your payments, NHG pays them for you – and becomes your creditor for this amount. The advantage to this system for the mortgage provider is that they are guaranteed payment, in return for which they offer a reduction in mortgage interest of anywhere between 0.3 and 0.7% (in some cases, even 0.9%).

An NHG mortgage loan can be taken out to a maximum of € 245,000 (2016), being € 231,132 for the home plus the remaining amount for civil law notary costs, advice and transfer tax. Note: as of July 1 of this year (2016), this maximum amount will be € 225,000 (or € 212,264 for the home). If you want to take out a higher loan, the related interest will be higher. You can also take out a second mortgage aimed at improving your home, buying land or for long lease. For further information on conditions, please consult a tax advisor.

OTHER MORTGAGES

With the following types of mortgage you will no longer be allowed to deduct the related mortgage interest from your taxable income. For this reason, they are basically no longer being offered. If you already have one of these types of mortgage and lower your mortgage interest, or change mortgage providers, you can keep it.

Endowment mortgage: No repayments are made during the term of the mortgage. Instead, the whole loan is redeemed in a single lump sum at the end of the term. The redemption is financed by means of a with-profits endowment policy that matures on the expiry date of the mortgage.

Special endowment mortgage (*Spaarhypotheek*): This is a variation on the Endowment Mortgage. It too provides for a lump-sum redemption of the mortgage loan at the end of the term. The distinguishing feature is that the interest rate on the loan is exactly the same as the gross rate of return on the investment under the endowment policy.

Banksparen mortgage (SEW): Seven years ago, this new type of mortgage was introduced; instead of an endowment policy, a special savings or investment account is linked to the mortgage. This type of mortgage is only possible in the case of immovable property and a related mortgage; at the end of the term, the savings must be used for paying off the mortgage; payments must have been made into the account for a period of at least 15 years, and the highest payment may never exceed ten times the previous payment.

Interest-only mortgage: Here, no redemptions take place during the term of the mortgage. It is usually part of an ordinary Endowment Endowment Mortgage and can only be taken out for a maximum of 50% of the value of the property or of the purchase price.

DUTCH TAX ISSUES FOR EXPATRIATES

In essence, a mortgage is a tax-driven product. Hence, to determine the most appropriate type of mortgage for you, it is necessary to first consider your tax status. In the Netherlands, the two major tax issues with which an expatriate is faced are the 30%-ruling and the choice between resident (*binnenlands belastingplichtige*) and partial non-resident tax status (*partieel buitenlands belastingplichtige*). Of which a more in-depth explanation can be found on page 106/108.

The 30%-Ruling

Simply put, the 30%-ruling allows an employer to grant an employee a tax-free allowance of up to 30% of his total remuneration to cover expenses related to his placement abroad that he would not have had had he not been sent abroad – such as, for instance, housing-related expenses. Your total gross remuneration is reduced by 30% and in return you receive a 30% tax-free allowance. The result of the 30%-ruling is a higher net salary. When applying for the 30%-ruling, the employee may choose to have resident or partial non-resident tax status, see the following paragraph (and page 106/108).

Looking for your rental property?

The biggest rental website in the Netherlands

Visit Pararius.com for the largest and most up-to-date overview for rental properties in the Netherlands. Pararius offers **more than 12.000 rental properties** in the Netherlands and only professional real estate agents can offer their rental properties on Pararius.

The website is available in six different languages and you are able to view all rental properties **completely free of charge.** Every month over 1 million people find their rental property via Pararius.

All properties contain pictures, a map showing exactly where the property is located and a detailed description of the property. Check out which real estate agent you are about to contact by viewing their profile on Pararius.

Sign up for free and receive all new listings matching your profile.

ENERGY LABEL

For quite a while now, cars and household equipment have been issued an 'energy label', ranging from A – G, to indicate how energy-efficient they are. A is the most efficient, G the least. All houses / apartments must also carry this same label (also called *energieprestatiecertificaat*), to be issued by a certified advisor, which is valid for a period of ten years and is handed over with the sale or renting out of the house / apartment. If you cannot show this label, you will not be able to sell your house, while renters will owe less rent. This is all part of the government's aim to become one of the cleanest and most energy-efficient countries within Europe. Measures that influence the classification of your house are, for instance: roof insulation, double glazing, and a ventilation that allows the recuperation of heat. Though you are not obligated to take measures to improve the rating of your house, doing so may contribute to increasing its value, while you might be able to get a more favorable mortgage.

On January 2010, a new type of energy label was introduced, that takes into account the type of house and that provides more information on how energy can be saved, making it easier to compare the energy efficiency of houses, and in January and February of last year, all homeowners in the Netherlands were issued a provisional label, aimed at encouraging them to look into how they can upgrade their energy efficiency. Anyone who wants to sell or rent out their house, will first have to arrange a definitive label – or risk a € 405-fine.

The cost of obtaining the energy label costs depends on the size and type of house. In the case of apartment buildings, a rebate may be possible, while, in the case of 'similar houses' an 'example house' of the series may be used as a basis. Nonetheless, a separate certificate must be issued for each house. A certified advisor can be found by visiting www.energielabelvoorwoningen.nl, and following the steps on this site. You will need your Digid (or digital identity) to do this. As the site is in Dutch, you might wish to enlist the assistance of your realtor to arrange the energy label.

Partial Non-Resident Tax Status

Expatriates who are partial non-residents owe taxes on income derived from certain sources specifically stated in the Dutch income tax legislation.

Partial non-residents are also entitled to tax deductions insofar as they relate to specific income sources, alimony payments and mortgage interest payments for their principal place of residence.

A final important observation regarding partial non-residents is that, contrary to resident taxpayers, net wealth (i.e. assets minus liabilities, taxed at 1.2%) is not taxed here. Hence, the ideal mortgage for a partial non-resident takes advantage of the fact that the interest payments on the mortgage are tax-deductible and that the investment income is not taxed. The corresponding mortgage is discussed further on.

Resident Tax Status

Unless an expatriate chooses to be treated as a partial non-resident taxpayer, he is viewed as a resident for Dutch tax purposes. He is then taxed just as any ordinary Dutch citizen. Resident taxpayers (as well as partial non-resident taxpayers) are only entitled to mortgage interest relief on the principal place of residence. The value of every other residence is subject to wealth tax (over, in principle, the fair market value of the property minus the mortgage loan – at a rate of 1.2%). Whether this also applies to a house abroad depends on whether this is dealt with in a tax treaty between the Netherlands and the country in which the house is situated.

EXPATRIATES: WHAT MORTGAGES ARE APPROPRIATE?

The recommended mortgage depends on your special tax position and whether you are likely to move again.

The ordinary and the Special Endowment Mortgage are not appropriate for a number of reasons. This has to do with the likely duration of your stay. If you leave within, say, seven years and upon leaving decide to surrender the endowment policy, you may receive back only the total of premiums paid. The reason why there will be hardly any investment return is that insurance companies write off all policy costs during the first years of the insurance. Hence, if you surrender within this write-off period, the investment return will only be marginal.

Most expats opt to pay off the mortgage amount (either through an annuity or straight line mortgage), or to accrue the related amount on a savings account – on a special 'Own Home Bank Savings Account', SEW, see earlier on – and sometimes they opt for an investment mortgage (investment account linked to a mortgage). The redemption-free mortgage is also a reasonably popular option. Generally speaking, mortgages that are linked to insurances are no longer taken out, especially not by expats.

YOU ARE A RESIDENT TAXPAYER

If you are benefiting from the 30%-ruling, this will mean that you have a high net salary. This will enable you to make repayments. At the same time, income from wealth is tax-free. For that reason, barring special circumstances, repaying the loan will usually not be tax-efficient.

YOU ARE A PARTIAL NON-RESIDENT TAXPAYER

In this case you need to find a mortgage which allows you to benefit from the tax-deductibility of the interest payments while at the same time allowing you to benefit from the tax-exempt investment income (since there is no 'wealth/box 3' tax for partial non-resident taxpayers). A special type of mortgage can be found, allowing you to fully benefit from these advantages: a redemption-free mortgage combined with a compulsory savings scheme. Since there are no repayments, you benefit to the full from the tax-deductibility of the interest payments.

And since the investment income on the savings scheme is not taxed, you can use this to generate capital with which all or part of the mortgage can be repaid once your partial non-resident tax status ceases to apply. Because the savings are not taxed, it is better to save than to make repayments: the after-tax effect of the repayments will usually be lower than the tax-free effect of the savings. It follows that it is advisable to borrow as much as possible provided that it can be demonstrated that the funds are used for the acquisition of immovable property in the Netherlands. Finally, as partial non-resident taxpayers benefit from the 30%-ruling; here too this allows you to make savings.

U.S. TAXPAYERS

Special provisions apply to U.S. taxpayers; these are not covered here, but can be discussed with your tax advisor.

LOCAL TAXES

The aim of local taxes is to improve the taxpayers' surroundings, such as maintaining the streets, canals and city gardens, but also in the form of an extra contribution to education. And then there are the fun things, such as sports and recreational activities, art and culture.

Local taxes are levied and collected by the municipality or other government organizations. The majority of the total amount collected is levied through municipal property tax (*Onroerend Zaak Belasting* – OZB), waste collection taxes, sewerage charges, water control authority assessments, and the pollution levy.

MUNICIPAL PROPERTY TAX

If you own a house, you owe municipal property tax. This is purely an 'owner's tax'; users owe nothing. When determining the amount due, the value of the property, or the woz-value, must first be determined. The municipality employs its own valuation surveyors to do this. This value is determined annually and is adjusted each year by applying an inflation rate that differs per municipality. When real estate prices go up, the municipalities generally lower their property tax rates to compensate for this. When they go down, the property tax rates are raised accordingly. Thus, in terms of euros, the height of the municipal property tax assessment is largely independent of the developments in the housing market. The woz-value forms the basis for calculating local taxes, such as OZB and the water board assessment, as well as the deemed rental value for income tax purposes (see page 90).

WASTE COLLECTION TAXES

This tax is levied to cover the costs of collecting and processing household waste. This includes the emptying of the glass, paper, plastics, and clothing containers that can be found in Dutch towns and cities. Processing waste is an expensive business. Environmental laws are becoming stricter and separating waste is a costly affair.

SEWERAGE CHARGES

These taxes are meant to cover the costs of maintaining the municipal sewage system. Everyone who makes use of this system, owes sewerage taxes. Only owners of immovable property have to pay it. You might notice that your sewerage charges increase each year, due to the arrears in the maintenance of the city sewage system.

WATER BOARD ASSESSMENTS

This is money spent for keeping the water level in, among others, rivers, canals, ditches and streams at a certain level and ensuring the quality of the surface water. During the wet season, the water systems are drained. During the dry season, if necessary and possible, more water is brought in. Thus the water boards play an important role in this wet country. Your water board assessment helps to pay for these services.

POLLUTION LEVY

The higher water control corporations, or Waterschappen, collect the pollution levy from all households. This levy is used for maintaining or improving the quality of surface water, while sewage treatment plants are used for cleaning waste water.

A COUNTRY OF TAXES

The Netherlands is truly a country of taxes. In order to guarantee or, where necessary, improve our enjoyment, local taxes are expected to continue to rise during the coming years. As they are levied locally, there are great differences between municipalities in the amounts due. The Consumentenbond (Consumers' Association), a Dutch organization that looks into and informs us on issues of importance to consumers, and Vereniging Eigen Huis (Association for Property Owners) investigate the local tax situation every year, to help ensure that these differences do not become too great. A few years ago, one of the major municipal authorities made a serious plea for more transparency when it comes to the calculation of local taxes per municipality. Hopefully the outcome will be in your favor.

These local taxes can also be seen as costs of living, along with fees for gas, electricity and water, insurances, as well as the deemed rental value and property transfer tax. The costs for gas, electricity, water, and insurances, as well as the local taxes, are charged by the municipality, the water boards or the government. Investigation shows that the costs for gas, electricity and water amount to 32% of the total costs for living, and local taxes; 25%.

DOG TAX

A very special tax is dog tax. Initially, the dog tax was a tax for companies that used dogs to pull carts. Now it is more of an environmental tax and is used to cover the costs of setting aside places for the dogs to run and play, and to clean up after them. Anyone who owns a dog must pay this tax, if they reside in a municipality that still levies it.

PAPER SERVICES

Also, we owe tax for the 'paper services' provided by municipalities. Some examples are:

- marriage license
- registration papers
- driver's license
- passport
- residence permit
- parking permit (in the larger cities).

Though municipalities and other government organizations are not allowed to make a profit on these services; they can pass on the costs in their entirety.

DENT

All these levies, added up together, can come to a considerable – and sometimes unexpected – amount and can put quite a dent in your vacation savings! So be sure to reserve at least € 2,000 a year for these taxes.

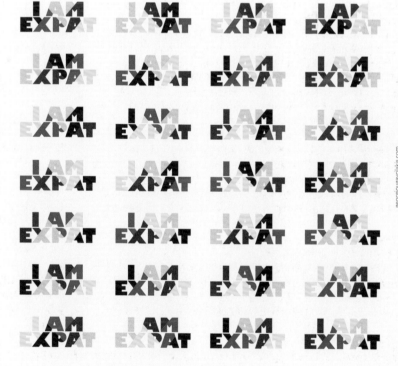

EXEMPTION FROM CUSTOMS DUTIES

If you transfer goods from a non EU-country to an EU-Member State (such as the Netherlands), you are subject to customs duties, VAT and other special taxes (for example excises and a special tax on cars). The taxation incurred upon importation can mean a great financial burden if you regularly change your place of residence for work or for other purposes. A special exemption can provide relief in these circumstances if you meet certain conditions.

EXTENT OF EXEMPTION

All EU-Member States provide an exemption if the imported goods form part of your household (personal) effects and they are transported as part of your change of fixed address. Usually the removal company will ensure that you make use of the exemption and will take care of administrative obligations. Whether you meet the related conditions is a question only the Customs Authorities can answer, however.

PERSONAL EFFECTS

These are effects such as clothing, furniture, linen, kitchen equipment, audio equipment, etc. Used cars, (motor) bikes, pleasure yachts and pleasure aircraft are also deemed to be personal goods. The exemption will be issued in the form of a permit (license). Usually the Customs Authorities will issue a license for the personal goods and a separate license for the car. To obtain the licenses mentioned above, you will have to fill out an application form. In certain circumstances, a car that is made available to a natural person by an employer, and that is used by that person for both business and private purposes, may be regarded as an item of personal property that is eligible for relief from customs duties.

CONDITIONS

When transferring your place of residence to any of the EU-Member States, certain conditions that must be met in order to successfully claim a relief from duties and tax:
- your usual place of residence must be transferred to an EU-Member State (in this case, the Netherlands)
- your usual place of residence must have been in a non-EU Member State for at least 12 months
- the goods to be transferred must have been in your personal possession, and must have been in your use during the last six months. In exceptional cases the authorities may grant an exception to this requirement
- you must apply for a permit in the Netherlands
- with the exemption request, you should submit a signed list of household effects and other goods to be moved
- you should fulfill the usual customs requirements upon importation
- the goods must be imported within 12 months of your actual change of residency. The importation may take place in separate transports but in each case there must be a direct link between the change of residency and the importation of the goods
- you must use the goods for the same purpose in the Netherlands and are not allowed to lend, hire out, transfer or otherwise dispose of the goods within a period of 12 months of the acceptance of the customs declaration by the Customs Authorities.

DETERMINING RESIDENCY

As mentioned above, the exemption can be requested if you change your place of permanent/usual residence from a non EU-country to the Netherlands and it will only be granted if you have been a resident of the non EU-country for at least 12 months preceding the move. If you do not have work connections here, or your work and personal connections are in different countries, then your home is considered to be where your personal connections are. It is up to you, when applying for the exemption, to prove the 12-month residency in the non EU-country. If you are deemed to have been resident in more than one country, the country with which your personal connections (family and/or social commitments) are, will prevail. If, for example your family remained in the Netherlands while you stayed in a non EU-country for a period of two years, the Customs Authorities will deem that you remained a resident of the Netherlands. Consequently, your 'return' to the Netherlands will not qualify as a change of residence either, as you will already be considered to have been a resident here.

Circumstances that prove personal ties with a particular country are: where your family/other personal relations live; memberships; municipal registration; a fixed home, either owned or rented; other sources of income; and nationality. Also the following issues can play a role: physical presence; other living space; where you carry out your work; financial interests; and your administrative ties with the government and other social institutes. In other words, if your family is not the deciding factor, there are several other circumstances that are also taken into account.

Based on recent case law, one can conclude that the Dutch Customs Authorities have become stricter, which is further supported by rulings issued by the Court of Haarlem and the Court of Justice in Amsterdam.

MOVING FROM AN EU-MEMBER STATE TO THE NETHERLANDS

If you import goods from another member state, you will have already paid EU VAT and the exemption will therefore not be of any use. This is different, however, for cars – for more information, see page 151).

REVOCATION OF THE EXEMPTION

After the permit has been granted and you have imported the goods, the exemption will be revoked if you lend, hire out, transfer or otherwise dispose of any of the household effects, including the car, to another party within 12 months. Therefore, if anyone borrows your car, even for a short while, during your first 12 months in the EU, you will be liable for duties and tax immediately. This condition is in effect for 12 months starting on the date on which the Customs Authorities accept the customs declaration.

LARGE SAVINGS ON DUTIES

The exemption for household effects, when you move your permanent place of residence to the Netherlands, is subject to a number of strict conditions but when applied provides worthwhile savings on duties upon importation.

ORGANIZATIONS

NEDERLANDSE VERENIGING VAN MAKELAARS, NVM
Dutch Association of Real Estate Brokers
Fakkelstede 1, 3431 HZ Nieuwegein
P.O. Box 2222, 3430 DC Nieuwegein
Tel.: 030 608 51 85
www.nvm.nl

VERENIGING EIGEN HUIS
Dutch Housing Association
Displayweg 1, 3821 BT Amersfoort
P.O. Box 735, 3800 AS Amersfoort
Tel.: 033 450 77 52
www.eigenhuis.nl

CENTRAAL BUREAU VOOR STATISTIEK, CBS
Central Bureau for Statistics
www.cbs.nl

CONSUMENTENBOND
Consumer Society
Enthovenplein 1, 2521 DA The Hague
P.O. Box 1000, 2500 BA The Hague
Tel.: 070 445 45 45
www.consumentenbond.nl

KONINKLIJKE NOTARIËLE BEROEPSORGANISATIE, KNB
Royal Dutch Notaries
Spui 184, 2511 BW The Hague
P.O. Box 16020, 2500 BA The Hague
Tel.: 070 330 71 11
www.notaris.nl

DOUANE NEDERLAND
Dutch Customs
Service desk: 0800 0143
www.douane.nl

TAX AND CUSTOMS ADMINISTRATION
Steenvoordelaan 370, 2284 EH Rijswijk
P.O. Box 3080, 2280 GB Rijswijk
Tel.: 070 372 49 05
www.belastingdienst.nl

RECOMMENDED READING

THE ACCESS GUIDE/HOUSING IN THE NETHERLANDS
useful information on renting and buying property, valuation and about choosing an agent
www.access-nl.org

WEBSITES

GENERAL HOUSE HUNTING WEBSITES
www.funda.nl
www.huislijn.nl
www.huizenzoeker.nl
www.jaap.nl
www.miljoenhuizen.nl
www.pararius.nl
www.vbo.nl
www.zah.nl

REAL ESTATE AGENTS PORTALS
www.makelaar.lokaalzoeken.nl: search for a listing of local agents
www.makelaars.net: real estate brokers portal
www.makelaars-nederland.nl: real estate brokers portal
www.mva.nl: Makelaars Vereniging Amsterdam
www.nvm.nl: Nederlandse Vereniging van Makelaars

HOUSING-/REAL ESTATE AGENCIES
The Hague Real Estate Services: www.thehaguerealestate.nl
Amstel Housing: www.amstelhousing.nl
Amsterdamse Maatschappij: www.amsterdamsemaatschappij.nl
Beeuwkes Makelaardij: www.beeuwkes.nl
Bosch & Duyn: www.boschenduyn.nl
Burger van Leeuwen: www.bvl-residential.nl
Buise van Soest: http://buisevansoest.nl
De Vries Robbe: www.vriesrobbe.nl
Direct Wonen: www.directwonen.nl
Estata Makelaars: www.estata.nl
Finsens Makelaardij: www.finsensmakelaardij.nl
Gravestate: www.gravestate.com
Haagen & Partners: www.haagen-partners.nl
Home in Amsterdam: www.homeinamsterdam.com
Housingonline: www.housingonline.nl
Housingsolutions: www.housingsolutions.nl
Inter Agency Holland: www.interagency.nl
Kimmel & Co: www.kimmel.nl
Local Home: www.localhome.nl
Luijckx Makelaardij: www.luijckx-mak.nl
Makelaars Associatie: www.makas.nl
Mie Lan Kok: www.mielankok.nl
Nelisse Makelaars: www.nelisse.nl
Pararius: www.pararius.nl
Perfect Housing: www.perfecthousing.nl
Plink Adviesgroep: www.plink.nl
Quality Rentals: www.qualityrentals.eu

Stoit Groep: www.stoit.nl
Tettero & Wetters: www.tettero-wetters.nl
TVN Real Estate: www.tvnsite.nl
Van Dorp Verhoog Makelaars: www.vandorpverhoog.nl
Van Paaschen Makelaardij: www.vanpaaschen.nl
Welp Makelaardij: www.welpmakelaardij.nl
Wobeco Housing: www.wobeco.com
Zeilstra Beheer: www.zeilstrabeheer.nl
The Hague Real Estate Services: www.thehaguerealestate.nl

TEMPORARY RESIDENCE
BizStay The Hague: www.bizstaythehague.com
Corporate Housing Factory: www.corporatehousingfactory.com
Hotel Residences: www.hotelresidences.nl
Htel Serviced Apartments: www.htel.nl
Prinsenhof: www.prinsenhof.info
Rien vd Broeke Village: www.village.nl
The Student Hotel: www.thestudenthotel.com

RENTAL FURNITURE
In-Lease Nederland: www.in-lease.com
Home Inspirations: www.home-inspirations.nl
Re-Place: www.re-place.nl

MORTGAGES
http://hypotheekvisie.nl
www.expat-mortgages.nl
www.huis-hypotheek.nl
www.hypotheekshop.nl
www.hypotheker.nl
www.independer.nl

BUILDING MARKETS
Fixet: www.fixet.nl
Gamma: www.gamma.com
Hornbach: www.hornbach.nl
Hubo: www.hubo.nl
Karwei: www.karwei.nl
Praxis: www.praxis.nl

This chapter covers the legal, tax and financial information you may need during your stay in the Netherlands, such as: money matters; where much of your hard-earned money goes (the tax man); obtaining permits; getting married in the Netherlands and its legal consequences; what to do when you want a divorce; the rules on inheritance; insurances you need to consider; where to go for legal assistance, and much more.

Legal, Tax and Financial Matters

CONTRIBUTING AUTHORS YOLANDA BOKHORST, STEPHANIE DIJKSTRA, ARJAN ENNEMAN, KEES DE GRAAF, EDITH VAN RUITENBEEK AND ROBIN SCHALEKAMP

MONEY MATTERS

THE EURO

Since January 2002, the monetary unit of the Netherlands has been the euro (or €), replacing 700 years of the guilder. The euro is also the currency in Andorra, Austria, Belgium, Finland, France, Germany, Greece, Ireland, Italy, Luxembourg, Monaco, Portugal, San Marino, Spain and Vatican City. Denmark, Sweden and the United Kingdom still make use of their own currency. Though ten new countries joined the EU in May 2004, this does not automatically mean they have 'acquired' the euro. In order to do this they must meet certain economic criteria. One of the first steps to be taken in the process towards introducing the euro in these countries is to join the exchange rate mechanism (which has replaced the EMS, or European Monetary System), linking the national currency to the euro. This has been done by Estonia, Lithuania, Slovenia, Cyprus, Latvia, Malta and Slovakia. Since then, all of these countries have adopted the euro as the national currency. Montenegro and Kosovo have unilaterally adopted the euro.

All EMU countries that have introduced the euro have the same bank notes and coins. These coins have two faces: the common euro face and a national face – though these coins look different, they can be used in any of the countries that have introduced the euro. There are seven bank notes: 5, 10, 20, 50, 100, 200 and 500 euros, and eight coins: 1 and 2 euros and 1, 2, 5, 10, 20 and 50 euro-cents.

Until January 1, 2007, you could exchange both guilder coins and bank notes at De Nederlandsche Bank for euros. As of then, you can only exchange bank notes, which you can do until January 1, 2032.

NUMBER PUNCTUATION

The Dutch way of punctuating numbers and decimals is exactly opposite to the English way, so that € 25,25 is 25 euros and 25 euro-cents, and € 10.000 is ten thousand euros. Round figures are written with a comma and a dash: e.g. 15 euros is € 15,-.

CHANGING MONEY

The introduction of the euro has made it easier to travel throughout most of Europe: you can go from country to country and use the same currency. However, for all other currencies, the issue of exchange rates is still an important one.

The exchange rate (*wisselkoers*) is fixed every day and will be posted wherever you exchange money. The rate does not vary from one bank to the next, although the charge for exchanging money may differ. The most common place to exchange money is a bank (such as ABN Amro, ING or Rabobank), or a GWK exchange office. You will find GWK offices at railway stations, the airport, and places where there are many tourists. If you can show an international student card at a GWK exchange office, you will be charged less.

In very heavily touristed areas you may see other types of exchange offices, but their charges could be higher, so it is best to wait until you see a bank or GWK office. There is no informal market for currency. Anyone who approaches you on the street with an offer to change money will be a thief or con artist, rather than a money-changer.

OPENING YOUR ACCOUNT

To manage your day-to-day finances, you will need a current account, called a *privérekening*. The former Postbank, which has now merged with the ING, referred to this account as the *giro-rekening*, so that you might still come across this name in certain documents.

To open an account, you must visit the bank in person, bringing along proof of identification (passport or EU identity card). Contrary to the past, you do NOT need a Citizen Service Number (*burgerservicenummer*, see page 66) to open a bank account. Most banks also like to see some type of proof of a regular income (such as a pay slip). Another option is to send an online request to open a bank account. In response, you will be sent a proposal which you can take with you to a bank, along with proof of identification, registration and, as the case may be, employment or registration with an educational institution, to finalize the opening of the account. Some banks will make an appointment for someone to pay you a house-call to verify matters, after which they will open a bank account for you.

While opening the account, you also arrange your bank card (see further on). Some banks offer a choice of cards, depending on whether you plan to use them abroad or not, other banks offer 'only' one type of card, all functions included. These cards allow you to withdraw up to several thousand euros a day at the bank or in the stores. For the use of these cards you pay a nominal annual fee. An account at a commercial bank is functional the same day that (or the day after) you open it. Most banks do not send statements anymore as almost everyone uses online banking nowadays. If you wish to receive 'paper' statements, you had best communicate this to the bank. With some banks, if you want to be able to overdraw your account ('go into the red'), you must bring proof of a source of regular income, so that you can determine together with the bank employee to what amount you can do this.

If you want to arrange a loan, the bank will check with the BKR (Bureau for Credit Registration) whether you are 'creditworthy'; here they keep records of your credit card and bank history. If the BKR issues a negative advice, the bank can refuse you.

Current accounts pay no interest, but you are charged interest if you overdraw from them: i.e., if you 'go into the red'. Various other types of savings accounts are available for other purposes.

BANK CARDS

When you open your account, the bank will offer you options regarding plastic cards. The basic card, or *bankpas, betaalpas* or *europas*, is used for making cash withdrawals from cash dispensers and for paying in stores using a *pinautomaat*. If you choose to have one – and we strongly recommend that you do, unless you want to have wads of cash in your wallet – you will receive notice in the mail when it comes in at the bank that you can come and collect and activate it (do not forget to bring proof of identity – passport or EU identity card), or they will send it to you by mail, in which case you follow the included instructions on how to activate it. You will be issued a four-digit *pincode* to be used every time you use the card to withdraw cash or make a payment. Be sure to memorize it so that a thief can never steal your card and find out your number at the same time. If you forget the number, you have to get a new card. If you want, you can change your *pincode* into any other four-digit combination you like, at the bank. If you receive a replacement card (for instance, every so many years, you are issued a new card), you activate the card by making a payment in a store, by making a withdrawal from an ATM, or be requesting how much money is in your account through the ATM.

Your basic card will have various symbols on it, indicating its various functions. One symbol matches the one on *pinautomaten* (for paying in stores), and others match symbols on cash dispensers. Most bank cards also work in ATMs abroad, a feature which, in most cases, must be activated online or through the bank. Before going on vacation, make sure this feature has been activated – and make sure it is set to 'worldwide' if you are leaving Europe. This can also be done temporarily.

Some banks offer variations on this basic card, which give it extra functions. They will tell you about these possibilities.

On www.mistermoney.nl/bankieren.asp, you will find an overview of what the various banks offer, in terms of Internet banking, a credit card, mobile banking, etc. (in Dutch).

CREDIT CARDS

A credit card is a separate card. In the Netherlands, the commercial banks mostly have an arrangement with either MasterCard or VISA. The money you spend with your Dutch credit card will be deducted on a monthly basis from your account or you will receive an invoice from the credit card company.

The main difference between your basic bank card and a credit card is that your basic card will refuse to make a transaction if your balance is insufficient, whereas a credit card will always work unless it has been blocked – following theft, for example. This is why banks will give their clients credit cards only after they have known them a while, and have been able to determine, for instance, if the client has a regular source of income – and why the use of a credit card costs more.

Paying by credit card is less common in shops – especially smaller shops and supermarkets – mainly because the shops must pay a percentage of each sale to the credit-card company. Restaurants, hotels and department stores generally accept all major cards, however. Look at the window beside the door to see which cards they will take. In some stores, they will ask you to present some form of identification before allowing you to use the credit card.

CASH DISPENSERS
(OR AUTOMATED TELLER MACHINES, ATMS)

You will find a *geldautomaat* or cash dispenser at every bank, and in railway stations and other public places where people are spending money. Dispensers will accept almost every kind of card, nowadays. You must find a match among the symbols on the dispenser and on your card.

To use a cash dispenser, you insert your card in the slot, and in most cases are given the option to select a language; Dutch, English, French or German. You type in your *pincode*, indicate that you want to withdraw money, select the amount, confirm it, and wait first for your card and then for your money. If a dispenser is not working it will say *buiten dienst*. If you do not have enough money in your bank account to cover your withdrawal, it will say *saldo niet toereikend*. If you type in the wrong *pincode* more than twice, the machine will swallow your card and you will have to go to the bank for a new one.

PAYING IN STORES

Paying with a bank card (*pin, pinpas*; the operative word being *pinnen*) has become the most popular way of paying – after all, many stores (even stores where you buy large amounts of large objects, such as furniture or other household goods) still do not accept credit cards.

Shops have a link to the bank system, and the amount due is deducted immediately from your account. You insert your card into a reader that looks like an oversized calculator and you type in your own secret four-digit personal identification number (PIN, or *pincode*), sometimes only after saying 'OK' to the amount they are about to deduct. The bank checks whether or not your balance will cover the amount; you verify the amount by pressing *ja* ('yes'), and the transaction is complete. If there isn't enough money in your bank account, you will have to find some other way to pay.

Also when goods are delivered to your home – if you have not already paid for them – you pay the delivery person in cash, or, if they have an 'ambulant' pin machine, with your bank card and pincode.

THE COIN ISSUE

In shops, clerks sometimes have trouble making change and will ask you for coins. During the last few years of the guilder, the use of the single cent was unceremoniously abolished and prices got rounded off to the nearest five cents. With the introduction of the euro, came the introduction of not only the one cent-coin but also the two cent-coin, much to the annoyance of shopkeepers and customers. Starting towards the end of 2004, it became common use again to round prices off.

BANK TRANSFERS / ACCEPTGIRO

Bills are generally paid by bank transfer, also known as the *giro* system. When bills are sent, they usually have a yellow *acceptgirokaart* attached to them. In the olden days, you filled in your own account number on it, signed your name, and sent it to your bank (either by means of the specially-provided postage-free envelope, or by depositing it in their mail box), which deducted the money from your account. Nowadays, most people pay the bill via Internet, entering the receiver's name and bank account number, as well as the *acceptgiro* number in the required spaces.

Your bank can also provide you with forms for paying bills that do not have an *acceptgirokaart* attached. These are called *overschrijvingsformulieren*. On these you fill in the amount, the account number and the city of residence or establishment of the recipient, indicate what the payment is for (where the form says *betreft*, *betalingskenmerk*, or *mededelingen*), and place your signature where it says *handtekening*. You can also take your bill to your personal bank and pay it there. However, since the introduction of Internet or online banking, hardly anyone ever makes use of this option anymore.

For bills that you have to pay on a regular basis, such as your monthly rent, you can go to the bank and fill in a form known as a *machtiging*. This gives the bank permission to transfer a certain amount from your account on a specific day of the month. *Machtigingen* can also be arranged online, if you have opted for Internet banking. This will continue until you tell them to cancel a payment or to stop altogether. If you buy something by mail, the order form will sometimes include such a *machtiging* for a one-time payment or an *acceptgiro*. Your signature and account number are all the seller needs to get his money.

ELECTRONIC BANKING

All Dutch banks offer you software that allows you to make payments from the comfort of your own home: electronic banking. Almost all banks offer this software in English – when you contact your bank, make sure to indicate that you would like to receive the English-language version. Most of these programs also have simple labeling options that allow you to keep itemized track of your spending habits.

INTERNET BANKING

More popular than electronic banking is Internet banking. It allows you to contact the bank via the Internet and – by means of an entry code – recall the amount on your bank account and carry out any payments. Furthermore, you can access an overview of your insurances and investments, and place orders for the buying and selling of shares, options, etc – also from abroad, of course. Contact your bank for information on what else they offer through Internet banking.

When you participate in an Internet savings 'plan', you save money on an account that you can only access via the Internet. The amount of interest you receive on this account is relatively high, as the margins can be kept low, due to the fact that you are the one managing the account and executing the moves.

PAYING ON THE INTERNET

Now that we do more and more virtual shopping on the Internet, we need a virtual purse. In this virtual purse, we of course find our credit card, but there are also alternatives. The two best-known ways of paying via the Internet are called PayPal and iDEAL. For more information, visit their websites. For prepaid payments – so that you need give neither your bank account number nor your credit card details – there is the paysafecard (www.paysafecard.com), or pre-paid credit cards.

MOBILE BANKING

Mobile banking (m-banking) allows you to access your bank services by means of your mobile phone (or tablet or laptop). You can find out how much money is on your account, make payments and look up your receipts and payments. Not only that, but you can also find out what the state of your investments is, inform yourself of the latest financial news and the stock market, and place orders on the Dutch and American stock markets. Among the banks that offer mobile banking are ABNAmro, ING, Rabobank and SNS.

The mobile banking market is a fluid and quickly developing one. We therefore suggest you check the banks' various websites for what they offer and who they are working with. Another player on this market is www.mobile2pay.nl, which offers you mobile banking services regardless of your bank (provided it is a Dutch bank) or your mobile phone service provider. Mobile2pay can be used anywhere where you cannot make use of your bank card (for instance when Internet-shopping or shopping from the comfort of the back seat of your car) and is currently also being introduced as a payment method in shops and restaurants across the country.

BANKING HOURS

Regular banks are open Monday through Friday, generally from 9 A.M. to 5 P.M. Many also open for a couple of hours on the one evening of the week that shops in the neighborhood stay open. This is usually a Thursday or a Friday. Due to the advent of Internet banking, there are fewer bank offices now than just a few years ago.

TAXES

For purposes of application of the tax laws, it is very important to know whether you are a resident of the Netherlands or not. If you are, you are regarded as a 'resident taxpayer'; if not, as a 'non-resident taxpayer' – though so-called qualified non-residents can also be treated as resident taxpayers. And then there is a fourth option: if you are benefiting from the 30%-ruling, you may opt to be treated as a partial non-resident taxpayer. As it would – not surprisingly – require at least one book to tell you about the tax treatment of these four categories, we have picked out a handful of subjects that could be of interest to you, as an expatriate. These have been divided into the following headings: Income Tax, Wage Tax, and the 30%-ruling.

INCOME TAX

ARE YOU A RESIDENT?

Under Dutch law, the question of a person's residence is determined 'according to the circumstances', focusing on with which country the ties are stronger. This is a question of facts, and in case law – among others – the following circumstances have been considered relevant when deciding on this issue:
- the place where you have your home
- the place where your family (partner) resides
- the place where you work
- the length of your stay in the Netherlands
- other personal ties with the Netherlands, such as (club) memberships, bank accounts, etc.

From this list it can be deduced that the existence of a lasting relationship of a personal nature with the Netherlands is regarded as an important factor when deciding whether or not you are a resident of this country.

THE TAX SYSTEM

There are different categories of income, each of which is treated differently for tax purposes, and these are the following:

Box 1: Income from work and home

This box includes, among others, income from employment, pensions, social security benefits, business income, periodic payments (e.g. alimony received), income from home ownership (*eigenwoningforfait*, if the house is your principal place of residence, see page 90) – less deductibles, for example mortgage interest (again, if the house is your principal place of residence), alimony paid, etc. The amount of tax due is calculated on the taxable income according to the progressive tax rates. The tax rates vary from 36.55% to 52%. Over the first two tax brackets (up to € 33,715) the social security contributions for those younger than the pensionable age (28.15% in total) are also calculated. The social security contribution-percentage for those of pensionable age is 10.25%. The tax brackets for those under the pensionable age are:

2016	Income	Wage Tax	Social Security	Total
Bracket 1	up to € 19,922	8.40%	28.15%	36.55%
Bracket 2	€ 19,923 – € 33,715	12.25%	28.15%	40,40%
Bracket 3	€ 33,716 – € 66,421	40,40%		40,40%
Bracket 4	€ 66,422 and more	52%		52%

Box 2: Income from substantial shareholding

If you own (possibly together with your partner) at least 5% of the shares in a Netherlands company (BV or NV) or in a similar foreign company limited by shares, this income is taxed at 25%.

Box 3: Taxable income from savings and investments

A notional income from investments is taxed, instead of the actual income. 30% is levied on 4% of the assets – after the deduction of debts and a personal allowance – the effective tax rate therefore being 1.2%. No taxes are levied over the first € 24,437 (2016).

FISCAL PARTNERS

Fiscal partners can allocate common sources of income and deductible items – such as mortgage interest for the principal place of residence, medical expenses or study costs – to each other's tax return in such a way that they can reap the maximum benefit from them. Without fiscal partnership, certain items could end up being deducted against lower tax rates (resulting in lower refunds), or certain levy rebates could be reduced.

Married couples and registered couples are automatically considered fiscal partners. Unmarried couples who are living together are only considered fiscal partners if they are registered at the same address with the municipal registration office, and meet one or more of the following conditions. They:

- have a civil partnership agreement drawn by a civil law notary (as of 2012 the contract must also include a mutual care stipulation)
- have a child together
- jointly own their principal residence
- are considered partners in a pension scheme
- were fiscal partners the previous year.

Contrary to the past, partners are no longer free to choose whether or not they wish to become fiscal partners. The law determines whether they are or not.

Retroactive Effect

If one of the aforementioned conditions is fulfilled during the course of the fiscal year, fiscal partnership will automatically apply as of that date. If you are already living together and then buy a house then you will be considered fiscal partners. Those who, during the course of a year, become fiscal partners can choose to have this status for the entire year. Those who were fiscal partners during the preceding year, are automatically fiscal partners as of January 1 of the next fiscal year.

LEVY REBATES

Instead of personal allowances, Dutch tax law contains levy rebates; rebates on tax and on the so-called general insurance contributions. Various levy rebates are available, depending on your personal circumstances. The general levy rebate, which has been created for those who either receive income from (self-)employment or a government benefit (it is taken into account when wage tax is withheld over these payments), is also available if you have no such income, provided you have a fiscal partner who pays taxes in the Netherlands as well as contributions for the national insurance schemes. All you have to do is submit a request with the tax authorities and – as there is nothing to deduct it from – the tax authorities will pay out the amount of the rebate.

FOUR TAXPAYER OPTIONS

Resident Taxpayers

If you are a resident taxpayer, you owe income tax on your entire, worldwide, income. In principle it makes no difference where in the world you earn your income (thus you may end up owing double taxes; see further on). The main sources of income that constitute taxable income are: business income, employment income, income in the form of periodic benefits (whether in cash or in kind) and notional investment income.

Non-Resident Taxpayers

If you are a non-resident taxpayer, you are only liable to pay income tax on your income from certain sources in the Netherlands, resulting in a limited tax liability. The main sources of income that are considered taxable are: Dutch business income, employment income, income from real estate in the Netherlands and income in the form of periodic benefits (whether in cash or in kind) and a substantial shareholding in a Netherlands company. In principle, employment income that you earn while you are physically not in the Netherlands is not taxable here (see further on).

Goodbye hassle, welcome WePayPeople

You are a contractor or knowledge migrant who is looking for a trusted partner to take care of all your payment affairs.

For two good reasons: you want to maximize your net pay and you want to be paid on time. Fast, easy and without the usual hassle.

Look no further. WePayPeople offers you a one-stop contact with all the required knowledge when it comes to payroll issues, such as taxes, the 30%-ruling, work permits and other related matters. Make it easy on yourself, check out our services and try our expat calculator at **www.dutch-umbrella-company.com**

WEPAYPEOPLE

Donauweg 1, 1043 AJ Amsterdam – The Netherlands. +31 (0)20 – 820 15 60

The Dutch Umbrella Company is a WePayPeople company

'Qualified' Non-Residents Treated as Resident Taxpayers

The scheme for qualified non-resident taxpayer status applies since January 1, 2015. You are a qualified non-resident taxpayer if you live in an EU country, Liechtenstein, Norway, Iceland, Switzerland, Bonaire, Sint Eustatius or Saba, and pay taxes in the Netherlands on more than 90% of your worldwide income. Do you meet all conditions of this new scheme? In that case, you are entitled to the same deductible items, tax credits and tax-free allowances as residents of the Netherlands. The same conditions apply to your partner.

Do you not meet all conditions? For instance, because you pay tax in the Netherlands on less than 90% of your worldwide income? In that case, you may, for example, no longer deduct the interest on the loan for your owner-occupied home on your tax return. You may no longer opt for resident taxpayer status either.

Partial Non-Resident Taxpayers

You only have the option of being treated as a partial non-resident taxpayer if you benefit from the so-called 30%-ruling (which will be discussed further on). When making use of this option, you are a resident of the Netherlands for income (and deductibles) in box 1, but you are treated – upon your request – as a non-resident in boxes 2 and 3. This option gives you the best tax position you can have in the Netherlands.

TAX REFUND

In order to realize the tax benefit from deductibles (such as your mortgage interest) at an earlier point in time than through the final income tax bill, you can request the tax inspector to pay the tax refund in advance during the current year through a negative preliminary tax bill. The tax refund is then transferred directly by the tax office to your bank account, on a monthly basis.

DOUBLE TAXATION

Resident Taxpayers

As a resident of the Netherlands, you have to pay tax on your worldwide income, as a consequence of which you may be faced with double taxation. After all, income earned abroad will often also be subject to taxation there. This situation is covered by the tax treaties that the Netherlands has entered into with many countries. In most of these treaties, income from employment in the Netherlands is tax-exempt in the Netherlands, provided all the following conditions are satisfied:

■ you are present in the Netherlands for a period or periods not exceeding in the aggregate 183 days in any 12-month period or in a fiscal year, and
■ the remuneration is paid by or on behalf of an employer who is not a resident of the Netherlands, and
■ the remuneration is not borne by a permanent establishment or permanent representative of the employer in the Netherlands.

If the cumulative conditions summarized above are not met, your income will be taxable in the Netherlands.

Please note that if you carry out work in the Netherlands via a foreign employment agency, you cannot always apply the '183-day rule'. The material relationship between you, the foreign employment agency, and the Dutch recipient will also have to be taken into consideration.

For countries with which the Netherlands has not entered into a tax treaty, there is a unilateral arrangement. This will often mean that income earned abroad is exempt from taxation in the Netherlands, although it will be taken into account for the purpose of calculating the (progressive) tax rate applicable to your further income, which is then taxed in keeping with the 'normal' rules.

Non-Resident Taxpayers

As a non-resident taxpayer, you generally owe tax in your country of residence on income earned in the Netherlands, as a consequence of which you may be faced with double taxation. This situation is also covered in tax treaties.

U.S. TAXPAYERS

If you are a U.S. citizen benefiting from the 30%-ruling and you opt for the status of partial non-resident taxpayer, you owe tax in the Netherlands over income earned on working days physically spent in the Netherlands only. Therefore, if you spend a lot of time traveling outside the Netherlands, this could clearly be to your advantage.

A lower tax credit may, of course, have a negative impact on your U.S. tax liability, but this will very likely be outweighed by the benefit. This rule does not apply to statutory directors.

WAGE TAX

PAYROLL DEDUCTION

The term 'wage' is interpreted very widely and includes cash benefits, benefits in kind, and also entitlements (such as pensions, which you can read about further on). In general, your employer is required to deduct the wage tax due from your wages and pay it to the Tax Office. The amount thus deducted can later on be credited with the income tax due. In some cases, no tax bill is imposed and thus the payroll deduction is the final tax due. If you are working for a non-Netherlands employer who does not have a permanent establishment, a deemed permanent establishment or a permanent representative in the Netherlands, your employer must register with the tax office as a foreign withholding agent and set up a payroll administration for the employees who are working in the Netherlands.

COST ALLOWANCES

The Netherlands wage tax law provides the following cost allowances for both resident and non-resident taxpayers:

■ cost allowances: allowances for all kinds of expenses, the (non) taxability of which is determined by the business or personal nature of the expenses; the same applies to income in kind. Business expenses cannot be deducted on your personal income tax return, with the exception of (fixed) public transportation costs – subject to certain conditions
■ 30%-ruling: under certain conditions, if you are an employee and have come to the Netherlands from abroad, extra expenses called 'extraterritorial expenses' can be reimbursed tax-free, either for the amount of the actual expenses or on a notional basis, being a maximum of 30% of your wage. The latter can be done if the Tax Office has issued an official approval (the actual 30%-ruling). Your employer can also decide to reimburse your real extraterritorial expenses instead.

PENSION

The term 'pension' has been strictly defined for tax purposes. A pension scheme that complies with this definition is a 'qualifying pension scheme'. If your pension scheme is indeed a qualifying pension scheme, your contributions are deductible and your employer's contributions are tax-exempt. The related benefits you will receive are subject to tax at the time of payment. However, if a pension scheme does not 'qualify', your contributions are not deductible nor are your employer's contributions tax-exempt.

The continuation of a non-Netherlands pension scheme requires particular attention, since it will often not satisfy the Dutch criteria. In order for your pension scheme to be considered a qualifying pension scheme, your employer will have to request the approval of the Dutch tax authorities. If you continue to contribute to a non-Netherlands pension scheme with a non-recognized foreign insurance company, you may receive a so-called 'protective tax bill'. This tax bill will only be 'cashed' if, according to Dutch law, improper use is made of the pension insurance. If you contribute to a (qualifying) Netherlands pension scheme, you will receive a protective tax bill upon emigration.

See more on pensions on page 70.

COMPANY CAR

The 'benefit' that you enjoy from the private use of a company car is taxable as income from employment (to be reported through the payroll administration) whether you are a resident or a non-resident taxpayer. If you drive fewer than 500 kilometers a year for private purposes, it could prove worthwhile to keep a daily log of your private and business kilometers, as the benefit will then not be added to your taxable income. If the benefit related to the use of the car is taxed through your payroll, the 30%-ruling applies to it.

THE 30%-RULING

30%-RULING/EXTRATERRITORIAL EXPENSES

The 30%-ruling is a tax facility that has been created for employees who have been posted from or recruited outside the Netherlands to work in the Netherlands. You do not need to be a resident of the Netherlands and you do not have to (physically) carry out work in the Netherlands for it to apply. The ruling can be found in the Wage Tax Act. The effect of this facility is that your employer can pay you a tax-free allowance of up to 30% of your wage for so-called 'extraterritorial expenses', as a result of which the effective rate of wage tax is reduced. Since January 1, 2012 there are new and revised conditions for the 30%-ruling. In these paragraphs, we will go into the new ruling. We will also discuss the transitional rules that apply to those who had already been granted the 30%-ruling on January 1, 2012.

THE CONDITIONS FOR THE 30%-RULING

Whether you satisfy the conditions for the 30%-ruling or not depends on the circumstances at the start of your employment in the Netherlands as an 'extraterritorial employee'. These conditions are:

■ Posted or recruited from abroad: you must have been posted to the Netherlands from another country or recruited abroad.

VAT AND REFUNDS

Everyone who purchases goods or services in the Netherlands, pays value added tax (VAT), known here as BTW.

The suppliers of these goods and services charge their clients/customers VAT over and above the price of the goods/services and pay it to the tax authorities – after offsetting it against any VAT they have paid themselves. The price you see on items in stores includes this tax, so that you are not in for a little surprise at the cash register, like you are in some countries. (Please note that, though in retail stores for businesses, the 'ex-BTW' price is quoted, you *do* pay BTW when checking out. However, you will be allowed to deduct this BTW on your quarterly or annual BTW-tax return, if you have your own business. You can read more about this on page 76). In the case of services, it is always advisable to ask whether the stated price includes VAT or not.

In the Netherlands, most goods and services are taxed at a rate of 21%, but some fall under the 6%-category – such as food, water, pharmaceuticals, books, magazines and newspapers, and services such as fixing a bicycle, repairs to shoes and clothing, and the hairdresser. For information on how much tax is due on Internet-purchases from abroad and what to do if you are overcharged, visit: www.belastingdienst.nl/wps/wcm/connect/nl/douane/douane.

Tourists and expatriates can receive a refund on the VAT they have paid. The refund can be arranged through some stores affiliated with a refund group, or by showing the tax receipts at Customs, where they stamp it and then send it back to the retailer with a request for a refund. There are also several organizations (see the reference pages) in the Netherlands that help you arrange your refund. The administration fee varies from 4% to 10% over a minimum expenditure of € 50. Note, however, that retailers are not obligated by law to provide this service and therefore in most cases will not cooperate; visit www.vatfree.com/en to find out who does.

Who can benefit from the services of these organizations?
1. travelers who live outside the European Union and purchase goods in the EU for personal use
2. expats who move back to a country outside of the European Union, on goods they have bought during the last three months preceding the move
3. (Dutch) persons who are emigrating to a non-EU country.

For more on the rules, contact the Dutch Customs Authorities (0800 0143) or the organizations listed at the end of the chapter, or visit their websites.

TAX ISSUES FOR U.S. CITIZENS

Living abroad gives rise to complex tax issues that often confuse expatriates. The following is a brief overview of the main issues affecting U.S. citizens or Green Card holders living in the Netherlands. The first item to note is that, if you are a U.S. citizen or Green Card holder, you are still required to file a U.S. tax return. There are, however, several provisions in the tax code and the tax treaty aimed at reducing your tax liability. Another thing to keep in mind is that your tax return can, and may have to be, extended beyond the original filing deadline.

EXCLUSIONS FROM TAX

The first of these provisions is the foreign earned income exclusion under which you can exempt up to $ 100,800 (2015 – $ 101,300 for 2016). To qualify for this exclusion, you must meet one of two tests – the Physical Presence Test (PPT) or the Bona Fide Resident test (BFR). To meet the PPT-requirements, you must be out of the country for 330 (not necessarily consecutive) days during any period of 12 consecutive months. It does not matter what the nature or purpose of your stay abroad is (employment as well as brief vacations qualify), the kind of residence you establish, or what your intentions are about returning to the U.S. The nature and purpose of your stay, however, *are* relevant when determining whether you meet the tax home test, which determines the place where you are permanently or indefinitely engaged to work in (self-)employment. (To make matters complicated, however, this 'tax home' is not necessarily your tax home for domicile or tax purposes.) You do not meet the physical presence test if illness, family problems, a long vacation, or your employer's orders cause you to be present in the other country for less than the required amount of time. To qualify for BFR you must be living outside the U.S. 'for an uninterrupted period that includes an entire tax year' – a tax year being from January 1 to December 31. As long as it is clearly your intention to return to this country, brief vacations and other trips will not jeopardize this status. In case of 'war, civil unrest, or similar adverse conditions', the minimum time requirements can be waived.

Your tax home is the general area of your main place of business, employment, or post of duty, regardless of where you maintain your family home. It is the place where you are permanently or indefinitely engaged to work as an employee or self-employed individual. Having a 'tax home' in a given location does not necessarily mean that the given location is your residence or domicile for tax purposes. If you do not have a regular or main place of business because of the nature of your work, your tax home may be the place where you regularly live. If you have neither a regular or main place of business nor a place where you regularly live, you are considered an itinerant and your tax home is wherever you work.

Another exclusion available to expatriates who qualify for the PPT or the BFR, is the foreign housing exclusion, under which you can deduct a portion of your housing costs such as rent, certain utilities, and other expenses associated with maintaining a home abroad.

If you are self-employed and work abroad, you can claim the foreign earned income exclusion and the foreign housing deduction. This reduces your regular income tax, but not your self-employment tax. The foreign housing deduction is not the same as the foreign housing exclusion, as the exclusion applies to amounts considered paid for with employer-provided amounts, while the deduction applies only to amounts paid for with earnings from self-employment.

FOREIGN-EARNED INCOME

For the specifics on what and who qualifies and what and who doesn't, visit www.irs.gov/publications and select the Tax Guide for U.S. Citizens and Resident Aliens Abroad (for tax year 2015, this was publication 54).

FOREIGN TAX CREDITS

Another strategy for reducing your U.S. tax liability involves the use of foreign tax credits. Foreign tax credits may be taken whether you qualify for the abovementioned exclusions or not. Dutch income taxes paid on income that is not already excluded can be used as a credit towards your U.S. taxes.

TAX TREATY

As mentioned above, the U.S. has entered into a tax treaty with the Netherlands that may exclude your income from either U.S. or Dutch taxation. Generally, a person on a short business trip to the Netherlands will not have to pay Dutch taxes. Numerous requirements are set forth by the treaty, so caution should be used before applying this broad statement.

FILING FOR EXTENSION

All Americans are familiar with the April 15 filing deadline. If you are living in the Netherlands on April 15, you are automatically granted an extension till June 15. For a variety of reasons, your U.S. tax return may be further delayed and can be extended up until October 15. The tax implications of a foreign assignment may seem confusing. The most important things to keep in mind are that there are provisions set up to avoid paying double taxes on the same income and that good record keeping is very important.

Dutch nationals coming in from abroad may also qualify. The Dutch tax authorities also want to know the date on which you signed the contract, as this could help determine the country you lived in before you accepted the employment position for which the 30%-ruling is being requested.

■ Netherlands payroll: for the ruling to apply, there must be a Netherlands withholding entity. This means that your employer must deduct wage tax (and general insurance contributions, if applicable) from any wages paid out to you (in principle including any salary earned abroad that is taxable here) and pay this to the Dutch tax authorities. A non-Netherlands employer can also act as a Netherlands withholding entity.

■ Specific expertise/scarcity: you must have 'specific expertise which is not or scarcely available on the Dutch labor market'. The condition that you have specific expertise, will (if you lived more than 150 kilometers from the Dutch border) normally be considered to be met if you earn a minimum salary of € 36,889 (excluding the tax-free allowance of the 30%-ruling). If you are younger than 30, have a master's degree and are recruited from abroad, a reduced salary threshold of € 28,041 applies. (When you reach the age of 30, the higher threshold applies.) Academic scientists are exempt from the salary norm. The condition that you have specific skills that are scarce on the Dutch labor market will only be assessed in exceptional cases or if you are part of a group of employees that is brought in.

■ 150 kilometer boundary norm: if you lived within 150 km from the Dutch border during two-thirds of a 24-month period before starting your activities in the Netherlands, you are not entitled to the ruling. This can affect you if you come to work here from, for instance, Belgium or Germany. If you had already been granted the 30%-ruling on January 1, 2012, transitional rules apply. If you are a doctoral student, the period of your doctoral research will not be taken into account, as long as you resided outside the 150-kilometer boundary before starting your doctoral research and on the condition that your employment in the Netherlands starts directly after you have completed your doctoral research. The question has been put to court as to whether or not this norm is in conflict with the EU rules on the free movement of workers. The court has stated that this is not the case, unless the 30% reduction of the 30%-ruling is far more than the reimbursement of the actual extraterritorial costs – a decision that is up to the Dutch court to make.

■ Request by both employee and employer: you and your employer must jointly file a request for the application of the 30%-ruling. The request must be submitted with the Tax Office for Non-Residents in Heerlen within four months after the start of your employment for the ruling to apply from day one.

EXEMPTION REGARDING THE 150-KILOMETER BOUNDARY NORM
In practice, the 150-kilometer boundary norm presented a problem for employees who left the Netherlands after having benefitted from the 30%-ruling, and then returned to the Netherlands, applying for the 30%-ruling again. For instance, if the previous employment in the Netherlands had lasted more than eight months of the preceding 24 months, the employee would theoretically not be entitled to the 30%-ruling upon return to the Netherlands. However, an exemption has been created for abovementioned situation. Now (with retroactive effect until January 1,

2012), the date on which the work activities were first carried out in the Netherlands is taken into account when determining whether or not the conditions for 150-kilometer boundary/two-thirds of 24 months norm have been met. The commencement date of the subsequent employment in the Netherlands is therefore not decisive. Please note that the maximum period for the 30%-ruling (see below) should still be taken into account.

THE 30%-RULING AFTER TERMINATION OF EMPLOYMENT
The 30%-ruling is – with retroactive effect to 1 January 2012 – only applicable till the last day of the wage tax period following the wage tax period in which the employment ended. For instance, if your employment contract ended July 8, 2016 and you receive an additional payment in September 2016, the 30%-ruling will not apply to this payment.

CHANGING EMPLOYERS
If you are benefiting from the 30%-ruling and you switch employers, you will be able to 'take it with you' to your new employment (if a new employer is found within three months and the other conditions are satisfied) though only for the number of months left of the maximum duration of the ruling. The request must be filed within four months of the change.

MAXIMUM PERIOD EIGHT YEARS
In principle, the ruling applies for a maximum period of eight years. At some point during the course of the 30%-ruling, your employer will have to check whether the 30%-ruling can continue to apply during the rest of the period. As soon as it becomes clear that the conditions are no longer met, the 30%-ruling will end. You should also keep in mind that previous periods of residence or employment in the Netherlands that ended less than 25 years ago will reduce the period of eight years.

EMPLOYMENT AGREEMENT
You may not simply split the gross salary for tax calculation purposes into a taxable part and a tax-free allowance. Your employment contract (or an addendum to it) should clearly indicate a reduced gross salary, any further taxable or tax-free benefits, as well as the fixed 30%-allowance to be paid on top of the salary and benefits. The Ministry of Finance has provided an approved draft that can serve as an addendum to the contract, for those who wish to have a clear idea as to how this can be arranged.

EXTRATERRITORIAL EXPENSES, NO 30%-RULING
If you do not qualify for the 30%-ruling, for whatever reason, your employer can reimburse your actual extraterritorial expenses, without any tax consequences. In this situation, you have to deliver proof of these expenses.

TRANSITIONAL RULES
As mentioned before, January 1, 2012 saw the introduction of a number of changes to the 30%-regulation. New conditions have been added and other conditions have been tightened. Starting January 1, 2012, if you have been granted the 30%-ruling, your employer will have to verify whether you qualify for the 30%-ruling according to the new rules – unless the transitional rules apply. One of the transitional rules is that, if you were granted the

30%-ruling more than five years ago on January 1, 2012, the 'old' terms and conditions of the 30%-ruling will continue to apply. If the 30%-ruling was granted five years ago or less on that date, the salary threshold must be met as of the 61st month of its application. Moreover, you will have to have met the 150-kilometer rule when your employment started. Please note, as mentioned above, the Dutch Court is currently judging whether the 150-kilometer boundary is in line with the European rules.

The following once again applies: if the criteria for the 30%-ruling are not met, subject to conditions, your actual extraterritorial expenses can be reimbursed, free of tax.

The new maximum period of eight years and the rule stating that a previous stay or employment in the Netherlands that ended within 25 years prior to a request for the application of the 30%-ruling will lead to a reduction of the maximum period of eight years will only apply to new cases. However, please note that if you do not meet the salary criteria and/or are (were) living within 150 kilometers of the Dutch border, you are no longer entitled to the 30%-ruling.

CONSEQUENCES FOR WAGE TAX PURPOSES
Basis for Taxation
Your taxable wage, after having determined the tax-free 30%-allowance, is assessed according to the normal legal wage tax rules, in the same way as they apply to all employees in the Netherlands. This means that your employer may provide tax-exempt allowances for certain expenses in addition to the 30%-allowance. On the other hand, certain allowances for expenses that qualify as extraterritorial will reduce the level of the net 30%-allowance or will be taxable, so that you do not benefit (doubly) from both tax-free opportunities.

School Fees International Schools
Your employer may pay a tax-free allowance for the school fees of children attending an international (primary or secondary) school or pay them directly. School fees that you pay yourself are not tax-deductible. Dutch schools with an international stream do not automatically qualify as international schools for purposes of the 30%-ruling.

Impact on Social Security and Pensionable Base
Employee insurance contributions and pension rights may be accrued on your contractual (lower) gross salary only! In order to avoid a pension gap, ask your employer or seek expert advice; a solution is available.

Partial Non-Resident Taxpayers
If you have been granted the 30%-ruling, then you may choose to be treated as a partial non-resident taxpayer on your Dutch income tax return (see page 106). The choice to be treated as a partial non-resident taxpayer will be made on the application form and can be changed every year.

As a partial non-resident taxpayer, you need not report any investment income on your Dutch income tax return (except for Dutch source income, such as Dutch real estate), but you can still deduct certain personal expenses (i.e. alimony payments, medical expenses, etc.).

PERMITS

SHORT STAY
If your stay in the Netherlands will not exceed three months, then most likely you will not need a visa to enter the Netherlands. In most cases a valid passport will be sufficient. You should check with the Dutch Embassy or Consulate in your home country whether or not a visa is needed. If you do, this type of visa is called a *visum kort verblijf*, or short stay visa.

LONGER STAY
If you will be staying longer than three months, then you might need one of the following permits:
- Authorization temporary stay (as the case may be; for highly skilled migrants) (*Machtiging tot Voorlopig Verblijf, or MVV*)
- Residence permit (as the case may be; for highly skilled migrants) (*Verblijfsvergunning*)
- Work permit (*Tewerkstellingsvergunning*) (not required for highly skilled migrants).

HEALTH INSURANCE
All residents of the Netherlands are obligated to arrange private health insurance. To this purpose, they will have to arrange a Citizen Service Number (*burgerservicenummer*) (see page 66) and a residence permit. EU/EEA nationals need a Citizen Service Number (*burgerservicenummer*) and a valid passport to do this.

AUTHORIZATION TEMPORARY STAY/RESIDENCE PERMIT

EU/EEA AND SWISS NATIONALS
If you are a national of any of the European Union (EU) or European Economic Area (EEA) member states or Switzerland, you will not need an authorization temporary stay prior to traveling to the Netherlands. Formally, EU/EEA and Swiss nationals also do not need a residence permit; however, if you intend to stay here longer than four months, you will have to register with the municipality.

Although EU/EEA/Swiss nationals will be entitled to reside and work in the Netherlands without any kind of permit, they will only be entitled to a residence permit – should they want one – if they have sufficient financial means, being at least the minimum social security norm (*bijstandsnorm*).

NON EU/EEA/SWISS NATIONALS
You are exempted from the need to arrange an authorization temporary stay if you are from the United States, Canada, Japan, South Korea, Monaco, Vatican City, Australia or New Zealand. In all other cases, you need an authorization temporary stay prior to traveling to the Netherlands as well as to be able to apply for a residence permit upon arrival. You cannot apply for a residence permit if you entered the Netherlands without making use of this entry visa.

ENTRY AND RESIDENCE PROCEDURE (TEV)
On June 1, 2013, the Modern Migration Policy was introduced. Immigrants no longer need to apply separately for an authorization temporary stay (MVV) and the residence permit, but instead can use the Admission and Residence procedure (TEV). With the TEV-procedure, you start with applying for the MVV with the Dutch

Embassy or Consulate in your home country/country of legal residence – or your prospective employer informs with the IND in the Netherlands as to whether there is any objection against issuing you one. If there is indeed no such objection, the IND sends an MVV-approval to the Dutch embassy in your home country/ country of legal residence and immediately issues your residence permit so that you do not need to apply for it separately.

Prior to traveling to the Netherlands, you collect the authorization temporary stay at the Dutch Embassy or Consulate in your home country/country of legal residence. Once you have arrived in the Netherlands you collect your residence document in person within two weeks at the IND desk. In order to be able to issue you your residence document, the IND needs your fingerprints, passport photo and signature. Please check with the IND as to how and where you can provide these.

An MVV must also be requested for your accompanying family members. Processing time is approximately 90 days.

RESIDENCE PERMIT (VVR-PROCEDURE)
If you are exempted from the need to arrange an MVV, you can apply for a residence permit with the IND. Or your prospective employer can apply for the residence permit while you are still living abroad.

REGISTERING WITH THE MUNICIPALITY
If you are planning on staying in the Netherlands longer than four months, you have to report with the municipality (*stadhuis* or *gemeentehuis*) to have yourself entered in the municipal register (*bevolkingsregister*). Please keep in mind that this procedure can only be executed when suitable housing has been arranged.

REQUIRED DOCUMENTS
The documents that you have to submit when registering and/or applying for a residence permit are, among others:
- a legalized certified copy of your birth certificate (also your spouse's or partner's)
- a legalized marriage license, if applicable
- if either you or your partner were previously married, a copy of the legalized divorce decree.

Whatever else you need depends on your circumstances and country of origin. Other documents, such as a passport, work permit and proof of insurance will be required at some later point, check with the IND what these are.

YOUR STAY EXCEEDS FIVE YEARS
If you are a national of an EU/EEA-country or a Swiss national and have legally resided in the Netherlands for a period of five years, you qualify for the residence document 'long-term residence of citizens of the Union'. Please note that you are not obligated to request this.

ECONOMICALLY NON-ACTIVE
If you are an economically non-active EU-citizen, you may come to the Netherlands to, for instance, spend your retirement years. However, you must have health insurance and have sufficient money, being the 'income norm' applicable to you for a minimum of one year (the applicable income norm can be found on the site

of the IND). This may also be your spouse's or registered partner's income. Citizens of the new members of the EU need to apply for a residence document for economically inactive persons (unless they are from Malta or Cyprus).

WORK PERMIT

EU/EEA/SWISS-NATIONALS
In principle, if you are a national of an EU/EEA member state or of Switzerland, you may work in the Netherlands without a work permit. Your EU/EEA/Swiss passport is enough proof that you are permitted to work in the Netherlands. Please note that at this moment, Croatians still need a work permit to work in the Netherlands.

To work here as a self-employed person, you do not need a work permit. For more on the applicable rules, visit the website of the IND.

NON EU/EEA/SWISS NATIONALS
If you are a non EU/EEA/Swiss national and wish to work in the Netherlands, even if only for one day, you must obtain a work permit, unless you are a so-called 'highly skilled migrant' in which case you only need a residence permit (see further on). It depends on your situation whether the employer should submit the application for the work permit with the IND or with the Employee Insurance Agency (UWV).

If you are a non EU/EEA/Swiss national and wish to work in the Netherlands for less than 90 days, you will probably need a work permit. Your prospective employer can apply for a work permit with the UWV.

If you are a non EU/EEA/Swiss national and wish to work in the Netherlands for more than 90 days, you will have to apply for a combined residence and work permit (GVVA), also known as the single permit. The employer applies for a single permit with the IND. Please note that the single permit does not apply to:
- seasonal workers
- students
- asylum seekers
- employees of an international company
- Croatians.

For these immigrants, the employer still needs to apply for a work permit with the UWV.

To work here as a self-employed person, you do not need a work permit. For more on the applicable rules, visit the website of the IND.

REQUIREMENTS
In general, the UWV only issues work permits if the employer has been able to convince them that there are no qualified individuals available on the EU/EEA labor market who can do the job. The employer should therefore submit proof that he has done everything in his capacity to find individuals on the EU/EEA labor market (i.e. by submitting copies of advertisements, statements from recruitment agencies, postings on the Internet, etc.). Several months prior to filing the work permit application, the vacancy must be reported with the local UWV. If this condition is not met, a work permit will not be issued. Furthermore, the permit may be granted on the condition that the employer provide retraining

opportunities for EU/EEA nationals seeking jobs, insofar as this can reasonably be requested of him.

An easier way to obtain a work permit is on the basis of a so-called inter-company transfer, see *Special Rules for Work Permits*, on page 128.

PROCESSING TIME

Theoretically, processing time for a work permit is five weeks after a complete application – together with the answers to possible additional questions raised by the UWV – has been submitted. The processing time for a so-called single permit is 90 days. During the application process, you will not be allowed to work in the Netherlands. Companies risk high penalties, and their directors even prison, if they break the law on this matter.

PERIOD OF VALIDITY

You will be issued a work permit or a single permit for the duration of one year. This period may be extended. A work permit or single permit is not transferable to another employer or to another position.

REFUSAL

A reason to refuse an employment permit is if there is a suspicion that the vacancy will not be filled by people from EU/EEA-countries who are seeking work because the terms and conditions of employment or the working conditions in the business concerned do not comply with the collective labor agreement or the law.

WHO DOES WHAT

The employer takes care of the work permit and single permit application. He can start the application procedure while you are still living abroad.

HIGHLY SKILLED MIGRANTS AND EUROPEAN BLUE CARD

In 2005, a policy that allows highly skilled migrants into the Netherlands was introduced. The aim of the policy is to simplify the entry of highly skilled people from outside the EU/EEA into the Netherlands in order to improve the position of the Netherlands as a knowledge economy and to make the Netherlands more attractive as a work location for highly skilled migrants. To this end, the work permit requirement for this category of persons has been abolished and replaced by a residence permit under the restriction of 'highly skilled migrant'.

Only companies that are established in the Netherlands can make use of the highly skilled migrant policy.

PROCEDURE

If your employer wants to bring you here as a highly skilled migrant, he must submit a 'request for advice about issuing a permit for temporary residence for a highly skilled migrant', the so-called TEV-procedure, with the IND. Once positive advice has been issued, your prospective employer will inform you of this and you will be able to pick up your MVV at the Dutch Embassy or Consulate in your

country of origin within three weeks. After this, you have three weeks to travel to the Netherlands, after which you collect your residence document at the IND office in person, within two weeks.

If you are a national of a country for which the Netherlands does not require an MVV, you may only start working once your residence permit for highly skilled migrants has been issued. To circumvent this wait, you can apply for an 'MVV for a foreign national who is not subject to an MVV requirement'.

DURATION PERMIT

This permit will be issued for a maximum period of five years if you have an employment contract for an indefinite period of time. If it is a fixed-term contract, the permit will be issued for the duration of the contract.

IND

The Immigration and Naturalization Service (IND) has sole responsibility for implementing the procedures for entry into the Netherlands / the Dutch employment market.

DEFINITION

Highly skilled migrants are defined as contracted employees who earn a minimum gross income of € 4,240 a month (2016; € 4,579,20, including the 8% holiday allowance), to be indexed annually. The annual income includes salary withholding tax, employee and social security contributions, the holiday allowance, and a monthly supplement (which must be guaranteed and paid every month), but excludes bonuses and payments in kind (e.g. company car). Employer charges are also not taken into account.

Since this income requirement is a considerable obstacle for young migrant workers, a lower threshold applies to them; persons under the age of 30 who earn a minimum of € 3,108 gross per month (2016; € 3,356.64 including holiday allowance) can also qualify as highly skilled migrants. Holders of a European Blue Card must have a salary of € 4,968 (€ 5,365.44 including holiday allowance) to qualify as highly skilled migrants. For recent graduates who have found employment in the Netherlands, the salary norm is adjusted to € 2,228 a month (€ 2,406.24, including holiday allowance).

STUDENTS

Foreign students who have obtained a bachelor's or a master's degree in the Netherlands and students that have obtained a master's degree or their Ph.D. at a qualifying university abroad, as well as scientific researchers and post-doctoral students, have three years to request a residence permit to dedicate a year to finding work as a highly skilled migrant in the Netherlands, to start a so-called 'innovative company' or to work without a work permit. Until such time as they find work, they are not eligible for a benefit and will therefore have to be able to provide for their own basic needs, nor are they considered highly skilled migrants (yet).

The aim of this Scheme – which was implemented in anticipation of the Modern Migration Policy – is to ensure that foreign ('exceptional') talents, who might represent added economic value, are admitted to the country.

CHANGE OF EMPLOYER

Highly skilled migrants are allowed to change employers while their residence permit is still valid. The IND will test the change to a new employer against the applicable conditions.

If you are dismissed, a reasonable term of three months will be granted to find another position that satisfies the conditions.

Should you accept a position that does not satisfy the wage requirement, you will have to apply for a work permit.

PARTNERS AND CHILDREN

Partners and children of highly skilled migrants will initially be granted a residence permit in keeping with the duration of the permit of the highly skilled migrant. Partners of highly skilled migrants can apply for a work permit without having to go through the labor market assessment described on page 112, under *Requirements*.

PRACTICAL ISSUES

Companies can enter into a standard contract with the IND, which can be found on www.ind.nl. Once the IND has authorized the company to make use of the new regulation, the company will be issued entry codes that will allow them to access the application forms that can be found on the IND website. This will help the IND process applications within two weeks.

ACCELERATED MVV-PROCEDURE

Employers who have been appointed as 'referent' are eligible for using the accelerated MVV-procedure for highly skilled migrants. A decision on such a request will basically be made within two weeks.

Part of the procedure requires that the identity of the highly skilled migrant and his/her relatives be confirmed on the basis of a passport. Marriage certificates and birth certificates of children will still have to be authenticated to show the family ties. The authentication requirements that apply to so-called problem countries do not apply.

EUROPEAN BLUE CARD

The European Blue Card has been created for non-EU employees who come to carry out highly qualified work in the EU. The conditions are stricter. They must:

- have an employment contact of at least one year
- earn a gross salary of at least € 4,968 a month (2016)
- have the required professional qualifications
- have followed at least three years of higher education
- have their diplomas valuated by Nuffic (see end of chapter)
- if they wish to carry out the profession of doctor or lawyer: be able to supply proof of the fact that they are legally qualified to carry out their profession
- have the right documents for entering the country
- not necessarily have a sponsor (recognized and registered with the IND), though the procedure will go faster if they do.

Family members, if they meet the general requirements for family 'reunion', may request to be allowed to enter the country as 'accompaniers' of a holder of a European Blue Card.

MARRIAGE

THE CEREMONY

Ja, ik wil – Marriage Dutch style

Imagine this scenario: you spent months arranging your wedding; you've stood up in church and declared 'I do'; you've celebrated with your nearest and dearest; only to discover down the track that your wedding was as valid as Mick Jagger and Jerry Hall's Bali nuptials. In the Netherlands, a church service alone does not satisfy the legal requirements for the state of marriage. A civil service is all that is deemed legally valid. This is actually the case in many countries, the difference being that in some other countries churches are licensed to register marriages. If you want a church wedding in the Netherlands you will first have to undergo a separate civil service.

CIVIL WEDDING

For most people the term 'civil' conjures up images of a hurried, impersonal service held in an ugly municipal building with couples queuing up for the privilege. In the Netherlands it doesn't need to be like this as there is a great variety of interesting locations available for a civil wedding. The municipality of The Hague alone offers many possible locations. Couples are not restricted to marrying within their own municipality (*gemeente*). They could, for instance, consider any of the following options: a theater in Leidschendam; the Rotterdam Zoo; the Huygensmuseum Hofwijck, Voorburg; a castle in the countryside; the Commandeurskamer at the Bataviawerf in Lelystad; or the *trouwzaal* of an historic *stadhuis* such as those in The Hague, Delft, Gouda or Middelburg.

WHO CAN GET MARRIED HERE?

Anyone of Dutch nationality can get married here, regardless of whether they live here and regardless of the nationality of their intended. Two foreign nationals may marry in the Netherlands on the condition that one of them legally resides in the Netherlands. If both foreign nationals live here and want to marry here, they must both reside here legally. The condition of having the right residence documents does not apply to EU/EEA nationals.

The above also applies to entering into a registered partnership.

IN CASE OF DOUBT

If one of the partners legally resides in the Netherlands or has Dutch nationality, then the question of whether or not this person is allowed to get married or enter into a registered partnership is answered in accordance with Dutch law. If the marriage is permitted in the Netherlands, then the fact that the national law of the non-Dutch partner does not allow the marriage (for instance, a same-sex marriage) will not influence their ability to get married in the Netherlands. However, this does not guarantee that the marriage / partnership will be recognized in the home country.

Non-Dutch nationals who are not allowed to get married / enter into a registered partnership according to Dutch law, can do this anyway in the Netherlands if they are allowed to do this according to their national law, and provided the marriage / partnership is not in violation of Dutch public order.

NOTIFICATION

Would you like to get married or enter into a partnership? Then you first need to notify the municipality. Before September 2015 this was called a 'notice of intent to marry' (*in ondertrouw gaan*). You can announce your intention in any municipality in the Netherlands. It is most practical to do this in the municipality where you will get married or enter into your partnership. You can arrange this online if both of you are registered with the Municipal Personal Records Database (BRP) and if all the required documents are okay. You need to produce passports (identity cards), birth certificates, witness forms (see next paragraph for more on witnesses), proof of single status and evidence of your Dutch residency. Documents from overseas require the appropriate *apostille* stamp (see International Certificate for an explanation of the *apostille* stamp), or other proof of legalization. If a foreigner is marrying a Dutch national or a resident of the Netherlands then the IND (Immigration and Naturalization Services) must issue a declaration (called M46), stating that they do not object to the marriage – which it sends directly to the municipality and which is valid for a period of six months. An M46-declaration is not required for EU/EEA/SWISS citizens or those who have a permanent residence permit.

If you wish to enter into a registered partnership (see further on, under *Age, Same Sex, Registered Partnership*), then you must also register for this in advance (minimum 14 days, maximum one year) and be able to produce the M46-declaration, with the same exceptions as stated above.

All required documents may not be older than six months.

WITNESSES
At least two witnesses or a maximum of four witnesses must sign the marriage certificate. Witnesses can be of any nationality, and you need to provide copies of their passports to the municipality where you are marrying. This is one document you don't need to have stamped with an *apostille*! If you are unable, or do not wish, to provide your own witnesses, the municipality can arrange witnesses for you.

INTERNATIONAL CERTIFICATE
A foreigner marrying in the Netherlands can pay a small sum extra to have an international extract of the marriage certificate (*Internationaal Uittreksel uit de Huwelijksakte*) issued. This certificate contains the most important details as well as an explanation in nine languages so it should save many people the cost of having the certificate officially translated for use in another country.

However, if the certificate is needed for official use in a country outside the Netherlands then it will need to be endorsed by the Dutch authorities with an *apostille* stamp. An *apostille* stamp is simply an internationally recognized certification of authenticity and is required by all countries on official documents issued in another country. In some cases, the international authorities will want a copy of the full certificate, in which case you will have to obtain a certified translation of the marriage certificate.

AGE, SAME SEX, REGISTERED PARTNERSHIP
18 is the minimum legal age for marriage, although a pregnant female may marry at 16 providing she has proof from her gynecologist and her parents/guardians have granted their permission. The same applies to the 16 or 17-year-old father. Same-sex marriages are also possible (since April 1, 2001).

Since 1998, it is also possible for two people of the same or the opposite sex to enter into an arrangement similar to marriage, known as a registered partnership. (Please note that a registered partnership is not the same as a cohabitation agreement.) The only differences between registered partnership and marriage lie in the area of children and dissolution. If the parents are married, a child automatically has two parents. If the parents are registered partners, the father must legally recognize the child first. And a marriage is dissolved in court, while a registered partnership can be dissolved by means of a written statement by a civil law notary or a lawyer (if both parties agree to the dissolution, and provided there are no children under the age of 18 involved). A registered partnership can be converted into a marriage.

Both the registered partnership and the marriage between two persons of the same sex afford nearly all the same rights as marriage and differ only in regard to children and adoption. They are not legally recognized outside the Netherlands.

WEEKDAY WEDDINGS
Many foreigners are surprised by the fact that Dutch weddings often take place on weekdays. This may have something to do with the costs involved. A free civil service wedding is possible, but it is usually only available between 9 – 10 A.M. on a Monday or Wednesday morning. Please note that, in the bigger cities, the dates for the free wedding or the unmarried partnership are often fully booked months ahead of time. It won't be conducted in an atmospheric *trouwzaal*, but in a small room at the *gemeentehuis*. The ceremony lasts 10 minutes; no speech will be given and no music will be played, and only a handful of guests will be allowed. Despite the fact that the service is free, it will still set you back some money as you are required to purchase a *registratieboekje* (a booklet in which your marriage is registered), and to pay for proof of registration with the municipality as well as for witnesses if you can't provide your own.

The costs for a civil wedding service range quite dramatically, starting around € 40 and going up to around € 1,200 – depending on the time and location chosen. Generally speaking Monday to Thursday between 9 A.M. and 4 P.M. is the cheapest time to marry, and (as mentioned earlier) in some municipalities you can get married free of charge on certain weekday mornings. After 4 P.M. weekdays and on weekends, the costs can increase substantially, the most expensive option being getting married on Christmas Day or New Year's Eve, after midnight. The cost for marrying on a

Saturday is approximately three times as high as a mid-week wedding, making it very attractive to marry on a Friday. For further information regarding times available for weddings, and the relevant costs involved, consult the *Huwelijksdata Gids*, available at your local town hall.

A ROOF OVER YOUR HEAD

If you have always dreamed of an outdoor setting for your wedding, and you are brave enough to try such a thing in the Netherlands, then you need to be aware of the fact that for a marriage to be legal it has to take place with a roof above your heads. In effect this means that you could have the ceremony conducted outdoors, but you would need to move inside for the signing of the registrar.

LAST NAMES

Once married, the couple has a number of choices regarding their last names. In the Netherlands, the husband can take his wife's surname after marriage, and vice versa. You can also choose to use your surname followed by your spouse's surname, or the reverse, your spouse's surname followed by your surname. And, a last option, both husband and wife may choose to keep their own surnames.

Children can be given either their father's or their mother's last name, or the two. Once a choice has been made, all the children of the same father and mother must carry the same last name. If the father has not legally recognized the child, it will be given its mother's surname.

RING FINGERS

If you are used to surreptitiously checking out a person's marital status by the sight of a wedding band on the ring finger of the left hand, be aware that in the Netherlands a wedding ring may be worn on the ring finger of either hand. During a civil wedding service the couple will place rings on their right hands. For a church wedding the tradition in this country is that Catholics wear their wedding ring on their left hand, whilst Protestants wear it on their right hand.

DUTCH LAW ON MATRIMONIAL PROPERTY

GENERAL COMMUNITY PROPERTY

The Dutch legal system determines that if you get married under Dutch law without having drawn up a marriage contract, in principle all property and debts that either of you had before the marriage, become joint property and joint debts once you are married. The same applies to property and debts that you acquire during your marriage. This legal system is called general community property.

Gifts and inheritances can be left out of the community property provided this is stipulated in the will of the testator or in the deed of gift. In the case of the death of one of the partners, then half of the community property will form the estate. The other half will already belong to the surviving partner.

MARRIAGE CONTRACT

You can deviate from the legal system before or after entering into marriage by means of a marriage contract (*huwelijksvoorwaarden*). The marriage contract has to be drawn up by a civil law notary who enters the deed containing the marriage contract in the public matrimonial property register at the District Court of the dis-

trict in which you were married. If you were married outside the Netherlands, it is entered in the matrimonial registry of the District Court in The Hague. This you do, in order to ensure that anyone can find out whether you have a marriage contract and what clauses it contains. The contract can help avoid that debts, incurred by you or your spouse, can be recovered from the other.

When moving to the Netherlands, if you do not have a marriage contract, it is always wise to seek the advice of a civil law notary or lawyer on whether unexpected Dutch rules of legislation might affect your matrimonial regime.

REGISTERED PARTNERSHIP AND SAME-SEX MARRIAGES

As mentioned earlier, instead of getting married, partners (also same-sex partners) can choose to become registered as common law partners in the civil registers. The consequences of such a registered partnership are (aside from the 'matter' of children) exactly the same as the consequences of an ordinary marriage, such as general community property in case a partnership contract is absent, and alimony in case of divorce. As of 2001, marriage is also available for people of the same sex.

Matrimonial property law also affects partnerships, in the sense that general community property can be avoided by means of a 'registered partnership agreement' drawn up by a civil law notary.

THE LAW ABROAD AND INTERNATIONAL PRIVATE LAW

Every country has its own rules on matrimonial property. International private law determines which legislation is applicable to a marriage with international aspects – for instance in the case you and your spouse were married abroad or do not have the same nationality. Every country has its own rules on international private law and the authorities of a country always apply the country's own rules of international private law. This can lead to different, conflicting results; international treaties are meant to avoid such conflicting results. Regarding the law on matrimonial property, the Dutch authorities apply the rules of the Hague Matrimonial Treaty 1978 to all marriages entered into after September 1, 1992.

THE HAGUE MATRIMONIAL PROPERTY TREATY 1978

At the moment, the Netherlands, France and Luxembourg are party to the treaty of 1978, which, with certain exceptions, is only applicable to you if you entered into marriage on or after September 1, 1992. The premise of the treaty is that if you have not stated a particular choice of law in a marriage contract, the law of the country in which you both settle directly after entering into marriage is applicable to the worldwide assets and debts in the case of divorce or death of one of the spouses, and other issues, such as bankruptcy. If you and your spouse have the same nationality, there are some exceptions to aforementioned premise.

The Treaty does not apply to registered partners and it is not yet clear whether it applies to same-sex marriages.

EMIGRATION, IMMIGRATION OR NATURALIZATION

Abovementioned treaty determines that during the marriage – due to emigration, immigration or naturalization – the originally applicable law on matrimonial property may be replaced by the law on matrimonial property of a different country. This is only the case if you entered into marriage on or after September 1, 1992 and did not explicitly state a choice of law in your marriage con-

tract. The replacement of the applicable law can have great consequences for, for instance, the extent and the division of the matrimonial property should you get divorced or either one of you die.

MOVING TO THE NETHERLANDS

If you got married on or after September 1, 1992, lived abroad at the
time of the marriage and subsequently moved to the Netherlands,
the matrimonial property system changes after ten years. Ten
years after you moved to the Netherlands, if you do not have a
marriage contract, you become married according to the Dutch
system of general community property. If you are both of Dutch
nationality at the time of the move, then the Dutch law of matrimonial property becomes applicable as of the moment you settle
in the Netherlands.

The change in system of matrimonial property also takes place
if you married on or after September 1, 1992 and both subsequently acquired Dutch nationality while living in the Netherlands. As
of the moment you acquire Dutch nationality, the Dutch legal system applies to your matrimonial property regime – unless you
have explicitly chosen another applicable law.

CHOOSING AN APPLICABLE LAW

By stipulating which law is to apply, you leave no doubt as to which
law of matrimonial property is applicable. Making such a choice is
of particular importance if your marriage has international
aspects. A choice of law helps to avoid that – due to emigration,
immigration or naturalization – a different law becomes applicable. However, beware of the fact that a choice made in the Netherlands does not always have the desired effect in a country that is
not a party to the Hague Matrimonial Property Treaty 1978. In
order to ensure that other parties are also bound by your choice,
you must have this choice registered; who does this and how this
is done, depends on the law that you have chosen. In such a situation it is best to seek advice on this matter in both countries.

MAKING THE MATRIMONIAL PROPERTY REGIME KNOWN

Third parties, such as creditors, are not always bound by your matrimonial property regime. If your matrimonial property regime is
not governed by Dutch law, a Dutch civil law notary can have the
regime entered in the Dutch matrimonial property register at the
court, so that the rules of your marriage system are binding for, for
instance, creditors in the Netherlands. If this has not been done, a
creditor may assume that you have been married according to the
Dutch legal system (which would be general community property) unless he knew or could have known to the contrary. However,
both you and your creditor had to have been living in the Netherlands at the time the debt was incurred.

DIVORCE

Dutch law distinguishes between a divorce by mutual request and
a divorce upon request of one of the spouses. The proceedings are
started by means of a (joint or unilateral) petition.

COMPETENCE OF THE COURTS

In the Netherlands you can file a petition for divorce before the
District Court of the district in which you and/or your spouse
live(s). The Dutch courts are competent if one of the following conditions is met:

- both of you have Dutch nationality
- the one requesting the divorce is Dutch and has been living
  here for a period of six months or more
- both of you legally reside in the Netherlands
- one of you legally resides in the Netherlands, and both of you
  submit a request for divorce
- one of you legally resides in the Netherlands while the other
  files for divorce here
- the one requesting the divorce has been living in the Netherlands for at least 12 months
- you and your partner legally resided in the Netherlands and
  one of you still lives here.

In all other cases, the Dutch courts are not competent and you cannot file for divorce in the Netherlands.

APPLICABLE LAW

Dutch law applies if the Dutch court is competent to decide on the
request for the dissolution of the marriage. Exceptions can be
made if both of you have a common other nationality and:

- you choose to apply the law of your common nationality or one
  of you makes this choice in the divorce proceedings and the
  other does not contradict this choice
- one of you chooses to apply the law of your common nationality and both of you have a real social connection with the country of your common nationality.

RECOGNITION

Whether or not the ruling of the Dutch court will be recognized
abroad depends on whether or not your country is a party to the
treaty that the Netherlands has entered into on this matter – the
Treaty on the Recognition of Divorces – and on your country's
national law. Be sure to get solid advice on this matter, particularly
on how you can make sure the divorce is recognized in your home
country.

UNILATERAL PETITION

Should you be the one filing the unilateral petition, the petition
should contain a request on how you would like the four consequences of the divorce (which you will find below) to be arranged.
Your spouse can lodge a statement of defense, containing his/her
wishes regarding the consequences.

In a hearing, the court will allow itself to be further informed
on these matters and will determine the date on which it will rule
on this matter. If the proceedings are likely to take a long time, the
court, if asked explicitly, will come up with provisional measures on
such pressing matters as child visitation rights, alimony, and child
support. If you or your spouse do not agree with the final ruling, you
or your spouse can bring an appeal before the Court of Appeals. No
appeal can be brought against the provisional measures.

JOINT PETITION

If both of you have come to an agreement regarding the four consequences of divorce, you can have these drawn up in a settlement.
This settlement can be drawn up by two lawyers – if each of you
has a lawyer – or by one lawyer, who is then the 'divorce mediator'.

This settlement is brought before the court, which rules in keeping with it, requiring no future hearing. Children age 12 and older are invited to come to court to give their opinion on the custody arrangements. However, they can also do this by means of a written statement. A hearing will then not be necessary.

MEDIATION

The purpose of a divorce mediator is to have both of you arrange the consequences of the divorce together, thus promoting the acceptation and durability of the agreement. The idea is that the discussion with the mediator provides you with better insight into the underlying emotional problems, allowing you to better describe your differences and see the merits of the various solutions that the mediator suggests. The settlement is submitted before the court along with the petition and the court rules in keeping with this settlement.

In the case of divorce, there are several reasonably diverse areas that the mediator should be able to advise you on, such as custody, alimony, and the division of marital property. If he (or she) cannot advise you on all these matters, he will be able to refer you to a specialist who can.

COLLABORATIVE DIVORCE

In order to avoid the uncertain outcome of a divorce court procedure and possible further litigation, a couple who wants to separate can also opt for what is referred to as a collaborative divorce. If this is the case, they work together with their lawyers and, if necessary, other family professionals, towards a settlement that best meets the needs of both parties and their children. To this purpose, they sign a contract (the 'participation agreement'), binding each other to the process and disqualifying their respective lawyer's right to represent either one in any future family-related litigation.

THE FOUR CONSEQUENCES OF DIVORCE

As of March 2009, the Dutch Continued Parenthood and Well-Planned Divorce Act provides that parents who are getting a divorce are obligated to draw up a parenting plan. The court will in general not pronounce the divorce requested by one or both of the parties with children under the age of 18 until a parenting plan has been drawn up. At the very least, this plan needs to contain arrangements concerning the following child-related issues: visitation rights, the way in which information will be exchanged and consultations regarding important matters will take place, and arrangements concerning the costs of care and upbringing. Also, the plan needs to outline the way the parents plan to involve the children in drawing up the plan.

1. Children

Custody. In principle both of you retain custody of the child(ren). This is only different if you both agree, or one of you is of the opinion, that it is in the interest of the children that only one of you has custody. In that case, you or your spouse should submit a request before the court to rule on this matter when ruling on the divorce.

Place of residence. When you both have custody, you need to agree on with which parent the children will have their main place of residence.

Visitation rights. The parents will have to agree on when the children will be with the one and when they will be with the other parent. If they cannot agree, the court can be asked to decide.

Child support and care. Child support is based on the idea that the children should be allowed to maintain the same 'standard of living' after the divorce. To determine the amount of financial support required, the court looks at the needs of the children entitled to the support and the financial capacity of the parent who has the duty to provide financial support. The needs of the children are based on the actual 'costs' that are related to the children and net family income before the divorce. You can find more information on the financial aspects of divorce in the brochure *Geldwijzer Alimentatie* (Money Guide for Alimony), which you can order from NIBUD (you will find the address at the end of the chapter).

Child support is due until the children reach the age of 21. As of their 18th birthday, the child support is to be paid out directly to the children and, until they reach the age of 21, aims to cover (a portion) of their study costs.

The parent with whom the child(ren) is/are registered will receive the Child Benefit (*kinderbijslag* – see page 193). When both of you are to share an equal part in the raising and maintaining of the children, then – unless you request otherwise – one of you will receive the Child Benefit, but you will be expected to divide it among the two of you. Furthermore, there are some other measures that pay out a monthly allowance but only to parents whose income lies below a certain maximum.

2. 'Partner' Alimony

The court will determine whether and to what degree you will have to support each other financially. In principle, 'partner alimony' will not be paid out longer than 12 years, however, the spouses can agree to a different period. If the marriage lasted shorter than five years and there are no children, it will only be paid out during a period equal in length to the marriage. This also applies to registered partnerships. When calculating the alimony, the court takes the following into account:

a. The needs of the one who has the right to alimony
Say, you are the one who needs alimony. To determine your minimum needs, the court will take into account the legal minimum income for those who are unemployed plus other, unavoidable, living expenses. However, your actual financial capacity, but also the fact that you could get a job, will also be taken into account – as well as the standard of living that you were accustomed to during the marriage. Despite the latter, the judge will also take into account the fact that you could move to cheaper living quarters, or rent out a portion of the house, or whether you have children living at home who could contribute to your family income.

b. Financial capacity of the other spouse
Having determined your needs, the court determines the amount that your (former) husband/wife can contribute, taking into account his/her income and financial needs.

c. New relationship
If you move in together with another person, get married or enter into a registered partnership, you lose the right to partner alimony.

d. Change of circumstances
If, after determining the amount of alimony you are to receive, you get a job and are capable of providing for yourself, your right to alimony may cease or be reduced to a lower amount. Conversely, should it be agreed that no one owes alimony, after which one of the two partners finds him or herself in a situation in which (s)he can no longer provide for him or herself, it can be determined that alimony is due after all.

Alimony paid to former spouses is entirely deductible, the amount of taxes thus saved is added to the amount of income available for partner alimony. The former spouse, however, owes the related income tax (taking into account this spouse's tax bracket, which could lead to a difference in income tax deducted and income tax paid – this is also taken into account when calculating the amount of alimony).

3. Division of the Marital Property
The ruling of the court on the divorce should contain instructions on how the marital property is to be divided (taking into account the fact that your marriage is governed by the Dutch rules on community property or that you have a pre or postnuptial agreement, see page 117). Legally, that which is part of the communal property should be divided equally among you, including the debts; however, you can agree otherwise. Be aware of tax complications if the worth is not shared 50/50. Also keep in mind that, if another country's law is applicable, the Dutch court may apply those rules.

4. Pension Rights
In the case of divorce, each of you has a right to a portion of the amount of old age pension accrued by the other during the period of marriage – provided the pension is covered by Dutch law – to be paid out as of the retirement of the person in whose name the pension has been built up. You can agree otherwise, allowing it to stay entirely with the person who built it up, or agreeing to a different division. The Dutch courts rarely rule on this matter. Either you decide to act in accordance with the law, or you agree not to.

If you are the partner of the pension receiver, the wisest would be to inform the pension provider of your divorce within two years after the date you are officially divorced; the provider is then obligated to pay out your half to you.

DUTCH INHERITANCE LAW

SUCCESSION BY WILL
In the Netherlands you can determine who your heirs are in a will (succession by will). If there is no will, then the law determines who your heirs are (succession by law/intestate succession). If you make a will in the Netherlands, according to Dutch law, it should be done by means of a deed made up by a Dutch civil law notary.

SUCCESSION BY LAW
Only blood relatives, spouses or registered partners are entitled to the inheritance. The (adopted) children and spouse or registered partner form the first group of heirs, each inheriting an equal share. The brothers, sisters (and their children) and parents form the second group of heirs. Grandparents and great-grandparents finally form the third and fourth group. If there are no relatives

within the first, second or third group respectively, then the relatives within the next group are eligible.

ALLOCATION BY LAW
If the spouse or registered partner, together with one or more children of the deceased, is the heir, then, by intestate succession, he or she will get all assets and debts of the deceased. The children will only have a monetary claim on him or her to the amount of their share, claimable at the time he or she dies or goes bankrupt. Should the spouse or registered partner remarry, the children are entitled to claim the proprietary rights of assets derived from the inheritance, to avoid that these assets end up with the stepfamily. The spouse or registered partner may retain the usufruct of these assets.

This allocation by law can be set aside in a will so that, for instance, the children also take part in the proprietary rights and liabilities as of the day of the devolution of the estate, instead of just having the monetary claim.

STATUTORY CLAIMS
Children always have a right to a fixed, minimum value of the estate of their parents, also referred to as the statutory claim. Even if, for example, a parent states in a will that a child is not to inherit anything, the child can make this monetary claim on the joint heirs anyway. The statutory claim amounts to half of the value of the portion which the child would have inherited had it not been disinherited. In a will, the parent can state that the statutory claim is not claimable until his or her spouse, registered partner or partner with whom the parent has a cohabitation agreement, dies.

If the spouse or registered partner is disinherited, he or she can claim the usufruct of the family dwelling and furniture and even of other assets, insofar as he or she is in need of this.

FOREIGN INHERITANCE LAW AND INTERNATIONAL PRIVATE LAW
Every country has its own rules on inheritance law. International private law determines which legislation is applicable to an estate of an international nature – for instance if the deceased did not have Dutch nationality or was not residing in the Netherlands at the time of his death. Every country has its own rules on international private law and the authorities of a country always apply the country's own rules of international private law. This can lead to different, conflicting results; international treaties are meant to avoid such conflicting results. Regarding inheritance law, the Dutch authorities apply the rules of the Hague Inheritance Treaty 1989.

THE HAGUE INHERITANCE TREATY 1989
According to the treaty of 1989, Dutch inheritance law is applicable to the worldwide estate if:
- the deceased was living in the Netherlands at the time of his/her death and was of Dutch nationality, or
- the deceased was living in the Netherlands at the time of his/her death and was not of Dutch nationality, but had been living in the Netherlands for more than five years before he/she died, or
- the deceased explicitly stipulated, in his or her will, that Dutch inheritance law was applicable. This is only possible if he/she had Dutch nationality or lived in the Netherlands at the time of his/her death.

THE ROLE OF THE CIVIL LAW NOTARY

In the Netherlands, there are several important moments when you will need the help of a so-called civil law notary. For instance, when you buy a house, when you draw up your (pre)nuptial agreement or cohabitation agreement, when you draw up a will and when you establish a corporation. In order for these documents to have legal effect, and to ensure legal certainty, the law states that you need a deed, drawn up by a civil law notary.

The original deed always remains in the files of the notary. Sometimes you are required to enter a copy of the deed in a public register.

Civil law notaries are lawyers who have specific tasks and competencies and who are appointed by the King. They play an impartial role in the drawing up of notarial deeds and can advise the parties in such a way that the interests of all parties are taken into account and that there are no unpleasant surprises. If one of you does not have Dutch nationality, then matters of international law enter the scene. Be sure to seek advice on these!

BUYING A HOUSE

The civil law notary takes care of all the legalities involved in the transfer of the ownership of the house, including the drawing up and execution of the deed of transfer. This can only be done by a civil law notary. He evaluates the transfer and looks into the background of the parties who are involved. If there is anything that seems not quite right, he will immediately freeze the process and – if possible – resolve the situation.

The civil law notary is the financial spider in the web. He makes sure that the bank, the seller and any creditors get the money they are due and that the transfer tax is paid. And it goes without saying that the payment of the house and the transfer take place at the same time; he carries out the payment on your behalf only once he is sure that you will become owner of the house.

It is also the task of the civil law notary to carry out a number of investigations – in the Land Registry, the Bankruptcy Registry, the Matrimonial Property Registry and, as the case may be, the registry of the Chamber of Commerce – to verify that the property is not in any way encumbered. He also consults the Land Registry to check if all the data on the house is correct and whether it is subject to a mortgage and/or attachments. If it is, then in most cases, its ownership cannot be transferred and he and the owner will have to find a solution. He also checks whether there are any impediments or possible servitudes, such as a right of way through the garden.

In the Matrimonial Property Registry, the civil law notary checks whether the seller has been divorced sometime between the purchase and the sale of the house, in which case the former spouse may have ownership rights regarding the house.

Should you take out a loan to finance the house, the civil law notary is responsible for drawing up the mortgage deed.

In principle, you can select whichever civil law notary you want. The real estate agent can draw up the purchase contract for you, but the notary can do that too. Once the contract has been signed, the notary has it entered in the Land Registry. This way, the seller cannot sell the property again to someone else, while it also protects you against his possible bankruptcy and/or attachments resulting from any financial problems he may have. Your notary can provide you with more information on these issues.

RELATIONSHIPS

You and your loved one can lay down certain agreements regarding your relationship in a contract. For instance, if you want to live together without getting married, you can draw up a cohabitation contract. Or, if you want to get married, you might want a prenuptial agreement.

These contracts will also have to be drawn up by a civil law notary, who can advise you on their content. As an impartial party, he will draw up a balanced agreement that will take into account all personal circumstances, of both you and your partner/spouse-to-be.

After talking to both of you, the civil law notary will make a draft of the contract. Once you agree on the content, the final deed will be drawn up and signed by the two of you and the notary. In case of a marriage, this will have to be done before the actual ceremony takes place. Though, of course, you can also arrange a post-nuptial agreement, if you are already married.

INHERITANCE / WILLS

You need a civil law notary if you want to draw up a (living) will. In a personal meeting, you will get together to discuss your wishes. In your will, you can state who your heirs are to be and make detailed legacies regarding leaving specific items or sums of money to specific persons or institutions. Should you wish to appoint an executor or, for instance, a guardian for your child(ren), then this must be included in the will.

Once you have signed the will at the office of the notary, he will enter it in the Central Registry of Wills. This way, the will can always be found.

The notary can also give you advice regarding the validity of a will drawn up abroad and whether or not it will be necessary to draw up a will in the Netherlands. Of note in this context is the fact that, on August 17 of 2015, the European Inheritance Law Regulation entered into force. The Regulation has been accepted in all countries of the European Union, except for the United Kingdom, Ireland and Denmark. The aim of this Regulation is to simplify successions – that have an international context – for European citizens, and to make the settlement of international inheritances within the European Union run smoother. Your civil law notary will be able to advise you as to how to set up your will, taking into account the rules of the Regulation.

CHOOSING AN APPLICABLE LAW

By stipulating which law is to apply, you leave no doubt as to which law is applicable to the inheritance. Making such a choice is of particular importance when the inheritance has international aspects. A choice of law helps avoid that – due to emigration, immigration or naturalization – a different law becomes applicable to the inheritance. However, though you might have explicitly made such a choice, it is not always recognized in other countries, especially regarding real estate outside the Netherlands. In such a situation it is best to seek advice on this matter in both countries.

SETTLEMENT OF THE INHERITANCE AND INTERNATIONAL PRIVATE LAW

The Dutch Inheritance Conflict Act determines that the settlement of an inheritance (for example: how the heirs should accept or refuse an inheritance, what powers the executor of a will has) is governed by Dutch law, if the deceased was residing in the Netherlands at the time of his death. If this is not the case, it is assumed that the settlement is governed by the law of the country of residence.

TAXES IN THE CASE OF DEATH

Nationality not Important

If you are a resident of the Netherlands when you die, then, in all likelihood, inheritance taxes will be due in the Netherlands. It does not matter what your nationality is: the entire worldwide estate of non-Dutch nationals who die while living in the Netherlands is (also) subject to taxation here. It also does not make a difference where your heirs are living at the time of your death.

Factual Situation

To determine whether you were living in the Netherlands, the factual situation is taken into account. If you had a house in the Netherlands and a family that also lived in the Netherlands for Dutch tax purposes, then you will most probably be considered to have been a resident of the Netherlands (and to have had resident tax liability). Also if you benefited from the so-called 30%-ruling and opted for the status of 'partial non-resident taxpayer' (see page 106) you will still be deemed to have been a resident taxpayer for inheritance tax purposes. In other words, the 30%-ruling has no bearing on this.

Double Taxation

As not every country applies the same taxation principles as the Netherlands, your passing away while living in the Netherlands could lead to double taxation. Some countries apply the principle of nationality of the deceased instead of the principle of residence. Furthermore, most countries levy inheritance tax on any portion of the estate located in that country (for instance immovable property). To avoid double taxation, the Netherlands has entered into tax treaties with a number of countries. In the situation in which there is no treaty, a national ruling aimed at the avoidance of double taxation can be invoked. However, this is no guarantee that double taxation will be completely avoided.

Exemptions

The inheritance tax law contains a few exemptions. The most important ones are (for 2016):

- the spouse / partner has an exemption of € 636,180. Also those who 'merely' live together can qualify for the exemption; be sure to have yourself informed
- children, grandchildren, and great-grandchildren have an exemption of € 20,148
- parents (regardless of whether one parent inherits, or both parents inherit together) have an exemption of € 47,715
- handicapped children who were largely supported by the deceased or that are not likely to be able to provide for themselves have an exemption of € 60,439
- donations for causes of a religious, life philosophy, charity, cultural, and scientific nature, as well as for causes for the general good are fully exempted
- all other situations: € 2,122.

These exemptions are subject, however, to certain deductions, such as for pensions.

Rates

Inheritances that exceed the exemption are subject to various rates. The rates in inheritance law are 'double progressive'. This means that the higher the value of the inheritance, the higher the rate; and the greater the (family) distance to the deceased relative, the higher the rate. Inheritances are divided into two categories, those that go up to € 121,903 (2016) and those that exceed this amount. Spouses, registered partners and children are subject to a rate of 10% for the first category and 20% for the second. Grandchildren and other descendants owe 18% over the first category and 36% over the second. All other heirs owe 30% over the first category and 40% over the second.

Law on Matrimonial Property

As you could read earlier in the paragraphs on marriage, the main rule in Dutch matrimonial law is that if you get married you do this in general community property. In other countries this is often the exception and, in many cases, you will have drawn up a marriage contract in accordance with your (foreign) law. You should be aware of the fact that, should you pass away in the Netherlands, the national law on matrimonial property can have several unexpected fiscal consequences. For instance, you may have included a survivorship clause or a settlement clause in your marriage contract, the aim of which is to avoid inheritance tax. However, you should take into account that it might not have the intended fiscal consequences as long as you are living in the Netherlands: the law contains what are referred to as 'fictions', pursuant to which taxes can be levied after all. 'Fictions' allow certain situations that might otherwise not be covered by a law to fall under its scope anyway.

Transfer Tax

Even if the deceased and the heirs were living outside the Netherlands at the time of death, Dutch transfer tax still could enter the picture. The criterion used to determine whether transfer tax is due is whether the goods had strong ties with the Netherlands. The most important items on which transfer tax can be levied are:

- a Dutch company that has a permanent establishment in the Netherlands
- the following assets belonging to a non-Dutch company:

- real estate situated in the Netherlands, after deduction of the mortgage debts
- the direct right to profits that a company owner has, without the benefit of shares, regarding profits or losses of this company which is established in the Netherlands, after deduction of any debts the company may have incurred
- shares in a company that primarily owns real estate.

There are no exemptions to the transfer tax. The rates are the same as the rates for inheritance tax.

WHAT TYPE OF INSURANCE IS AVAILABLE

Perhaps you have not even thought about insurance at this stage. It is, however, of the utmost importance for a safe and healthy stay abroad. You could fall off your Dutch bicycle, have appendicitis, or have your house broken into. It is, therefore, advisable to arrange your insurance, if possible before you leave your home country or immediately upon your arrival in the Netherlands.

What exactly do you have to insure yourself against? Here is an overview of a few of the standard insurances available in the Netherlands, either through private insurance companies, banks, or your employer. Keep in mind that if you take out all insurances with the same insurance company, they may offer you a rebate on the entire package. You can also arrange your insurances through an insurance broker. You can find more information on brokers' associations and the Dutch insurance situation on the websites listed at the end of the chapter.

MEDICAL
Medical insurance is perhaps the most important insurance you can arrange. The last thing you want to deal with, when you are battling the local flu, is that your visit to the doctor and your medication are not covered.

What's more, as of January 1, 2006, all residents of the Netherlands are obligated to arrange health insurance in order to be able to legally reside in the Netherlands. To pay for this, everyone pays a fixed contribution of approximately € 1,450 and an income-dependent contribution. This income-dependent contribution is compensated by your employer, who pays it directly to the tax authorities. If you are unemployed or self-employed, you receive no such compensation. You receive an annual preliminary assessment for the amount you owe, which is based on what the tax authorities estimate you will be earning that year (in the case of self-employment). If you end up paying too much, you will be reimbursed after the final tax assessment over the year in question. Also if you are receiving a benefit or old age pension, you pay an income-dependent contribution – whether this is compensated, depends on your social security institution or pension plan. Children are covered free of charge and the government offers financial assistance (called *zorgtoeslag*) to persons (also self-employed) whose income lies below a certain level, to help pay the premium. There is a fixed deductible (see further on); by increasing the amount of the deductible, you can decrease the income-independent part of your contribution.

All insurance companies are obligated to accept all applications, regardless of age, gender or health. The cost of a basic insurance is pretty much the same across the board; doing a little comparative shopping becomes worth your while if you are interested in additional coverage – or eliminating certain coverage. However, keep in mind that insurance companies are not obligated to take you on for additional coverage – in other words, they may refuse you for an additional health care package. You can change insurance companies every year; visit www.independer.nl, www.zorgkiezer.nl or kieszorg.nl to compare insurance companies and coverage. English-language information can be found on www.zorgwijzer.nl/zorgvergelijker/english.

Issues that are of interest to look at when doing comparative shopping are: the amount of the deductible (*eigen risico*, or 'own risk'), what the coverage is if you are abroad and fall ill or otherwise require medical care, level of dental care offered, alternative therapies, etc. Another very important issue is described in the next paragraph. Also; if you are traveling within Europe, ask your insurance company to issue you your European Health Insurance Card, which will allow you to receive free medical care (or at a reduced cost) in any of the other EU/EEA countries and Switzerland, if treatment becomes necessary during your visit or you are suffering from an existing chronic condition. Keep in mind that it has not been created for those who go abroad specifically to receive medical care. Be sure to ask your insurance company what, if any, further conditions apply.

INSURANCE IN KIND OR RESTITUTION
When you are arranging your insurance, you will run into the terms '*natura polis*' or '*restitutie polis*'. If you take out a *natura* policy, your insurance will pay your medical bills directly. However, they will only pay out these bills to medical service providers they have entered into a contract with (you are free to select your own *huisarts*, or GP), which means that you must verify that such a contract exists between the medical care provider you wish to select and your insurance company before you make use of his or her services – or else run the risk of paying the bill yourself.

The *restitutie* policy is slightly more expensive, but does give you freedom of choice as to whom you wish to turn to for medical assistance. With the restitution policy, you pay the bill yourself and then submit it with your insurance company, for restitution.

Some insurance companies offer a combination of the two types of insurances, and with many insurance companies you will find they are not excessively strict about the existence of an actual contract between them and the care provider, provided he is recognized by a professional organization.

DEDUCTIBLE – 'OWN RISK'
The no-claim rule that existed until January 1, 2008, was replaced by an 'own risk' clause. For 2016, it amounts to € 385. The own risk does not apply to children until the age of 18, visits to the GP, visits to the midwife, maternity care (see page 233), care covered by voluntary additional insurance or dental care for children / persons until the age of 21. You can also opt for a voluntary deductible of up to € 885 a year.

EXCEPTIONAL MEDICAL EXPENSES
Long-term medical care
The WLZ (Wet Langdurige Ziektekosten, or Long-Term Medical Care Act) has replaced the AWBZ as of 2015. It is a national insur-

ance scheme that insures persons against risks that cannot be covered by individual insurance. Everyone who legally resides and works in the Netherlands has a right to coverage by this insurance. You can read more about it on page 71. Its premise is that everyone should be able to stay living at home with the support of their social network or the assistance of the municipality, though it also covers care in an institution. It is meant to cover steep medical expenses that are not covered by a regular health insurance and that are simply not affordable. The same health care insurance company with which you have placed your 'regular' health insurance also takes on your personal coverage by this insurance. You owe a social security contribution to pay for the WLZ, which is calculated over – and withheld from – your salary and some types of benefits. You also owe a contribution for this insurance over income from self-employment.

A special aspect of exceptional medical expenses is the PGB (*persoonsgebonden budget*, or personal budget): you are granted a certain amount of money, which you can use to 'purchase' personal care, care by a nurse or other personal assistance. PGB-WMO helps cover assistance if you want to stay living at home but cannot live fully independently, PGB-WLZ is for long-term care, PGB-jeugdwet is for children, and PGB-ZVW is medical care at home. A combination of multiple PGB-budgets is possible.

DENTAL CARE

We mention dental care here separately because it is no longer included in any basic package (with the exception of dental care for children up to the age of 18 and 'specialist' dental care, including dentures). You must take out an additional dental policy to cover standard dental care.

MEDICATION

Also medication deserves special attention: in your policy you are likely to find something along the lines of "we only cover GVS medication". This is a consequence of an arrangement whereby types of medication have been 'clustered', after which a maximum price has been determined for this cluster. If you are prescribed medication, then the cluster-specific maximum price is covered by the insurance. If your medication is more expensive than that, you will have to pay the difference. If this is the case, then you can also discuss with your doctor and/or pharmacist whether a cheaper – and equally as effective – alternative is available. Homeopathic medicine is not covered by the 'GVS'-system, so that you will have to pay for it yourself, unless you arrange additional insurance to cover it.

Check with your insurance company whether you can take out an additional policy to cover these extra costs as well as the cost of homeopathic/alternative medication.

On the website www.medicijnkosten.nl you can check whether your medication is covered by your insurance company. You fill in the name of your medication, then on the next page other specifics (such as g/ml), and then it tells you how much of it will be covered and how much you have to contribute to paying the costs.

PREGNANCY AND CHILDBIRTH

During pregnancy, you visit a midwife with increasing frequency up to and including delivery; this is covered by your insurance. At least two ultrasounds, if they are medically required, are also covered.

In principle, in the Netherlands, a 'normal' childbirth takes place in the home, with the help of a midwife (in actual fact, only about 18% of the deliveries take place at home); this is covered by your insurance. The costs of a hospital delivery are fully covered if your midwife, GP or specialist has determined that, for health and safety reasons, the baby should be delivered in the hospital. This is called a *bevalling op medische indicatie*. If you voluntarily choose to have your baby in the hospital (called a *poliklinische bevalling*), you will have to contribute towards the costs of your hospital delivery – though some insurance companies also cover these costs. You can find more on having a baby on page 230.

Kraamzorg (Maternity Home Care, see page 233) is also covered by the basic insurance package, though you have to pay a contribution towards the costs.

STUDENTS

Students will often find that their host institution has made sure that they are insured – as everyone is required by law to have health insurance – though you should verify this, of course. Special packages for students are available. For more information, see page 217. Furthermore, under certain conditions, if you are insured under the public health care scheme in your home country (EU/EEA/Switzerland), you can request to be issued the European Health Insurance Card, proving that you are covered by this insurance policy, in which case you do not have to arrange insurance here. However, once you take on a job or start an internship in the Netherlands, you may have to arrange health insurance here.

SELF-EMPLOYED PERSONS
Disability

Employees are covered by the employee insurance schemes for the consequences of disability. Self-employed persons are not, and have to arrange private insurance to cover these consequences.

When selecting this type of insurance, you can take the following issues into account: when you wish the payments to cease (for instance, when your pension starts to pay out), your job level (the amount of premium you owe depends on your job level), as of which percentage of disability you want the insurance to start paying out, the degree of disability it is meant to cover (for instance, inability to do the same work, similar work, or any type of work), and whether or not you want the payments indexed over time.

The payments will amount to 80% of your average income over the last three years, however, you can insure a lower amount. Some insurance companies offer a lower premium to beginning entrepreneurs.

You should investigate your options carefully when deciding whether you want to take out the insurance or the insurance with the higher premium / exclusions as the latter may, in fact, turn out to be more attractive, despite its financial drawbacks. And you may simply opt not to insure yourself at all; this particular insurance is not obligatory. The premiums you pay for this insurance are tax-deductible, you will pay taxes over the payments you receive should be you become disabled for work.

If you are considered a high-risk client (due to a chronic disease, or a physical challenge, or health issues in the past), the insurance company you approach may charge a higher premium or refuse to insure you at all. For these people, a so-called alternative insurance (called *vangnetverzekering* – safety net insurance) has been created. To make use of this possibility, you must request this disability insurance within 15 months of starting your own company.

Pregnancy
As of June 4, 2008, pregnant self-employed mothers have a right to 16-weeks of paid pregnancy leave, based on the Zelfstandig en Zwangerregeling (Self-Employed and Pregnant Regulation). (See more on pregnancy leave on page 191.) How much you receive depends on the number of hours you worked in self-employment the previous year. If you worked 1,225 hours or more, then you will receive a benefit equal to the minimum wage. If you worked fewer than 1,225 hours, then your benefit will be less and will depend on your profits / income over the previous year. You also have a right to this benefit if you work for your partner / spouse ('s company).

HOUSE
You've finally settled for that beautiful house in the center of Amsterdam or out in the woods. Just putting your key in the lock makes you feel happy. Now you want it insured!

A house insurance generally covers the financial consequences of fire, breaking and entry, as well as unexpected events such as storm, fire, lightning, theft, vandalism, explosions and more.

HOUSEHOLD CONTENTS
And how about that beautiful, expensive couch, or your antique dining room, or Dutch painting? A household contents insurance covers virtually everything you have in your house against fire, theft, water damage, storms and more. For possessions that are especially valuable, such as jewelry, antique musical instruments or your stamp collection, you can take out additional insurance for Valuable Possessions. Some insurance companies offer a 'Home Electronics' insurance, to ensure coverage of your computer, television and sound installation, among others.

TRAVEL
You've finally booked that wonderful trip to Singapore, but you are worried about whether your luggage will come back in one piece, or that you might be pickpocketed, or lose your camera! Or maybe you've decided to go skiing instead, but are worried about what type of costs you might incur if you fall and break a leg. In that case, you might want to contribute to your peace of mind (and what else are vacations for?) by taking out travel insurance (which can include cancelation insurance). You might find it economically more interesting, even, to take out year-round travel insurance; it often costs little more than the insurance for a three-week vacation.

CAR
Driving around in the Netherlands can be risky business. Though the Netherlands is considered one of the safest countries when it comes to driving, the Dutch are not the gentlest of people behind the steering wheel. Particularly tail-gating and claiming the right of way (which they have when coming from the right, unless indicated otherwise) can lead to some hair-raising situations. In short, if you own a car here, you will want to take out car insurance. Furthermore, car owners are obligated by law to have minimum liability coverage, called a *wa-verzekering*. If you take out car insurance, this will automatically include minimum liability insurance (which can be extended upon for a fee). For the various types of insurances

available (for instance, covering damage to your car, theft, joyriding, etc.), contact your insurance company. You can also opt to include legal aid insurance, if you do not already have a general one.

PASSENGER
Other drivers claiming their right of way can be particularly unnerving for passengers. Should anything happen to one of your passengers, this is most often not covered by your regular car insurance and therefore it is advisable to take out this additional insurance. It covers not only the situation in which you are 'rolling', but also when you are on the side of the road because your car has broken down, or when you are filling your gas tank. You will probably have two choices: a 'damages' insurance and an 'accidents to passengers' insurance. The former pays out damages, including a certain amount of emotional damages, the latter pays out a fixed amount in the case of death or permanent disability.

ACCIDENT
This insurance covers any type of accident (not only those on the road), such as falling off the stepladder, or dislocating your arm playing rugby. Those who take out this insurance are paid a lump sum if something goes wrong, to cover any large expenses that may be the consequence of the accident. You can take out individual or family insurance.

LIABILITY FOR PRIVATE PERSONS
Say, the little apples of your eye have decided to play soccer in the front yard after all and have kicked the soccer ball not through your window, but your neighbor's. Or that you drop a can of paint on the car parked next to yours. To cover the expenses related to any of these accidents, you can take out liability insurance for private persons, which will then cover the bills. You can take out individual or family insurance.

DISABILITY INSURANCE FOR EMPLOYEES
The days that you could count on the government to guarantee you a lifestyle as the one you were used to before you became disabled for work are over.

The government has had to introduce a few changes in its spending pattern too, so that, should you end up with a disability, chances are that your benefit-related income will be far below the level of income you were accustomed to receiving. To help cover this difference you can take out additional private disability insurance. There is, however, the possibility that your employer has made additional arrangements. Please ask your employer about this before arranging your own additional insurance.

LEGAL AID
You might end up having to deal with the situation in which a person you have held liable will not pay, or your kitchen has not been delivered, or your boss is not sticking to what you agreed to in your employment contract. This can be very tough to cope with and quite time-consuming, especially in another culture, language and legal system – and is hardly something you can deal with without legal aid. To this end, you can take out legal aid insurance, which will not only provide you with the aid you need, but will also cover your legal aid expenses. Family members are often automatically included in this insurance.

MOTOR AND 'SCOOTER'

Maybe you want to go touring around the country and actually feel the wind in your face. Then you might choose to buy a motorcycle or a moped. For these types of vehicles there is a separate insurance, called the Motor and Scooter Insurance. Also for motorcycles and mopeds, you can take out additional Passenger Insurance.

BICYCLE

One of the thriving black markets in the Netherlands is that of stolen bicycles. After a few months of watching those happy Dutch cyclists, you may succumb to the temptation of buying one of those environment-friendly contraptions yourself, only to have it stolen! Or damaged. It's a good thing you can take out bicycle insurance.

LEGAL PROBLEMS

Legal problems are always on the lure: for example, your rental agreement could be canceled, you could be fired, or your landlord could refuse to make important repairs. You could have problems with the tax authorities or with receiving your benefits. Repairs to your washing machine were not done properly. Your divorce is pending or, following an accident, your damages have not been reimbursed. In other words, since there are many kinds of legal problems, chances are that you might have one or two of your own.

You might want some legal advice as well, before making an important decision. For example, before accepting a job, borrowing money or renting a house. In all such cases, it is good to know where you can go for legal advice.

ADVICE

All legal aid agencies offer advice. These include legal counters, trade unions, lawyers and municipal social service counselors. For more on these, read on.

LEGAL PROCEEDINGS
Civil Law

There is no obligation to have legal representation before the subdistrict sector of the District Court. Cases involving amounts lower than € 25,000, employment law cases, and cases involving rent law, light misdemeanors and consumer credit are to be brought before the subdistrict sector of the District Court and therefore do not require representation by a lawyer. You can choose between representing yourself, or letting yourself be represented by a person with legal training, such as a process-server.

In all other situations, legal representation is mandatory before the District Court (with the exception of administrative law cases), the Court of Appeals and the Netherlands Supreme Court. If you have not arranged it, the magistrates will not accept the case.

ADMINISTRATIVE LAW

Administrative law applies to governmental decisions, for example relating to building permits or benefit payments. A lawyer is not required for administrative law issues. Also here, you may represent yourself. For more complex matters, however, it would be wise to consult an expert – for example, a lawyer.

CRIMINAL LAW

In principle, criminal law does not require legal representation. You, as a defendant, may defend yourself. If you are taken into custody, you are automatically assigned a lawyer. However, you are free to change lawyers if you wish. If you face criminal charges but are not in custody, you can consult a lawyer.

SUMMARY PROCEEDINGS

If you initiate a summary proceeding, you will need to use the services of a lawyer. If you are a defendant in such a proceeding, you are not obligated to employ the services of a lawyer.

FEES

There are no flat rates for the services of lawyers. The rates vary not only from one law office to the other but also according to the type of case. Therefore, it is worth the trouble to inquire at several law offices about their (hourly) rates for the type of case, and about the amount of time the lawyer expects to dedicate to the case.

No cure, no pay is not allowed by the code of conduct all lawyers have to abide by.

FINANCIAL ASSISTANCE

For many people, legal fees can be a problem. If you wish to start or are facing legal proceedings but cannot pay for them (entirely), you can ask your lawyer to request government-financed legal aid (*toevoeging*). If it is granted – and this depends, among others, on your income and financial means – the government will pay part of your legal fees. *Toevoeging* is only granted to pay your lawyer's fees – and not related expenses, such as court registry fees, extract fees, process server expenses, etc. (it therefore usually does not cover what is normally charged). It can also be used to help cover the costs of mediation. The income limits in question are fixed and are regularly adjusted (see www.st-ab.nl, and click on *normbedragen*, then *Wet op de Rechtsbijstand*, or Legal Aid Act).

If your income is high or you have sufficient financial means and do not qualify for government-financed legal aid, you must pay the legal fees yourself. You can, however, take out legal aid insurance to help pay for lawyers' fees. There may be a first risk clause.

SPECIAL RULES FOR WORK PERMITS

TEMPORARY WORK
In the case of temporary work, a work permit can be issued for a maximum period of 24 weeks. The work must then be carried out by a non-Dutch national who has lived outside the Netherlands during a period of 14 weeks preceding the issuing of the work permit. This type of work permit, it follows, cannot be extended. These permits are usually issued for seasonal work.

INCIDENTAL WORK
Those who have 'regulated' professions (such as a lawyer or a professor) and want to come to the Netherlands to carry out their work temporarily and/or incidentally, must report this in advance (*verklaring vooraf*). Regulated professions are professions that are carried out by persons who must meet specific legal requirements, such as a university title, a diploma or a certificate of experience. Whether or not their stay is 'temporary or incidental' is evaluated per request, taking into account the length, frequency, regularity and continuity of the work for which this person is coming to the Netherlands.

Temporary and incidental work on the basis of a 'regulated' profession, to be carried out in the Netherlands, is possible if:
■ the employee is an EU/EEA/Swiss resident
■ the profession is regulated. If it is not, it must have been carried out during at least two years of the ten years prior to the arrival in the Netherlands.

In some cases, an advance verification is carried out; this is the case if the profession is in the areas of national health or public order. When applying for approval, the employee must submit a number of documents, such as proof of nationality, professional qualifications and experience. Other professions might require more papers.

INTER-COMPANY TRANSFER WITHIN A GROUP OF COMPANIES
1. *High Management Position or Highly-Qualified Position*
For a work permit to be granted in the case of an inter-company transfer, proof must be delivered of the fact that the employee fills a high management position or highly-qualified position and has that specific specialist knowledge that is essential for the company. Furthermore, the employment conditions must be in keeping with the function

requirements that are applicable in the Netherlands. The company in question must be a large, independent company or group of companies whose aim it is to make a profit. It must also have an establishment in the Netherlands and an annual turnover of at least € 50 million. The salary of the employee must be at least € 4,579.20 gross per month (€ 4,240 excluding holiday allowance).

2. *Trainees*
There are special rules for employees of an international group of companies who have a university or higher professional (HBO) education who wish to come here to work (as the case may be; as a trainee). Again, the company in question must be a large, independent company or group of companies whose aim it is to make a profit. It must also have an establishment in the Netherlands and an annual turnover of at least € 50 million. In the case of traineeships, the employer must submit a program, showing the need for placing the employee in the Netherlands (the learning objectives should be formulated). The salary of the employee must be at least € 3,108 (€ 3,356.64 including the holiday allowance). Furthermore, in connection with the fact that the trainee is apparently not being sent to the Netherlands to fulfill a permanent position, the period of the traineeship must be shorter than three years.

3. *Trainer/specialist*
This is the case if an employee is transferred within the group to pass on specific knowledge and technological know-how within a group of companies. The employee needs to have a degree from a university or higher professional (HBO) education. The salary of the employee must be at least € 4,240 (€ 4,579.20 including the holiday allowance). Furthermore, in connection with the fact that the trainer is apparently not being sent to the Netherlands to fulfil a permanent position, the period of the traineeship must be shorter than one year.

WORKING VIA AN EMPLOYMENT AGENCY
If an employee is hired via another company or an employment agency, the employer need not arrange the work permit; this must be done by the other company or the employment agency. The employer should, however, ask for and keep a copy of the work permit in his administration.

INTERPRETERS
The Dutch courts make use of interpreters in the case of (criminal) law proceedings, police hearings and for asylum seekers – but you can also request the assistance of an interpreter if you feel you need one in any other type of case. If the court requests the assistance of an interpreter, the costs are in principle carried either by the state or by the party who is ordered to pay the costs in a civil case. If you need the use of a translator/interpreter, ask your legal aid agency where you can find one and what the costs will be. Beware that price and quality are not always consistent. As of January 1, 2010, the Dutch Ministry of Justice will in principle refer everyone seeking the assistance of an interpreter to the Concorde Group, www.concorde.nl.

WHERE TO OBTAIN LEGAL AID ASSISTANCE
Juridisch Loket – **Legal Counter**
The Juridisch Loket has been created to provide you with free legal information and advice on matters regarding employment issues, family issues, social security (benefits), rent and housing law, alien affairs, problems regarding products bought or services rendered (consumer issues), criminal law, neighbor problems, permits and driver's licenses. If you require actual legal assistance, the Juridisch Loket can recommend a lawyer or mediator and can inform you of whether you qualify for subsidized legal aid from either one of these. To find a Juridisch Loket near you, visit www.juridischloket.nl and click on *bezoek een vestiging*.

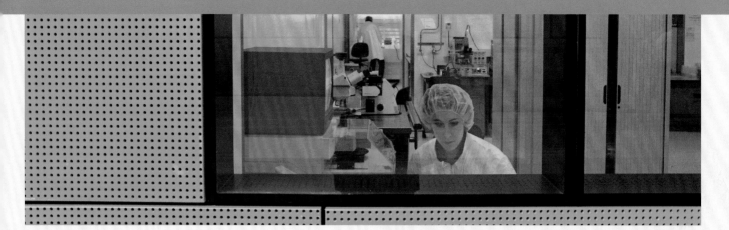

JOURNALISTS / MUSICIANS

Journalists and musicians do not need a work permit, if their principal place of residence is outside the Netherlands and they come here to work on an incidental basis and stay here for a short period of time (up to three months). A maximum of five fixed counselors, who are employed by the artist or journalist, are also exempt from the work permit requirement if the activities are related to the care and support of the artist / journalist.

GUEST LECTURER

Work permits are not required for those who come as guest lecturers to universities, universities of applied sciences (*hogeschool* or HBO), institutions for higher international education, or research institutions that are connected to, or operate in the area of, one of these universities/institutions – under the condition that the lecturer has his principal place of residence outside the Netherlands and works and stays here on an incidental basis.

SCIENTIFIC RESEARCHER / DOCTOR IN TRAINING

Scientific researchers, paid or unpaid, do not need a work permit to work here. Unpaid scientific researchers do not need a formal employment agreement, merely a so-called Guest Agreement. Once they receive remuneration for their efforts, however, they do need an employment agreement. Furthermore, certain requirements apply to their academic background, while research must be their main task and their employer / host institution must be registered with the IND, which means that the accelerated procedure is available to them.

Those working on a Ph.D. at a university or research institution and medical doctors in training can come to the Netherlands as highly skilled migrants; the minimum income does not apply to them, though it may not lie below the minimum wage.

FOREIGN SERVICE PROVIDERS

Foreign service providers from within the EU / EEA / Switzerland do not have to request a work permit when working with non EU-citizens in the Netherlands. For instance, a French service provider does not need a work permit when bringing in an employee from Finland. However, the service provider must provide the UWV with information on the company, the nature of the services, and the identity of the employees.

ASYLUM SEEKERS

Asylum seekers may work in the Netherlands 24 weeks a year, provided they are not on the deportation list and have been under the care of COA (Central Organization for Asylum Seekers) or a municipality for at least six months. Their employer must request a work permit for them from the UWV.

Legal Aid Bureaus

For more information on organizations providing subsidized legal aid, and to find one close to you, visit www.rvr.org (Raad voor Rechtsbijstand), or www.rechtsbijstand.nl. More sites can be found at the end of the chapter.

Lawyers

It is usually wise to seek advice or legal representation, especially if the other party already has. If you do not qualify for subsidized legal aid, then you will likely turn to a lawyer. Most lawyers specialize in certain types of cases or legal areas. You can approach the Netherlands Bar Association – an organization to which all lawyers in the Netherlands belong – for a recommendation. As mentioned earlier, a Juridisch Loket can sometimes recommend a particular lawyer, depending on your case. Another useful source of legal advisors and/or lawyers, as well as basic legal information, is www.jurofoon.nl.

Many lawyers offer free introductory consultations. The first consultation lasts about thirty minutes, during which the lawyer will examine your case and recommend any steps you should take. Be sure to ask in advance whether – and what – the lawyer charges for the first consultation.

Mediators

The option of mediation first noticeably entered the 'conflict scene' in divorce cases, but is now rapidly gaining popularity in other

STUDENTS

When coming to the Netherlands as a non-EU citizen, special immigration procedures apply. Which specific requirements are to be met depend on your nationality and the purpose of your stay. Some nationals need an entry visa plus residence permit, while other nationals only need a residence permit. Upon arrival, other procedures must be completed, such as your registration in the municipal population register (BRP/*bevolkingsregister*). For more on this, see page 111.

ENTRY VISA: MVV / SHORT STAY VISA

If you are a national of an EU/EEA member state, Switzerland, Monaco, Canada, the U.S., Japan, Australia, South Korea, New Zealand, or Vatican City you will not need an authorization temporary stay (MVV) to study in the Netherlands; you only need a residence permit (see further on). You may enter the Netherlands without a visa.

If you are from any other country and you intend to stay here longer than three months, you will need an authorization temporary stay (MVV) to enter the country. As of August 1, 2008, all Dutch educational institutes are required to apply for the MVV on behalf of their foreign students. This means that you, as a student, can not apply for the MVV yourself. Please contact your Dutch university for more about their MVV application procedure.

If you will be here shorter than 90 days, you may need a 'short stay visa' (*visum kort verblijf*). You can apply for this visa at the Dutch embassy or consulate in your home country.

RESIDENCE PERMIT / REGISTRATION GBA

As it has also been determined that all Dutch educational institutes are required to apply for the residence permits on behalf of their foreign students, which means that you are not allowed to do this yourself. Upon arrival you will need to pick up your residence permit – as the MVV merely allows you to enter the country and is only valid for 90 days. You will also have to register with the municipality (registration BRP/*bevolkingsregister*).

EU/EEA/SWISS nationals do not need a residence permit, but if they stay here longer than four months, they too need to register with the municipality. Also, once you are a resident of the Netherlands, in principle you are obligated to arrange private health insurance, pursuant to the Health Insurance Act (perhaps your host institution has arranged a collective insurance in which you can participate). In order to be able to do this, you will have to obtain a Citizen Service Number (*Burgerservicenummer*, see page 66) and provide proof that you are staying here legally, such as a residence permit or, if you are an EU/EEA citizen, a valid passport. You obtain the Citizen Service Number (BSN) when you register with the municipality. Note: people under the age of 30 who are in the Netherlands solely for the purpose of studying, do not need to take out Dutch health care insurance. Also, if you have an EU Health Insurance Card, which you can get if you are insured under the public health care scheme in your (EU) home country and your stay abroad is temporary, you will be continued to be covered by this insurance policy. It is up to your health insurance provider to determine what constitutes a temporary stay.

REQUIREMENTS FOR ADMISSION TO UNIVERSITY

To be granted a residence permit for study purposes, you must follow a study at a recognized school or university (of applied sciences). It is not enough just to be taking Dutch language lessons. However, if you do not meet all the requirements for admission to a university/program or you need only to pass the language proficiency test, you can stay in the Netherlands for a period of one year to follow a customized preparatory program, to which purpose the university can – and must – request a residence permit for you.

Many educational institutes offer a year-long 'familiarization and language' course (called a *schakeljaar*, or link-year), created specifically for students from non-European, non-Western countries who come to the Netherlands to follow an education at HBO or university level. You can read more about this in chapter 9. Be careful when googling the

legal areas as well, such as commercial law (including 'business mediation'), family law, labor law, inheritance law and administrative law. It is, of course, an attractive approach that can save you both time and money – as it is more likely to result in a solution that is a viable compromise reached by the parties involved, rather than one that is chosen for you by an emotionally distant judge.

Also once a case has gone to court it is not too late to enlist the help of a mediator: either you and the other party together can decide to go to a mediator or, either before or during the court hearings, the judge can evaluate with you whether employing the services of a mediator might be preferable.

For more information, visit www.gecertificeerdemediators.nl.

Fees
No cure, no pay does not apply if you enlist the help of a mediator: you will owe his or her fees and the reimbursement of any expenses he/she may have incurred. In some cases, the first 2.5 hours of consultation are free. Rest assured, the total costs will almost always be considerably less than what you would end up paying in legal fees if you went to court. In principle, both parties carry an equal share in the expenses, but you may choose to allocate the costs differently. In many cases, a mediator can also request a *toevoeging* for you, allowing your mediation expenses to be subsidized.

Municipal Counselors

Many municipalities have municipal counselors (*Sociaal Raadslieden*) – ask at your municipality whether this is the case where you live. These councilors can answer many questions regarding social security, taxes, legislation, regulations and (semi)governmental institutions. They can also help you write letters, draw up notices of objection as well as mediate on your behalf, free of charge. For more information, or to find one, visit www.mogroep.nl/thema/sociaal-raadsliedenwerk-srw.

Process-Servers

Also process-servers offer legal aid, particularly, of course, when it word *schakeljaar*; the same term has been introduced for third-year medical master's students who will be entering further training.

INTERNSHIP

If you have a residence permit for studying in the Netherlands, and you have to do an internship here, you do not need an employment permit (*tewerkstellingsvergunning*). You do need to arrange the standard internship agreement, however, on which you can find on: www.studyinholland.nl. This agreement has to be signed by three parties: yourself, your employer, and the educational institution.

If you are not studying in the Netherlands, and want to come here to do an internship or to acquire work experience, then if you are a non-EU/EEA/Swiss national, you will need a work permit. You must be able to demonstrate that you need this work experience for your job in your country of residence or, as the case may be, as part of your studies, and that you will be resuming your studies once you return to your home country.

A JOB ON THE SIDE

Being enrolled as a student in the Netherlands, you are allowed to work a maximum of ten hours a week, or full-time during the months of June, July and August. Your employer will need to apply for a work permit. Note that EU/EEA/Swiss students can work as many hours as they like, without the need for a work permit – with the exception of Croatian students, who will need a work permit during their first twelve months on the Dutch labor market.

GRADUATES

If you are a graduate of a foreign university, you can come to the Netherlands for a period of one year to find work as a highly skilled migrant. You have to apply for the Orientation Year for Highly Educated Persons Residence Permit within three years of graduating. You must have at least a master's degree or a Ph.D. from a qualifying uni-

versity, and your diploma must be valuated by Nuffic (see chapter 9). For further conditions, please check the website of the Immigration and Naturalization Services (IND).

If you have graduated from a Dutch higher education institution with either a bachelor's or a master's degree, you have three years to apply for a change in the purpose of your stay from 'study' to 'orientation year for graduates in the Netherlands'. During one year you are free to take up any job, traineeship or placement to gain work experience without the need for a work permit, but after that year you must change your residence. The terms for changing it into a permit for a highly skilled migrant are more lenient, as a lower minimum salary requirement applies: € 2,228 (excluding the holiday allowance) gross a month (2016).

It is very important to comply with the rules stated in the Act on Employment for Foreigners (WAV) and Aliens Act (VW). If you are convicted of illegal employment or do not comply with the arrangements made with the IND, you might not be able to arrange a residence permit for knowledge migrants or a work permit for your employees in the future. A risk you cannot afford to run if you are dependent on personnel that you bring in from abroad.

---

comes to collecting your debts (up to € 25,000), but also with financial questions. As mentioned earlier, there where you are not required to have yourself represented by a lawyer in civil cases, you can request the assistance of a process-server.

Unions

All unions have a legal department that you can consult for information and advice if you are a member. They offer assistance in employment law cases and social security cases – all free of charge, if you are a member.

Legal Advice Centers

Anyone can go to a Legal Advice Center, for information and advice. They are usually manned by volunteers, mostly law students.

Other Organizations

There are a number of organizations you can turn to for advice and aid as well, if you are a member. Some of the more useful ones are:

- the Consumers Association (Consumentenbond): this association offers advice on consumer issues, such as the renting or buying of products and/or services. Though they do not offer legal-procedural aid, they can mediate in conflicts with manufacturers or those who provide services.
- ANWB: members of the ANWB are given free legal advice on issues regarding transportation, recreation and tourism. You do not have to be a member if you call in for legal advice following a traffic accident. The ANWB offers its members full legal aid in the case of accidents abroad.
- Vereniging Eigen Huis (Homeowners' Association): Vereniging Eigen Huis offers its members advice on issues involving home ownership, such as financing, building and legal matters.
- If you have taken out legal aid insurance, the organizations that provide the insurance often also offer legal aid.

MAJOR BANKS

ABN AMRO BANK
www.abnamro.nl or www.abnamro.com (international)

ASN BANK – www.asnbank.nl

ING BANK
www.ing.nl or www.ing.com (international)

RABO BANK
www.rabobank.nl or www.rabobank.com (international)

SNS BANK – www.sns.nl

TRIODOS BANK – www.triodos.nl

TAXES

BELASTINGDIENST
National Tax Office
Central website: www.belastingdienst.nl
National Tax Information, tel.: 0800 05 43

INTERNATIONAL TAX OFFICE HEERLEN
Postal address: P.O. Box 2865, 6401 DJ Heerlen
Visiting address: Kloosterweg 22,
6412 CN Heerlen (by appointment only)
Tel.: 0800 05 43 (National telephone number)

MINISTERIE VAN FINANCIEN
Ministry of Finance
Korte Voorhout 7, The Hague
P.O. Box 20201, 2500 EE The Hague
Tel.: 070 342 80 00
www.government.nl/ministries/fin

DOUANE
Tax and Customs Administration
Steenvoordelaan 370, 2284 EH Rijswijk
P.O. Box 3080, 2280 GB Rijswijk
Tel.: 070 372 49 05
www.belastingdienst.nl

PAYROLL SERVICE

Dutch Umbrella Company (a WePayPeople company)
Donauweg 10, 1043 AJ Amsterdam
Tel.: 020 820 15 60
www.dutch-umbrella-company.com

IMMIGRATION/PERMITS

GENERAL
www.immigratiedienst.nl

www.newtoholland.nl: the official website of the Netherlands on immigration

IMMIGRATIE EN NATURALISATIE DIENST, IND
Immigration and Naturalization Service
Various locations: www.ind.nl

MINISTERIE VAN BUITENLANDSE ZAKEN
Ministry of Foreign Affairs
Bezuidenhoutseweg 67, The Hague
P.O. Box 20061, 2500 EB The Hague
Tel.: 070 348 64 86
www.government.nl/ministries/bz

DIGID
Digital Identity
To digitally authenticate the identity of a person who applies for a transaction service via www.digid.nl/english

UWV
Tel.: 079 750 29 03
www.uwv.nl

PERMITS FOUNDATION
An international corporate initiative aimed at promoting the improvement of work permit regulations for the spouses of expatriate employees.
www.permitsfoundation.com

WORK PERMITS
www.workpermit.com/netherlands

EXPAT FOUNDATION
An independent interest organization for expatriates and their Dutch based employers.
www.expatfoundation.org

LEGAL

MINISTERIE VAN VEILIGHEID EN JUSTITIE
Ministry of Security and Justice
Schedeldoekshaven 100, 2511 EX The Hague
P.O. Box 20301, 2500 EH The Hague
Tel.: 070 370 79 11
www.government.nl/ministries/venj

INSTITUTE FOR INTERNATIONAL PRIVATE AND PUBLIC INTERNATIONAL LAW
T.M.C. Asser Instituut
R.J. Schimmelpennincklaan 20-22,
2517 JN The Hague
P.O. Box 30461, 2500 GL The Hague
Tel.: 070 342 03 00
www.asser.nl

KONINKLIJKE NOTARIËLE BEROEPSORGANISATIE, KNB
Royal Dutch Notaries
Spui 184, 2511 BW The Hague
Tel.: 070 330 71 11
www.notaris.nl

RECHTSHULP NEDERLAND
Legal Aid Netherlands
www.rechtshulpnederland.nl

DE NOTARISTELEFOON
The Notary Helpline
Tel.: 0900 346 93 93 (0.80 € per minute)
www.notaris.nl

NEDERLANDSE ORDE VAN ADVOCATEN
Netherlands Bar Association
Neuhuyskade 94, 2596 XM The Hague
P.O. Box 30 851, 2500 GW The Hague
Tel.: 070 335 35 35
www.advocatenorde.nl

VERENIGING VAN PERSONEN- EN FAMILIERECHT ADVOCATEN
Association of Family Lawyers
P.O. Box 65707, 2506 EA The Hague
Tel.: 070 427 12 63
www.vpfa.nl

DE NATIONALE OMBUDSMAN
National Ombudsman
An independent institution that investigates citizens' complaints about improper conduct on the part of government and police authorities and officers
P.O. Box 93122, 2509 AC The Hague
Bezuidenhoutseweg 151, 2594 AG The Hague
Tel.: 0800 335 55 55 (toll free)
www.nationaleombudsman.nl

CONSUMENTENBOND
Consumers Association
www.consumentenbond.nl

RAAD VOOR DE KINDERBESCHERMING
Child Care and Protection Board
www.kinderbescherming.nl

NEDERLANDS MEDIATION INSTITUUT
www.gecertificeerdemediators.nl
and specifically for divorce mediation:
www.vas-scheidingsbemiddeling.nl

THE ROYAL DUTCH TOURING CLUB (ANWB)
Wassenaarseweg 220, 2596 EC The Hague
General tel. no for members: 088 269 22 22
Legal Assistance, tel.: 088 269 72 05
Specially for victims of traffic accidents,
tel.: 088 269 77 66 (also for non-members)
www.anwb.nl

EMBASSIES BY COUNTRY

AUSTRALIA
Carnegielaan 4, 2517 KH The Hague
Tel.: 070 310 82 00
www.australian-embassy.nl

BELGIUM
Alexanderveld 97, 2585 DB The Hague
Tel.: 070 312 34 56
www.diplobel.org

BRAZIL
Mauritskade 19, 2514 HD The Hague
Tel.: 070 302 39 59
www.brazilianembassy.nl

CANADA
Sophialaan 7, 2514 JP The Hague
Tel.: 070 311 16 00
www.canada.nl

CHINA
Willem Lodewijklaan 10, 2517 JT The Hague
Tel.: 070 306 50 61
www.chinaembassy.nl

DENMARK
Koninginnegracht 30, 2514 AB The Hague
Tel.: 070 302 59 59
www.danishembassy.nl

FINLAND
Groot Hertoginnelaan 16, 2517 EG The Hague
Tel.: 070 346 97 54
www.finlande.nl

FRANCE
Smidsplein 1, 2514 BT The Hague
Tel.: 070 312 58 00
www.ambafrance.nl

GERMANY
Groot Hertoginnelaan 18, 2517 EG The Hague
Tel.: 070 342 06 00
www.duitse-ambassade.nl

GHANA
Laan Copus van Cattenburch 70,
2585 GD The Hague
Tel.: 070 338 43 84
www.ghanaembassy.nl

GREECE
Amaliastraat 1, 2514 JC The Hague
Tel.: 070 363 87 00
www.greekembassy.nl

INDIA
Buitenrustweg 2, 2517 KD The Hague
Tel.: 070 346 97 71
www.indianembassy.nl

INDONESIA
Tobias Asserlaan 8, 2517 KC The Hague
Tel.: 070 310 81 00 – www.indonesia.nl

IRELAND
Dr. Kuyperstraat 9, 2514 BA The Hague
Tel.: 070 363 09 93 – www.irishembassy.nl

ISRAEL
Buitenhof 47, 2513 AH The Hague
Tel.: 070 376 05 00 – www.israel.nl

ITALY
Alexanderstraat 12, 2514 JL The Hague
Tel.: 070 302 10 30 – www.italy.nl

JAPAN
Tobias Asserlaan 2, 2517 KC The Hague
Tel.: 070 346 95 44 – www.nl.emb-japan.go.jp

NEW ZEALAND
Eisenhowerlaan 77, 2517 KK The Hague
Tel.: 070 346 93 24 – www.mft.govt.nz

NORWAY
Lange Vijverberg 11, 2513 AC The Hague
Tel.: 070 311 76 11
www.noorwegen.nl

PAKISTAN
Amaliastraat 8, 2517 JC The Hague
Tel.: 070 364 89 48
www.embassyofpakistan.com

PORTUGAL
Zeestraat 74, 2518 AD The Hague
Tel.: 070 328 12 39
www.portugalglobal.pt

RUSSIAN FEDERATION
A. Bickerweg 2, 2517 JP The Hague
Tel.: 070 345 13 00
www.netherlands.mid.ru

SAUDI ARABIA
Alexanderstraat 19, 2514 JM The Hague
Tel.: 070 361 43 91
www.saudiembassy.nl

SOUTH AFRICA
Wassenaarseweg 40, 2596 CJ The Hague
Tel.: 070 392 45 01
www.zuidafrika.nl

SPAIN
Lange Voorhout 50, 2514 EG The Hague
Tel.: 070 302 49 99
www.exteriores.gob.es

TURKEY
Jan Evertsenstraat 15, 2514 BS The Hague
Tel.: 070 360 49 12
www.turkishembassy.nl

SWEDEN
Burg. van Karnebeeklaan 6a, 2585 DB The Hague
Tel.: 070 412 02 00
www.swedenabroad.com/thehague

UNITED KINGDOM
Lange Voorhout 10, 2514 ED The Hague
Tel.: 070 427 04 27
www.gov.uk/government/world/organisa-
tions/british-embassy-the-hague

UNITED STATES OF AMERICA
Lange Voorhout 102, 2514 EJ The Hague
Tel.: 070 310 22 09
http://thehague.usembassy.gov

**FOR A COMPLETE LIST OF EMBASSIES AND
CONSULATES**
www.government.nl/issues/embassies-
consulates-and-other-representations

CHAPTER 6

Getting around in the Netherlands is quite simple, the road networks are good and the public transportation system, which includes several airports, is excellent. All you need to know is how the system works. This chapter goes into the public transportation system, how to get a Dutch driver's license, the system of vehicle approval, the idiosyncrasies of Dutch drivers, whether or not you should buy a car here, the fact that you have to pay road tax, the Dutch automobile association, cycling and walking through the country, and last but definitely not least, the Dutch airports.

CONTRIBUTING AUTHORS DANIËL VAN APELDOORN, STEPHANIE DIJKSTRA AND JACOB VOSSESTEIN

THE SPIDER IN THE INTERNATIONAL WEB

In many ways, the Netherlands is like the spider in the web of Europe. Rotterdam, the largest seaport in the world, is the place where millions of goods enter and leave Europe; the International Court of Justice is in The Hague; Amsterdam is one of the diamond capitals of the world; there are excellent international universities in the various cities of the Netherlands; world-renowned museums can be found here; unique exhibitions are arranged on a regular basis; and cultural events lure tens of thousands visitors to the country every year. Several multinational companies have their offices in the Netherlands, and a lot of international business is negotiated in this little country, facilitated by the fact that almost everyone here speaks at least one other language – in most cases English. In short, millions of people enter and travel around the country, either on business, on vacation or to set up home here.

All this requires a lot of traveling and could not be achieved without an excellent infrastructure: Schiphol is the fourth largest airport on the European mainland, the Thalys-train takes you from Amsterdam to Paris in a mere four hours, the Betuwe train-line – set up to transport goods to the east (particularly Germany) – opened in June 2007, the public transportation system, including not only trains, but buses, trams and metros, offers an extensive and detailed network, there are several regional airports that also offer international connections, and the roads promise a comfortable cruise to your destination...

AIR TRAVEL

SCHIPHOL

As mentioned earlier, Schiphol is the third largest airport in Europe, through which approximately 65 million passengers and approximately 1.65 million tons of freight pass per year. Aside from its logistic uses, it is also a prime business location, with a World Trade Center, a number of hotels, recreational activities, over 560 companies that employ almost 60,000 people, and, of course, its booming duty-free shopping business. (Though there is no longer such a thing as duty-free shopping in Europe, it still applies to passengers shopping at Schiphol Airport, regardless of their destination, with the restriction that tax-free shopping is not possible for alcohol and tobacco if you are traveling to a destination within the EU, unless you subsequently leave the EU within 24 hours.)

SECURITY

Those who are departing from Amsterdam are advised to arrive three hours in advance in connection with the added security measures after September 11, 2001.

TRAVELING BY TRAIN FROM SCHIPHOL

Amsterdam is 15 minutes away; Rotterdam and Utrecht 45 minutes; Brussels two hours; Cologne and Paris three. The train station is located right underneath the Arrivals Hall, allowing you to catch the various Intercity and high speed-lines to these, and countless more, destinations.

REGIONAL AIRPORTS

The Netherlands boasts many regional airports, such as Eindhoven, Groningen, Maastricht, Rotterdam, Enschede and Lelystad, which offer both direct flights abroad, as well as flights to Schiphol airport. The advantages of making use of one of these airports are not hard to think of: often they are closer to your home or office; they are easily accessible by car, taxi or bus; parking is cheap; the walking distances are short; check-in times are brief; and there are special services for business travelers. If you use them as a start-out point from which to go to Schiphol, there are additional advantages: check-in time is considerably less time-consuming at the regional airports and most often you do not have to go through this procedure again at Schiphol, greatly reducing your total check-in and transfer times, as your luggage is automatically labeled onward. Often there are special through-connection fares for those who wish to make use of this option.

TRAIN TRAVEL

The Netherlands has a dense railway network that offers frequent service, as well as the quickest way to travel between city centers. The carriages are modern and clean and, although many Dutch people complain about delays, the trains usually run on time. (Everything is relative!)

HIGH-SPEED TRAVEL

As mentioned above, you can travel by high-speed train (the Thalys or the TGV) from Amsterdam, Schiphol or Rotterdam to Belgium and – final destination – Paris. If you are going to Germany or Switzerland, you can take the high-speed ICE train, and if you are going to London, there is the Eurostar. These high-speed trains are really only a worthwhile option if you intend to travel all the way to these far-away destinations as, within the Netherlands, they still travel at regular speeds through the densely populated areas. Only once they reach France, do they pick up speed. In other words, don't count on cutting time by taking the high-speed train from Amsterdam to Rotterdam.

Note, however, that you may only travel on a high-speed train if you have bought a special (more expensive) ticket for this train and have made a reservation. If you inadvertently board the Thalys in Amsterdam to go visit you friend in Rotterdam and you are caught, you could find yourself paying a hefty fine!

OPTIONS

On the train you have a choice of first or second class, which is indicated with a large 1 or 2 painted on the outside. First class costs about 50% more and gives you a slightly larger seat in a compartment that is less likely to be full. Though smoking and no-smoking compartments are indicated, this is no longer of relevance as, as you can read further on, you are no longer allowed to smoke on the trains.

TICKETS

Regular train travel is either one-way (*enkele reis*) or return (*retour*). You cannot buy 'paper' tickets anymore, instead you purchase either an *OV-chipkaart* (Public Transportation Card) or a one-time *chipkaart*, which you can buy at a ticket window or at a yellow ticket machine, which you will find either in the main hall of the station or on the platform. The ticket machine – which, at many stations, is starting to replace ticket windows altogether – takes either cash, or a bank card. You can read more about the *(ov-)chipkaart* further on.

Note: even though you now use the same pass to travel by train, bus and tram (metro), you need to check out of each one before you get on another one! Largely, this does not apply if you switch trains, but it does apply if you go from traveling by train to say, traveling by bus. When does it apply when traveling by train? When you switch companies: to a regional train company, such as Arriva or Connexxion.

PASSES

There are a wide variety of passes and special tickets that can save you money. Which type you choose depends on the kind of traveling you will be doing – frequent or infrequent, long distances or short, alone or in a group, during rush hour or not, and your age. The clerks at the ticket windows can advise you and will be especially helpful if you choose a time of day when they are not busy. Also one-day *OV-chipkaarten* are available, which can be used for traveling by bus, tram, metro or train.

If you wish to look into your options online, visit www.ov-chip-kaart.nl and click on *English* to enter the English-language section. By clicking on the various card types, you can read more about them and find out which one will best suit your needs. The Netherlands has a general public transportation card, called the *ov-chipkaart*, which can be used on trains, trams, and buses, as well as to arrange – see later on – a public transportation bicycle. For more on how the card works, see *The Public Transportation Card*, on page 138.

Students are issued a public transportation pass for traveling at a reduced price, called the *Studenten ov-chipkaart*. You can choose whether you want to travel for free between Monday morning 4 A.M. and Saturday morning 4 A.M. (and at a reduced price during the weekends, on holidays and during summer break) or for free between noon Fridays and Monday 4 A.M., as well as holidays and summer break, and at a reduced price on weekdays. This choice is marked on the *chipkaart* and is referred to as the *studentenreisproduct*.

INSPECTORS

You will often travel on the train without anyone ever looking at your *ov-chipkaart*. If the conductor catches you without one, however, you will be fined. In the larger cities, the railway is trying to reduce the number of people who hang around at the stations without any particular purpose. For this reason you might be asked to show your public transportation pass on the platform. In fact, it is increasingly becoming impossible to make it inside and to the platform without swiping your card first.

TIMETABLES AND INFORMATION

You can buy the complete railway timetable at the station and at most magazine/bookstores. A much abbreviated version that lists only the major so-called Intercity trains is also available. However, most likely you will simply check your connections online, by visiting www.ns.nl. This site offers more than just train schedules, it also includes information on how to get to and from the station, in Dutch and in English. Another option is to download the app: 9292.

You can also call the general number for information on public transportation: 0900 9292, or visit www.goabout.com for travel advice that includes bus, tram and metro lines.

As of July 9 of 2014, train travelers will no longer be able to use 'paper tickets'; only their personal or anonymous ov chip cards that are valid for as long as the money on them stretches (they are both rechargeable). An exception applies to tourists and incidental train travelers: they can purchase a one-time ov chip card, though they will have to pay the full rate plus an additional 1 euro. The cards can be bought at an NS Service Window (at a train station, tobacco or magazine store or supermarket, as well as in the tram or bus).

SMOKING

You are not allowed to smoke on trains – not even on the balconies. This ban also applies to all areas you might be in while waiting for, or walking to, your train; halls, stairs, flyovers, elevators and covered platforms – though restaurants and cafeterias will continue to have 'smoking/non smoking' areas. Despite this general rule, covered platforms have a designated smokers' area, indicated by a pillar with an ashtray, a 'smoking' sign and the words *rookzone* – and you are still allowed to smoke on open-air platforms, just not in their closed waiting areas.

Only on international trains, as the situation differs per country, will the division 'smokers' vs. 'non-smokers' be maintained, with the exception of trains with a Benelux destination.

ONCE YOU GET THERE

Once you arrive at your destination, you have a few options for how to get where you are going. These you find in the following paragraphs.

TAXI SERVICES

Say you want to visit your long-lost cousin in the remote, but picturesque village of Cothen. You find out that you can take a train to Zeist – which you courageously do – but what do you do once you get there? Cothen would constitute a brisk, say, two-hour walk from there. Or perhaps you've agreed to meet your friends in Amsterdam, and need to get from Central Station to the Rijksmuseum within half an hour?

TAXIS

You cannot hail taxis on the street in the Netherlands like you can in many parts of the world. You must either request one by phone, or go to a taxi-stand where taxis wait. All major railway stations have a taxi-stand. Hotels and restaurants are always happy to call a taxi for you if you ask.

The regular Dutch taxis use meters and charge roughly the same rates. When you start, the meter will already show a balance of several euros. This ensures the driver a minimum fare. Only for very long distances is it sometimes possible to negotiate a fare in advance. Otherwise you pay what the meter indicates. It is customary to give taxi drivers a tip, which usually means increasing the amount up to a round figure.

SHARE TAXIS

At many train stations, there are special taxi services, offered at a reduced rate as, in most cases, you share these taxis with other passengers. Below, we have included a list of these taxis – which one you will end up using, depends on where you will be requiring its services; the province of North Holland, or Gelderland, or South Holland, or one of the major cities. You can also visit www.ns.nl, click on *English*, and then on *Door to door*, under *Our products*.

These taxis are available at almost all train stations in the Netherlands, but not in the biggest cities. As they are useful mostly for reaching the smaller towns, the idea is that you take a train to a location close to your place of destination and arrange to have a share taxi pick you up there. Share taxi numbers and sites for information depend on where you will be traveling; there is no central

- There are about 22.5 million bicycles in Holland, making that more than one for every inhabitant
- About 1.1 million new bicycles are sold every year
- The Dutch cycle approximately 1,000 kilometers per year, per person
- The percentage of bicycle owners is the highest among those with the highest income
- There are 2,655 bicycle shops in Holland
- There are 35,000 kilometers of bicycle paths and lanes, and 116,500 kilometers of paved roads (including 2,235 kilometers of expressways)
- There are approximately 8 million registered cars in the Netherlands
- The Netherlands has one of the lowest car density percentages in the whole of the EU: 44.4%
- In the provinces of Drenthe and Noord-Brabant there are relatively more cars, due to the fact that distances are greater and public transportation is not quite as omnipresent
- Conversely, the number of cars in the bigger cities is relatively low
- Almost 15% of the Dutch households have two or more cars, while fewer than one family in ten does not have a car
- Holland is the fourth safest country to drive in. Only the U.K., Sweden and Norway have lower numbers of fatalities
- There are 5,046 kilometers of waterways navigable for ships of 50 tons
- There are approximately 162,000 recreational boats in the Dutch harbors / water sports companies
- In Drenthe, there are 1,000 recreational boats, in the provinces of North Holland and South Holland, there are 32,000 each
- There are 2,808 kilometers of standard gauge railways
- On average, the Dutch travel a little over 30 kilometers a day: 22.5 by car (either as a driver or a passenger), 3 by train and 2.5 by bike
- 8.6 of these kilometers are work-related, 6 are for social purposes (visiting other people's homes), and 5.5 for sports, hobbies or going out.

TIP If a stranger offers to sell you a bicycle for less than € 40, don't buy it. It's probably stolen, and you too are violating the law if you take possession of it.

telephone number or site for this service. If you call 0900 9292, they can tell you which number to call for travel within your region or put your call through to the available taxi services in your area.

- Zone taxis: You can step into an NS Zone Taxi simply by showing your public transportation card *(ov-chipkaart)*. You pay based on the number of zones you travel through; for trips up to two kilometers, you pay € 6; for trips up to four kilometers, you pay € 9; and for trips up to six kilometers, you pay € 12. Longer trips (maximum 30 kilometers) will cost you € 3 per two kilometers. Reservations are made online or by telephone (0900 679 82 94), using your *ov-chipkaart*-number (mijn.nszonetaxi.nl), and the taxi will be ready at the station, or pick you up where you are and take you to the station. You can also use the Reisplanner Xtra app to book a Zone Taxi. The price for the trip is automatically deducted from your account.
- Train taxi: perhaps you have heard of the train taxi. In case you're wondering why you can't find one: they no longer exist.
- Share taxi: though all these types of taxis are share taxis, there is also simply the share taxi that goes by the name *deeltaxi*.
- Regio taxi: This is a cross between public transportation and taxi services that take you from door to door. Special taxi services are available for persons with physical disabilities.

SCHIPHOL AIRPORT TAXI

And last, but not least, there are several Schiphol taxi services to take you to and from all Dutch airports, saving you the hassle of arranging long-term parking, dragging your luggage to the connecting bus and worrying about your car while away. For more information visit www.schiphol.nl/Travellers/ToFromSchiphol/SchipholTravelTaxi.htm, or www.taxi.connexxion.nl.

The Schiphol Hotel Shuttle will take you to more than 100 hotels in Amsterdam. You can buy a ticket at their service desk in Arrivals 4 (across from *Starbucks*) at Schiphol airport; follow the signs to Amsterdam Shuttle Desk. For more information visit www.airporthotelshuttle.nl. In the arrivals hall of Schiphol airport, you will also find the Schiphol Business Taxi. They can be reached by phone at 088 339 47 41.

'CORPORATE' TAXIS

For 'top managers and policy makers', Connexxion offers a variety of services, available 24 / 7, visit http://taxi.connexxion.nl/directievervoer/649.

BUSES AND TRAMS

If you are looking to make your way through the larger cities, or from one town to the next, the Dutch transportation companies provide frequent services on buses and trams. Amsterdam and Rotterdam also have a subway (called the metro). Rural communities are linked by bus.

BUS SERVICES

There are two types of buses; city buses and regional buses. Depending on the area they operate in, they go by different names. City buses operate within towns and cities and stop frequently. Regional buses take you from town to town and cover considerable distances between stops once they have left a town.

FIGURING IT OUT

Visit www.connexxion.nl to find out which lines operate in your region and to plan your trip. Unfortunately, as of 2012, the English-language pages of the site appear to have been discontinued. However, on the home page, you will find *Waar wil je heen?* (Where do you want to go?) *Plan uw reis* (Plan your trip), where you can fill in where you are leaving from under *van*, where you are going to under *naar*, followed by the date and the time. Or, visit www.goabout.com. You can also download the public transportation schedule of your area (*Zoek dienstregeling*), or download the app: CXX. In the larger cities, the local transportation companies have their own office window at the railway stations where they sell the schedule. Otherwise try either the VVV tourist office or the municipal offices (*gemeentehuis, stadhuis* or *stadskantoor*).

In the larger cities, you will find a map of the city – dotted and lined with the bus, tram and subway (metro) lines – at many of the tramstops, allowing you to figure out just where you can go and how to get there. Or you can download the 9292-app.

THE PUBLIC TRANSPORTATION CARD – *OV-CHIPKAART*

There two types of public transportation card, or *ov-chipkaart*: the personal *ov-chipkaart* and the so-called anonymous *ov-chipkaart*. The personal *ov-chipkaart* is a plastic credit-card shaped public transportation card with your photograph that contains information on the amount of credit it still has on it, on whether you have a right to certain reductions, and on whether you are traveling on the basis of a public transportation 'subscription', or pass. You can find travel discount products on www.ov-chipkaart; click on *English, Reloading*, and *Subscriptions and Travel Products*.

When entering the tram, bus or metro, you hold the card against the card reader. When you leave, you again hold the card against the card reader and it will tell you how much the trip cost and how much credit remains on the card. When traveling by train, you hold the card against the card reader on the platform before entering the train and, upon arrival, before leaving the platform. This way you pay for your travel based on the number of kilometers you travel rather than based on the number of zones you travel through (though the zone system may remain in place in some areas). The 'anonymous' *ov-chipkaart* does not have your photograph and is issued without the option of an automatic 'refill' or the use of subscription or (age-related) reductions. For one-time use, for tourists for instance, there are 'disposable' one-day cards – to be bought from an NS ticket automat or NS service window at the train station – that are only valid on the day of purchase (unless they are traveling to Germany or Belgium). Students are issued a public transportation pass.

More information on the *ov-chipkaart* can be found on www.ov-chipkaart.nl. This site also has English-language information and is where you can order your card (and upload your photograph), as well as arrange travel credit and fix things if you forgot to check out at the end of your trip. Travel credit can also be arranged at, for instance, supermarkets and magazine/bookstores where you will find the yellow automats for transferring money (credit) onto your *ov-chipkaart*, using your bank card. For some or other reason, you cannot buy a train 'ticket' online via this site, however; you *can* buy one via www.ns.nl. You click on *English*, and the on *Single ticket*. Check out the *Amsterdam Travel Ticket* while you're at it.

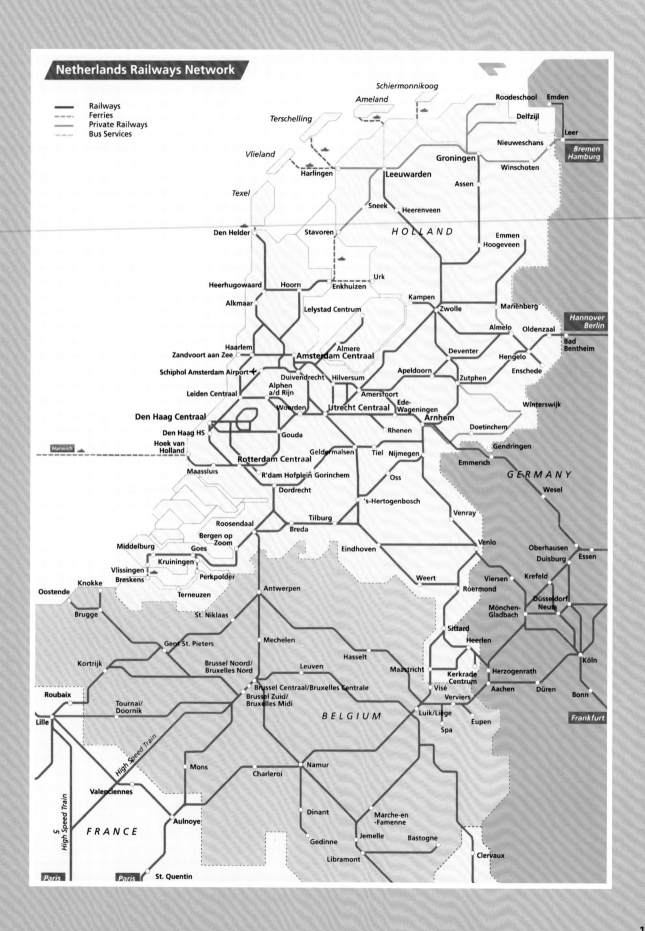

Netherlands Railways Network

— Railways
- - - Ferries
— Private Railways
·-·-· Bus Services

PASSES

If you will be using the buses and trams four days a week or more, it might be more economical for you to buy a monthly pass. To arrange a pass, visit a Connexxion booth at the bus stations outside the train stations.

Again, students are issued a public transportation pass, called the *Studenten ov-chipkaart*. As a student, you can choose whether you want to travel for free between Monday morning 4 A.M. and Saturday morning 4 A.M. (and at a reduced price during the weekends, on holidays and during summer break) or for free between noon Fridays and Monday 4 A.M., as well as holidays and summer break, and at a reduced price on weekdays.

INSPECTORS

Though you have been given the responsibility of swiping the *ov-chipkaart* yourself – and might find that you can generally elude inspection – sooner or later, a team of inspectors will suddenly appear in the bus or tram, and if you are caught traveling without a swiped *ov-chipkaart*, you will be fined.

GREENWHEELS SHARE CAR

On 1,700-plus locations – including 90 train stations – in the Netherlands, including Amsterdam, The Hague, Rotterdam and Utrecht, you can find Greenwheels Share (rental) cars. Both individual and shared subscriptions are possible, provided all (maximum three) drivers are at least 24 years of age. Gas is included in the rent and you pay a security of € 225. There are three types of subscriptions; you can find them on the site, as well as information on what type of driver's license you need to drive a Greenwheels Share Car. NS travelers enjoy a discount.

If you 'subscribe' to a Greenwheels car, this car is parked on a fixed location and is available 24 / 7, though you must not forget to reserve it in advance – something you can do just a few minutes before picking it up, provided the car is available, of course – by visiting their site, using the app or calling their telephone number. When you arrange your subscription, you are issued a personal 'chip' card with which you open the car. You can also open the car using your cell phone. After entering your pin code on the on-board computer, you can drive away. You can also use a Greenwheels tank card to fill your fuel tank. Greenwheels pays the bill and charges you for the actual amount of kilometers you've driven. Once you return, you log out and the computer automatically registers the time and the kilometers. Every month, you receive an overview of your use. The amount due is deducted from your bank account a few days later. Visit www.greenwheels.nl for more

information, for instance to see on which non-Dutch driver's licenses you may drive one of their cars.

Greenwheels cars can also be used by companies who want to make them available to employees. For instance, employees who come to work by public transportation or bicycle, but need a car every now and then to visit a client or attend a meeting at another office.

PUBLIC TRANSPORTATION BICYCLE

One final way to get to your destination once you have arrived somewhere by train is by Public Transportation Bicycle (*ov-fiets*). To rent one of these, you pay € 3.35, allowing you to use the bicycle 24 hours. If you keep the bicycle 72 hours, you pay 3 x € 3.35, after that you start paying € 5 per 24 hours. You can also rent a scooter, paying € 7.50 a day. You can request a public transportation bicycle pass (*ov-fietspas*) or have your public transportation pass (also the *Studenten ov-chipkaart* student pass qualifies) registered, either of which you can then use to pick up a bike. Payments are done after the fact (there is an annual subscription fee of € 10), by means of an automatic payment (*automatische incasso*). Bicycles are available on more than 275 locations throughout the country (approximately 100 towns/cities), including various locations within the bigger cities of Amsterdam, The Hague and Rotterdam. For more information, visit www.ov-fiets.nl.

More than 150 train stations also offer the possibility of renting a bicycle, on a non-public transportation basis; the costs for this are between € 7.50 and € 15 a day, plus a security deposit of € 50. More information can be found on www.nederlandfietsland.nl.

WATER TRANSPORTATION

If there is one thing that we have in abundance in the Netherlands, it's water. So it would be only logical to expect a public water transportation net – which there is. There is the ferry service between Hoek van Holland and the Maasvlakte; a waterbus in the Dordrecht / Rotterdam area (www.waterbus.nl); and a watertaxi / maastaxi in Rotterdam. The former two are very convenient for commuters while the water and maastaxi in Rotterdam offer a much-needed connection between the two city shores.

There are also plenty of non-public transportation and very picturesque (and cheap) ferries across the many rivers and canals of the Netherlands. Sometimes it could be well worth your while (it could save you time as well as stress!) to get off the highway, out of the traffic jam and take an inland road to a ferry across the river.

DRIVING YOUR CAR

Remember the bumper sticker: 'If you don't like my driving, get off of the sidewalk'? Well, sometimes partaking of the road system here feels that way too. All of a sudden, you are supposed to know that any car *coming from the right* has the right of way, unless specifically indicated otherwise. This means not only developing rightview paranoia, but also rearview paranoia; if you do not take your right of way, you are almost sure to incur the wrath (if not the

INFORMATION NUMBER

For information about public transportation anywhere in the country you can telephone 0900 9292. You will first get a recorded message in Dutch, but if you wait, a live person will come on the line who can also speak English, French or German. You can also download the app; 9292.

Else, you can visit www.ns.nl or www.nshispeed.nl, which also have an English-language section (just click on *English*), to plan your trip.

The number for information on international buses and trains is 0900 9296.

AMSTERDAMSE VEREN

The Amsterdamse veren offers six ferry services across the IJ. Three leave from the De Ruijterkade behind Amsterdam Central Station, one leaves from a little further east – traveling back and forth from Azartplein – and two from a little further west – back and forth from the Houthaven. All six are free of charge for pedestrians, cyclists, mopeds, scooters and vehicles for disabled persons. It's also a great idea for those who want to 'cruise' the IJ for free; you can get on and off wherever you want, and spend a wonderful 30 minutes on the water.

front bumper) of the car behind you. It is also important to know that the window of opportunity for taking your right of way is about a second-and-a-half, after which you might as well settle for letting the other car go first – in other words, there is lots of potential for upsetting at least one other person!

Also, slowing down to see if this is the street you want to enter – or parking space you wish to take – is almost certain to guarantee an irritated passing by (either left or right, depending on where there is more space) so that it is best to check before making your definite turn. Since we're on the subject of checking, be sure, before making any turn, that there are no bicycles going straight ahead as they have the right of way over you (even if you 'are' the car).

Other, guaranteed, sources of irritation to Dutch drivers are: lingering in the left-hand lane on the highway if you are only planning on exceeding the speed limit by a mere 10 kilometers, taking more than two seconds to get your car rolling once the light turns green – and driving an obviously very expensive car (but that is a whole other issue).

Having said all these deliciously unkind things about the Dutch drivers, fairness requires us to point out that the Netherlands is statistically one of the safest countries in the world to drive in.

MOTORCYCLE

Everything written in the following paragraphs also applies to having a motorcycle. Only, the rules on exchanging a license might vary on certain points; for more information, contact the RDW (see further on).

OWNING A CAR

Once you plan on owning a car, keep the following in mind. You must:

- have a valid driver's license (see *Driver's License*)
- know the rules of the road (you will find a few further on)
- arrange a periodic check-up of the car (Vehicle Approval – APK, see further on)
- have the registration certificate of the car transferred to your name (see the next paragraph)
- take out car and liability insurance (more on insurances in chapter 5)
- pay road tax (see *Road Tax*).

THE VEHICLE REGISTRATION CERTIFICATE / CARD

Previously, when you owned a car, three important documents came with it, called *deel IA*, *deel IB* and *deel II* (parts IA, IB and II) – which, together, constituted the *kentekenbewijs* (vehicle registration certificate). *Deel IA* contained all the technical information on your car, such as brand, type and number and was called the *voertuigbewijs*. *Deel IB* contained the name and address of the owner of the car and was your proof of ownership / registration. It was called the *tenaamstellingsbewijs*. Whoever was driving the car had to carry *deel IA* and *IB* with him at all times. You could not buy a car from someone who cannot produce this document and you could not sell your car without it. *Deel II* was the proof of transfer, or *overschrijvingsbewijs*. Ownership was transferred, making use of this document, at the post office (or a store offering post office services). In vehicle registration certificates issued before June 1, 2004, these documents were called *deel I*, *II* and *III* (corresponding to *deel IA*, *IB* and *II*, respectively).

As of 2015, the RDW no longer issues paper registration certificates – only credit-card sized registration cards (*kentekencard*). These have a chip and have replaced parts IA and IB of the certificate. Part II, the proof of transfer, has been replaced by a code. This code consists of nine numbers; you receive the first part of this code when you transfer ownership of the car, you receive the second part with the registration card. Added together, these form the code which can be used when selling, exporting, suspending or otherwise disposing of the car. If you want, you can exchange your certificate for this new card. In any case, any car you buy – whether it be new or 15 years old – will come with this new *kentekencard*.

IMPORTING A CAR

In the following paragraphs you can read about the steps you must take to obtain a registration certificate for your car.

VEHICLE TAX – BPM

BPM is a vehicle tax that is due by the first person to register a car or motorcycle in his name in the Netherlands. If you buy a car in the Netherlands, the official car importer takes care of it (the tax is included in the price). If you bring your car/motorcycle in from abroad, convert a non-passenger car into a passenger car, or drive a car/motorcycle with foreign license plates in the Netherlands, then you have to take care of it yourself. See the following paragraphs.

The amount of BPM you owe, depends on the CO_2 emission of your car. This is determined by the RDW. They issue you a form stating your car's CO_2 emission, which is based on the European Type Approval of your car. In the absence of such a a form, a fixed emission rate is determined based on the type of fuel you use. If you want, you can have an individual test carried out on your car, to determine its particular emission rate.

APPROVAL RDW

To register your car for the BPM, you must have your car approved by the RDW (see page 149). To this purpose, you visit an RDW-vehicle approval center (call 0900 0739 to find the one nearest you), bringing:

- the vehicle
- proof of identity (passport, ID card or Dutch driver's license)
- foreign vehicle registration certificate
- the Individual Approval Certificate (APK-rapport), European Type Approval, or Certificate of Conformity.

In principle, a vehicle that was registered in an EU-country, Andorra, Monaco, San Marino, Vatican City, Switzerland, Norway, Liechtenstein or Iceland, or that forms part of your moving inventory will be allowed into the country, provided it meets the APK-requirements (see page 149). When importing a car from an EU/EEA country, you make an (online) appointment with the RDW to have the car approved – though you can also go without making an appointment. If you want it to undergo an APK-test (the general technical test), you can have the RDW carry this out simultaneously. If you already have a foreign APK, this can be adopted. On the day of your appointment, you bring the items listed above. The RDW will then determine whether the car can be registered. A Certificate of Conformity (*Certificaat van Overeenstemming*), lists all specifics related to the car and you can request it from the manufacturer of the car or their representative in the Netherlands.

If you import a car from outside above countries, you cannot have the approval carried out at an RDW approval center; you will

The new E-Class.
Masterpiece of Intelligence.

Traffic and Safety

For years, measures implemented by the authorities succeeded in structurally reducing the number of fatal accidents, which were reduced from 1,088 in 2003 to 570 in 2014 (data for 2015 as yet not published). It appears that these are largely caused by cyclists as well as senior citizens riding 'scootmobiles' and electric wheelchairs. There were fewer deaths among younger people. The Ministry points a finger at the municipal roads as it has observed that the greatest number of victims are to be found within the country's city limits. The VVN (Veilig Verkeer Nederland, or organization for Safe Traffic in the Netherlands) organizes annual theory lessons and practical exams for children in the last two years of elementary school (either fifth grade or sixth grade), as a consequence of which children the age of 11 are already familiarized with important rules regarding the right of way (for buses, pedestrians, horses, cyclists, etc.), traffic signs, using a cell phone while cycling, and being sure they are seen in traffic.

MOST FREQUENTLY ASKED QUESTIONS FOR THE 3VO: WHAT IS THE PERMITTED BLOOD ALCOHOL LEVEL?

The law says 0.5 promille is the limit for all drivers (except for those who have just acquired their license, see further on). This does not translate into a fixed number of glasses of a particular type of alcohol – it depends on weight, age, sex, stomach content, etc. During the first five years after obtaining your driver's license, the permitted blood alcohol level is 0.2 promille. The limit is not only for the drivers of cars, but also of (motor)cycles and mopeds! The limit of 0.2 promille applies to moped and motorized bicycle riders until the age of 24.

On the water, the permitted blood alcohol level is 0.5.

Twelve years ago, the BOB-campaign was introduced, aimed at encouraging partiers to always select one person who will not drink and who will do the driving. This campaign has proven successful: over the course of ten years, the number of drunk drivers has been reduced by almost half.

MAY I USE A MOBILE PHONE IN THE CAR?

Not while driving. It is permitted if you are standing still in a traffic jam or at a red light. See page 148. The same applies to moped riders.

SHOULD MY CHILD USE A BICYCLE HELMET?

Though they are not obligatory, there is no doubt that they can help avoid serious head injury, if worn correctly (which also means using the right size). There are many bicycle riders in the Netherlands and every year, there are 26 fatal accidents involving children; 14,000 children end up in the hospital and 23,000 have to see a doctor due to biking accidents.

WHERE SHOULD MOPEDS/SCOOTERS RIDE?

Mopeds ride in the regular car lanes within city limits, unless there is a blue, round sign with both a bicycle and a moped on it; this sign means that mopeds must ride on the bicycle path. Outside city limits, mopeds must ride on the bicycle paths, unless there isn't one. For further information, we refer you to the road signs and their explanation.

Scooters and motorized bicycles (snorfiets) may make use of bicycle lanes. Helmets are not required for motorized bicycles, but they are for scooters. The drivers must have passed a theoretical traffic exam and must have taken out insurance.

WHAT ABOUT CAR LIGHTS?

During the day, if you cannot see clearly, and after dark, you use regular headlights. In the case of fog, snow or rain, you should use your fog lights front and back. If you are stopped by the police because one of your car lights is not working, you must have reserve bulbs with you so that you can replace the broken one. If you don't have any with you, you will be fined either € 90 or € 140, depending on whether you are outside or within city limits.

For more information, visit:
www.vvn.nl

SPEED LIMIT

Maximum speed limit	End maximum speed limit zone	Maximum speed limit on electronic sign	Advised speed limit	End advised speed limit

CLOSED

Closed in both directions	One way only, no entry	One way

Priority road	End of priority road	Priority intersection	Entry permitted	Limited to vehicles with 2 wheels

Closed to all vehicles	Closed to mopeds	Closed to bicycles

Priority intersection incoming road to the left	Priority intersection incoming road to the right	Give way	Stop!, give way	Traffic circle / roundabout

Signs indicating direction of traffic	

No parking	No stopping

RIGHT OF WAY

DIRECTION

PARKING AND STANDING STILL

PARKING AND STANDING STILL

No bicycles and mopeds parking

Parking

Taxi stand

Immediate loading and unloading of goods

Permit parking only

Parking for carpoolers

City limits

End of city limits

ALLOWED AND NOT ALLOWED

No passing

End no passing zone

Oncoming traffic must get off road. Traffic moving in this direction has right of way

No U-turns

End of all indicated directions

End of all directions given on electronic signals

WARNING

Bad road conditions

Right-hand curve ahead

Left-hand curve ahead

Traffic under restrictions

End of traffic under restrictions zone

RULES OF THE ROAD

Highway

End of highway

Motor vehicles only

End of motor vehicles only zone

Sidewalk

End of sidewalk

S-curve

Dangerous intersection

Traffic circle / roundabout

Guarded railroad crossing

Bicycle path

End of bicycle path

Bicycle / moped path

End of bicycle / moped path

Unguarded railroad crossing

Tram crossing

Road works ahead

Road narrowing ahead

Slippery when wet

Children crossing

Pedestrian crossing

Pedestrians

Bicycles and mopeds

Quay or riverside

Oncoming traffic

Possible wind gusts

Traffic lights

Traffic jam

Bus / tram stop

Rest area, food, fuel

Route indicators (national and European)

Local signs

Signs for bicycles and mopeds

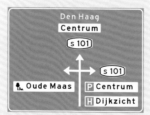
Directions within city limits

District directions within city limits (names)

District directions within city limits (numbers)

Choose lane Number of lanes

Dead end

Countries on whose license you are allowed to drive in the Netherlands for a period of ten years after issuance (or, if it is valid for a shorter period of time, until the expiration date): Austria, Belgium, Bulgaria, Croatia, (the Greek part of) Cyprus, Czech Republic, Denmark, Estonia, Finland, France, Germany, Greece, Hungary, Iceland, Ireland, Italy, Latvia, Liechtenstein, Lithuania, Luxembourg, Malta, Norway, Poland, Portugal, Rumania, Slovakia, Slovenia, Spain, Sweden, Switzerland, and the United Kingdom (including Northern Ireland). On a license issued in any other country, you are allowed to drive during a period of 6 months.

THE ANWB

Almost all Dutch drivers are members of the ANWB, the Royal Dutch Touring Club. As befits this country of cyclists, the ANWB started — more than 125 years ago — as an organization for cyclists. Though they still offer, for instance, recreational maps to cyclists and hikers, they were clever enough to expand their services to include car drivers. Members of the ANWB are offered the following:

ROAD SERVICES — WEGENWACHT
The ANWB Road Services offer members of the ANWB 24-hour breakdown assistance (called Wegenwacht) on the Dutch roads (and for an extra fee: in your driveway), and even European roads. Help usually arrives within 30 minutes, though this of course depends on road, traffic and weather conditions, as well as the number of breakdowns on the route. If the repair service cannot repair your vehicle on the spot, ANWB offers free transportation of your vehicle and the passengers. Furthermore, members who make use of Road Services also have the option of the Car Replacement Service and a replacement driver in case of illness or accident. With this service you are loaned a car if yours cannot be repaired within the hour. It offers three levels of service; the third level includes legal assistance in certain circumstances. Membership fees are cheaper for those younger than 24 and for those whose partner is already a member.

SERVICES WHEN TRAVELING ABROAD
When traveling abroad, ANWB membership (Wegenwacht Europa Service) also offers you certain benefits, such as an internationally recog-

have to go to the RDW test center in Lelystad. In the following instances, however, you can nevertheless go to an RDW approval center. Namely, if the car:
- is part of your household goods
- has had a Dutch license plate in the past
- has European Type Approval
- was manufactured before January 1, 1998 — though it will have to undergo further tests. You can find information about this on the RDW site under Individual Vehicle Approval (*Individuele Goedkeuringen*).

Registration
If the RDW approves your car, it will issue you a form for BPM-registration (*Document voertuiggegevens voor de BPM-aangifte*), which you deposit in a special Tax Office mailbox at an RDW center. Depending in the situation, it will have to be accompanied by a number of additional forms — please be sure to contact the Tax Office to ask which these are. You can also mail it all in to the Tax Office of your district; you can find the addresses on the site of the Tax Office (www.belastingdienst.nl), or by calling them.

The Tax Office / Customs Authorities will determine how much BPM you owe and send you a payment notice. Once you have paid this, the Customs Authorities will send proof of payment to the RDW, after which the RDW will send you your vehicle registration card within five to seven weekdays, and the car will have been registered in your name.

Exceptions
Under certain conditions, you do not owe BPM. The most important one is covered in *Should You Keep Your Car?*, further on. Other exceptions include if you will be here temporarily, or certain conditions subject to which you may continue driving with your foreign license plates. If you export your car, you can, subject to conditions, request a restitution of the BPM you paid for your car. More information can be found on the website of the tax authorities: www. belastingdienst.nl (under *Auto en vervoer*, then BPM.

License Plates and Insurance
You have now successfully imported your car, but first you need to arrange license plates — ask with the RDW where you can have this done. Don't forget to arrange insurance! You will need to arrange minimum (statutory liability) insurance, as well as any other type of voluntary insurance you wish to arrange. For more on this, see page 126.

nized credit card to give you access to cash in the case of an emergency, legal help, car replacement, assistance from foreign road services organizations, and more – such as, for instance, a replacement driver should you fall ill or become injured. Fees vary, according to the level of service, so be sure to check the website.

LEGAL SERVICE
The ANWB legal services department provides its members with advice and information by phone, including mediation should problems arise concerning travel insurance or in case of an accident. If you have a (legal) question – for instance regarding the rental of a vacation home abroad – you can contact the Legal Department of the ANWB via e-mail or by phone, and they will let you know whether and how they can help you. Non-members can contact this ANWB legal information line for a first opinion in the case of personal injury due to an accident.

INSURANCE
You can take out a variety of insurances with the ANWB, such as, among others, travel insurance, cancelation insurance, car, bicycle, motorcycle, house, household content, and boat insurance.

STORES AND PUBLICATIONS
Members of the ANWB are issued membership cards which offer them special discounts on books, maps, guides, and other items sold at the special ANWB stores – including travel pouches, car seats for children and outdoor clothing.

MEMBERSHIP CARD
Showing your ANWB-membership card will also provide you with a discount on fuel prices at more than 600 gas stations across the country, as well as a discount on entrance fees to amusement parks and museums; on hotel and shop prices; and on fees for rental cars.

OTHER TAXES
When importing a car or motorcycle, you owe the customs department import duties and VAT. No VAT is due for a car that that has driven more than 6,000 km, or whose license plates were issued more than six months ago and no customs duties are due over cars bought in the EU. See page 151 on possible exemptions from these taxes and the BPM. And do not forget about Road Tax, on page 152.

BUYING A CAR HERE
If you buy a car, either second-hand or new, in the Netherlands, all that has been described above has been taken care of – all you need to do is have the car's registration card put in your name. To do this, you (and the former owner) go to a store offering post office services. Here they will enter your information into the system, after which you will receive your *kentekencard* in the mail one or two days later. You must bring proof of identity: a valid Dutch driver's license that was issued no more than ten years ago or a valid (Dutch or foreign) passport, EU ID-card, Dutch travel document for aliens, or NATO ID-card. You also need to bring along proof of registration in the municipality in which you live (except if you bring a Dutch driver's license), which was issued no more than three months ago. For a more in-depth explanation of this process, see *Road Tax – Declaration and Payment*.)

RULES OF THE ROAD
Here, in summary, are a few main traffic rules for cars:
- traffic coming from the right has the right of way (unless you are driving on a priority road, indicated by an orange diamond for you and 'shark's teeth' for the incoming roads)
- cars turning off a road must give right of way to cyclists and pedestrians who are continuing straight ahead on it
- traffic entering a roundabout (traffic circle) has the right of way unless indicated otherwise
- the speed limits, unless otherwise marked, are 50 kilometers an hour in cities and towns, 60 or 80 on secondary roads, and 100 or 120/130 on the motorways
- until the age of 18, children who are not taller than 1 meter 35 must use a booster seat when sitting in the passenger seat or in the back
- when crossing railroad tracks: as soon as the bells start ringing and the lights start flashing, get off. You may only proceed across the tracks once the lights have stopped flashing
- seat belts are mandatory.

A CHILD IN THE CAR
Everyone traveling by car must use a seat belt. Children who are not yet 1 meter 35 tall, are legally obligated to make use of a car

seat. If they are taller than 1 meter 35, they have to make use of a seat belt and, if possible, a booster seat. For children who weigh less than 13 kg, you must use a baby seat (in most cases, these are referred to as a Maxi Cosi). Children who weigh between 9 and 18 kg are to be put in a car seat that is secured in the car by means of the seat belt and that has a five-point belt to secure the child. Children who weigh between 15 and 36 kg should make use of a booster seat. Clearly, the weight categories overlap and it is up to you which solution you opt for if your child is in more than one weight category. Both the car seats and the booster seats must be approved, which can be verified by checking a sticker placed on the seat, stating ECE R44/03 or ECE R44/04, or else that the seat meets the i-Size norm. The sticker also indicates the weight category for which the seat has been created. An important rule is that children up to the age of 13 months (this will become 15 months) must be transported facing backwards. This way, in case of a collision, they are pushed back into the chair, rather than flung forwards.

There are no approved seats for children who weigh more than 36 kilos. These children are expected to use a seat belt, and, if they are not yet 1 meter 50 tall (the same applies to adults), a seat belt clip to ensure that the seat belt runs across their shoulder and not their neck – or a booster seat.

You may not transport more passengers than there are seats and seatbelts. The only exception to this rule is if your car was built before 1971. The only exception to the obligation to use a booster seat (aside from traveling by taxi or bus) is if you pick up your children at school and are taking home a playmate, or are taking children to a party or to participate in a sports event; in that case, you must put your own child in the car seat and may transport the other child (using a seat belt) for a maximum distance of 50 km. Also, if you already have two car seats in the back and are transporting a third child while there is no space for a third car seat, you can use a seat belt for this child. You may never transport a child under the age of 3 if you do not have a seatbelt for it, also not if your car is from before 1971.

If transporting a child / adult who is not yet 1 meter 50, make sure you deactivate the airbag on the passenger side, as your passenger might suffocate if it inflates. If you have no other recourse, put the seat as far back as possible or, preferably, use a booster seat. You should not travel in the front seat with a child on your lap.

USING A MOBILE PHONE

Drivers/riders of motorized vehicles, mopeds and vehicles for people with disabilities may not call or receive calls on their mobile phones without an aid, such as a headset or car kit. Nor may they send or read text messages, e-mails or WAP messages. If you need to talk, you must stop your vehicle, though you may briefly make use of your phone while waiting at a traffic light or standing still in a traffic jam.

This legislation does not apply to cyclists, horse riders and driving instructors in passenger seats. Nor does it apply to the use of equipment such as radiophones in cabs and 27 MC communication equipment. However, if your behavior has contributed to an accident or a (potentially) dangerous situation in traffic, you run the risk of being prosecuted.

Violation of this prohibition carries a minimum fine of € 230 (€ 160, if you are riding a moped). In addition, your cell phone may be confiscated. The cost of arranging hands-free calling is less than the fine, so it is a smart move to just do about it. In all likelihood, what with Bluetooth, the ability to make hands-free calls has already been taken care of.

TRAFFIC SIGNS

In general, blue signs tell you what is permitted, and red signs warn you of a restriction. A red circle indicates that something is forbidden, and a red triangle tells you something about the road conditions. A yellow or orange diamond indicates that you are on a road with priority (in which case, cars coming from the right do not have the right of way). An English-language explanation of the Dutch traffic signs and regulations can be found on the website of Rijkswaterstaat. However, navigating the site to where it is, proved a challenge: easiest is to simply google 'Rijkswaterstaat' and 'Road traffic signs'.

PARKING

Parking regulations vary from city to city, so you should ask a local what they do about parking. A local map will have carparks marked with a blue symbol and a P. Carparks with controlled entry have various payment systems.

Sometimes streets and carparks look as though you can park in them for free, but in fact there is a ticket dispenser (it will have a blue sign with a white P on it) nearby. Look for signs that say *betaald parkeren* (paid parking), and *parkeerautomaat*. During certain hours, which are posted on the dispenser, you must pay enough (using your bank card and pin code) to cover the period you will be parked. You then place the ticket that comes out of the dispenser of your car so that the parking inspectors can read it. In some cases, you are not given a ticket, but instead enter your license place number in the dispenser. You can also download the ANWB or Yellowbrick app (the ANWB and Yellowbrick work together on this), and – after registering with them – order a transponder sticker for behind your windshield. Through the app, you enter the zone code (which you find on the parking automat) and then press 'start'. When you return, you press 'stop' – your charges are automatically deducted from the bank account you have linked to the app. They also provide you with a Q-Park card, which you use when entering a Q-Park parking garage and once again when leaving it.

Also beware, particularly in the inner cities, of signs saying *Parkeren voor vergunninghouders*. These are placed few and far between, but usually indicate that the entire area, if not neighborhood, is reserved for car owners holding a parking permit. If you live in this area, you can get one of these permits at the *gemeentehuis* or the local *Dienst Parkeerzaken* (parking department). Prices vary per city. Sometimes you can 'park & pay' in these areas; this is indicated by one of those blue signs with a white P, with an automat underneath. Whether you can get a permit if you work in one of these areas, depends on the city's rules.

In some of the smaller towns, you will see blue lines painted along where you park. This means that you need to place a *parkeerschijf* (parking disc) on your dashboard, indicating your time of arrival. On signs along the street (usually at the beginning) you will see how long you may remain parked there (the sign will say, for instance, 'max. 30 min.' or 'max. 2 uur'). You can buy a *parkeerschijf* at newspaper stores, gas stations and automobile accessory stores.

Parking violations are punished rather severely. Fines start at € 90, but what can make it seriously costly is the fact that, in some places, the inspectors will attach a wheel clamp or tow away your car, generating a nasty bill for you.

THE RDW

If you own a car, you will soon find out about the organization we referred to earlier on; the Rijksdienst voor Wegverkeer, or RDW. The RDW is the Dutch Road Traffic and Transport Authority. A government-commissioned body, it produces technical and administrative regulations aimed at making Dutch road traffic and transportation as safe and effective as possible. Its vehicle registration system enables the administration of the country's vehicular details, making it possible to quickly locate the owners or holders of vehicles and to call their attention to tax, insurance and APK obligations (see the next paragraph), for instance. This system is also indispensable when following up traffic offenses.

Besides the vehicle registration system and the approval of imported cars, the RDW also manages the Central Driver's License and Moped Certificate Register, and the exchange of Dutch driver's licenses for those issued outside the Netherlands.

VEHICLE APPROVAL – APK

Before a vehicle is allowed onto the Dutch roads, and at intervals during its use, the RDW (Vehicle Technology and Information Center) ensures that the vehicle meets environmental, safety and economic demands. This work includes providing vehicle type approvals, carrying out certain independent tests, and supervising the Dutch *Algemene Periodieke Keuring*, or APK (annual general technical test), after which you are issued the Individual Approval Certificate. For cars that run on gasoline and that were manufactured more than four years ago, an APK is carried out once every two years until the car is eight years old – after which it is carried out annually. Cars that run on any other type of fuel require an annual APK once they have been manufactured more than three years ago. This can be done by specialized centers, called *keurings-stations*, or by a local garage that has been recognized by the RDW. There is no fixed price for this test, and prices vary greatly. If you do not agree with the outcome of the test, you can submit a request for a renewed test with the RDW.

It is your responsibility to remember to have the APK done; the RDW will not remind you (beware that they have been known to carry out random tests and that you are obligated to cooperate!). As an extra service, your garage may send you a letter of reminder. When your car has been APK-tested, the garage notifies the RDW of this and of the outcome. If the RDW receives no such notification, because you failed to have your car tested on time, they will send you an invoice with a fine.

As you could read in the preceding pages, if you want to import a car that was manufactured more than three / four years ago (depending on the type of fuel), then it must be APK-approved. A car that is imported from outside the EU or the EEA (see inset on page 146) will have to meet stricter codes. Which these are, depends on the year of manufacture. In some cases, the certificate of conformity will suffice (see earlier on).

IF YOUR CAR BREAKS DOWN

There are a variety of services available for those of you who need roadside assistance in the case of a car breakdown. For 60 years, the ANWB (see page 146) held the monopoly on offering road-side car-breakdown services. Recent years saw the introduction of a number of competitors to the market, such as Route Mobiel, Euro-cross and SOS Pechhulp, Allianz Global Assistance, as well as individual insurance companies that offer cheaper membership – while still providing help within 30 minutes, as well as assistance abroad. The difference in price lies in the variety of services; you can find their websites at the end of the chapter for more information.

EXPORTING YOUR CAR

If you are moving out of the Netherlands and want to take your car with you, you must de-register it with the RDW. To do this, you visit the RDW, bringing along proof of identity (passport or Dutch driver's license, or a valid travel document), proof of registration (*tenaamstellingsbewijs*; *deel 1B* of the registration certificates), the transfer certificate (*overschrijvingsbewijs*; *deel II* of the certificates), and the most recently issued license plates of the car. If you have a vehicle registration card, you bring it and the nine-digit code, as well as proof of identity and the license plates.

The RDW will give you a *vrijwaringsbewijs* (proof that the vehicle is no longer registered with the RDW), and return to you the proof of registration (*tenaamstellingsbewijs*; *deel 1B* of the registration certificates), and the transfer certificate (*overschrijvingsbewijs*; *deel II* of the certificates). You use the proof of registration and the transfer certificate, as well as *Deel 1A*, with the technical information on your car, to register your vehicle abroad. If you already have a vehicle registration card, you will receive the *vrijwarings-bewijs*, as well as the card, with one of the corners cut off, and a paper *deel II*. You will use the latter two to register your card abroad. In both cases, they will keep the license plates.

Once exportation has been accepted by the RDW, you can no longer drive your car on the public roads. If you need to do so, you can ask the RDW to issue you special exportation license plates, which are valid for a period of 14 days (do not forget to arrange insurance for this period).

For more information, contact the RDW. They can also provide you with more information if you wish to export a car that is already physically located abroad.

DRIVER'S LICENSE

As a rule, residents of the Netherlands are required to have a Dutch driver's license in order to drive a motor vehicle. You are a resident if you spend at least 185 days per calendar year in the Netherlands. There are, however, a number of exceptions to this rule. If you have a driver's license that was issued before January 19, 2013 and that was issued in the countries listed on page 146, you are entitled to drive in the Netherlands on your foreign license for ten years after it has been issued, unless it expires earlier, in which case you can use it until that date. If it is over nine years old and you have registered with a Dutch municipality, you can use it another two years as of the date of registration. If it was issued after January 19, 2013, you can use it for 15 years, provided it is still valid. After this period, you will have to get a Dutch driver's license – to which purpose you can exchange it. You can also opt to exchange it for a Dutch license straight away.

If you have a driver's license that has been issued in any other country, you may drive in the Netherlands on your foreign license for a period of six months (185 days) after registering as a Dutch resident. During this period, you have to take a driving test in the Netherlands to acquire a Dutch driver's license. Also for some of these countries it has been determined that you do not have to take the test and can simply exchange your license; in the following paragraph you can see for which countries this is the case.

Special rules apply to those who have been accorded diplomatic or consular staff status, as well their families. Contact the RDW (Dutch Road Traffic and Transport Authority – see the end of the chapter) or the Ministry of Foreign Affairs, Protocol Department, for more information. Special rules also apply to those who benefit from the 30%-ruling, see further on.

Furthermore, you must be at least 18 years of age to drive a car in the Netherlands.

OBTAINING YOUR LICENSE

As of the age of 16, you can do your theoretical exam, while as of the age of 16-and-a-half you may start taking driving lessons. When you are 17, you can take the road test. If you pass before the age of 18, you will be allowed to drive, but only if you are accompanied by an adult who must be registered as an 'accompanier' (*begeleider*). You will be issued a *begeleiderspas* (accompanier's document) along with your driver's license, both of which you must always have with you.

EXCHANGING A FOREIGN DRIVER'S LICENSE

If you live in the Netherlands and possess valid residential status you may trade in a valid driver's license issued by the countries listed in the inset on page 146, as well as Aruba, Monaco, Isle of Man, Netherlands Antilles, and the State of Jersey for a Dutch license.

Driver's licenses issued in the following countries can only be exchanged if they cover the categories listed here: Taiwan, B (passenger car); Israel, B (passenger car); Japan, 1B (passenger cars and motorcycles of more than 400cc); Singapore, Class 2 (motorcycles of more than 400cc) and Class 3 (passenger car), Andorra (license for passenger cars); South Korea, second class ordinary license; the Quebec province of Canada, Class 5; and all categories of licenses from Aruba, Netherlands Antilles, Jersey, Isle of Man, and Monaco.

If you had a Dutch driver's license that was valid after June 30, 1985, then in most cases you can exchange your foreign driver's license, no matter which country issued it, for a new Dutch license.

You cannot exchange a so-called international driver's license for a Dutch license, as it is merely considered to be a translation of the national driver's license.

The driver's license must also have been issued in a one-year period during which the holder resided at least 185 days in the issuing country.

More information can be found on www.rdw.nl, click in *Information in English*.

The 30%-Ruling

If you are benefiting from the 30% tax ruling, you and the other member(s) of your family can simply exchange your license, no matter where you are from. Ask for an exchange form for your foreign driver's license at your local municipal office.

License Verification

As so many different types of driver's licenses from various countries are submitted for exchange, the validity or authenticity of every document has to be verified. The Department of Road Transport may therefore ask you to have the validity and significance of certain information confirmed by the Consulate or Embassy of the country that issued the foreign driver's license. You may also be required to have the content of the foreign driver's license translated by an approved interpreter/translator. For Japanese, Taiwanese and Chinese licenses, this is obligatory.

The Procedure

In order to exchange your foreign driver's license, you must go to your local municipal office. There, if required (see below) you request (and pay for) a health form (called *eigen verklaring*). Once this has been completed, you mail it to the CBR (Centraal Bureau Rijvaardigheid – Central Road Aptitude Bureau) which, on the basis of this form, decides whether or not to issue you a Certificate of Fitness. If you are granted one, they note this fact in the license registry, after which they send you notice of the fact that they have done this. Once you have received this notice, you go back to the local municipal office to request the driver's license, where you submit:

- one recent color passport photograph (old rules say two, so it may be best to verify this)
- the original, valid foreign driver's license (EU/EEA licenses that have expired may be exchanged if you submit a copy issued by the relevant authority abroad that there is no objection against exchanging the license)
- for non-EU/EEA citizens: a residence permit
- for students: proof of registration with institute of education
- proof of identity
- for non-EU/EEA citizens: the certificate of fitness
- the exchange form, which has been partially filled in by you and partially by a civil servant from the municipal office
- (if you are benefiting from the 30%-ruling:) a copy of a statement issued by the Tax Office in Heerlen proving that you or the other member(s) of your family are benefiting from the 30% tax-ruling.

As soon as the municipal fees have been paid, the municipal office issues you a certified copy and proof of receipt. It then sends the entire application, your original license, and the papers, to the RDW, who evaluate the request and – if they grant it – send you a notice stating that you can pick up your Dutch driver's license at the municipal offices. If you want to keep your original license, rather than hand it in, you need to deliver proof of the fact that you will be needing it.

You cannot exchange your driver's license if you do not live in the Netherlands.

Certificate of Fitness / Medical Check-Up

If you are from an EU/EEA country or Switzerland, then you will not need a Certificate of Fitness unless your license has been issued for a shorter period of validity than usual (for the country issuing the license) or if it contains annotations that are not recognized within the EU. Nationals of all other countries need a Certificate of Fitness and, as the case may be, a medical check-up (note: the rules are often subject to change, so it is always best to check with the CBR – 0900 0210 – which rules currently apply, to be on the safe side). A medical check-up is required:

- when trading in a license issued by certain countries
- when certain medical issues are involved
- when the license has been issued for a shorter period of validity than usual (for the country issuing the license)
- when you are older than 70 and your license expires the day (after) you turn 75
- if you are older than 75
- when it contains unrecognized limitations
- when the license concerns certain categories
- when the validity of the license in the Netherlands has expired or you have driven on it for a longer period than permitted
- if the license has not been registered and you have been here longer than one year.

Also when arranging a medical check-up, you have to obtain the *eigen verklaring* (health form) at the municipal office. Once this has been filled in by a doctor other than your GP, you send it to the CBR for evaluation. If they feel it is necessary, they will ask you to visit a specialist for further check-up. Depending on the outcome of this visit, the medical advisor of the CBR will decide whether or not you will be allowed to drive. For more information, you can approach the CBR or the RDW.

Return of Your Original Driver's License

The original driver's license will be returned to the embassy or country of origin of the license. Depending on the legislation of the country that has issued the license, you can then have it returned to you.

RETAKING THE TEST

If your driver's license cannot be traded in, you will have to take a theory test and a road test at the Central Road Aptitude Bureau (Centraal Bureau Rijvaardigheid, or CBR). More information on this subject can be obtained from calling the RDW (0900 0739). If you visit www.rijbewijs.nl or www.rdw.nl and click on *English Information*, you can read about exchanging your license; however, when this issue of *The Holland Handbook* went to print, you could not find any information on taking the test on these sites, or the option of taking it in English – which *is* possible.

The test consists of questions on traffic rules and questions on the recognition of dangerous situations (and how to act). Unless you take the test in English – an option which is available for selection when you make your online reservation – or Dutch, if you want to take the test in another language, you have to arrange an interpreter at least two weeks in advance. To arrange the theory exam, you visit the site of the CBR to select a location, time, and to make a reservation. The road exam has to be booked for you by a driving school, you cannot do this yourself. You do have to authorize them to do this, which you do on the CBR-site as well. On www.traffictrainer.nl you can take theoretical practice exams in English.

SHOULD YOU KEEP YOUR CAR?

When moving to another country there is always the question of what to do with your car. Should you keep your old car, buy a new one in the country you are leaving or buy a new one in the country you are going to? All these options have their own merits for tax purposes. And, when returning to your native country, the same questions arise.

In these paragraphs you will find a brief overview of some of the issues you should be aware of. These paragraphs are based on the premise that the Netherlands is your new country of residence, however the same principles are applicable in every country of the European Union. In the Netherlands the taxes involved when importing a car are the Value Added Tax (VAT/BTW), the *Bijzondere Verbruiksbelasting van Personenauto's* (BPM – see page 142) and import duties.

COMING INTO THE NETHERLANDS
From a European Union Member State
When it comes to taxes, if you are coming from another member state there are no special requirements for bringing your old car with you.

If you are considering buying a new car, you should be aware that the taxes levied on a new car in the Netherlands are extremely high. They can amount to up to 45% of the list price. In view of the fact that there is hardly any country in the European Union that levies the same amount of taxes on new cars, you might therefore want to buy your new car in the country you are coming from. Keep in mind that if your car is less than six months or 6,000 km old, or its license plates have been issued within the last six months, you will have to pay VAT in the Netherlands. Check whether you can get a (partial) refund of the VAT/BTW paid when the car was delivered to you in the country where you bought it.

For the rules on importing a car, read the first paragraphs under *Driving Your Car*.

From a Non-European Union Member State
If goods are imported into an EU-member state, customs duties are due. However, for your household effects – that includes cars – there can be an exemption from customs duties (see page 98). Some of the conditions to be met are that you must have lived in a non EU-member state for a period of at least 12 months and that you must have had the car in your possession for at least six months.

We will look at these two requirements in the following two paragraphs.

WHERE DO YOU LIVE?

Your usual place of residence is the place where you normally live for at least 185 days of each calendar year for personal and professional reasons. If there are no professional reasons, evidence must be produced proving that personal commitments lead to close ties between yourself and your place of residence. If you are living in a country in order to carry out an assignment, the usual place of residence is the country where you have your personal commitments. Personal commitments mean family and/or social commitments, such as:

- the place of residence of your family, your children or other people with whom you have a personal relationship
- the place with which you have social ties (e.g. cultural activities societies, sports clubs, committees).

POSSESSION FOR A PERIOD OF SIX MONTHS

You must have had the car in your possession for at least six months and you must have used it in the non EU-member state from which you are moving. This condition is very important. Generally speaking, if your employer has put a car at your disposal, the customs authorities are of the point of view that the car has not been in your possession. The same applies if you have leased a car in the country from which you are moving. In these cases, the exemption from customs duties is not granted for your car.

CONDITIONS AFTER THE EXEMPTION IS GRANTED

After the customs authorities have granted an exemption and you have imported the car, you may not lend out, hire out or sell your car within a period of twelve months after the customs have accepted your customs declaration. In short, you should keep the full power of use of the car for twelve months.

If the twelve month-condition is not met, you will be liable to pay taxes immediately and even be fined for misuse of the rules. Even if the car is stolen or badly damaged and the insurance company sells the wreckage, the exemption will be revoked. In those cases you will have to pay duties for a car you do not and could not own anymore!

LEAVING THE NETHERLANDS

When leaving the Netherlands, the first question of importance is: am I going to another member state of the European Union, or am I leaving the European Union altogether.

Going to Another Member State

When you are going to another member state there are also no special requirements for taking your old car with you. Via the website of the Dutch tax authorities, you can request a (partial) refund of the BPM – visit the site for more information. As you read earlier, the taxes levied on a new car in the Netherlands are extremely high, amounting up to 45% of the list price, and there won't be any refund of these taxes either. In view of the fact that there is hardly any country in the European Union that levies the same amount of taxes on new cars as in the Netherlands, it is advisable to buy your new car in the country you are going to.

Another option would be to buy it in the Netherlands when you are already living in the other country. In that case you might even be cheaper off altogether, because then you do not have to pay

VAT/BTW and BPM in the Netherlands, but only the taxes in the country you are then living in and the list prices here are relatively cheap. If you live in the United Kingdom, for instance, this could lead to a price difference of € 2,300 and more – *and* you can easily arrange for the steering wheel to be placed on the right-hand side.

Mind you, when your car is less than six months or 6,000 km old, you will have to pay VAT in the member state you are going to. On the other hand, you can get a (partial) refund of the VAT/BTW paid when the car was delivered to you.

Leaving the European Union

When leaving the European Union altogether there also are no special requirements for taking your old car with you. However, you can request a (partial) refund of the BPM – see the website of the tax authorities. When you buy a new car in the Netherlands and it is exported within 30 days, you can buy the car duty-free. In effect it is the same procedure as described before for buying a car in the Netherlands whilst living in another member state. You have to be able to prove that the car actually left the European Union within 30 days. The tax authorities can demand that you produce evidence of the importation and the car duties paid in your new country.

Of course the country you are moving to might levy import duties on your car. However, in general they will grant you an exemption if you have owned the car for more than six months. Clearly, it is vital that you get detailed information on the applicable rules before you move.

TAKE CARE OF BUSINESS BEFORE YOU MOVE

There are plenty of possibilities for reducing the tax burden on your car when you are leaving or returning to a country. Because of the detailed rules on this issue, you should take care of business before you actually move. Preferably you should seek professional assistance at least six months before moving. That will give you the opportunity to use the rules to your advantage.

ROAD TAX

As mentioned earlier, if you own a car, delivery van or motorcycle in the Netherlands, you must pay road tax. Cars are 'vehicles with three or more wheels, designed for transporting a maximum of eight persons, excluding the driver'. A delivery van is a vehicle with cargo space and also a maximum permitted loaded weight of 3,500 kg. Other regulations apply to vehicles with cargo space and a higher maximum permitted loaded weight. They are covered in a separate brochure entitled *Zware Bedrijfsauto's, Bussen en Opleggers* (*Heavy Commercial Vans, Buses, Trailers and Semitrailers*).

WHEN DO YOU HAVE TO PAY?

You have to pay road tax from the time your name is transferred to the vehicle registration card (*kentekencard*, see page 142). Regardless of whether you are temporarily unable or unwilling to use your vehicle, you are always required to pay road tax. You pay for possession of a vehicle, even if it remains parked on private premises. (See further on, for suspension options.)

If you are a resident of the Netherlands, but driving a car that is registered abroad, you still have to pay road tax and vehicle tax (BPM) – unless you use the car fewer than two weeks. For those two weeks you will still have to request an exemption from the RDW.

DECLARATION AND PAYMENT

When you buy a vehicle, from a private person or a garage, he will give you either the proof of registration (*tenaamstellingsbewijs, deel 1B*) and the proof of transfer (*overschrijvingsbewijs*) or the credit-card sized *kentekencard* and code, which you will take to a RDW-window (or store offering postal services), plus proof of identification and of your address (a driver's license will suffice). There the vehicle will be put in your name and you will be handed a document that will prove that the transaction has taken place, plus the first four digits of the registration code. Within one or two days, the RDW will send you your new *kentekencard*, plus a five-digit code. These five digits, plus the four on the transaction document, are what you will need to sell the car again. They will also issue you a document stating that the vehicle is no longer register in the name of the seller (*vrijwaringsbewijs*, or warranty against liability); this you give to the seller. It will allow him to prove that he is no longer responsible for the vehicle. For more on this see page 149. Once your name is transferred to the registration certificate, this also serves as a road tax declaration. You must indicate whether you want to pay for each three-month period separately or for four consecutive periods at once. Soon afterwards, you will automatically be sent a bill and *giro* payment slip (*acceptgiro*) for the road tax for which you are liable (if, for some or other reason you don't receive one, contact the Central Tax Office). Thereafter, the bills will be posted to you on a periodic basis. The period for which you must pay road tax is stated on the bill, as is the due date.

You can also arrange to have the bills paid automatically by means of a *machtiging* (authorization). However, in order to effectuate these automatic payments, you must request permission to do this from the Tax Office/Central Administration. If you send in a *machtigingsformulier* (authorization form, authorizing the Tax Office to automatically deduct the periodic payments), which you will receive along with your first *acceptgiro*, this is considered a request for permission. If granted, the payments will be collected automatically. This option is available for quarterly and monthly payments.

ROAD TAX RATES

The amount of road tax you pay depends on the following:
- the type of vehicle (i.e. passenger car, delivery van, motorcycle)
- for passenger cars and delivery vans: tare weight. This is stated on the registration certificate (under *massa ledig voertuig*)
- for passenger cars: the fuel used (gasoline, diesel, LPG or a combination of gasoline/LPG)
- the province in which you live
- whether your vehicle is equipped and intended to be powered by an electric motor or hydrogen fuel only: in that case you do not owe road tax
- the amount of CO_2-emission of your car
- the age of your car; if it is 40 years old or older, then you do not owe road tax
- whether you have a physical disability – in that case, you do not owe road tax. Contact the tax authorities for more information.

You do not have to pay additional road tax for a caravan (camper), collapsible caravan or static caravan, even if their maximum permitted loaded weight exceeds 750 kg. For campers that are not pulled by a car, but that can be driven independently, you owe road tax; however, subject to conditions, you can arrange to owe only a quarter of the amount of road tax due. For cars with a low CO_2-emission, you do not owe any road tax – the exact conditions for this changed as of January 1, 2014, so be sure to verify these as this date approaches.

You can always inquire at any large post office (or a store offering post office services) or the Tax Department offices of the Central Office for Motor Vehicle Taxes, if you want to know precisely how much road tax you have to pay for your vehicle. (You can calculate how much you will owe if you visit www.belastingdienst.nl/rekenhulpen/motorrijtuigenbelasting.)

TRAILERS

As of January 1, 2007, you no longer owe road tax for trailers attached to your car, based on the rule that this tax is no longer due for light-weight trailers.

NO ROAD TAX

No road tax is due for cars that run on electric motors, whose energy is generated by a battery or fuel cell, a motor that can run on hydrogen and for cars that emit 0 CO_2.

VEHICLE MODIFICATIONS

You may have to pay more, or less, road tax if you modify your vehicle. For example if:
- modification of your vehicle results in a change in its tare weight. As a result, your vehicle may then fall under a different weight category
- you change the type of fuel you use in your passenger car. If you modify your vehicle in this way, you must have your registration certificate adjusted. For this, contact the RDW Centrum voor Voertuitechniek en Informatie (0900 0739). They will inform the Tax Department of the change
- vehicle conversions: for instance, from van to camper or to regular car.

If you have made these changes, you also must have the vehicle re-inspected by the RDW. If the changes lead to a change in weight or fuel, you must have *deel 1A* of the vehicle registration papers or your *kentekencard* adjusted accordingly by the RDW. The vehicle does not need to be re-inspected by the RDW if the car has been converted to run on gas by a recognized garage. They will also arrange the new registration papers for you.

As of the next road tax period, you will owe the new amount, for which you will automatically be billed. If you paid road tax for a full year in advance, you will receive an additional assessment or a reimbursement, depending on the situation.

MOVING WITHIN THE COUNTRY

If you move within the Netherlands, you register with your (new) municipality. They will pass on the new address to the Tax Office, who will send the bills to your new address.

SALE OF YOUR VEHICLE

When you sell your vehicle, you must pay road tax over the period during which it was sold, but you can be reimbursed. If you have yet to receive a bill for the tax, you will be sent one for a lesser amount. If you have already paid it, you will be reimbursed. Automatic payments will be stopped automatically.

BICYCLES, THE HEART OF DUTCH CULTURE BY JACOB VOSSESTEIN

Ah, the bike, the Dutch bike, *de fiets*. Pity it wasn't invented in the Netherlands, for wouldn't it be a far better symbol of this nation than the tulip or the wooden shoe? It conjures up the very essence of Dutch culture, and I will tell you why.

Not all immigrants / expats appreciate Dutch bikers, whichever background they may have. Foreign visitors find their behavior unpredictable, dangerous, and anarchistic – with bikers suddenly popping up when you least expect them. And I agree, it is all true, but let me take you along another line of thought which may be worth considering too...

To my idea, the Dutch bike – the simple, sturdy, run-of-the-mill black bike, omnipresent in Dutch cities – reflects several traditional Dutch characteristics.

Obviously, in a flat and very crowded country, it is a pragmatic means of transportation that gets you everywhere in no time, certainly when you ignore traffic signs and other silly official obstructions which, as a tax-paying citizen, you may question and toss aside. In applying a riding style that foreigners tend to describe as 'suicidal', a Dutch city biker will reach his / her destination far sooner than when using the tram, let alone a car.

Another plus: everyone can afford a bike, be it new or second-hand. Not generally employed in any status games, it is a very egalitarian means of transportation. As bikers are exposed to rain and wind and the laws of gravity on steep bridges, any difference in status or social stature between them is soon eradicated, revealing the essence of life: a body struggling against the forces of nature. Office clerk, bricklayer, human resources manager or secretary of state, all bikers have to bow to the elements. And toiling against gale force 8 on an unsheltered dike road or a straight-as-a-ruler suburban street will encourage modesty in anyone, making him equal to his fellow human beings who suffer likewise. Well, theoretically, that is.

The bike also satisfies the Dutch inclination to not waste any resources. It is not only a cheap means of transportation, it also improves one's general shape, thus reducing medical expenses. On a slightly more abstract level, bikers can also congratulate themselves on the fact that their effort is for the good of the planet as a whole: no fumes, no noise, no use of exhaustible resources, no great amount of unnaturally paved space needed. What could be more satisfying than a good conscience combined with excellent health and a well-filled wallet?

But that is not all. Riding a bike could be seen as having a touch of philosophy to it, even spirituality. It teaches the rider balance, and we're not only talking about physical balance. Riding along during rush hour at about 20 km/h among scores of other bikers doing likewise, all – well, most of them – waiting for the red light to turn green, trying to find a clear section of road to cross, cycling through the pouring rain... Things like that produce a certain equilibrium with your fellow bikers, peace of mind almost, to quote a Hindu term. It makes you realize the true size of your ego: just a small flame among many, hardly more than that of a match, nothing special really.

Besides balance, biking teaches you alertness. Though the race may not be about winning, it's challenging nonetheless: avoiding the carefully parking truck, calculating whether you can still pass just in front of that car that has no right whatsoever to be going so fast, racing for a minute to catch the bridge just before it closes (or is it: opens?) for a ship, catching the orange light nanoseconds before it turns red and when this fails, scanning the surroundings for any signs of police presence.

So with eyes on all sides and ears open to the sounds of car tires, tram bells, moped noises and of course each other's ringing bells, bikers wind their way through the ever-changing river of traffic where they may physically be the weaker party but morally speaking are superior by far: unpretentious, silent, un-polluting, utterly democratic, going with the flow and yet self-willed. This feeling of modest self-righteousness gets stronger when the bike is used for the transportation of items such as the daily shopping, the two children, a dog, or a pile of wood for some do-it-yourself job.

There are a thousand and one subtle effects and conditions which become part of your delicate existence when you bike. In a densely populated nation, give and take are essential, and biking may be a good preparation for the bigger podium of life. Royalty, prime ministers and captains of industry have preceded you, so what's keeping you from joining the steel-framed army when going to work, school or the supermarket? If you can't beat us, join us. See you at the traffic light!

Jacob Vossestein is the author of a.o. the bestselling books Dealing with the Dutch *and* The Dutch and their Delta. *For more information on Jacob see: www.jacobvossestein.nl.*

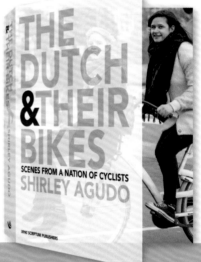

You deliver proof of the sale of your vehicle by means of the *vrijwaringsbewijs* (warranty against liability), which you will either receive from the dealer to whom you sell it, or from the buyer, who is issued this document when he registers the car in his name at the post office (or a store offering post office services).

GOING ABROAD TEMPORARILY

If you temporarily go abroad, you are still required to pay road tax on time for the duration of your absence, regardless of whether you take your vehicle with you (however, see following paragraph on *Suspension*). There are three ways to ensure that the road tax is paid on time. You can:

- pay the bill(s) for the duration of your stay abroad in advance. For this, contact the Central Office for Motor Vehicle Taxes
- authorize someone to pay the bill(s) for you
- arrange a *machtiging*, allowing the Tax Office to collect the payments automatically. To do this, you contact the Tax Office/Central Administration.

SUSPENSION

If you will not be using your vehicle for an extended period of time (for instance because you are going abroad), you can apply for suspension of the registration certificate at a large post office (or a store offering post office services) – for a fee. To this purpose, you must bring along proof of identification and *deel IB* (see page 142 under *Vehicle Registration Certificate*) and *deel II* with you – or your *kentekencard*. You will not owe road tax as of the date of suspension (provided the period of suspension lasts at least a month) and will automatically be reimbursed for amounts already paid. If you end the suspension before month has passed, then you will owe road tax over the entire month. Suspension is granted for a maximum period of one year, but can be extended after this period has passed. During the period of suspension you will not be allowed to drive your vehicle on a public highway and you must inform the Tax Office of its physical whereabouts during this period.

You can also arrange the suspension online, on the website of the RDW. To this purpose, you must have a DigiD (digital identification code), which you can read more about on page 72.

You can read more about this in the brochure entitled *Uw Auto of Motor en het Kenteken* (*Your Car or Motorcycle and its Registration*), available, among others, at stores offering post office services.

SUSPENSION AND APK

While your road tax payments are suspended, your car might still have to undergo the APK-test to make sure it is APK-approved before you start driving it again. In that case, an exception is made to the rule that you may not drive your car out on the road. You must, however, request a one-day dispensation from the tax authorities before you do this. And make sure that your car is insured! Call 0800 0749 (the Central Office for Motor Vehicle Taxes) to enquire as to what your best course of action is under the circumstances.

SUSPENSION AND INSURANCE

Once you have suspended the payment of road tax, you can use proof of this suspension to suspend your car insurance are well. It might be useful to continue to insure it against theft and damage, however.

REACTIVATING THE PAYMENTS

If you want to start using your car again, after a period of suspension, then you go back to the store offering post office services with the same papers to reverse the situation. Regardless of whether you had a paper proof of registration (*tenaamstellingsbewijs*) or *kentekencard*, you will be sent a new *kentekencard* by the RDW. If the full 12 months have gone by, the suspension ends of its own accord and the RDW will automatically send you your new proof of registration. As mentioned above, if you want to extend the suspension, you have to go back to store offering post office services to arrange this. You can also do all of this online, via www.rdw.nl.

YOUR VEHICLE LEAVES THE COUNTRY PERMANENTLY

If your vehicle leaves the country permanently, you must arrange its deregistration with the RDW (see page 149). Once you have taken care of these formalities, you will automatically receive a road tax reimbursement for the period after which your car is no longer in the Netherlands. If you paid road tax for four consecutive periods at once, you will also receive a tax reimbursement for the periods that have not yet taken effect.

FREQUENT CHECKS

The Central Office for Motor Vehicle Taxes closely monitors the payment of road tax. Photographs, customs data and police information, such as fines and records, are also utilized. If it is discovered that you have not paid road tax, or have paid too little, you will receive an increased assessment.

BICYCLES AND MOPEDS

THE BEST WAY TO GET AROUND

If you really want to sample Dutch life, and get around quickly and easily, buy yourself a bicycle – Dutch-style: a sturdy, no-nonsense bike, preferably not too expensive so that if it gets stolen you will not feel too bad. Fancy, 10-speed bicycles are relatively rare, and used only for recreational cycling.

A new bicycle, made by one of the better-known manufacturers and sold at a bicycle shop, costs between € 275 and € 500. A discount store will sell you a new, imported bike for as little as € 175, but you must examine it to make sure the quality is alright.

BUYING A SECOND-HAND BICYCLE

Most students (and foreign visitors) buy second-hand bicycles (*tweedehands fietsen* or *tweedehands rijwielen*). A reasonable one will cost you between € 75 and € 175. You can find them at (second-hand) bicycle shops, at the bicycle parking facilities near railway stations or on www.marktplaats.nl. They will also be advertised in the small ads at the back of the local newspaper under *Rijwielen*, or on the notice board at the supermarket or anywhere students congregate. (A woman's bike is a *damesfiets* and a man's bike is a *herenfiets*. Dutch men are not embarrassed to ride women's bicycles – and vice versa.)

Since the second-hand bicycle market is different in different towns, you should ask a local for advice. They may know of an especially good place, and, if you're lucky, may even help you to pick your bicycle and negotiate the price.

When you buy a bicycle, make sure that its lights work and that it has a sturdy lock (*slot*). Even better is to buy a chain and padlock so you can fasten your bicycle to something when you park it (secure parking for bicycles is available at most railway stations and in some city centers. Look for the signs for *rijwielstalling* or *fietsenstalling*).

TOURING THE COUNTRY
The Netherlands is one of the most cyclist-friendly countries in the world. Crisscrossing the country are well-kept cycling paths, running straight through areas that are not accessible to anything with an engine, offering you the beautiful, quiet enjoyment of Dutch nature, unhindered by anything other than fellow nature lovers and nature itself. You can pick up great guide books and maps at the VVV or the ANWB and plan long or short trips anywhere you like. Trains have special bicycle compartments, so that you can travel clear across the country and then take off from there.

RENTING A BICYCLE
You can also rent bicycles by the day from the parking facility at many railway stations, under payment of a deposit. It is wise to telephone in advance to make a reservation. Ask at the railway station for the free booklet. In certain places, such as Veluwe National Park, bicycles are available, free of charge, to roam the beautiful woods at your leisure.

For more on renting a bicycle and on the Public Transportation Bicycle, see page 140.

TRAFFIC RULES FOR CYCLISTS
As a cyclist, you too must obey the traffic signs and rules, and stay in the bicycle lanes marked on the street. As a rule, cars that are turning across your path are supposed to stop for you, but it is wise to watch out. You should also signal with your arm if you are planning to turn. You can be fined for riding at night without lights, and for drunken cycling as well as for reckless endangerment when using your mobile phone while on the bike. Contrary to the situation in many countries, you may *not* ride your bicycle on the sidewalk.

MOPEDS
As of January 1, 2008, anyone riding a moped (*brommer* or *bromfiets*), motorized bicycle (*snorfiets*), light vehicle, light vehicle (*brommobiel*) or quad (*vierwielige brommobiel*) needs a moped license, called the AM-license. If you have a driver's license for automobiles or motorcycles, you do not need to get one. You can take the theoretical exam as of age 15-and-a-half and the practical exam as of age 16. If, for medical reasons, your driver's license is no longer valid, you can still obtain or retain an AM-license for the purpose of driving a light vehicle.

You take the exam at one of the CBR (Centraal Bureau voor Rijvaardigheid, Road Aptitude Bureau or www.cbr.nl) 'theory centers'. Once you have passed the theoretical exam, you can go to the municipality and request them to issue you the so-called AM-license. They will check with the CBR whether you have indeed passed your exam, which will remain valid for a period of six months. Within five days, you can go pick up your license, bringing along a passport photograph, proof of identity and the required payment.

When riding a moped, keep in mind that you must always wear a (suitable) helmet, and carry with you your moped certificate/license and proof of insurance. Failure to do either of these will result in a fine of € 90. Riding without having obtained a license will cost you € 240, and without having arranged insurance; € 370.

Mopeds must also have a license plate. The process of arranging this is comparable to the process for a car; it takes place via the RDW. For more information, please check page 150, on how to go about this and whom to contact. Failure to be able to present one will also result in a € 45-fine. And, as with a car, you may not make any 'hand-held' calls on your mobile phone while riding your moped; the fine will be € 160.

BEING A PEDESTRIAN

Tourists have been known to take a seat in the window of a café at a busy Amsterdam intersection just to watch the show of Dutch traffic interaction. All pedestrians jaywalk, none of the bicycle riders pay any attention to the color of their traffic light, trams trundle along and stop within an inch of all cars' lives (be they Mercedes or Toyota), buses wheeze their asthmatic way through this all with an inch to spare, and cars ... well, cars take whatever space everyone else deigns to grant them.

In all this mess, being a pedestrian is by far the most convenient. Riding a bike is faster, but pedestrians can squeeze through, around or over any obstacle and, if it starts to rain, they can hop on a tram or bus and get out of there high and dry.

BLIND PEDESTRIANS
Luckily, this does not mean that those of us who cannot see had best stay home. In many cities and towns, there is a whole intricate system in place to help the blind navigate their way. For instance, the pedestrian lights produce a variety of ticking sounds, depending on whether they signal *walk* or *don't walk*. Also, hidden among the regular sidewalk tiles, are special ribbed or rubber tiles (also in place at railroad stations), indicating where the sidewalks end. And fellow-pedestrians, but also other road users, have an eye out for the special white sticks with red rims, used by the blind – and often take the time to lend a helping hand.

TOURING THE COUNTRY
Just as is the case for cyclists, there is a wonderful network of pedestrian paths running across the entire country. Visit any VVV or ANWB-store to pick up a guide book on walking routes and local sites of interest to visit.

RULES
Jaywalking may be quicker, but, if you want to make sure you make it across in one piece, it's nice to know that cars must yield to pedestrians on zebra crossings (but don't be naïve; car drivers are not naturally inclined to yield to anyone who isn't at least half way across – they expect you to 'wait your turn'). Cars making a turn on a green light must yield to pedestrians going straight ahead on a zebra crossing. Don't expect them to wait till you have made it all the way across, though; just out of their way gives them plenty of room to proceed, as far as the Dutch drivers are concerned.

Also make sure that you don't mistake a bicycle path (*fietspad*) for a pedestrian path, they often look very much the same and at times run parallel. Generally speaking, the path closest to the road is the bicycle path.

Trams have priority over everyone, no matter where they are coming from.

GENERAL

MINISTERIE VAN INFRASTRUCTUUR EN MILIEU
Ministry of Infrastructure and Environment
Plesmanweg 1 – 6, 2597 JG The Hague
P.O. Box 20901, 2500 EX The Hague
Tel.: 070 456 00 00
www.government.nl/ministries/ienm

DOUANE
Dutch Customs
www.douane.nl

PUBLIC TRANSPORTATION

GENERAL
Prices, departure and arrival times
Tel.: 0900 92 92
www.9292ov.nl
9292ov app: available at the App Store

OV CHIPCARD
www.ov-chipkaart.nl

NEDERLANDSE SPOORWEGEN, NS
Dutch Railways
Prices, departure, arrival times and travel
planner – www.ns.nl
Reisplanner app: available at the App Store

NS INTERNATIONAL
www.nsinternational.nl

PLAN YOUR JOURNEY
http://9292.nl/en#
9292 app: available at the App Store

DRIVER'S LICENSE

GENERAL ENGLISH-LANGUAGE INFO
www.rijbewijs.nl

CENTRAL OFFICE FOR MOTOR VEHICLE DRIVING TESTING, CBR
Centraal Bureau Rijvaardigheidsbewijzen
Head office, Sir Winston Churchilllaan 297,
2288 DC Rijswijk
Postbus 5301, 2280 HH Rijswijk
Tel.: 0900 02 10
www.cbr.nl

DRIVER'S LICENSE INFORMATION FOR PERSONS HOLDING DIPLOMATIC OR CONSULAR STAFF STATUS
Ministry of Foreign Affairs, Protocol Department
Tel.: 070 348 64 86
www.government.nl/ministries/bz

TRAFFIC RULES

GENERAL
www.veiligverkeernederland.nl

ROAD TAX

CENTRAAL BUREAU MOTORRIJTUIGEN-BELASTING
Central Office for Motor Vehicle Taxes
Tel.: 0800 0749
P.O. Box 9047, 7300 GJ Apeldoorn
www.belastingdienst.nl

RIJKSDIENST VOOR HET WEGVERKEER
(National Traffic Authority) Vehicle technology and information center
Head office: Europaweg 205, Zoetermeer
P.O. Box 777, 2700 AT Zoetermeer
Tel.: 0900 0739
www.rdw.nl

THE ROYAL DUTCH TOURING CLUB (ANWB)
P.O. Box 93200, 2509 BA The Hague
Wassenaarseweg 220, 2596 EC The Hague
General tel. no for members: 088 269 22 22
To become a member: www.anwb.nl/lidmaatschap
Roadside Assistance Service (Wegenwacht),
tel.: 088 269 28 88
Legal assistance, tel.: 088 269 72 05
Specially for victims of traffic accidents,
tel.: 088 269 77 66
Traffic information, tel.: 0900 96 22
General website: www.anwb.nl
Route Planner: http://route.anwb.nl/routeplanner
General information: www.anwb.nl
ANWB traffic app: available at the App Store

ROADSIDE ASSISTANCE

AA Team: www.aa-team.nl
ANWB: www.anwb.nl/wegenwacht
Routemobiel: www.routemobiel.nl

CAR RENTAL

Auto Europe: www.autoeurope.nl
Avis: www.avis.nl
Budget: www.budget.nl
Europcar: www.europcar.nl
Hertz: www.hertz.nl

CYCLING

THE DUTCH & THEIR BIKES
SCENES FROM A NATION OF CYCLISTS
By Shirley Agudo
Published by XPat Media
With almost 700 photos it's the definitive
photo guide to the world's best bicycle culture
www.dutchandtheirbikes.com

BICYCLE TOURING HOLLAND
By Katherine Widing
Published by Van der Plas Publications
This book treats you to 50 wonderful bike
tours into 'every corner of the country, and
sometimes beyond into some of the most picturesque destinations in neighboring Belgium
and Germany'
www.cyclepublishing.com

IN THE CITY OF BIKES
The story of the Amsterdam Cyclist
By Pete Jordan
Published by Harper Collins
A funny, engaging and exhaustively tribute to
Amsterdam's unique biking history
www.cityofbikes.com

CYCLING TOURS IN THE NETHERLANDS
www.bike-netherlands.com
www.cycletours.nl
www.fiets.amsterdam.nl
www.fietsen.123.nl
www.fietspad.nl
www.holland-cycling.com
www.nederlandfietsland.nl
www.rotterdambycycle.nl
www.totzo.org
www.tulipcycling.com
Fiets! app: available at the App Store

BICYCLE AND PUBLIC TRANSPORTATION
www.ov-fiets.nl
www.nsfiets.nl

CHEAPER TRAVEL BY PUBLIC TRANSPORTATION

BIKE RENTAL
www.bikecity.nl
www.bicycleholland.com
www.macbike.nl
www.orangebike.nl
www.rentabike.nl
www.tulipcycling.com
www.yellowbike.nl

SHOPS TO BUY DUTCH STYLE BICYCLES
www.workcycles.nl
www.bakfiets-en-meer.nl
www.dutchbicyclegroup.nl
www.hansstruijkfietsen.nl
http://vanmoof.com

AIRPORTS

SCHIPHOL AMSTERDAM AIRPORT
Evert van de Beekstraat, 1118 CP Schiphol
Tel.: 0900 0141
www.schiphol.nl
Schiphol app: available at the App Store
Schiphol flight information app:
available at the App Store

ROTTERDAM THE HAGUE AIRPORT
Rotterdam Airportplein 60, 3045 AP Rotterdam
Tel.: 010 446 34 44
www.rotterdamthehagueairport.nl

MAASTRICHT AACHEN AIRPORT
Vliegveldweg 17, 6191 SB Beek
Tel.: 043 358 99 99
www.maa.nl

EINDHOVEN AIRPORT
Luchthavenweg 25, 5657 EA Eindhoven
Tel.: 040 291 98 18
www.eindhovenairport.nl

GRONINGEN AIRPORT EELDE
Machlaan 14, 9761 TK Eelde
Tel.: 050 308 08 50
www.groningenairport.nl

LELYSTAD AIRPORT
Tel.: 0320 284 775
De Zwaluw 2, 8218 PD Lelystad
www.lelystad-airport.nl

Presumably, starting June 1 2016, tourists can make use of a new public transportation pass, called the Holland Travel Ticket. For either € 59 or € 39, they can use this ticket on the train, bus tram and metro – without limitation, for an entire day. The cheaper version will allow travel only after morning rush hour is over and in the weekends. If the card proves a success, it will be introduced permanently starting next spring. Where exactly it can be bought was not yet clear at the time this *Holland Handbook* went to press, but presumably at train stations, certainly at Schiphol Airport and eventually online, before coming to the Netherlands.

Tourists visiting the province of South Holland (which includes The Hague and Rotterdam) can buy a Tourist Day Ticket for € 13.50. This can be used on buses, trams, the metro and the waterbus – not the train. When you buy this ticket, you are given a free map with information on places to visit in the region. You can find an overview of where to buy a Tourist Day Ticket on www.touristdayticket.nl.

Visitors of Amsterdam can buy the Amsterdam Travel Ticket, which includes travel by train between Schiphol Airport and any train station in the city, as well as on the Amsterdam Airport Express bus, and unlimited travel on buses, trams, metros and ferries operated by GVB. It costs € 15 for one day, € 20 for two days, and € 25 for three, and comes with a map with highlights of the city. Sales points are: Schiphol Airport, Amsterdam Central Station and various other locations in the city.

If all you are planning on doing is traveling by train, and you are feeling adventurous, you can also opt for a so-called 'day ticket' (*dagkaart*), which can be bought at certain chain stores and supermarkets (such as *Albert Heijn*, *Blokker* or *Hema*) and is often offered in combination with a reduced price for, for instance, a zoo, a museum, a day of wellness, or a special lunch. These are temporary offers and an overview of what is available on a given day can be found on www.treinreiziger.nl. Click on *reizen*, then *kortingsacties*, then *overzicht goedkope treinkaartjes*.

AIRLINES FLYING TO AND FROM THE NETHERLANDS

Aer Lingus: www.aerlingus.com
Aeroflot Russian Airlines: www.aeroflot.com
Air Canada: www.aircanada.nl
Air France: www.airfrance.com
Alitalia: www.alitalia.nl
Arkefly: www.arkefly.nl
British Airways: www.britishairways.com
British Midland Airways: www.flybmi.com
Cathay Pacific Airways -
www.cathaypacific.com
China Airlines: www.china-airlines.nl
Cityjet: www.cityjet.com
Continental Airlines: www.continental.com
Corendon: www.corendon.nl
Delta Airlines: www.delta.com
Easyjet: www.easyjet.com
Finnair: www.finnair.com
Fly BMI: www.bmiregional.com/en
Iberia: www.iberia.com
Japan Airlines: www.jal.co.jp
KLM Royal Dutch Airlines: www.klm.nl

Lufthansa: www.lufthansa.com
Martinair Holland: www.martinair.com
Northwest Airlines: www.nwairlines.com
Qantas Airways: www.qantas.com
Ryanair: www.ryanair.com
SAS Scandinavian Airlines: www.flysas.com
Singapore Airlines: www.singaporeair.com
Transavia.com: www.transavia.com
Turkish Airlines: www.turkishairlines.com
United Airlines: www.unitedairlines.nl
US Airways: www.usairways.com
Virgin Atlantic: www.virgin-atlantic.com
Vueling: www.vueling.com

FLIGHT BOOKING

www.cheaptickets.nl
www.ebookers.nl
www.skyscanner.nl
www.vliegtickets.nl
www.vliegwinkel.nl

Once you have solved the more pressing matters, there are many other things you will need to know about living in the Netherlands, such as shopping hours and customs, how to arrange household help, safety, taking care of your pets, Dutch gardens and family life, (mobile) telephone and Internet Service Providers – not necessarily in that order. You will find answers to such 'pressing' questions as 'Why do the Dutch leave their curtains open?', but also on how to get your telephone service started and whether the Netherlands is a safe country to live in.

CONTRIBUTING AUTHORS STEPHANIE DIJKSTRA, CONNIE MOSER

SHOPPING

OPENING HOURS

Shopping hours in the Netherlands for a long time were based on the idea that people who work in shops should be able to live according to much the same pattern as other people. Nearly all shops were therefore closed on Sundays and in the evenings. This started to change during the '90s and in 1996 the government made it official by extending the number of hours shops are allowed to stay open. The pattern has therefore become much more variable, in order to meet the shopping needs of the many double-income households.

In general, shops in the Netherlands are open Monday through Saturday from 9 A.M. to 6 P.M., with the following most common exceptions:

- many shops (at least in the smaller villages) are closed on Monday mornings to enable shopkeepers to stock the shelves and do their administration
- small shops often close an hour or two early on Saturdays
- one evening each week, all shops in an area will either stay open until 9 P.M., or open again from 7 – 9 P.M. This is called *koopavond*, and is usually on a Thursday in cities and a Friday in towns and villages
- small shops might close at other times – at lunch-time, or on Wednesday afternoon, for example, when children are free from school
- the bigger supermarkets open an hour earlier and stay open a few hours longer in the evening to give people time to shop before or after work
- all stores in an area may decide to open their doors on Sundays, particularly in the bigger cities
- in the big cities you might be able to find a small grocery shop that is open late in the evenings and on Sundays. This is called an *avondwinkel*, and its prices will be higher than prices elsewhere
- mini-markets carrying a small selection of goods can be found at some gas stations, larger train stations and at Schiphol airport.

THE OPEN-AIR MARKET

Once or twice a week, each town or district will have an open-air market, often in the central market square. This starts at about 8 / 9 A.M. or 1 P.M. and closes between 4 and 6 P.M. Here you can buy fruit and vegetables, fish, sweets, bakery products, fabric, clothing, bedding, cosmetics and many other items. Excellent bargains can be found, but you must have a critical eye for quality.

Especially in the big city markets, products are available from all across the world in stalls that cater to the tastes of customers from, among others, the Caribbean and Mediterranean regions.

Keep in mind that the rules regarding starting and finishing hours can be applied so strictly that a market salesman will refuse to sell you his goods 15 minutes before 'opening time', even though it is pouring rain and you have a cantankerous baby with you and chances are absolutely nil that you will return at any other point during the day.

APPLIANCES

The current used in the Netherlands is 220 volt, so – unless you are inclined to import a shipload of converters or are moving here from another 220-volt country – you are most likely going to be looking for a small army of appliances when you move here.

The good news is that there are several chains for buying household appliances. They usually sell all that you need in one place: refrigerators, washing machines, dryers, dishwashers, vacuum cleaners, toasters, coffee machines, deep-frying pans, televisions, radios, heaters – that sort of stuff. Prices among these chains can vary considerably, so have a good look around before you spend a whole lot of unnecessary euros.

One tip is that little stores that reek of exclusivity – in towns filled with expats and other high-spenders – are bound to have a nice little margin on top of the purchasing price. On the other hand, they are also more likely to have someone who is willing to come over and help you install it all and to offer service with a smile, during your appliances' life-time. This is worth looking into and may even be worth that margin.

Another thought is that, as expats often move on to other countries where the current is different again, you could try the various clubs and your (spouse's) employer's Intranet-bulletins for second-hand goods.

The most common place in the Netherlands to go for second-hand goods nowadays is www.marktplaats.nl.

For buying a telephone, see further on, in *Being Connected*.

COMPUTERS AND SOFTWARE

Computers and software can be bought at larger and smaller computer, electronics and appliance (chain) stores, or via the Internet.

On rare occasions, certain supermarkets or large drugstore chains will offer a computer (or printer, or DVD-player)-bargain. There's no way to predict the likelihood of this, so it is a matter of chance – and luck – whether you will run into such an offer just as you are looking for a computer – or printer, or DVD-player.

FURNITURE, BEDS

Furniture can be bought in any number of places, from tiny, exclusive little shops to big well-known chains. The Netherlands has two names for its furniture conglomerates, being either *meubelboulevards* or *woonboulevards* (furniture or living boulevards). Some are huge indoor malls with stores of all levels of exclusivity, some are geographic locations where a sizeable collection of larger stores are all located. There are also *brocante*-stores (where they sell furniture and other more decorative items that do not yet quite deserve the name antique, but are already in the 'nostalgic'-category) as well as, of course, antique stores (see more about these in Chapter 11, under *For Antique Lovers Only*). In Chapter 9, under *Living On A Shoestring*, you will find more on low-budget spending.

Beds can be bought at either certain furniture chains or stores as well as in specialized stores.

BOOKS

With the exception of the bookstores in possibly the littler towns, they almost all carry a selection of English-language books. In the bigger cities, there are specialized English-language bookstores such as the American Book Center or Waterstone's – and then there are the large bookstores that carry not only English-language books, but also, for instance, French, German and Spanish.

A CLEAN HOME AND SELF

Detergents, floor polishers, carpet cleaners and the like can be bought both in supermarkets (again, prices can vary considerably, so if you have a tight budget, shop around!), but also at the drugstore (*drogisterij*) – where you will also find drain de-cloggers, stain removers, mold removers and some of the more chemical products.

Soaps, shampoos, toothbrushes, toothpaste, shaving cream, hand cream and sanitary items can also be bought at supermarkets and *drogisterijen* – while at the latter you will also find make-up, homeopathic medicines, dietary supplements, bubble baths, some toys, travel kits, mosquito repellent and a range of massage oils, for starters.

Baby necessities, including food and formula, can also be bought at either type of store.

SHOPPING ETIQUETTE

Take one or more shopping bags with you when you go to buy groceries. Even in the supermarket, you must pack your groceries yourself. While you already paid for the sturdier plastic bags at the supermarket, as of this year, shops must charge you for the smaller bags they pack your groceries in, too. This way, the government hopes to make consumers more aware of plastic pollution and to thereby protect the environment. The really thin bags for meats, fruits and vegetables will remain free, the rest can cost anywhere between two and 25 cents. All supermarkets have shopping carts handy at the entrance, but in most supermarkets they are interlocked with chains and it takes a 50-cent or one-euro coin to unlock the connection. You get your coin back when you re-connect the cart.

Payments can be made with cash, but shops also accept PIN or bank debit cards.

GETTING SERVED

The Dutch do not queue, as you will soon notice. You must learn the art of gently but firmly pushing your way into the bus or train, for example. You must also learn the art of getting served in a shop. Look first to see if there is a system by which people take numbers from a small dispenser at the entrance. This makes it easy; you need only watch for your number to come up. Otherwise you are expected to keep track of who was waiting before you and to speak up when it is your turn. A trick, used by many Dutch, is to enquire: '*Wie was de laatste?*' (Who came in last?), this way, you only have to keep an eye on this person to know when your turn is. This takes practice (and patience).

BARGAINING

This is not customary. You are expected to pay the price that is marked, especially for new items. If you are buying something second-hand – at a flea market, for example – you can try making

- the Dutch consume an average of 7.7 kilograms of coffee per person per year. This makes the Dutch the fourth biggest coffee drinkers in the world, after Finland, Norway and Sweden
- 91% of the population (15 years old and over) drinks coffee
- the Dutch drink an average of 84 liters of beer per person per year
- there are 1.2 million milk cows in the Netherlands. They produce 10.5 billion liters of milk
- over half of all the milk produced in the Netherlands is turned into cheese
- the Netherlands is the world's largest exporter of cheese, butter and powdered milk

- Dutch exports of milk and dairy products total approximately € 3.6 billion
- the Netherlands exports 1 billion kilos of tomatoes, or 62 kilos per person
- 5% of 12-16 year-olds has occasionally smoked, and 27% of 16-20 year-olds
- Dutch libraries lend out 85.2 million books a year; 40.8 million of these are for young readers
- one out of ten Dutch adults is left-handed
- 19.5% of the Dutch population does not drink alcohol (drinking, on average, one glass of alcohol a day); 80.7% of those between the ages of 12-16 don't drink.

an offer. The answer will be an angry 'no', however, if you drop the price by more than about 25%.

EYE CONTACT AND GREETINGS

When Dutch people enter and leave a small shop, they generally greet the shopkeeper ('*Goede dag*' – good day – is always a friendly greeting). It is important in any case to acknowledge the shopkeeper's presence by at least establishing eye contact.

FOOD

The Netherlands is a former shipping and colonial power that had interests in Indonesia, South Africa and the Caribbean. Many people from these countries eventually came to live in the Netherlands. They were later joined by guest workers from the Mediterranean countries and by international businessmen and women and their families as the Netherlands became the hub of their business interests in Europe. Thus, the Netherlands is a truly international country and it is relatively easy to find supermarkets and delicatessen / gourmet food shops that cater to most culinary needs.

DUTCH WAY OF EATING

The Dutch usually only eat one hot meal a day; it can be served for lunch or dinner, but it is generally served as the evening meal. Breakfast may consist of fresh breads or open-faced sandwiches made of bread, fresh from the bakery, or Dutch rusks (*beschuit*), rolls, or croissants topped with butter, jams or jellies, cheese, sausages or cold cuts. Lunch is usually more of the same, but it might include a small cup of hot soup (this does not qualify as a hot meal), fruit, a *kroket* (croquettes – *kroketten* are shaped like a fat hot dog, but are made with a soft, meat-based filling, covered in bread crumbs and fried), a mixed salad, or an *uitsmijter* (two fried eggs on

a layer of ham, roast beef and/or cheese on two slices of bread). The meal is accompanied by milk, coffee or tea. There are coffee and/or tea breaks in the mornings and afternoons that are sacred in the Netherlands (also in the offices) and the piping hot beverages are served with cookies – or pastries or cakes, if there is a special occasion. In the evening, there might be a *borrel* or drink consisting of, in most cases, beer, and a snack such as *bitterballen* (little round croquettes) before dinner – though, again, this is most often saved for a special occasion. Dinner is heartier with vegetables, meat and a healthy serving of the ubiquitous potato side dish like *patat frites* (French fries) or merely potatoes that are boiled or steamed. Sometimes, the vegetables and potatoes are mashed together to create the traditional Dutch *stamppot* dishes (see next paragraph), which are served with some delicious *rookworst* (smoked sausage) or *draadjesvlees* (simmered beef). There is also some kind of dessert, usually yogurt that comes in a variety of tastes, or *vla* (custard), fruit or sometimes cheese. To accompany the meals, the Dutch usually stick to water or milk or maybe soft drinks – wine is more often saved for special occasions.

When the Dutch eat out, they will eat the foods they don't cook at home, in other words, Indonesian, Italian, French, and Chinese, among others.

TYPICAL DUTCH FOODS

While the local cuisine is rich in variety due to the inclusion of many recipes that criss-cross international borders, there is a basic Dutch cuisine that is best described as 'home cooking'. It is the 'comfort food' that most Dutchmen crave when away from home

for prolonged periods or after a summer of light meals.

If you were to ask a Dutchman to name one national dish, he would probably mention *erwtensoep* (pea soup). Next would come the *stamppot* dishes of *boerenkool met worst* (curly kale with sausage), *hachée* (beef and onion stew), *zuurkool met worst* (sauerkraut with sausage) and *witlof met ham en kaas* (Belgian endives with ham and cheese sauce). In May and June, everyone eats *asperges met ham en eieren* (asparagus with ham and eggs).

Other goodies that are generally the first to be consumed by the Dutch who have been away for a while are: a *boterham met hagelslag* or *vlokken* (sandwich with chocolate sprinkles or flakes), *bitterballen* or *kroketten*, *stroopwafels* (fine waffles, filled with syrup) and raw herring with chopped onions.

INDONESIAN/CHINESE FOOD & SPICES

At last count, there were over 900 Chinese/Indonesian shops in the Netherlands. Thus it is safe to say that virtually everyone in the Netherlands eats Indonesian food in what has become known as the Indonesian *rijsttafel*, where rice is the central dish with any number of side dishes. These may include three different types of rice, several fish, meat, poultry and vegetables dishes, and condiments. The *rijsttafel* may be prepared at home, eaten at restaurants or carried home from Indonesian or Chinese/Indonesian takeouts.

If you are thinking of preparing some of these dishes yourself, then it is good to know that since the 16th century, when the Dutch explorers started to return from the orient with exotic spices, these spices have had an important place in the Dutch kitchen cabinet. Most are available in the supermarkets. If you don't find what you are looking for there, almost all of the herbs and spices known to man are sold in Indonesian shops or *tokos*, and Chinese supermarkets.

ETHNIC SHOPS

Also in the big cities you will find shops specializing in foods and other products for specific ethnic groups, such as a *Turkse slager* (a *slager* is a butcher) or a *Turkse winkel*, where they sell products from Turkey and the eastern Mediterranean. You can buy meat that is *halal* at an *Islamitische slager*. In Amsterdam you can find kosher (Jewish) meat markets, and in Amsterdam, Rotterdam and The Hague there is a small Chinatown. And there are more possibilities: Moroccan, Japanese, Indian, etc. Also available are the Tex/Mex dishes popular in America; most supermarkets have a small Tex/Mex department.

If you are looking for something from a specific culinary/geographic area, check the Internet.

SUPERMARKETS

Dutch supermarkets carry the basic groceries, such as baking and cooking ingredients, dairy products (including cheese), herbs and spices, bakery goods, some health foods, 'exotic foods' (such as Japanese, Moroccan, Tex/Mex, Indian and Indonesian), fruits and vegetables, meats, fish and poultry, baby foods and pet foods, along with daily house and kitchen supplies (such as detergent, toilet paper and cleaning supplies). The selection of frozen foods is proportionate to the capacity of the store; the larger the supermarket, the more goods there are on offer.

At the supermarkets you can browse at your leisure while getting acquainted with the local products, and buy the basics to stock your pantry. If you feel shy or awkward about the language, contact can be kept to a minimum. The check-out system is relatively simple and not all that different from the systems in other countries. However, there will come a time when you will overcome your fears and be lured by the sights and smells of the neighborhood specialty shops, or stalls at open markets.

DAIRY PRODUCTS

Of all of the wonderful foodstuffs produced in the Netherlands, the Dutch are probably most proud of their milk and milk products. The ubiquitous purveyor of this life-sustaining substance, the Holstein Frisian cow, grazes everywhere. The Gouda and Edam cheeses are so well-known around the globe that wherever cheese is sold, Gouda and/or Edam are always present.

While the supermarkets offer a good selection of fresh and processed cheese, serious cheese lovers and connoisseurs shop at their local cheese specialist or *kaasspecialist*. He not only has the largest selection of cheeses, but he ages his Dutch cheeses naturally to obtain the optimum taste and perfection, and his cheeses never hit the shelves until they are least two months old. And, since most Dutch cheeses are classified according to age, he keeps a watchful eye on the aging process. The cheese shops and supermarket cheese departments are also well-stocked with imported cheeses from among others France, Italy, Spain, Belgium and England.

Generally, the place to buy your milk and other dairy products is in the supermarket; however, you might also consider buying directly from the cheese farms that sell fresh farmer's milk, buttermilk, eggs and cheese – and of course from the cheese specialist.

BAKERY – *BAKKERIJ*

The shops that probably delight foreign residents most are the bakeries (*bakkerijen*) that turn out those mouth-watering fresh breads, rolls, cookies, pastries and creamy bon-bons. At Christmastime they have a full range of seasonal breads and cookies, then at Easter-time they outdo themselves with a stunning array of brilliant, foil-wrapped chocolate bunnies, bon-bons, marzipan animals and fruits and cakes decorated for the season.

The bakeries often also offer breads baked according to French, Italian and Middle Eastern tradition. Bread is baked fresh daily and is often still hot when you get home from your shopping.

THE FISH SHOP – *VISHANDEL*

Although not the great seafaring nation it once was, the Netherlands still retains its reputation for being a purveyor of fine sea-

ALCOHOL USE

SALE OF LIQUOR

From the age of 18 onwards you may legally buy beer, wine and liquor. Until recently, beer and wine could be sold to kids as of the age of 16, however, in order to protect their developing brain, the government decided to raise the age limit. Alcoholic beverages are for sale in liquor stores and supermarkets, though supermarkets only sell beer, wine and alcoholic beverages with an alcohol percentage up to 12 to 13%.

Bartenders, liquor dealers and cashiers must ask youngsters who are buying alcohol from them to submit proof of their age, such as a passport, ID-card or driver's license. If either of these cannot be supplied, they are not allowed to sell it to them.

DRINKING AND DRIVING

You may not drive if you are over the 0.5-blood alcohol level or, during the first five years after you have been issued a driver's license, 0.2. This latter limit also applies to drivers of mopeds and motorized bicycles until the age of 24. Driving under the influence is a criminal offense and applies to driving a car and riding a motorcycle, scooter, moped or bicycle. You risk a fine running from € 360 to € 1,100 (€ 125 to € 700, if you are riding on a moped or a scooter), depending on your blood alcohol level, plus a possible ban on driving of up to almost a year and possible incarceration. In some cases (for instance, if your blood alcohol level is between 1.3 and 1.8, or as a 'beginning' driver, over 0.8), you may be required to take a two-halfday (€ 546) or four-halfday (€ 870) course (to be paid for by you), which, if you do not take it (from start to finish) could lead to the loss of your driver's license. If your blood alcohol level exceeds 1.8, you may also be required to take a € 1,056 alcohol dependency test. Also drunk cyclists can expect a fine anywhere between € 100 and € 200.

If you are caught driving under the influence of soft or hard drugs, you run the risk of three months of incarceration, having your driver's license suspended for five years, or a fine of up to € 7,800.

DRUG USE

For the record, trafficking in (importing or exporting), selling, producing and processing either hard or soft drugs are offenses in the Netherlands. The possession of soft drugs (up to 30 grams) or hard drugs (0.5 grams) for personal use is a summary, non-indictable offense. Anyone under the age of 18 caught with 5 grams of soft drugs will have to hand them in, pay a fine of € 60 and do 12 hours of community service. If they have between 5 and 30 grams, the fine goes up to € 65.

COFFEE SHOPS

Coffee shops can sell soft drugs without being prosecuted, pro-vided they observe strict rules. The aim of this policy is to prevent users of soft drugs from becoming marginalized or being exposed to more harmful drugs.

A coffee shop can best be described as a café that does not sell alcoholic beverages (except in Amsterdam, where some do), and in which, subject to certain restrictions, soft drugs may be sold. Although the sale of soft drugs is an offense, low priority is given to the prosecution of coffee shop owners, provided they sell small quantities only and meet the following conditions:

- no more than five grams per person may be sold in any one transaction
- the stock may not exceed 500 grams
- no hard drugs may be sold
- drugs may not be advertised
- the coffee shop must not cause any nuisance
- no drugs may be sold to persons under the age of 18, nor may minors be admitted onto the premises.

Municipalities may set up extra rules, for instance regarding the proximity to schools, the presence of informational material and the required physical presence of the proprietor. Agreements are made with the local police regarding routine checks and the mayor of a city has the authority to close coffee shops that do not meet these conditions.

For those of you who think coffee shops can only be found in the bigger cities: there are somewhere in the vicinity of 900 coffee shops, spread over 100-plus municipalities. As this is more than 25% of all Dutch municipalities and only a handful of these are 'big' cities, don't be surprised if your sleepy little village has one too. Incidentally, three-quarters of the cannabis they sell is of the home-grown variety (referred to as 'nederwiet').

LEGAL GYMNASTICS

The Dutch government has to perform legal gymnastics in order to make the sale of soft drugs in 'coffee shops' possible. First of all, clearly, the sale of soft drugs is not allowed. Secondly, nor is the culturing of soft drugs. To nonetheless make the existence of coffee shops possible, two terms have been introduced: 'gedoog-beleid' (policy of tolerance) and 'lage opsporingsbeleid' (policy of low investigational priority). The sale of soft drugs in coffee shops is tolerated and, provided the conditions are met, the culturing of soft drugs to be sold via coffee shops will not be prosecuted. If is often remarked that the words 'tolerance' and 'flex-ibility' well describe the Dutch mentality – and there is no better example than this, some might say. Another interesting observation is that, though shop owners may not charge VAT over their sales, they do owe income tax over their income; generating a pleasant calculated € 400 million a year for the state coffers.

DRUG TOURISM

For a short while, the government managed to introduce a law stating that, if you were planning on getting a taste of the mellow side of Dutch life and joining the crowd in a coffee shop for a little recreational consumption, you had to become member of the shop – including membership card, only available to those who could demonstrate that they were living in the municipality in which the coffee shop is established. This is no longer the case. Now, theoretically, all you have to do is prove you are a legal resident – but already several municipalities have announced that they will not be enforcing this rule. Coffee shop owners, meanwhile, are expected to destroy their 'membership' lists.

food. The quality and quantity available here are excellent. Supermarkets may carry a small variety of fish and seafood but the seafood specialists in the shops called *vishandel* offer by far the largest selection. Not every village has one, so look in the larger towns for the best selection.

Much of what is on sale is cold water fish but occasionally you will see some excellent fish from the Mediterranean. In addition to the fish you buy to prepare yourself, the fishmonger will have some pre-fried haddock and codpieces, raw and pickled herring and some excellent prepared dishes such as fish salads, jambalaya and paella. The fishmonger will also cut or fillet your fish to your specifications.

THE CHICKEN OR POULTRY SPECIALIST – *POELIER*
While most supermarkets and butcher shops and some stalls at open markets carry whole chickens, chicken parts and eggs, there are also shops that specialize in all kinds of poultry and eggs and, in the late autumn and winter months, game birds and game. The signs outside their establishments either read *kip specialist* or *poelier – wild en gevogelte* (venison and fowl). Most of these shops have a selection of chicken and turkey parts, rolled roasts, ground chicken and turkey, and prepared foods such as chicken *saté* and grilled chicken, as well as (prepared) rice and vegetable dishes.

GREENGROCERY – *GROENTEBOER*
Dutch farmers provide this country with a stunning variety of fruits and vegetables. There is a large concentration of apple, pear and cherry orchards in the Betuwe region while vegetable gardens and greenhouses dot the landscape. To supplement these locally-grown products, fruits and vegetables are imported from as far away as China and South America.

Vegetables play a central role in the Dutch meal, so you can expect them to be fresh and tasty. Supermarkets all have a fruit and vegetable department, but for the best selection and personal service, you might want to try the independent greengrocer known as *groenteboer* and his/her shop, called the *groentewinkel,* while often the local Turkish/Moroccan store will also carry an excellent selection of fresh fruit and vegetables. Many greengrocers also offer prepared *rauwkost* (cut fruits or salad material ready for mixed salads), soups, stews and casseroles. In the late autumn and winter months they sell packets of pre-cut vegetables for the famous Dutch pea soup and *stamppot* dishes.

THE BUTCHER'S – *SLAGER*
Dutch farmers produce very fine beef, pork, lamb, veal and poultry. However, if you have been raised on succulent marbled steaks and roasts carved from grain-fed beef cattle, the local beef may be disappointing; it is lean – but it *does* have a fuller flavor than its grain-fed cousins. Thus, a good butcher is invaluable. You will find him behind the butcher counter in butcher shops and supermarkets. He is called a *slager* and his business is called a *slagerij*. Visit him on a quiet day and he will usually be willing to give advice on how to cook the Dutch meats. Notice the singular way he trims and presents his meats. Almost all fat and bones are removed from the beef and if you want the bones for soups and stews, you will have to pay extra.

A good, innovative butcher prepares the meats for barbecues, fondues and snacks and sells prepared salads and sauces as accom-

CONVERSIONS

DIMENSIONS

AMERICAN	METRIC
0.03937 in	1 millimeter [mm]
0.3937 in	1 centimeter [cm]
39.37 in / 1.094 yard	1 meter [m]
0.621 mi / 3281.5 ft	1 kilometer [km]

AMERICAN	METRIC
1 inch	2.54 cm
1 foot	0.3048 m
1 yard	0.9144 m
1 mile	1609 m

DRY MEASURES

AMERICAN	METRIC
1 ounce	30 grams
1/2 pound	225 grams
1 pound	450 grams
2.2 pounds	1 kilogram

AMERICAN	DUTCH
3 1/2 ounces	1 ons = 100 gram
1.1 pounds	5 ons = 500 gram= 1 pond
2.2 pounds	10 ons = 2 pond= 1 kg
1/2 cup + 1T	1 kopje
1T	1 eetlepel [el] = 15 gram
1/2 t	1 theelepel [tl] = een lepeltje

LIQUID MEASURES

AMERICAN	DUTCH
1 quart + 3T	1 liter
3T + 1t	1/2 deciliter [dl]
6T +1t	1 deciliter = 1/10 liter
1/2c + 2t	2 deciliter
3/4c + 2t	2 1/2 deciliter
1 1/3 c	3 deciliter

TEMPERATURE

Fahrenheit to Celsius
• Substract 32 and multiply by 5, then divide by 9
• Example: 68°F: 68-32=36, 36x5=180, 180/9=20°C

Celsius to Fahrenheit
• Multiply by 9, divide by 5 and add 32
• Example: 20°C: 20x9=180, 180/5=36, 36+32=68°F

OVEN TEMPERATURES

FAHRENHEIT	CELSIUS
300	150
325	165
350	180
375	190
400	205
425	220
450	230
475	245
500	260

paniments. He might also have some delicatessen dishes such as quiches and savory meat pies. He most certainly offers some delicious locally-made sausages and cold cuts from all across Europe.

CHILDREN'S FOODS
Everything is in place for raising healthy babies in the Netherlands. Supermarkets, drugstores (*drogisterijen*) and pharmacies (*apotheken*) all carry baby foods in jars, as well as vitamins and infant formulas. Your *huisarts* (GP) or the doctor at the *Consultatiebureau* (Well-Baby Clinic, see page 234) can also recommend foods for your baby and will refer you to a specialist if required.

HEALTH AND VEGETARIAN FOODS
The Dutch are very aware of the benefits of eating well and there are health food departments in every supermarket. There are also health food stores (*reformhuizen* or *reformwinkels*) in most cities and villages. Theirs are natural products with no chemicals added that are made from organically grown or *biologische* materials. Many greengrocers also sell prepared vegetarian foods and organically-grown or eco foods. At least one health food company offers boxes that are delivered to your home, together with recipes, saving you the effort of planning and shopping for dinner. These are also available from non health-food affiliated stores/supermarkets.

QUANTITIES TO BUY
Food sold in bulk is advertised by the piece (*per stuk*) or by weight:
- kilo = 1,000 grams = 2.2 (US) pounds
- pond = 500 grams = 1.1 (US) pounds
- ons = 100 grams = approx. 3.5 ounces

HOUSEHOLD HELP

Quite a few Dutch households make use of a household help / cleaning lady, most often referred to as *hulp in het huishouden* – lit-erally 'household help' – or a *werkster*. Cleaning ladies are very hard to find, but there are a few ways in which you can go about this: you can hang a little card on the notice board of your local supermarket (while you're at it, check and see if someone hasn't hung up a card, offering their services) or you can place an ad in the local newspaper. Most newspapers have an item called *Kleintjes*, which means 'little ones', that has been created specifically for short notices and ads. The card or ad should state: *hulp in het huishouden gezocht* and you might want to add the fact that it would be helpful if (he or) she spoke English – or some other common language. A third, and probably best, way to find household help is through friends, neighbors and other acquaintances, as this way you are more likely to find a reliable, dependable and honest one.

The per-hour price for household help is usually around € 10-15, plus sometimes their public transportation fare. Contrary to what was the case for a long time, if you hire household help, you are not expected to withhold wage tax and social insurance contributions on the wages you pay out to them – provided they do not work for you more than three days a week. They are then expected to declare their own earnings on their income tax return. Once they work for you more than three days a week, you are expected to withhold wage tax and social insurance contributions – though special rules apply. Make sure you have yourself informed by a tax specialist, before you tread on slippery ground!

In the bigger cities, you will find commercial cleaning companies for businesses that offer an on-the-side service of household help. Their hourly rate is a bit higher, as the company pays their taxes and contributions. To find one of these companies, you can check the Yellow Pages or Internet under *Schoonmaakbedrijven*, and see if one of them offers *Huishoudelijk werk*. Or else just select one of the bigger-looking companies and call and ask. Beware of the fact that they may have long waiting lists! On the Internet, you might wish to give www.ikzoekeenwittewerkster.nl a try – with 'wit' (white), they mean that your household help owes taxes over her earnings!

SAFETY

The Netherlands is a safe country to live in. Your children can safely ride their bikes to school (the impatience of the average Dutch driver being the greatest threat) and you can safely go out to dinner – even in the 'big' cities and even after dark. In the smaller towns, this is even more so.

Drug-related crime, murder and other forms of human aggression are at a low level here. But let's remain realistic: they do, of course, take place and you must always keep your eyes and senses (particularly your common sense) open. Do not go walking in deserted (woody) areas after dark. Do not use the cash dispenser, when the only other person around is a nervous, strung out-looking individual. When walking alone, search for well-lit areas. Keep your eye on your child. And no matter where you are, do not leave your mobile phone, computer or other obvious valuables behind in the car, where everyone can see them.

BEING IN THE BIG CITIES

It goes without saying that, as in any big city, you should keep your eye on your purse, bags, cameras and whatever else you might have on you. And that you should not wander alone into a dark alley-way. And that if you do not like the looks of certain characters hanging around the street you want to go into, you should walk down the next, if you have that option. It also goes without saying that it is always better to have the look of a worldly-wise, undaunted cosmopolitan – rather than a frightened, hunted deer. It is human nature for con artists, thieves and other unpleasant folk to zero in on a person 'asking' to be a victim. But that goes for walking around in Atlanta, Santiago, Seville and Singapore too.

A MYTH OR TWO

Now that we are talking about the big cities, this is a good oppor-tunity to deal with a myth or two about the Netherlands. Yes, the government hands out drugs – for free – to so-called 'incurable' drug addicts. As you might know, the Dutch are big on helping the underdog, and assistance is given to drug addicts to promote their rehabilitation, to improve their physical and mental condition and to improve their social circumstances. However, when 'free' drugs are handed out, this is not so much to make life easier for the drug users, but rather to decrease crime in the streets. Instead of having desperate junkies roaming the streets, looking for someone to mug, the government has chosen to hand out drugs, which they do in fixed places in the big cities – away from the crowds – where the addicts know where to find them.

And yes, there are areas in the cities where prostitution is condoned. One of these areas, the so-called red-light district in Amsterdam, is famous for it. It might interest you to know that this can be considered one of the safest areas of Amsterdam: it is always well-lit, well-patrolled by the police and never deserted, as the prostitution industry is one that operates 24 hours a day – particularly at night, of course. However, should you wish to visit the area, a daytime visit may be a better idea as this will reduce the risk of being targeted by the nevertheless ever-present pickpockets or other questionable characters with dubious intentions. If there is ever any problem, you can rest assured that there is nothing the police hasn't seen or dealt with – so don't hesitate to enlist their help.

REPORTING A CRIME

Should you become a victim of crime, locate the nearest police officer or police station to report it. The police will take your statement, give advice on canceling credit cards and provide you with helpful phone numbers and addresses. Be sure to give a description of the culprit and the location. In the Netherlands, good citizens turn in found wallets or purses to the police. Thieves remove the cash, bank cards and credit cards and toss the rest.

OBLIGATION TO CARRY ID

Everyone over the age of 13 must carry some form of legal ID at all times; this being a passport (for EU nationals) or a valid aliens document (for non-EU nationals). Dutch nationals may show either a driver's license, a passport, or an identity card. Photocopies are not allowed, nor is inviting the police officer to your home to check your documents. Children over the age of 13 must have their own papers; inclusion in their parents' passport is not enough.

Who is authorized to ask you to show your papers? The police are, as well as parking inspectors, officers of the Health and Safety Inspectorate, inspectors from the Building Control Department, tax inspectors, customs inspectors, forest rangers (whom you will meet while walking your dog), school inspectors, etc. And, of course, but this is a totally different type of situation, you show your ID when opening a bank account, requesting a government benefit, starting a new job, etc. – AND when attending a soccer game...

The purpose of this obligation is to help combat crime and you may only be requested to show your documents if there is a valid reason – for instance, if you have committed a (traffic) offense or crime, are using public transportation without having paid for it, or if the police needs your assistance, for instance to help solve a crime, or to maintain the public order. The request must be in keeping with the position of the person asking you for your ID. In other words, a tax inspector cannot detain you for this purpose in connection with running a red light.

If you refuse to comply, you may be taken to the police station for identification and run the risk of owing a € 45 fine, for those younger than 16, and € 90 for those older than 16.

Store and building security officers may ask you for your ID, but you do not have to show it. However, they are then allowed to deny you entry or to escort you out of the building.

Confirm the loss or theft in writing to your insurance company, including a copy of the police report. It is always a good idea to have copies of your travel documents and/or important papers in case something unfortunate does happen.

LOCK YOUR DOOR

Streets are generally well-lit in the cities and towns in the Netherlands, so that you can safely let out your dog in the evening, run to the supermarket or walk to your friends' house a couple of streets away. When you leave the house, however, it is always best to lock the door, particularly if you live in a reasonably well-to-do neighborhood. There is always the chance that there is a certain individual out there, waiting for you to leave the house.

Make sure you have good locks on your doors and windows. Double locks on doors, or dead bolts, can offer additional protection. A *dievenklauw* is a special lock that prevents entry. A locksmith can install these for you, or you can purchase the locks yourself at a hardware or do-it-yourself store.

A SAFE HOME

Although it is customary for the Dutch to leave their curtains open, it is generally not a good idea to show off too many possessions. Having expensive television, stereo and computer equipment out in full view might prove to be too tempting. Likewise leaving a pocketbook or wallet on the table, or jewelry you have removed from your person, could pique the interest of a potential thief.

There are security systems companies (*beveiligingsbedrijven*) with specialists who can install security systems for you. They can help you with alarm systems, video cameras, fences, electronic eyes, movement detectors, lighting, etc.

In order to ascertain that you are dealing with a reputable agency for your security needs, look for the *Preventiecertificaat* or *Politiekeurmerk* registration. Not only does this guarantee the reliability of their personnel and the quality of the work, it is also recognized by insurance companies, so that you may be entitled to discounts on your personal property and home owners' insurance (*inboedel* and *opstal verzekering*). A list of companies with these certifications can be found on www.preventiecertificaat.nl and www.politiekeurmerk.nl. Always ask if a company has this certification before doing business with them.

If you would prefer not to leave behind an empty house, but can't find anyone who'd be willing to watch over it for while, you could always try to find someone via a house-sitter organization. One such organization is Holiday Link, which you can find on www.holidaylink.com (click on *Vakantieoppas*), while there is also www.huisoppas.nl, www.huisoppasser.nl or www.homecare-oppas.nl. House-sitters will even take care of your pets, if you want.

FIRE PROTECTION

All homes should have smoke alarms, and they are easily installed. If you are renting, ask your landlord to do it. If he is unwilling, you can do it yourself. Smoke alarms can be bought at do-it-yourself/hardware stores or department stores. Small fire extinguishers can also be purchased at do-it-yourself/hardware stores, while fire blankets for kitchens and powder extinguishers are also available.

OCCUPANT IDENTIFICATION CARD

Special red, white and blue identification cards can be filled in listing the names of all of the occupants of the house (including pets). In Dutch, these are called *Meterkast Identificatie Kaart*. This ID-card is then hung in your meter closet (*meterkast*) in the hallway. In the event of an emergency, or a fire, the police and fire department will first look here for any information on the inhabitants of the house. Cards are available at your local police bureau.

EMERGENCY!

Should you have an emergency and need the police, the fire department or an ambulance, the national number for all services in Holland is: 1-1-2.

You can stick a 1-1-2 sticker on your phone and let all family members know this is the number to call if a serious emergency arises. The operator will send the services you need, or all three if required.

If there is a problem that does not constitute an emergency, 0900 8844 will connect you to your local police.

RECYCLING AND WASTE MANAGEMENT

In general the Netherlands is considered to be a very 'green' country; not just for its wide-open fields, but also for the mentality of the Dutch in protecting their environment. The vast majority of the population takes part in various recycling efforts. From the organic waste, which is collected separately, compost is made which is then reused in gardens and agriculture. Of the more than two million tons of paper and glass collected, close to 90% is recycled and used for new products.

The Ministry of Infrastructure and Environment (Ministerie van Infrastructuur en Milieu) works in close cooperation with international and domestic partners on improving the living environment of this country. There are many organizations working to monitor issues such as living space, respect for nature, space and raw materials and over 4,000 people are concerned with issues of living space, housing and environment. An additional task is to plan, conduct and supervise the building of projects in government housing, and to develop a sustainable environmental policy. There are also numerous programs and activities that citizens can get involved in aimed at helping to preserve and improve the environment.

To foreigners coming to live in the Netherlands, the rules and regulations may seem to be bewildering in their detail, so here is a basic guideline to the most common recycling practices.

1. Recycling tax: upon purchasing new electronic and household equipment, you will automatically be charged a recycling tax or removal tax known as *verwijderingsbijdrage*, regardless of whether you are handing in an old appliance or not. The assumption is that, for each new appliance purchased, the old one will have to be environmentally disposed of or recycled at some point in time. A list of rates is available from the store.

2. Household waste: outside of Amsterdam, households are usually furnished with two, or sometimes three, separate waste containers (a green *groenbak* for garden, fruit and vegetable waste, a gray *grijs container* for all remaining waste, and, as the case may be, a third container for paper). As of 2015, many municipalities have issued their inhabitants yet another container: for plastics, metal, and drink packaging (PMD), encouraging consumers to separate these *before* they are taken to the waste separation facilities. These containers are emptied on alternating weeks. Pay attention – if you place the wrong container at the curbside it will not be emptied. In some cities the city provides a multi-purpose waste container, a so-called *duobak*. This is one container with a separation inside. The smaller part in the back is intended for 'green' waste, the larger part in the front for all other waste. If you feel the container(s) provided is/are not sufficient, you can always contact the city council for an additional one. This will entail an additional yearly contribution, as the additional waste also needs to be disposed of. Make sure you do not leave your containers on the street at the end of the day. You can be fined for not returning them to your property. There are a few municipalities where glass and paper are also collected curbside, usually in wealthier suburban areas.

3. Groenbak: cat litter and used baby diapers are not considered organic waste for the *groenbak* and should be placed in the gray container. Milk packages, plastic bags, large pieces of wood and thick tree branches, the ashes from your fireplace, sand, dog and cat hair and the contents of your vacuum cleaner are also NOT to be placed in the green container. 'Green waste' is vegetable, fruit, and potato peels, leftover cooked food, fish and meat leftovers with bones (wrapped in newspaper in the summer months), nut shells and eggshells, hardened cooking fat, tea bags, coffee filters with coffee grains, small garden trim-

mings, mowed grass and leaves, weeds, flowers and house-plants, straw and the contents of your hamster or rabbit cages.

In some cities, due to the lack of space, there unfortunately is no separation of waste, other than what a private individual brings to the separate waste disposal stations and/or containers. Most towns publish a calendar, distributed around November (regarding the following year) to each household, of contact addresses for properly disposing of all types of waste, as well as pick-up dates for waste containers and locations for *chemokars* (chemical cars – see further on, under chemical waste). If you don't have one of these calendars, you can request one from your *gemeentereinigingsdienst* (sanitation department) or download it from your municipality's website.

4. Refunds on bottles: most glass soft drink bottles, the large acrylic plastic *euroflessen* and some small glass bottles or jars have a deposit that is paid upon buying them. The word *statie-geld* (deposit) and an amount will be listed on the label. Once you return these to the store for recycling (there are special bottle stations for these at most supermarkets), the deposit is returned to you by way of a *bonnetje*, or paper receipt, after you have placed the bottles into the bottle return machine. This receipt can be redeemed when you pay for your groceries or at the *klantenservice* (customer service).

5. Glass: all glass that does not have a deposit can be dropped in special containers which are usually placed at convenient locations throughout the town (such as in the supermarket parking area). There is often a symbol on the label showing a hand with a bottle and the word *glasbak*. These 'glass collectors' (*glasbakken*) are often, but not always, yellow. Some cities allow for the separation of white, green and brown glass. The containers will stipulate *bont* (white), *groen* (green), or *bruin* (brown). Since this effort was started, the Dutch have come to recycle more than 89% of their glass.

6. Paper: often placed near to the glass recycling containers you will find the blue paper collectors (*papierbakken*). Again, most of the paper in the Netherlands is recycled. You may recycle newspapers, magazines, junk mail, envelopes, paper packaging, and wrappers. Don't forget to remove all plastic first. As mentioned earlier, in a number of municipalities, houses are provided with a separate paper container.

7. Batteries: most supermarkets and some stores and schools have special containers for collecting old batteries. Often these are located by the bottle recycling station at the grocery store or at the checkout counter of stores; the *batterijenbak* is usually red or blue. If none are available close by, you can ask at the supermarket or inquire with the city council where the nearest collection points are (batteries can also be handed in with other chemical waste – see next point).

8. Chemical waste (paint and painting materials, toners, printer cartridges, batteries, oil, turpentine, nail polish, and caustic cleaning agents, etc.): many cities have a special car (*chemokar*) that comes by every three months to collect chemical waste. You can check with the city council on collection dates and

times or request the calendar listing all relevant contact information for the year.

Alternatively, you can dispose of these materials, as other large pieces of rubbish (construction waste, car tires, etc.), at the waste separation and recycling station that is available in nearly every city and town.

9. Medicines: outdated prescriptions and any overdue non-prescription medicine can be handed in at most pharmacies for proper disposal. Pills, cough syrup, suppositories, antibiotic ointments, etc. should all be disposed of via the pharmacy.

10. Clothing: some cities and towns have a large container for clothes and shoes, generally placed by local organizations, and most often located close to a shopping area. During the year there are often also special initiatives by schools or churches to collect clothes for specific charities. Aside from the Salvation Army (*Leger des Heils*) you can contact the following organization to get information on addresses to hand in clothes: Sympany, or www.sympany.nl.

11. Large waste (*grof vuil*): any furniture (if not recycled through second hand shops) and large household debris can be collected by special appointment through the city's waste collection department. Within certain volume limitations, this waste will be collected free of charge, but it has to comply with certain regulations, e.g. wooden parts have to be gathered and tied with rope. Anything outside city regulations is best brought to the municipal waste separation and recycling station (*afvalscheidingsstation*, see next point) or, alternatively, one could order a private container to collect and dispose of all waste. This *puinbak* waste container (generally used during construction for large amounts of debris) can be ordered for a fee covering the delivery and removal. Contact your town hall and ask for *gemeentereiniging grof vuil*.

12. *Afvalscheidingsstation* (waste separation and recycling station): anything that is too large or specific (e.g. chemical waste) to be put in your regular waste container can be taken to a waste disposal station. For private individuals the rules here are pretty lax, as opposed to business disposal of waste, which usually comes at a price. You will usually be questioned upon entering the station as to what kind of waste you want to discard and will be directed to the right locations. There are, for instance, separate containers for wood, cardboard, tires, stones and construction rubbish, and chemical waste.

It bears to be kept in mind that any soil and earth removed when redoing a garden is generally not accepted unless a special government inspection (at a price) has taken place to ensure that it is not polluted by contaminants such as oil, lead or chemicals.

13. Computers, printers and scanners: if you need to dispose of ICT equipment in working order you can contact IT RECYCLING, or www.it-recycling.nl, and ask about *grijsgoed* (gray goods) recycling.

If you wish to become involved in a local environmental group you may check with your municipality. There are 'eco-teams' in many neighborhoods who work to increase awareness of the necessity to recycle and to protect the environment that carry out local projects.

For additional information on environmental policy and recycling contact VROM, the Ministry of Spatial Planning, Housing and Environment (Ministerie van Infrastructuur en Milieu (www.rijksoverheid.nl/ministeries/ienm).

PETS

DOG TAX

If you have been living in the Netherlands for a while, you have undoubtedly taken a slip over *hondenpoep* – dog poop. Rather than enjoying the beautiful architecture of the Dutch cities, you find yourself staring at the sidewalks, navigating your way around the deposits of our furry friends. How can it be that this nation of clean, hygienic, well-educated people can live with sidewalks pockmarked with *hondenpoep*? If we had an answer, we'd tell you. There is, however, an ongoing campaign to have dog owners train their dogs to leave their mess in the roadside gutters (watch out when stepping out of the car!) and, as you can read elsewhere in this book, dog owners pay taxes for their hounds. This tax used to be a 'corporate' tax, but is now levied on private dog owners, the proceeds of which are used to create areas within the cities and towns that can be considered public dog toilets or to put of dog-poop baggy dispensers at regular intervals within town and keep these well-stocked. This is the only pet-related tax there is, so maybe there is some justice after all.

FAVORITE PETS

And then there is a whole array of other favorite pets: cats, canaries, parrots and fish, for instance. Also rabbits, guinea pigs and hamsters are very popular. In some gardens, you will find the occasional goat, miniature pony or pot-bellied swine and in some children's bedrooms; rats, snakes, spiders, turtles, and the occasional bat.

PET CARE

Pets have a position in Dutch households that is very similar to that of the children. Some are served the best cut of the rarest beef, others are given the best chair, with the best view of the TV – and, naturally, access to the accompanying snacks. And the care provided is top-notch: the veterinary services (a vet is called a *dierenarts*) are excellent in the Netherlands, and include animal hospitals, ambulances and even crematoriums. There are also dog-walking services (*honden uitlaat service*) for those who can't imagine life without Whoofy, but unfortunately have to spend the whole day in the office. And last but not least, the pet stores in the Netherlands offer a wonderful array of toys, cushions, cages, leashes, snacks, top-of-the-line food, and... pets, of course.

FINDING A PET

If you want to buy a dog, however, it is always better to do this via a recognized breeder rather than through a pet store. Breeders can be found through the Raad van Beheer op Kynologische Gebied in

Nederland, the phone number of which you will find at the end of the chapter. For any other type of animal (other than the household rodent type – for which the pet store, or the petting farm, called *kinderboerderij*, will do fine) – you can best ask the local vet where you can find one. If you are looking to save an unwanted cat or dog, there are kennels, called *dierenasiel,* where 'lost and found' or otherwise homeless animals are brought. These kennels are well-run and most of the time have a good profile of the animals they are trying to place. Often, they have to find a new home for the pets of families who have to go abroad, or who have family member who is allergic to animals and find it greatly rewarding to have found such a loving pet a new home.

RELOCATING YOUR PET

The family pet has relocation needs as well. Each year more than 750,000 animals are transported around the world. For admittance to the Netherlands, cats and dogs must have a health certificate in Dutch, English, French or German, legalized by the Veterinary Service in the country of origin, stating a complete description of the animal (genus, age, breed, color, hair, marks – this part must be laminated in passports issued after December 12, 2014), the name of the owner, and that a complete vaccination against rabies has taken place with the date, type of vaccine used, expiry date, batch number and manufacturer, which must have taken place at least 21 days before entry into the Netherlands. As puppies, kittens and baby ferrets must be at least 12 weeks old to receive this vaccination, this means that they must be at least 15 weeks old when they enter the country. The maximum amount of time that is allowed to pass between a vaccination and your pet's entry into the country depends on the make of the vaccination and can be read in its information leaflet. Animals must be de-wormed and checked for ticks. Some countries have quarantine regulations. It is best to check with the Dutch Consulate well in advance what the requirements are so that you can make sure you meet them (see the website at the end of the chapter).

Furthermore, when transporting dogs, cats and ferrets (yes, ferrets...) within Europe; you must arrange a European-style animal passport, arrange a rabies-vaccination and make sure they have identification (a chip / microtransponder – tattoos are no longer accepted as of July 2011 for animals coming from outside the EU / EEA). At the moment, the European Commission is working on a veterinary certificate for other pets, but as this has not yet been finalized, rabbits, small rodents, birds, fish, amphibians and reptiles usually only need a declaration of health issued by a vet. For more information, visit the (Dutch-language) website of the Landelijk Informatiecentrum voor Gezelschapsdieren (National Information Center for Pets) at www.licg.nl. Click on *Praktisch, Reizen en vakantie*, *Invoereisen per land – Europa*, then on *Nederland*.

ADVICE ON ANIMAL TRANSFER

A professional organization such as KLM Cargo, specialists in animal transfer, can inform you on all regulations, provide you with helpful travel tips for your pet and arrange suitable transportation for your animal. They also operate a 24 hour-a-day animal hotel at the Schiphol airport (their website and phone number can be found at the end of the chapter). KLM Cargo transports a wide variety of animals and if you have one they don't transport, they will likely be able to inform on you whom to contact for the transportation of other animals. Else contact the airline you will be traveling with. Or visit www.klm.com, click on *Prepare for Travel*, and then on *Travelling with Pets*.

IDENTIFICATION AND REGISTRATION

In order to simplify the identification and registration of pets in case of loss or theft, identification microchips can be easily implanted by a veterinarian. The site www.stichtingchip.nl (which also has English-language pages) makes it possible to find information on where the lost animal is. The site www.chipnummer.nl provides you with a number of pet registration sites.

ANIMAL BOARDING

Though you love your animals and have brought them all the way here, traveling back and forth may not be something you wish to subject them to on too regular a basis. Should you be leaving the country on vacation (or for work) you might wish them the same comfort and care that you hope to enjoy during your trip. Look in the Yellow Pages or Internet under *dierenpension* to find a list of 'animal hotels' (a *hondenpension* is specifically for dogs, a *kattenpension* for cats). There is no surefire way to find out whether you can expect your family pet to be happy there – the best you can do is visit the place itself to discuss your (animal's) needs, check out the conditions and see whether you have a good feeling about the place and the owner in general. Maybe a trial run over a weekend will give you some peace of mind.

GARDENS AND CURTAINS

Ask the Belgians what they find typical of the homes of their Northern Neighbors and they will mention two things. One is their gardens, and the other is their curtains. In Belgium, family life is for the family: there are virtually no front yards (the garden is in the back) and huge, no-nonsense blinds go down as soon as the first lights go on inside the house.

Not so the Dutch. The Dutch are very proud of their gardens, be they postage stamp-size or park-size – particularly their front yards, as these are what everyone sees. They love a cozy (*gezellig*) neighborhood with flowers, flowering bushes, little rock gardens and – yes – the occasional garden gnome or even windmill. It is not without reason that Dutch flower bulbs are exported all across the world and that the hub of the world's flower industry is near Schiphol airport: the Netherlands is where the flowering heart of the world beats.

The neighborhoods in the Netherlands can look very prim and proper: there are special rules about not building too many different types of houses in one street (this is of course different in the very expensive areas, where the houses are so far apart – if they are even visible – that no one really cares). So what you get is a row of well-kept, dime-a-dozen houses, with picture-perfect front yards and... uncurtained windows.

If you take an evening stroll after sunset, you get a chance to admire family life, Dutch style. Grandma and Grandpa are sitting behind a steaming cup of coffee, savoring their evening ration of one cookie. Or Mom and Pop are reading a magazine, with one of their teenage children surreptitiously eyeing the TV over their homework. Or the living room is empty and upstairs you see Mom dressing baby on the dressing table, while Pop is chasing their three-year-old from room to room. Later in the evening, Mom and

Dad will settle down to their well-deserved cup of coffee – still to be admired through open curtains. Only once they go to bed, will the curtains downstairs be closed. For those of you who were wondering: bedroom curtains are always closed once the lights go on.

The Dutch do not feel self-conscious about what goes on behind their front door and feel comfortable with their curtains open. The rule of Dutch behavior is *doe maar gewoon, dan doe je gek genoeg* – act normal and you will be acting crazy enough. What this boils down to, basically, is modesty. Act modest, live modestly: do not buy expensive cars, do not have any airs, decorate your home simply, and don't do anything I wouldn't do. If you close your curtains, you probably have something to hide. Which is why many Dutch families leave their curtains open: so that everyone can see for themselves; look, we are 'normal'.

THE MEDIA

THE PRINTED MEDIA

In the Netherlands, 11 independent companies publish 27 daily newspapers – nine nation-wide and 18 regional – each with its own editorial staff and amounting to a daily total of 3.1 million papers. The five major *nationwide* newspapers (there are a few regional newspapers whose number of subscribers exceeds those of some of the larger nationwide papers) in the Netherlands are *De Telegraaf* (circulation 430,686), *De Volkskrant* (237,409), the AD (340,209), NRC *Handelsblad* (154,986) (NRC also had a morning paper, NRC.Next, for a younger public, but they ceased to publish it

last year), and *Trouw* (98,259). Popular among those who are active in the business world is the *Financieele Dagblad* (46,557), which has economic news and stock market analyses. These numbers do not include online subscriptions (you can find the websites at the end of the chapter), which are usually the number of subscribers multiplied by five and which are growing. Fifty households in 100 receive a daily newspaper; of the 3.1 million newspapers distributed per day (54% national, 46% regional newspapers), 92% goes to subscribers – giving the Netherlands the highest percentage of subscribers in the world. (Incidentally, approximately 23% of the subscribers share their newspaper – for instance, with their neighbors.)

As mentioned above, there are many regional newspapers, which can provide you with important information on what is going on in your region. And if you want to know what is going on in your town, you can take out a subscription to the local town paper. The Netherlands also has many magazines; for art lovers, computer fanatics, travelers, feminists, men, children, animal lovers, garden lovers and just about any other type of hobby. Do not despair, however, that you will have to wait until you speak Dutch before you can read about what is going on in the world, as sometimes even in the smallest towns you will find such magazines as *Newsweek*, *Time Magazine*, *The Economist*, *The Financial Times* as well as the newspapers *El País*, *The International New York Times*, USA *Today* and more (such as German, Italian, Turkish, French magazines and newspapers, to name but a few).

There is one subscription-free newspaper, *Metro*, which you can pick up, among others, on the train.

POST OFFICES A THING OF THE PAST

This country's last remaining post offices closed in 2012. Mail services are now carried out under the banner of PostNL and are offered through post office ticket windows in regular stores, such as bookstores, tobacco stores, and supermarkets. These services also include paperwork services, such as the issuing of fishing licenses, vehicle registration cards, and public transportation passes. Full-time mail delivery jobs no longer exist either; the work is now carried out by a team of cheaper flex workers. For more information, for instance to find out where you can buy stamps near you visit www.postnl.nl.

In order to cut costs, PostNL will has also removed more than half of the existing mailboxes, leaving 8,700 across the country. The number of stores offering mail services is being brought back from 2,500 to 1,000.

TELEVISION AND RADIO

Dutch television will also not present much of a problem as it is subtitled, leaving all foreign movies, series and other programs in their original language. The Netherlands has a plethora of television channels to choose from available through cable, including British, Belgian, French, Spanish, German, Italian and Turkish television as well as CNN (news) and MTV (music) – but keep in mind that the cable package available depends on where you live.

The main Dutch broadcasting companies are: TROS (general), VARA (social-democratic), AVRO (general), NCRV (Protestant), KRO (Catholic), VPRO (progressive), BNN (general, young audience) and EO (evangelical Christian) who all work together in the NOS (Netherlands Broadcasting Corporation). The fact that these companies have a certain denomination does not mean that you will watch solely Catholic programs on the KRO, or social-democratic programs on the VARA: these denominations are to be considered from where the broadcasting company originated and dictate only a certain percentage of the types of program you will see (with the exception of the EO, whose character is most clearly noticeable in the type of programs it broadcasts). In fact, some of them have merged to form KRO-NCRV, AVROTROS, and BNN-VARA. The broadcasting companies share broadcasting time on Nederland 1, 2 and 3, but there are more Dutch channels, such as RTL 4, RTL 5, RTL 7, RTL 8, Net 5, SBS 6, SBS 9 and Veronica, which mainly broadcast popular (often U.S. or U.K.-purchased) programs. For more viewing pleasure there is Discovery Channel, Nickelodeon, National Geographic, Animal Planet, MTV, TMF, CNN and EuroSport, as well as German, Belgian and British channels. Children's programming is available daily from 7 A.M. on several of the Dutch channels as well as on Nickelodeon, Ketnet/Canvas (Belgium) and on BBC 2. For an overview of what's on, go to www.tvgids.nl. If 60 channels is not enough, or you cannot be connected to the cable lines because you bought a farm house way out in the middle of nowhere, then, of course, you can solve this problem by purchasing a satellite dish or digitenne (for both, see further on). Satellite TV will bring you many more international channels, as well as movie channels – though increasingly these are becoming available through cable TV as well.

Furthermore, the Netherlands has five national radio stations and several regional ones, but the fun thing is, of course, that certainly when it comes to radio, you can listen to broadcasts from just about anywhere in the world.

KIJKWIJZER

The NICAM or Netherlands Institute for the Classification of Audiovisual Media has developed the *kijkwijzer* (whose principle is *weet wat je ziet* or know what you see), a system using pictograms to rate the content of films, DVDs, television programs, and computer games. The picture symbols indicate violence, sex, fear, discrimination, drug and alcohol misuse, and rough language. Also shown are age limit recommendations of AL (all ages), MG6 (watch with children under 6), 12 (not younger) and 16 (not younger). Any media items with a 16 year-advice should not be rented out to or sold to minors under 16, and movie theaters may refuse entrance to those who appear to fall outside the age category.

For more information, visit www.kijkwijzer.nl and view the icons or pictograms.

BEING CONNECTED

STARTING YOUR TELEPHONE SERVICE

Although efforts have been made to introduce competition in this market, KPN is still the main company providing fixed phone lines in the Netherlands. Despite this fact, however, it does not have a monopoly on these lines; other companies have bought up the rights to a certain number of the KPN lines and offer cheaper rates (also when phoning abroad) if you make use of their lines. Still, you have to keep in mind that you will have to pay a subscription to KPN, for which you will receive a bi-monthly bill. The good news is that the existence of these companies has forced KPN to reduce their rates. You therefore might want to compare the rates, before choosing to register with one of these companies. For more information on calling via cable, see page 183. If you opt for 'Internet en bellen' (Internet and telephone), you eliminate the need for a separate KPN subscription. Currently, there are approximately 5.5 million digital phone lines, more than 2 million DSL-lines, and 750,000 glass fiber lines. For a complete overview of discount providers, also for mobile phone services, see: www.bencom.nl.

SUBSCRIPTION

In the Netherlands, you are not only charged per telephone conversation (depending on the length of the call), but you also have to pay a 'subscription' to make use of the telephone lines (unless, as indicated above, you opt for 'Internet and telephone'), the amount of which you will find on your bi-monthly telephone bill. In most cases, you will have to 'subscribe' for a minimum period of one year, even if you only want to subscribe for a shorter period of time. At least one of the telephone companies provides the option of paying a fixed amount per month, which will entitle you to unlimited calling locally but also to a great deal of other countries.

To arrange payment of your bills, you can provide the company with your bank account number and they deduct the payment automatically every month.

OTHER CHEAP CALLING OPTIONS

0900 Access Numbers: One option is to make use of 0900 access numbers: for instance, you dial 0900, followed by the country's so-called service number. Once you have connected to this number, you dial the country code, followed by the person's telephone number. You do not have to register to make use of this option, but you should verify that you have not blocked the use of 0900-numbers (which some people do, as they also provide access to more dubious – and expensive – options). The costs of making this type of call are a connection rate and a per-minute fee, or really per second, as minutes are not rounded off. Before being put through to the person you are calling, you will automatically be informed of the rate for this call – a service for which you are not charged. Visit www.televergelijk.nl for up-to-date information on the most attractive 0900-providers per country that you want to call. You can also make use of the Belo900-app for mobile phones.

Other access numbers: You can also dial a local number, for which you are charged a local rate (or, if you have taken out a subscription that allows unlimited calling with the Netherlands for a fixed fee per month; the call is included in the fee). Once you have dialled this number, you enter your personal code, after which they tell you how many cents you will be paying for the connection (just a few cents). Once you have completed this process, you dial the number you want to dial abroad. This service is not available for all countries, but if it is, this means the entire call, no matter how long, will cost you no more than the connection fee of a few cents.

Carrier (Pre)Select: With Carrier (Pre)Select, you dial 16xy (representing the two digits of the carrier) and then the number of the person you want to call. The carrier offers you cheaper rates. With

EXPATICA
LIVE. WORK. LOVE.

"Excellent news and analysis aimed at the English-speaking community"
THE GUARDIAN

Moving abroad?

New country, new culture, new friendships, Expatica.com is your complete resource for international living.

Expatica.com offers:

Comprehensive resource to cover all aspects of moving to and living abroad

Engaged international community with active forum discussions and events

Facebook, Twitter and Newsletter daily updates

- **Daily Local News & Content**
- **Survival Guides**
- **Daily & Weekly Newsletters**
- **Jobs & Housing**
- **International Dating**
- **Forums & Discussions**
- **Signature Events & Fairs**
- **Expat Blog & Experiences**
- **Special Expat Offers**

Expatica.com - The international community's home on the web. Helping Internationals Worldwide in 11 countries.

 the Netherlands Belgium Germany France Spain Switzerland United Kingdom Moscow Portugal South Africa Luxembourg

 facebook.com/ExpaticaInternational
 twitter.com/Expatica

 ADVERTISE WITH US Looking to reach 5 million expats?
Email: advertise@expatica.com

PreSelect, the number is automatically put before the number you dial. With this option, you pay KPN a subscription for your telephone line, and for all calls made without using 16xy.

Call cards: These cards can be purchased at supermarkets, kiosks, telephone stores, and online. You scratch off a protective layer from the card to reveal your access code, which you enter after calling a computer free or at local rates, followed by the number you want to call. More information can be found (in Dutch) on www.ibeltegoed.nl.

MORE CHEAP CALLING

In some places, it is possible to make phone calls over the wireless WiFi-net, while retaining your own number and telephone. This way you can call anywhere in the Netherlands at local rates and in the rest of the world at *very* cheap rates. Or, you just call over Whatsapp, using your mobile phone – for free.

Furthermore, MSN, Skype and VoipBuster allow you to make free telephone calls to another Skype, etc.-user (also abroad), via your computer – or, for a small fee, to a fixed or mobile telephone (visit www.msn.com, www.skype.com or www.voipbuster.com for more information or to download the software needed). For more information on calling via the Internet, visit www.bellenviainternet.net.

DIGITAL MAIL BOX

Banks, utilities, KPN telephone, health insurers, gas stations, cable companies, and a host of other companies can send their bills to a digital mail box that you can set up via your bank (so nothing ever gets lost in the mail!). ABN Amro, ING and the Rabobank offer you this service. On the banks' sites, you select which companies are to send their invoices online. You receive notice of received mail by e-mail and with one click you can open, look at and pay your bills online. For more information, visit your bank's website, or www.finbox.nl.

MOBILE TELEPHONES

Despite its relatively modest size, the Netherlands has the highest number of mobile operators in Europe. This makes the mobile phone market highly fluid and sometimes a bit confusing, what with the numerous special promotions and mobile telephone options.

CHOOSING A MOBILE PHONE SERVICE

There are several criteria that are important to consider when choosing a mobile phone service. The total number of minutes per month that you use, the amount of data you will need to satisfy your mobile Internet needs, and the need for additional services such as voicemail, SMS text messages, calling long distance, and using the mobile phone when abroad. Depending on your needs, you will use one of the following three possibilities:

- subscription services with a contract, which includes a certain number of minutes that you can call, text messages you can send, and data. You receive a monthly bill (for the subscription and, if you have exceeded your contractual number of minutes, a fee for these minutes). Subscription services will charge an initial connection fee, but there are many special offers available aimed at attracting new customers – so shop around
- a pre-pay service based on buying a card with call units and no subscription fee. You can read more about this below.
- sim-only; you buy your own mobile phone (make sure it's simlock-free; *simlock-vrij!*) and take out a 'sim-only' subscription, which means that you are sent a sim-card, without an accompanying mobile phone. This can be a financially quite attractive option. To compare rates, visit www.sim-only-vergelijk.nl.

Virtually all the mobile phone operators cover the entire country. For an overview of these providers, and to help you make your choice, we advise you to visit www.bencom.nl. Be sure not to miss the smaller, less-profiled companies that offer financially attractive pre-pay and/or subscription services. You will also find a list of websites at the end of the chapter.

Most consumers make use of the service providers of these network operators, however, there is also Ortel Mobile, where you can obtain a pre-paid sim-card without needing a contract, allowing you to make use of the KPN-work.

PRE-PAID CALLING
This is a popular choice among Dutch users, particularly young people. One reason is that the pre-pay phone allows users to pay for their calls in advance, and thus avoid subscription fees and hefty unexpected bills. They are cheap, convenient and provide enough coverage for most Dutch users in the Netherlands.

Each pre-pay phone will only be suitable for that particular network, for example, if you buy a T-Mobile phone, you are restricted to using that phone and buying call units for the T-Mobile network. However, the networks are so extensive and so many agreements have been reached with other companies (abroad), that you will likely experience very little hinder in making local calls or calls from abroad – see further on in *Free to Roam?*

Pre-pay cards are available in denominations of 10, 20, 25, 40, and 50 euros and can be bought at a variety of locations, such as supermarkets and drugstores, as well as the phone company-stores. For more on the various arrangements offered by the mobile phone companies, visit their websites, as they are continually subject to change.

BUYING A MOBILE PHONE
If you are buying a (subscription, pre-pay or sim-lock free) mobile phone, you can do this at the larger department stores, electronic chains, brand stores, non-brand telephone stores, or, simply, via the Internet. It is always worth your while to shop around, as both the brand stores and the non-brand stores may offer certain reductions and other special promotions. Most mobile phone companies include a mobile phone in their subscription package.

Be sure to bring your passport / driver's license and proof (such as a bank statement) of your most current address if you are planning on buying a mobile phone with a subscription in a store.

SWITCHING
Once you have chosen a particular mobile phone company for your phone with subscription, you are not stuck for life. You can switch companies and even keep your own phone number. Check with your company to see what the rules are (on giving notice and over what period), if you are not yet sure which one to go for. The same goes for pre-pay phones, whereby you can also switch from pre-pay to subscription and vice versa. In most cases, the phone company that you are planning on switching to, arranges the switch. You wait for a message from them that they have completed the switch and they terminate your contract with your former provider.

FREE TO ROAM?
From the expat's perspective, perhaps the most important issue is being able to make and receive calls in other countries. Through international 'roaming' agreements, cellular operators allow foreign operators to use their networks so that they have broader international coverage. Mobile phone services are available in

another region or country if there is a company that has a roaming agreement with the user's GSM network operator. Unsurprisingly, the cost of using a mobile for international and overseas calling can be high.

Also, mobile telephone companies increasingly have their own international network, allowing you to call from wherever you are, simply using their network, whether it be by pre-pay or subscription.

Whereas before, travellers were challenged by the incompatibility of mobile phones and networks, this is largely no longer an issue. If you are faced with this problem, keep in mind that some mobile phone companies offer the possibility of placing the SIM-card (containing your phone's memory, including your own phone number) of your Dutch mobile phone in a phone that will work in the other country – this can be done at the Airport Telecom at Schiphol Airport or Rotterdam Airport (www.airporttelecom.nl, also for satellite phones) or you can visit www.onesimcard.com. Do keep in mind that you will have to deposit a considerable guarantee for this and that the phones rates will be *steep*; if you place a call within the U.S., you will first be calling back to the Netherlands and from there back again to the U.S.

If you want to keep things simple, you can also just buy a cheap pre-pay phone in your country of destination if you travel frequently to a particular country, or rent one.

MOBILE PHONE TECHNOLOGIES
As the technology and the possibilities offered by the various mobile telephone companies are continuously changing, we recommend that you visit the various mobile phone company websites to see what they have to offer.

MOBILE PHONE USE IN THE CAR
You may not use a mobile phone while driving unless you are using a hands-free device. You can read more about this on page 148.

INTERNET SERVICE PROVIDERS AND CONNECTIVITY

A study, carried out in 2013, yielded that the number of fixed telephone lines in the Netherlands is decreasing (from 10 million in 2000 to 7.2 million in 2013), while the number of mobile telephone connections reached 21 million that year. Ninety-five percent of all Dutch households had either a desktop or a laptop as well as access to the Internet, whereby an increasing amount of connections to the Internet takes place via a laptop or some other device (such as a tablet or mobile phone; in fact 78% of those who accessed the Internet used a laptop and 59% of them a mobile phone). In that year, 88% of those who used the Internet did so on a daily basis.

In short, the Netherlands is connected: 71% of the Dutch population is active on social media, whereby 93% of all those between the ages of 12 and 25 had a social media account (but also 30% of those between the ages of 65 and 75!). Internet is used for obtaining information, for joining political / societal discussions and for communicating – 95% of all communication via the Internet involves e-mail. So it is only logical that all companies offering television and telephony services focus on offering Internet services as well – or else they would be missing out on a lot of action! At least the four largest Dutch cable companies offer digital TV and high-speed Internet services to their subscribers now and have

hollands
nieuwe.

hollands
nieuwe.

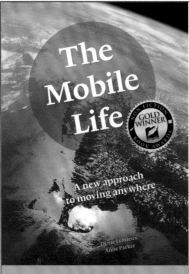

considerably expanded services, including discounted telephony. Also certain telephone companies offer Internet, television and telephone services via cable – please check their websites, or visit www.prijsvergelijken.nl www.providercheck.nl, or www.adslwinkel.nl for more information. One of the more interesting services they offer is that of being able to create your own website and/or customized e-mail addresses – so if that is something that is of interest to you, be sure to check out what is on offer.

TELEVISION

DENSELY CABLED/DIGITAL

Ninety-eight percent of the Dutch homes have television and more than 8 in 10 households watch digital TV, or 6.5 million people. Only 8 years ago, this was 2 in 10 homes. More than half of these connections are digital cable, which supplies both digital and analog TV, whereby Ziggo, KPN, UPC and CanalDigitaal are the four largest providers.

The impact of Internet on television watching has of course been significant. You can now watch TV live or you can choose to catch missed episodes or movies on the computer, your tablet, or your TV. Of course, prime time remains prime time, that much is evident from research – but now you can spread prime time across your day: watching your favorite series while it is being aired, and watching that movie you've always wanted to see again on your tablet the next day.

For only € 18 a month, you can already watch 60 digital channels, making access is so cheap that you probably won't even know that you're paying for it. If you opt for Internet and TV, you pay anywhere between € 30 and € 55, depending on the options you choose: watching missed programs, TV on your tablet, being able to pause your program, multiple TVs, On Demand Films, etc. An excellent overview of the various providers and their packages can be found on www.prijsvergelijken.nl and clicking on *Internet, bellen en TV*.

While consumers may assume that this means they have no choice if they are not happy with their service and that they are at the whim of the cable companies, this is not the case; consumers are protected by heavy regulations on cable TV companies.

DIGITAL TV

Currently, there are four ways to receive a digital TV signal; via cable, ether, the Internet (IP, it requires an ADSL-connection), or via satellite. The option of receiving your signal via the ether (digitenne) allows you to place a simple receiver in your windowsill, tent, or car, and watch TV anywhere you like!.

For more on who is on the market, what they are offering, and what is available where you live, visit www.digitaaltvkijken.nl or www.bencom.nl.

EXPANDED SERVICES

Over the years, the standard number of channels available to the cable TV subscriber has jumped to around 60. As mentioned earlier, there are now ready-made interactive capabilities and expanded channel options available through digital TV, as well as high-speed Internet and local and long-distance telephony. For more channels, you might want to consider installing a satellite on your roof; see further on.

ADSL AND BROADBAND

The providers of ADSL high-speed Internet can be found on www.adslwinkel.nl, or www.breedbandwinkel.nl (type in your postal code, and it will tell you what is available in your area).

The list of those offering high-speed capabilities is ever-changing, so rather than list the ones that can be found at the time of typing this contribution, we recommend you visit these sites.

FAST-MOVING INDUSTRY

Once again, this is a fast-moving industry and, as this book appears only once a year, we have found ourselves limited to describing the situation as it was at the start of 2016. For more up-to-date information, we advise you to call the cable net-companies or visit their websites, which you will find at the end of the chapter.

THE ALTERNATIVE: SATELLITE TV

If you do not have cable (by choice or because you live in a remote area) or want to see channels not available through cable, you can opt for satellite TV. This involves finding an electronics store or other distributor who sells satellite dishes, and arranging for its installation. Canaldigitaal offers an impressive range of channels (more than 400), which you can receive by making use of a special decoder. For an additional charge, you can choose from several other packages (Basis, Family, Entertainment, etc.).

Visit www.canaldigitaal.nl for more information on – and to order – the equipment necessary for hooking up to them.

SAFETY

NATIONAL EMERGENCY NUMBER: 112

TO CONTACT THE POLICE
Emergencies: 112
Central National Police Information Number,
tel.: 0900 8844
www.politie.nl

TO CONTACT THE FIRE DEPARTMENT
Emergencies: 112
General website: www.brandweer.nl
Amsterdam, tel.: 020 555 66 66
Rotterdam, tel.: 010 446 89 00
The Hague, tel.: 088 886 8000
Utrecht, tel.: 030 286 00 00

AMBULANCE
Emergencies: 112
Amsterdam, tel.: 020 555 55 55
Rotterdam, tel.: 010 433 33 00
The Hague, tel.: 070 322 21 11
Utrecht, tel.: 030 233 22 22

NEWS IN DUTCH

MAIN DUTCH NEWSPAPERS
Algemeen Dagblad: www.ad.nl
De Telegraaf: www.detelegraaf.nl
De Volkskrant: www.volkskrant.nl
Het Parool: www.parool.nl
NRC Handelsblad: www.nrc.nl
NRC Next: www.nrcnext.nl
Trouw: www.trouw.nl

MAIN DUTCH NEWS WEBSITES
www.nieuws.nl
www.nu.nl
http://nos.nl/nieuws

DUTCH NEWS IN ENGLISH

Dutchnews.nl
English-language news from business and politics to sport. Plus features, opinion and debate
www.dutchnews.nl

Expatica: English-language news and information source for expatriates living in, working in or moving to the Netherlands
www.expatica.com/netherlands

IamExpat Dutch News
www.iamexpat.nl/read-and-discuss/news

UTILITIES

TO ARRANGE YOUR UTILITIES
Iedereen Bespaart: www.utility-provider.nl

MAIN MOBILE TELEPHONE SERVICE PROVIDERS
HI: www.hi.nl
KPN Mobile: www.kpn.com
Ortel Mobile: www.ortelmobile.nl
Telfort: www.telfort.nl
T-mobile: www.t-mobile.nl
UPC: www.upc.nl
Vodafone: www.vodafone.nl

INTERNET / CABLE TV / TELEPHONE
12move: www.12move.nl
Chello: www.chello.nl
Essent: www.essent.nl
Het Net: www.hetnet.nl
KPN: www.kpn.com
Online: www.online.nl
Tele 2: www.tele2.nl
Telfort: www.telfort.nl
UPC: www.upc.nl
Ziggo: www.ziggo.nl
Vodafone: www.vodafone.nl
XS4ALL: www.xs4all.nl

SATELLITE TV
www.canaldigitaal.nl
www.skydigibox.nl

MAIN ENERGY SUPPLIERS
Overview of licensed energy suppliers:
www.energieleveranciers.nl
Price comparisons: www.energieprijzen.nl,
www.energievergelijken.nl
Eneco: www.eneco.nl
Energiedirect: www.energiedirect.nl
Essent: www.essent.nl
Greenchoice: www.greenchoice.nl
Homestroom: www.homestroom.nl
Nederlandse Energie Maatschappij:
www.nederlandenergie.nl
Nuon: www.nuon.nl
Oxxio: www.oxxio.nl
Qurrent: www.qurrent.nl

PETS

ANIMAL AMBULANCE
Tel.: 0900 0245

LOST PETS
To report lost animals (chip registration)
Tel.: 0900 40 40 456

AMIVEDI NEDERLAND
To registrate lost animals: www.amivedi.nl

EUROPEAN PET NETWORK
www.europetnet.com

NDG – STICHTING DATABANK GEZELSCHAPSDIEREN NEDERLAND
Central Identification Database
Tel.: 0900 40 40 456
www.databankgezelschapsdieren.nl

PET MOVING SERVICES
Air Animal: www.airanimal.com
Air Pets Oceanic: www.airpets.com
International Animal Transport DTC:
www.dtciat.com
KLM Cargo: www.klmcargo.nl

SHOPS FOR PRODUCTS FROM HOME

KELLY'S EXPAT SHOPPING
Zoutmanstraat 22a, 2518 GP The Hague
Tel.: 070 346 97 53
Luifelbaan 50, 2242 KV Wassenaar
Tel.: 070 511 87 29
www.kellys-expat-shopping.nl

MARKS & SPENCER
Grote Markstraat 32, The Hague
Tel.: 070 302 01 02
Kalverstraat 226, Amsterdam
Tel.: 020 330 00 80
www.marksandspencer.eu

ONLINE SHOPS FOR PRODUCTS FROM HOME

British Cornershop:
www.britishcornershop.co.uk
The English Shop: www.english-shop.com

Food from Home: www.foodfromhome.de
Kelly's Expat Shop: www.kellys-expat-shopping.nl
Marks & Spencer: www.marksandspencer.eu

TYPICAL DUTCH PRODUCTS

Dutch Heritage webshop:
www.dutchheritage.eu
Holland at Home: www.holland-at-home.com
Typical Dutch Stuff:
www.typicaldutchstuff.com

DUTCH SELLING AND BUYING WEBSITES

Marktplaats: www.marktplaats.nl
Tweedehands: www.tweedehands.nl

RECOMMENDED READING

FOOD SHOPPERS' GUIDE TO HOLLAND
By Ada Henne Koene
Published by Eburon
A comprehensive review of the finest food products in the Dutch marketplace and a very useful food dictionary.
www.eburon.nl

DUTCH CULINARY ART
By Janny de Moor, Nico de Rooij and Albert Tielemans
400 years of festive cooking in the Netherlands.
www.dutchculinaryart.com

DUTCH COOKING TODAY
Published by Inmerc
This book has typical Dutch dishes, honest stews, juicy one-pan dishes, the best snacks, the tastiest cakes and the yummiest desserts. It allows all – from lovers of the *Hollandse Pot* (Dutch Pan) to admirers of trendy cuisine – to become acquainted with old and new dishes of the Netherlands.
www.zoekboeken.nl

DUTCH DELIGHT
Text by Sylvia Pessiron
Photography by Jurjen Drenth & friends
Published by Nilsson & Lamm
Learn what the Dutch eat and drink, graze through their eating habits and recipes, and when you're done, try them.
www.dutchshop.nl

THE NEW DUTCH CUISINE
Text by Albert Kooy
Photography by Pieter Ouddeken
Published by KM Publishers
This basic cookbook offers possible guidelines for the contemporary cook.
You'll find some old-fashioned Dutch dishes like hodge-podge, scrapple, head cheese, sausage rolls etc. The beautiful photo's sometimes show a complete dish, more often they are taken while cooking so they show the method of preparation.
www.newdutchcuisine.eu

ONLINE BOOKSHOPS BASED IN THE NETHERLANDS
www.abc.nl
www.boek.net
www.bol.com
www.hollandbooks.nl
www.libris.nl

BOOKSTORES FOR ENGLISH LANGUAGE BOOKS

THE AMERICAN BOOK CENTER
Spui 12, 1012 XA Amsterdam
Tel.: 020 625 55 37
www.abc.nl

THE AMERICAN BOOK CENTER
Lange Poten 23, 2511 CM The Hague
Tel.: 070 364 27 42
www.abc.nl

WATERSTONE'S BOOKSELLERS
Kalverstraat 152, 1012 XE Amsterdam
Tel.: 020 638 38 21
www.waterstones.com

THE ENGLISH BOOK SHOP
Lauriersgracht 71, 1016 RH Amsterdam
Tel.: 020 626 42 30
www.englishbookshop.nl

PUBLIC LIBRARIES

General: www.bibliotheek.nl
Rotterdam: www.bibliotheek.rotterdam.nl
Amsterdam: www.oba.nl
The Hague: www.bibliotheekdenhaag.nl
Utrecht: www.bibliotheek-utrecht.nl

Children are very important members of the expat population, as the success of a placement abroad depends largely on whether the children (the family as a whole) manage to feel at home in their new country. Luckily, the Netherlands is probably one of the smoothest countries to ease into. There are a lot of fun attractions, parks, activities and other sources of entertainment, several child-friendly festivities and plenty to stimulate the curious mind of the child, and perhaps one of the most charming aspects; children still come together to play outdoors here.

Read on through this chapter to learn about day care, the Child Benefit, parental leave, birthday parties, Sinterklaas, shopping, general entertainment and a host of other subjects.

CONTRIBUTING AUTHOR STEPHANIE DIJKSTRA

DAY CARE

Although the Dutch government is keen on keeping women in the work force, the current demand for day care far outweighs availability, particularly in the western part of the country. Though the number of children going to day care has been decreasing (fewer births, other alternatives), waiting lists remain long in certain areas, and though official figures are unavailable, we advise you to register early on (preferably as soon as you are pregnant) and still be prepared to wait anywhere between six to 18 months before your child is placed.

Kinderopvang is the general term used in Dutch to cover childcare. In the following paragraphs you will find a brief description of the various options available to you as a (working) parent. Though every type of *opvang* has its own approach, it might be reassuring to know that every municipality has a legal obligation to ensure that minimum rules regarding the following issues are implemented: hygiene, safety, size of groups, sleeping space, toys, insurance, and sick children (they must stay home).

KINDERDAGVERBLIJF

Kinderdagverblijf, or *crèche*, is a cross between a day care center and nursery school and is available for children between the ages of 0 and 4 (infants as of six weeks). Approximately 754,400 children currently make use of the various types of day care available in the Netherlands, though with the rising prices of *kinderopvang*, parents are increasingly going in search of cheaper alternatives – all of which are listed in this chapter as well. Drop-off time is between 8 and 8:30 a.m., pick-up time between 5:30 and 6 p.m., though some centers offer more flexible hours; even 24 hours non-stop. You can place your child there for a number of mornings and/or afternoons a week (called *dagdelen*; day-portions) or for a full week, if necessary. Some of the *kinderdagverblijven* also have arrangements for older children (until the age of 12) for pre and after-school hours and school holidays.

Finding a Kinderdagverblijf

One of the largest day care organizations in the Netherlands, Partou (www.partou.nl), offers more than 300 day care centers across the country and – for your convenience – has English-language web pages, or www.kinderopvang-spot.nl. The sites provide an excellent explanation of how the system works – in Dutch – as well as a list of day care centers by province or type of day care.

Cost

Fees vary from municipality to municipality, from one day care center to another and of course depending on whether you receive a subsidized spot. Expect to pay approximately € 210 (net) per two fulls day per month to € 1,300 for five full days per month. The maximum government subsidy (*kinderopvangtoeslag*, see further on) you will receive is € 6.89 per hour, for a maximum of 230 hours per month.

See the following paragraph on government subsidy. Visit www.kostenkinderopvang.nl to calculate what your approximate expenses will be.

Regulations and Subsidy

Parents who place their children in day care, receive an income-independent and an income-dependent contribution, the amount of which also depends on the number of children and the actual costs of the day care or after-school care for elementary-aged children, whereby the amount you receive is determined by the child for whom you pay less (fewer hours or cheaper care). The employer is obligated to contribute in the costs of the income-independent portion, but you *receive* the contribution from the tax authorities. Parents receive the income-dependent contribution from the government. Together, this is referred to as *kinderopvangtoeslag*.

To arrange it, you visit www.toeslagen.nl, click on *kinderopvangtoeslag* and follow the instructions. If you have already arranged the *toeslag*, it will automatically be extended. If there are any changes in your situation – moving in together, marriage, divorce, more or fewer children in day care, a change in income or in bank account number, etc. – you have to notify the tax authorities on this same site. Check the website of the tax authorities: subject to conditions, you can receive *kinderopvangtoeslag* if you live abroad (under *Kinderopvangtoeslag als u in het buitenland woont*).

To qualify for *kinderopvangtoeslag*, you and your partner must meet the following requirements:

- you have Dutch nationality, or legally reside in the Netherlands
- you have one or more children registered at your address for whom you receive *kinderbijslag* (see page 193), a foster parent contribution, or whom you largely support financially
- the day care center your child attends (be it day care, after school care, or a host family) is registered with the municipality in which it is located as an acknowledged organization, to which purpose it must be meet certain criteria. If they are indeed registered, they will have been issued a statement saying so – so be sure to ask to see it. You can also visit the website of the National Register for *kinderopvang* (www.landelijkregisterkinderopvang.nl) to verify whether the day care center is registered there
- you have entered into a written agreement with the facility offering *kinderopvang*
- the child does not yet attend middle or high school
- you or your partner pays for the day care

- you work in employment, are self-employed, work for your partner's company, are a student, are following an *inburgerings-cursus* (cultural familiarization course), or
- you receive a benefit that includes the right to a contribution by the municipality towards the day care payments. This is the case, for instance, if you are: rejoining the labor market after a long period of time (combined with either a benefit or a registration with the Center for Work and Income); a student; (as above) following a cultural familiarization course (*inburgerings-cursus*), etc.

Single parents can apply for additional financial support, to the effect that they receive the same income-independent contribution as a two-working-parent family (1/3 of the total costs). Under certain conditions, your municipality might contribute to paying the costs of day care. For instance, if you are an artist and are looking for work based on the Work and Income for Artists Act (WWIK), if you are younger than 18 or if you are still a student. For the applicable conditions, please contact your municipality.

The amount of *kinderopvangtoeslag* you receive is based on the number of hours worked by the partner who works the least. So if you work five days a week and your partner three, then you receive an amount based on those three days. Your partner is expected to be able to take care of the child(ren) on the other two days. If you lose your job, you retain your right to the *kinderopvangtoeslag* for a period of six months, to allow you to find another job.

PEUTERSPEELZALEN (TODDLER GROUPS)

Peuterspeelzalen are toddler groups for children age 2 – 4 and are usually open in the mornings although some municipalities now offer afternoon programs. Technically speaking, the *peuterspeel-zaal* is not a day care facility and should be seen more as a pre-school, especially since opening hours are limited. Often, they are liaised with (and on the same premises as) a primary school, which allows an easy transition from the *speelzaal* to the school. There are approximately 15 children in a group to two teachers. Typically, children are accepted two or three fixed mornings per week. You will find *peuterspeelzalen* in the *gemeentegids* – a guide published by your municipality with useful addresses – or in the telephone book.

Cost

The cost of sending your child to a *peuterspeelzaal* may be income-indexed. Expect to pay anywhere from € 45 to € 150 per month for two mornings a week.

Recognized and registered *peuterspeelzalen* also qualify for employer or government contributions, see the rules explained above.

BUITENSCHOOLSE / NASCHOOLSE OPVANG (AFTER-SCHOOL DAY CARE)

Both the *buitenschoolse opvang* (BSO) as well as the *naschoolse opvang* provide day care during after-school hours and holidays to children between the ages of 4 and 12. The BSO also offers an additional service during pre-school hours. These services are, as you can imagine, in great demand. To find out who provides 'non-school-hour care' near you, visit www.kinderopvang-spot.nl. Additional options include: day and night care (single parents with night-time shifts might benefit from this), and 'teen'-care. Your municipal guide or municipal website will provide you with more information on these options.

Elementary schools are obligated to arrange BSO for their pupils, either on or off-premise.

Cost

The fee structure is much the same as for the *kinderdagverblijf*. We refer you to our explanation under *Regulations and Subsidy*, on page 187, regarding employer and government contributions. Also here, the rule applies that the organization providing the *buiten-schoolse opvang* and *naschoolse opvang* must be registered as an acknowledged organization. This maximum amount of government contribution you can request is € 6.42 per hour.

GASTOUDER (HOST PARENT) /TEACHER AT HOME

A host parent usually has children of her own (in most cases, the host parent is a woman) and cares for up to six children at her home. In some cases, the *gastouder* will come to your house. Another option is to have a *leidster* (preschool teacher) or *oppas* (sitter, who must meet certain requirements) come to your house.

There appears to be a growing demand for this type of day care. Look in your local telephone book or *gemeentegids* (municipal guide) under *kinderopvang* to find a *gastouder / leidster / oppas* in your neighborhood. We have included a number of websites at the end of the chapter through which you can arrange a *gastouder / leidster / oppas*; these sites also help you arrange the government contribution to help cover the costs. Word-of-mouth is also a good source of sitters of either type; plenty of excellent sitters are not officially registered, but rely on the mommy network. Also the website www.oudermatch.nl/en (for English) is a very helpful site, providing you with the opportunity find other parents in your vicinity to connect and find a child care solution together, or else you can visit www.gastouderland.nl, or www.gobmare.nl.

Cost

The *gastouderbureau / kinderopvang aan huis* maintains strict guidelines regarding fees and responsibilities. The cost of making use of these options is usually income-indexed and currently ranges around € 4.50 to € 9.50 per hour, depending on the number of children, whether the person in question has experience and whether you expect her (him) to do some (light) household work.

Parents can only request a maximum of € 5.52 government subsidy and this only for *gastouders* who have been entered in a national registry, and they cannot make the payments directly; this has to take place via a *gastouderbureau*.

Note!: Sending your child to a *gastouder* or making use of a *leidster / oppas* is also covered by the legislation regarding employer and government contributions as described on page 187. In order for you to qualify for a government contribution, the *gastouder-(bureau) / leidster / oppas* must be officially registered. If you already have a favorite child-sitter, then in order for this person to qualify, he or she has to register with the National Register for *kinderopvang*. To do this, they have to meet the following conditions:

- they must be 18 years of age or older
- they, and anyone they share the home with who is 18 years of age or older, must have a valid Statement of Good Behavior
- they must have a valid EHBO (first aid) for children diploma
- they must have a 'good parent' certificate
- they must have a degree (or a so-called 'experience degree') in Health and Care (MBO2 in Helpende Zorg en Welzijn) or one of the diplomas listed on the Ministry of Education's site (under *diploma's gastouderopvang*)
- they must have a risk inventory carried out for their home.

These, and possible further, conditions can also be found on www.gastouderland.nl.

PARENT PARTICIPATION DAY CARE

A relatively new phenomenon is the Parent Participation Day Care (*ouderparticipatiecrèche*); whereby the children rotate among the parents of the group. This is an accepted form of day care according to the new day care laws described earlier in this chapter, which means that the parents qualify for government support in the costs, provided the group is registered and recognized.

FERTILE STORKS

During the 17th century, there was no such thing as the sexual revolution. Babies and the conception thereof were shrouded in mystery. In order to answer such painful questions as 'Where do babies come from?' the Dutch came up with the following, absolutely plausible, explanation: babies were brought by the stork. If this failed to impress the children, other, equally plausible, explanations were available: babies were found among the beets, or they were found in wells or in hollow trees.

Why, of all birds, did the stork get to be the one to deliver this precious freight? In the Netherlands, storks were always considered harbingers of good luck. Therefore, it was only logical that they would be the ones to bring proof of the fact that the mother was fertile, the marriage fruitful and the father a real man.

Nowadays, if you pass a front yard with a stork in it, you can be sure that this is the announcement of the birth of a new world citizen. The use of storks is also very popular on birth announcements.

Cost
It's hard to predict what the costs will be of this type of care, as it will likely depend on the agreement the parents reach among themselves. The fact that it qualifies for subsidy will probably influence what the parents ultimately agree upon. In order to ensure quality child care, the government has created stricter rules regarding this type of care, such as regarding the type of (child care) diploma the parents have (see above, where the conditions are listed). If these requirements are not met, this type of care will no longer qualify for subsidy.

AU PAIR

Au pairs in Holland receive room and board and, in exchange, their primary responsibility is child care. In addition, the au pair may be required to help with light housekeeping duties. In most cases, you select an au pair with the help of an intermediary or au pair organization. Their responsibilities include interviewing and selecting qualified host families and au pair candidates, drawing up contracts, helping with the visa process and assisting with adjustment difficulties. As of June 1, 2013, you are obligated to arrange an au pair via a recognized bureau.

Cost
Room and board amounts to approximately € 450 to € 850 per month, while the host family is also responsible for covering visa, permit and insurance expenses. Furthermore, you will pay the au pair organization a one-time interview, registration and placement fee. Some organizations also charge a monthly management fee, so be sure to check out several organizations (see the list at the end of the chapter) before signing on the dotted line.

OPPAS (BABY-SITTER)

Planning a quiet evening out with your partner? A neighborhood high school or university student is probably your best bet. Although some communities maintain an *Oppascentrale* (central listing of local baby-sitters and telephone numbers – check your local telephone book), often the best way to locate a reliable sitter is through your local network or by word-of-mouth.

Cost
Depending on age, experience and geographic region, fees can range from € 3.50 to € 6 per hour (depending, also, on the number of children). Other rates apply should you decide to employ a babysitter on a permanent basis in your home. In this case, an hourly fee of around € 5 to € 7.50 is paid for basic child-care responsibilities. Another fee schedule applies if housekeeping duties are also required (approximately € 7 to € 10 per hour).

LESS RUN-OF-THE-MILL OPTIONS

1. *Flexibel Kindercentrum / Kinderdagverblijf (Flexible Child Center)*: This is a type of child care center that is open 24 hours a day, 7 days a week, but receives no government support. You will find them in the larger cities in the Netherlands. To find one, check your *gemeentegids*. The cost depends entirely on the center, and the number of days/hours that you place your child(ren) there. Fifty-two weeks of 11-hour days should cost you approximately € 23,000 (based on a charge of € 6.10 – € 7.14 an hour), 40 weeks should cost you approximately € 19,450.

2. *Nanny*: Visit www.some-buddy.nl or www.nanny.nl for more information on nannies, housekeepers, baby-sitters, care-takers and chauffeurs.

3. *International Women's Clubs*: Many international women's clubs have their own Moms and Tots Groups and will be happy to have you join the group. Although this is not, per se, a day care option, it is a great way to meet other parents and to network. For a list of (women's) clubs, see page 260. ACCESS also maintains a list of non-Dutch day care options (toddler playgroups, pre-schools, international day care centers, etc.). You can find their number at the end of the chapter.

PARTY TIME

Life is a party! Here are a few festivities in honor of children:

KRAAMBEZOEK
(Visiting the New-Born Child)
In the Netherlands, when a child is born, you send out announcements (called *geboortekaarten*, or birth cards) to just about anyone you know: 90-year-old aunts, colleagues you haven't seen in five years, uncles you never really liked, your best friend from nursery school. And they all respond! You might end up sending out 150 announcements – but beware! The Dutch interpret this is an invitation to come and admire the little tyke; so be sure you stock up on some *beschuit met muisjes* (rusks covered with sugared aniseeds – pink aniseeds for a girl and blue aniseeds for a boy) as your 90-year-old aunt, your ex-colleagues, your unpleasant uncle and your best friend from nursery school will be arriving shortly (that is, assuming you have any of these people 'on supply' in the Netherlands). This is why so many birth announcements contain the short sentence: *Moeder en kind rusten van 13.00 – 15.00 en ná 20.00 uur,*

(Mother and child will be resting ...) or *Bezoek is welkom, maar bel even* (Visitors are welcome, but please call in advance).

Often the question is asked: 'How so rusks with aniseed?' – well; eating aniseeds will do the mother a lot of good as tradition has it that they stimulate her milk production. That explains why mommy is eating them, but not why everybody else has to...

VERJAARDAG (BIRTHDAY)
Kids' birthdays are, of course, Very Important Events. Luckily, the Dutch think so too. So, how do they celebrate them? On the day of the birthday, the birthday boy or girl gets to *trakteren* at school. This means that at some point in the morning, he or she hands out little items of food to his or her classmates. There are about 30 children per class; consequently this happens, on average, two or three times a month. For this reason, many teachers prefer that you bring something other than sweets, such as tangerines, cheese or *worst* (slices of sausage) on a toothpick, an apple or maybe even little boxes of raisins. Some parents put a lot of effort into making these packages look fun: they make bugs or boats or dolls by arranging the cheese, pickles or carrots just so.

Dutch children also get to give birthday parties, to which they invite a couple of their best friends from school and/or the neighborhood. Interestingly, kids often have *two* birthday parties: one with fun and games for the kids from school and the neighborhood and one for the extended family and other grown-ups (including *their* kids). The latter is usually without organized fun and games and mostly involves the receiving of gifts, the eating of cake and cookies and putting up with aunts and uncles saying how much everybody has *grown* since the last time they saw them. What you organize for the former (more official) party more or less depends on your budget and your imagination (a visit from a clown, a treasure hunt, dressing up and making a movie, visiting a circus, visiting a puppet theater, you name it). Ask other parents about what is popular among the children in your child's age group.

If your kid is invited to a Dutch birthday party, the invitation will state when and where it is taking place and what to bring in terms of, for instance, a bathing suit or a dress-up costume. The Dutch are not into big expensive gifts: generally speaking something in the price range between € 7.50 and € 15 will suffice. If you bring something more expensive, they might feel a little embarrassed. And of course: do not forget to arrive ON TIME. This is Holland, remember? Plus, chances are the actual party will be somewhere else (like the pool, or the woods), so coming late means your child might miss out on all the fun!

SINTERKLAAS (SAINT NICHOLAS)

You will find more about Sinterklaas on page 44, however, he is definitely worth mentioning here as he is *the* children's friend in the Netherlands.

St. Nicholas, or Sinterklaas, is considered the patron saint of children. Every year on December 5th, in honor of his birthday, he makes children happy by giving them lots of gifts. Contrary to Christmas, the festivities surrounding this important event are not limited to one single day. Somewhere halfway November already, Sinterklaas arrives on his steamboat from Spain, accompanied by his helpers, Zwarte Pieten. The Zwarte Pieten (Black Petes) are his Moorish helpers, colorfully dressed and made up with shiny black faces, curly black wigs and golden hoops in their ears. Sinterklaas has one major arrival date and point in the Netherlands that is covered extensively on television. However, after this day, he makes a grand entry into almost all towns and cities, parading down the main street with his energetic Zwarte Pieten and waving royally at his little fans.

The Zwarte Pieten are the ones who know who's been good and who's been bad and who have the sooty task of climbing down the household chimney to deliver gifts to those who have been good. Again, contrary to Christmas, these gifts are not delivered merely on December 5th. Any time between Sinterklaas's arrival in November and his departure in December, he and his helpers may decide to pay a kid's home a surprise visit at night. In order to limit the excitement, parents usually compromise to having him visit twice a week, say on Tuesday night and Saturday night, in order not to be dragged out of bed at 6 o'clock *every* morning to see if there are any surprises. During these weeks, Sinterklaas also pays a visit to offices, schools, day care centers, old age homes, department stores and private homes, bringing little gifts, cookies (*per-pernoten* and *kruidnoten*; ginger and cinnamon cookies), candies (*schuimpjes* – sugary cushions) and chocolate coins, which are handed out to the attending crowd.

When the children are told they can anticipate a nighttime visit from their friend, they place a shoe by the chimney, often with a little note in it, explaining what they hope to receive or thanking Sinterklaas for their previous gift, plus a little present for Sinterklaas or Zwarte Piet and sometimes a carrot for Sinterklaas's white horse, Amerigo. And then they sing a little song, aiming the notes up the chimney. It is a heart-warming, Norman-Rockwell-type of moment that makes your heart sing too.

The festivities change, as the children get older, or if Sinterklaas is celebrated among only grown-ups – because, yes, this is something the grown-ups enjoy doing long after they've stopped believing in fairytales. The older age group arranges a type of lottery, in which they each draw one other person in the group to make a gift for, and a poem. 'Make' a gift being the operative word here, because in most cases, the real gift is disguised, hidden or incorporated into a much bigger playful contraption, designed and created by the giver. Also the poem has its specific elements; in particular, humor and a little bit of leg-pulling, often listing memorable moments of the past year including, preferably, the receiver's mishaps and gaffes. The reader has to be able to abandon taking him or herself too seriously for the occasion, though the poems are ultimately written with much affection.

Most families try to have the main celebration on December 5 itself, regardless of the day of week. On this day, called *pakjesavond* (or gift evening), families and friends get together for the exchanging of gifts. In the case of families with littler children, the parents often arrange either a personal visit from Sinterklaas, or else for a big bag of gifts to be deposited at the front door by a friendly neighbor, who will then bang on the door and the windows as a cue for the parents to exclaim: "Oh, there's Zwarte Piet! Quick, let's see whether he's left us any gifts!"

The rest of the evening is spent enjoying this unique Dutch family tradition (most schools start an hour later the next day, to allow the children to catch up on the sleep they inevitably missed due to the excitement of *pakjesavond*).

KERSTMIS (CHRISTMAS)

Does all this mean that there is no Christmas in the Netherlands? Not at all. Though the celebration of Christmas, as many know it, is based on the Dutch tradition of Sinterklaas (and is therefore really a 'repeat' just three weeks later), this does not mean that, come December 25, everyone will be going about their daily routine. Kerstmis is definitely a time of *gezelligheid* (a unique Dutch word for what can best be described as coziness) when friends and family get together to enjoy each other's company and a good meal, and companies organize Christmas celebrations for the entire staff. Increasingly, the Dutch are taking to whipping out all sorts of outdoor decorations to lighten up the dreary December days, and, while they are at it, buying each other gifts to put under the tree – though some Dutch purists limit the gift-giving to only Sinterklaas. And so, even among the most die-hard purist families, Christmas remains a very important day on the kiddie calendar, with families traveling across the country to visit grandma and grandpa and all the favorite aunts and uncles – who can seldom resist the temptation to give a little something to the children.

LEGAL ISSUES

ZWANGERSCHAPSVERKLARING – 'STATEMENT OF PREGNANCY'

If you are pregnant, currently working and plan to do so following delivery, you will need to obtain a *zwangerschapsverklaring* (or 'statement of pregnancy') from your midwife or gynecologist. This document confirms your estimated due date and will be used to determine when you will be eligible for *zwangerschapsverlof* (pregnancy leave), which you can read about in the next paragraph.

ZWANGERSCHAPSVERLOF AND BEVALLINGSVERLOF –
PREGNANCY LEAVE AND BIRTH LEAVE

In the Netherlands, women have a right to 16 weeks' paid leave, divided into 4-6 weeks of pregnancy leave and 10 weeks of birth leave. Pregnancy leave may be initiated between 4-6 weeks prior to the estimated due date, but no later than that, as Dutch law states that you may not work from 4 weeks before, until 6 weeks after, delivery. *These latter 6 weeks are referred to as birth leave. When you take up your leave should be determined together with your employer.* Starting with due dates on or after May 26 of this year, if you are expecting twins (or more) you will get 2-4 weeks more leave and it will have to start at least 8 weeks before your due date. As of last year, you can go back to work after the legally required 6 weeks have ended, and spread the remaining 4 weeks of birth leave over a period of a maximum of 30 weeks.

During pregnancy leave you receive 100% of your normal wages – either directly from the Social Security Institution or via your employer – up to a maximum of € 202.17 (the so-called daily wage) a day, though some employers pay out the gap between this and your full last-earned salary. Should the baby arrive early, you still have a right to the full 16 weeks. If it is late, and you have used up the 6 weeks beforehand, you still have the right to a 10-week leave (birth leave) following the baby's birth. If your child has to stay in the hospital for an extended period of time then, as of last year, the mother has a right to a maximum of 10 additional weeks of birth leave to take care of her child once it returns home.

If, prior to the start of your pregnancy leave, you are unable to work due to a pregnancy-related illness and must stay at home, then you have the right to 100% of the official daily wage. If you are unable to *return* to work due to medical reasons secondary to pregnancy and/or delivery, then you also have a right to up to 104 weeks of benefits at 100% of the daily wage. Both of these benefits are based on the Sickness Benefits Act and not on the Pregnancy Leave-regulation. If you become ill more than six weeks before your due date, then your pregnancy leave officially starts six weeks before your due date, regardless of any agreement you have reached with your employer. During the days preceding the official leave, if the illness is not due to pregnancy, you will receive at least 70% of your personal wage.

Would you like to take more than the government-stipulated 16-week leave? In order to do so you need to apply for a voluntary *Ziektewet*-insurance at your Social Security Institution (UWV) within four weeks of discontinuing your work activities.

Pregnancy Leave for Self-Employed Mothers
The Zelfstandig en Zwangerregeling (Self-Employed and Pregnant Regulation) gives self-employed mothers a right to a 16-week pregnancy leave. In the case of pregnancy-related illness, you will have to have arranged voluntary insurance in order to receive anything during this period.

How much you receive depends on the number of hours you worked in self-employment the previous year. If you worked 1,225 hours or more, then you will receive a benefit equal to the minimum wage. If you worked fewer than 1,225 hours, then your benefit will be less and will depend on your profits / income over the previous year. You also have a right to this benefit if you work for your partner's / spouse' company. If you are both employed and self-employed, you receive a benefit from both sources, to a total of no more than your normal earnings, and no more than the minimum wage.

You request this benefit by contacting the Social Security Institution (UWV).

Pregnancy Leave if You Are Receiving a Benefit
If you are receiving the unemployment benefit (WW), Sickness Benefit (ZW), or a benefit due to disability for work, then the pregnancy leave payments will temporarily replace these payments. You should arrange this yourself with the UWV (Social Security Institution).

YOUR RIGHTS AS A PREGNANT EMPLOYEE
You are not obligated to tell a prospective employer that you are pregnant, but if you choose to do so, he may not turn you down for this reason. You *do* have an obligation to tell your current employer that you are pregnant, however – at the latest three weeks before your pregnancy leave is due to start. You may not be fired during pregnancy or within 12 weeks following the birth of your child. Only under very special conditions, for example in the case of bankruptcy, may your employment be terminated. Should your contract end during pregnancy, for instance, at the end of a contract for a limited period of time, you have the right to unemployment (WW) and sickness benefits – and therefore also pregnancy leave. Should you quit your job and your baby is due or born within ten weeks, then you have a right to pregnancy leave as well.

During pregnancy, your employer is obligated to protect your safety and health, and you are eligible for certain additional rights. Discuss these with your employer. If you do not tell your employer that you are pregnant, you cannot exercise these rights. A few examples of your rights are: the right to regular working and resting hours, extra breaks and a suitable, closed-off space to rest (and where you can lie down). You are under no obligation to work overtime or at night. These rights are applicable up until six months after delivery. You also have the right to other working hours or other work if your current work is unsafe or hazardous to your health. If neither option is available, you have the right to be exempted from work. There are also special regulations regarding nursing, hard physical labor, stress, chemicals, radiation, risk of infection, noise, extreme vibrations, extreme heat or cold, etc. Check the website of the Ministerie van Sociale Zaken en Werkgelegenheid (Ministry of Social Affairs and Employment) for details.

'DELIVERY LEAVE' AND SHORT PARENTAL LEAVE
Daddies have a right to stand by their wife/partner while she gives birth (this is covered by the fascinatingly misnomered 'calamity leave'), followed by two days of paid 'delivery leave' (*kraamverlof*), which can be used up at any point within four weeks after the birth of the child(ren) (if the child is born in the hospital, this is within four weeks after the child comes home). Under this same banner of 'calamity leave', daddies may also take time off to register the birth of their child – not a full day, but for however much time is needed to do this. As of January of this year, the mother's legal partner also has a right to three days parental leave right after the birth of the child (whether or not you will receive wages over three days depends on your employer). For more on long-term parental leave, see further on.

REGISTRATION
Within three working days (not including the day of birth) your baby has to be registered at the *gemeentehuis* (town hall). This must take place at the town hall of the municipality in which your baby

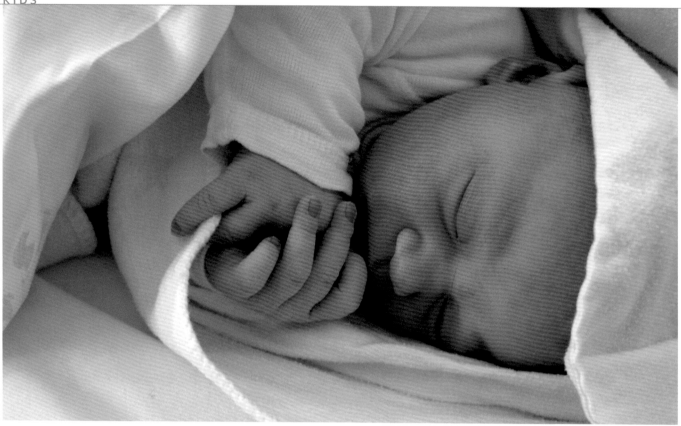

was born – not your home town, if different. The father usually performs this task. If this is not possible, then it must be done by someone who was present during the birth of the baby – or, of course, by the mother. Necessary to register the baby are; valid proof of identity of the person registering the birth, valid proof of identity of the mother, a certified copy of the marriage license (if applicable), proof of recognition of the baby (if applicable), the certificate of birth supplied by the doctor, hospital or midwife, and a certificate containing the choice of the last name of the child (if applicable). In order to avoid undue hassle, check with the *gemeentehuis* in question prior to registration as to what is needed, as requirements may vary from one municipality to another. Also ask for an International Birth Certificate (for an additional fee) at this time. This document will come in handy when registering your baby with your embassy or consulate and when applying for a passport. Being born in the Netherlands does not give your baby the right to a Dutch passport – that is unless one, or both, of the parents is/are Dutch (see the following paragraph, however!).

LEGALLY RECOGNIZING BABY

If you and your partner are not married, the father may choose to legally recognize the baby either prior to birth, at the time of registration at the town hall or at a later date. In most cases, the mother must be present for this. This must take place in the town hall where you reside – not where you register the birth (unless of course this is one and the same). Check with your municipal offices or lawyer to verify which documents are necessary and what other possible requirements there may be. If the mother is not Dutch, while the father is, the baby will only acquire Dutch nationality automatically at birth if he/she was legally recognized by the father prior to his/her birth. After that, until the age of 7, the child will acquire Dutch nationality once the Dutch father recognizes it. Children older than 7 acquire Dutch nationality after recognition by a Dutch father and a DNA-test, establishing the fact that the 'recognizer' is indeed the biological father.

If the father legally recognizes the baby, then this determines that there is a family relationship between the father and the child, a duty to support the child and a right for the child in the inheritance, should the father pass away. However, it does not mean that the father automatically has parental authority. Parental authority is only automatic if the parents are married or registered partners. In all other cases, a request to this effect must be brought before the court.

If the father does not have Dutch nationality, then the civil servant of the municipality will have to check whether recognition is possible. Make sure you are well-informed of the consequences of recognition for the baby's nationality, name and military duties (at a later age), as well as the father's obligation to support it.

KINDERBIJSLAG – CHILD BENEFIT

If you are living in the Netherlands and/or are employed and pay Dutch wage taxes, then you are entitled to *kinderbijslag*. This holds true not only for your own (adopted) children, but also step and foster children and other children you raise and care for as if they were your own. Following the registration of your child's birth, the municipal offices forward your data to the Sociale Verzekeringsbank (the Social Insurance Bank). Within a few days you receive a registration form for the benefit. Payment is made on a quarterly basis directly into your bank account up until your child is 18 years of age. The amount paid out is based on the age of your child and is currently set at € 197.67 for children between the ages of 0-5, € 240.03 for children between the ages of 6-11, and € 282.39 for children aged 12-17 (2016). Children age 16 and 17 must be attending school (either HAVO, VWO or MBO – for more on these acronyms, see chapter 9). For more information, visit www.svb.nl.

If you already have children when you move here, you can request the *kinderbijslag* by contacting the SVB (Sociale Verzekeringsbank).

CHILD ALLOWANCE

January 1, 2009, saw the introduction of the *kindgebonden budget*, or Child Allowance, to be paid out by the tax authorities. The amount paid out depends on the parents' income and the number of children in the family, and runs from a maximum of € 1,032 per year if there is one child, to € 2,316 for four children (with € 177 per year per subsequent child). To qualify, parents must either have Dutch nationality or a valid permit. The *kindgebonden budget* does not affect the payment of the *kinderbijslag* (see above), which is an income-independent allowance. As of 2016, single parents receive a maximum *kindgebonden budget* of € 3,050, instead of an income tax deduction.

OUDERSCHAPSVERLOF – PARENTAL LEAVE

The law stipulates that both working parents have the right to take an unpaid leave of absence to care for a child (adoption, step or foster child included) as of their first day of employment (it used to be that they had to have been in employment for at least one year). Leave may be taken either by both parents together or one after the other, at any time during the first seven years of the child's life. A request for leave must be submitted at least two months before the intended first day of leave. In the case of twins, leave is available for each child. The legal amount of time allotted is based on the number of contractual hours per week that you work, times 26 – and the standard rule is that you will work 50% during a period of one year. For instance, if you work 32 hours a week, this means you work 16 hours a week during a period of one year. As the rules are not always practical – for either the employee or employer – other conditions may be agreed upon, such as taking up 100% leave over a period of six months, working at 75% of your normal working hours over a period of two years, or spreading your leave over six periods. As of 2015, parents can decide for themselves when and how they take up this leave. Check whether a collective labor agreement applies to you, in which there may be further, more beneficial, rules on parental leave. Although not required by law, some employers continue to pay up to 75% of the wages during parental leave. If you become sick during this leave, your employer must pay wages over the hours during which you would otherwise have worked. If you switch jobs, you can take your remaining parental-leave days with you to your new employer.

As it is unpaid leave, you might experience financial hardship during Parental Leave. Single parent families can request government support during this period based on the *Bijstand* (welfare) regulations, via the Sociale Verzekeringsbank (SVB). Two-parent families are expected to be able to solve this by means of an income earned by the other parent.

BORSTVOEDING – BREAST-FEEDING

Employers must provide breast-feeding employees with a quiet area in which to breast-feed or express – not the restroom! If this is not feasible, then the employer must allow the employee to find an appropriate spot or to go to the baby in order to do this. Feeding / expressing time is considered work time and may therefore not lead to a reduction in your wages. A maximum of one quarter of normal working hours may be used for this purpose, up until the child is nine months old. Discuss the various options with your employer prior to initiating pregnancy leave.

ADOPTION / FOSTER LEAVE

If you adopt a child, you and your partner individually have a right to four consecutive weeks' adoption leave surrounding the arrival of the child (if you adopt more than one child at once, the period of leave is still four weeks). This leave may be taken up anywhere between four weeks before the arrival of the child and 22 weeks after his or her arrival and can be spread out over these 26 weeks. During the period of leave, you will receive 100% of your wages, up to a maximum of € 202.17 (the 'daily wage') a day. Self-employed persons do not have a right to a benefit in connection with unpaid leave for adoption.

Under certain conditions, this same leave is available to persons taking in a foster child.

ZORGVERLOF – SHORT CARE LEAVE

By law, a full-time employee has the right – per year – to take a maximum of two times the number of hours he or she works in a week, in order to care for a sick (foster) child, partner or parent (if you work 36 hours a week, you have a right to 72 hours, with 32 hours you have a right to 64 hours, and so on). There are two conditions for this: one is that the care is really necessary and two is that you are the one who must provide this care. Your employer may ask for proof of this and he may only refuse to grant you this leave on substantial company grounds. This type of leave does not have to be taken up in one go. The employer is obligated to continue to pay at least 70% of your wages during this period, but no less than the minimum wage. Your industry's CAO (Collective Labor Agreement) or the company's regulations may contain additional rules, so be sure to check what these may be.

If your child / partner / parent suddenly falls ill and you have to leave your work immediately, this first day is covered by the rules on Calamity Leave. Short Care Leave starts the next day.

LANGDUREND ZORGVERLOF – LONG CARE LEAVE

You have an annual right to take up leave to care for a terminally ill or terminally threatened (foster) child, partner or parent for a longer period of time. As of 2015, you can also use this leave to care for grandparents, grandchildren, siblings, other people living with you (such as an uncle), and people with whom you have a social relationship who rely on you for help (such as a neighbor or a friend). Also the state of the person needing your help need not be so critical: 'simply' being ill or in need of your help is sufficient. The right amounts to – in total, per year – six times the number of hours you work per week. If you work 40 hours a week, this means that you have a right to 240 hours of long care leave per year. You cannot take up leave for more than 12 consecutive weeks, and you will have to work at least 50%. As is the case with Parental Leave,

you can reach an agreement with your employer based on which you take up a full 100% leave over six weeks, or you take up your leave in 'chunks', provided it is taken up within 18 weeks in total. Again, this can only be refused on substantial company grounds. In principle, you have no income over the hours you don't work, unless this has been specified otherwise, for instance in a collective labor agreement (CAO).

CALAMITY LEAVE
Calamity leave has been created for unforeseen situations in which you have to act immediately and personally, for instance, to find a baby-sitter for your suddenly sick child, to find a plumber if the water pipes have burst, in the case of sudden death in the family or, as mentioned above, to register the birth of your newborn child. In principle, this leave is granted for a couple of hours, though it could be extended to a couple of days, during which period your employer is to continue 100% payment of your salary. If the circumstances are such that they qualify for Short Care Leave, your leave will automatically be converted into this type of leave after 24 hours. For the rules on this type of leave, see above.

UNPAID LEAVE – SOCIAL SECURITY AND PENSION
Before taking up any kind of unpaid leave, be sure to inform yourself of the consequences for your build-up of social security benefits and your pension.

TAKING CARE OF A HANDICAPPED CHILD
The TOG, Support in the Household Expenses for Those Taking Care of Handicapped Children, had been created to provide financial assistance to those parents who have a (mentally or physically) handicapped (foster) child between the ages of 3 and 17 living at home. This benefit has been abolished as of 2015; instead, parents receive double *kinderbijslag*, depending on conditions set by the Social Insurance Bank (SVB – www.svb.nl) – for instance to help cover expenses due to the fact that the child cannot live at home.

Children who, since before they reached the age of 18, or while following a higher education, have become sick or disabled in such a way that they are permanently disabled for work, receive the Wajong-benefit independently. As of this year, if a child is partially disabled for work, they have a right to assistance from the municipality in finding work.

LAST WILL AND TESTAMENT
Preparing a will is probably one of the most important steps you will take to ensure the future well-being of your newborn. Although not common knowledge, not all foreign wills are valid in the Netherlands. This depends, among others, on your country of origin (what are the requirements for a valid will there?), how the will has been drawn up and whether the Netherlands has entered into a treaty on the matter with your country of origin.

If something were to happen to both parents, the courts will appoint a guardian; most often the person mentioned in the will. If the will states nothing on this matter, a relative in the country of origin will be appointed. In order to guarantee that the *voogdij* (guardianship) of your child is given to the person of your choosing, it would be best to have a testament drawn up, or at least checked, by a Dutch *notaris* (civil law notary) – to be on the safe side. Check the Yellow Pages or get a referral from a friend for the name of a civil law notary in your area.

VACATION

According to Dutch law, all children as of the age of 5 are *leerplichtig* and must attend school (unless they are sick). Exceptions may be made for parents who are required to work during standard school holidays and vacations, generally up to a maximum of 10 days. Extraordinary family situations such as special birthdays, anniversaries, illness or death are other exceptions. Dutch schools are very strict about this and a formal request in writing is required prior to taking your child out of school. International schools may have their own set of regulations – so when in doubt, ask!

SHOPPING

BABY FOOD AND FORMULA

Baby food (*babyvoeding*) can be purchased at all supermarkets and most *drogisterijen* (drugstores) and *apotheken* (pharmacies). You can also find formula (*opvolgmelk*, treated milk for babies) in these stores, though the very specialized types of formula for babies with allergies (soy-based products) are often only available through the *apotheek*. Also health food stores (*reformhuizen* or *reformwinkels*) carry their own baby foods and formula.

You will be advised as to what kind of formula to try by the *Consultatiebureau* (Well Baby Clinic, see page 234).

BABY CARE PRODUCTS

(Popular) baby care products – baby shampoos, soaps, ointments, etc. – can be found at the *drogist* (drugstore), while a smaller selection is available in supermarkets. Brand name and own label diapers are available at the *drogist* and the supermarket.

CLOTHES

Clothes for babies and children can be found in the larger department stores, certain brand stores and, of course, stores specializing in baby and children's items. Virtually every main shopping street in every little town has a store that carries a large variety of children's clothing. Children's shoes can be bought at almost any shoe store. At the end of the chapter you will find a list of shops.

MATERNITY CLOTHES

Maternity clothes are called *positiekleding* or *zwangerschapskleding*. Many department stores carry maternity clothes, as do the specialty shops listed at the end of the chapter. You can also purchase very stylish 'oversize clothes' at an Extra Size (*grote maten*) woman's shop or in the XL larger sizes sections of most clothing stores. Many second-hand clothing shops (*tweedehandswinkels*) have a selection of maternity clothes, too. *Zwangerschapszwempakken* (swim suits) can best be purchased at a specialty shop.

FURNITURE

There are large chains of stores as well as smaller shops, all across the Netherlands, that carry or specialize in baby furniture. Here you can also find cribs, strollers, car seats, high chairs, lamps, bottles, baths, clothes, toys, the works. Check the Yellow Pages or Internet under *Babyartikelen* and check the list at the end of the chapter.

TOYS & GAMES

Speelgoedwinkels are toy stores carrying a wide selection of toys and games, but toys and games can also be found in department stores and even in a few of the household chains. Second-hand children's shops carry playthings as well as children's books. Often they will have a message board where you can post larger items for sale such as carriages, cribs, furniture, etc. Furthermore, there are splendid toy stores all across the country that do not belong to any chain and that sell some of the more old-fashioned variety of (wooden) toys.

FUN THINGS TO DO

EXTRACURRICULAR ACTIVITIES

Some of you may be used to extracurricular activities arranged by the school... unfortunately, most Dutch schools do not have such a program. On the other hand, tuition is free if you send your child to a local school, so this may have something to do with it. Yet this does not mean that your child has to twiddle his or her thumbs all day, once school is out. In almost all municipalities you will find an organization or private persons that offer all sorts of activities, such as carpentry, painting, music, dancing, art, cooking, etc. Just ask around, check your *gemeentegids* or give your municipality a call. And, perhaps even the best fun of all, is simply being able to go out and play with the kids in the neighborhood – something that is still very popular here.

Furthermore, there are several sports organizations; the more popular ones being for tennis, field hockey and gymnastics – though there is also judo, basketball, baseball, soccer, dancing, horseback-riding, cycling (of course) and much, much more.

SWIMMING

One very important extracurricular activity (that is sometimes arranged through schools) is swimming, which should come as no surprise in this country of canals, rivers, lakes and the sea. Though your child does not *have* to take swimming lessons, there is a well-regulated system of classes to take and diplomas to aspire to – a program that virtually every child follows and takes pride in completing.

SCOUTS AND OTHER CAMPS

Boy and Girl Scouts (called *scouting*) clubs are very popular here. The kids get together almost every Saturday afternoon, and engage in fun and educational activities. Occasionally, the groups go camping for an entire weekend, while they organize week-long summer camps during summer vacation. Check the telephone book or your *gemeentegids* for the local chapter, or visit www.scouting.nl/english.

Other popular camps are for horseback-riding and sailing and you could of course also ask among the international schools whether they are arranging anything for the summer (or know of someone who is). Some municipalities arrange a day-camp during the summer vacations with a full program of activities for the children; drop-off time early in the morning, pick-up time late afternoon. Once again, your *gemeentegids* or someone at the municipal offices should be able to tell you whether there's something like that going on in your town or one nearby.

FILLING YOUR DAYS

A very popular item of entertainment for younger kids in the Netherlands is the petting farm, to be found in almost every town and city. They usually have goats, sheep, rabbits, guinea pigs, chickens, ducks, pigs, a pony, some cats and the occasional donkey. Kids love it, and often learn something about the animals while they are there. Also, if you are looking for a rabbit for the family, this is a place to try out as they tend to have a few extra hopping around. Aside from the petting farm, you'll be surprised to find that many towns also have a so-called *hertenkamp*; an enclosed area with deer who peacefully graze their way through life, and who enthusiastically welcome a handful of leftover bread should you and the kids care to bring them a visit. It is not quite clear what the origin of these deer camps is; are they a reminder of the days when deer roamed around freely? Or were they once the private parks of the well-to-do at a time when it was the thing to do to populate these parks with something a little more dainty than a woolly sheep? The answer to this question remains a little elusive, but the sight of these elegant animals is nonetheless a pleasant one – and they are quite friendly.

Playgrounds are also to be found on various locations in towns and cities, with swings, slides, seesaws, a sand box, and more. And, of course, most zoos also have *great* (and large) playgrounds for your children to let off steam, while you sit and enjoy a well-deserved cup of coffee. You can find more on zoos a little further on in this chapter.

Another staple activity of Dutch summer time are the traveling circuses and fairs (*kermis*), whose arrival is announced well in advance so that you can set aside time for a fun day out with the kids. You buy an admission ticket to the circuses. The fairs sometimes charge an entry fee, but mostly you pay for the rides and attractions you choose to enter.

For rainy days (of which there will be plenty), there are the covered playgrounds – called Ballorig, Playcity, or Kidzcity – which are huge covered areas with a great variety of things to enjoy: humongous slides, intricate rope-climbing structures, merry-go-rounds, trains, you name it. In some of the bigger cities you will find activ-

ity centers, where children learn to build tree houses, floats and other complicated contraptions. A valuable source of information on these activities and centers is: www.uitmetkinderen.nl (a day out with children), where you can search for museums, amusement parks, pools, zoos, playgrounds, etc. according to age, postal code, price range, and alphabet.

AMUSEMENT PARKS AND MUSEUMS

The Netherlands has some great amusement parks and museums, such as:

- De Efteling: a huge park offering several days' worth of entertainment in fantasyland, with fairytale woods, wild rides on rollercoasters, castles, fairytale figures and more.
  Europalaan 1, Kaatsheuvel (near Tilburg)
  www.efteling.com.

- Corpus: a 'journey through the human body' during which the visitor can see, feel and hear how the human body works and what roles healthy food, a healthy life and exercise play. It offers education and entertainment, as well as a vast number of permanent and variable exhibitions.
  Willem Einthovenstraat 1, Oegstgeest
  www.corpusexperience.nl

- The Open Air Museums (Openluchtmuseum): where you can make a trip through time. There are many, including, among others:
  - *Nederlands Openluchtmuseum* (daily life in the Netherlands between 1600 and 1970).
    Schelmseweg 89, Arnhem
    www.openluchtmuseum.nl
  - *Orientalis* (Open Air Museum, for a glimpse of the world 2,000 years ago in the Middle East, focusing on Judaism, Christianity and Islam).
    Profetenlaan 2, Heilig Landstichting
    www.museumparkorientalis.nl
  - *Zuiderzeemuseum* (life in a fishing village around 1900).
    Wierdijk 12-22, Enkhuizen
    www.zuiderzeemuseum.nl

■ NEMO: a scientifically oriented play / educational center; offering a discovery trip through fantasy and reality.
Oosterdok 2, Amsterdam
www.e-nemo.nl

■ Safari Park Beekse Bergen: a place where you can take a drive (or walk) among more than 100 wild animals, a trip that could take more than a day!
Beekse Bergen 1, Hilvarenbeek (near Tilburg)
www.safaripark.nl

■ Duinrell: a fantastic water festival, with attractions, a ski valley, a wild pool and lots of entertainment.
Duinrell 1, Wassenaar
www.duinrell.nl

■ Pony Park Slagharen: a place where you can experience life in the Wild West, with an amusement park, a shopping street, Wigwam World, Colorado City and lots of entertainment.
Zwarte Dijk 37, Slagharen
www.slagharen.com

■ Planetarium Franeker, where, more than 200 years ago, Eise Eisinga made a scale model of the solar system in his living room, with a mechanism that keeps planets and pointers in motion and that works to this day.
Eise Eisingastraat 3, Franeker
www.planetarium-friesland.nl

■ Children's Museum at The Tropical Institute (Koninklijk Instituut voor de Tropen), where contemporary non-Western cultures are brought to life for children between the ages of 6 and 12. Also available for children's parties.
Linnaeusstraat 2, Amsterdam
www.kit.nl

■ Walibi World: a huge outdoor swimming and water paradise, with more than 50 attractions and shows, offering entertainment and adventure.
Spijkweg 30, Biddinghuizen
www.walibi.nl

■ Louwman Museum: the national automobile museum. For anyone who is car crazy and interested in the history of automobiles from the first horseless carriages through subsequent models of motorized, steam and electric vehicles.
Leidsestraatweg 57, The Hague
www.louwmanmuseum.nl

■ Madurodam: a miniature version of the Netherlands, including Schiphol airport, the Delta works, the center of Amsterdam and more.
George Maduroplein 1, The Hague
www.madurodam.nl.

This is but a small selection (see Chapter 11 for more tourist attractions). Ask around among other parents or at the vvv (Tourist Information Office; there is one in almost every municipality, but you will find a list of vvvs at the end of chapter 11) what other tips they may have.

ZOOS

Animals are always a great success with children and what makes the Netherlands such a wonderful 'zoo country' is that there are so many of them, and that a lot of effort is put into recreating the natural habitats of the animals – so that both we and they can enjoy their stay here. As mentioned earlier, the zoos all have extensive playgrounds, for when your kids need to blow off steam, as well as indoor facilities for rainy days, and child-friendly cafeterias.

■ Amersfoort Zoo: This large zoo near Amersfoort has provided its animals with increasingly spacious and comfortable habitats over the last two decades, bringing it on a par with all the other large zoos in the Netherlands. It has a Savannah, encircled all the way around, allowing you to circumnavigate the area and enjoy the animals as they graze and drink peacefully; a Japanese Garden; and lots of daytime activities.
DierenPark Amersfoort, Barchman Wuytierslaan 224, Amersfoort
www.dierenparkamersfoort.nl

■ Apenheul: Apenheul has 30 species of apes, monkeys and prosimians – some of which are allowed to roam free! Their group areas are extensive and imaginative, providing them with familiar surroundings and all manner of activities to keep them occupied. But monkeys and apes are not the only animals you will meet at Apenheul. The 'zoo' also provides a home to macaws, pudus, anteaters, gundis, tortoises, and many other creatures. Note: Apenheul closes for the winter.
Apenheul, J.C. Wilslaan 21, Apeldoorn
www.apenheul.nl

■ Artis Zoo: Artis was founded more than 160 years ago, and its winding paths, majestic trees and the monumental historical buildings still give it a special, 19th-century atmosphere. There are more than 8,000 animals in the zoo, as well as the Geological Museum, a very sophisticated Planetarium, a magnificent, recently renovated Aquarium, and Micropia: the only microbe-museum in the world.
Artis, Plantage Kerklaan 38, Amsterdam
www.artis.nl

■ Avifauna: Avifauna is one of the largest bird parks in the world. The birds come from the tropics to the cold Northern Hemisphere. There are more than 450 species of birds, in beautiful settings, which are expertly and lovingly taken care of. Avifauna is not only a bird 'zoo', it is actively involved in endangered species breeding programs and bird protection activities, and educates children on nature protection programs. It also has a special Cuba section and Asia bird cages.

Vogelpark Hotel Rederij Avifauna, Hoorn 65, Alphen aan den Rijn
www.avifauna.nl

■ Blijdorp Zoo: At Rotterdam Zoo you can walk from continent to continent, meeting fascinating animals that feel perfectly at home in the surroundings that emulate their natural habitat. The covered facilities, in case of rain, include Taman Indah, Oceanium, with sharks, king penguins, sea lions and and jellyfish, while you can also visit Gorilla Island, travel up Crocodile River and visit the African Vulture Rock.

Rotterdam Zoo / Blijdorp, Blijdorplaan 8, Rotterdam
www.rotterdamzoo.nl or www.diergaardeblijdorp.nl

■ Burgers' Zoo: Burgers' Zoo is a modern, but genuine jungle! This zoo, located near Arnhem, covers more than 45 hectares and houses more than 3,000 animals. It has a spectacular tropical rain forest, a living desert and a large animal population, such as bighorns and red lynxes, to be admired in their natural surroundings. Furthermore, a large number of hoofed animals and birds live with the lions in the 'Safari Park' and there is a wonderful indoor water world.

Burgers' Zoo, Antoon van Hooffplein 1, Arnhem
www.burgerszoo.nl

■ Dolfinarium Harderwijk: At Dolfinarium, you can visit the Lagoon, a biotope with dolphins, fish, seals and sea lions all living together. The Lagoon is a 15 million-liter closed saltwater ecosystem. Also, you can visit Aqua Bella, the dolphin show, as well as visit the modern rescue and research center for sick or injured dolphins or see the walrus and seal shows. Weather permitting, you can sunbathe, swim or ride in a paddle boat near the Park Beach. Dolfinarium's program is continually changing, so be sure to check the website to see what's going on.

Dolfinarium Harderwijk, the World of the Sea, Strandboulevard Oost 1, Harderwijk
www.dolfinarium.nl

■ Emmen Zoo or Wildlands: Emmen Zoo is famous for the manner in which the park's habitats reflect the continents of the world. The animals reside in that part of the world where they belong. The zoo has a very spacious feel about it and all the animals enjoy a great amount of freedom in their enclosures, allowing them to behave as naturally as possible. You can spend hours enjoying the Jungola jungle, the Serenga Savannah, or to the cold rocks of Nortica.

Noorder Dierenpark Emmen, Hoofdstraat 18, Emmen
www.wildlands.nl

■ Naturalis: At v, nature is exhibited in all its colors and diversity. The museum is a combination of natural history and high-tech multi-media in a modern, artistic and technologically advanced setting, representing but a selection of two centuries' worth of collecting animal and plant specimens, fossils, stones and minerals. Exhibition rooms have seven permanent displays (including a walk through the Ice Age, with dinosaurs), while Naturalis hosts many fascinating temporary displays as well. There is also a Nature Information Center where amateur researchers can search through a wide range of books, magazines, slides, photographs, videotapes, computer files and reference collections.

Naturalis, National Museum of Natural History, Darwinweg 2, Leiden. Museum entrance: Pesthuislaan 7, Leiden
www.naturalis.nl

■ Ouwehands Dierenpark in Rhenen: This is a wonderful family zoo, close to Arnhem, but off the beaten track. It was established more than 75 years ago and has retained that early-20th century cozy feel. It has a huge bear habitat with rescued circus bears, and a gorgeous polar bear pool, where kids can press their noses up against the glass and be inches away from these huge white animals, a seal show, and much more. Extra-special is its huge, indoor, all-wood-mulch-and-sand playground for children (RavotAapia), with rope-bridges, sand games, waterplay, huts, caves and slides – at no extra charge. Even if the weather doesn't clear up all day, making it impossible to see the animals, you can still spend a full day in this indoor children's habitat and have the children begging you to go back soon!

Ouwehands Dierenpark, Grebbeweg 111, Rhenen
www.ouwehand.nl

RECOMMENDED READING

THE ACCESS GUIDE/FAQ SHEET ON HAVING A BABY IN THE NETHERLANDS
Information for expectant parents, parents of babies and toddlers. Topics include pregnancy, child health and safety, insurances, support groups, childcare services
www.access-nl.org

HOW TO BE A GLOBAL GRANDPARENT
Living With the Separation
By Anne Huscroft and Peter Gosling
Published by Zodiac Publishing
www.theglobalgrandparent.com

THIRD CULTURE KIDS
The Experience of Growing up Among Worlds
By David C. Pollock and Ruth E. Van Reken
www.nicholasbrealey.com

RAISING GLOBAL NOMADS
Parenting in an On-Demand World
Published by Expatriate Press
By Robin Pascoe
With contributions from Barbara F. Schaetti, PhD and Lois J. Bushong, MS, LMFT
www.expatexpert.com

KIDS LIKE ME
Voices of the Immigrant Experience
Published by Intercultural Press
By Judith M. Blohm and Terri Lapinsky
www.nicholasbrealey.com

DAY CARE

ACCESS
Provides a free guide/FAQ sheet "Your Child" on issues relating to day-care options for expats
www.access-nl.org

KINDEROPVANG, AFTER-SCHOOL HOURS CARE
www.afterscool.nl
www.eigenoppas.nl
www.gastouderservice.nl
www.regeltante.nl

1OFORKIDS
Paulus Buijsstraat 51, 2582 CH The Hague
Tel.: 06 109 366 80
www.1oforkids.nl

BLUE UMBRELLA
Weesperstraat 106, 1018 DN Amsterdam
Tel.: 020 468 75 60
www.blueumbrella.nl

COMPANANNY
English-language day care for children 0 to 4 years, and after school care for children 4 to 12 years
Several locations in Amsterdam, The Hague, Rotterdam and Oegstgeest
Tel.: 020 417 01 17
www.compananny.nl

COMME A LA MAISON
International day care for children 0 to 6 years
Duinweg 1, 2585 JT The Hague
Tel.: 070 404 97 50
www.commealamaison.nl

CRECHE HERMELIJNTJE
Headoffice: Hoge Prins Willemstraat 266, 2584 HX The Hague
Tel.: 070 306 27 71
www.hermelijntje.nl

PARTOU KINDEROPVANG
Headoffice: Hullenbergeweg 379, 1101 CR Amsterdam
Tel.: 020 398 61 00
www.partou.nl

TRUE COLORS
Part of the Stichting Rijswijkse Kinderopvang with 25 locations in Rijswijk and Ypenburg
Karel Doormanlaan 1, 2583 AG Rijswijk
Tel.: 088 00 173 62
www.truecolorschildcare.eu

VILLA BLOOM
Loosduinse Hoofdstraat 536, 2552 AP The Hague
Tel.: 070 820 05 42
www.villabloom.nl

STICHTING KINDEROPVANG HUMANITAS
Has approximately 70 kinderdagverblijven in the Netherlands as well as *gastouder* centers. It also has a national registration point for *kinderopvang* (Landelijk Meldpunt Kinderopvang) that can help you find a day care spot
Headoffice: Meezenbroekerweg 1a, 6412 VK Heerlen
Tel.: 045 561 53 70
www.kinderopvanghumanitas.nl

STICHTING KINDEROPVANG NEDERLAND (SKON)
Has a national network for *kinderopvang*, *naschoolse opvang* and *buitenschoolse opvang*
Headoffice: Energieweg 1, 3542 DZ Utrecht
Tel.: 0346 55 95 00
www.skon.nl

TRIODUS KINDEROPVANG
Has approximately 50 *kinderdagverblijven* in The Hague
Koninginnegracht 10, 2501 ED The Hague
Tel.: 070 312 00 00
www.triodus.nl

ZEIN INTERNATIONAL CHILDCARE
Jozef Israelsplein 36, 2596 AV The Hague
Tel.: 070 326 82 63
www.zeinchildcare.nl

ZO KINDEROPVANG & BSO
Scheveningseweg 46, 2517 KV The Hague
Tel.: 070 345 85 63
www.zokinderopvang.nl

PLAYGROUPS/KINDERGARTENS

THE ACTIVITY SHOP
Private English Language
Pre-School/Kindergarten
Hallekenstraat 28A, 2242 VD Wassenaar
Tel.: 070 514 67 38
www.tasid.nl

THE CLOWN CLUB
Johan de Wittstraat 33, 2242 LA Wassenaar
Tel.: 07 514 09 81
www.theclownclub.com

ENGLISH-SPEAKING PLAYGROUP
Sixlaan 4, 2252 CG Voorschoten
Tel.: 071 576 56 64
www.english-playgroup-voorschoten.nl

KINDERGARDEN
Herengracht 244, 1016 BT Amsterdam
Tel.: 020 423 54 22
www.kindergarden.nl

ROBBEBURG INTERNATIONAL PLAYGROUP
Jekerstraat 84, 1078 MG Amsterdam
Tel.: 020 640 56 47
www.robbeburg.com

AU PAIRS/NANNIES

WORLD WIDE AU PAIR AND NANNY SEARCH
www.findaupair.com

AU PAIR NEDERLAND
Maashegeweg 79a, 5804 AB Venray
Tel.: 0478 551 910
www.aupair-nederland.nl

AUPAIR AGENCY MONDIAL
Van Boetzelaerlaan 42, 2581 AK The Hague
Tel.: 070 365 14 01
www.aupair-agency.nl

NANNY ASSOCIATION
Heuvelpoort 310, 5038 DT Tilburg
Tel.: 013 543 78 85
www.nanny.nl

AU PAIR SELECT
www.aupairselect.nl

AU PAIR INFORMATION
www.aupairinformation.nl

YES AU PAIR
www.yesaupair.com

FINANCIAL ISSUES

NIBUD
National Budget Institute
P.O. Box 19250, 3501 DG Utrecht
Tel.: 030 239 13 50
www.nibud.nl

KINDEROPVANG
www.skon.nl

SOCIALE VERZEKERINGSBANK
Social Insurance Bank
For the Child Benefit (kinderbijslag)
Tel.: 071 512 90 00 – www.svb.org

SPECIAL NEEDS CHILDREN

**AUTISM ASSOCIATION FOR OVERSEAS
FAMILIES (NL)**
Parents and professionals working together
for children with autism
www.aaof.info

**LIGHTHOUSE SPECIAL EDUCATION
(PRIMARY)**
Individual SEN-program taught in English
Amalia van Solmsstraat 155, 2595 TA The
Hague
Tel: 070 335 56 98
www.lighthousese.nl

**SPECIALIZED AUTISM SERVICES
(THE HAGUE)**
www.specializedautismservices.com

DOWN'S SYNDROME FOUNDATION
Hoogeveenseweg 38, 7943 KA Meppel
Tel.: 0522 281 337
www.downsyndroom.nl

DYSLEXIA PARENT SUPPORT GROUP
www.aaof.info/dyslexia

THINGS TO DO

AMSTERDAM MAMAS
Community of mothers in Amsterdam
organizing all kinds of activities
www.amsterdam-mamas.nl

VINEA
summer camp activities for children age 7-20
Tel.: 026 384 83 38
www.vinea.nl

SWIMMING LESSONS

SWIMKIDS
English and Dutch spoken swimming lessons
for children from three to ten years.
www.swimkids.eu

ZWEMSCHOOL MAX, The Hague
www.maxzwemschool.nl

The first part of this chapter has been written for parents of either elementary or secondary school-children. It goes into the types of international education available, followed by what can be of importance to children when they move abroad, in terms of belonging and continuity, preparing for university, fees and taxes. Then it describes the Dutch school system.

The second part has been written with university-level students in mind. It describes the types of university – research-oriented 'traditional' universities and 'universities of applied sciences' – as well as the international programs and courses available in the Netherlands. Here you will also find information on qualifications for entering a university program, the credit system and the type of degree students obtain. Next, this second part goes into student life in the Netherlands; eating out, socializing, sports, as well as finding suitable housing, a job on the side and arranging a student grant. The final part describes 'Life on a Shoestring'; how to survive on little while either studying or otherwise living in the Netherlands on a modest income.

Education

CONTRIBUTING AUTHORS ANNEBET VAN MAMEREN, STEPHANIE DIJKSTRA, WILLEMIJN VAN OPPEN AND EP-NUFFIC

SENDING YOUR CHILDREN TO SCHOOL

WHAT SCHOOL SHOULD I CHOOSE?

When moving from one country to another, there are several issues that come to mind when trying to decide on what type of school to send your children to. Not only do you want to make the transition a smooth one, you also want to ensure that should they decide to go to university, they have the right diplomas. And, last but not least, you want to keep your children's emotional well-being in mind.

There are several factors you can take into account when choosing your children's new school, such as language, your child(ren)'s age, culture, curriculum and, of course, what's available. If your children are young and you intend to stay in the Netherlands for a longer period of time, you might consider a Dutch national school. If your children are older, or will stay here temporarily, an international school might be a better option. A word on all these matters in the following paragraphs.

INTERNATIONAL EDUCATION OPTIONS

In the Netherlands, you will find private international schools as well as subsidized international education at the so-called 'Dutch International Schools' which are spread throughout the country and feature an international curriculum taught in English according to the international standard, at a relatively low, but mandatory, fee. The Dutch International Schools are part of the Dutch school system and thus bound by ministry rules, while others are privately operated.

The subsidy provided by the Dutch Ministry of Education makes it possible for these schools to offer a good quality international education at a reasonable fee. The fees range from € 3,500 to € 6,500 for primary schools and from € 5,500 to € 8,000 for secondary schools and are non-negotiable (although extra fees may be charged for, for example, projects or field trips). Fees at private international schools can go up to € 12,000 a year.

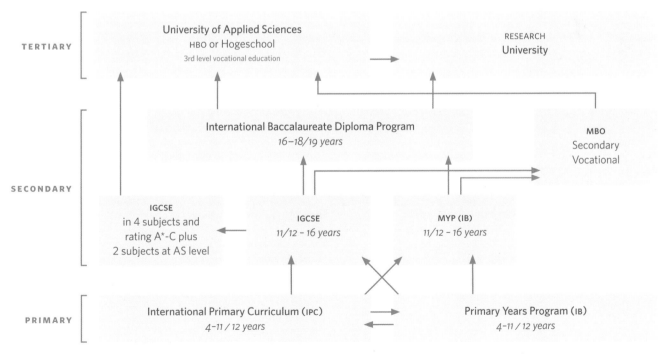

Table by Willemijn van Oppen, Educaide

QUALIFICATION FOR ADMISSION

The qualifications for admission to these schools are set by the Dutch Ministry of Education. The following students may be admitted to these schools:

- children from a non-Dutch family with an expatriate status that will be staying in the Netherlands for a limited period of time
- children from an internationally mobile Dutch family, who have largely been educated abroad, and for whom an international education will be more advisable in order to ensure continuity
- children from a Dutch family that is bound for an international assignment, and who will be switching from education in Dutch to English. This transitional period is limited to a period of one year.

In general, Dutch and private international schools only offer English-language education, but the so-called 'Foreign National Schools', such as the French, German, Indonesian and Japanese schools, teach their national curricula in their native tongue.

PRIMARY INTERNATIONAL EDUCATION

Primary education starts at the age of 4 and continues up until the age of 11 or 12. The Dutch International Primary Schools and the private international schools use either the International Primary Curriculum (IPC) or the International Baccalaureate Primary Years Program (IBPYP). For children with special educational needs, there is Lighthouse Special Education school in The Hague. For more information, we refer you to our reference page at the end of the chapter.

SECONDARY INTERNATIONAL EDUCATION

During the first four to five years of international secondary education, the Dutch International Secondary Schools prepare their students for either the International Baccalaureate Middle Years Program (IBMYP) or the International General Certificate of Secondary Education (IGCSE). The IGCSE is the globally recognized equivalent of the British GCSE. If at least four (I)GCSE subjects with marks ranging from A*-C plus a GCE in two subjects at AS level are obtained, the Dutch Ministry of Education validates it at the same level as the Dutch HAVO, which entitles a student to an entry ticket to the universities of applied sciences.

Students who have successfully completed the IBMYP or the IGCSE can be admitted to the two-year International Baccalaureate Diploma Program (IBDP). The IB-diploma is widely recognized as providing a well-balanced pre-university education. It is an accepted entrance qualification for top universities around the world.

Private so-called foreign national schools may have different curricula for both junior and senior secondary school. The American Schools in Wassenaar and Rotterdam as well as the British School in the Netherlands also offer students the option of following the IBDP in the final two years of high school.

SECONDARY LEVEL VOCATIONAL SCHOOLS

If a student has successfully completed the IGCSE or IBMYP (Middle School), but is not admitted to the IB-Diploma Program, either the MBO OR THE IBCP might be a good option. MBO offers 3-4 years of secondary vocational training and in the Netherlands students can take several English-language programs in, for instance, Business and Hospitality, but also in agriculture (www.mboraad.nl). With an MBO-4 diploma, a student can be admitted to a University of Applied Sciences.

The IB Organization has developed a new curriculum for the final two high school years; the IBCP (International Baccalaureate Career-Related Program), as an alternative to the IBDP. It offers secondary general and vocational education, and the diploma has been validated by the Dutch authorities to be comparable to at least a Dutch HAVO-diploma with vocational subjects. The IBCP incorporates the IB-principles in a program created for students who want to focus on career-related learning, thus providing them with both an academic and practical foundation. The British School in the Netherlands offers the IBCP, making them the first – and so far only – school in the Netherlands to offer this program.

EUROPEAN BACCALAUREATE

For children of staff of the European Union, 14 European schools have been created, offering the European Baccalaureate, which is taken at the end of the seventh year of secondary education. The EB is not the same as the International Baccalaureate or the various national Baccalaureates. It supports a rounded knowledge of all subjects and allows students – who must have strong skills in at least two languages as well – to specialize in individual fields.

Currently there are two European Schools in the Netherlands, one in Bergen (Noord-Holland), and one in The Hague.

BILINGUAL EDUCATION

In August 2014, twelve Dutch Primary Schools joined a national pilot offering bilingual primary education, where between 30 to 50% of the time the pupils are taught in English. Six more schools started in August 2015. The children who wish to follow this curriculum need to master the Dutch language at (near) native level. This pilot will last through 2019.

An increasing number of Dutch Secondary Schools (HAVO and VWO) also offer TTO; *tweetalig onderwijs*, or bilingual education, in which some of the courses are offered in Dutch and others in English. This is, of course, only an option if your child has a sufficient command of the Dutch (and English) language. Also many of these schools award an IB-certificate English A-2 upon graduation. TTO-students can also opt to follow the IB-diploma program at one of the Dutch international secondary schools instead of the VWO 5 & 6, subject to the same conditions that are applicable to the international students, which are non-negotiable.

To explain the acronyms HAVO and VWO: HAVO is an equivalent of General Secondary Education and prepares students for either the MBO (2nd level vocational education) or the University of Applied Sciences (HBO, 3rd level vocational education), where as the VWO, which stands for pre-university education, leads to either the University of Applied Sciences or the University (Academic).

The third type of secondary education, VMBO (1st level vocational education), last four years and prepares students either for senior secondary vocational education and training (MBO, *middelbaar beroepsonderwijs*), or HAVO. Also a number of VMBO AND MBO-schools now offer the option of a bilingual program.

PREPARING FOR UNIVERSITY

If it is likely that your child is planning on going to university abroad after graduating from high school, then your best bet would be to find out whether there are any national schools from that country here and, if not, what the additional requirements are to be admitted with either a Dutch VWO diploma, the IB diploma, or the EB diploma to the university/universities of your pref-

ISA

The **International** School of **Amsterdam**

50 YEARS

Education for International Understanding

For over 50 years, the International School of Amsterdam (ISA) has been a global leader in the international education community fostering curiosity, creativity and a passion for learning.

Serving 1200 students from over 50 countries, ISA combines a rich cultural heritage with world-class faculty and staff, inspiring students to look beyond simple answers and facts and to pursue a genuine understanding of the world.

We have built a tradition of excellence by pursuing innovative, research-based approaches to teaching and learning, such as our long-standing partnership with Harvard University's Project Zero. At ISA, we develop student's thinking skills and help them learn *how to learn*.

ib · COLEGIO DEL MUNDO · WORLD SCHOOL · ECOLE DU MONDE

erence, before your child starts with the final two years of high school. As there are so many different types of international and nationality-based schools in the Netherlands, it is impossible to provide you with information on each and every one of them. We therefore advise you to contact the various international schools directly for more information on their program. For a list of all international schools in the Netherlands, visit the following website: www.educaide.nl. You can also find their addresses through the websites listed at the end of this chapter.

If there are no schools that offer the national program of your home country, or if you are going to be moving on to other countries later on, check whether the school you are considering for your child offers the IB (International Baccalaureate)-Diploma Program, as almost all universities accept the IB-diploma. The IB-program is offered at all international schools in the Netherlands as well as at the American Schools of The Hague and Rotterdam and the British School in the Netherlands. You can find an overview of the schools that offer the IB-program on www.educaide.nl.

FEES AND TAXES

It must be noted that the fees of the various non-Dutch schools vary considerably. In order to obtain information on these fees, please contact the schools in question. Many companies pay or reimburse the tuition fees for expat children, and the payments and reimbursements are often exempted from income tax. Tuition fees and taxes are a complicated issue, as there is also the 30%-reimbursement ruling, under which most tuition fees are deductible, to be taken into account. To be brought entirely up-to-date on this issue, we advise that you contact your tax consultant.

WAITING LIST

As many schools (Dutch and international) may have a waiting list, you are strongly advised to register your child with the school of your liking well in advance if possible.

OTHER CONSIDERATIONS

IDENTITY

It has been said that one of the unanticipated complications of moving abroad with children is their adoption of 'other' – or better said, 'unfamiliar' – norms in terms of social interaction as well as expectations of life, creating a culture clash within the own home. Rather than opposing this and asking your children to stick to who and how they were, it is best to realize that they are going through an internal struggle themselves. They are trying to understand the rules of interaction of this new world they are expected to find a place in – and are trying them on for size as it were. Perhaps you can remind yourself that what your children are going through is a very valuable experience; they are learning one of life's most important lessons, namely the relative value of a culture's norms. They will benefit from this lesson for the rest of their lives. Of course, you do not have to accept everything they do just because they are going through an assimilation process; part of the process they are going through is figuring out a compromise between the two cultures. By making clear what is and is not acceptable to you and your family, you can help them find their way.

It is understandable that you might want your children to retain their national identity and that you hope to circumvent the culture clash problem by sending your children to a nationality-based school in the Netherlands. Of course, the chances that your children will retain their, say, French identity is greater if they go to a French school. However, even if you were to move *within* your own country, the school *will* be different and your children *will* have to adapt – and change. The culture that so defines Bordeaux will not be found in Arras, nor will the dialect, colloquialisms or rules of interaction. In short, you might as well prepare for some adaptation issues even if you send your French children to the French school in The Hague or Amsterdam, as differences are unavoidable.

LOCAL SCHOOL OR INTERNATIONAL SCHOOL?

There are two other significant factors that can be taken into account when deciding on what type of education to choose for your child: belonging and continuity. Depending on the age of the child, either the one or the other could play an important role in your decision whether to send your child to an international or a local school.

BELONGING

Elementary school age is an age in which belonging to the local (international) community is very important. Riding their bicycle around and knowing (and communicating with) every schoolchild, shop owner and parent in the neighborhood creates a sense of community. At that age, for their basic sense of security in later life, belonging is what matters. In principle, this is best achieved by attending a 'national' school, speaking the local language and playing with local children. However, this does not mean you will be doing your child a disfavor if you send him to an international school; there are plenty of other ways to achieve a sense of belonging among students at an international school as well – through extracurricular activities or by living nearby other international children or the school. As with many things you will be deciding on when moving abroad: a lot depends on the child, your circumstances and your options. A word of advice: should you choose to send your children to a local school, you are advised to continue speaking your native language within the family, so that your children can continue to communicate with their friends back home – another community that is very central to their sense of belonging and identity.

TEENAGERS: CONTINUITY

The world at large, with raging hormones, a body that is spinning out of control, new expectations when it comes to dress codes and behavior, and new standards of coolness, are strange and bewildering enough at home. They are almost insurmountable in a new country, where culture and language are 'undecodable', and your child will almost certainly be at a total loss. At this age, therefore, continuity is of importance. In this context, if this is your first move, it would be advisable to place your child in a foreign national school if available. Particularly if you expect to go back to your home country after your stint here is over. If there is no such school, and there is no way to guarantee continuity, then perhaps your best option would be to send your child(ren) to an international school where they will meet companions in the same position and where there are special immersion courses for children who do not speak the English language well or at all. And naturally, sending your child to a local school with an international department (referred to as a Dutch international school) or to just plain a local school also has its merits. All of this depends, of course, on factors such as location, scholastic and language aptitude, whether you want to become a part of the local community, whether and where your child wants to study after completing high school, how long you will be here, and of course, whether you expect to be transferred to yet another country after this.

If your move to Holland is one in a chain of transfers, and you want to keep the aim of achieving continuity at the basis of your decision, you will most likely end up placing your child(ren) in an international school – or, if you are confident that you will find a nationality-based school in your subsequent countries, a nationality-based or foreign national school. Your career path, and particularly the countries you will move to next, will be of influence on this decision. Even so, continuity will only be partly achieved: without a doubt, international schools and nationality-based schools also differ (to a greater or smaller) degree from country to country.

And then there is one final issue to consider here, and that is the issue of geographical, and thus social, isolation: whichever school you choose to send your child to, but particularly if you are going to send your child to an international school, try to live close by it, so that your child lives close to friends.

THE NATIONAL EDUCATION SYSTEM

In these paragraphs, you will find a description of the Dutch primary and secondary school system.

PRIMARY EDUCATION

In the Netherlands, most children start primary school (*basisschool*) the day after their fourth birthday. The *leerplicht* or compulsory education age applies as of age five, meaning that you cannot keep children out of school and take them back to your home coun-

try for extended periods of time, outside of school vacations, without the school inspector's permission. It also means that home-schooling is only rarely permitted – and under strict conditions.

Primary education lasts eight years (including two years of kindergarten), usually until the age of 12. In the final year ('group 8') pupils are advised as to the type of secondary education they should pursue. This advice is based largely on the *leerlingvolgsystem* (pupil monitoring system) which is used to register the achievements of the pupils during their entire elementary school time, and an aptitude test (often referred to as CITO-*toets*). In this test, children answer questions in the areas of Dutch language, math, and optionally; world-orientation (which can been seen see as a combination of history, biology, geography and world religions). Since the 2014/2015 school year, all Dutch schools are obliged to apply one of the three end tests that have been approved by the Ministry of Education. Also since last school year, the teacher's high school advice is leading. The teachers base their advice on the above-mentioned pupil monitoring system, as well as other characteristics such as the pupil's eagerness to learn, attitude, interests, and level of maturity. The end test now comes after the teacher's advice, and has become more of a second opinion. If the test scores come out higher than the teacher's advice, the pupil will be able to go to a higher level of high school education. If the test results are lower, the teacher's advice stands.

The following three types of Primary Education are subsidized by the Ministry of Education:

- Approximately one-third of Dutch children goes to *openbare school*, or public school. These schools are run under the authority of the municipality and are not based on any particular religion or conviction, though they do optionally teach religion-related subjects upon request. For more information on these schools, you can contact the Association for Public Education (Vereniging voor Openbaar Onderwijs); see the telephone number at the end of the chapter.

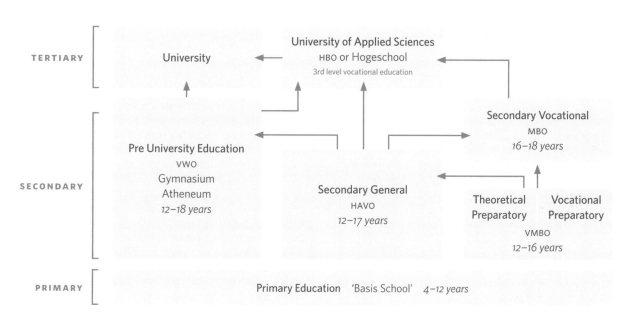

Table by Willemijn van Oppen, Educaide

- Approximately two thirds of the Dutch children go to a *bijzondere*, or 'special', school. These schools are run by their own board, which is usually a group of parents or a foundation. They often reflect a particular denomination or philosophy, such as Roman Catholic or Protestant. There are also Jewish, Islamic, Hindustani, Humanistic and so-called Waldorf schools (or 'Free' schools, as they are called here).
- Some other 'special' schools are based on a particular educational philosophy, such as Montessori, Jenaplan, Dalton, and Freinet. Combinations of denominational schools and a particular educational philosophy can also be found.

FOREIGN LANGUAGE TEACHING IN DUTCH PRIMARY SCHOOLS
By law, all Dutch schools are obliged to start teaching English by group 7 (about age 10) at the latest. An increasing amount of schools has decided to start with English earlier; sometimes even starting in group 1 (kindergarten). You'll also find a few primary schools that teach French, German, or Spanish. The schools that offer early foreign language education are called VVTO (Vroeg Vreemde Taal Onderwijs) schools. A list of all participating schools and some more useful information you can find here: www.europeesplatform.nl/vvto. There are also a few Dutch schools that have recently introduced the theme-based International Primary Curriculum (IPC).

CHILDREN REQUIRING SPECIAL CARE
In the Netherlands, in principle all primary schools are 'inclusive' – meaning that children with mild deviations such as e.g. dyslexia will be admitted to a regular primary school. For children who need additional special care and attention, there are both public and denominational schools, for instance for children with physical disabilities, for children who are sick for a long period of time and schools for children with learning or behavioral problems.

DUTCH IMMERSION CLASS
In Dutch schools, the language of instruction is Dutch. Non Dutch-speaking four and five-year-olds usually ease in pretty easily. If your child is six years old or older, and doesn't speak Dutch, you could still enroll him or her in a Dutch school. However, many schools will require attendance of a Dutch immersion class (called *schakelklas* or *nieuwkomersklas*) first. After approximately one year of immersion class, the child will transition to a regular school, when possible to a class that corresponds with his/her age group. Some schools have their own, internal newcomer class, but usually these are dedicated, specialized separate schools. Also on the secondary level there are Dutch immersion classes, the so-called *internationale schakelklas*.

Some cities also offer a *kopklas*. This class is meant for highly-motivated children who have finished primary school with high grades for math, but much lower ones for the Dutch language. The aim is for these pupils to follow a higher level of secondary education compared to their initial high school advice, after one year of *kopklas*.

GOVERNMENT FUNDING
Primary school is funded by the government. Each child costs the government approximately € 5,500 per year (more in the case of special needs schools). Parents are only asked to pay a contribution for certain special activities such as events arranged by the school, field trips, swimming or cultural activities. The amount of the parent contribution varies per school and lies between approximately € 40 to € 700 per year.

PRIVATE DUTCH SCHOOLS
In the Netherlands, there are also a few private (non-government funded) primary and secondary schools. These schools typically have smaller classes compared to the regular schools, and are often experienced in supporting pupils with minor behavioral issues, or learning difficulties like dyslexia or dyscalculia. The fees of these schools start at € 10,000 per year.

SECONDARY EDUCATION

In the Netherlands, after a child has completed primary school, the parents and child together choose what type of secondary school the child will go to. This decision is based, for the most part, on the recommendation given by the primary school during the final year (see the information provided in the previous section).

There are three types of secondary school pupils can choose from and they go by the following acronyms: VMBO, HAVO and VWO. All three start with a sort of 'basic package' – adapted to the level of education, see further on – that usually lasts two years and consists of subjects that generally all students follow. At the end of the first year (called the *brugklas*, or 'transition class'), a final decision is usually made regarding the type and level of secondary education in which the student will continue until graduation. Many secondary schools offer a mixed *brugklas* (VMBO/HAVO or HAVO/VWO), giving the pupils one year to make up their minds and to demonstrate the level at which they are capable of performing. In some secondary schools, this decision is made after two years. In the third year of secondary education, the three types of schools become quite different, see the following paragraphs.

For children requiring a less challenging type of secondary education there is a so-called 'practical' learning path, focusing on practical skills and the competencies necessary for employment.

GENERAL SECONDARY EDUCATION: HAVO AND VWO
The two programs of secondary education that grant admission to higher education are HAVO, which lasts five years, and VWO, which lasts six years. Pupils are enrolled according to their ability, and VWO is considered more rigorous. The VWO curriculum prepares pupils for university (also known as WO), while the HAVO-diploma prepares students for admission to a university of applied sciences, also known as HBO.

The last two (for HAVO) or three (for VWO) years are referred to as the exam preparation phase, or upper secondary education. During these years, pupils focus on one of four subject clusters (*profielen*), each of which emphasizes a certain field of study in addition to satisfying general education requirements and allowing them to take a number of electives. A pupil enrolled in VWO or HAVO can choose one the following subject clusters: 1) Science and Technology (*Natuur en Techniek*); 2) Science and Health (*Natuur en Gezondheid*); 3) Economics and Society (*Economie en Maatschappij*), and; 4) Culture and Society (*Cultuur en Maatschappij*).

Learning is the Heart

innovative international education for children aged 4-18

Proudly Hosting:

TEDˣ
Youth@ISH

 MODEL UNITED NATIONS
THE INTERNATIONAL SCHOOL OF THE HAGUE

The International School
of The Hague
www.ishthehague.nl

As mentioned earlier, an increasing number of Dutch Secondary Schools (HAVO and VWO) also offer TTO; *tweetalig onderwijs*, or bilingual education, in which some of the courses are offered in Dutch and others in English. Also many of these schools award an IB-certificate English A-2 upon graduation.

VOCATIONAL SECONDARY EDUCATION: VMBO/MBO

VMBO last four years and offers a choice of four 'learning paths' (or 'routes' as the Dutch call them): theoretical, mixed, vocational and basic profession-oriented – each of which offers a choice out of four further sectors: Economics, Technology, Social Sciences (including Biology), and Agriculture. Also a number of VMBO-schools now offer the option of a bilingual program.

Students who have completed VMBO have the option of either going on to HAVO (if he or she has completed the theoretical or the mixed 'route') or senior secondary vocational education and training (MBO, *middelbaar beroepsonderwijs*). The latter is offered in the areas of economics, hospitality, technology, services, social welfare and agriculture. MBO programs vary in length from one to four years as well as in level (1 to 4). Completion of a level-4 MBO program qualifies pupils for access to HBO.

CAMBRIDGE CERTIFICATE

Some schools also offer the Cambridge Certificate in English. This additional diploma offers proof of proficiency in reading, writing, listening, speaking and "English in Use" (idiom and grammar). This certificate is well appreciated by schools of further education and future employers.

TYPES OF SCHOOLS

As is the case for primary schools, the majority of secondary schools are subsidized and can be divided into public schools and schools based on a particular denomination (for instance, Roman-Catholic, Protestant, Jewish or Islam) or educational philosophy (for instance, Montessori or Dalton). Of course, there are also schools for students requiring special care, often in combination with an educational philosophy, such as Montessori, Jenaplan or Dalton.

COMPULSORY EDUCATION AND GOVERNMENT FUNDING

Education is compulsory until a student reaches the age of 18, or has obtained the so-called *startkwalificatie (*basically a VWO, HAVO or MBO level 2 diploma*)*. This obligation to pursue and education is referred to as the child's *leerplicht*, or period of compulsory attendance.

Until the age of 16, children are fully *leerplichtig*. After that, the obligation focuses not so much on attending school full-time as on obtaining a secondary school-diploma. This is also referred to as their *kwalificatieplicht* (until the age of 23), during which time they are allowed to combine school and work.

Schools are required to allow children to take a day off on days that their parents' religious or 'life' convictions require that the children stay home from school.

Secondary education is government-funded and each child costs the government approximately € 7,600 per year. Parents can also be asked to make a contribution to the school, but this is a voluntary contribution and is meant to cover festivities and excursions.

GOING TO UNIVERSITY

The higher education system in the Netherlands is based on a three-cycle degree system, consisting of a bachelor's, master's and Ph.D. degree. It is offered at two types of institutions: research universities (WO) and universities of applied sciences (HBO). Whereas research universities are primarily responsible for offering research-oriented programs, universities of applied sciences are primarily responsible for offering programs of higher professional education, which prepare students for specific professions. These tend to be more practice-oriented than the programs offered by research universities.

Approximately 32% of the population between the ages of 15 and 64 has a higher education degree (this percentage is on the rise: 40% of those between 25 and 34 have a higher education degree, being 37% of men and 44% of women). On www.studyin-holland.nl/education-system you can find more information on the Dutch higher education system.

Research Universities

Academic education (*universiteit*) is offered to students with an IB-Diploma or the Dutch VWO by universities in Maastricht, Eindhoven, Tilburg, Nijmegen, Wageningen, Enschede, Groningen, Utrecht, Amsterdam, Leiden, Delft, and Rotterdam. Some of these universities also have faculties in other cities.

The university programs are organized around a bachelor's or undergraduate phase that lasts three years and a master's or graduate phase that lasts one to two years. These universities (including the Open University) are primarily responsible for offering research-oriented programs (*Wetenschappelijk Onderwijs*, WO) and the possibility to conduct research in a wide range of disciplines: language and culture, behavior and society, economics, law, medical and health sciences, natural sciences, engineering, and agriculture. All research universities also offer Ph.D.-programs.

As many Dutch universities have partner institutions in other countries, students can follow part of their course abroad. Your university can tell you with which universities it has an exchange agreement.

Hogescholen or 'Universities of Applied Sciences'

Higher professional education (*Hoger Beroepsonderwijs*, HBO) is offered by universities of applied sciences to students with an IB-diploma (and in some cases the IGCSE-diploma with two additional subjects at GCE-level, or an MBO-diploma, or the Dutch HAVO/VWO-diploma). HBO programs focus on applied arts and sciences in one of the seven HBO sectors: agriculture, engineering and technology, economics and business administration, health care, fine and performing arts, education/teacher training, and social welfare.

The universities of applied sciences offer four-year bachelor's degree programs as well as master's programs lasting one to two years. All degree programs focus on preparing students for particular professions. They tend to be more practically-oriented than programs offered by research universities. In addition to lectures, seminars, projects and independent study, students are often required to complete an internship or work placement (*stage*) which normally takes up part of the third year of study, as well as a final project or a major paper in the fourth year.

INTERNATIONAL EDUCATION
Next to the research universities and universities of applied sciences, Holland has a third and smaller branch of higher education, officially known as 'International Education' (IE). International education offers advanced training courses, taught in English, originally designed for people from developing countries whose jobs require highly specialized knowledge. Most of the IE institutions are part of a research university and focus on courses relevant to developing countries.

STUDYING IN ANOTHER LANGUAGE / COUNTRY
Across the country, the Dutch higher education institutions are offering a growing number of courses in English, both specialized courses as well as entire bachelor's, master's and Ph.D.-programs. In total, there are over 2,100 international courses on offer, taught entirely in English. The site www.studyfinder.nl offers international students a complete, independent, reliable and up-to-date overview of all the international study programs offered by the Dutch higher education institutions, ranging from short training seminars to full-fledged bachelor's and master's degree programs.

As Europe's higher education market is unifying rapidly, European students are increasingly investigating their study options across national borders – while Europe is becoming more attractive for students from overseas too. Unfortunately, most information resources still focus on the national level so that students are often not aware of what their options are. The sites www.bachelorsportal.eu, www.mastersportal.eu and www.phdportal.eu fill this information vacuum for the different degrees and help students find and choose an equivalent study program across Europe. On www.scholarshipportal.com you will find an overview of the financial support available from many different sources for those who want to study in Europe, while www.shortcoursesportal.com lists the options for short-term programs in Europe, such as summer and winter schools, and www.distancelearningportal.com lists distance learning courses. Together, these portals are the European study choice platform, listing over 20,000 study options in 37 European countries and more than 1,000 scholarships – aimed towards stimulating student mobility and promoting European Higher education.

Even though there are many degree programs taught entirely in English, you may want to take on the challenge and do a study program in Dutch. If you are looking for a program or course conducted in Dutch, you can check the following websites: www.studiekeuze123.nl and www.duo.nl. A number of university centers offer Dutch as a second language-courses. The courses are specially designed for foreign students who have otherwise qualified for admission to Dutch higher education, but must first prove that they have mastered the language sufficiently.

REQUIREMENTS FOR ADMISSION TO HIGHER EDUCATION
As mentioned earlier, for access to wo bachelor's programs, students are required to have an IB-diploma, a vwo-diploma or to have completed the first year (60 ECTS, see further on) of an HBO program. The minimum access requirement for HBO is an IB-diploma (and, in some cases, the IGCSE-diploma with two additional subjects at GCE-level), the Dutch HAVO/VWO-diploma or a level-4 MBO-diploma. When applying for WO or HBO, students are required to have completed at least one of the subject clusters (in Dutch: pro-

fielen) that fulfils the requirements for the higher education program in question. A quota, or numerus fixus, applies for access to certain programs, primarily in the health sector, and places are allocated using a weighted lottery. Potential students older than 21 years of age who do not possess one of the qualifications mentioned above can qualify for access to higher education on the basis of an entrance examination and assessment. The only access requirement for the Open University is that applicants be at least 18 years of age.

To determine whether your diploma qualifies, if you have a non-Dutch secondary school-diploma or an IB-diploma, you must have your diploma evaluated by your prospective educational institute.

DEGREES
Bachelor's degrees are awarded by universities and universities of applied sciences. An HBO bachelor's degree program requires four years of study to complete, at the end of which graduates obtain the degree 'Bachelor of ...', indicating the professional field of study. A wo-bachelor's degree requires three years of study to complete, and graduates are awarded the degree 'Bachelor of Science / Bachelor of Arts'. The same distinction is made for the names of master's degrees awarded by universities and universities of applied sciences.

The first year of every HBO and WO-program is known as the propedeuse. Once you have your HBO-propedeuse, you have a choice: you can either continue in the bachelor's program at the university of applied sciences, or you can begin in the first year of a WO (university) program. This is a way for HAVO-students, who are not qualified to enter a wo-university program, to enter one after all, after 'investing' a year in obtaining an HBO-propedeuse. Many programs have the same propedeuse, which means that obtaining it gives you the option of choosing among several programs in which to continue.

Once a wo-bachelor's has been obtained at a particular university, this automatically qualifies the student to continue on to at least one master's program (usually) at the same university. In some cases, this can also be at a different university – in the Netherlands or in a foreign country. Should the student choose to 'switch' directions and apply to a different master's program at the same university, the university could set additional requirements.

Associate Degree
The associate degree (it goes by the same name in Dutch) program is a two-year 'short cycle' degree program offered by universities of applied sciences. It enables students to obtain a professional qualification in a shorter period of time and can help them learn the skills and competencies needed to improve their chances on the job market. Access requirements to an associate degree program are the same as for an HBO bachelor's program. Once they have obtained an associate degree, graduates can seek employment or continue in the last two years of an HBO-program, to obtain a bachelor's degree.

International Secondary Vocational Education
There is a growing number of MBO-schools (secondary vocational education) in the Netherlands that offer not only the Dutch MBO-4 diploma, but also the BTEC level 3 diploma. The BTEC diploma is

composed of several units with themes such as Accounting, Marketing, and Management, and focuses on the future profession of the student. Within the chosen direction, 18 units need to be completed successfully. The program is bilingual for now, meaning that students must master both Dutch and English.

The following courses are offered at BTEC 3 level: Business and Fashion, Hospitality, Horticulture, Aviation, Tourism and an Extended Diploma in Business.

Within the BTEC International Branch, the IVS-Alliance is the largest player in the Netherlands with more than 4,500 students who study at the 14 MBO schools. For more information regarding this topic and participating schools, you can visit www.ivs-alliance.nl, though this site still is in the Dutch language only. There are also MBO schools that offer the BTEC3 in combination with the Dutch MBO4, which are not member of the IVS alliance. In all cases, the BTEC3 diploma is internationally recognized, and offers plenty of opportunities to study and/or work abroad. It is issued by the British organization EDEXCEL.

Graduates with a BTEC extended Diploma can follow an accelerated program within the third level vocational schools (University of Applied Science or HBO) in the Netherlands and also abroad. There are good partnerships of the MBO-schools with other third level vocational schools (HBO) or Universities of Applied Sciences, that offer, among other, courses in International Business & Management Studies (IBMS), Small Business, Asian studies and International Business & Language (IBL).

As the BTEC diploma program is not subsidized, it needs to be financed by (the parents of) the student.

European Business Baccalaureate Diploma

Recently, a new program has been developed: the European Business Baccalaureate Diploma (EBBD), which is recognized all across Europe. In the Netherlands, the Summa College in Eindhoven currently is the only school that offers this program. For more information check www.eurobacdiploma.eu.

CREDIT SYSTEM

The ECTS credit system is used by all higher education institutions in the Netherlands. The focus of degree programs determines both the number of credits required to complete the program and the degree that is awarded. A WO bachelor's program requires the completion of 180 credits (3 years), an HBO bachelor's program requires the completion of 240 credits (4 years). An associate degree requires the completion of 120 credits.

In most cases, a WO master's program requires the completion of 60 to 120 credits (1 or 2 years). In engineering, agriculture, dentistry, math, and the natural sciences, 120 credits are always required. For medicine, veterinary medicine and pharmacy, 180 credits are required. An HBO master's program requires the completion of 60 to 120 credits.

DOCTORATE

The third cycle of higher education, leading to a doctor's degree, is offered only by research universities. All research universities in the Netherlands are entitled to award the country's highest academic degree, the *doctoraat* or Ph.D., which entitles a person to use the title *doctor*, abbreviated to *dr*. The process by which a doctorate is obtained is referred to as the *promotie*. The doctorate is primarily a research degree, for which a dissertation based on original research must be written and publicly defended. The minimum amount of time required to complete a doctorate is four years.

Most students working on doctorates are in fact paid employees rather than students. They apply for positions as AIOs, or research assistants. These positions are advertised in the same way jobs are, and candidates approach the supervisor directly. Candidates with foreign qualifications may apply for these positions and ask for permission to write their dissertation in another language. Candidates may also contact a university faculty independently, and write their own research proposal. Sometimes the research for a dissertation can be conducted in the candidate's own country.

It is not necessary to take on a position as an AIO in order to get a Ph.D., it merely enables candidates to have a source of income while working on their Ph.D.

GRADING

The grading system has been the same for several decades: the scale is from 1 (very poor) to 10 (outstanding). The lowest passing grade is 6; 9s are seldom given, 10s are extremely rare, and grades 1-3 are hardly ever used.

CHOOSING A UNIVERSITY

The Dutch system of quality control guarantees that the education

offered at all the institutions meets the same high standards. When Dutch students choose where they want to study, they are not thinking of which research university or university of applied sciences is best, but instead are looking at which specializations are offered and which emphasis or academic tradition is featured. Each institution has its own atmosphere and style. They distinguish themselves in this way, and not through any absolute measure of quality. For these reasons, employers in the Netherlands look first at the degree a person has earned. Where this degree was earned is not so important.

On www.studyfinder.nl you can search and compare study programs based on the criteria that matter to you. This can be the city where the institution is located or the study subjects that are taught.

QUALITY CONTROL

How do you know for sure that your course or program is of the right quality? Find out whether it has been accredited by the Accreditation Organization of the Netherlands and Flanders (Nederlands Vlaamse Accreditatie Organisatie, www.nvao.com), which has been appointed by the Dutch and Flemish government for the purpose of monitoring the quality of the higher education courses and programs on offer. Most institutions that offer English-language education have been required to sign a special Code of Conduct. This code sets out standards for the Dutch higher education institutions in their dealings with international students. By signing the Code of Conduct, the institutions guarantee international students that they will adhere to rules regarding the quality of programs, student recruitment policy, selection, and counseling procedures. Find out more which institutions have signed the Code of Conduct on www.internationalstudy.nl.

LANGUAGE

To enroll in a program or course that is conducted in English, you must have the appropriate level of command of the English language. To determine this, you must take an English language test, such as TOEFL (Test of English as a Foreign Language, see www.ets.org) or IELTS (International English Language Testing System, see www.ielts.org). Additional language requirements can be found by visiting the database of international courses that can be found on www.studyinholland.nl.

MAKING THE TRANSITION

In principle, if you want to come to the Netherlands as a student, you can only come here to follow a particular course (or full study program) and you must meet all requirements. There are, however, three exceptions to this. The first is: if you meet all requirements for studying in the Netherlands, you are allowed come here for a year first to study Dutch. The second is: if you do not meet all requirements, you can come here for a year to follow a preparatory program for the particular studies of your choice. The third option, which you can read more about on page 218, is the so-called *schakeljaar*; a transitional year that has been created for specifically for non-European, non-Western students to help them prepare for their studies here.

TUITION

There are two types of institutions that offer higher education in the Netherlands: government-funded and government-approved. Studying at a government-funded institution will cost anywhere upwards from € 1,984 a year (for 2016/2017), for EU/EEA/Swiss/Surinam-students. Students of all other nationalities generally pay higher fees; the average tuition fee for bachelor's programs being between € 6,000 and € 15,000, and for a master's program between € 8,000 and € 20,000.

As of 2009, the Netherlands government no longer funds study placements occupied by non-EU/EEA/Swiss students. Nonetheless, tuition fees in the Netherlands can be considered reasonable, compared to international education options in other countries, while the level of education is excellent. Furthermore, there are plenty of grants available, which you can read about further on. EU/EEA/Swiss students can still apply for the *studiefinanciering*-loan, which will replace it.

You can find more about student grants further on, or by visiting www.studyinholland.nl/scholarships/find-a-scholarship or www.scholarshipportal.com.

PERMITS

See page 130 for the rules on permits when coming here to study.

COSTS OF DAILY LIVING

If you come to study in the Netherlands, you will need to take into account such issues as tuition, rent and daily expenses, as well as basic health insurance, obtaining a permit, transportation (though, if you qualify for the study loan – *studiefinanciering* – you are offered a public transportation pass), books, notebooks and perhaps membership fees for student (sports) organizations. You can expect all this to amount to approximately € 800 – € 1,300 a month, though this of course depends on the amount of tuition you owe. Housing will cost you between € 300 and € 600 a month. For more information on this, visit www.studyinholland.nl/practical-matters/daily-expenses.

PROOF OF SUFFICIENT FINANCIAL MEANS

Foreign students from outside the EU – in order to be issued a (provisional) residence permit – must prove that they have sufficient financial means to cover the study expenses and to provide for themselves, being € 35 net a day. This means that you must have access to a monthly amount that has been determined in the *Studiefinanciering* Act 2000, and depends on what you will be studying. For university (of applied sciences) studies, this is approximately € 863 (excluding tuition fees) per month, or € 1,500 (excluding holiday allowance) per month, if you are bringing your family. You must either have this amount in your bank account (multiplied by 12, proving that you can afford living here for a year), or you must deliver proof of the fact that you have arranged a bank loan or found a guarantor in the Netherlands. This person must also prove that he or she can provide for you (and your family, if there is one) and meet the *studiefinanciering* finance requirements.

STUDENT GRANTS

In many cases, you will qualify for a restitution of your tuition fees. For more on student grants, tuition fee restitution, as well as financial assistance for refugees and asylum seekers, see page 217. Also contact your university (of applied sciences) to see whether they offer any grants.

STUDENT LIFE

TYPES OF STUDY UNIVERSITY TOWNS

There are more than 703,000 students in the Netherlands. To recap, the term 'students' covers two types: those who attend a research university (referred to as *Wetenschappelijk Onderwijs* or WO – 36%) and those who attend a university of applied sciences (referred to as *Hoger Beroeps Onderwijs, hogeschool* or HBO – 64%).

There are 12 cities in the Netherlands that have a research university: Amsterdam, Rotterdam, Delft, Leiden, Utrecht, Wageningen, Groningen, Enschede, Nijmegen, Tilburg, Eindhoven and Maastricht. Some of these universities are very old, with ancient jails, court houses and convents acting as university buildings – which are naturally also filled with the required amenities for modern-day students.

On the other hand, there are more than 50 universities of applied sciences. They are more recent than the classical universities, but because of the sheer numbers of their students, they generate the feel of a student town in many of their home locations. Universities of applied sciences, incidentally, often share a city or town with a classical research university, while other cities house only universities of applied sciences, such as Arnhem, Leeuwarden, 's-Hertogenbosch, Sittard, Breda, Diemen, Alkmaar and Haarlem. Almost all the student towns have a genuine student atmosphere; student cafés, restaurants, etc., making it easy to have a 'cheap' night out on the town.

HOUSING

All student towns share one problem: it is hard to find proper housing. It is already hard enough for Dutch students, let alone for foreign students who do not have their own network and who will not be staying here long. If you are participating in an exchange program or are enrolled in an international course, it is quite possible that housing has been arranged for you by the institution. You should consider accepting it immediately, or you might regret it later. If your institution has not actually arranged housing for you, they often have special departments for foreign students that help them find a suitable place to live. The best thing to do would be to contact your faculty and/or to visit the university's/faculty's website, which you can find at the end of the chapter.

A few websites where you can look for more on housing are: www.kamernet.nl, www.easykamer.nl, www.housinganywhere.com, and www.kamers.nl (where you click on the town or city in which you are looking for a place to live). Though the information may be in Dutch, they are fairly simple to navigate. Housing is *huisvesting*, *huur* means rent, and anything with the word *kamers* – meaning 'rooms' – also refers to housing.

Once you have found a place to live, what can you expect? In Holland, students usually have their own room. You might have to share the shower, toilet, kitchen and living room with other students, and it is common for men and women to live together in a shared house. If this is a problem for you, you should make this known as soon as possible. Given the shortage of good accommodation, you may find the room you are offered rather small and below the standard you expected. Usually, there is not much you can do about this, as most institutions are glad they have found accommodation for their students at all.

STUDENT ORGANIZATIONS

Not many Dutch institutions of higher education have a campus whose atmosphere is dominated by the local fraternities/sororities and student organizations. This does not mean to say, however, that student life does not influence the atmosphere in these student towns. The cities are not very big and the student population is always relatively large enough to allow its presence be felt when downtown, or in certain neighborhoods. And though there may not be large campuses, every student town has a number of student organizations that do or do not have their own 'club houses', and that have their own traditions, rules, atmosphere and culture which can also be felt outside their walls. The advantage of joining one of these organizations is that you meet many new people in a short period of time and that their club houses provide a regular place to meet up with your friends when going out. Young students become a member of these organizations to find a network for having fun now – and for their career later on.

Becoming a member does, however, often include going through hazing. If you are studying here for just a short period of time, you might prefer to check out the smaller student organizations that do not have any hazing traditions, or only a short one. Many student organizations have been founded by the institutions of higher education themselves, but there are also organizations that are organized around a sport, religion or other common interest. It would be virtually impossible to list them all here, but you can visit the following website: studenten-verenigingen.start-

pagina.nl, which will give you an overview of all the student organizations per city and most international student organizations. And of course, you can ask anyone at your institute of higher education what they recommend.

Aside from the so-called free time organizations (*gezelligheidsverenigingen*) there are the faculty organizations (*studieverenigingen*). Also these organize many activities, only more related to the subject of your studies. They organize lectures, workshops and, for instance, the sale of textbooks at a reduced price. These organizations are faculty-based and can be found via the institute of higher education. They are definitely worth visiting, as they allow you to meet many people who can help with and advise you on your study and other important student life issues. Check with your institution for an up-to-date overview of the *studieverenigingen*.

And last but not least, there are a few national and international student organizations that can help you find internships, work placements and temporary jobs as well as fun and interesting activities. The most important ones are AEGEE and AIESEC. AEGEE is a general European student organization, while AIESEC helps students find international internships in a global learning environment. Their websites are www.aiesec.nl and www.aegee.nl, respectively.

HOLLAND ALUMNI NETWORK

As an international student, you can also join the Holland Alumni Network. It offers services to international students in the Netherlands, Holland Alumni, Holland Alumni associations, Dutch higher education institutions and other relevant organizations – and allows you to connect with and join 62,000 fellow students and alumni. You can register with the Holland Alumni network at www.hollandalumni.nl/register.

SPORTS FOR STUDENTS

All student towns have facilities for the more popular sports, which are sometimes a part of a regular sports organization, but are sometimes affiliated with the institute of higher education. The Dutch student sports organizations are about sporting together rather than about competition. Membership is often quite affordable, especially as most organizations offer a student discount.

One of the most important and more competitive student sports in the Netherlands is rowing. Most Dutch rowing clubs are student clubs, either affiliated with the larger student organizations, or independent. Many students take up this sport during their first year and stop after graduating. Its main event is the Varsity, a huge rowing tournament to which the larger student rowing clubs send their best teams to compete. While all the competing is going on, thousands of students sit and stand by the water to watch, picnic, drink and party – a party which continues until deep in the night on the premises of the student organization of the winning team of the so-called Old Four Race.

However, rowing is not all there is. There is soccer, hockey, rugby, tennis, and more – most of which have their own organization. You can find out more about these at your university/faculty or you can visit the website of Studentensport Nederland (SSN), at www.studentensport.nl.

A NIGHT OUT ON THE TOWN

Where to go for fun and socializing? Some of the Dutch student towns are also the largest towns/cities in the Netherlands and have enough to offer in terms of cafés, restaurants, dance clubs and other places. The answer to the question of where to go is obvious: wherever you want. Still, the most fun would be to go where you find other students and where things are not too expensive. Luckily, there are many student cafés and restaurants and designated student cafeterias, where, at little cost, you can buy a meal. But don't overlook the so-called 'eet-cafés', which have a pleasant atmosphere and cheap food. Go out and investigate, and ask others what they recommend. This search alone is already half the fun.

If you are looking for a cultural night out on the town, you might be interested in obtaining a CJP (pronounced say-yay-pay: *cultureel jongeren paspoort*, or cultural youth pass). The CJP is the Dutch equivalent of the Euro <26 card, costs € 17.50 for those under 30 and € 25 for students (more discounts!) and can be bought via www.cjp.nl (click on *Koop je pas*). With this you not only obtain reductions on tickets for theater and concert events, but also on the entrance fee for exhibitions and films. If you visit www.cjp.nl and look for the *kortingen*, you can click on an event and it will tell you how much rebate your CJP pass will get you. You can also download their app. The card is part of ISIC (International Student Identity Card, www.isic.org) and EYCA (European Youth Card Network, www.eyca.org), meaning that students can benefit from discounts at restaurants, cinemas and shops around the world.

FINANCES

The word alone is intimidating, because who wouldn't want more spending money? Here is some advice on arranging a loan, taking out insurance, finding a job, and on grants and scholarships.

Banks

Most banks will probably be willing to support you financially and to answer any finance-related questions you may have. Ask about their loans. At least the following banks have special programs for students: ABN Amro, ING, Rabobank and SNS. These programs can include special interest rates, a maximum loan, the use of a credit card, special repayment programs, health insurance for those who cannot take out a health insurance in the Netherlands, and other insurances.

Several banks (certainly in the cities where there is a substantial international student population) understand the situation of foreign students and are quite flexible about working out an arrangement that will help you cover your costs and pay back your loan once you have completed your studies and have a job. The banks will certainly ask to see your student registration and for you to find a guarantor. Approaching one of the banks listed earlier would be your best bet.

Insurance

Students under the age of 30 who are in the Netherlands solely for study purposes (and are not in a part-time job or paid internship) are exempt from the general requirement to take out Dutch public health care insurance; however, they will have to make alternative arrangements. Perhaps you are covered under a public health care insurance plan at home. If this is the case, make sure this provides adequate coverage during your stay in the Netherlands. If you are from an EU-country, your insurance company can provide you with an EU Health Insurance Card – proof of your insurance. Otherwise, you will have to make other arrangements, for example by taking out a private insurance policy. There are private packages on the market, created especially for international students, visit AON (www.students-insurance.eu), whose packages also include liability insurance, household content insurance, legal advice, etc., or studentsinsured.com.

You can find more about insurances in the insurance section on www.studyinholland.nl/practical-matters.

Jobs

If you would like to take on a paid job alongside your studies, you are allowed to do so – however, keep in mind that you will need a residence permit and a *burgerservicenummer* (Citizen Service Number)! You can read more about these on pages 66 and pages 111 and 130. For more on working here as a foreign student, go to page 130. Depending on your nationality, you can only work for a limited number of hours per week and only if your employer has applied for a work permit for you – always make sure you check the applicable regulations. This can be either full-time seasonal work in June, July and August, or part-time work of no more than 10 hours a week outside the summer period. Though your Dutch employer will have to apply for a work permit for you, this process will be relatively uncomplicated as your employer will not need to prove that there are no EU/EEA/Swiss nationals capable of doing the job. EU/EEA and Swiss nationals are free to work as many hours as they like, alongside their studies. Do not forget that you will have to take out health care insurance if you take on a job, as you risk a hefty fine if you don't.

Many students have on-the-side jobs in cafés and restaurants. However, you can also go to one of the employment agencies you will find listed at the end of chapter 3. Of course, you can also try to find a job without their help. If you feel your Dutch is not up to snuff then you can certainly try the bigger multinational companies in the Netherlands: they often have international projects that can be carried out without having to speak any (or faultless) Dutch. You can find these companies on www.intermediair.nl. Another site to visit, though you mostly will be required to be able to speak some Dutch, is www.studentsforstudents.nl.

When the full *studiefinanciering* grant existed (see further on), there was a limit on how much you would be allowed to earn while receiving this grant. This limit has been abolished.

A CAREER IN HOLLAND AFTER GRADUATION

If you are considering starting your career in the Netherlands after graduating from your Dutch institution, visit www.careerin-holland.nl and find all the information you need.

GRANTS

Scholarships

A lot is already taken care of for EU-students who come to the Netherlands as part of an EU exchange program, such as acceptance at the education institution, funding and housing. To find out more about this, you can look into the Erasmus program (www.erasmusprogramme.com).

To find out more about scholarships, also for non-EU students, and whether you qualify, visit www.studyinholland.nl/scholarships/find-a-scholarship. Here you can enter your field of study and your country of origin and see for which grants or scholarships you might qualify. Also check scholarshipportal.com or contact your university in the Netherlands to find out whether it has a grant for international students, as some have their own grant programs.

Refugees and Asylum Seekers

Those who have refugee status or are asylum seekers and are starting a higher education, can approach Stichting UAF Steunpunt (www.uaf.nl) for more information on the possibilities of a grant. On their website, click on the little British flag in the top right-hand quarter to access a leaflet listing the conditions you must meet.

Studiefinanciering

As of September 2015, the law on the *studiefinanciering* changed. As of that date, students no longer receive a grant from the government with which to pay for their studies; instead, they can take out a maximum loan of € 1,024 (including a tuition fee loan) – it is up to the student him or herself to determine exactly how high they want the loan to be. If your parents are of limited financial means, you can apply for an additional grant of € 383.77 a month, which will be converted into a gift if you obtain your diploma within ten years. You will have 35 years in which to pay off the loan. There are no longer any limits as to the amount of money you are allowed to earn while receiving the *studiefinanciering* loan. If you enter a Dutch university (of applied sciences) between 2015-2016 and 2018-2019, and obtain your diploma, you will be issued a € 2000-voucher for further studies. Note: the old system will continue to apply for students following secondary vocational education (MBO): more information can be found on www.duo.nl.

If you have a right to the *studiefinanciering*-loan, you also have a right to the *Studenten ov-chipkaart*, with which you can travel by

SCHAKELJAAR – LINK YEAR

Refugees, asylum seekers and other non-Dutch nationals who come to study in the Netherlands often go through a period of cultural and language adjustment that conceivably prevents them from getting everything they can out of their studies – or giving it all they have. For this reason, a number of institutes of higher education now offer a so-called *schakeljaar* (link year), created specifically for non-European, non-Western students, who are planning on following a study at a Dutch university (of professional education).

The course is divided into two parts: a basic program and a follow-up program. During the 'link' year, you are offered a Dutch language course (including the specific terminology that you will come across during the course of your studies), informatics, and study techniques, as well as a preparatory course for the study of your choice. Furthermore, you are familiarized with the Dutch culture and university system; for instance, how you are expected to approach your studies, how classes are given, how to give a presentation and how to work on group assignments.

Schakeljaren are offered in a.o. Rotterdam, The Hague, Roermond, Amsterdam, Utrecht, Groningen, and Windesheim. For more information, visit www.uaf.nl/mijnuaf/mijnuaf_studie/voorbereiden_op_een_studie/schakeljaren.

What the costs of the *schakeljaar* are, depend on your personal situation, as well as any agreements reached between your university and the municipality on financing and whether you have a right to the *studiefinanciering*-loan. For more information, approach your university.

public transportation for free either during the weekend or on weekdays (your choice) and at reduced rates during the other days. This public transportation pass is also subject to the condition that you complete your studies within ten years. If you do not, then, retroactively, you owe a monthly amount for the possession of this card. You are granted a *Studenten ov-chipkaart* during a maximum of five years. If you do not wish to take out a loan, you can still make use of the free *Studenten ov-chipkaart*.

Visit www.duo.nl and click on *Foreign Student* for more on study grants, the restitution of tuition fees and other information. Note: be sure to arrange a DigiD (see page 72), in order to arrange your *studiefinanciering* / tuition fee loan online!

Studiefinanciering for Non-Dutch Nationals

If you are a non-Dutch national, legally residing in the Netherlands, you can apply for the *studiefinanciering*-loan if:

- you are an EU/EEA/Swiss national and lived in the Netherlands for five consecutive years with a maximum interruption of six months, or if you (or your non-Dutch parent or partner) work here at least 56 hours a month (either on a temporary contract, permanent contract, on call, free-lance or self-employed) – check the website for further applicable rules.

- you have a type I (temporary) residence permit issued on a variety of grounds (for an overview, please visit the site of the IB Groep)
- you have a type II (permanent) residence permit
- you have a type III (temporary) residence permit or type IV (permanent) residence permit, for asylum seekers
- you or your parents (on your behalf) received a study allowance (granted, under specific conditions, to parents of children younger than 18) during the school year in which you turned 18, and you meet all other conditions. You are advised to contact the DUO if this is the case, for further information
- you have a residence permit type V (EU residence permit for long-term residents).

DUO strongly advises foreign EU-students (if you have not been living in the Netherlands for five consecutive years or more) to contact one of their support offices. They can provide you with further information.

EU/EEA/Swiss nationals who do not qualify for the *studiefinanciering*-loan, can, however, apply for a tuition fee loan, to be repaid upon completing their studies, see the following paragraph.

Loan Tuition Fees

If you are an EU/EEA/Swiss national (listed below), but do not qualify for the *studiefinanciering*-loan, you can receive a loan to cover your tuition fees. In the case of legal tuition fees paid in connection with a government-funded institute of higher education, the total annual amount of the loan is € 1,984 (academic year of 2016-17). In the case of tuition fees paid in connection with a non-government-funded institute of higher education, you can apply for a loan for the total amount of fees, up to a maximum of five times the so-called legal tuition fees. An interesting impending change is the shifting of the age limit: you no longer have to be younger than 30 to apply for a tuition fee loan; as of August 2017, you can request it until you reach the age of 55.

To qualify for this, you must meet the following conditions:
- you are between the ages of 18 and 30
- you are from: Austria, Belgium, Bulgaria, Cyprus, the Czech Republic, Denmark, Estonia, Finland, France, Germany, Great Britain, Greece, Hungary, Iceland, Ireland, Italy, Latvia, Liechtenstein, Lithuania, Luxembourg, Malta, Norway, Poland, Portugal, Rumania, Slovakia, Slovenia, Spain, Sweden or Switzerland
- you are enrolled as a full-time student in an accredited course at a funded or recognized institute of higher education or university, senior vocational education (MBO), or secondary vocational education for adults (VAVO).
- you have a *burgerservicenummer* (see page 66)
- you have your own bank account in the Netherlands
- you have completed a 'Restitution of tuition fee'-form – for MBO and VAVO, there is a separate form.

Forms can be downloaded from www.ib-groep.nl. Apply for restitution before January 31, of the school year in which you wish to continue receiving it. For the 2016-2017 school year, this means you must have applied for it by January 31, 2017.

study in holland

study in holland
open to international minds

More than 2,100 study programmes taught in English

www.studyinholland.nl

Five Years of Legal Residence

To prove that you have been living here for at least five years (with a maximum interruption of six months), you must be able to submit the document 'long-term residence of citizens of the Union' or else your history of registration in the various municipalities that you have lived in.

Going Abroad

If you have a right to the *studiefinanciering*-loan, you can take this right abroad with you, provided you have 'demonstrable' ties with the Netherlands. This could be because you legally resided in the Netherlands during three of the preceding six years (there are other ties, as well as exceptions to the need to have lived here three of the preceding six years, so be sure to visit the DUO-website to find the exact conditions), do not receive a grant abroad, and follow a study abroad that is considered of 'sufficient quality'. This can be for a temporary period abroad or for a full study program.

Parents

Under certain conditions, parents who have a type I, II, III or IV residence permit or are EU/EEA/Swiss nationals also qualify for a parental grant for tuition fees and school expenses for children who are going to school full-time and who are younger than 18 years of age, paid out by the DUO. The amount depends on the joint income of the parents and the type of school attended. You can find out more about this grant on the DUO-website, under *Tegemoetkoming ouders* (financial support for parents).

LIVING ON A SHOESTRING

WELL-FED AND WELL-DRESSED

It would be nicest, if your employer were to send you to the Netherlands within the context of a jointly agreed career move in order to hone and show your professional talents at a local branch. Then, you would be welcomed by the Human Resource Department who would probably arrange suitable (though maybe comparatively cramped, compared to your home country – the Dutch are not into huge houses) housing for you and help you with your accommodation expenses. Many employers contribute to the tuition fees of your children. And a lease car – maybe not as large and comfortable as you are accustomed to (the Dutch are not into showy cars, either) – would be waiting for you.

THE OTHER EXPAT

However, most of you who come to the Netherlands will not enjoy such luxuries. You might have come here, driven by ambition; to study, or to find a job. Or possibly to seek protection from persecution. Or because your multinational employer has not yet caught on to your talents.

A SHOE AND A SLIPPER

As the Dutch would say: you've come here on a shoe and a slipper. And it's going to stay that way, for the time being – also financially. Your income will lie somewhere between € 500 and € 1,100 a month, sometimes less. This will indeed quite likely be the case if you have come here as a student.

If this is your situation, how do you deal with it? In giving you the following tips, we are working on the assumption that you do have a place to live and, therefore, a mailbox. Many of the following tips may not be new to you, but to be complete, we will list them anyway.

YOUR MAIL BOX

For starters, you will find that your mailbox is full of publications that you have not asked for. In most cases, this will be promotional material for your local stores and supermarkets. Furthermore, you will receive one or two local (regional) newspapers. These are called 'house-to-house' papers (*huis-aan-huis bladen*), and contain, aside from local news, a lot of locally relevant advertising.

Don't throw them away; pay attention to them, as they can mean savings for you, even if your Dutch is still somewhat rocky. Here are a few words to remember:

■ *Reclame*. This means that the product (of which there is hopefully a picture) is being sold at a reduced price
■ *Aanbieding*. Same thing
■ *Korting*. Also same thing
■ *Bon, kortingsbon, coupon*. You are to fill in the coupon and take it to the store, where they will give you a reduction on the products advertised
■ *Op = op, weg = weg*, or *op is op, weg is weg* (finished = finished, gone = gone). This means that a limited amount of a certain product is being sold at a reduced price
■ *Occasion*. This is a second-hand (or 'pre-owned') item, such as furniture, or cars.

FOOD

It is a good idea to take a look at above publications before going shopping. Most Dutch people shop for their daily needs at supermarkets that, in the '60s and '70s, chased away the local mom and pop stores. They are part of the larger chains – such as Albert Heijn, Aldi and Jumbo – and focus on a particular segment of the market. If you want to spend less money, go to a supermarket that targets a wide segment of the consumer market that has relatively little spending money. The quality of the products will be comparable, as the Netherlands has a very strict and effective Inspectorate for Consumer Goods. The things that will tip you off in your selection of a supermarket are through-put, variety and presentation. Luxurious-looking supermarkets are usually more expensive than their modest-looking competitors.

In the store, always be on the look-out for the word *aanbieding*. And check whether the supermarket sells goods under its own label, as these are usually cheaper than other, world-renowned, brands. The quality will almost always be the same; only the packaging will be cheaper. Pay attention if there is a reduction for buying more than one package (2 *halen, 1 betalen* – buy two, pay for one).

When buying food, pay attention to the 'best before'-date: *ten-minste houdbaar tot*, sometimes merely *t.h.t.*

STREET MARKETS

But don't limit yourself to the supermarkets; the local street markets, which are organized once or twice a week, have plenty to offer. As they say in the Netherlands: at the street market, your guilder is worth one-and-a-half (the same, presumably, applies to your euro). Also here, shop around and compare.

The Dutch go to the street markets to spend less money and the market vendors know that. There are two main segments at the market: food and textile (but also flowers and plants – to buy those, you should go at the end of the day, when the vendors want to 'get rid' of their stuff and sell it at greatly reduced prices). You can also buy quite a decent wardrobe at the street market.

SMALLER SHOPKEEPERS

A third, excellent, source of supplies is the local 'exotic' food stores. Already since a long time, this country has had a good supply of *tokos* (Indonesian) and Chinese stores and supermarkets. Since it has become even more multi-cultural, the smaller shopkeepers have been making an admirable niche for themselves, especially those from the Middle and Far East. They have taken on the challenge of opening small butcher stores, bakeries and grocery stores – with success. With the added advantage that they often sell goods and spices that cannot be found in the traditional supermarkets (but can sometimes also be found at the street markets).

GOING OUT TO EAT

The best way to save money on food is by doing your own cooking, of course. But this is not always as much fun as going out for a bite to eat. If you decide to go out, focus on *eet-café's* rather than restaurants and check out the price of their *dagschotel* (meal of the day), which should not be more than € 15. They are served on a large plate and are sufficiently filling and nutritious. Even cheaper are the Surinam take-outs, which you can find in most big cities, and their Turkish and Moroccan competitors, who mostly advertise their *shoarma*. Or you can go to the traditional Dutch *patatzaak*, where they sell French Fries (*patat*), *kroketten* (which have a soft, meat-based filling, rolled in bread crumbs and fried) and other fried meat products. McDonald's can also be found in almost any city or larger town, though they are not necessarily the cheapest.

DURABLE GOODS

But food is not all you want. You also want durable goods, such as a radio, a television and perhaps a DVD-player. You want to furnish your apartment. You might, one day, want a car. When it comes to owning a car, do not forget that the Netherlands is a country of traffic congestion and traffic jams. Buy a car only if you really need it, as taxes are high (both on the purchase price and on fuel) and the road tax (which is unavoidable) is considerable. The amount of road tax you pay depends on where you live, and the weight and fuel of your car. If you live in a city, be prepared to walk long distances as you can seldom park near your destination (or home). Consider whether you might not be better off with a bicycle (and public transportation) – in which case, don't forget a sturdy lock as bicycle theft is a thriving industry in the Netherlands! Stall your bicycle inside if you can. If you want a car anyway, check out the used cars market: www.gaspedaal.nl.

TRANSPORTATION

Don't forget that students who qualify for the *studiefinanciering*-loan receive a public transportation pass. See more on page 138.

CLASSIFIED ADS

For the purchase of durable goods, you can check out the classified ads in newspapers. Here, you can also place your own ads, offering whatever you want (including your services if you want to start a – free-lance – business from home). They even have a romantic section. The ads are classified and most often mention the price and the telephone number of the seller. You name it, you can find it. Cars, televisions, furniture, dishwashers, dryers, bicycles, gardening tools, baby items, pets, toys, computers, printers... But be careful that you are not taken advantage of. And you can try to bargain, but keep in mind that not all Dutch people are used to bargaining and will tenaciously stick to their original price.

If the ads don't yield anything, another great source of 'pre-owned' goods is www.marktplaats.nl, where you type in the brand name or simply the item you are searching for, indicate in which area of the Netherlands (if necessary all of the Netherlands) you wish to find it, and wait for the results. Keep a dictionary at hand, as it is in Dutch and you will not find anything in the category 'couch', but will have more success looking under *zitbanken*.

THRIFT SHOPS

In so-called working-class neighborhoods you can find many stores for used items, including clothing, though you should always check the quality. And there are the so-called recycle-centers (thrift shops), called *kringloopwinkels*, an initiative of the environmental organizations. These organizations object to the throw-away mentality of the well-to-do. You can fill your house with very useful items with the help of these organizations. And you might pick up a thing or two, of which you recognize the value and significance that the seller might not have.

BEWARE OF VERY CHEAP PRICES

One final word of warning: many drug-addicts support their habit by selling stolen goods. Since the arrival of hard drugs, many people have installed extra locks and safety-locks – as should you. There are quite a few stolen goods on the market, such as electronic ware, scooters and bicycles – and their prices are very attractive. But beware of the fact that there are often well-concealed registration numbers on these items and that if the police find such a number (corresponding to a stolen good) on your purchase, then you have a problem. *The buyer of stolen goods is worse than the thief*, is their motto and they – nor the judge – will be much impressed by your defense that you bought the item in good faith. They operate on the principle that if an item has been sold at a 'ridiculously' low price, then you should have known better and cannot have been acting in good faith.

HEALTH INSURANCE

In order to register in the Netherlands, you have to show that you have a valid health insurance, which is not always cheap. You pay a nominal contribution and an income-dependent contribution, however, if your income is below a certain level, you can request government support (called *zorgtoeslag*) to help pay for the nominal contribution. If you are employed or receiving a government benefit then, in most cases, your employer or social security institution will pay the income-dependent portion. The basic health care insurance package covers: visits to your GP (*huisarts*), specialists, physical therapy, pregnancy and childbirth costs, home care

after birth, hospitalization, most prescription drugs and medical equipment. As you can read earlier in this chapter, students under the age of 30 who are here solely for study purposes are exempt from the obligation to take out health insurance with a Dutch insurance company, though they will have to make other arrangements to make sure they are insured.

You can read more about insurances on page 124. For more on the *zorgtoeslag*, visit www.toeslagen.nl.

PAYING THE RENT

If you are 18 years or older (subject to conditions, you can be younger than 18) and reside here legally (the same applies to anyone you are sharing a house with; partner, roommates) you have right to rent subsidy (*huurtoeslag*) if:

- you rent an 'independent' accommodation, that is, with its own front door, bed/living room, toilet and kitchen
- there is a rental contract, indicating that your stay is not temporary
- you (and the persons with whom you are sharing the accommodation) are registered at this address with the municipality
- you have Dutch nationality or reside here legally
- the rent is not too low (the amount can be found on the site of the tax authorities (www.belastingdienst.nl, under *Huurtoeslag*); it depends on your age and on whether you are living on your own
- the rent is not too high (see above point)
- you have a certain maximum income, which differs depending on your age and whether you are living on your own
- you have no income from savings or investment that exceeds a certain amount
- the rules regarding the maximum rent are more flexible for disabled persons.

To apply, or to find out how much subsidy you qualify for, contact the tax authorities. You can find more information on www.toeslagen.nl. On this site you can also apply for the *huurtoeslag*, as well as find certain exceptions / additional rules.

STUDENT LOANS

If you have come here as a foreign student, keep in mind that you can approach many of the larger banks for (low interest) loans and a student insurance package (if your educational institution has not already arranged one for you).

LEGAL AID

If you are in need of (cheap) legal advice, you can approach a so-called *Juridisch Loket*, which offers free consultation on elementary issues that can be dealt with in less than an hour, or else answers legal questions and then sets you up with legal aid. You can read more about the Juridisch Loket, and financial aid when dealing with legal issues, on page 127.

COLD AND LONELY?

And if there is a lot of month left, after your change purse has been depleted of its last dime and you are feeling cold and lonely? Go to a library; entry is free and you can read anything you want, in several different languages. When reading, you are never alone and... there's central heating.

WEBSITES

STUDY IN HOLLAND
www.hollandalumni.nl
www.studyinholland.nl
www.studyfinder.nl

LISTINGS OF INTERNATIONAL SCHOOLS
www.educaide.nl: a brief outline of the
educational system in the Netherlands

MASTER PROGRAMMES
www.theofficialmasterguide.nl: for a complete overview of the master's degrees
available in the Netherlands

HOUSING FOR STUDENTS
Easykamer.nl: www.easykamer.nl
DUWO: ww.duwo.nl
Erasmate: www.erasmate.com
Housinganywhere:
www.housinganywhere.com
SSH: www.sshxl.nl

INTERNATIONAL EDUCATION SUPPORT

Educaide: www.educaide.nl
Edufax: www.edufax.nl
New2NL: www.new2nl.com

STUDENT ORGANIZATIONS

FULBRIGHT CENTER
Netherlands America Commission for Educational Exchange
Westerdoksdijk 215, 1013 AD Amsterdam
Tel.: 020 531 59 30
www.fulbright.nl

AIESEC
Enables contact between students and companies to do an international internship in
over 100 countries.
AIESEC is located in 10 main university cities
in the Netherlands -- www.aiesec.nl

AEGEE
A network of 253 student organizations in 42
countries with over 17,000 members
www.aegee.nl

INTERNATIONAL VOCATIONAL EDUCATION

MBO RAAD
Organization of secondary vocational education
For more information on English Language
MBO programs that are offered in your region
check: www.mboraad.nl

IVETA
*International Vocational Education And
Training Association*
www.iveta.org

INTERNATIONAL HIGHER EDUCATION

VERENIGING HOGESCHOLEN
Prinsessegracht 21, 2514 AP The Hague
Postbus 123, 2501 CC The Hague
Tel.: 070 312 21 21
For a complete overview of government funded universities of applied sciences in the
Netherlands
www.vereniginghogescholen.nl

VERENIGING VAN UNIVERSITEITEN (VSNU)
*The Association of Universities in the Netherlands. For a complete overview of government
funded research universities in the Netherlands*
Lange Houtstraat 2, 2511 CW The Hague
Tel.: 070 302 14 00 – www.vsnu.nl

EP-NUFFIC, THE NETHERLANDS ORGANIZATION FOR INTERNATIONAL COOPERATION IN HIGHER EDUCATION
For information on internationalization in
higher education
P.O. Box 29777, 2502 LT The Hague
Kortenaerkade 11, The Hague
Tel.: 070 426 02 60
www.ep-nuffic.nl
www.studyinholland.nl

EUROPEAN ASSOCIATION OF INTERNATIONAL EDUCATION
The EAIE is a non-profit organization whose
main aim is the stimulation and facilitation
of the internationalization of higher education in Europe and around the world
www.eaie.org

DUTCH RESEARCH UNIVERSITIES

Delft University of Technology: www.tudelft.nl
Eindhoven University of Technology:
www.tue.nl
Erasmus University Rotterdam: www.eur.nl
Eindhoven University of Technology:
www.tue.nl
Leiden University: www.leiden.edu
Maastricht University:
www.maastrichtuniversity.nl
Nyenrode Business Universiteit:
www.nyenrode.nl
Radboud University Nijmegen: www.ru.nl
Open University: www.ou.nl
The Protestant Theological University:
www.pthu.nl
TiasNimbas Business School:
www.tiasnimbas.edu
Tilburg University:
www.tilburguniversity.edu
University of Amsterdam:
www.english.uva.nl
University of Groningen: www.rug.nl
University of Twente: www.utwente.nl
Utrecht University: www.uu.nl/EN
VU University Amsterdam: www.vu.nl
Wageningen University:
www.wageningenuniversity.nl

UNIVERSITIES OF APPLIED SCIENCES

Universities of applied sciences offering international degree programs and short courses:
www.studyinholland.nl/education-system/
dutch-institutions/universities-of-applied-
sciences

INTERNATIONAL SCHOOLS

ALKMAAR AREA
The European School
Molenweidtje 5, 1862 BC Bergen NH
Tel.: 072 589 01 09
www.esbergen.eu

ALMERE
Letterand International (Primairy Dep.)
Roland Holststraat 58, 1321 RX Almere
Tel.: 036 536 72 40
www.letterland.nl

Secondary Dept at Int. School Almere
Heliumweg 61, 1362 JA Almere - Poort
Tel.: 036 760 07 50
www.internationalschoolalmere.nl

AMSTERDAM AREA
Amsterdam International Community School
Prinses Irenestraat 59-61, 1077 WV Amsterdam
Tel.: 020 577 12 40
www.aics.espritscholen.nl

British School of Amsterdam
Anthonie van Dijckstraat 1, 1077 ME Amsterdam
Jan van Eijckstraat 21, 1077 LG Amsterdam
Fred. Roeskestraat 94A, 1076 ED Amsterdam
Tel.: 020 679 78 40
www.britams.nl

International School Amsterdam
Sportlaan 45, 1185 TB Amstelveen
Tel.: 020 347 11 11
www.isa.nl

Annexe du Lycée Français Vincent van Gogh
Rustenburgerstraat 246, 1073GK Amsterdam
Tel.: 020 644 65 07
www.lyceevangogh.nl

The Japanese School of Amsterdam
Karel Klinkenbergstraat 137
1061 AL Amsterdam
Tel.: 020 611 81 36
www.jsa.nl

ARNHEM / NIJMEGEN
Arnhem International School
Primary Dept. at Dr. Aletta Jacobsschool
Slochterenweg 27, 6835 CD Arnhem
Tel.: 026 323 07 29
Secondary Dept. at Lorentz
Groningensingel 1245, 6835 HZ Arnhem
Tel.: 026 320 28 40
www.arnheminternationalschool.nl

BREDA
International School Breda
Mozartlaan 27, 4837 EH Breda
Tel.: 076 560 78 70
www.isbreda.nl

BRUNSSUM (LIMBURG)
Afnorth International School
Ferdinand Bolstraat 1, 6445 EE Brunssum
Tel.: 045 527 82 20
www.afnorth-is.com

DELFT
International School Delft
Jaffalaan 9, 2628 BX Delft
Tel.: 015 251 1447
www.isdelft.nl

EERDE
International School Eerde
Kasteellaan 1, 7731 PJ Ommen
Tel.: 0529 451 452
www.eerde.nl

EINDHOVEN
International School Eindhoven
www.isecampus.nl
Oirschotsedijk 14b, 5651 GC Eindhoven
Primary Dept
Tel.: 040 251 94 37
Secondary Dept
Tel.: 040 242 68 35

ENSCHEDE
International School Twente
www.istwente.com
Tiemeister 20, 7541 WG Enschede
Tel.: 053 482 11 00

GRONINGEN
Groningse Schoolvereniging
Primary Dept. at Groningse Schoolvereniging
Sweelinckklaan 4, 9722 JV Groningen
Tel.: 050 527 08 18
www.g-s-v.nl
Secondary Dept. at IS Groningen
www.maartenscollege.nl
Rijksstraatweg 24, 9752 AE Haren
Tel.: 050 534 00 84
www.g-s-v.nl

THE HAGUE AREA
HSV International Schools
Tel.: 070 318 49 65
International Primary Departments HSV
Nassaulaan 26, 2514 JT Den Haag
Tel.: 070 318 49 50
Koningin Sophielaan 24a
2595 TG Den Haag
Tel.: 070 324 34 53
Van Nijenrodestraat 16
2597 RM Den Haag
Tel.: 070 328 14 41
www.hsvdenhaag.nl

Lighthouse Special Education (Primary)
Amalia van Solmstraat 155, 2595 TA Den Haag

Tel.: 070 335 56 98
www.lighthousese.nl

The International School of The Hague
Wijndaelerduin 1, 2554 BX Den Haag
Primary Dept.
Tel.: 070 338 4567
Secondary Dept.
Tel.: 070 328 14 50
www.ishthehague.nl

The European School of The Hague
Houtrustweg 2, 2566 HA Den Haag
Tel.: 070 700 16 00
www.eshthehague.nl

The American School of The Hague
Rijksstraatweg 200, 2241 BX Wassenaar
Tel.: 070 512 10 60
www.ash.nl

The British School in The Netherlands (BSN)
Admissions: Tel.: 070 315 40 77
Junior Schools BSN
Age Range: 3-11
Vlaskamp 19, 2592 AA Den Haag
Diamanthorst 16, 2592 GH Den Haag
Vrouw Avenweg 640, 2493 WZ Den Haag
Senior School BSN
Jan van Hooflaan 3, 2252 BG Voorschoten
Tel.: 071 560 22 22
Age range: 11-18
www.britishschool.nl

Deutsche Internationale Schule (German School)
Van Bleiswijkstraat 125, 2582 LB Den Haag
Tel.: 070 354 94 54
www.disdh.nl

Le Lycée Français Vincent van Gogh
Scheveningseweg 237, 2584 AA Den Haag
Tel.: 070 306 69 23 / 070 306 69 30
www.lyceevangogh.nl

The Indonesian Embassy School in the Netherlands
Rijksstraatweg 679, 2245 CB Wassenaar
Tel.: 070 517 88 75
www.sekolahindonesia.nl

HILVERSUM
International Primary School Hilversum
Rembrandtlaan 30, 1213 BH Hilversum
Frans Halslaan 57A, 1213 BK Hilversum
Violenstraat 3, 1214 CJ Hilversum

Tel.: 035 621 60 53
www.ipsviolen.nl

International School Hilversum
Alberdingk Thijm (Secondary Dept)
Emmastraat 56, 1213 AL Hilversum
Tel.: 035 672 99 31
www.ishilversum.nl

LEIDERDORP
Leiden International Primary School
at Elckerlyc Montessori
Klimopzoom 41, 2353 RE Leiderdorp
Tel.: 071 589 68 61
www.elckerlyc.net

OEGSTGEEST
International Secondary Dept. at
Het Rijnlands Lyceum
Apollolaan 1, 2341 BA Oegstgeest
Tel.: 071 519 35 55
www.isrlo.nl

MAASTRICHT
United World College Maastricht
Discusworp 65, 6225 XP Maastricht
www.uwcmaastricht.com
UWCM Primary School:
Tel.: 043 356 11 00
UWC Maastricht Secondary School
Tel.: 043 367 46 66
www.uwcmaastricht.com

ROTTERDAM
De Blijberg–International Primary Department
Graaf Florisstraat 56, 3021 CJ Rotterdam
Tel.: 010 448 22 66
www.blijberg.nl

Rotterdam International Secondary School
at Wolfert van Borselen
Bentincklaan 294, 3039 KK Rotterdam
Tel.: 010 890 77 44
www.wolfert.nl/riss

American International School of Rotterdam
Verhulstlaan 21, 3055 WJ Rotterdam
Tel.: 010 422 53 51 – www.aisr.nl

UTRECHT
International School Utrecht
Van Bijnkershoeklaan 8, 3527 XL Utrecht
Tel.: 030 870 04 00
www.isutrecht.nl

SCHOOL HOLIDAYS
PRIMARY AND SECONDARY SCHOOL VACATIONS

MAY 2016
All regions: April 30 – May 8

SUMMER 2016
Northern Region: July 16 – August 28
Middle Region: July 9 – August 21
Southern Region: July 23 – September 4

FALL 2016
Northern and Middle Regions: October 15-23
Southern Region: October 22-30

CHRISTMAS 2016
All Regions: December 24 – January 8, 2017

SPRING 2017
Northern Region: February 18-26
Middle and Southern Regions: February 25 – March 5

MAY 2017
All regions: April 22-30

SUMMER 2017
Northern Region: July 22 – September 3
Middle Region: July 8 – August 20
Southern Region: July 15 – August 27

Note: The dates for the short holidays may differ from one school to another. For further information concerning holidays, you should consult the school your child is attending

Few things are more distressing than becoming sick abroad. Do the doctors have the same wealth of knowledge as they do in your home country? Will you be able to communicate with them? What are the health facilities? It is undeniably hard to qualify medical care, as it depends on so many factors, but the general consensus – though there will always be someone who has a different opinion or experience – is that, whether you have the common cold, a serious illness or are expecting a baby, you are in good hands in the Netherlands.

There are, of course, differences, as this is a different culture. For this reason, we have selected a number of relevant topics (finding a family doctor, going to the hospital, having a baby and other medical issues) to help familiarize you with the careful, caring, though nonetheless Dutch approach to health care. And what always helps: (almost) all doctors speak English here.

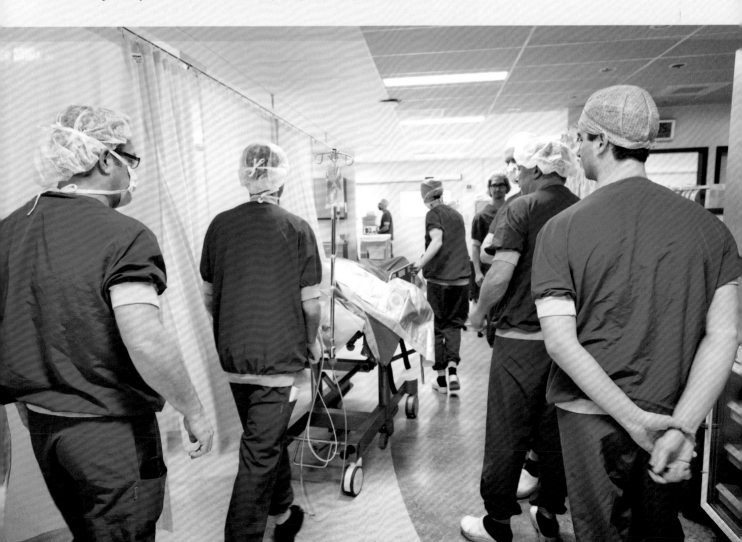

CONTRIBUTING AUTHOR STEPHANIE DIJKSTRA AND CHRISTINE HOUSER

THE FAMILY DOCTOR

HUISARTS — FAMILY DOCTOR, OR GP

The Dutch word for family doctor or GP is *huisarts* – which literally translates into 'house doctor'. This does not mean that he or she will come to your house if you are sick; you are expected to make an appointment and go see him (or her). *Huisartsen* do make house calls in the case of emergencies; either after hours or during specifically allotted hours in their schedule. The name 'neighborhood doctor' would have been closer to the truth, as most people in the Netherlands go to a GP in their neighborhood. Many doctors share an office location and take turns covering after hours and weekends. Some of these offices are located near (or even in) a hospital, for your convenience.

FINDING A GP

The best place to start looking for a GP is in fact in your neighborhood – and the way to find out which doctor lives in your neighborhood is to visit your *gemeentehuis*, or city/town hall. There you can ask for a *gemeentegids* (a booklet issued by your municipality containing information on just about everything relevant to the town or city you live in, such as doctors, schools, lawyers, health clubs, day care, churches, etc.), which will have a list of all the local GPs. If you feel a bit hesitant about leafing through this booklet and finding your way unassisted, someone at the *gemeentehuis* will probably be glad to help you out. Of course, you can also simply ask those living in your neighborhood or other expats which doctor they go to. Or you can check the Yellow Pages or Internet for *Artsen – huisartsen*.

In no way are you *obligated* to go to the GP who lives nearest to you. Nor can you expect him (or her) to accept you, should you approach him. Some GPs have more patients than they can handle and find themselves forced to turn down new ones, at least for a while. Once you have settled on a GP, ask him if you can meet to discuss your needs and expectations and to establish compatibility – especially as you are from abroad and might have different expectations. You must register in advance with a GP, as otherwise you may have difficulty finding someone who can see you on short notice, should you become ill.

SPREEKUUR — VISITING HOURS

If you have any medical or psychological questions, ailments, or if you need help, your GP will be the first one you call. Some GPs have walk-in consultation hours, usually early in the morning; you simply go to the GP's office, sit down in the waiting room with the other patients, and await your turn. Other doctors only see you by appointment. You call in, make an appointment for the same or the next day – and come at the agreed hour. Unless the doctor has been called out on an emergency, you will probably not have to wait more than 15 minutes. Sometimes you can only call to make an appointment in the morning. However, if you are taken miserably ill in the afternoon, it is best to simply be persistent about wanting to at least make an appointment for the next day. If you are scheduling your appointment, you have the opportunity to request a double slot. You will need to explain this to the *receptionist* (assistant) who answers the phone. A double appointment means the GP will have 20 minutes to spend with you, instead of the usual 10. The extra time is often needed given the differences in culture, language, and expectations, and will help both you and the GP feel less rushed.

For simple questions, or to request a refill for your prescription, most doctors have a *telefonische spreekuur*, whereby you can call in and speak to the doctor (or, at times, his assistant, who has followed special training) with your question or request.

Speaking of questions, most GPs do not necessarily volunteer any extra information. They like to keep things short. If you are feeling a little insecure about your illness, or would like some background information, do not hesitate to ask your questions, as this is likely the only way you will be getting any extended answers. The Dutch GPs are also less likely to (refer you to a specialist to) run a battery of tests 'just in case'; if you have decided you want to rule something out then you should mention this. Unless you happen to have a cranky one (which could happen in any country and, in which case, you are free to go in search of a different doctor), the GPs here are quite understanding of your fears.

IF YOU NEED TO SEE A SPECIALIST

The GP, if he thinks you need more specialized expertise (or if you think you do), will refer you to a specialist. Most often, this will be someone at the nearest hospital. He will give you a referral notice (containing, among others, a history of your ailment) for the hospital and specialist he feels you should see. This does not mean that you do not have a say in what (type of) specialist you get to see or which hospital you would like to go to. Most GPs are quite flexible and all you have to do is say what (or who) it is you want.

Keep in mind that, for your insurer to cover the expenses involved in your visit to the specialist, they will want to see a copy of the referral notice (see page 229) – so you have no choice but to visit your GP first! If you want to see a specialist without a referral, this is possible, but it might be more difficult to schedule an appointment and you might need to cover the costs yourself. International insurance policies (rather than local Dutch ones) may have different rules regarding specialist referrals, so consult your specific policy to be sure of what to expect.

EMERGENCIES

Should you have a medical emergency of the type that requires first aid, you can go straight to the hospital to the SEH (Spoedeisende Hulp), or in some hospitals that have not yet updated to the current term, EHBO (*Eerste Hulp bij Ongelukken* – First Aid) for assistance. Nowadays, certain regional hospitals no longer offer first aid services. They expect you go to your GP who will do the stitching up or – in case of procedure he cannot perform, such as putting on a cast – will send you to a hospital that *does* do this. In the case of other types of emergencies, you can either dial 1-1-2 (the emergency telephone line), or you can call your GP, who – if he feels you should indeed head straight for the hospital – will call ahead to the hospital and make sure someone is aware of the problem and is ready to receive you.

IF YOUR DOCTOR IS AWAY

If your GP is away on a skiing vacation in the Austrian Alps or is out for an evening at the opera, he will leave a taped message in Dutch giving you the number of an on-duty doctor. The taped message might also give you the number of the emergency line, the *doktersdienst*. The actual name of the *doktersdienst* depends on where you live, as does the telephone number. Once you dial this number, they will ask what your problem is and where you live, after which they will give you the telephone number of a doctor on duty near you, or have a doctor call you.

THE REGIONAL DOCTOR'S OFFICE

Another alternative is the so-called *Regionale Huisartsenpost*. Often, (most of) the GPs in a particular regional area have joined forces to cover the evenings, nights and weekends. To consult a doctor outside of office hours, all you need to do is call one central number. The phone will be answered by a doctor's assistant or GP, and together you can determine if you need to see a doctor. In that case, you can visit the *Huisartsenpost* or, if this is not possible, a doctor will visit you.

MEDICATION

The GP can recommend medication and give you a prescription (*recept*). If you live in a country where you leave the doctor's office with a prescription for at least three types of medicine no matter what you have, then you had best be prepared. Chances are, your doctor will recommend that you simply go home and go to bed with some toast and a cup of hot tea, which is the Dutch panacea for most minor illnesses. He probably will not prescribe antibiotics, as Dutch doctors are of the opinion that the more frequently you take them, the less effective they become. Furthermore, if truth be told, the thought that suppressing the symptoms (in the case of the millions of cold viruses running rampant in the winter) might bring you more comfort is not something that occurs to most of them.

If you would very much like to be given medication, the best thing is for you to say so. Your doctor might not be in complete agreement, and might make you feel like a bit of a wimp, but to clear away any misunderstandings, you can explain that this is the treatment you receive in your home country and that it makes you feel more secure (or better!).

For medication refills, simply call your GP. In most cases, his or her assistant will be able to write out the prescription and will forward your request to the pharmacy of your choice. You can also choose to pick it up at the doctor's office. Some doctors charge (a portion of) the consultation fee for this service.

Medications available in Netherlands are regulated via a central, national, service. In some cases, this means that the medication you are accustomed to may not be available in Netherlands (sometimes it is, it is just not what the doctor is used to prescribing, so be sure to ask about it). A substitute medication will be available, but in some cases special procedures have to be followed to obtain a medication that works best for you – and these are often complex and time-consuming, so it is best to be prepared for that, should special medication be needed.

CHECK-UPS

Another thing to be aware of is that general medical check-ups are, on the whole, not carried out in the Netherlands. There are no annual blood pressure, cholesterol, or blood-sugar tests. You can request them, if you like, but you would have to list exactly what you want – and sometimes even argue your case. This may be surprising, but rather than expending your energy on being frustrated, you might as well do the practical thing: either persist, or have these tests carried out while you are visiting your home country.

In the bigger cities, you may perhaps be able to find (an international) medical center that does offer these tests.

PAYMENT

Under the new insurance law, you have a choice between taking out health care insurance 'in kind' (*natura*) or based on 'restitution' (*restitutie*). In the latter case, you will have to pay your medical bills yourself and then ask you insurance company for a restitution, in the former, the insurance company will pay your medical bills directly. Be aware that Dutch insurance policies always include an amount that you will need to pay yourself, in addition to your monthly or yearly premium (a deductible, called *eigen risico*). The specific amount changes every year. For more on this, see page 124.

OTHER SERVICES

If you need to see a dentist, eye doctor, physical therapist, need other help with physical disabilities, or need advice on your sexual health, ask your GP for recommendations. See more about these topics further on.

THE SPECIALIST

If you have been given a referral from your GP to see a specialist, you will then have to make an appointment. Usually, your GP will have written down the relevant phone number on the referral notice. Depending on the type of specialist you need to see and the urgency of your condition, you can see him/her the same day or only months hence (there has been great dissatisfaction in the Netherlands regarding waiting lists and considerable effort has been put into reducing these, so with any luck, the wait will be reasonable).

THE REFERRAL NOTICE – INSURANCE COMPANY

As mentioned under *The Family Doctor*, do keep in mind that, for your insurer to cover the expenses involved in your visit to the specialist, they will want to see a copy of the referral notice (proving that your doctor thought it was necessary for you to see the specialist). Often, the hospital keeps your referral notice – which you hand in to the specialist's assistant when you come in for your appointment – and forwards a copy to the insurer along with the bill they submit on your behalf. If, however, you declare your own expenses with the insurer (either after paying them yourself, or along with a request for your insurer to pay the bill), then you will have to send (a copy of) the referral notice yourself. Without this referral, the insurer will likely not pay the bill.

POLIKLINIEK AND PONSPLAATJE

In the Netherlands, most specialists work out of hospitals and not private clinics. When you come to visit him/her at the hospital, you look for the sign *Poliklinieken*, and the correct department. If this is your first visit to the hospital, you register at the front desk. There you will be asked a few initial questions (your name, address, insurer, GP, and a few other questions). This information will go into the computer and also onto a little credit card-sized plastic card, called a *ponsplaatje*, which you must bring with you every time you go to the hospital as it is used, among others, to find your records, mark forms, send your bills to your insurance company, and to print out labels for lab tests.

Many hospitals are in the process of replacing the *ponsplaatje* with an electronic card, called the *electronische patiëntenpas*. This card contains all medical data on the patient in question. Some hospitals have neither – so it is best to ask at the information desk the first time you go to the hospital.

ASSISTANT

Once you arrive at the hospital for your appointment, you give the referral notice to the specialist's assistant. Along with the referral notice you might also have to hand in an envelope containing a short description of your ailment, allowing the specialist to gain some preliminary insight into your condition.

YOUR VISIT WITH THE SPECIALIST

When you visit the specialist, he will read the note provided by your GP, discuss your situation with you, arrange the necessary tests and prescribe a possible treatment. In most cases, you will not be filling out four pages of your own (and your entire family's) medical history before the visit – but this really depends on the medical problem at hand. If there is anything potentially of impor-tance, be sure to mention it – such as former illnesses, hereditary afflictions and allergies to medication – as the history taken is often minimal. And, as with the GP, if you have any questions, ask. Or, if you expect a particular treatment or medicine, discuss this. Dutch doctors are not circumspect out of orneriness; they simply believe that the patient will ask what he wants to know.

Be aware that although you have been referred to a specialist, in many cases the doctor you see at least initially will be an assistant doctor (either one in-training or one just working as an assistant in the practice, without specialty training). Usually, you will not know this unless you ask, so don't feel rude about asking. It is often better for you, as the patient, to know with whom you are speaking and what their level of expertise is.

Depending on the seriousness of your illness and the urgency of your lab tests, you may be referred to an emergency room of the hospital or be sent straight to the laboratories for blood tests.

ARRANGING HOSPITALIZATION

If your illness requires immediate hospitalization, the specialist calls ahead and makes the appropriate arrangements, ensuring that the doctors on duty will be waiting for you. If he is of the opinion that he will want to see you again, that you need to see a different specialist or that you require hospitalization at some point in the future, he will send you to either his secretary or the central appointment office to make your next appointment. If you have been admitted to hospital, in addition to the hospital doctors, your GP might check on you from time to time, though he might wait till you have come home from the hospital and pay you a house call.

HOSPITALS

GENERAL

There are many hospitals – eight of them are university hospitals and the others are run by the community or religious organizations. Once you are referred to a specialist or hospital, be sure to ask your GP whether there is a hospital that specializes in your condition.

Though waiting lists are being worked away, keep in mind that for some surgeries there might be a long waiting period.

BEING ADMITTED TO THE HOSPITAL

We mentioned earlier that you should not expect to go through your entire medical history when visiting the specialist. This does happen, though, when you are admitted to a hospital, particularly if you are going to be operated on. You may even find yourself going through your whole history three times: with the admitting doctor, with the anesthesiologist and with the doctor who will be operating you. Anything vital, such as allergies to medication, is definitely worth repeating each time.

ROOMS

Don't expect a private room during your hospital stay. You might be offered a double room but also be prepared for a room for six. The rooms here can also be co-educational so don't be surprised if they ask you if you object to sharing a room with patients of the opposite sex.

Take your pajamas, toothbrush, toothpaste and other toiletries that you might need for any overnight or weekend stay. Also take along your prescription medicines.

Most, if not all, hospitals allow you to have your own telephone line and have a television set hanging over your bed. If you choose to use these, you are charged a daily fee (and given headphones for the television).

Dutch hospital roommates can be quite chatty so that, if you are fond of your privacy and want your curtains closed all the time, they might be a bit disappointed. This could particularly be the case if they find out you are a foreigner, as they are naturally curious to start with and even more so when they find out you are from another country. They not only want to know more about where you're from, they also want to be sure that you appreciate what a fine country you have come to live in.

CHILDREN'S HOSPITALS
While all hospitals have children's wards, there are also several excellent children's hospitals throughout the country. You can give your GP your preference. Don't forget to take your records along that describe the child's previous illnesses and a list of immunizations given. Children's hospitals put a lot of effort into keeping the children entertained and many offer long-term patients the opportunity to keep up with school, if need be.

LODGING FOR THE RELATIVES
Some hospitals, but particularly children's hospitals, have lodging possibilities if you or your relatives want to be nearby. This is of particular importance if you are still nursing a baby that is being hospitalized. There are also Ronald McDonald houses (for parents of sick children) in the larger cities.

VISITING HOURS
Do not forget to check the visiting hours, as they are different in every hospital. Some hospitals can be very strict about enforcing these hours.

HAVING A BABY

SAFE
Many newcomers to the Netherlands are taken aback by the non-interventionist approach to perinatal care and are often told that everyone delivers at home with the help of a midwife. In fact, only about 18% of deliveries take place at home, the rest take place in a hospital under the guidance of a midwife or gynecologist. Mothers-to-be are monitored regularly throughout pregnancy, labor and delivery as well as during the postpartum period – as are their babies.

Despite the fact that, in general, mothers are satisfied about perinatal care in the Netherlands, there was nonetheless a relatively recent report (December 2009) stating that the incidence of still-born babies is relatively high here, particularly compared to other EU-countries. How can this be explained? According to the Dutch medical world, this is not due to the quality of the medical care provided here, but rather to the risks inherent in having your baby at home. With their 18%-rate of home births, the Dutch are still outliers in the home-birth statistics, presenting a sometimes risky delay when it comes to the urgent need for medical inter-

vention when things are not going as they should. The Dutch often say: 'Having a baby is not a disease'. And they are right. Yet, everyone knows that the hours or minutes during which a child chooses to enter the world can be very critical. And having the full spectrum of medical care available straight away is crucial. Also the fact that expectant mothers only visit a midwife – who generally speaking does not perform ultrasounds – during pregnancy contributes to the risk of infant death, according to Dutch medical specialists. Visiting a specialist and having at least one ultrasound carried out would allow the timely detection of growth deficiencies, heart problems and other potential threats to the babies' health while still in utero – all of which the Dutch specialists are more than equipped to deal with. Therefore, if you want to minimize the risks, visit the gynecologist at least once, and have your baby in the hospital, where you are assured of the correct, and complete, medical care.

In the following paragraphs, you will find a description of the system as it currently is in the Netherlands.

SO YOU'RE PREGNANT...
Congratulations! The first step is to make an appointment with your local *verloskundige* (midwife) or gynecologist. Make sure to call by week 8-10 as most practices are quite busy. Look in the Yellow Pages under *verloskundigen* or confer with your GP to find either a midwife or a gynecologist. Although you do not officially need a referral to visit a midwife, your GP will be able point you in the right direction. If you go straight to a gynecologist, you need a referral for the costs to be covered by your insurance.

PRENATAL CARE
The Midwife
A midwife is an independent practitioner who can legally practice obstetrics without the supervision of a medical doctor. And unless complications arise or there is a previous medical problem – in which case you will be referred to a gynecologist – once you have opted for a midwife, she will be your sole health care provider during pregnancy, labor, delivery (also when you have your baby in the hospital: see page 230, *Where Will You Have Your Baby?* for more on this) and the initial postpartum period. Midwifes work alone or in a group practice, in which case you will be seen by different midwifes during routine check-ups. One word of advice: as the Dutch feel that pregnancy and childbirth are very normal, natural occurrences, they might not anticipate your need for information or reassurance. Make sure you have a list of questions ready and don't let yourself be thrown by what might appear to be a casual approach to and/or dismissal of your concerns. If need be, explain that there is more (hospital) guidance in your country, and stand your ground.

As mentioned earlier, it is advisable to visit a gynecologist at least once to make sure the baby is healthy and growing – discuss this with your GP and/or midwife so that you can obtain a referral notice to send to your insurance company.

The Gynecologist
Although it is not standard Dutch practice, should you prefer to be cared for by a *gynaecoloog* (gynecologist) from day 1 (or starting early on during your pregnancy), then this can be arranged, but you will need a referral from your midwife or GP in order for the

costs to be covered by your insurance. It may not be standard practice, but it is not very likely that they will refuse to give you one.

If at any time your midwife feels that you or the baby are at medical risk, she will also refer you to a gynecologist, under whose treatment you will, if necessary, be for the remainder of the pregnancy. In that case, this will be fully covered by your insurance.

The GP
Though it is very rare, an expectant mother is sometimes cared for by her GP. This holds true in small villages where there is no midwifery practice. The GP, in effect, takes over the midwife's normal responsibilities.

ROUTINE CHECK-UPS
Your first visit to the gynecologist / midwife will take place around week 12. They will note down your and your partner's medical history as well as that of your respective families. Your weight and blood pressure as well as fetal growth, position and heart beat will be monitored. Blood iron levels will also be checked and you will discuss whether you plan to have a *thuisbevalling* (home birth) or a *ziekenhuis bevalling* (hospital birth). You will visit the midwife / gynecologist approximately 12 times during pregnancy and, except for the first visit which should last about half an hour, most visits will be no longer than a quarter of an hour. As most midwifes do not have ultrasound equipment, you will be referred on to a hospital should an ultrasound prove necessary or, as mentioned earlier, upon your request. It is also possible to have a so-called *pret-echo* (an ultrasound for fun) or video made of your baby *in utero*. Enquire about this option during your routine visit.

It is important that you feel at ease and that you can communicate your needs to your practitioner – whether this be a *verloskundige*, GP or gynecologist. Should you feel that your best interests are not being met, move on. There are other midwifes and other doctors.

PRENATAL TESTING
Prenatal testing and genetic screening are not performed on a routine basis in the Netherlands. Genetic screening, for example, is generally conducted only when the pregnant woman is found to be in a high-risk category for fetal chromosomal defects such as Down Syndrome, Cystic Fibrosis, Spina Bifida or Muscular Dystrophy. In the Netherlands, a pregnant woman is considered at high risk if she is 36 years or older, if she has previously had a child with a congenital defect or if there is a history of chromosomal problems in either her or her partner's family. Should you not fit into one of the above categories but have personal concerns, discuss this matter with you midwife or gynecologist.

The following are the most standard tests available:
- *Echoscopie (Ultrasound)*: An ultrasound is used for screening for fetal defects between 16-20 weeks, whereby an image of the fetus is projected onto a screen by means of sound waves. It can diagnose some, but not all, fetal abnormalities. If in doubt, it can also be used to detect twins or to determine the due date.
- *The Double test*: This test is carried out at 8 weeks' pregnancy, allowing ample time to do any follow-up testing in case of doubt. It is only suitable for calculating the chances that the baby has having Down Syndrome – and not for detecting (the chances of) other chromosomal defects.
- *The Triple (Screen) Test*: This is a blood test done between 14-16 weeks to measure three different protein levels associated with

fetal abnormalities, by drawing blood from the mother. This test can only estimate the risk of a woman having a baby with a chromosomal defect, such as Down Syndrome or Spina Bifida. Should the results of the Double or Triple Test be positive for an increased risk, one of the following two tests may be advised. They are not done on a routine basis.
- *Vlokkentest (Chorionic Villi Sampling)*: This can be done through the cervix at 11-14 weeks or through the abdomen at 12-13 weeks, whereby they aspirate chorionic villi – minuscule, naturally occurring, finger-like projections – from the placenta. The test is used to check the chromosomes and DNA and to test for genetic abnormalities. It cannot be used to test for Spina Bifida. The results are back within 7-10 days. This test can be performed at any major medical center, such as a hospital.
- *Vruchtwaterpuntie (Amniocentesis)*: This test is done after 15 weeks of pregnancy, by aspirating amniotic fluid through the abdomen. It tests for genetic abnormalities and the chances of Spina Bifida. It takes several weeks to get the test results back. This test must also be performed at a major medical center. Since there are potential risks involved with both chorionic villi sampling and amniocentesis, you should discuss these options with your practitioner.
- *Nekplooimeting (Neck Fold Measurement)*: The measurement of the fetus's neck fold is performed during an ultrasound at around 10-14 weeks, when the fetus is 4-8 cm long. Research has shown that an enlarged neck fold may be indicative of chromosomal defects such as Down Syndrome. This test may be performed in conjunction with a blood test, carried out between 9 and 14 weeks of pregnancy. Together, they are referred to as the Combination Test.
- *NIPT-test*: blood is drawn from the mother as of the 10th week of pregnancy, allowing an analysis of the unborn child's DNA. This test is only available to mothers with an increased risk based on the Combination Test, or if there is some other medical indication for carrying it out. It estimates the chances of certain abnormalities and is therefore not conclusive. For absolute certainty, if it indicates that there is indeed an increased risk, chorionic villi sampling or an amniocentesis will still have to be carried out.
- *Doptone (Fetal Heart Monitor)*: The heartbeat of the baby can be monitored for irregularities. This is also carried out during routine check-ups and is therefore not only used to detect potential abnormalities.
- *Fetoscopy*: A flexible fiberoptic device is inserted through the abdomen of the mother to observe the baby and withdraw blood for testing.
- *Cordocentesis*, or Percutaneous Umbilical Cord Blood Sampling: A testing of the blood from the fetal umbilical cord to detect abnormalities. Usually used when useful information cannot be obtained from one of the above tests. This test also carries significant risks and should be thoroughly discussed with your practitioner.

ZWANGERSCHAPSCURSUSSEN (CHILDBIRTH PREPARATION CLASSES)
The Netherlands offers several types of prenatal exercise and birthing classes. Here is a list of the most common approaches to preparing for childbirth:
- *Zwangerschapsgymnastiek (Childbirth Gym)*: This 8-10 week class is given by a physical therapist and is usually offered

through your local *Thuiszorg* organization (for more information on this organization see page 235). A combination of exercises, breathing and relaxation techniques and informal lectures is used to help prepare you for the big day. One of the classes is a 'partner' evening where spouses/birthing coaches can learn hands-on techniques useful during labor and delivery. Classes start in the last trimester.

- *Yoga*: The emphasis of this course is on mastering simple yoga positions, increasing body awareness and learning breathing techniques to promote relaxation in order to better deal with labor pain. (Coaching) partners can also attend a number of sessions. This course is usually offered as of the second trimester.
- *Lamaze / Psychoprofylaxis*: Lamaze focuses primarily on your mind rather than your body, and on how you can learn to deal with (your fear of) pain. It can be taken separately or as part of the course *Samen Bevallen*.
- *Samen Bevallen ('Delivering Together')*: This nine-week course helps couples prepare for labor and delivery. The role of the partner as well as breathing and relaxation techniques are covered.
- *Haptonomie (Haptonomy)*: Haptonomy is the art of touching and feeling. Through stroking and rocking, couples learn to make contact with their baby in utero. Breathing and relaxation techniques are also taught in order to better cope with labor pain. These private lessons usually start in the fourth or fifth month and are given by a physical therapist specialized in Haptonomy.
- *Mensendieck / Cesar*: This group class focuses on exercising muscle groups stressed during pregnancy and delivery. Emphasis is placed on improving postural awareness and movement in order to avoid discomfort or pain which may occur during pregnancy. Breathing and relaxation techniques are also thoroughly covered. This course is made up of 8-10 lessons with one partner evening and one postpartum session and is usually initiated by the sixth month. Cesar is similar to Mensendieck, but pays additional attention to the delivery itself, in particular its emotional aspects, and can be continued after having given birth.
- *Zwangerschapszwemmen (Swimming)*: Most local pools offer special classes for expectant mothers. The water temperature is usually warmer, which promotes general relaxation.

WHERE WILL YOU HAVE YOUR BABY?

As previously mentioned, there are two options available when giving birth in the Netherlands: you can do this either at home under the guidance of a midwife (or, very rarely, your GP), or in the hospital, assisted by either a midwife or gynecologist.

At Home

Keep in mind that if you decide to have your baby at home, this is not irreversible. You have the right to change your mind at any point during pregnancy or delivery, although the latter may be more difficult to execute. You will be taken to the hospital by ambulance should the midwife detect any complications during the delivery.

At the Hospital

If you have been under specialist (hospital) supervision during your entire pregnancy, then you will most likely deliver your baby at the hospital. If you have been under non-hospital *verloskundige* supervision, you will only deliver in the hospital if there are complications (detected either prior to or during delivery). However, you can also opt for what the Dutch call a *poliklinische bevalling* (out-patient hospital delivery) attended either by a midwife or gynecologist; you then voluntarily have a hospital delivery, but are in and out of the hospital within 24 hours – barring complications. You will be required to stay longer in the case of medical complications or a (planned) Caesarean section.

As mentioned earlier, for a hospital delivery to be covered by your insurance, there must have been a medical reason for the baby to be born there, which arose either during pregnancy or delivery. If you opt for a voluntary *poliklinische bevalling*, the insurance company will cover a portion and you will be expected to pay a contribution. Sometimes the insurance covers all costs – so be sure to ask. If, in the case of a *poliklinische bevalling*, you have to stay on longer, due to medical complications or the need for a Caesarean, this will always be covered by your insurance. Home deliveries are fully covered by the insurance policy.

ZWANGERSCHAPSVERLOF (PREGNANCY LEAVE)

If you are currently working and plan to do so following delivery, you will need to obtain a *zwangerschapsverklaring* ('pregnancy

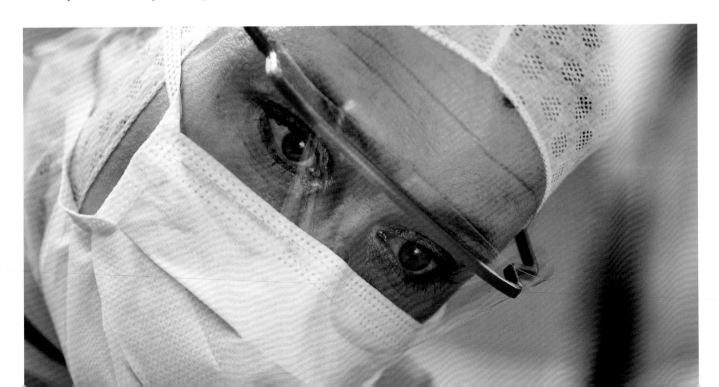

statement') from your midwife or gynecologist. This document confirms your estimated due date and is used to determine when you are eligible for *zwangerschapsverlof*. In the Netherlands, women have the right to 16 weeks' paid leave. This may be initiated between 4-6 weeks prior to the estimated due date. The law states that you may not work from four weeks before, until six weeks after delivery. Should the baby arrive early, you still have a right to the full 16 weeks. If it is late, and you have used up the six weeks beforehand, you still have the right to a ten-week leave following the baby's birth. As of 2008, a similar leave exists for pregnant self-employed mothers.

You can read more about pregnancy leave on page 191.

And don't forget, dads/partners also have their own *verlof* (leave). The law stipulates that fathers are entitled to paid leave on the day the baby is born, two paid days following the birth of their child (see page 192, under *Delivery Leave*), and a further three days (paid or unpaid) Parental Leave to stand by the mother right after birth. For more on long-term Parental Leave, see further on.

THE BIG DAY HAS COME!

Call the midwife or hospital once your waters have broken and/or your contractions have reached a certain frequency. In the case of a *thuisbevalling* (delivery at home), the midwife will either come right over or within a few hours, depending on the stage of labor you are in. She will stay with you throughout the delivery, and once the baby is born, will examine the baby and perform the APGAR-test. During delivery, the midwife is assisted by a *kraam-verzorgster* (maternity aid – see further on). Generally speaking the midwife will leave your house within an hour of the delivery. The *kraamverzorgster*, on the other hand, will stay on to dress and care for the baby, prepare the crib, help the mother take a shower, and clean up the house a bit. If the baby was born during the night, she will take care of mother and baby and leave a list of instructions and her phone number – urging you to call if you have any questions. (See section *Kraamzorg* for more details).

If it has been determined that you are to give birth in the hospital (*bevalling op medische indicatie*) or if you have opted for a *poliklinische bevalling* (out-patient hospital delivery), then you will have to phone either your midwife or the hospital directly – depending on the situation or what has been agreed upon. The hospital will discuss with you whether or not you should come in straight away. Once in the hospital, you will be given a birthing room and they will palpate and examine you to determine how much you are dilated. The heartbeat of the baby will also be monitored. Depending on how busy it is, and how your delivery is going, be prepared to spend much of the time on your own with your (coaching) partner – another reason to take a childbirth class to prepare you both for this period of waiting and coping with contractions. You will of course be checked on regularly, but it is usually not until the actual delivery – attended by either an in-house midwife, your own midwife, or a gynecologist – that you will have full-time supervision. And keep in mind that you may be assisted by the midwife or gynecologist on duty, and not the practitioner who followed you throughout your pregnancy.

PAIN MEDICATION DURING DELIVERY

As mentioned earlier, the Dutch have a rather 'level-headed' attitude towards pregnancy and delivery and feel that it is a natural process that should not be interfered with. Consequently, pain medication is not offered during a home birth and only rarely during delivery in a hospital. Midwifes, on the whole, are not even allowed to administer pain medication. To avoid unpleasant surprises, be sure to discuss with your doctor or midwife what types of medication or pain relief options are available. Be tactful, but persistent! If need be, explain your concerns and let them know that labor and delivery are handled differently in your home country.

Learning to deal and cope with pain is one of the keys to a successful labor and delivery. Research has shown that the more you know about labor and delivery, the better you are able to deal with both pain and any complications which may occur. So sign up for a childbirth preparation class early on – and take your partner along!

Other so-called 'alternative' pain relief options are hypnosis, acupuncture and TENS (Transcutaneous Electrical Nerve Stimulation). Ask your doctor or midwife or call the phone numbers at the end of the chapter for details.

KRAAMZORG (MATERNITY HOME CARE)

The Netherlands provides wonderful maternity home care subsequent to either a home birth or hospital delivery. It is, in fact, obligatory, so if you are from a culture in which you do not expect strangers in your home just after delivering, it can be a bit of a (hopefully pleasant) shock.

Depending on your insurance coverage, you are entitled to approximately a week of home care provided by a *kraamverzorgster* (maternity aid). For an overview of who covers this and whether you have to pay a contribution in the costs, visit www.independer. nl and enter *Kraamzorg* in the search window). You have a legal minimum right to a total of 24 hours of *kraamzorg*, spread over eight days, though your insurance policy may cover, for instance, 80 hours over a maximum of ten days. If there is a shortage of maternity aids, then, under circumstances, you can hire private assistance and have this covered by your insurance company. The maternity aid will visit daily to assess the health status of both mother and child. Part or full-time care is available (spreading the total number of hours over several days, for instance; 2 – 8 hours per day) although full-time care is becoming more and more difficult to book due to a shortage of *kraamverzorgsters*. Check the Yellow Pages under *kraamzorg* or with friends and/or your midwife or gynecologist for a list of organizations in your area. And be sure to apply during the first trimester – you certainly do not want to miss out on this unique care.

The *kraamverzorgster* teaches parents/care-givers how to bathe, change and care for the baby. She will also assist with breastfeeding and will, depending on how many hours per day she works, tend to housekeeping, cooking, shopping and caring for the other members of the family.

An excellent source of (Dutch-language) information and websites is www.kraamzorg.nl.

BABY IN THE HOSPITAL

If your baby needs to stay in the hospital for a while, check with your hospital what options are available in terms of lodging for you. Also check with your insurance provider what is covered. Many hospitals have some type of maternity lodging option whereby you do not officially take up a hospital bed but still can spend the night – and nurse/be there with your baby.

THE FIRST WEEK AFTER BIRTH

During the first week at home you will be visited 2-3 times by your midwife and/or GP to check on the health status of you and your baby. They will also confer with the *kraamverzorgster*. You must arrange for this service prior to delivery, especially if you are planning to give birth in a hospital – the gynecologist does not make house calls! Between day 4 and day 10, they will also administer the *hielprik* ('heel prick' or Guthrie test) to check for several metabolic and thyroid diseases – whereby a small amount of blood is drawn from your baby's heel and sent to a laboratory for testing.

Within the first 3-14 days, the *Consultatiebureau* (Well Baby Clinic, see next section) will send a *wijkverpleegster* (neighborhood nurse) to your home to check on the baby. Depending on where you live, the *hielprik* may be performed by this nurse, rather than by your midwife or GP.

As you can see, you will have quite a full house that first week: the *kraamverzorgster*, the *verloskundige*, the GP, the *wijkverpleegster* and last but not least, the *kraamvisite* (visitors). And believe me, they will come in droves! In the Netherlands, once a baby is born, everyone comes to admire your new family member: neighbors, colleagues, friends, relatives...

THE CONSULTATIEBUREAU (WELL BABY CLINIC)

Whereas in most countries, routine check-ups are carried out by a GP or *kinderarts* (pediatrician), in the Netherlands this service is provided by the local *Consultatiebureau* up until a child is 4 years of age. The *Consultatiebureau* is a community-based, country-wide network of clinics providing preventative health care to infants and toddlers. Through screening – motor and cognitive development, speech, hearing and sight – abnormalities can be detected early on and monitored. However, the *Consutatiebureau* doctor may not treat your child; if need be, your child will be referred to your GP who, in turn, will refer you to a specialist when appropriate. One of the more important responsibilities of the *Consultatiebureau* is carrying out The Ministry of Health, Welfare and Sports' vaccination program. Although it is not mandatory, 95% of all par-

ents do indeed opt to have the clinic perform this service.

Your first contact with the *Consultatiebureau* will take place by phone with the registration of your infant. This should be done soon after delivery. The local office will follow up by sending a *wijkverpleegkundige* (neighborhood nurse) to your home within 3-14 days after delivery. During this initial visit the nurse will observe your baby, discuss with you your initial experiences with (breast)feeding and schedule the first check-up at your local clinic. You will also be given a *Groeiboek* (Growth book), which you should take with you to each appointment at the *Consultatiebureau*. An English-language version is available, so be sure to ask for one at the time of registration. During the first year, you will visit the *Consultatiebureau* approximately eight times, and you will be seen by the *Consultatiebureau* doctor and/or the nurse, who will – among others – weigh and measure your infant. You will also have sufficient time during these visits to discuss any other issues of concern (nutrition, parenting issues, etc.).

After that initial year, you and your child will visit the *Consultatiebureau* on a yearly basis until it reaches the age of 4. Prior to each visit you may be asked to complete a questionnaire regarding your child's health, living situation, development and behavior. The results are discussed during your visit with both the doctor and the nurse.

SCHOOL-AGE CHILDREN

Once your child has reached school age, this health service (including the carrying out of the vaccination program) is transferred to the local health office of the *Gemeentelijke Gezondheidsdienst*, better known as the GGD (Municipal Health Service). In 2009, they introduced the (voluntary) vaccination against cervical cancer for girls, to be administered in the year in which they turn 13. Both the *Consultatiebureau* and the GGD-services are offered free of charge.

REGISTERING YOUR BABY

Your baby needs to be registered within three working days after birth at the *gemeentehuis* (town hall) in the city or town where the

baby was born – not where the baby lives, unless this is the same. You can read more about this on page 192.

POSTPARTUM CLASSES

Postpartum exercise classes are available through the *Thuiszorg* organization (see the section on *Medical Organizations*). If you participated in their *zwangerschapsgym*-program (childbirth gym) during pregnancy, you will be invited to attend these classes. During these sessions you will have the opportunity to strengthen muscles which have taken a beating during pregnancy and delivery (abdominals and pelvic floor) as well as all other major muscle groups. Both the *zwangerschapsgym* and the postpartum classes present a wonderful chance to exchange pleasure and pain. In most cases the group of women is the same, so that you get to see and talk with the mommies you went through the last trimester of pregnancy with. The first class is usually a 'baby show' where you come together with all the babies and show off your new off-spring!

English-language postpartum classes are offered through ACCESS (see the information section at the end of the chapter).

SIX-WEEK CHECK-UP

You will go back to either your midwife or gynecologist for a check-up around six weeks postpartum. They will examine the position of your uterus, the healing of any ruptures or exterior incisions and – if you had any medical complications – discuss your general recovery. This is a good time to bring up any particular issues of concern such as postpartum blues and anti-conception, although these may also be discussed with your GP.

OUDERSCHAPSVERLOF (PARENTAL LEAVE)

The law stipulates that both working parents have the right to take a non-paid leave of absence to care for a child (step, adoption or foster child included). You can read more about this on page 194.

MEDICAL ORGANIZATIONS

THUISZORG (HOME CARE) ORGANIZATION

Thuiszorg (literally meaning: home care) has been created to help inform, care for and prevent complications among those who require assistance at home, such as the elderly, people who are chronically ill, people who have just come home from the hospital and people with physical or mental disabilities. Caring for them at home allows home care providers to reach people who might otherwise not have the opportunity to ask for information or advice. Annually, approximately 600,000 people make use of these services. If you require any of these services, including those leading up to the birth of your baby and for follow-up care (*kraamzorg*), check out your local *Thuiszorg* organization.

Among the services *Thuiszorg* offers, aside from the prenatal and postpartum courses we already mentioned, are:
- rental of *bedklossen* (metal frames that raise the bed; required for home birth/first week following delivery) and baby scales
- home care following a serious illness or accident
- home care for the elderly or handicapped
- meal services
- rental of crutches, wheelchairs, special beds, bed pans and lift-ing devices (these will be brought to your house and installed if necessary)
- household help, if due to illness or handicap you are no longer able to do this yourself
- hairdresser and pedicure at home, plus the possibility of buying new clothing from your home
- dietary and nutritional advice.

The *Thuiszorg* system is divided into geographic regions, with services and costs differing from one organization to another. In most regions the *Consultatiebureau* falls under the responsibility of the *Ouder en Kind* (parent and child) department of the *Thuiszorg* organization. To find your local *Thuiszorg office*, check the telephone book or ask your GP or *midwife*, or visit www.zorgkaartnederland.nl/thuiszorg (see also the listing at the end of this chapter). Keep in mind that, whereas some lectures are offered to the general public free of charge, others must be paid for.

Depending on the type of care you require, either the municipality will fund the care you receive, or your insurance policy (as of last year, this is covered by the WLZ – Long-Term Care Act). You will, in most cases, have to contribute in the expenses; check with your insurance company whether you can arrange additional insurance to cover this.

MEDICATION

THE PHARMACY AND THE DRUGSTORE

Prescription drugs are filled at an *apotheek* (pharmacy or apothecary). They computerize your prescriptions and keep a close watch on the drugs you are taking in order to avoid drug interaction. Many bill your insurance company directly for the costs of prescription medicine.

Opening hours are much the same time as for other establishments, but there is always an *apotheek* open in the evenings and on weekends. The name of the nearest *apotheek* that is open during after-hours is posted on your *apotheek*'s door, in the local newspaper, or you can obtain a copy of their schedule at any local pharmacy.

Pharmacies also carry over-the-counter (non-prescription) drugs, vitamins, homeopathic medicines, infant formulas and some baby foods as well as medical supplies such as bandages and thermometers. Drugstores, on the other hand, do not carry prescription drugs, but handle over-the-counter remedies such as throat lozenges, syrups, homeopathic medicines, and pain relievers, as well as toiletries, cosmetics, cleaning supplies and baby formulas and foods.

ALTERNATIVE MEDICINE

Alternative medicine such as acupuncture and homeopathy are also very popular in the Netherlands. For more information, get in touch with the *Alternatieve Geneeswijzen Infolijn* (www.infolijn-ag.nl) or look in the *Gouden Gids* (Yellow Pages) under *Alternatieve Geneeswijzen*. More sites can be found at the end of the chapter.

Homeopathic medicines can be purchased at either an *apotheek*, *drogisterij* or a *reformhuis* (health food store). For more on the insurance coverage of medication, we refer you to page 125.

DENTAL CARE IN THE NETHERLANDS

In the Netherlands, dental care is provided by university-educated dentists, all of whom are government-registered. The quality of the care provided, compared to other countries, is without a doubt, excellent. Of course there are exceptions in both directions but, this being the Netherlands, these are never very extreme.

The Dutch visit their dentist on a regular basis – approximately 85% go once or twice a year – so you won't see many people with poorly cared-for teeth.

TYPES OF PRACTICES
Almost all dental practices in the Netherlands are private, and there are no state practices. Most of them (about 65%) are modest undertakings, with one dentist and one assistant. In the larger cities, there are larger groups, including dentists, assistants, and so-called mouth (dental) hygienists (*mond hygienisten*), who check the state of your teeth and gums and refer you to the dentist if necessary. This allows the practice to diversify its services. In the larger cities there are also separate dental hygienist practices. You can visit these without a referral from your dentist.

RATES
The government determines the rate for services rendered, which makes these rates, generally speaking, lower than in most wealthy countries. All dentists who work in the Netherlands must adhere to these codes. Anything they do is described in uniform (so-called UPT) codes that allow the insurance company to determine the related costs.

INSURANCE
Dentistry is privatized in the Netherlands, meaning that you are responsible for paying for the related costs and not your insurance company. Your insurance company will fully carry the costs of dentistry *for your children* until the age of 18, as well as approximately 75% of

their orthodontic care, and dental surgery for adults. All other dental care (the majority of the care you receive!) can only be insured by taking out additional insurance. Whether or not visits to the dental hygienist are covered by dental insurance, depends on your policy.

SPECIALIZATIONS
In Netherlands you can find all regular dental specializations. The best-known are dental surgeons, who are usually affiliated with a hospital, and orthodontists, who usually have a private practice, though the number of paradontologists (who specialize in gums), endodontologists (root canal specialists), implantologists and children's dentists is increasing. You can only visit one of these if you have been referred to them by a regular dentist.

OTHER ISSUES OF INTEREST
All dentists in the Netherlands must comply with the rules set by the Dutch government on hygiene – you will have little to worry about there. Most dentists will give you a local anesthetic before a painful treatment. Laughing gas is seldom used and, if so, only by a limited number of specialized dentists.

FINDING A DENTIST
New practices, that still take on new patients, often have a website. Make sure to do some comparison shopping before you decide on one. Issues to take into consideration are: philosophy of the dentist / practice, opening hours, is there a dental hygienist, do they remain abreast of new developments, what do they specialize in, does the staff speak English, etc.

This having been said, all Dutch dentists follow a thorough training, make use of modern equipment and run a clean shop. If the Netherlands turns out to be your new location, dental care should be the least of your worries.

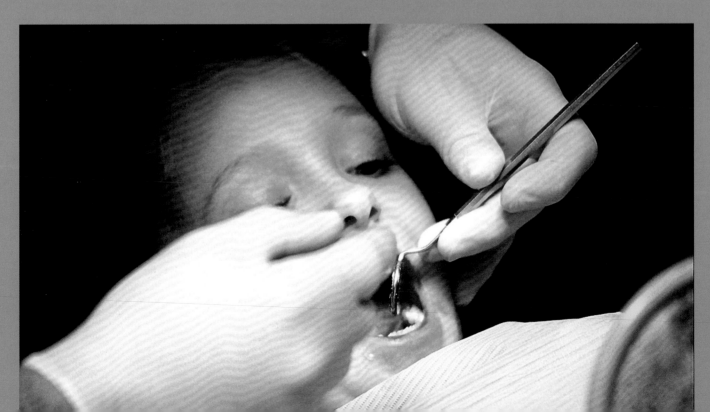

OTHER MEDICAL ISSUES

DENTIST

Many expats save their visits to the dentist for when they go back 'home'. However, also dental emergencies cannot be predicted and it is better to know whom you want to call *before* your gums have decided to call it quits. As when looking for a GP, the *gemeentegids* is a good source of addresses. However, now that you have a GP, you can also simply ask him to recommend you a dentist. Other sources are the Yellow Pages under *Tandartsen*, or colleagues, friends or neighbors. In the Yellow Pages you will also find orthodontists (*Tandartsen – specialisten orthodontie*) and dentists specializing in surgery and other mouth afflictions (*Tandartsen – specialisten mondziekten en kaakchirurgie*).

As is the case with your GP, if you have an emergency after hours (evening, night, weekend), simply call your dentist and you will hear a recording telling you which dentist in your neighborhood is on duty.

Dental care is not covered by the basic insurance you take out in the Netherlands. Children's dental care, however, is covered until age 18. No premium is due for children's health insurance. Please check page 12 and see the insert on page 236 for more on dental care.

PHYSICAL THERAPY / ALTERNATIVE THERAPY

For physical therapy, manual therapy, haptonomy, chiropractics, cranial-sacral therapy and more, check the Yellow Pages under *Fysiotherapeuten*, or ask your GP. Alternative medical care is not covered by the basic insurance policy (see page 125 for more on this subject). You have to take out additional insurance to cover this type of care – and while arranging this, you should check whether you are taking out a *natura* or *restitutie* policy. This in connection with the fact that, in the case of a *natura* policy, you have to make use of a(n) (alternative) medical care provider with whom your insurance company has reached an agreement, in which case the insurance company will pay your bills directly. You are free to select your own medical care provider in the case of a *restitutie* policy, but then you will have to pay your own bills first and request restitution from your insurance company (see page 124).

If you have an existing insurance policy, or are participating in a collective (company or educational institute) policy, make sure you check with your insurance company whether they cover your particular health cost needs and have a contract with the medical care provider of your choice. And do not forget that they often require that you hand in a referral notice from your GP, stating that you need this type of therapy, before they are willing to cover the costs (see page 229).

PHYSICAL DISABILITIES

The Netherlands has an excellent record when it comes to assisting individuals with physical disabilities. If you are in this position and require special help, contact the city hall (*gemeentehuis*) to see what they can do for you. For instance, depending on your situation or disability, they can help you finance the adaptation of your home to meet your needs. There are also many ways in which other organizations in the Netherlands, such as *Thuiszorg* (see earlier on), can assist. All you have to do is ask.

As for insurance coverage when it comes to physical disabilities, check not only with your insurance company, but also look into what the municipality covers, as they help cover non-medical expenses, such as assisted living, protected living and occupational activities.

PUBLIC AND SEXUAL HEALTH

If you are traveling to Third World countries and need injections before you go, you will get them at the city clinics/Municipal Health Service (referred to as the GGD – *Gemeentelijke Geneeskunde Dienst* – or GG&GD – *Gemeentelijke Gezondheid & Geneeskundige Dienst*). They will advise on what is required as opposed to what is recommended plus they are responsible for advising the community at large on PAP smears, mammograms, sexually transmitted diseases and vaccinations for babies and older children. You can also visit the Travel Clinic in several of the bigger cities or the KLM Travel Clinic at various locations for information on traveling to Third World Countries – you can find their websites at the end of the chapter.

For information on sexual health and birth control, you can contact the Rutgers organization, which has branches in several of the bigger cities across the Netherlands and has an international, English-language website. For information on AIDS and STDs, you can contact SOAAIDS, see our list of resources at the end of the chapter, SOA is the Dutch acronym for STD, or sexually transmitted diseases.

For more information on the public health program of the Netherlands, including the immunization program for children, visit www.rivm.nl and click on *English*.

MENTAL HEALTH CARE AND ADDICTIONS

Mental health care is available for children and young people, adults, the elderly, addicts, and so-called forensic-psychiatric patients. For more information on the services available, you can contact the Regional Institutions for Ambulatory Mental Health Care (RIAGG). They have several offices in the Netherlands; check your local telephone book to see if they have a listing where you live, or ask your GP. If you wish to see a private psychologist or psychiatrist, you can also ask your GP to refer you to one, or you can find one yourself that feels right to you. Don't forget to ask for a referral notice!

For problems with addictions, there are also several options: there are ambulant centers for alcohol and drugs (Consultatiebureau voor Alcohol en Drugs), institutions for social work that focus on offering care to people with drug problems, clinics for treatment, and outpatient clinics with special departments for addicts. Other options are the Arta Lievegoed Zorggroep, which has an anthropological basis and is for both mental health care, physical disabilities and addictions, or the Jellinek Clinic. Ask your GP for more information.

DEATH

In case of death in the family or a visiting friend, it is best to call your GP, who can certify the death. He can walk you through what is required in the Netherlands. Then you will have to call the embassy or consulate of the country of which the deceased is a passport holder. They will help take care of the required formalities of their country and help notify the next of kin, if necessary.

EMERGENCIES

In case of an emergency, call the national emergency number 112.
State whether you need an ambulance, the police or the fire department and they will connect you with the correct department

GENERAL

MINISTERIE VAN GEZONDHEID WELZIJN EN SPORT
Ministry of Health, Welfare and Sports
Parnassusplein 5, 2511 vx The Hague
P.O. Box 20350, 2500 ej The Hague
Tel.: 070 340 79 11
www.government.nl/ministries/vws

THE ACCESS GUIDE/FAQ SHEET ON HEALTH CARE IN THE NETHERLANDS
This publication concisely covers a wide range of health topics from birth to death, insurance to legal rights, home care to hospitals, and special services to social services
www.access-nl.org

EXPAT MEDICAL ADVISOR
Contact Christine Houser MD
Tel.: 06 28 616 818
www.expatmedicaladvisor.com

INTERNATIONAL HEALTH CENTERS

INTERNATIONAL HEALTH CENTRE THE HAGUE
Prins Willemstraat 41, 2584 ht The Hague
Tel.: 070 306 51 11
www.ihch.nl

BRONOVO HOSPITAL
Bronovolaan 5, 2597 ax The Hague
Tel.: 070 312 41 41
www.bronovo.nl /expats

WASSENAAR HEALTH CENTRE
Rijksstraatweg 324, 2242 ab Wassenaar
Tel.: 070 512 72 00
www.bronovo.nl

CENTRE MEDICAL FRANCOPHONE
Laan van Middenburg 2, 2275 cc Voorburg
Tel.: 070 386 21 91
www.cmfonline.nl

HEALTHCARE FOR INTERNATIONALS
Gebouw Strijp-Z
Tilburgseweg-West 100, 5652 np Eindhoven
www.h4i.nl

FOR TRAVELERS

LANDELIJK COÖRDINATIECENTRUM REIZIGERSADVISERING (LCR)
National Coordination Center for Traveler's Advice
The central organization in the Netherlands that occupies itself with the prevention of disease among travelers
P.O. Box 1008, 1000 ba Amsterdam
Tel.: 0900 95 84
www.lcr.nl

KLM HEALTH SERVICES
Gebouw 133
Stationsplein N.O., 1117 bv Schiphol-Oost
Tel.: 020 649 51 87
www.klmhealthservices.com

TRAVEL CLINIC HAVENZIEKENHUIS
Haringvliet 2, 3011 td Rotterdam
Tel.: 010 412 38 88
www.havenziekenhuis.nl

TROPENCENTRUM AMC
For vaccinations and medical examinations
Meibergdreef 9, Amsterdam
Tel.: 020 566 38 00
www.tropencentrum.nl

DEREISDOKTER.NL
medical information for travelers
www.dereisdokter.nl

HUISARTSEN (GP) SEARCH ENGINES

www.huisartsen.nl
www.huisarts-gids.com
www.zorg.independer.nl/huisartsen
Medische Gezondheid Nu app: available in the App Store

HAVING A BABY

THE ACCESS GUIDE/FAQ SHEET ON HAVING A BABY IN THE NETHERLANDS
Information for expectant parents, parents of babies and toddlers. Topics include pregnancy, child health and safety, insurances, support groups, childcare services
www.access-nl.org

INTERNATIONAL CONFEDERATION OF MIDWIVES
Supports the interests of pregnant women, mothers and midwives
Laan van Meerdervoort 70, 2517 an The Hague
Tel.: 070 306 05 20
www.internationalmidwives.org

STICHTING KNOV
Midwifery in the Netherlands
Mercatorlaan 1200, 3528 bl Utrecht
Tel.: 030 282 31 00
www.knov.nl

ZWANGERSCHAPSYOGA
Pregnancy Yoga
Central Registration of yoga-teachers qualified to teach pregnancy course Samsara
www.yoga-nl.nu

ACUPUNCTURE

NEDERLANDSE VERENIGING VOOR ACUPUNCTUUR, N.V.A.
Dutch Association for Acupuncture
P.O. Box 2198, 3800 cd Amersfoort
Tel.: 033 461 61 41 – www.acupunctuur.nl

MEDICATION

APOTHEEK
Pharmacies per location
www.apotheek.nl

CONSUMED
www.consumed.nl

TO ORDER MEDICINES ONLINE
www.dokteronline.com
www.kring-apotheek.nl
www.medicijnen.nl
www.docteronline.com

INSURANCE

www.independer.nl
www.kiesbeter.nl
www.zn.nl
www.zorgverzekering.org/eng

ALTERNATIVE MEDICINE

NEDERLANDSE VERENIGING VAN KLASSIEK HOMEOPATHEN
Dutch Association for Classic Homeopathy
P.O. Box 710, 2400 AS Alphen aan den Rijn
Tel.: 0172 49 96 95
www.nvkh.nl

VERENIGING VOOR NATUURKUNDIG THERAPEUTEN
Association for Natural Therapists
Liendertseweg 112-2, 3815 BJ Amersfoort
Tel.: 033 472 60 03
www.vnt-nederland.nl

ALTERATIVE MEDICINE/CARE
www.infolijn-ag.nl

SEXUAL HEALTH

SOAAIDS FOUNDATION (ALSO FOR STDS)
Keizersgracht 390-394, 1016 GB Amsterdam
Tel.: 020 626 26 69
www.soaaids.nl
www.aidsfonds.nl

RUTGERS INTERNATIONAL
P. O. Box 9022, 3506 GA Utrecht
Oudenoord 176-178, 3513 EV Utrecht
Tel.: 030 231 34 31
www.rutgers.nl

DIET

NEDERLANDSE VERENIGING VAN DIËTISTEN
Dutch Association for Dieticians
De Molen 93, 3995 AW Houten
Tel.: 030 634 62 22
www.nvdietist.nl

MENTAL HEALTH

NEDERLANDS INSTITUUT VOOR PSYCHOLOGEN
Dutch Institute for Psychologists
P.O. Box 9921, 1006 AP Amsterdam
Tel.: 020 410 62 22
www.psynip.nl

NEDERLANDSE VERENIGING VOOR PSYCHIATRIE
Dutch Association for Psychiatry
Mercatorlaan 1200, 3528 BL Utrecht
Tel.: 030 288 84 00
www.nvvp.net

PSYQ
International Mental Health Services (IMHS)
Overschiestraat 61, 1062 XD, Amsterdam
Tel.: 088 357 46 00 - 06 12 21 52 55
Carel Reinierszkade 197, 2593 HR The Hague
Tel.: 088 357 34 78 - 06 52 56 83 82
Torenallee 20, 5617 BC Eindhoven
Tel.: 088 357 36 95
www.psyq.nl/expatriates/expats

PARNASSIA
Psycho medical centers in the Hague region
Tel.: 070 391 63 91
www.parnassia.nl

U CENTER
Julianastraat 23a, 6285 AH Epen
De Horst 1, 3971 KR Driebergen
www.u-center.nl

ADDICTION

ADDICTION AND MENTAL HEALTH
Trimbos Instituut: www.trimbos.nl

ALCOHOLICS ANONYMOUS (AA)
Tel.: 020 625 60 57
www.aa-nederland.nl

NATIONAL DRUG INFORMATION
www.drugsinfo.nl

AUTISM

AUTISM ASSOCIATION FOR OVERSEAS FAMILIES (NL)
Parents and professionals working together for children with autism
Berglustlaan 15b, 3054 BA Rotterdam
www.aaof.info

SPECIALIZED AUTISM SERVICES (THE HAGUE)
Coordinator: Kelly Lynn Redden
www.specializedautismservices.com

PHYSIOTHERAPY

KNGF
DE FYSIOTHERAPEUT
P.O. Box 248, 3800 AE Amersfoort
Stadsring 159b, 3817 BA Amersfoort
Tel.: 033 467 29 00
www.fysionet.nl

DUTCH ASSOCIATION FOR MANUAL THERAPY, NVMT
Orthopedic Manipulative Therapy
P.O. Box 248, 3800 AE Amersfoort
Stadsring 159b, 3817 BA Amersfoort
Tel.: 033 467 29 00
www.fysionet.nl

DENTAL CARE

www.tandarts.nl
www.tandarts.pagina.nl
www.tandartsplein.nl

CHAPTER 11

From world-famous museums to an ice-skating extravaganza equaled by none, the Netherlands is one of the best-kept travel secrets and, now that you're living here, it's all right at your doorstep. Considering that the entire country is only 310 kilometers at its longest stretch, you should have no excuse for not exploring this rich cultural realm from top to bottom. This chapter will set you on your way with an up-to-date selection of events for 2016 and beyond, the top ten tourist attractions, an exclusive list of extra haunts favored by the Dutch themselves, plus two special sections; one for antique lovers intent on pursuing the perennial trail of the Netherlands' treasures, and the other for outdoor-lovers.

Veel plezier ! (Enjoy!)

Things to do in Your Free Time

CONTRIBUTING AUTHORS SHIRLEY AGUDO, STEPHANIE DIJKSTRA, CONNIE MOSER AND STEVEN STUPP

CULTURAL LIFE

Small on land but big on culture, the Netherlands is filled to the brim with a rich blend of visual and performing arts steeped in history. Home to almost 1,000 museums, the most famous of which are the Rijksmuseum and the Vincent van Gogh Museum in Amsterdam, the Kröller-Müller Museum in Otterlo, and Boijmans van Beuningen and the Kunsthal in Rotterdam, the Netherlands offers a cultural pick-me-up just waiting for you to imbibe. With such a rich history of Golden Age painters and other artists, including Rembrandt, Vermeer, Van Gogh, Jan Steen, Frans Hals, M.C. Escher, Karel Appel and Piet Mondriaan, Dutch museums are bulging with homegrown legacies. Even the small Mauritshuis Museum in The Hague, which is known for, among others, the famous 'Vermeer' and 'Rembrandt by Himself' exhibitions, has made a name for itself.

From the artist's palette to the architect's drawing table, the Netherlands is home to no less than 55,000 historic monuments and buildings officially protected by preservation laws. These ancient buildings, some several centuries old, can be found not only in the larger inner cities of Amsterdam, Leiden, The Hague and Delft, but virtually everywhere. At the other extreme, the Netherlands is also renowned for its modern architecture, and there are many modern-day architects such as Rem Koolhaas, Herman Hertzberger, Aldo van Eyck and Jo Coenen, whose designs are admired by people the world over.

Performing arts venues, such as various theater groups, both 'mainstream' and experimental, are active all year round in theaters, parks and on the streets. Dance groups that are invited to perform across the globe include the Nederlands Dans Theater, Scapino Ballet and the National Ballet. Every year, The Hague hosts the Cadance Festival and Utrecht hosts the Spring Festival. Every other year, you will also find the Holland Dance Festival in The Hague.

Throughout the whole month of June, you can visit the Holland Festival in Amsterdam, combining all of the performing arts, while the Early Music Festival in Utrecht is famous for its medieval, renaissance and baroque music. All the major cities have concert halls (such as the Concertgebouw in Amsterdam), where you can enjoy classical concerts and operas. And then there is Pinkpop, Paaspop and Parkpop, all three for popular music, and last, but definitely not least, the wild and woolly North Sea Jazz Festival.

And for movie buffs who want to see more than just the commercial blockbusters, there are film festivals, such as the International Film Festival Rotterdam in February, the Dutch Film Festival in September, the World Wide Video Festival in April, and the International Documentary Film Festival in December.

And while you're on the 'expat' trail, be sure to catch a glimpse of the busiest seaport on earth in Rotterdam. Nearly destroyed in World War II, the city's modern splendor is a striking testimony to Dutch ingenuity.

GETTING IN

Information about what is happening in the Netherlands is available on a variety of websites and English-language print media, a list of which is available in the reference section at the end of this chapter. Tickets for most entertainment and cultural events are available through the network of local information offices (vvvs) throughout the country, or through www.ticketmaster.nl, or www.ticketline.nl. A list of these organizations can also be found at the end of this chapter. Tickets can also be purchased at the respective theaters. For the more popular shows you should reserve tickets long in advance. For movies, you can find an overview for the whole of the Netherlands on the website listed at the end of this chapter.

If you are particularly interested in museums, you might want to buy a *museumkaart* (museum pass), which is available at all participating museums (or via their website, www.museumkaart.nl – Dutch language only). This card gives you either free or discounted admission to more than 400 museums throughout the country, plus, in most cases, it allows you to cut the line. If you are older than 19, it will cost you € 59.50. A youth pass (under 19) costs € 32.45. There is a € 4.95 administration cost the first year you buy the card.

In order to encourage younger people – ages 12 through 30 – to take an interest in culture, the *cultureel jongeren paspoort* (CJP – Cultural Youth Pass) has been introduced. It costs € 17.50 and can be bought at several locations including the Uitburos, the vvv offices and through their website (www.cjp.nl – you can click on *English* at the bottom of the web page. To buy it, click on *Koop je pas* on the home page). The CJP offers you considerable reductions for many of the events listed above, and on their website you will find an overview of what is happening on the cultural scene.

SELECTED CULTURAL EVENTS IN 2016 – 2017

One of the major advantages of expat life in the Netherlands is the number of cultural activities that non-Dutch speakers can enjoy. The following selected cultural events for 2016 through 2017 are sure to please everyone regardless of their linguistic abilities.

NATIONAL MUSEUM WEEK
Dates: Apr. 16–24, 2016 (April 8-16, 2017)
This is a weekend in which many museums open their doors to the public. There will be more than 100 organized excursions. Furthermore, there will be free films, slide shows, extra tours, a look behind the scenes, demonstrations, workshops and treasure hunts for children. You can recognize the participating museums by the special red-white-and-blue flags of the Museum Week.
Across the country, various museums
www.nationalemuseumweek.nl

TONG TONG FAIR
Dates: May 28-Jun. 5, 2016
For 12 days, the Eurasian cultures and their global contexts are put in the spotlight on a 20,000 m² festival site in The Hague. It is a combination of music festival and large indoor market, highlighting 3 food halls, 5 stages, presentations, workshops and artists from Asia and Europe.
The Hague, Malieveld
www.tongtongfair.nl

HOLLAND FESTIVAL
Dates: Jun. 4-26, 2016
Innovative stage performances in Amsterdam. The world's most celebrated artists perform one whole month in, among others, the Stadsschouwburg, the Muziektheater and the Concertgebouw. Visitors can enjoy opera, theater, music, dance and film.
Various theaters in Amsterdam
www.hollandfestival.nl

PINKPOP
Dates: Jun. 10-12, 2016
This year is the 46th edition of what is touted as the world's oldest pop music festival. It is a pleasant, if packed, international open-air affair with various pop artists performing their hits.
Landgraaf Megaland
www.pinkpop.nl

OEROL FESTIVAL
Dates: Jun. 10-19, 2016
10 days of theater on location: street theater, world music and visual arts.
Various locations on Terschelling (one of the Wadden Islands, north of the Netherlands),
www.oerol.nl

FESTIVAL CLASSIQUE
Dates: Jun. 10-19, 2016
5 days of classical concerts for all ages and tastes.
Various locations: Scheveningen
www.festivalclassique.nl

FESTIVAL MUNDIAL
Dates: Jun. 25-26, 2016
Multicultural festival with, among others, theater and music from all corners of the world, as well as world art and culture.
Tilburg Leijpark
www.festivalmundial.nl

PARKPOP
Date: Jun. 26, 2016
The largest free open-air pop festival in Europe with local and foreign pop groups on two stages. There will also be a pop market and a playground for children.
Zuiderpark, The Hague
www.parkpop.nl

NORTH SEA JAZZ FESTIVAL
Dates: Jul. 8-10, 2016
One of the largest and best-known international jazz festivals in the world which has, in its decades-long history, enjoyed performances by virtually all the jazz and contemporary music heroes of all time. More than 8 hours of music on 15 stages per day, with contributions by more than 1,300 jazz musicians.
Ahoy Rotterdam
www.northseajazz.com

DELFT CHAMBER MUSIC FESTIVAL
Dates: Jul. 28-Aug. 7, 2016
A unique chamber music festival with a variety of concerts.
Museum Het Prinsenhof, Delft
www.delftmusicfestival.nl

SUMMER CARNIVAL
Dates: Jul. 29-30, 2016
An exotic music, dance and float parade, which turns the inner city of Rotterdam upside down. Dancers in fantastic costumes and many swinging orchestras on decorated floats are followed by thousands of dancing visitors. Includes the queen election on the 18th, the Battle of Drums on the 29th and the street parade itself on the 30th.
Center of Rotterdam
www.rotterdamunlimited.com/zomercarnaval

CANAL GAY PARADE
Date: Aug. 6, 2016
Amsterdam's celebration of all things Gay, Lesbian, Bi, and Transgender, which has grown into one of the world's premier Pride parades.
Amsterdam canals
www.canalparade.nl

LOWLANDS
Dates: Aug. 19-21, 2016
Lowlands is Holland's biggest and most adventurous outdoor music festival. It offers a choice of the best alternative music, theater, film, stand-up comedy, visual arts, literature and more.
Walibi World, Biddinghuizen
www.lowlands.nl

PREUVENEMINT
Dates: Aug. 25-28, 2016
Four-day culinary event, with over 30 stands acting as restaurants. Beer and soft drinks available at separate stands. Live music on a permanent open-air stage.
Vrijthof Square, Maastricht
www.preuvenemint.nl

UITMARKT AMSTERDAM
Dates: Aug. 26-28, 2016
Opening of the new cultural season with shows on indoor and outdoor stages. Also an information market and a book market.
Museumplein and Leidseplein, Amsterdam
www.uitmarkt.nl

WORLD HARBOR FESTIVAL
Dates: Sep. 2-4, 2016
Experience daily life in the biggest harbor in the world. This festival is all about maritime, educational and cultural activities in which the harbor of Rotterdam and its industrial area are the main feature.
Harbor of Rotterdam
www.wereldhavendagen.nl

HAAGS UIT FESTIVAL
Date: Sep. 3-4, 2016
At this festival, music ensembles, dance companies, orchestras and theater groups give you a taste of what is to come in the new season. The performances are held on various stages of the theaters on the Spui and there is a literary, cultural, theater and information market.
Lange Voorhout and Spuiplein, The Hague
www.haagsuitfestival.nl, see also www.denhaag.com

CROSSING BORDER FESTIVAL
Dates: Nov. 2-6, 2016
A refreshing look at poetry, writing and music, with approximately 120 performances on various stages by poets, writers and musicians.
Koninklijke Schouwburg and Het Nationale Toneelgebouw in The Hague
www.crossingborder.nl

INTERNATIONAL DOCUMENTARY FESTIVAL (IDFA)
Dates: Nov. 16-27, 2016
One of the biggest documentary film festivals in the world, with more than 150 documentaries and an extensive workshop program.
In and around Pathé Tuschinsky and Pathé de Munt Theaters, Amsterdam
www.idfa.nl

INTERNATIONAL FILM FESTIVAL ROTTERDAM
Dates: Jan. 25-Feb. 5, 2017
International film festival with non-commercial films from all across the world, amounting to approximately 200 movies, documentaries, short films and videos.
Center of Rotterdam
www.iffr.com

FOR ANTIQUE LOVERS ONLY

The Netherlands is replete with a regular cache of antique fairs, exhibitions, shopping routes and auctions (*veilingen*) sure to satisfy the most discriminating antique lover and buyer. In fact, certain venues are world-renowned meccas for museum-quality pieces. Whether you're a professional buyer, an amateur with deep pockets and good taste, or you just enjoy looking at beautiful old things, you won't want to miss these annual events.

Here are a few of our favorites, beginning with the two biggest and best:

PAN AMSTERDAM
Date: Nov. 20-27, 2016
Known as the best national arts and antiques fair with prominent dealers and gallery owners from the Netherlands and Flanders, PAN Amsterdam is regarded as the most important fair in the world for Dutch glass and silver. Equally attractive is its reputation for an excellent price/quality ratio, in other words, good value for your money.
RAI, Amsterdam
www.pan.nl

OUTDOOR ACTIVITIES

Once you've expanded your cultural horizons, you will need to save some of your spare time to improve your physical well-being while living in the Netherlands. This may be one of the most populated countries on the planet, but there is still plenty of space and activity for the outdoor enthusiast, including cycling, running, hiking, wave- and kite surfing, wall climbing, horseback riding, parachuting, mini-golf, archery, bird watching, camping or aerobics. This country being as small at it is, the majority of these activities will not make the outing much more than a day trip...

Leisure time can be filled with easy access activities such as cycling along the 35,000 kilometers of bicycle paths in the country, either as a slow-going family activity or on a race bike for a real workout. The ANWB and VVV sell useful and detailed maps of the whole country as seen from the cyclist's and the hiker's needs. They – and the site www.recreatienoordholland.nl – can also provide you with information on a whole host of recreational activities in and around the Dutch coast, such as in-line skating, mountain-biking, kite-flying, horseback riding, wind surfing, canoeing, sailing, and off-shore fishing, to name a few.

For the intrepid walker, flower parks and gardens are popular, as are walks through castle gardens, sand dunes, mud flats and the numerous parks in the country. Visit www.natuurlijkwandelen.nl for inspiration on beautiful walks through the Dutch countryside. The pinnacle of the walking frenzy is probably the *vierdaagse* in Nijmegen where more than 45,000 hikers converge for a four-day-long hike in July (see www.4daagse.nl for information and registration in English). Also Holland.com is a good site for ideas and the VVV offices also offer detailed information, guides and maps.

For the avid golfer there is a large selection of golf courses in the country (see the reference pages at the end of the chapter for more information), however do not forget that, to play on the Dutch courses, you must have a golfing permit, called GVB (*Golf Vaardigheidsbewijs*), a registered handicap, or a course permit (*baanpermissie*; permission to play on a specific course, issued by the course itself, subject to conditions). For more information, check www.ngf.nl for the Netherlands Golf Federation. For those looking for something a little spicier on the course, Farmersgolf is the latest variation on the classic game of golf. Played on pastures, over ditches, through forests and amongst the cows, the game was invented in the Netherlands on the pastures of the Weenink Cheese Farm in Lievelde. For more information, see www.farmersgolf.com.

Below are two intrinsically Dutch outdoor activities, popular among young and old, that allow you to explore a part of the country that not many people take the time to see, but that none of those who do ever forget:

NORTH TO SOUTH ON FOOT: THE PIETERPAD ROUTE
Bicycling is not the only cross-country sport in the Netherlands; walking on a well-laid-out path is another – 490 kilometers worth of walking, that is, from Pieterburen in the northern province of Groningen to the Pieterberg (Pieter Mountain) in Maastricht in the southernmost province of Limburg. Objective: to experience all that the Netherlands has to offer under one low sky and, of course, to commune with nature while getting a hearty dose of exercise.

Different routes are detailed in a guidebook, a prerequisite for your journey and available at the VVV or ANWB offices. If you are feeling really ambitious, an extension of the trail continues on through France all the way to the Mediterranean Sea.

The Pieterpad has been divided into a number of *etappes*, 26 in total. The distance of each *etappe* varies anywhere from 15 to 20 kilometers and can easily be covered in one day (even by inexperienced walkers). It is also possible to walk the *etappes* in two directions, as in from North to South or from South to North; the guide book describes both options.

There are actually two guide books; the first, *Pieterpad Deel I*, maps out the 13 different *etappes* from Pieterburen to Vorden (somewhere in the middle of Holland); the second, *Pieterpad Deel II*, maps out the next 13 *etappes* from Vorden to St. Pietersberg. Unfortunately, this guide has not yet been translated into other languages, nonetheless, the maps are pretty self-explanatory – in fact, essential.

Keep in mind that you will presumably be walking from point A to point B. This requires parking your car in the one spot and using public transportation to get to the other – or to get back to where you parked your car after you have completed the walk.

For more information, visit the sites at the end of the chapter.

THE ULTIMATE ADVENTURE: MUD-FLAT WALKING TO THE ISLANDS

To the north of the Netherlands lie the five *Wadden Islands*: Texel, Vlieland, Terschelling, Ameland and Schiermonnikoog. Between these islands lie the famous Wadden, the sea-beds of the Wadden Sea – together with the German and the Danish section, this is one of the UNESCO World Heritage sites, measuring 11,500 km² in total. Twice a day, thousands of cubic liters of North Sea water stream through the Wadden, accounting for the tremendous riches of sea life present here.

During low tide, it is possible to walk across the sea-bed and experience the abundance of mussels and oysters and clams, amongst other life forms residing here. This is the famous 'Wadlopen', which is commonly translated into 'mud-flat walking' – not to be confused with mud-walking which takes place in the Northern tip of Friesland.

The simple algorithm of high and low tides are best not left to the uninitiated: visitors are advised to never venture off into the rich life of the Wadden unattended, as it may cost you your life. The tide has been known to rise within minutes, leaving you to the torrents of the seas without warning. Fortunately for us city, or other, folk, there are many guides who have lived their whole lives on these wet planes and who can safely let you in on the treasures of the Wadden Sea bottoms.

Wadlopen takes place from mid-March to early October. To arrange a tour, visit the sites at the end of the chapter.

TEFAF MAASTRICHT

Date: Mar. 10-19, 2017

In the very southeast corner of the Netherlands in the city of Maastricht, The European Fine Art Fair (TEFAF) is an annual blockbuster event drawing more than 74,000 visitors from around the world. A paradise for antique buffs and buyers, the TEFAF is one of the world's most prestigious arts and antiques fairs, and a trendsetter in the field. The works presented by the 275 art and antiques dealers from around the world are museum-quality and unrivaled anywhere in scale and diversity.

MECC, Maastricht

www.tefaf.com

AUCTION HOUSES

For those of you who prefer the fast-action bidding scene, the Netherlands offers monthly opportunities to attend both major and minor auctions or *veilingen*. Christie's (www.christies.com) and Sotheby's (www.sothebys.com) lead the pack in Amsterdam. Watch for notices of their *kijkdagen* (open viewing days) where you can survey what will be auctioned in forthcoming days. Some of the smaller houses are also well worth a visit, such as De Zwaan in Amsterdam (www.dezwaan.nl) and the VendueHuis in The Hague (www.venduehuis.nl).

ANTIQUE SHOPPING

While delftware is often foremost on the shopping list for visitors, the Netherlands offers a plethora of antique treasures for every budget. In almost every major city, the VVV information office has a brochure with antique shopping routes or, at the very minimum, suggestions on what streets have the largest concentration of such shops.

A good example of this is the world-famous *Spiegelkwartier*, a very historic and picturesque neighborhood just across the bridge from the acclaimed Rijksmuseum in Amsterdam. Featuring over 80 specialized art and antique shops, this area has been the heart of the national art and antiques trade for more than 100 years. From archaeological finds to 17th-century furniture, glass and Dutch delftware, from oriental art to art nouveau, from tribal art to contemporary art, from old medical instruments and clocks to jewelry, icons, paintings and Old Master prints, the Spiegelkwartier has it all. It even has its own website at www.spiegelkwartier.nl.

Another great venue is the summer-long antique and book market held on the *Lange Voorhout* plaza in The Hague where, on Thursdays (10 A.M. to 6 P.M.) and Sundays (10 A.M. to 5 P.M.) from mid-May to the beginning of October, you can immerse yourself in leisurely antique browsing with some requisite café-sitting on the perimeter (www.haagseantiekenboekenmarkt.nl). According to the VVV of The Hague, the street with the largest concentration of antique shops in the city is the *Denneweg*, a curiosity-seeker's paradise, and also a very popular restaurant and bar area. The *Frederikstraat* is also known for its proliferation of antiques shops – including antiquarian bookshops – as is the *Javastraat*.

TOP TEN TOURIST ATTRACTIONS

THE TOP TEN PLACES THAT DRAW THE MOST FOREIGN VISITORS
Tourists and expatriates alike come to the Netherlands to admire its cultural heritage, with lyrical windmills, spectacular fields of tulips and renowned Dutch artists such as Van Gogh, Rembrandt, Vermeer, Hals and Steen completing the picture.

Below you will find the ten most popular sites frequented by visitors. While Amsterdam remains the biggest draw with its rock-and-roll reputation, some of the best-kept travel secrets lie well beyond this hub, and there's much more to see within a very short reach.

To locate these attractions, simply refer to the map on this page. For the main zoos and other children's attractions, see Chapter 8.

1. VAN GOGH MUSEUM
Amsterdam's top tourist attraction is devoted almost entirely to the work of one of the most popular artists the world has ever known, spanning his early years in South Holland, through his Impressionist years in Paris, to his last years in St. Rémy. This museum is the perfect size for those short on time.
Paulus Potterstraat 7, Amsterdam
www.vangoghmuseum.nl

2. ANNE FRANK HOUSE
Possibly the most deserving of all the Netherlands' major tourist attractions, the Anne Frank House, provides fascinating insight into the Frank family's life in hiding from 1942 until 1944, during the Nazi occupation. The museum also provides information on the plight of the 100,000 Dutch Jews who were killed in the Holocaust and hosts a variety of other exhibitions, focusing on such issues as persecution and the repression of freedom of expression, both past and present. Note: entrance tickets are bought online!
Prinsengracht 267, Amsterdam
www.annefrank.org

3. RIJKSMUSEUM AMSTERDAM
This largest museum in the Netherlands, which recently reopened its doors after a complete renovation, houses an internationally renowned collection with paintings from the 17th-century Dutch

TOURIST ATTRACTIONS

1. DE EFTELING, KAATSHEUVEL [NEAR TILBURG]
2. KINDERDIJK, KINDERDIJK
3. KEUKENHOF, LISSE
4. VAN GOGH MUSEUM,
   ANNE FRANK HOUSE,
   THE TROPEN MUSEUM, AMSTERDAM
5. ZUIDERZEE MUSEUM, ENKHUIZEN
6. MADURODAM, THE HAGUE
7. DELFT

8. DELFSHAVEN, PORT OF ROTTERDAM
9. THE KRÖLLER-MÜLLER MUSEUM, OTTERLO [NEAR ARNHEM]
10. BIESBOSCH NATIONAL PARK
11. DE HAAR CASTLE, HAARZUILENS
12. FRANEKER PLANETARIUM, FRANEKER
13. THORN [NEAR ROERMOND]
14. BOSCHPLAAT NATURE RESERVE, TERSCHELLING
15. PALEIS HET LOO, APELDOORN
16. WATERLAND NEELTJE JANS, BURG-HAAMSTEDE
    [BETWEEN THE ISLANDS OF SCHOUWEN AND NOORD-BEVELAND]
17. NOORBEEK [NEAR MAASTRICHT]
18. HUNNEBEDDEN/DOLMENS, BORGER [BETWEEN ASSEN AND EMMEN]
19. VEERE [SOUTH-WEST PROVINCE OF ZEELAND]
20. WESTEREMDEN [GRONINGEN]

Republic, the 'Golden Age', including works by Rembrandt (the most famous of which is the imposing *Night Watch*), Johannes Vermeer, Frans Hals and Jan Steen. Silver, delftware, doll's houses, prints, drawings, Asiatic art and Dutch history are also featured.
Museumstraat 1, Amsterdam
www.rijksmuseum.nl

(In inimitable Dutch style, the Rijksmuseum, in conjunction with Amsterdam Airport Schiphol, has opened the world's first, permanent airport museum exhibition center. A fly-through peek at Dutch art history features exhibits by the masters themselves, including Jan Steen, Pieter de Hoogh, Jacob van Ruisdael and, of course, Rembrandt. Entrance is free to this 'art on tap' situated behind passport control on the 'Holland Boulevard', the corridor between the E and F Pier. Due to renovations, this exhibition is closed and hopes to reopen in the fall of 2016).

4. KEUKENHOF
From late March through the end of May, visitors come in droves to see the display of over 7,000,000 flowers in the famous Keukenhof Gardens. The 70-acre gardens offer a breathtaking, immaculate display of tulips, hyacinths, daffodils and amaryllis planted by the Netherlands' leading flower growers. Not to be missed.
Open: Mar. 24 - May 16, 2016
Stationsweg 166a, Lisse
www.keukenhof.nl

5. DELFT

Famous for its distinctive blue and white porcelain, Delft continues to charm visitors – and shoppers. Once home to Dutch artist Vermeer, it has an abundance of beautifully preserved 17th-century buildings (including the imposing Town Hall and the Old Church), requisite tree-lined canals and a daunting array of porcelain shops.
www.delft.nl

6. THE KRÖLLER-MÜLLER MUSEUM

Located in the wooded parkland of De Hoge Veluwe National Park, you can either drive your car or borrow the white bicycles available at the park gates, free of charge, to travel the couple of kilometers to this museum, which ranks as the third most important collection of art in the Netherlands. Over almost 90 paintings and over 180 drawings by Van Gogh (roughly 50 of which are on display at any given time) and other artists such as Seurat, Monet and Picasso are featured, including a Sculpture Garden second to none and worth the trip in itself.
Houtkampweg 6, Otterlo
www.kmm.nl

7. DELFSHAVEN / PORT OF ROTTERDAM

Delfshaven is where the Pilgrim Fathers departed for the New World in 1620. The tiny harbor has been preserved to look much as it did in centuries past, with the addition of some trendy waterfront restaurants. Across the road at the Spido Landing Stage, tours by boat offer unique insight into modern life in the world's busiest seaport.
Delfshaven/Spido Cruises: www.spido.nl
www.rotterdamhistorischdelfshaven.nl
Historisch Museum Rotterdam, Korte Hoogstraat 31, Rotterdam
www.hmr.rotterdam.nl

8. MADURODAM

'All Netherlands in a day' is how to best describe this miniature scale-model town where you can see all of the Netherlands' major cities and landmarks up close and personal, with many mechanized exhibits, including busy motorways and sailing ships.
George Maduroplein 1, The Hague
www.madurodam.nl

9. KINDERDIJK

A UNESCO World Heritage Site and the most archetypal of all Dutch scenes, with 19 windmills idyllically situated along a broad canal. The Visitors' windmill opens April 1, with canal cruises beginning on the same day. During July and August the mills are put into action on Saturdays (In 2016, the National Windmill Days, when most windmills across the country are open to the public, will be on May 14-15. Presumably, in 2017, they will be on May 13-14.)
By the Lek River, southeast of Rotterdam
www.kinderdijk.nl

10. THE ARCHEON

This archaeological theme park in Alphen aan de Rijn in South Holland is world-renowned among history buffs. There are reconstructions of villages from three major time periods: Prehistory, the Roman Period, and the Middle Ages. It is a 'live' museum where people in period dress live and work, and is therefore a pleasantly participatory way to see and learn about history.
Archeonlaan 1, Alphen a/d Rijn
www.archeon.nl

PLACES UNDISCOVERED BY THE MASSES

Expatriates and tourists are not the only ones who like to enjoy the sights in the Netherlands. The following are places recommended by the Dutch themselves. (Be sure to check the websites or call for opening times, as some places are closed, for example, on Mondays.)

TEYLER'S MUSEUM IN HAARLEM

Aside from being the very first museum in the Netherlands, Teyler's Museum was the third museum in Europe, following in the footsteps of the Oxford Ashmolean and the British Museum. It was once a living theater; a place to discuss, with colleagues, the inventions of the times, to hear speakers and to chew over the discoveries of science and art, as well as a laboratory for experiments and demonstrations. Today we can peer into the past through the collection of microscopes and telescopes, Newtonian measuring equipment, fossils, rocks and gems and, of course, paintings, drawings, etches and sketches, or visit its library with its Travel and

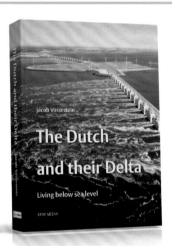

Important Documents such as the Diderot Encyclopedia (the first in Europe), James Cooks' travel journals, Darwin's scribbles and the works of others of world-renown.
Spaarne 16, Haarlem
www.teylersmuseum.eu

BIESBOSCH NATIONAL PARK
7,000 hectares of winding gullies, deep creeks and fields of rushes. The park was created in 1421 when the St. Elizabeth flood washed away 16 villages and turned a prosperous agricultural region into a freshwater tidal area. Today, visitors can explore the park on foot or by boat and observe a unique range of plants, animals and birds.
near Dordrecht
www.np-debiesbosch.nl

THE SINGER MUSEUM
Laren (near Hilversum in the province of North Holland) became fashionable with painters in the 1870s, notably those of the Impressionist Hague School. The Singers, an American couple who moved to Laren in 1901, collected the paintings of visiting artists, and this delightful museum – situated in the residential area of a very chic town – is based on their collection. Upscale local shops complete the experience.
Oude Drift 1, Laren
www.singerlaren.nl

FRANEKER PLANETARIUM
In 1774, Eise Eisinga, an amateur scientist, built a planetarium in his living room in order to calm the villagers' fears about the end of the world. Despite his limited knowledge about the conjunction of the planets, the planetarium is a masterpiece of engineering that still functions perfectly after 200-some years, making it the oldest in the world.
Eise Eisingastraat 3, Franeker (Friesland)
www.planetarium-friesland.nl

RECREATIONAL AREA SPAARNWOUDE
In 1969, the government, five municipalities and the province of North Holland decided to keep the area between Amsterdam and Haarlem 'green'. Thus the recreational area 'Spaarnwoude' was launched, covering a total landmass of over 6,178 acres. Located just outside Haarlem, Spaarnwoude has become one of the most popular recreational areas in North Holland. It is considered a pocket of peace and tranquility, offering its visitors the opportunity to hike, cycle and inline skate, while taking in the area's natural beauty. But that is not all: other activities/attractions include parks, play areas, a golf course, a scaling wall, an educational farm, canoe courses, 'adventureland' and... the opportunity to go skiing at Snowplanet.
just outside Haarlem.
www.spaarnwoude.nl

THORN

A favorite subject for posters advertising the province of Limburg, but a village relatively undiscovered by foreign visitors. Thorn is a wonderfully picturesque town with cobbled streets and white-washed houses and farms that intrude right into the main or 'high' street, giving the town a very rural atmosphere. The local abbey was founded towards the end of the 10th century.
Thorn, near Roermond.
www.vvvmiddenlimburg.nl

PANORAMA MESDAG

Panorama Mesdag is a cylindrical painting, more than 14 meters high and 120 meters in circumference. The vista of the sea, the dunes and Scheveningen village was painted by one of the most famous painters of the Hague School, Hendrik Willem Mesdag. It is the oldest 19th-century panorama in the world in its original site, and a unique cultural heritage.
Zeestraat 65, The Hague
www.panorama-mesdag.nl

BOSCHPLAAT NATURE RESERVE (ISLAND OF TERSCHELLING)

Situated on the marshy land of the southern shore of Terschelling, one of the five 'Wadden' islands, this is where thousands of water-fowl and migrating birds gather. Nearby you'll also find lovely beaches where the sand is golden and the water clean.
Terschelling
www.natuurlijkwandelen.nl/boschplaat

THE TROPEN MUSEUM

Not as crowded as Amsterdam's other large museums, here you can discover the culture of New Guinea; learn about art, culture and colonialism; travel through Africa and South-East Asia; or visit Latin America and the Caribbean, discovering a world apart. An excellent restaurant serves unusual dishes from around the world, and temporary exhibits, are also featured. The adjacent Tropen-theater presents a mind-boggling selection of cultural performances from around the world.
Linnaeusstraat 2, Amsterdam
www.tropenmuseum.nl

WATERLAND NEELTJE JANS (THE DELTA PROJECT)

In a fascinating exhibition and tour, find out about Zeeland's endless fight with the sea and the pragmatic Dutch response – a massive dam and flood barrier that literally closed off the sea. From April-October you can visit a dolphin station and make a round-trip on the Oosterschelde (a portion of the sea that once stretched into the province of Zeeland, but that now, due to the dikes, has become brackish water and a unique nature area). Don't miss the hurricane simulator!
Island of Neeltje Jans, Faelweg 5, Vrouwenpolder
www.neeltjejans.nl

NOORBEEK

Popular with Dutch hikers, this tiny village nestles cozily in a valley (yes, they do exist) in Limburg and still retains its authentic atmosphere with tractors chugging down the high street to deposit hay in the lofts above the farms.
Noorbeek near Maastricht
www.noorbeek.nl

ZUIDERZEE MUSEUM

This living museum of 130 buildings built on the banks of the IJsselmeer provides a snapshot of life between 1880 and 1932. The original houses, school, church and shops have been transported from 39 locations in the IJsselmeer region.
Wierdijk 12-22, Enkhuizen
www.zuiderzeemuseum.nl

OPEN AIR MUSEUM (NEDERLANDS OPENLUCHT MUSEUM) – ARNHEM

A 44-acre park representing a time capsule of Dutch provincial life with all the inherent customs and traditions in a living history setting, complete with a cross-section of real historic buildings and houses literally transported from their original location. Windmills, fully furnished thatched-roof farmhouses and craft shops complete the melting pot.
Schelmseweg 89, Arnhem
www.openluchtmuseum.nl

FOAM FOTOGRAFIE MUSEUM – AMSTERDAM

FOAM aims to inform and inspire the audience by presenting all facets of contemporary photography and exhibits world-famous photographers alongside emerging artists, ranging from historical to contemporary work. Includes major exhibitions and discussion forums.
Keizersgracht 609, Amsterdam
www.foam.org

EYE FILM INSTITUTE NETHERLANDS

EYE Film Institute is completely dedicated to film and the moving image. Film is exhibited as art, entertainment, cultural heritage, and a conveyor of information. It offers exhibitions, programs, films for children, educational programs and activities for all ages.
IJPromenade, Amsterdam
www.eyefilm.nl

GRONINGER MUSEUM – GRONINGEN

This eclectic museum juts out into the canal and defies description, with exhibits ranging from arts and crafts to fashion. If the drawbridge entrance happens to be raised for a passing boat, be sure to look at the tongue-in-cheek tiles underneath. A zany place through and through.
Museumeiland 1, Groningen
www.groningermuseum.nl

HUNEBEDDEN (DOLMENS)

One of the largest concentrations of Stone Age boulder formations exists in the idyllic province of Drenthe in the northeast, where 54 dolmen configurations, one with a capstone weighing an incredible 20,000 kilos, are scattered throughout the countryside, which

are believed to be the megalithic skeletons of burial tombs used by farmers in this most ancient area of the Netherlands. Amazingly, these Fred-Flintstone-like structures are almost 2,000 years older than the famous Stonehenge in England, and 1,000 years older than the pyramids in Egypt.

Even more amazing is how they were transported and lifted into place. The Nationaal Hunebedden Informatiecentrum (National Dolmen Information Center) in Borger, where you can also see the largest hunebed, is the perfect place to get the lowdown on theories. Information center: Hunebedstraat 27, Borger (between Assen and Emmen)
www.hunebedcentrum.nl

INTERNATIONAL CLUBS

The real estate agents have found you the ideal place to live, the movers have brought over your possessions from another part of the world, an acquaintance or two at work has shown you the places around town, and you think you are on the road to settling in – but not quite! For those who like the company of others, either occasionally or often, it's the circle of like-minded friends that one needs in order to be able to enjoy the fairly long blustery winters of the Netherlands. Social clubs are a great place to meet other expatriates who have recently arrived, as well as those 'expats' and other members who have been around for a while – as well as locals, of course.

In the Netherlands, those looking for a place to network are sure to find something that will meet their needs: for professional women, there are WIN (Women's International Network) in Amsterdam that provides women with a forum for meeting, networking, and getting down to business, and, along similar lines, Connecting Women, in The Hague. Then, of course, there are International Rotary Clubs, for both men and women. Those who are looking for a nationality-based club, there are plenty on offer, as well as clubs based on a particular hobby, such as dance, drama or art. For those who are simply looking for a group of friends, or a source of fun family outings, there are also several clubs to join, in places as diverse as Eindhoven, Maastricht, Breda, Dordrecht, Enschede, Groningen, and more – and, of course, the cities of Amsterdam, The Hague, Rotterdam and Utrecht. For more information on clubs in the Netherlands, check the reference pages at the end of the chapter.

SPORTS CLUBS

As you'll quickly realize, the hardy Dutch are avid sports enthusiasts with well-organized leagues and clean, modern facilities. Whether it's a bike touring group or a competitive, high-profile sport that you fancy, there's something for everyone here. As an expat, you'll have no excuse not to be fit during your sojourn in this country.

WHY JOIN A SPORTS CLUB?

Sports clubs offer a great outlet for meeting new people, staying (or getting) in shape, practicing the Dutch language and, in many cases, providing an indoor venue when the weather outside is frightful. The question is: what's the best way to find a sports club in your area that suits your interests and budget?

HOW DO I FIND THE RIGHT CLUB?

Depending on where you live:

- find out if your community publishes a guide titled *stadsgids* or *gemeentegids*, or visit the local city hall, *gemeentehuis*. The sports clubs will be listed under *sportverenigingen*. Most of the titles should be understandable, but you may have to use your dictionary. Telephone the club's chairperson, secretary or contact person. Chances are good that they will speak English if your Dutch is not yet up to speed
- contact ACCESS, www.access-nl.org
- search the Internet, as most clubs have their own websites
- drop in on the sports facilities or gym in your area to pick up some information. You can also check bulletin boards within the facility for club announcements
- visit visit www.sport.nl to find a sports club near you.

Once you have found one or more clubs in the sport you like and have made contact, ask if you can try out the training sessions a couple of times before you must become a member. There is no harm in shopping around if the community you live in has more than one club offering a particular sport. Once you join, you are usually committed financially for a year.

COMPETITIONS

Dutch sports are unified into national 'bonds' or governing sports bodies, and competitions follow international rules and regulations.

JUST FOR KIDS

In the Netherlands, sports are not really as much part of the Dutch school curriculum as they are in many other countries. If students want to be active in sports, they must find a venue outside of school. International and American schools in the Netherlands, however, generally provide more opportunities. Additionally, this being a country where most people live below sea level, children are (informally) required to earn a swimming diploma. Many clubs and pools offer such a program. A good source of information on sports clubs (for kids) is the *gemeentegids* (or *stadsgids*), which you can pick up at your municipality (*gemeentehuis*).

AMERICAN BASEBALL FOUNDATION

For nostalgic Americans and all those interested in 'batting up', the American Baseball Foundation has its own clubhouse and has even branched out to feature interims of football, basketball and softball. For more information, see the reference pages. Or visit ABF International Sports Club, www.abfsport.nl. Baseball is also gaining in popularity across the Netherlands, among kids and adults; visit www.knbsb.nl for more information.

STUDENTS

For more information on sports activities for students, see page 216.

WEBSITES

More sports-sites can be found on the reference pages at the end of the chapter.

SELECTED SPORTS EVENTS

SNEEKWEEK

An annually recurring sailing event – that in some or other form has been taking place since 1814, when the people of Sneek went out sailing to celebrate the fact that a local hero had deserted the French army and made it home safely – that spans an entire week. There are sailing races every day, in various categories, as well as festivities and a fair.
Aug. 6-11, 2016
Sneekermeer, Sneek
www.sneekweek.nl

SKÛTSJESILEN

Skûtjesilen is the name for sailing races between old freight ships, or flat-bottom boats, that were used towards the turn of the 19th century to transport turf, fertilizer and other goods to isolated farms. Their bottoms were flat, allowing them to navigate the shallow waters when approaching their destination. These boats are a sight to behold; beautiful, old-fashioned, lovingly-constructed wooden testaments to a practical, sea-faring nation.

Jul. 30 – Aug. 12, 2016
Frisian Lakes
www.skutsjesilen.nl

DAM TO DAM LOOP

A 16km-course from Dam Square to the center of Zaandam through the IJ-tunnel. In total 60,000 runners from across the world singed up last year, of which approximately 20,000 sign up for the Business Run (Business Loop). Participants are encouraged to run in support of a charity; these charities are given extra publicity preceding the Run. There are bands and small orchestras lining the course, along with hundreds of thousands of spectators, creating a festive atmosphere.

Sep. 17-18, 2016
Amsterdam
www.damloop.nl

JUMPING AMSTERDAM

One of the largest international equestrian events in the Netherlands, that attracts approximately 50,000 visitors a year and includes a.o. dressage, jumping, ponies, juniors, and driving – as well as entertainment.

Jan. 26-29, 2017
Amsterdam RAI
www.jumpingamsterdam.nl

ABN AMRO TENNIS TOURNAMENT

An increasingly famous tournament, which has become one of the 10 worldwide '500 points tournaments', allowing the players to accumulate more 'ranking points'.

Feb. 13-19, 2017
Rotterdam Ahoy
www.abnamrowtt.nl

ABN AMRO CPC LOOP

An international city-pier-city half-marathon that takes place annually in The Hague, attracting over 18,000 participants every year. The course is flat, fast and traffic-free. The race begins in the city center, heads out to the pier at the coastal resort of Scheveningen and then returns to where it started. There is also a 10km fun run and other recreational walking and running events varying in distance – also two for kids.

Mar. 5, 2017
The Hague/Scheveningen
www.nncpcloopdenhaag.nl

ROTTERDAM MARATHON

Thanks to the three World records that have been established on this course, the Rotterdam marathon has attained (inter)national fame. The ABN Amro Marathon Rotterdam has become the biggest marathon in the Netherlands. The course is fast, the crowds are great and the atmosphere on the Coolsingel is unique.

Apr. 9, 2017
Rotterdam
www.nnmarathonrotterdam.nl

SPORTS IN HOLLAND BY STEVEN STUPP

Sometimes in the Netherlands it feels as if the world you know has been turned inside out. Consider sporting events. In countries such as the United States, these are family outings. A fight in the stands during a game is a major news story; reports of injuries are greeted with shock and outrage. People bemoan the loss of innocence. Outside the stadium, all bets are off. While the death of some of the spectators in a drive-by-shooting a few days later would still be awful, people would shake their heads and agree that these things happen.

REVERSE SITUATION
In the Netherlands, the situation is reversed. In spite of Dutch concerns that the country has become less safe, street violence remains rare. Whenever the odd incident of the much-feared – and redundant – *zinloze geweld* ('senseless violence') occurs, the country has a collective nervous breakdown, with governmental hearings, newspaper editorials, massive protest marches and national moments of silence. On the other hand, news that fans rioted at a football (soccer) match would come as no surprise. If people were injured or even killed in such an incident, everyone would agree that, while it was a tragedy, these things happen.

UNCHARACTERISTIC
Sadly, violence at football matches in the Netherlands is not uncommon. If this seems strangely uncharacteristic, it is. While the perpetrators are a very small minority of the Dutch populace, they have made their presence known. Only English hooligans exceed the Dutch in their reputation for violence. As a consequence, a massive police presence that is just short of a major military operation helps keep the peace at games. This includes the *Mobiele Eenheid* ('Mobile Unit') or *ME*, the bad dudes of the normally pleasant Dutch police force: the riot police. Meanwhile, the fans, busy celebrating and singing their team's fight songs, seem oblivious to all of this. The collective atmosphere is bizarre: a festival parading through the middle of an armed camp. It is strange what people grow accustomed to.

HOBBIES
Given this level of enthusiasm for football, you won't be surprised to learn that sports in general are very popular in the Netherlands. During your stay in this country, you'll have the opportunity to take advantage of this at one of the seemingly innumerable local sports clubs and associations, which allow athletes of every age and caliber to participate in their favorite hobby, or simply socialize.

NATIONAL PASTIMES
Alternatively, you can partake in one of the national pastimes, such as a pleasant bicycle ride. The Netherlands is filled with scenic routes running through forests or next to canals that practically beg to be peddled down – and, invariably, lead to one of the bars and cafés that dot the countryside. Another perennial favorite is *wandelen* or walking, be it across the mud flats on the North Sea coast or during the *Vierdaagse van Nijmegen* (The Four Days in Nijmegen), an annual walking event. Or, if the local pond freezes over in the winter, you can dazzle (amuse) your neighbors with your ice-skating prowess (ineptitude).

FRISIAN SPORTS
Other options are provided by activities that are unique to the Netherlands. The northern province of Friesland is home to several. *polsstokhoogspringen* (pole-jumping) is a sort of aquatic pole vault where you try to jump over a canal – to a dry victory. Another is the *Elfstedentocht* (Eleven City Tour). This classic Dutch event is a 125-mile (200-kilometer) ice-skating race across the frozen lakes and canals of Friesland. During the most recent *Elfstedentocht* (in 1997) all other activity in the country came to a halt. The live television broadcast attracted almost three-quarters of the Dutch population! Never a people to let an excuse for a party pass, tens of thousands celebrated the whole weekend long. The race itself is not for the faint-hearted. For many it is a grueling experience. As a consequence, the winner is an instant, albeit temporary, national hero.

GO HOLLAND!
If you're less ambitious or a couch potato at heart, television offers an easy way out. The Netherlands provides numerous athletes and

teams for you to cheer on. At the international level, the country is surprisingly competitive in a number of sports. Historically, notable areas of excellence include volleyball, field hockey, tennis, bicycle racing, football, sailing and speed skating.

THE 'CLAP' SKATE

In the last category, the Dutch are currently nothing less than a world superpower. Thanks in part to their invention of the so-called *klap* ('clap') skate, which has a hinged blade, they have dominated the longer distance events in recent years. To give you an idea of how strong the Dutch skaters are, they won eight gold, seven silver, and eight bronze medals at the 2014 Olympics!

FOOTBALL/SOCCER

Football/soccer, however, is the sport the Dutch have consistently excelled at for the longest time, including nine World Cup appearances and three trips to the finals; but lacking the crucial final victory, the Dutch are still known as the best team never to win the World Cup. (Team sport or not, internal rivalries have on occasion been the Achilles heel of the Dutch squad.) It helps that football is immensely popular in the Netherlands, with numerous amateur and professional teams throughout the country. Allegiance varies from city to city: Rotterdam has Feyenoord, Amsterdam has Ajax and Eindhoven has PSV (the Philips Sports Vereniging, or Union). Dutch football stars are definitely in vogue these days; there are Dutch players on professional teams throughout the world.

TEMPORARY NATIONAL PRIDE

Dutch fans are no less legendary than the teams they support, although some are infamous, as we have seen. With the notable exception of the hyperactive hooligan minority, the Dutch bring a festive atmosphere to any sporting event. Stadiums resound with the sounds of '*Nederland, o Nederland*' ('Netherlands, oh Netherlands'), a fight song sung to the tune of '*Auld Lang Syne*' that is played by the small band of drums and trumpets that inevitably accompanies the Dutch fans. Now and then, you'll hear cries of '*Oranje boven!*' ('Orange Above!' or Orange Will Triumph!) and '*Hup Holland hup!*' (Go Holland!). This team spirit is reflected on the streets of the country in a sort of micro-nationalism phenomenon. Normally the Dutch aren't openly proud about their nationality, but on the day of a major contest or tournament there is an explosion of pride in the form of the royal color orange on the flags, balloons, shirts and hats that suddenly blanket the land. These disappear with equal rapidity after the game.

SMALL COUNTRY

But for all of their talent, the size of the country provides Dutch athletes and fans with one overriding advantage, a secret weapon for sporting events: no matter what you do, you just can't win. If you beat them, they will solemnly tell you, "What do you want from a small country?" If you lose, they will gleefully cry out, "See what a small country can do?!"

'CUTE AND QUAINT VILLAGE' DESTINATIONS

While there are plenty of picturesque villages or *dorpjes* throughout the country, *The Holland Handbook* award goes first and foremost to five in the northern and heartland provinces: Sloten and Hindeloopen in Friesland, Giethoorn and Staphorst in Overijssel, and Bronckhorst in Gelderland. SLOTEN, about the size of a panoramic snapshot, is the epitome of charm with its gabled houses along a central canal. HINDELOOPEN is famed for its ornately hand-painted furniture and interiors, as well as its ice-skating museum glorifying the Elfstedentocht race (a race course that runs along the canals and lakes that connect 11 towns in the country which can only be held when weather permits). The town clings to the IJsselmeer, cut off and preserved from its sailing prosperity by the construction of the *Afsluitdijk*, or Enclosing Dike, in 1932. GIETHOORN, the 'Venice of the North' where transportation is limited to boats and bikes in the old part, is a punter's paradise and one of the most stunning thatched-roof villages in all of the Netherlands, despite the yearly onslaught of camera-happy gawkers. STAPHORST, where locals still don their traditional garb, wins the time warp prize of the bunch for its fierce adherence to Calvinistic ways. (Be wary of pointing your camera at the traditionally outfitted residents here though, as they consider it a serious invasion of privacy.) BRONCKHORST, officially the smallest town in the Netherlands, is a precious mix of cobblestone streets, farmhouses and local artisans, accented, oddly enough, with a museum devoted to Charles Dickens, and a Christmas festival bar none.

Other prizewinners in this category include Veere, in the southwest province of Zeeland, and the previously-mentioned Thorn, in the southeast province of Limburg. VEERE was a former sailing port of major significance, although it's now blocked off from the sea by a dike and sits ever-so-quietly but elegantly on the shore of the Veerse Meer, one of the largest lakes in the Netherlands. THORN, in contrast, is a rural haven known as the 'white village' for its abundance of white-washed, 18th-century houses. It makes for a pleasant respite on your journey either into or out of the bustling metropolis of Maastricht.

And for the quintessential daytrip, offering a combination of village charm and infusion of art, don't miss the glorious studio and gallery of destined-for-eternal-fame, Dutch still-life artist Henk Helmantel. His spectacular, 13th-century parsonage home in WESTEREMDEN lies in the northern province of Groningen. Open to the public on certain afternoons only from May through October (and by appointment throughout the year), the Helmantel gallery is a work of art in itself. (www.helmantel.nl). His home is open to the public (during which a tour of the premises is given) every Thursday, Friday and Saturday afternoon, May through October (2016: May 5 – October 29). Groups can also make appointments for other dates.

For more information on all of the above villages, contact the pertinent vvvs (whose phone numbers you can obtain from your local vvv or via 0900 8008).

TOURING THE LAND OF CASTLES

In a country as rich in history as the Netherlands, it shouldn't surprise you that there are a multitude of castles to visit and explore; in fact there are over 300 castles, manor houses and estates. Wander into one of these impressive structures and, without even having to close your eyes, you can imagine yourself transported to the times of princes, knights and damsels in distress. Or, at least, in love.

Below, four of the best-known castles – but keep in mind, there are 296 more!

One of the most famous castles that are open to the public is the MUIDERSLOT, in Muiden, built in 1280 by Count Floris, a man who was, to use a Dutch expression 'stone rich', which meant that he could afford to build a castle of stone, rather than using the wood that poorer people used to build their houses. The furniture, objects and paintings that are now found in the castle stem from the 17th century, the time when the famous Dutch poet and writer P.C. Hooft lived there. Three different tours of the castle can be taken; the Knight's Route, the Tower Route and the Guided Route – each providing you with insight into a different aspect of life in the castle.

Also well worth a visit is PALACE HET LOO, in Apeldoorn, which, for three centuries, was the summer palace of the Dutch Royal Family and has since been converted into a museum, illustrating life as it was lived by the royals over the centuries. Particularly the gardens of this palace are famous and have attracted countless visitors.

CASTLE DE HAAR, in Haarzuilens, is the Netherlands' fairytale castle; built in the 14th century and surrounded by a park, water fountains and a garden reminiscent of Versailles, as well as boasting an interior filled with richly colored Flemish tapestries and delicate paintings depicting religious themes, it is a place where weddings are held, as well as children's parties – dressed up as knights and princesses, they make their fantasy come true.

LOEVESTEIN CASTLE, built around 1368, is located strategically in the heart of the Netherlands. In 1673, it became part of the Dutch Water Line, created to protect the Netherlands against Louis XIV's French troops. The concept was simple, but extremely effective; by flooding a 3-5 km stretch of land, the Water Line successfully kept the troops from advancing any further. In fact, in times of floods, the only access road to the castle still becomes untraversable.

Would you like to immerse yourself in the world of kings and dragons? Wake up in a room that held queens and princesses, whose ladies-in-waiting were standing at attention with corsets in hand? Visit www.kasteel.nl for an overview of castles that have chosen to continue the age-honored tradition of hospitality, in style...

WEBSITES

OFFICIAL HOLLAND WEBSITES
www.holland.com: the official website of the
Netherlands Board of Tourism
www.lekkerweg.nl: Dutch-language website
on tourism and recreation in the Netherlands

WEBSITES WITH NATIONAL EVENT
DIARIES IN ENGLISH
www.expatica.com
www.iamexpat.nl
www.xpat.nl

ONLINE TICKET SALES
www.belbios.nl: cinema reservations
www.museumtickets.nl: ticketing portal for
museums, exhibitions and tourist attractions
www.ticketmaster.nl

MUSEUM WEBSITES
www.museum.nl: an overview of all the
museums in the Netherlands
www.museumserver.nl: portal website for
museums in the Netherlands

AUCTIONS
Christie's Amsterdam: www.christies.com
Sotheby's Amsterdam: www.sothebys.com
Venduehuis The Hague: www.venduehuis.com
Veilinghuis Onder de Boompjes, Leiden:
www.onderdeboompjes.nl

CASTLES
http://kastelen.startpagina.nl
www.kasteleninnederland.nl
www.kasteel.nl

OUTDOOR ACTIVITIES
De Keukenhof: www.keukenhof.nl
Mud flat walking: www.wadlopen.org
National Park De Biesbosch:
www.biesbosch.org
Nederlands Openlucht Museum:
www.openluchtmuseum.nl
Recreational Area Spaarnwoude:
www.spaarnwoude.nl
South Limburg: www.noorbeek.nl
The Groene Hart (Green Heart):
www.vvvhetgroenehart.nl
The Pieterpad: www.pieterpad.nl
The Veluwe: www.develuwe.nl
Wetlands Safaris close to Amsterdam:
www.wetlandssafari.nl
Windmills of Kinderdijk: www.kinderdijk.nl

DINING OUT

IENS INDEPENDENT INDEX
Offers an up-to-date and objective restaurant
survey for the Netherlands
IENS makes use of more than 100,000 assessors
and offers a database of more than 20,000
restaurants
www.iens.nl
IENS Toppers app: available in the App Store

SPECIALBITE
Guide to Special Dining
Visit this website when you are looking for
restaurants that are rated as 'special' by well-
informed locals
www.specialbite.com

DINNERSITE.NL
A complete restaurant guide for the
Netherlands
www.dinnersite.nl

RECOMMENDED READING

THE HOLLAND GUIDE APP
Published by XPat Media
The Holland Handbook on your iPad
With interactive maps, almost a thousand live
references and hundreds of stunning photos
Available in the App Store
www.xpat.nl/hollandguide

HERE'S HOLLAND
By Sheila Gazaleh-Weevers
with Shirley Agudo & Connie Moser
Published by Eburon Academic Publishers
Colorful two-in-one guide to Holland for travelers and expats alike. Features out-of-the-way
places, museums, gardens, castles and more –
along with cultural and historical background
www.heresholland.com

THE NETHERLANDS
By Jeremy Gray & Reuben Acciano
Published by Lonely Planet Publications
For curious and independent travelers
www.lonelyplanet.com

THE NETHERLANDS – THE ROUGH GUIDE
By Martin Dunford and Phil Lee
Published by Rough Guides
Distributed by Penguin Travel Guide
www.roughguides.nl

THE NETHERLANDS – EYEWITNESS
TRAVEL GUIDE
By Gerard Harmans.
Published by Dorling Kindersley.
www.traveldk.com

OVER HOLLAND
Photography Karel Tomeï
Published by Scriptum
Previously unpublished work by Holland's
most renowned aerial photographer, Karel
Tomeï. Humorous and refreshingly different:
spectacular and surprising photographs are
combined with work by Dutch writers, cabaret artists, poets, actors and aphorists
www.scriptum.nl

HOLLAND FROM THE TOP I, II, III, IV AND V
Photography Karel Tomeï
Published by Scriptum.
This book gives you wings
www.scriptum.nl

AMSTERDAM CITY GUIDE
Published by Lonely Planet Publications
By Jeremy Gray
A smart, stylish and streetwise guide which
helps to connect with the real Amsterdam
www.lonelyplanet.com

CLOUDLESS AMSTERDAM
Published by Bas Lubberhuizen
Photography by Peter Elenbaas
Text by Lambiek Berends
Stunning aerial photographs provide an un-
expected view of the changing city Amsterdam.
Journalist Lambiek Berends wrote a brief
history to accompany them
www.lubberhuizen.nl

ATLAS OF AMSTERDAM
Published by Noordhoff Uitgevers
The atlas tells you everything you always
wanted to know about Amsterdam, and
everything you never knew you wanted to
know too.
www.bosatlas.nl
To order: www.hollandbooks.nl

THE DUTCH AND THEIR DELTA
Living Below Sea Level
By Jacob Vossestein
Published by XPat Media
The fascinating account of how the Dutch
manage to live below sea level

www.jacobvossestein.nl
To order: www.hollandbooks.nl

THE DUTCH & THEIR BIKES
Scenes from a Nation of Cyclists
By Shirley Agudo
Published by XPat Media
With almost 700 photos it's the definitive
photo guide to the world's best bicycle culture
www.dutchandtheirbikes.com,
www.shirleyagudo.com
To order: www.hollandbooks.nl

THE XPAT JOURNAL
Published since 1998 by XPat Media
A lifestyle magazine packed with information
of interest to expats in the Netherlands. Articles cover topics such as legal affairs, taxes,
housing, health care, leisure activities as well
as reviews of local sites of interest, culture
and upcoming events.
Available by subscription
www.xpat.nl - www.thexpatjournal.nl

HOLLAND BOOKS
Features a wide range of books and travel
guides on Holland: www.hollandbooks.nl

INTERNATIONAL CLUBS

ENGLISH-LANGUAGE GROUPS AND CLUBS
ACCESS: www.access-nl.org
American Women's Club Amsterdam:
www.awca.nl
American Women's Club The Hague:
www.awcthehague.org
Andrew's Society of the Netherlands:
www.standrews.nl
Aussies in Holland:
http://aussieclouds.appspot.com/hollandsite
British Club The Hague:
www.britshclubthehague.nl
British Society of Amsterdam:
www.britishsocietyofamsterdam.org
CADS (Commercial Anglo Dutch Society):
www.cads-amsterdam.org
Club of Amsterdam:
www.clubofamsterdam.com
Connect International, Groningen:
www.connect-int.org
Connecting Women, The Hague:
www.connectingwomen.nl

Democrats Abroad Netherlands:
www.democratsabroad.nl
English Speaking Community in the
Netherlands: www.elynx.nl
International Almere:
www.internationalalmere.com
The International Rotaract Club in
Amsterdam: www.rotaract.nl
International Women's Club of Rotterdam
(Pickwick): http://iwcr.blogspot.nl
International Women's Contact The Hague:
www.iwcthehague.nl
International Women's Contact Amsterdam:
www.iwcamsterdam.nl
International Women's Contact Breda:
www.iwcbreda.nl
International Women's Contact South
Limburg: www.iwc-sl.nl
International Women's Contact Utrecht/
Amersfoort: www.iwcu.nl
The Irish Club-Netherlands: www.irishclub.nl
Kiwi Expat Association:
www.keanewzealand.com/europe
Legal Aliens: www.legalaliens.eu
The Netherlands England Society:
www.nederlandengeland.nl
Netherlands-India Association:
www.netherlands-india.nu
Newcomer's Club:
www.newcomersclub.com/nl.html
Petroleum Wives Club, The Hague:
www.pwc-thehague.com
Republicans Abroad Netherlands:
www.republicansabroad.nl
Rotary International, Amsterdam:
www.amsterdamrotary.org
South African Club: www.southafricanclub.nl
Toastmasters in the Netherlands:
www.toastmasters.nl
The Hague Online Social Club:
www.thehagueonline.com
Women's International Group Zeeland:
www.wigz.nl

FRENCH-SPEAKING CLUBS
Accueil des Francophones de La Haye:
www.accueillahaye.com
Alliance Française: www.alliance-francaise.nl
Institute Français: www.institutfrancais.nl
Union des Français à l'Étranger:
www.ufepaysbas.nl

GERMAN-SPEAKING CLUBS
Deutscher Klub in den Niederlanden:
www.deutscherklub.nl
Deutsch-Niederländischer Verein:
www.deutsch-nl-verein.nl

SPANISH-SPEAKING CLUB
Asociación Hispánica De La Haya:
www.asoha.nl

CULTURAL INSTITUTES

The John Adams Institute, Amsterdam,
Herenmarkt 97, 1013 EC Amsterdam
Tel.: 020 624 72 80
www.john-adams.nl

Goethe-Institut Amsterdam
Herengracht 470, 1017 CA Amsterdam
Tel.: 020 623 04 21
www.goethe.de

Goethe-Institut Rotterdam
Westersingel 9, 3014 GM Rotterdam
Tel.: 010 209 20 90
www.goethe.de

ART CLUBS

The Decorative & Fine Arts Society (DFAS)
of The Hague
Schoolstraat 23, 2271 BZ Voorburg
Tel.: 070 387 26 06
www.dfas.nl

International Art Club
Weimarstraat 49c, 2562 GR The Hague
Tel.: 06 2913 2776
www.iacdenhaag.nl

Images International Photo Club
English speaking photography club
of The Hague
www.imagesphotoclub.com
Studio Jean
Drawing and painting lessons
Thomsonlaan 65, 2565 HX The Hague
Tel.: 070 392 16 72
www.studiojean.nl

Marcello's Art Factory
Drawing and painting lessons, clinics and
events
Kon. Emmakade 148/149, 2518 JK The Hague
Tel.: 070 363 40 47
www.marcellos.nl

The British Choir of The Hague
Tel.: 070 328 28 03
www.cecilia-choir.com

ENGLISH-SPEAKING THEATER GROUPS
The In-Players International Drama Group,
Amsterdam,
Tel.: 020 770 49 84
www.inplayers.org

International Drama Group of English Speaking
Associates (I.D.E.A)
Tel.: 078 617 04 65
www.idea-panto.nl

Stichting The English Theatre (STET)
Tel.: 06 3005 0018
www.theenglishtheatre.nl

Anglo-American Theater Group (AATG)
P.O. Box 10239, The Hague
Tel.: 070 394 59 88
www.aatg.nl

Leiden English-speaking Theater (LEST)
Oude Singel 290, 2312 RK Leiden
Tel.: 071 513 00 02

International Drama Group of English
Speaking Associates (IDEA)
Tel.: 078 617 04 65
www.idea-panto.nl

ENGLISH-SPEAKING COMEDY
Boom Chicago
Not cabaret, and not stand-up, Boom Chicago
is a mix of sketches and pure improvisation.
Rozengracht 117, 1016 LV Amsterdam
Tel.: 0900 266 62 44
www.boomchicago.nl

SPORTS

ENGLISH-SPEAKING SPORTS CLUBS
The American Baseball Foundation
P.O. Box 133, 2240 AC Wassenaar
Tel.: 070 514 65 15
www.abfsport.nl

The Hague Hash House Harriers
www.haguehash.nl

Hash House Harriers Amsterdam
www.harrier.nl

The Hague Road Runners
Groenendaal 11, 2244 BK Wassenaar
Tel.: 070 328 10 25
www.hagueroadrunners.nl

Gaelic Football: www.denhaaggaa.com
Hague Rugby Club: www.haagserugbyclub.com

The Randstad Harings Diving Club
www.randstad-harings.nl

CRICKET
Qui Vive
Sportpark de Eendracht, Amsterdam
Tel.: 06 2508 83 01
www.ccquivive.nl

De Kieviten Cricket Club, The Hague
Tel.: 070 354 23 14
www.kieviten.nl/cricket

Voorburg Cricket Club, Voorburg
Tel.: 070 386 26 78
www.voorburgcc.nl
General info and clubs in the Netherlands
www.cricket.nl

GOLF
Nederlandse Golf Federatie, De Meern
Tel.: 030 662 18 88
www.ngf.nl

Amsterdamse Golf Club, Amsterdam
Tel.: 020 497 78 66
www.amsterdamsegolfclub.nl

For more golf clubs in the Netherlands:
www.golf.nl

ROWING
Rowing Center Berlagebrug
Weesperzijde 1094, 1097 DS Amsterdam
Tel.: 020 468 32 41
www.roeicentrumberlagebrug.nl

RUGBY
Amsterdam Sevens Rugby Tournament
Nationaal Rugby Centrum Amsterdam
Bok de Korverweg 6, 1067 HR Amsterdam
http://a7.amsterdamsevens.com

Amstelveen RC 1890 (ARC 1890)
Sportlaan 25a, Amstelveen
Tel.: 020 643 89 79
www.arcrugby.com

Dutch Australian Football Association (DAFA)
www.aussierules.nl

Rugby Club 't Gooi
Sportpark Naarden
Amersfoortsestraatweg 14, 1411 HC Naarden
Tel.: 030 272 51 11
www.rugbyclub-gooi.nl

SAILING
Watersports Center Sloterplas
Christoffel Plantijngracht 4, 1065 DA Amsterdam
Tel.: 020 617 58 39
www.wscsloterplas.nl

Zeezeilschool Scheveningen
RYA Training Center. All RYA classes are
in English.
Dr. Lelykade 22, 2593 CM Scheveningen
Tel.: 070 351 48 58
www.zeezeilschool.nl

TENNIS
Berg en Dal
Daal en Bergselaan 13, 2565 AB The Hague
Tel.: 070 325 13 33

De Uithof
Jaap Edenweg 10, 2544 NL The Hague
Tel.: 070 404 44 59

Mets Tennisbanen
Berk Blokstraat 103, 2586 HG The Hague
Tel.: 070 355 98 49

REFERENCES

Haagsche Lawn Tennis Club Leimonias
Klatteweg 103, 2597 KA The Hague
Tel.: 070 355 76 76
www.leimonias.nl

Westvliet Welness & Racquet Club
Westvlietweg 55, 2267 AC Leidschendam
Tel.: 070 386 44 44
www.westvliet.nl

Tennis Club Amsterdam
Nieuwe Kalfjeslaan 19A, 1182 AA Amstelveen
www.tcamsterdam.net

VVV TOURIST INFO

Tourist Information Office
General – www.vvv.nl

VVV AMSTERDAM
Stationsplein 10, 1012 AB Amsterdam
Tel.: 0900 400 40 40
www.vvvamsterdam.nl

VVV THE HAGUE
Hofweg 1, 2511 AA The Hague
Tel.: 0900 340 35 05
www.vvvdenhaag.nl

VVV MAASTRICHT
Kleine Staat 1, 6122 ED Maastricht
Tel.: 043 325 21 21
www.vvvmaastricht.nl

VVV ROTTERDAM
Coolsingel 67, 3012 AC Rotterdam
Tel.: 0900 403 40 65
www.vvvrotterdam.nl

VVV UTRECHT
Vredenburg 90, 3511 BD Utrecht
Tel.: 0900 128 87 32
www.utrechtyourway.nl

CITY INFO

AMSTERDAM
www.amsterdamsuitburo.nl
outings and events in Amsterdam

www.amsterdam.com
Offers an overview of museums, restaurants,
hotels, events and shops in Amsterdam

www.amsterdam.nl
This website is in Dutch and English and
provides everything you need to know about
Amsterdam

www.amsterdam.info
Informative website on Amsterdam in more
than 20 language

www.iamsterdam.com
A portal website on Amsterdam, Almere,
Amstelveen and Haarlemmermeer with
information on Nature and Geography,
People and Culture, Business, Government
and Politics and more

www.dutchamsterdam.nl
The no-nonsense travel guide to Amsterdam

THE HAGUE
www.haagsuitburo.nl: outings and events in
The Hague

The Hague City Council official website offers
city news, events and information in Dutch,
with a version in English
www.thehague.com

The Hague Online
Local daily news a weekly calendar of events
in the The Hague area and views for expats
by expats
www.thehagueonline.com

ROTTERDAM
www.rotterdamsuitburo.nl: outings and
events in Rotterdam
Event calendar with events, exhibitions,
festivals, general information, tips etc.
www.rotterdam.info

WE'D LIKE TO THANK THE FOLLOWING COMPANIES AND ORGANIZATIONS
FOR THEIR INVALUABLE CONTRIBUTIONS TO THIS BOOK

BDO ACCOUNTANTS & ADVISEURS
Robin Schalekamp, Kees de Graaf
K. P. van der Mandelelaan 40
3062 MB Rotterdam
Tel.: 010 242 46 00
robin.schalekamp@bdo.nl
www.bdo.nl

VAN BUTTINGHA WICHERS NOTARISSEN
Yolanda Bokhorst
Lange Voorhout 24
2514 EE Den Haag
Tel.: 070 356 68 00
y.bokhorst@vbwnotarissen.nl
www.vbwnotarissen.nl

C&G CAREER SERVICES
Peter Kranenburg
Hoogoorddreef 9, 1101 BA Amsterdam Z.O.
Tel.: 020 312 05 40
mail@cg-services.com
www.cg-services.com

EDUCAIDE
Willemijn van Oppen-Stuyt
P.O.Box 96911, 2509 JH The Hague
Tel.: 06 559 88 998
info@educaide.nl
www.educaide.nl

EXPATAX
Bart van Meijl, Arjan Enneman
Keizerstraat 3, 3512 EA Utrecht
P.O. Box 9310, 3506 GH Utrecht
Tel.: 030 246 85 36
bart@expatax.nl
www.expatax.nl

EXPAT MEDICAL ADVISOR
Christine Houser MD
Grotekerksbuurt 29, 3311 CA Dordrecht
Tel.: 06 286 168 18
info@ExpatMedicalAdvisor.com
www.ExpatMedicalAdvisor.com

EXPAT MORTGAGES
Henk Jansen
Roerstraat 133, 1078 LM Amsterdam
Tel.: 020 717 39 08
henk@expat-mortgages.nl
www.expat-mortgages.nl

EXPERTISE IN LABOUR MOBILITY
Nannette Ripmeester
Mathenesserlaan 255, 3021 HD Rotterdam
Tel.: 010 477 68 16
info@labourmobility.com
www.labourmobility.com

NEW2NL
Annebet van Mameren
Tel.: 06 2909 39 33
annebet@new2nl.com
www.new2nl.com

EP-NUFFIC
The organisation for internationalisation
in education
P.O. Box 29777, 2502 LT The Hague
Kortenaerkade 11, 2518 AX The Hague
Tel.: 070 426 03 99
www.epnuffic.nl

VAN HILTEN DE VRIES VAN RUITENBEEK
Attorneys and mediators
Edith van Ruitenbeek
Nassaulaan 15, 2514 JT The Hague
Emmalaan 25, 1075 AT Amsterdam
Tel.: 070 361 70 02
edithvanruitenbeek@hvradvocaten.nl
www.hvradvocaten.nl

RELOCATION CARE
Annette de Vreede
Blokstallen 2b, 4611 WB Bergen op Zoom
P.O. Box 152, 4650 AD Steenbergen
Tel.: 0167 56 52 48
annette@relocationcare.nl
www.relocationcare.nl

VDS AUTOMOTIVE SERVICES
Daniël van Apeldoorn
Heerewegh 28, 2731 BM Benthuizen
Tel.: 079 593 94 45
vanapeldoorn@vdsautomotive.com
www.vdsautomotive.com

VÉDÉVÉ LEGAL
Liane van de Vrugt
A. J. Ernststraat 595C, 1082 LD Amsterdam
P.O. Box 87250, 1080 JG Amsterdam
Tel.: 020 772 23 34
lvdvrugt@vedeve.com
www.vedeve.com